ook must be mailed back to th
the latest date shown bel

ECONOMIC GEOGRAPHY OF THE USSR

WORKS TRANSLATED UNDER THE RUSSIAN TRANSLATION PROJECT OF THE AMERICAN COUNCIL OF LEARNED SOCIETIES, AND PUBLISHED BY THE MACMILLAN COMPANY

W. CHAPIN HUNTINGTON, EDITOR

TOLSTOY AS I KNEW HIM,
My Life at Home and at Yasnaya Polyana
By T. A. Kuzminskaya, sister-in-law of Leo Tolstoy

THE LAW OF THE SOVIET STATE
By Andrei Y. Vyshinsky, Deputy Minister for Foreign Affairs

HISTORY OF EARLY RUSSIAN LITERATURE
By N. K. Gudzy

HISTORY OF THE NATIONAL ECONOMY OF RUSSIA
By P. I. Lyashchenko, member Academy of Sciences of the USSR

ECONOMIC GEOGRAPHY OF THE USSR
By S. S. Balzak, V. F. Vasyutin, and Ya. G. Feigin

NATURAL REGIONS OF THE U.S.S.R.
By L. S. Berg

Economic Geography of the USSR

Edited by

S. S. BALZAK, V. F. VASYUTIN, *and* Ya. G. FEIGIN

American Edition Edited by CHAUNCY D. HARRIS
Professor of Geography, The University of Chicago

Translated from the Russian by ROBERT M. HANKIN *and* OLGA ADLER TITELBAUM

Preface by JOHN A. MORRISON *Consultant on Soviet Geography; Formerly Chief, Eastern European Branch, Division of Research for Europe, Department of State*

1949 • THE MACMILLAN COMPANY • NEW YORK

First Printing

PRINTED IN THE UNITED STATES OF AMERICA

Foreword

THE Russian Translation Project of the American Council of Learned Societies was organized in 1944 with the aid of a subsidy from the Humanities Division of the Rockefeller Foundation. The aim of the Project is the translation into English of significant Russian works in the fields of the humanities and the social sciences which provide an insight into Russian life and thought.

In the difficult problem of the selection of books for translation, the Administrative Committee has had the counsel and cooperation of Slavic scholars throughout the United States and Great Britain. It is thought that the books chosen will be useful to general readers interested in world affairs, and will also serve as collateral reading material for the large number of courses on Russia in our colleges and universities.

Since Russian history is a continuum, the volumes translated are of various dates and have been drawn from both the prerevolutionary and postrevolutionary periods, from writings published inside and outside of Russia, the choice depending solely on their value to the fundamental aim of the Project. Translations are presented in authentic and unabridged English versions of the original text. Only in this way, it is believed, can American readers be made aware of the traditions, concepts, and ideologies by which the thinking and attitudes of the people of Russia are molded.

It should, of course, be clearly understood that the views expressed in the works translated are not to be identified in any way with those of the Administrative Committee or of the Council.

THE ADMINISTRATIVE COMMITTEE
JOHN A. MORRISON, *Chairman*
HAROLD SPIVACKE
SERGIUS YAKOBSON
MORTIMER GRAVES
W. CHAPIN HUNTINGTON

Foreword to the American Edition

[illegible]
[illegible]
MORTIMER GRAVES
W. CHAPIN HUNTINGTON

Preface to the American Edition

PRIOR TO World War II the American student wishing to inform himself about the economic geography of the vast portion of the world comprised within the Union of Soviet Socialist Republics and who could not read Russian, had to depend on more or less popular travel accounts (generally covering the Intourist prescribed tours) and on the scattered regional data contained in the more serious economic and political studies of the USSR. The greatly increased interest in the country resulting from the war and the emergence of the Soviet Union therefrom as the world's second greatest power has resulted in the publication of general geographic treatises on the country by American, British, and French geographers. But even the better of these have the weaknesses which necessarily result from the restrictions imposed by the Soviet Government on travel and field work within the country, from the official policy of restricting publication of many of the data needed by the economic geographer, and from the difficulty of obtaining the materials which are published. No other part of the world presents the foreign geographer with so many restrictions, obstacles and frustrations as does the USSR.

Yet few will now question the importance—even the vital necessity—for knowing as much as we can about the Soviet lands, their characteristics, their resources, their utilization, and the manner of that utilization as it is taught in the Soviet schools.

Economic geography is a subject well developed in the USSR. It is natural, therefore, to look to the Russians for a comprehensive treatment of the economic geography of their country. In selecting a Russian text for translation the Russian Translation Project of the American Council of Learned Societies was confronted at the outset with two difficult problems. The first of these arises from the fact that economic geography, being one of the social sciences, falls squarely within the arena of Marxist dialectic. Hence, any economic geography by a Soviet author will contain much which the non-Marxist is likely to regard as special pleading, distorted argument, and unnecessarily fervid praise of the Soviet leaders. These qualities make a Soviet economic geography of the USSR less valuable as geography to the Western reader than, say, an economic geography of France by a French geographer. Nevertheless, even with all the trappings of Soviet ideology, such a book is bound to contain material which cannot be found in foreign geographies of the USSR and if it is read with discrimination and sophistication the many grains of geographic fact can be winnowed out from the dogma of Marxist-Leninist-Stalinist dialectic. Moreover, since the purpose of the series in which this volume appears is to acquaint the American reader with Russian thinking, the inclusion of the dialectic is a necessary part of the presentation.

The second problem arose from the fact that while much has been written in the Soviet Union in the field of economic geography, most of the textbooks on the economic geography of the USSR are on the secondary school level. As the editors of the present work point out in their foreword, there was, at the time it was written, no textbook in the subject suitable for use in Soviet institutions of higher learning. And so far as is known to the writer of this preface to the American edition, no other of like suitability has been published since the appearance of the Russian edition of this book in 1940. It was thus a matter of choosing between the best of the several secondary textbooks available and the only text written for students in Soviet universities and higher professional schools. The problem was further complicated by the fact that the latter is but the first volume of a two-volume work, the second volume of which was not obtainable.

In addition to the preference of the Russian Translation Project for translating books of college rather than secondary school level, the present work recommended itself because of its detailed treatment of the areal distribution of the principal economic activities, agriculture, mining, manufacturing and transportation. Also, the number and detail of the maps in the Russian volume exceed that of any other available publication on the Soviet Union with the exception of the *Great Soviet World Atlas,* only the first volume of which is generally available in this country.

Since the book was written near the end of 1939 it necessarily does not not take into account the immense changes in the economic geography of the USSR occasioned by destruction in the invaded areas and the greatly stepped-up tempo of economic development in the regions east of the Volga. However, in view of the increasingly stringent censorship, it is extremely unlikely that a book of comparable detail covering the war and postwar changes in the economic geography of the USSR will be published in the foreseeable future. It is believed, therefore, that the volume will be the most comprehensive Soviet economic geography for some time to come.

In making this book available to English-speaking students of geography and to the interested public, those responsible for its selection and translation adhered strictly to the statement of principles early adopted by the administrative committee responsible for the Russian Translation Project and which appears on page v. It is recognized that adherence to these principles has, in the case of the present work, required the inclusion of many passages which are likely to strike most non-Marxist readers as Communist dogma having little or nothing to do with economic geography as the subject is understood outside the Soviet realm. However, in view of the intimate connection between the teachings of Soviet economic geography and the planned economic development of the country (a number of economic geographers are employed by the State Planning Commission), it is important that the foreigner seeking to comprehend the nature of Soviet economic development should be familiar with the peculiarities of the Soviet approach to economic geography as well as with its content. It is believed that the discrimination of the American reader will be a fully adequate shield against conversion to an alien philosophy.

Even with allowance for the repetition inevitable in a work by several authors, the non-Soviet reader will probably feel that the number of citations from Stalin's writings and speeches is excessive for an economic geography, though it deal only with the USSR. They begin in the first paragraph of the Introduction and, together with similar citations from Lenin, Marx, and Engels and from resolutions of Party congresses, are scattered liberally throughout the entire text. Other citations are rare. These genuflections to official dogma are coupled with fervid praise of the Soviet brand of socialism and unrestrained denunciation of all who disagree with it. Readers unfamiliar with the inner-Party strife which raged in the mid-1930s may be somewhat puzzled by the intemperate nature of the discussion in Chapter II on the socialist distribution of productive forces. The references to Trotskyists "foaming at the mouth" as they argued that a uniform distribution of productive forces was conceivable only on a world scale is reminiscent of the Moscow trials of 1937 and 1938. "Contemptible enemies of the people," "rightist capitulationists," "saboteurs"—maledictions applied to those who opposed construction of the Dnepr hydroelectric plant and favored developing industry where optimal conditions existed—are terms unknown to the lexicon of non-Soviet economic geography. In the Soviet Union it apparently is not enough for the economic geographer to give a factual account and reasoned explanation of the distribution of economic phenomena; like other social scientists, he must hew to the "Party line" and demonstrate his orthodoxy by frequent use of the official eschatology.

Students of geographic theory will be especially interested in the Soviet view of the science of economic geography expressed in the Introduction. To judge from the citations, the author considers Lenin and Stalin to be the chief philosophical architects of the science. The violence of the attack on Hettner (who is most certainly quoted out of context) is probably due to the fact that this "bourgeois" geographer at one time had many followers among Soviet geographers. Equally intriguing is the long attack in Chapter III on Alfred Weber's "bourgeois apologetic" theory of industrial location (Standortstheorie), an assault which ends with the curious assertion that "Marxist abstractions represent actual reality and are not far-fetched," while Weber's abstractions are held to be "an absolute fantasy, having nothing to do with actual reality." Unfortunately for Weber's standing in the Soviet Union, the "enemies of the people" used his theory in arguing against the creation of a second coal-metallurgical base in the Soviet East and against the industrialization of the national republics.

The American reader will thus find in this book much that is exasperating. But he will also discover a wealth of detail regarding the economic geography of the USSR which he will find nowhere else. The insight into the thinking and performance of leading Soviet economic geographers which the book provides may lead the geographer of the Western world to wonder what his Soviet colleagues could produce were they free to write without the restrictions imposed by the official ideology. Certainly, the few Western geographers who have had the good fortune to "talk shop" with those of the Soviet Union have found them professionally their equals in every respect. Those who have participated in placing this book before the American reader—be he student of geography or interested layman—are confident that he will find in it much that will lead to a better appreciation of the strength and the weaknesses of the land empire which covers so large a part of the Eurasian Continent.

The value of the book to the non-Russian reader is greatly enhanced by the addition of numerous explanatory footnotes, maps, and appendices to the American edition. These were prepared by the editor, Professor Chauncy D. Harris of the Department of Geography, University of Chicago, who is also responsible for the excellent reproduction of the maps which accompanied the Russian edition. The writer of this preface feels a special sense of gratitude to Professor Harris who took over the heavy responsibility of supervising the preparation of the American edition when other duties made it impossible for the writer to undertake it.

J. A. MORRISON, *Chairman,*
Administrative Committee,
Russian Translation Project

Washington
April 1948

Editorial Note to the American Edition

EDITING THE AMERICAN EDITION

IN THE preparation of the American edition, the original Russian text has been followed as exactly as possible, even to paragraphing and arrangement. No material whatever in the original has been omitted and editorial additions have been carefully noted as such. Editorial textual additions have been placed within brackets, either as short notes within the running text, or as longer footnotes. Asterisks indicate maps, tables, appendices, or indexes not found in the Russian edition.

Since the Russian text was prepared for citizens of the Soviet Union and not for foreigners, its authors assumed a knowledge of places and persons not likely to be possessed by the average non-Soviet reader; in order to aid the American or British reader, a number of indexes and other aids have been added to the American edition. Thus, a gazetteer provides an index to each place name mentioned in the text or depicted on a map; an index of plants and animals identifies each by its proper scientific name; an index of persons has a short biographical note on each individual; and an index to citations is accompanied by a bibliography of readings in the economic geography of the USSR, largely in English. It is hoped that the detailed table of contents may serve as a subject index. Other added aids include a table of equivalents, a list of abbreviations, a transliteration table, and a glossary of Russian terms. It should be noted that in this edition certain common terms such as oblast, kray, sovkhoz, and many others, have been considered as Anglicized and therefore as forming plurals with an "s" (Appendix V-A). In order to facilitate reference to tables and maps, they have been numbered and have been listed in the front of the volume.

The most arduous task, aside from the translation itself, was the drafting and checking of the maps. Since maps serve as a basic geographic tool, the quality of a geographic work often may be judged by the detail and accuracy of the maps. In the cartographic representation of distributions of physical and human data the present work ranks high among economic geographies. The sixty-five maps in the original Russian text were worthy of careful attention since they formed the best available black-and-white book-sized series of maps on the economic geography of the USSR. For example, Figures 27 and 28, folded to face pages 200 and 201, display magnificently the industrial production by branches of industry for the important cities of the Soviet Union, and Figure 18, folded to face page 89, presents the distribution of mineral deposits with a wealth of detail usually restricted to specialized atlases.

An attempt has been made in the American edition to locate on an appropriate map every place name mentioned in the text. This has necessitated the addition of names to existing maps in some cases and the compilation of entirely new maps in other cases. For example, 177 place names were added to Figure 16, Natural Zones, from the corresponding section of the text. Other maps with similar extensive additions include Figures 5 and 6, depicting water routes of the European and Asiatic sections of the USSR, Figure 70, Railroad Lines, and Figures 79 and 80, Automobile Routes, European USSR, and Asiatic USSR.

Among the nineteen new maps compiled especially for the American edition, the following form an important set of basic references for the location of frequently used physical, regional, and administrative names not located on any map in the original Russian edition: Figure 4, Surface Configuration; Figure 7, Statistical Regions; Figure 22, Administrative and Statistical Divisions, 1913; Figure 82, Census Regions and Administrative Divisions, 1926; Figure 83, Administrative Divisions in 1939 (at the time of the writing of the book); and Figure 40, Administrative Divisions, 1948. Other new maps help to clarify specific segments of the text: Figure 1, Boundaries and Limits of the USSR; Figure 3, Tectonic Zones; Figure 19, place names mentioned in Chapter II; Figure 20, place names mentioned in Chapter III; Figure 21, Density of Population, 1913; Figure 71, Railroad Systems; and Figure 81, Air Routes, 1937.

One particularly vexing problem has been the rendition of hundreds of place names that occurred only in the running text in the Russian edition. Usually these names appeared in adjectival forms, often in cases other than the nominative. Unfortunately no simple rules exist for the transformation of such names into the nominative noun form, which is preferred for transliteration and map representation. The only safe method of determining the proper form was to locate the name on a Russian map; this involved long and tedious search through many maps, particularly those in the two volumes of the *Great Soviet World Atlas,* though often the Gazetteer to Volume I saved a longer search. The system of translating the generics (for example, Ladozhskoye Ozero as Lake Ladoga, see Appendix V-B) also presented some problems and resulted in some inconsistencies. Even the transliteration of the names that existed on the maps in the original Russian text was no easy task since about ten thousand names had to be read from fine print on partially illegible photostats.

Acknowledgments

The translation was made first by Robert M. Hankin and a number of his associates. For various reasons it seemed desirable to make a thorough check and revision of the translation and this arduous undertaking was carried out ably and cheerfully by Olga Adler Titelbaum, who, on the basis of her translation of Berg's *The Natural Regions of the USSR,* prepared also the Index of Plants and Animals (with Identification by Scientific Names). Final typing of the manuscript was done by Carolyn Neller Winget.

A large number of cartographers worked on the maps, but unfortunately none was able to carry on throughout the project. Robert L. Carmin helped set up specifications for the maps. Glenn Wray drafted a few of the bases. Alfred Harris and Charles Richard Jones, however, did most of the drafting (excluding the place names and legends). The place names were applied to most of the maps by Louis Sokol, though Richard Forstall helped on a few. The legends were added principally by Lillian L. Peters and Lucille Rust Wyant, but Minnie Lee Van Tilberg and Don Edward Totten also helped with legends and did some other drafting. Stanley F. Smith helped with a few last-minute suggestions and corrections. Translations of legends, transliterations of place names, additions of place names from the text, and compilation of new maps for the American edition were the work of the editor.

Special thanks are given to Leonard Dykes, Allen K. Philbrick, John A. Morrison, and the Map Library of the University of Chicago for the use of materials without which much of the map work would have been impossible, and to the American Geographical Society and Theodore Shabad for permission to reproduce Figure 40.

William Horbaly did most of the work in the preparation of the indexes.

A word of sincere thanks goes to the editors of the Macmillan Company, whose experience, skill, and cordial cooperation added to the quality of the American edition.

Much credit for the successful completion of the book should be given to Mortimer Graves, who had general charge of the Russian Translation Project at the office of the American Council of Learned Societies, to Dr. John A. Morrison who initiated the translation of this particular work, and to Dr. W. Chapin Huntington, the general editor of the Project.

CHAUNCY D. HARRIS

Department of Geography
The University of Chicago

Contents [DETAILED TABLE OF CONTENTS OF TEXT MAY BE FOUND ON PAGE XIX]

* An asterisk marks items not in the original Russian edition.

INDEXES

* An asterisk marks items not in the original Russian edition.

Detailed Table of Contents of Text

List of Maps

* Maps compiled especially for the American edition are marked by an asterisk.

Figure

* Maps compiled especially for the American edition are marked by an asterisk.

Figure

* Maps compiled especially for the American edition are marked by an asterisk.

List of Maps

Figure

* Maps compiled especially for the American edition are marked by an asterisk.

List of Tables

* Tables not in the original Russian edition are marked by an asterisk.

* Tables not in the original Russian edition are marked by an asterisk.

Foreword [to the Russian Edition]

THE economic geography of the USSR is taught in many institutions of higher learning in our country. In spite of this, until now students have been not only without a textbook but even without materials for the course, and have been forced to use magazine articles or, at best, manuscript materials pertaining to other fields.

The present work is the first attempt to offer a textbook on the economic geography of the USSR for institutions of economics.

This textbook consists of two parts (or volumes). The first part [included in this book] is devoted to a general survey of the distribution of the productive forces of the USSR as a whole. It includes the character of the natural conditions and natural resources of the Soviet Union, the principles of socialist distribution of productive forces, and the distribution of population, industry, agriculture, and transport. The second part of the textbook [not available] is devoted to the nature of the Union republics and the basic economic regions of the USSR.

The editors consider it necessary to note that for technical reasons the Western Ukraine and Western Belorussia, which are included in the Soviet Union, have not received sufficient economic-geographic discussion in the appropriate division of the first part of the textbook [since the original Russian edition was printed in 1940 only a few months after the occupation in September, 1939, of these areas formerly in Poland]. In particular, the economic nature of these parts of the USSR is not given in the maps of the first part of the text. Therefore, in the second part, the Western Ukraine and Western Belorussia are treated in greater detail, as integral parts of a single Ukrainian state and of a single Belorussian state.

As is indicated by the treatment of several fundamental questions in the textbook, the authors, in compiling the text, encountered special difficulties because of the absence of monographs and up-to-date maps on many extremely important problems of economic geography.

The published cartographic materials and accompanying economic information cite data from 1935, as a rule. The editors, wherever possible, have brought up to date the economic indices indicated on the maps, making use of various sources.

The editors request teachers and students to make critical observations of the textbook for consideration in future revisions.

The following persons contributed to Part I of the *Economic Geography of the USSR*:

FEIGIN, Ya. G., Corresponding member of the Academy of Sciences of the Ukrainian SSR	Introduction Chapters II and III
KUDLENOK, P. I.	Chapter I
MARKUS, B. L., Doctor of Economic Sciences	Chapter IV
VASYUTIN, V. F.	Chapter V (General Nature of Industry and Secs. 1, 2, 4, 8, and 11)
GALITSKY, M. I., Professor	Chapter V (Secs. 3, 5, 6, 7, 9, and 10)
LIBKIND, A. S., Candidate in Economic Sciences	Chapter VI
KHACHATUROV, T. S., Lecturer	Chapter VII

The editors of the present work are:

FEIGIN, Ya. G., Institute of Economics of the Academy of Sciences of the USSR
VASYUTIN, V. F., Institute of Geography of the Academy of Sciences of the USSR
BALZAK, S. S., Socio-Economic Publishing House.
POMUS, M. I., Map Editor

In compiling the maps the following took part: O. A. VORONTSOVA, E. M. DAVYDOV, and M. I. POMUS. Maps were put into final form under the supervision of G. A. MOCHULSKY.

Introduction [A Soviet View of the Science of Economic Geography]

ECONOMIC geography is the science of the areal distribution of production and of the conditions of its development in different countries and regions. Production ". . . encompasses the productive forces of society as well as the producing (economic) relationships of human beings, and is thus the embodiment of their unity in the process of production of material goods." [1]

In studying where something is produced, economic geography, proceeding from basic laws of political economy, must set forth the conditions of development and distribution of productive forces in particular countries and regions.

In order to obtain this information, economic geography investigates the distinguishing features of the contemporary economic development of different countries and regions, the natural-geographic conditions of their economic development, and also the economic interrelations among countries and regions.

Economic geography not only describes the distribution of production, but by means of analysis and generalization of concrete material, studies those specific principles according to which this distribution occurs in a particular country, region, or branch of the economy.

The principles of the distribution of production cannot be separated from the general laws of the development of a given socio-economic system. Consequently, attempts to prove the non-historical nature of the principles of distribution, and the applicability of these very same principles of distribution to all socio-economic systems, in all countries and regions, is unscientific, and basically contradicts Marxism-Leninism. "The conditions under which people produce and exchange products," wrote Engels, "are not the same for different countries, and in each country change from one generation to the next. . . . Consequently, the man who would

[1] Stalin, *Questions of Leninism,* 11th ed., p. 551.

wish to apply the same principles to the economy of Tierra del Fuego and to the economy of contemporary England obviously will bring nothing to light other than the most common hackneyed position."[2]

The capitalist means of production of material goods is linked indissolubly with the fundamental, extremely uneven, inefficient distribution of productive forces. The distribution of capitalistic production is founded on the capitalist's pursuit of profit, and on anarchy, competition, and the law of unequal development of capitalism, the operation of which is reinforced particularly during the epoch of imperialism.

The international division of labor in the capitalist world, and the distribution of production, are based on the oppression of some countries by others, and on the forced conversion of a majority of countries and regions into agrarian raw-material colonies for the highly developed mother countries.

The basis of the distribution of productive forces in the USSR is the program of building a communist society. For the realization of this program the historic decisions of the 18th Party Congress, which gave a detailed plan for the distribution of productive forces in the Third Stalin Five-Year Plan, have great significance. As a result of the realization of this plan, there is being created a new economic geography for the Soviet Union, with a more uniform distribution of production throughout the country. More and more, industry is being located near both the sources of raw materials and the regions where the manufactured goods are consumed. The former backwardness of the national republics is being eliminated. The distribution of agricultural production is becoming more uniform. Regions previously exclusively consuming are becoming producing regions, and the complex development of production in the economic regions is being assured.

In studying the conditions of the development and distribution of production, economic geography gives an important position to the natural conditions of countries and regions.

However, the Marxist-Leninist understanding of the role of the natural-geographic environment has nothing in common with crude geographic theories according to which the natural-geographic environment is considered as the determining factor in the develop-

[2] Marx and Engels, *Works*, Vol. XIV, p. 149.

ment and distribution of productive forces. The economic characteristics of countries and regions, and also the territorial division of labor are explained by bourgeois geographers and economists on the basis of natural-geographic conditions. Thus, for example, the important German bourgeois geographer A. Hettner considered that the characteristics of the economy, way of life, and political structure of a particular country are all determined exclusively by its natural-geographic conditions.[3] With the aid of this premise, Hettner justified colonial oppression by imperialist countries, since colonies, according to Hettner, by virtue of their natural-geographic conditions are not capable of developing independently and need the assistance of "civilized" countries.

The American professor Huntington, author of a textbook of economic geography widely used in the United States, goes even further than Hettner. He explains the distribution of population, industry, and agriculture, and also the level of development of particular countries by climatic conditions alone.[4]

The errors advanced by G. V. Plekhanov concerning the role of the geographic environment in the development of productive forces achieved wide circulation among the economists and geographers of the USSR. Plekhanov maintained that the development of productive forces is determined by the geographic environment. This position led him in practice to underestimate the decisive role the particular methods of production of material goods prevailing in a given country play in the development and distribution of productive forces. The natural-geographic environment and natural resources play an important role in the development of productive

[3] [This statement is hardly an adequate summary of the views of Hettner; it probably reflects an internal dispute in the Soviet Union over the principles of the distribution of production, a dispute in which the views of Hettner may have been quoted by a group whose views did not prevail. Hettner himself stated that the consideration of natural factors can "arrive only at possibilities; the decision lies with man." (Alfred Hettner, "Die Geographie des Menschen," *Geographische Zeitschrift*, Vol. XIII, 1907, p. 413, as quoted by Richard Hartshorne, "The Nature of Geography," *Annals of the Association of American Geographers*, Vol. XXIX, 1939, p. 299.)]

[4] [It is true that Ellsworth Huntington lays great stress on the climatic factor; but the assertion that he explains "by climatic conditions alone" shows only a superficial acquaintance with his writings. His *Principles of Economic Geography* (New York: John Wiley, 1940, 715 pp.) reveals an appreciation of the complex physical, economic, political, and historical factors involved in the analysis of patterns of distribution of economic activities. Furthermore, his analysis of physical factors includes location, relief, soil, vegetation, and minerals, as well as climate.]

forces of particular countries and regions, but the utilization of these natural resources to raise productive forces depends on the social structure which prevails in a particular country. Thus, Tsarist Russia, for example, was not able to increase the use of its natural resources. Under conditions of socialist construction, however, their study and utilization has reached unheard-of levels.

"The geographic environment," writes Comrade Stalin, "is incontrovertibly one of the unchanging and indispensable conditions of the development of society and, of course, it influences the development of a society—it either accelerates or retards the course of development of that society. But its influence is not *the determining* influence, since society changes and develops incomparably faster than does the geographic environment."[5]

With the growth of productive forces and the perfection of productive techniques, human society increasingly recognizes the laws of nature and increasingly subordinates them to society itself, using natural resources for developing social productive forces.

Under conditions of a socialist economy the utilization of natural resources is planned and systematic, whereas under capitalism it is most inefficient and ruthless.

Nor are density of population and its growth decisive factors in the development and distribution of productive forces, although without a certain minimum population the development of productive forces is impossible. The decisive factor in the distribution of productive forces is the means of production of material goods, the means of acquiring the necessities of life required for the welfare of the people.

Each branch of the national economy, and even each branch of industry and agriculture, in addition to over-all general traits, has its own specific distributional characteristics. But these characteristics are indissolubly linked with the socio-economic and natural geographic conditions in particular countries and regions. For this reason the distribution of production must be studied not only by countries and regions, but also by branches.

The principles of distribution of socialist production, differing basically from the principles of capitalist distribution, necessitate a study of the economic geography of the socialist country and of the

[5] Stalin, *Questions of Leninism*, p. 548.

capitalist world, as two independent branches of the same scientific discipline.

In economic geography it is of utmost importance to study the details of the economic development of the different industrial sections of the country—the economic regions.

In his work, *The Development of Capitalism in Russia,* Lenin presents the results of studies of the economy of Tsarist Russia, not only by branches of the economy, but also by economic regions. He repeatedly emphasizes the need for study of specific characteristics of different regions.

In another of his works, *New Facts Concerning the Laws of the Development of Capitalism in Agriculture* (1914–1915), Lenin again emphasizes the full importance of studying economic regions, especially in the United States of America.

"The enormous area of the United States, only a little smaller than the area of all Europe, and the great variety of economic conditions in various parts of the country all prove the absolute need for separate investigation of the principal regions, essentially heterogeneous economically."[6]

An economic geography of the USSR is concerned with the distribution of the entire national economy and its particular branches throughout the territory of the USSR. It also studies the distinguishing characteristics of socialist construction in the different regions of the country, their productive forces, the dislocations which occur in them, and also the possibilities and avenues of their future development.

Lenin and Stalin repeatedly emphasized the need to study the variety of conditions in different regions and to take them into account in the practice of socialist construction. They pointed out that without knowledge and consideration of local conditions it was impossible to guide socialist construction.

At the 8th Party Congress (March, 1919) Lenin said, "It would be an error if we were simply to copy decrees for all parts of Russia according to a set pattern, if bolshevist-communist Soviet workers in the Ukraine and on the Don were to spread the decrees wholesale and without discrimination to other provinces."[7]

At the 10th Party Congress (1921) Lenin again emphasized this

[6] Lenin, *Works*, Vol. XVII, p. 577.
[7] *Ibid.*, Vol. XXIV, pp. 125–126.

thought, pointing out, "To standardize Central Russia, the Ukraine, and Siberia, and to subject them to a set pattern would be the height of folly."[8]

Comrade Stalin has often emphasized the importance and necessity of taking into account local peculiarities in conducting Party policies. Thus, in his report at the 10th Party Congress, in speaking of the need for the people of the Soviet East to shift to a Soviet economy and forsake industrial capitalism, Comrade Stalin pointed out that to accomplish this extremely important measure "it is necessary to take into account all the distinctive characteristics of the economic circumstances, even of the historic past, way of life, and culture of these nationalities. To transplant into the areas of these nationalities those procedures which are effective and significant here, in Central Russia, is unthinkable and dangerous."[9]

The Lenin-Stalin Central Committee of the Communist Party of the Soviet Union and Comrade Stalin himself gave daily instruction to Party and Soviet workers to take thoroughly into account local conditions in putting Party measures into effect. In his historic article "Reply to the Comrade Collective Farmer," Comrade Stalin pointed out that one of the chief reasons for mistakes made in the collective farm movement was the fact that local workers completely overlooked specific local conditions and worked according to a stereotyped pattern, a procedure which the Party has always condemned. Comrade Stalin wrote that local workers "violated Lenin's principle of taking into account the diversity of conditions in different regions of the USSR as applied to collective farm development. They forgot that among these regions there are advanced, average, and backward regions."[10]

Without considering the individualities of the regions—natural conditions, economy, way of life, etc.—the planning of their economic and cultural development is impossible. That is why a thorough study of the regions of our country is needed as one of the most important tasks of economic geography.

Among economic geographers of the USSR, various bourgeois theories have had wide circulation—the teachings of Hettner, the German

[8] *Ibid.*, Vol. XXVI, p. 243.
[9] Stalin, *Marxism and the National-Colonial Question*, p. 77.
[10] Stalin, *Questions of Leninism*, p. 308.

geographer and the location theories of Weber,[11] von Thünen,[12] and others.

These would-be "scientific" and "objective" theorists, minimizing contradictions of distribution of capitalistic production, set out to prove its "rationality," to justify colonial plunder by the "harmony" of international division of labor, etc. Among bourgeois economists and geographers "disinterested research"—to use an apt expression of Marx—"yields to the quarrels of hack writers, and impartial scientific investigations are supplanted by prejudiced, officious apology." [13]

To justify the separation of economic geography from other sciences, bourgeois scholars present the special, so-called "chorographic" (purely spatial) approach to the phenomena under study. The basis of "chorography" is the artificial separation of time and space, and examination of all economic-geographic manifestations only in terms of space, excluding the time factor. The German geographer, Hettner, developed most fully this "chorographic" point of view in economic geography with all the ensuing consequences. "The examination of objects and processes of the earth's surface from the chorographic point of view," writes Hettner, "is the interpretation of them not as objects in themselves, and not in relation to their development in time, but in their association in space." [14] Hettner's concept of space and time is purely theoretical, that is, he considers them only as a form of perception and not as existing in reality independent of our consciousness.

Hettner in essence defines existence, not in terms of time, but only in space. As a matter of fact "existence without time is as absurd as existence without space" (Engels). A genuine study of the distribution of production of various countries and regions is excluded by Hettner by virtue of this concept. Economic geography is concerned not only with

[11] [Alfred Weber's theories are available in English in *Alfred Weber's Theory of Location of Industries*, ed. by Carl Joachim Friedrich (Chicago: University of Chicago Press, 1929), 256 pp.]

[12] [Johann Heinrich von Thünen, *Das Isolierte Staat*, 2nd ed., 1842.]

[13] Marx, *Capital*, Vol. I, 1935, p. xix.

[14] Hettner, *Geography: Its History, Nature, and Methods*, p. 164. [The quotation apparently is from a Russian translation of Hettner's work. The original appears in Alfred Hettner, *Die Geographie: Ihre Geschichte, Ihr Wesen und Ihre Methoden* (Breslau, Germany: Ferdinand Hirt, 1927), p. 217. Hettner viewed reality as having three coexisting aspects, all of which are essential to an understanding of the whole: (1) the analysis of similar objects and processes by the systematic disciplines such as chemistry, botany, economics, or sociology; (2) the interpretation of objects or events in their time setting by history; (3) the interpretation of objects in their space associations by geography.]

facts coinciding in space, but also, as is the case with other economic sciences, it is concerned with facts which are constantly changing in time. According to Hettner, the economic geographer must study economic phenomena in a static frozen aspect. Thus, at the basis of Hettner's teaching of economic geography lies antihistoricism. The antihistoricism of Hettner, as of other bourgeois scholars, is one of the means used to immortalize capitalism and to defend its existence. Hettner openly declares that geography must be geared to serve the interests of the bourgeoisie.

Together with "chorography," as has already been shown above, the basis of Hettner's teaching is crude environmentalism.

Bourgeois professors, many of whom were revealed to be enemies of the Soviet people, tried by all possible means to popularize and implant the teachings of Hettner in the USSR. Using the teachings of Hettner, they showed that the Soviet Union by virtue of its natural conditions and geographic position should remain an agrarian country, and in the international division of labor must fulfill the role of an agrarian raw-material subsidiary to the industrially developed West European countries. On this basis they demanded the abolition of the monopoly over foreign trade. The teachings of Hettner were widely distributed throughout the economic-geographic literature. Several authors showed themselves to be followers of the antiscientific, theoretical conceptions of Hettner. They were preaching attitudes of crude environmentalism and attributing to the geographic environment the decisive role in the development and distribution of productive forces, and in the development of particular countries and regions. Another, no less harmful, point of view on the question of the role of the geographic environment was widespread. Several woebegone authors completely ignored the natural-geographic conditions of the development of particular countries and regions. By every means they minimized the role of natural-geographic conditions in the development and distribution of productive forces. In practice this was expressed by a disdainful neglect of the study of natural resources and of natural-geographic conditions for the development of countries and regions.

It is necessary also to note two other extremely harmful tendencies which have held sway over students of economic geography. The first is the excessive methodizing of economic geography, which ignores much concrete material and map work. The other tendency consists of reducing all economic geography to a list of facts, figures, geographic points, etc., without generalizing them into a definite system. Both extremes are equally alien to Marxist-Leninist economic geography. Without a study of the wealth of concrete material, and without representing it on maps, serious economic-geographic work is impossible. On the other hand, it is also impossible without proper corresponding analysis or without theoretical generalization of the huge body of concrete material.

The Party and the Government have attached great significance to economic geography as a science and as a subject to be taught. The decree of May 16, 1934, of the Council of People's Commissars and the Central Committee of the Communist Party of the Soviet Union speaks eloquently concerning the teaching of geography in elementary and secondary schools. The basic deficiencies of geographic instruction in elementary and secondary schools noted in this decree were present also in the higher schools (colleges) and to this day have not yet been eliminated. These deficiencies are: abstract and dry presentation, inadequate physical-geographic material, weak orientation through map presentation, and overloading the instruction and the textbooks with statistical material and general schemes. Hence the problem of completely eliminating these deficiencies in the teaching of economic geography is of utmost importance.

I Natural Conditions and Natural Resources of the USSR

SECTION 1. GEOGRAPHIC POSITION, SIZE, AND BOUNDARIES OF THE USSR

Position and Size

THE USSR occupies the eastern part of Europe and the northern and central part of Asia, extending north and south from Cape Chelyuskin (77° 44′ N. Lat.) to Kushka (35° N. Lat.) [Fig. 1]. West and east the territory of the USSR extends approximately from 21–22° E. Long. to Cape Dezhnev on the Chukotsk Peninsula near 169° 30′ W. Long.[1] From north to south the territory of the Union extends more than 4,500 km., and from west to east 11,000 km.

The USSR occupies an area of 21,300,000 square km., one-sixth of the habitable land of the earth.[2] In extent of territory the USSR takes second place in the world, ranking after the British Empire with an area of 34,300,000 square km. However, the possessions of the latter are scattered in all parts of the earth, while the territory of the USSR forms one huge continuous block of land. In the compactness of its territory the USSR is first in the world and is a

[1] [In 1947 the western limit of the Soviet Union was on the Bay of Danzig about 20° E. Long. Kaliningrad (Königsberg) is 20° 31′ E. Long.]

[2] [The area of the Soviet Union in 1938 was 21,170,000 square km. (8,176,000 square mi.), to which was added during the period 1939–45 about 670,000 square km. (260,000 square mi.). In 1946 the area thus was about 21,840,000 square km. (8,436,000 square mi.). The total land area of the world free of icecaps is 132,020,000 square km. (50,973,000 square mi.). The Soviet Union occupies 16.0%, or almost exactly one-sixth of the land surface of the earth not covered by icecaps, or about one-seventh of the total land surface of the earth (including Antarctica and Greenland). TABLE 1. AREAS ADDED TO THE SOVIET UNION 1939–1945 is Appendix VI, and may be found on page 543.]

tremendous country with vast territory and a population of more than 183 million.[3]

Geographically the USSR is distinguished by a number of peculiar characteristics. About 23% of the entire area of the USSR lies beyond the Arctic Circle, where the duration of day and night is measured not in hours but in days, weeks, and months—a fact which affects the climate, the soil and vegetation, and the fauna of the wide expanses of that part of the country.

The USSR lies in those latitudes of the globe where land predominates over water. These are between the parallels of 40° and 70° N. Lat.; along the 65th parallel North America and Asia have their greatest breadth. This fact is one of the reasons for the continental climate of our country.

The USSR extends farther north than any other country lying in the Northern Hemisphere. The mainland of the USSR reaches to 77° 44′ N. Lat., that of North America to 71° 50′ N. Lat., and that of Europe to 71° 10′ N. Lat.

Along almost all its southern frontier, the USSR borders on the greatest belt of mountain ranges and highlands in the world.

The Soviet Union lies in almost all the climate zones of the earth—from the Frigid to the Subtropical, the Tropical Zone alone not occurring. This fact is largely responsible for the great diversity in natural conditions in our country. Approximately 16% of the country belongs to the Frigid Zone, and only 4% to the Subtropical Zone. Four-fifths of the territory of the Union lies in the Temperate Zone.

The USSR is divided into two parts, European and Asiatic, the dividing line between which is determined variously by different authors. The eastern slope of the Ural Mountains, the Ural River, the Caspian Sea, and the southern slope of the Great Caucasus are regarded as the boundaries between the European and Asiatic parts of the USSR.

[3] [The population was 170 million by the Census of 1939 in the boundaries at the beginning of 1939. With adjustment for war losses of 20 million, for natural increase of 19 million, and for population of new territories added to the Union of 24 million, the 1945 population may have been in the neighborhood of 193 million. Only the Oriental countries of China and India have larger populations. The population of the Soviet Union greatly exceeds that of Western countries; it is about 50% greater than that of the United States, four times that of the United Kingdom, France, or Italy, and three times that of Germany before World War II.]

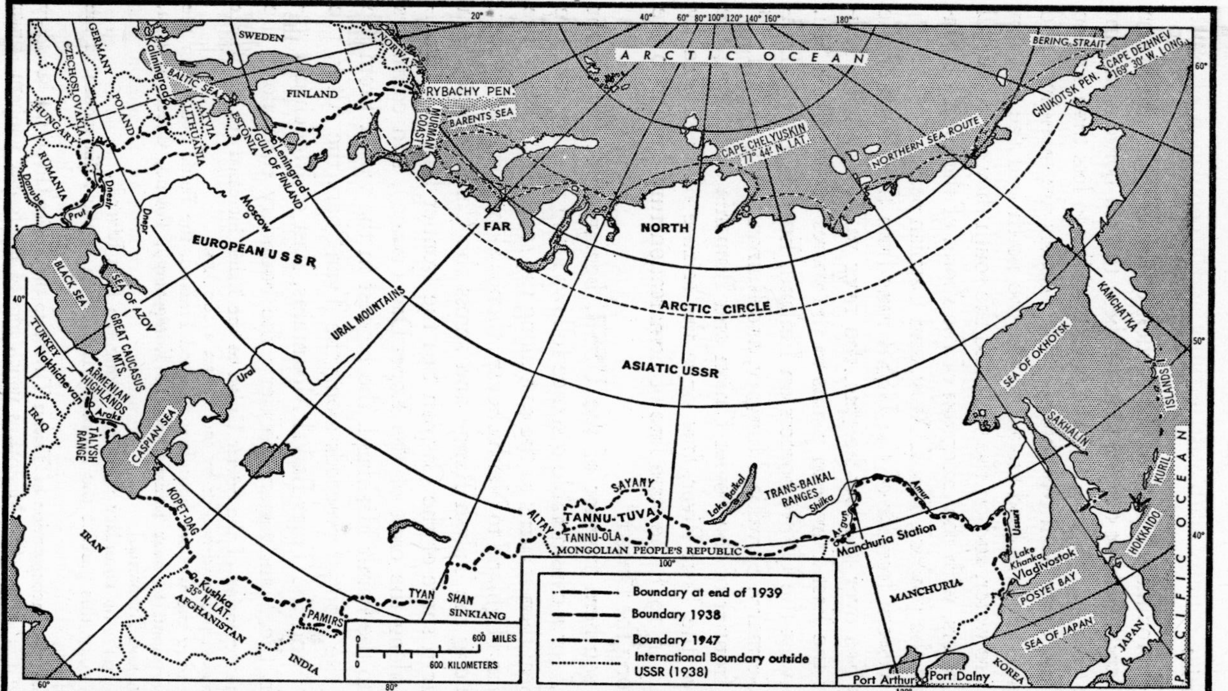

*Fig. 1. Boundaries and Limits of the Soviet Union (The 1938 boundary is separately indicated only in places where it differs from the 1947 boundary; the boundary at the end of 1939 is indicated only where it differs from both 1938 and 1947. See Fig. 2 for greater detail on the western boundary.)

Boundaries

The approximate length of the borders of the USSR, both by sea and by land, is about 60,000 km.; of these the sea borders amount to more than 43,000 km., and the land frontiers to less than 17,000 km.[4] Thus, more than two-thirds of our borders are maritime, and about one-third are land frontiers. On the north and the east our borders are water, and on the west and the south they are almost all land frontiers, with the exception of the shores of the Gulf of Finland, and the [Baltic], Black, Azov, and Caspian seas.

The western frontier of the USSR runs from the shores of the Barents Sea over the low heights, the river valleys, and the lowlands of the East European plains to the shores of the Black Sea. On the west the USSR borders on Finland, Estonia, Latvia, Lithuania, Germany, Slovakia, Hungary, and Rumania [Figs. 1 and 2].[5]

The frontier of the Soviet Union and Rumania runs along the course of the Prut River, but since the seizure of Bessarabia by Rumania in 1918 the state line of demarcation runs farther to the east—along the Dnestr.[6]

The southern frontier of the USSR, beginning at the Dnepr estuary,[7] for a considerable distance follows along the shores of the Black Sea; then it turns to the east along the southern limits of the Armenian Highland to Nakhichevan, thence along the Araks River, south along the Talysh Range and across the Caspian Sea. From the eastern shore of the Caspian Sea the frontier follows approximately along the crest of the Kopet-Dag (range), and continues east onto the Pamir Highland, the highest in the world. From the Pamirs the frontier proceeds along the Tyan-Shan, the Altay, the Sayany[8] and the Trans-Baikal Mountains. East of Manchuria station [on the Manchurian frontier], the boundary runs along the

[4] [The expansion of the Soviet Union to the Baltic increased the sea border and decreased the land border by more than 1,000 km.]

[5] [In 1947 the western boundary touched Finland, the Baltic Sea (from the Gulf of Finland to near Kaliningrad, or Königsberg), Poland, Czechoslovakia, Hungary, and Rumania.]

[6] [In 1947 the boundary again ran along the Prut River.]

[7] [In 1947 this part of the boundary line began at the Kilia mouth of the Danube.]

[8] [After the incorporation of Tannu Tuva into the Soviet Union the boundary ran along the Tannu Ola Mountains which formed the former southern border of the Tannu Tuva People's Republic. The Sayany, which formed the northern boundary of that republic, are now almost entirely within the Soviet Union.]

*Fig. 2. Changes in the Western Boundary of the USSR 1939–1947 (See Table 1, p. 544) (Adapted in part from U.S. Department of State, Division of Map Intelligence and Cartography. *European USSR Administrative Divisions, July 1, 1946*, Map 10414.1, Oct. 1946. Scale 1:5,000,000)

Argun River to its confluence with the Shilka and thence along the Amur River to its junction with the Ussuri. Here the frontier turns to the south along the Ussuri River, continues to Lake Khanka and thence proceeds to the shore of the Sea of Japan.

On the south the USSR borders on Turkey, Iran, Afghanistan, Western China (the province of Sinkiang), the Mongolian People's Republic, the Tannu Tuva People's Republic, Manchuria, and Korea.[9]

The southern frontier is the longest of all the frontiers of the Soviet Union and is almost entirely a land border.

The eastern border, from Posyet Bay (south of Vladivostok) to Bering Strait, is, with the exception of the island of Sakhalin, entirely a sea border, and follows the shores of the Great, or Pacific, Ocean and its seas which wash the shores of the Soviet Union.

The northern frontier of the USSR extends along the shores of the Arctic Ocean, from Rybachy Peninsula on the Murman Coast in the west to Bering Strait on the east. This frontier is a sea frontier for its entire length (about 25,000 km.). Through the Arctic Ocean along the shores of the Far North of the USSR passes the Northern Sea Route, which in the Third Five-Year Plan is being transformed into a normally functioning sea route, providing a regular connection with the Far East.[10]

The geographic position of the USSR, in comparison with other countries, is especially favorable for the development of productive forces. No other country in the world has frontiers so enormously long, or is so diverse in natural conditions, as the USSR. It is also especially important to note that the position of the USSR among other countries is not merely a geographic fact. The Soviet Union is encircled by capitalist countries, which makes it necessary to strengthen by every means the defensive potentiality of our frontiers.

[9] With Japan the USSR has a short land frontier on the Island of Sakhalin, running along 50° N. Lat. [This land frontier was eliminated in 1945.]

[10] In the Arctic Ocean the extreme limits of the western and eastern frontiers of the USSR are indicated on maps by imaginary lines which converge at the North Pole.

SECTION 2. THE GEOLOGICAL STRUCTURE AND LANDFORMS OF THE USSR

Geological Structure of the USSR

The territory of the USSR has had a complicated geological history, and its various parts differ sharply one from another according to the geological age of the underlying strata.

Geologically the territory of the USSR may be divided into distinct, very large regions called tectonic zones, which differ from one another in a number of fundamental geological characteristics. Five such zones may be distinguished: (1) Pre-Cambrian, (2) Caledonian, (3) Hercynian, (4) Mesozoic, and (5) the zone of Alpine folding.[11]

The tectonic zones are distinguished by the basic criterion—the age during which folding took place.

The zones in which folding was completed in the Pre-Paleozoic [Pre-Cambrian] Era are the oldest tectonic zones of the earth's

[11] The geological history of the earth is divided into eras, to which correspond certain groups of rock strata which compose the earth's crust. Five such eras are distinguished, from the oldest to the most recent: (1) Archaean, (2) Proterozoic, (3) Paleozoic, (4) Mesozoic, and (5) Cenozoic.

The eras in turn are divided into periods, to which certain systems of deposition correspond. The oldest eras—the Archaean and the Proterozoic—do not have general subdivisions. Their subdivision into periods has only local significance. The Paleozoic Era is divided into five periods: (1) Cambrian, (2) Silurian [including the Ordovician], (3) Devonian, (4) Carboniferous [Mississippian and Pennsylvanian in the United States], and (5) Permian. The Mesozoic Era is divided into three periods: (1) Triassic, (2) Jurassic, and (3) Cretaceous. And finally the Cenozoic Era, into three periods: (1) Paleocene, (2) Neocene (these two are commonly grouped as the Tertiary Period), and (3) Quaternary.

These subdivisions in the geological history of the earth are according to relative age; i.e., they indicate which layers of the earth's crust are old and which are young.

In the geological history of the earth there are distinguished also periods during which the internal forces of the earth were violently active, leading to fundamental reconstruction of the earth's crust; these are called periods of mountain formation (orogenesis).

Five epochs of powerful orogenesis are distinguished. The repeated processes of orogenesis which occurred in the Archaean and Proterozoic eras correspond to the epoch of Pre-Cambrian folding. The mountain-forming movements that occurred at the beginning and close of the Paleozoic Era correspond to the epoch of Caledonian and Hercynian folding [The Caledonian folding actually occurred well within the Paleozoic Era]. And finally, the mountain-forming processes that took place in the Mesozoic and Cenozoic eras correspond to the Mesozoic and Alpine foldings.

crust. In the succeeding geological periods these areas underwent exceedingly slow and weak movements, which created gently sloping synclines and broad anticlines, in places broken by joints and faults, along which there occurred sinking or raising of one part with relation to another, and also the extrusion of igneous (magmatic) rocks.

In the Soviet Union the zone of Pre-Cambrian folding is represented by the East European Platform, or block, which occupies almost all the area of the European part of the USSR, with the exception of the Urals and the Donets Ridge, and also by the Siberian Platform which includes the broad Aldan and Anabar shields. [A in Fig. 3; other references in brackets in the following few pages identify areas on Fig. 3.]

In the structure of plateaus two parts are distinguished: the foundation, composed of much folded, shattered, and usually highly metamorphosed rocks, and the mantle of deposits composed of younger rocks lying horizontally in layers, and scarcely metamorphosed at all.

In some places the ancient foundation outcrops on the surface or comes close to it, forming so-called "crystalline" shields and blocks. Such, for example, are the territory of the Karelian ASSR and of Murmansk Oblast (which is part of the Baltic Shield) [1a in Fig. 3], the Ukrainian [1b], Aldan [2b], and Anabar [2a] shields, and the Voronezh Block [1c]. In other places the foundation lies at a depth of from one thousand to two thousand meters or more, and is overlain by beds of sedimentary strata which form great depressions (synclines) or basins. Such basins are the North Ukrainian [1e], the Black Sea [1d], the East Russian [1f], the Caspian [1h], the Moscow [1g], and the Tungus [2c] depressions of the East European and Siberian platforms.

The second zone, that of Caledonian folds, occupies a relatively smaller area of the territory of the USSR [B in Fig. 3]. Within the area of this zone the folding processes in the main had been completed by the middle of the Paleozoic, at the beginning of the Devonian Period. Pre-Baikalia [3a], the ranges of western Trans-Baikalia [3b], and the regions adjoining the Siberian Platform on the southwest (the Yenisey Range [4a], the Sayany [4b], and the Minusinsk [4c] and Kuznetsk [4d] basins) belong to this zone.

The third zone, that of Hercynian folding, occupies a rather sizable area within the limits of the Soviet Union [C]. Within the area of this zone the folding processes were completed by the end of the Paleozoic Era. The following parts of the USSR belong to this zone: Novaya Zemlya [5a], the Urals [5b], Central Kazakhstan [5c], the Altay [5d], the northern and central crests of the Tyan-Shan [5e], Taimyr [5f], and Severnaya Zemlya [5g]. Part of this zone lies at a considerable depth and is covered by a thick deposit (of from one to two thousand meters) of Mesozoic and Tertiary age. The Ural-Siberian [6a], the Irtysh [6b], the Turgay [6c], the Syr-Darya [6e], the Amu-Darya [6d], the Fergana [6f], the Chu [6g], the Balkhash [6h], the Khatanga [6i], and other basins are regions of this sort.

The fourth zone, that of Mesozoic folds, has its greatest development in the Yakut ASSR and in the Soviet Far East [D]. This is a zone of recent folding, which in the main was completed at the end of the Mesozoic Period, but with subsequent weak movements continuing in it later as well. The Verkhoyansk [7a], Chersky [7b], Anadyr [7c], Kolyma or Gydan [7d], and Dzhugdzhur [7e] ranges and the Maritime Kray with the Sikhote-Alin Range [7f] and Eastern Trans-Baikalia [7g] belong to this zone. It extends into the European part of the USSR and Central Asia. Here it occupies regions adjoining the Caspian Sea on the northwest and on the east, the Mangyshlak Mountains [8a], Bolshoy Balkhan [8b], and other regions.

Finally, the fifth, youngest zone, that of Alpine folding, in which the processes of folding ended at the close of the Tertiary Period, lies along the edge of the territory of the Soviet Union [E]. The Crimea [9a], the Caucasus [9b], Kopet-Dag [9c], the Pamirs [9d], Sakhalin [9e], Kamchatka [9f], and the Koryak Range [9g] belong to this zone. In large part the great regions of earthquakes and volcanic eruptions belong to this zone, which indicates that the movements of the earth's crust continue here even at the present time.

These briefly characterized geological regions in some localities are composed of strata of exceptional thickness, measured in tens of thousands of meters. Regions with such large-scale sedimentation could have been formed under conditions of exceedingly great subsidence and downward flexures of the bottoms of vanished seas, subsequently encompassed by folding processes and uplifted to a considerable height.

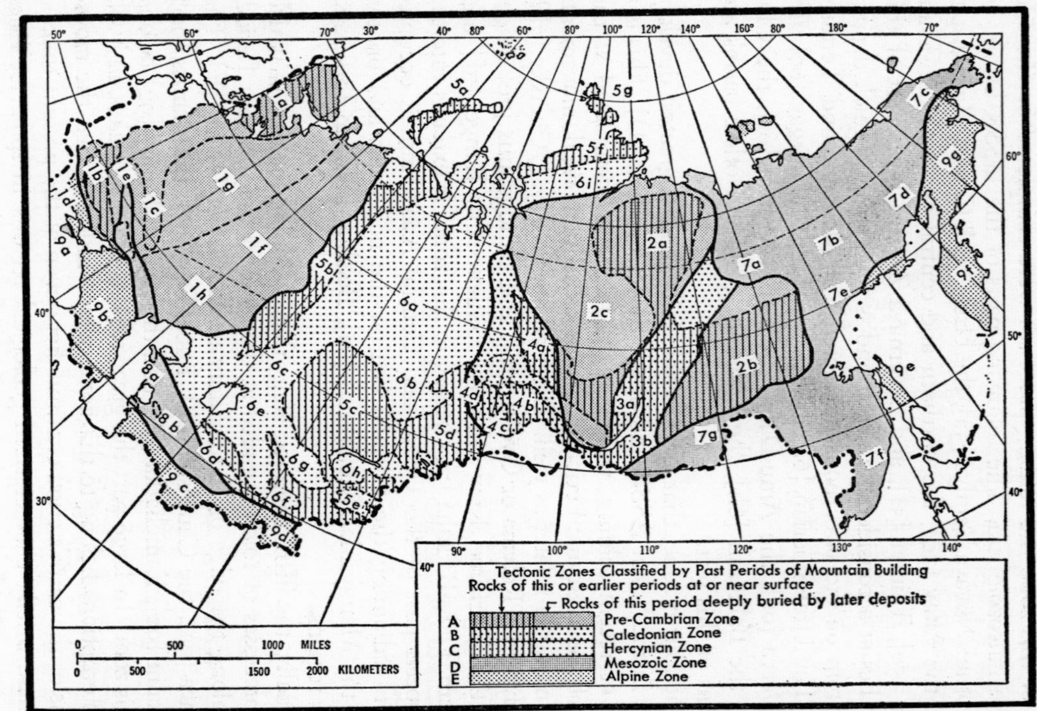

*FIG. 3. Tectonic Zones (adapted from *Great Soviet World Atlas*, Vol. I, Plate 90V)

KEY TO FIG. 3

A. Pre-Cambrian Zone
- 1. East European Platform
  - a. Baltic Shield
  - b. Ukrainian Shield
  - c. Voronezh Block
  - d. Black Sea Basin
  - e. North Ukrainian Basin
  - f. East Russian Basin
  - g. Moscow Basin
  - h. Caspian Basin
- 2. Siberian Platform
  - a. Anabar Shield
  - b. Aldan Shield
  - c. Tungus Basin

B. Caledonian Zone
- 3. Eastern Section
  - a. Pre-Baikalia
  - b. Western Trans-Baikalia
- 4. Western Section
  - a. Yenisey Range
  - b. Sayany (Mts.)
  - c. Minusinsk Basin
  - d. Kuznetsk Basin

C. Hercynian Zone
- 5. Uplands
  - a. Novaya Zemlya
  - b. Ural Mountains
  - c. Central Kazakhstan
  - d. Altay
  - e. Tyan-Shan
  - f. Taimyr Peninsula
  - g. Severnaya Zemlya
- 6. Lowlands
  - a. Ural-Siberian Depression
  - b. Irtysh Basin
  - c. Turgay Depression
  - d. Amu-Darya Basin
  - e. Syr-Darya Basin
  - f. Fergana Basin
  - g. Chu Basin
  - h. Balkhash Basin
  - i. Khatanga Depression

D. Mesozoic Zone
- 7. Siberia and Maritime Kray
  - a. Verkhoyansk Range
  - b. Chersky Range
  - c. Anadyr Range
  - d. Kolyma Range
  - e. Dzhugdzhur Range
  - f. Sikhote-Alin
  - g. Eastern Trans-Baikalia
- 8. Central Asia
  - a. Mangyshlak Mountains
  - b. Bolshoy Balkhan Range

E. Alpine Zone
- 9. Mountain Border
  - a. Crimea
  - b. Caucasus
  - c. Kopet-Dag
  - d. Pamirs
  - e. Sakhalin
  - f. Kamchatka
  - g. Koryak Range

These are the chief characteristics of the geological structure of the territory of the USSR.

Landforms

The surface of the USSR is characterized by a great variety of landforms, which are a result of the complicated interaction of the geological structure, of the geological history of the different parts of the Soviet Union, and of the nature of the action of external forces.

This variety of landforms exercises great influence on the character of the climate, on the distribution of the soil and vegetation cover, on the fauna, and also on economic development.

The plains of the USSR are physically suitable for the construction of railways and highways. The rivers which flow over such plains are in large part navigable; but on the other hand they possess smaller reserves of "white coal" than do mountain rivers.

The high mountain regions of the Caucasus, Tyan-Shan, the Pamirs, and the Altay are powerful condensers of atmospheric moisture. In mountain regions this moisture is turned into perpetual snows and glaciers, which feed numerous mountain rivers and form the source of their high water in summer. In the mountain regions the soil and vegetation cover varies considerably. Mountain pastures play a large role in the development of livestock raising. The numerous deposits of various metalliferous ores and other mineral resources are also associated chiefly with mountain regions.

The character of the topography in many cases influences the economic activity of man. The development of gullies, landslides, and karst phenomena sometimes causes damage to roads, bridges, and other economic installations.

Climate, soils, vegetation, and also fauna are closely related to the topography, as relief is one of the most important factors which determine the distribution of these natural phenomena on the earth's surface.

Within the limits of the Soviet Union there are considerable expanses lying below present sea level. The Caspian Lowland is among these [Fig. 4]. The levels of the saturated salt lakes located in this wide depression (Baskunchak and Elton) are 18 and 17.5 meters below sea level. The depression of the dry Lake Batyr (or

Karagie) descends to 130 meters below sea level; the Sarykamysh Depression, lying southwest of the Amu-Darya Delta, is 39 meters below sea level.

In the territory of the Soviet Union the greatest heights are in Central Asia in the Tyan-Shan and Pamir ranges. The highest point in the USSR is Stalin Peak [1 in Fig. 4],[12] 7,495 meters, at the junction of the Peter the First [3] and the Academy of Sciences [4] ranges; next comes Lenin Peak [2], 7,127 meters, in the Zaalay (Trans-Alay) Range [5].

Plains, Lowlands, and Uplands

Wide lowlands occupy more than half the surface of the USSR. Almost all the European part of the USSR is occupied by the East European Plain with an average elevation of 175 meters. In places this plain reaches elevations over 200–300 meters above sea level. These are the elevations which serve as watersheds for the principal rivers of the European part of the USSR. Such highlands are the Valday Hills, whose highest point is Kamennik (321 meters); the Volga Upland [Volga Heights] with the highest elevations rising to 400 meters between Syzran and Saratov; the Central Russian Upland, whose highest point is not over 310 meters; the Lithuanian-Belorussian Upland [6], with its highest point at 343 meters; and the Volyno-Podolsk Upland—the watershed between the Dnepr and the Dnestr. The Severnie Uvaly form the watershed between the Upper Volga system and the Severnaya (Northern) Dvina; they reach heights of 250 meters, but are only slightly dissected and are partially waterlogged.

On the surface of the East European Plain there are separate heights, so-called *gryady* [ridges], long and relatively narrow. In most cases these ridges are terminal moraines that were formed by the Quaternary icecap. One such is the Smolensk-Moscow Ridge, or *gryada,* which extends from Borisov by way of Smolensk across the central part of Moscow Oblast and then proceeds in the direction of Vologda. The part of this ridge which lies within the Dmitrov and Klin raions of Moscow Oblast is called the Klin-Dmitrov Ridge [7]. It reaches an elevation of 316 meters in Dmitrov Raion.

[12] [Other numbers in brackets in the following pages on relief also refer to locations on Fig. 4.]

Extensive areas within the East European Plain consist of lowlands and depressions, for the most part along the river courses. Examples are the Dnepr and the Oka-Don lowlands, and the Polesye, Meshchora, and Sukhona lowlands. The part of the East European Plain lying along the shores of the Black Sea and the Sea of Azov is called the Black Sea Lowland.

The East European Plain also has separate uplands, the remnants of ancient worn-down mountain ranges. Among these are the uplands and hills of the Kola-Karelia area, with the highest elevations up to 1,240 meters in the region of the Khibin Massif; also the Timan Ridge, stretching from Cheshskaya Bay to the sources of the Vychegda; and the Donets Ridge, located in the basin of the upper course of the Severny (Northern) Donets, whose highest point reaches 369 meters. The Zhiguli Hills [8] form the precipitous right [west] bank of the Volga from the mouth of the Usa [9] to the mouth of the Samara [10], with the highest point 371 meters above sea level, and 354 meters in local relief above the level of the Volga at the mouth of the Samara River. In origin the Zhiguli are faulted hills. In the Trans-Volga the Belebey Upland forms the watershed between the Belaya [11] and Kama rivers and reaches a height of 449 meters.

On the east the East European Plain is bounded by the Ural Mountains, and on the southeast, beyond the flat uplands of the Obshchy Syrt, it merges into the broad Caspian Lowland. On the south it is separated from the Caucasus by the Kuma-Manych Depression, and across the narrow Perekop Isthmus [12] between the Sea of Azov and the Black Sea it merges into the low-lying part of the Crimea; here at the edge of the sea it is bordered by the Crimean Mountains, which drop sharply to the sea.

Between the Urals on the west and the Yenisey on the east stretches the wide West Siberian Lowland. On the south it is limited by the fault line of the Kazakh Upland.[13]

In origin this very level lowland with an exceedingly slight slope to the shores of the Arctic Ocean is a depressed portion of the earth's surface, which was occupied later by a sea which subsequently vanished. On the divide between the Ob and the Irtysh the lowland is a vast waterlogged area, the so-called "Vasyuganye," no parts of which exceed 125 meters above sea level.

[13] The Kazakh Upland is usually designated in geographical literature and on maps as the "Kazakh Folded Country."

On the southwest the West Siberian Lowland is connected by the Turgay Lowland with the level expanses which lie north of the Aral Sea.

Southeast of the Aral Sea lies the Turanian Lowland, watered by the Amu-Darya, the Zeravshan, the Syr-Darya, the Chu, and the Ili rivers. To the south and east the Turanian Lowland extends to the slopes of the Kopet-Dag and the western Tyan-Shan; on the north and the northeast this lowland is limited by the Bedpak-Dala Plateau. The desert regions of the Kara-Kum and Kyzyl-Kum are located within the Turanian Lowland.

Between the Caspian and Aral seas lies the flat Ust-Urt Plateau, bordered on all sides by escarpments called *chinki*. The cliffs on the shores of the Aral Sea in places attain about 190 meters in local relief.

East of the Yenisey extends the Central Siberian Plateau. On the south the plateau is bordered by the Sayan ranges. To the east it extends beyond the Lena into the basins of the Aldan and Maya rivers and to the foothills of the Verkhoyansk Range; on the north it is limited by the line of the bench which runs approximately along 70° N. Lat. from the place where it cuts the Pyasina River in the region of Norilsk to the lower Olenek River. North of this line lies the North Siberian Lowland with an elevation of 50–70 meters above sea level, merging into the Byrranga Plateau on Taimyr Peninsula.

Along the upper Lena the watersheds reach absolute elevations of 600–700, and the river valleys 150–250 meters. In the basin of the Vilyuy River the plateau gradually merges into the wide Lena-Vilyuy Lowland, filled with numerous lakes and swamps.

In the basin of the Zeya and Bureya rivers lies the Zeya-Bureya Lowland, and along the lower course of the Amur, the Lower Amur Lowland.

Mountains, Mountain and Piedmont Plains

Along the southern and eastern borders of the USSR lie the Crimean Mountains, the Caucasus, the Kopet-Dag, the Pamir and Tyan-Shan system, the folded mountains and the massifs of the Altay, the Sayany system, the Trans-Baikal Ranges, and the system of ranges located in the Amur basin, including the Sikhote-Alin. In northeastern Siberia this belt of frontier mountains includes the broad folded highland composed of the Verkhoyansk, Chersky,

Kolyma, Anadyr, and Koryak ranges. The mountains of Kamchatka are also included in the frontier mountain zone.

On the border between Europe and Asia the Ural Range extends in a north-south direction for more than 2,500 km.

The Urals are divided into three parts:

1. The Northern (Severny) Ural begins at Konstantinov Kamen (elevation 454 meters, 68° 30′ N. Lat.), and ends at Isherim Peak (980 meters, 61° N. Lat.), not far from the sources of the Pechora. The highest point of the Northern Ural (and of all the Urals) is Narodnaya Mountain (1,885 meters, 65° N. Lat.).

2. The Middle (Sredny) Ural extends from Isherim Peak to Yurma Mountain (1,030 meters, 55° 25′ N. Lat.), located somewhat to the north of the parallel of Zlatoust [13]. Low passes are very characteristic of the Middle Ural. Thus, for example, the pass by which the Perm [Molotov]-Sverdlovsk Railway crosses the range reaches an elevation of only 410 meters.

3. The Southern (Yuzhny) Ural extends from Yurma to the middle course of the Ural River (52° N. Lat.) i.e., where the river changes its north-south direction to east-west. Yaman-Tau (mountain), 1,639 meters, is the highest point of the Southern Ural.

The Northern and Middle Urals consist basically of two parallel ranges; the divide is not the western or higher range, but the eastern one. The Southern Ural, however, consists of three main parallel ranges. The Ural-Tau Range [16], attaining 950 meters in elevation, and lying to the east, is the divide for the Southern Ural. West of it is located the Taganay [14] Range, with an elevation of over 1,200 meters.

The eastern slopes of the Urals are steep, and bear traces of the action of the sea; the western slopes are very gentle and deeply dissected by river valleys.

Joining the Northern Ural almost at a right angle and extending northwest to the shores of the Strait of Yugorsky Shar, is the low Pay-Khoy Range, averaging some 300 meters in elevation. Vaigach Island and Novaya Zemlya are its prolongation. To the south the low and flattened Mugodzhary Range forms a continuation of the Southern Ural.

In the southern part of the Crimean Peninsula there is a zone about 150 km. long and 50 km. wide, consisting of three parallel ranges in the west and two in the east. The Southern, or coastal, range is the highest (the highest elevation is Roman-Kosh [17], 1,543 meters) and bears the name Yaila, which is the Tatar word for "pasture." The summit of the Yaila has a relatively level surface, and a width of from 3 to 4 km. (on the Karabi-Yaila [18] up to 7 km.). In places the Yaila drops steeply to the sea, forming cliffs 300 to 600 meters in height.

Between the Black and Caspian seas lies the Caucasus. It can be divided into the following major parts: (1) the pre-Caucasus, comprising the Kuban-Azov Plain, the Stavropol Upland, and the foothill plains along the Kuma and Terek rivers; (2) the Main Caucasus Range, or Great Caucasus; (3) Dagestan; and (4) the Trans-Caucasus with its component parts—the Armenian Highlands, the Colchis Lowland, the Kura Lowland, and the Talysh Range with the adjoining Lenkoran Coastal Lowland [19].

In its central part, between the meridians of Elbrus and Kazbek [20], the Great Caucasus attains its highest elevations. Here the peaks of the Caucasus are sharply defined and covered with perpetual snow and glaciers: Elbrus (5,633 meters), Kazbek (5,043 meters), Dykh-Tau [21] (5,198 meters), Kashtan-Tau (5,145 meters), Shkhara (5,148 meters), and a number of other summits which rise to more than 4,500 meters. These are the cones of extinct volcanoes. The passes in this part of the Caucasus rise to elevations of 3,200–4,000 meters, and all except the Mamison Pass [22] [2,911 meters] are above the snow line.

East of the Caspian Sea, in Turkmenia, the Kopet-Dag Range extends along the boundary between the USSR and Iran in an easterly direction to the Tedzhen River. The main part of the range lies in Iran; only its borderland belongs to the USSR.

In Takzhikistan from the Zaalay (Trans-Alay) Range [5] on the north to the Hindu-Kush on the south extends the mountain land of the Pamirs, "the Roof of the World," with the highest mountain summits Stalin Peak [1] and Lenin Peak [2]. Topographically, the Pamirs may be divided into western and eastern sections. The western section is a highly dissected mountain country, the eastern is a high plateau.

East of the Amu-Darya the wide mountain country of the Tyan-Shan reaches east to Lake Zaisan. It lies south of the sources of the Ili River and north of the Zaalay Range in the Pamirs.

The highest summit of the Tyan-Shan is Khan-Tengri (6,995 meters).

Most of the summits of the ranges of the Tyan-Shan are flat; they are called *syrts* (pastures). Syrts are found especially in the ranges south of Issyk-Kul [lake] and in the Dzhungarian Ala-Tau.

Northeast of Lake Zaisan, extending to the sources of the Maly [Little] Abakan River [23] (a left tributary of the Yenisey), lies the mountain country of the Altay, which reaches across the frontier into the Mongolian People's Republic. The Altay, like the Tyan-Shan, is a system of ranges formed in ancient geological times. One-third of the total area of the Altay is occupied by level summits, the upper surfaces of separate massifs. In the Altay system, ranges of the Alpine type occupy one-tenth of the total area; the Katun [24], the North Chuya [25], and the South Chuya [26] *belki* (snowcapped mountains) are of this type. The Alpine topography of these ranges developed under the action of Quaternary glaciation and of present-day erosion, which, as a result of the weathering and abrasion of friable strata, gave the summits an Alpine form. Deep and steeply cut river valleys are characteristic of the Altay. For considerable distances the valleys of the Biya [37], the Katun [38], and the Bukhtarma [27] are of this sort, in which the rivers have carved deep gorges.

The Altay is divided into four parts:

The Southern Altay forms the divide between the Cherny (Black) Irtysh River, the basin of Lake Zaisan and the Bukhtarma River System. It extends from the mountain complex of the Tabyn-Bogdo-Ola [28] (which in Kiityn summit attains 4,500 meters) to the west as far as the Narym Range [29] on the left bank of the Narym River, and ends in the Kalbin Range [30] on the left bank of the Irtysh.

The Inner Altay (with Belukha, 4,620 meters, the highest summit) consists of the Katun Belki [24], the Chuya Belki [25, 26], and the Terektin Belki [31]. To the west the Kholzun Range [32], which attains 2,200–2,400 meters, is a continuation of the Katun Belki.

The Eastern Altay forms the divide between the Ob and Yenisey river systems. It begins at the Tabyn-Bogdo-Ola Massif [28] and extends as the Sailyugem Range [33] along the state frontier of the USSR to Chapchal (Shapshal) Pass [34] (3,177 meters). The Gorbu Range [35] belongs to the Eastern Altay.

The Mongolian Altay lies within the Mongolian People's Republic.

The snow line in the Southern Altay is at an elevation of 2,600–3,000 meters, and in the Eastern Altay at 3,000 meters.

From the sources of the Maly [Little] Abakan River [23] eastward as far as the western end of Lake Baikal extends a mountainous country called the Sayany, forming an arc convex to the north.

The highest point of the Vostochnie [Eastern] Sayany is Munku-Sardyk Peak, 3,491 meters in elevation. Mountain massifs with flat domelike summits predominate in the topography of the Sayany. Between the northern slopes of the Zapadnie [Western] Sayany on the south and southeast, the Kuznetsk Ala-Tau on the west, and the Vostochnie Sayany on the northeast lies the Minusinsk Basin, cut almost through the middle by the Yenisey.

Trans-Baikalia, located to the east of Lake Baikal, is a broad mountainous country in which lie the upper sources of the Amur and the Lena.

The mountain ranges of Trans-Baikalia have an easterly and northeasterly orientation, and are of fault origin. Of these, the Yablonovy Range stands out. It is, roughly speaking, the divide between the rivers of the Arctic and Pacific oceans. The highest points of the Yablonovy Range reach 1,610 meters. The highest point in all Trans-Baikalia is Sokhondo Peak, which reaches 2,508 meters and lies not far from the Mongolian frontier, at the sources of the Ingoda River.

To the northwest of the Yablonovy Range, in the basin of the upper Vitim, lies the rather wide Vitim Plateau, and in the basin of the Patom River, the Patom Upland.

The wide expanse located east of the middle course of the Lena River in large part is occupied by comparatively young mountain systems.

Formerly it was believed that from Trans-Baikalia to Bering Strait lay a mountain divide called the Stanovoy or Yablonovy. The Verkhoyansk Range was considered as a direct offshoot of the Stanovoy or Yablonovy Range. Actually no such long divide as the Stanovoy Range exists. Only in some places do parts of this chain (in Trans-Baikalia known under the name of Yablonovy) serve as a divide; and most of it belongs to the system of the upper Lena and is cut by its tributaries. The system of the Stanovoy Range proper, situated between the Aldan and Maya rivers, has been found to lie almost *in toto* within the basin of the Lena River.

Moreover, the Verkhoyansk Range ends approximately at the 62° parallel N. Lat. instead of joining the Stanovoy Range.

On the shores of the Sea of Okhotsk, between 142° and 152° E. Long. there are no clearly defined mountain ranges, and this region is an upland country occupied by spurs of the Chersky and Tas-Kystabyt ranges and the low coastal ranges of Tertiary age from Okhotsk to the western shores of the Gulf of Shelekhov. The Anadyr Range, the Yukagir Plateau, and the Kolyma Range are the divides between the basins of the Pacific and Arctic oceans. Southwest of the Oimyakon Plateau the Dzhugdzhur is the watershed range, on the western end of which abuts the system of the Stanovoy Range proper, located between the right tributaries of the Aldan and the left tributaries of the Amur.

In the basin of the middle and lower Amur lie the mountain systems of the Bureya Range, and between the Ussuri River and the shore of the Sea of Japan, the Sikhote-Alin. The Bureya Range begins at the headwaters of the Selemdzha River, where its elevation is highest (over 2,000 meters). Beyond the point where it is cut by the upper part of the Bureya River, the Bureya Range extends to the Amur, which cuts across it, forming a narrow gorge with sheer cliffs. Beyond the Manchurian frontier the Bureya Range is called the Maly [Little] Khingan. The Sikhote-Alin consists of a number of ranges, extending northeast from Vladivostok to the lower reaches of the Amur River.

Kamchatka is a country of young mountains. In surface structure it is clearly divided into two parallel ranges, extending in a northeasterly direction and separated by a lowland along the valley of the Kamchatka River. The Zapadny [Western] or Sredny [Middle] Range reaches its highest point in Belaya Sopka [Volcano] [39] (Ichinskaya), 3,840 meters in elevation. This peak is the only active volcano in the Zapadny Range. In the Eastern [Vostochny] Range and along the shore of the Bering Sea there are about twenty active volcanoes, of which the most important are Klyuchevskaya Sopka [40] on the lower Kamchatka River, with the highest elevation in all Kamchatka, 4,778 meters; Avachinskaya Sopka, 30 km. northeast of Petropavlovsk [41]; Kronotskaya Sopka [42] on the shore of Kronotsk Lake; and the northernmost peak, Shiveluch Sopka [43], 3,298 meters, located approximately at 56° 30′ N. Lat.

Such are the basic characteristics of the topography of the USSR, examined from the point of view of its major elements.

The contemporary topography of the Soviet Union is a product of the complex external and internal forces of the earth.

The Quaternary icecap, which embraced vast areas of the Soviet Union, had the most pronounced influence on the present topography. Almost all the northern zone of the European part of the USSR and considerable parts in the north of Western and Eastern Siberia were covered by glaciers.

The southern limit of the icecap reached the parallel of Zhitomir and Kiev, after which it veered sharply to the south, covering the Dnepr Lowland almost to the parallel of Dnepropetrovsk. Thence the edge of the glacier turned north to Bryansk and proceeded south of Kaluga to Belev, and then again turned sharply to the south, covering the Oka-Don Lowland approximately to the junction of the Don and Medveditsa rivers. Thence it proceeded sharply to the north along the western slopes of the Volga Heights to intersect the Volga east of the mouth of the Sura and Vetluga, to the confluence of the Vyatka and Kama, and thence to the Urals, cutting them at the parallel of 61° N. Lat.[14]

In Western Siberia the southern limit of the icecap has not yet been definitely determined; however, it proceeded approximately from the 61st parallel at the Urals to the junction of the Ob and the Irtysh and then almost in an east-west direction to the mouth of the Srednyaya [Middle] Tunguska; thence, bending around the Central Siberian Plateau along the Yenisey valley, it proceeded to the north onto the North Siberian Lowland. The northern part of Eastern Siberia was also occupied by the icecap, but its southern limit has not been established yet.

As a result of the action of the icecap upon the topography, terminal moraine ridges, lowlands called "forest areas" (*polesye*) filled with sandy-clayey material, and many lakes of glacial origin were formed. The icecap also left its mark on the surface deposits, which in different places attain different thickness. These glacial deposits are exceedingly diverse in their composition: they include glacial (boulder) clays, used for brick production, and glacial sands, which in some places provide excellent raw materials for glass-

[14] [Maps of glaciations show the southern limits as near the sources of the Vyatka and Kama rivers rather than at the confluence.]

making. The action of the glaciers is apparent in the accumulated boulders, pebble beds, rubble, and gravel, which furnish high-quality construction materials; on the other hand, they prevent the use of considerable areas of land for agriculture.

The mark of the icecap on the soil and vegetation cover is observable not only in the past, but also in the present period. The soil and vegetation cover to a large degree depends on the character of the glacial deposits, which form the parent material of the soil.

The territory of the Soviet Union which was not subjected to glaciation is characterized chiefly by an erosive form of topography. Here gullying and ravining, landslides, and karst phenomena are common. These are found also in moraine regions, but they are most typical of and predominant in the unglaciated regions beyond the moraines.

Gullying and ravining in the main are associated with the character of the surface strata, with their height, and with the character and intensity of the precipitation. The most favorable conditions for gullying and ravining are present in elevated sections covered with loess and other friable strata. Such conditions are found in the southern sector of the European part of the USSR, where there are extensive loess deposits, easily washed away by surface and ground waters. Destructive land use, the cutting down of timber stands, and the plowing of the slopes of gullies and ravines under Tsarism facilitated the formation of gullies.

The territory of the USSR covered by gullies and ravines, according to far from complete data, amounts to more than one million hectares. The development of gullying and ravining is harmful to agriculture: the rich chernozems are washed away by rapid streams. Typical regions of gullies and ravines are the Central Russian and Volyno-Podolsk uplands, the Volga Heights, and the Trans-Volga. In the USSR, in the interest of agriculture a planned struggle is being waged against gullying.

In regions composed of limestone and fissured strata, easily dissolved by ground water, karst phenomena are developed, which are detrimental to agriculture and the construction of railways, highways, and hydroelectric stations. Karst phenomena are most widespread in the region of the Onega-Dvina divide, the Ufa Plateau [45] in the Bashkir ASSR, the region of the Samara bend of the Volga [at Kuibyshev], Ivanovo and Perm [Molotov] oblasts, and in some other regions. Karst manifestations take the form of underground caverns, sinks, vanishing rivers, and so on. In this connection such phenomena as the settling of the ground, landslides, and lowering of the water table also occur. The regions where the Kuibyshev hydroelectric system is under construction are for a considerable area composed of limestones, dolomites, and other fissured strata, with which karst phenomena are associated. To avoid the consequences of karst manifestations in the construction of that system, appropriate scientific and practical measures are being taken.

Landslide phenomena depend upon the character of the stratification of the rocks and upon the erosive action of ground water.

Usually landslides are distributed along the shores of seas, rivers, lakes, gullies, and ravines, and are connected with definite hydrogeological conditions. Construction in such regions cannot be undertaken without considering the harmful effects of landslides. Frequently large creeping masses of earth completely destroy buildings, wharves, port installations, and bridges. The most typical regions of landslides are the right bank of the Volga, certain parts of the Central Russian, the Volga, and other uplands, and also the Black Sea coast in the neighborhood of Odessa and the south shore of the Crimea.

Thus, topography plays an important part in different branches of the national economy of the USSR.

SECTION 3. SEAS, RIVERS, AND LAKES

SEAS

The USSR is washed by three oceans, which form twelve seas, in whole or in part entering into the territorial waters of the Soviet Union. In addition, there are two seas within the USSR, which are of great significance for transport and industry. No other country in the world possesses water expanses so broad and so rich in fish and other marine animals as the Soviet Union.

Seas of the Arctic Ocean

On the north the seas of the Arctic Ocean wash the territory of the USSR: the Barents, White, Kara, Laptev, East Siberian, and Chukotsk seas [Fig. 5].

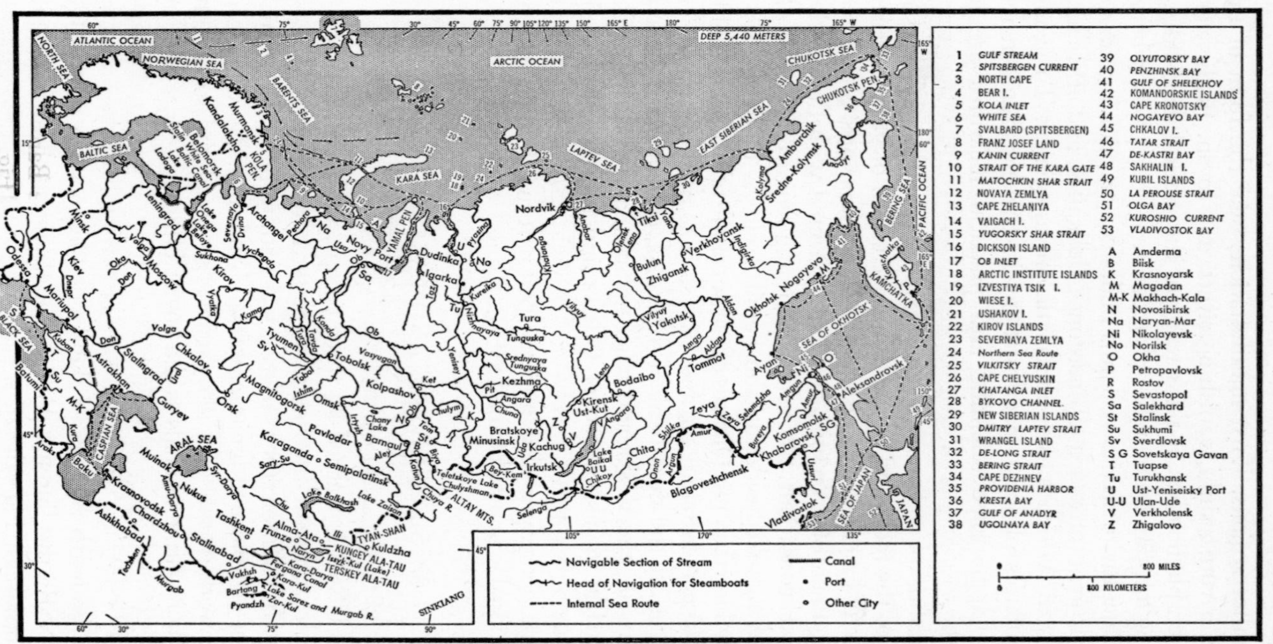

Fig. 5. Water Routes of the Asiatic Part of the USSR

The Arctic Ocean is connected with the Pacific Ocean by the narrow Bering Strait [33].[15] It is connected with the Atlantic Ocean through the Barents and Norwegian seas, and also through the Stalin White Sea to Baltic Canal.

The depths in the central part of the Arctic Ocean reach more than 4 thousand meters. According to the data of the I. Papanin expedition, the depth from the North Pole to 86° 40′ N. Lat. ranged from 4,300 to 4,400 meters. The greatest depth, 5,440 meters, is north of Wrangel Island, at 77° 45′ N. Lat. and 175° E. Long.

In the Arctic Ocean there is a cold current flowing from the northeast shore of Siberia westward to the eastern shores of Greenland and the northern part of the Atlantic Ocean. The existence of this current can be judged on the basis of the famous drift of the ship *Fram* and the remains of the ship *Jeannette*, and also the path followed by the drifting "North Pole" station and the drift of the icebreaker *Sedov*.

From the Atlantic Ocean the warm Gulf Stream [1] enters the Arctic Ocean, where it forms several branches.

Almost all the central part of the ocean is covered by ice, the thickness of which in the course of a winter reaches two to three meters. The ice, as it increases and fuses, forms ice fields. The piling up of ice floes forms the very uneven polar pack, which is difficult for ships to traverse, and extensive piling up of ice forms ice packs which usually attain four to five meters and in some cases seven to nine meters above the surface of the sea.

Exploration and study of the Arctic Ocean has been connected basically with two practical problems: the development of marine products and the discovery of the shortest sea route from the countries of Europe to Asia along the northern shores of Asia and North America. The latter problem, which was posed at the end of the sixteenth century, required more than three centuries for solution.

The Soviet expeditions, through the combined use of icebreakers and aviation, have made a number of remarkable voyages and have achieved great scientific progress; they have been and still are of decisive importance in exploring the Arctic basin. As a result of numerous heroic voyages and expeditions, the Barents, Kara, and Chukotsk seas have been investigated. In the Kara Sea, numerous islands have been dis-

[15] [Numbers in this section refer to locations on Fig. 5.]

covered, among them Kirov [22], Wiese [20], Ushakov [21], Izvestiya Tsik [19], and Arctic Institute [18].

The strictly scientific treatment of all work in the study of the ocean and the territories of the Far North guaranteed brilliant execution by Soviet aviators and scientists of the very important missions of the Party and the Government–missions of deep scientific and practical significance. Among these were the flight on July 20–22, 1936, by Chkalov, Baidukov, and Belyakov along the Stalin Route: Moscow to Franz Josef Land [8], Severnaya Zemlya [23], Kamchatka, and Chkalov Island [45]; the conquest of the North Pole by an expedition of four planes under the command of O. Yu. Schmidt and the setting up on the drifting ice on May 21, 1937, of the polar station "North Pole," with a staff consisting of I. Papanin, P. Shirshov, E. Krenkel, and E. Fedorov; the flights on June 18–20, 1937, of Heroes of the Soviet Union, Chkalov, Baidukov, and Belyakov, and on July 12–14, 1937, by Gromov, Yumashev, and Danilin, from Moscow to North America over the North Pole; and the heroic drift of the icebreaker *Sedov* from October 23, 1937, to January 13, 1940.

The Barents Sea extends from Spitsbergen [Svalbard, 7], Bear Island [4], and North Cape [3] eastward to Vaigach Island [14], the strait known as the Karskie Vorota [Kara Gate, 10], and Novaya Zemlya [12]. In the north, it reaches to Franz Josef Land [8], and in the southeast to the Strait of Yugorsky Shar [15] and Vaigach Island.

This sea is under the direct influence of the warm Gulf Stream. To the north of Norway and the Kola Peninsula the warm Atlantic Current divides into two diverging branches; the stronger branch proceeds to the north along the western shores of Spitsbergen, forming the so-called Spitsbergen Current [2], which curves around Spitsbergen on the north; the other branch, less strong, passing between Norway and Bear Island, is called the North Cape Current, and has considerable salinity (up to 3.45% and more). East of the 35th meridian this current in turn divides into three branches: one goes to the northeast, another to Novaya Zemlya, and the third (the so-called Kanin Current [9]) from Kola Inlet [5] to the southern island of Novaya Zemlya. Observations for the last fifteen years have indicated a noticeable rise in the temperature of the sea, which in turn has affected the migration of fish and other marine animals.

Thus, for example, the cod now moves in quantities large enough for commercial purposes as far as the northwestern shores of Novaya Zemlya (in the region of Cape Zhelaniya [13]). Likewise a connection has been discovered between the temperature of the warm Atlantic Current and the course of the weather in the North European part of the USSR. Over huge expanses of the northwestern and the central sections of the European part of the USSR, spring depends on the warm regime and also on the condition of the ice in this sea.

With respect to ice conditions, the Barents Sea is in a more favorable position than the other Soviet Arctic seas. In the western part, it is open to navigation throughout the year. Hence the ice-free shores of this sea in the region of the Murman Coast are very important for navigation.

The Barents Sea is rich in commercial fish, especially cod and bass.

The White Sea [6] penetrates into the continent and is connected with the Barents Sea by a rather wide and shallow strait, the so-called *gorlo* [throat] of the White Sea. This sea, which penetrates far into the continent, becomes very cold during the winter period, and is covered with ice, which remains solid for six to seven months each year on the average. It is relatively shallow. The greatest depths are in the region of Kandalaksha Bay, reaching 340 meters.

The White and Baltic seas are joined by the Stalin White Sea to Baltic Canal. This waterway shortens the route between the two seas by almost 4,000 km. In addition, it joins the White Sea with the internal basins of the Volga, the Kama, and other rivers by means of the Mariinsk system.

The White Sea to Baltic Canal is tremendously important in the freight movement of northern Karelia, which is rich in timber and mineral resources.

The Kara Sea extends from Novaya Zemlya and Vaigach Island on the west to Severnaya Zemlya [23] and Boris Vilkitsky Strait [25] on the east. It is connected with the Barents Sea by shallow and narrow straits—Matochkin Shar [11], the Karskie Vorota [10], and Yugorsky Shar [15].

This is one of the most difficult Artic seas to navigate because of ice conditions. The warm current seldom enters the Kara Sea, except for a weak branch which passes along the northern shores of Novaya Zemlya. On three sides the sea is surrounded by land, which has a marked effect on its climatic peculiarities, on the temperature of its waters, and on its ice conditions. On the other hand, the Ob and Yenisey, which bring to it considerable amounts of warm fresh water, also have a great influence on its climatic conditions.

In the western part of the sea, the currents move in a closed circle, counter-clockwise, caused by the prevailing northeasterly winds and the currents of the Ob and Yenisey. In the northeastern part of the sea, a current flows northeast from the estuary of the Yenisey to Cape Chelyuskin [26]. Farther to the north a cold current predominates, proceeding from the central part of the sea near Novaya Zemlya. These currents affect the movement of the ice.

The greatest depths are in the northwestern part of the sea, attaining 300 meters and more. Elsewhere the sea has depths reaching 200 meters, but almost half of the area is no more than 50 meters deep.

The ice of the Kara Sea is basically of local origin. It is mostly along the shores, forming the so-called land floe, of different widths in different parts of the sea. Thus, the width of the land floe on the western shores of the Yamal Peninsula is about 5 to 6 km., and on the northern shores of Ob Inlet, about 4 to 8 km. The land floe extends along the entire coast from Vaigach Island to the islands in the Yenisey estuary. The straits are frozen approximately from the first half of August until the middle of July.

The Laptev Sea extends from Severnaya Zemlya and Boris Vilkitsky Strait on the west to the New Siberian Islands [29] and Dmitry Laptev Strait [30] on the east; the East Siberian Sea, from the New Siberian Islands and Dmitry Laptev Strait on the west to Wrangel Island [31] on the east; the Chukotsk Sea, from Wrangel Island on the west to the region of Bering Strait on the east. These are shallow and brackish seas. Ice forms in them quickly, as a result of the relatively low salt content of their shallow waters and their proximity to continental expanses with a markedly continental climate. Ice forms at the end of September and from this time on it remains solid. The coastal land floe in these seas attains large dimensions. Thus, in the western part of the East Siberian Sea the land floe reaches a width of more than 300 km., and in the eastern part more than 130 km.

Winds and currents often cause the ice to recede from the shore, forming patches of open water, and these in turn freeze over, so that these seas are centers of formation and accumulation of ice in the Arctic Ocean.

The coasts of these seas throughout almost their entire extent are little indented and low-lying, with offshore shoals, with the result that conditions for navigation are unfavorable; only at the mouths of rivers are there natural harbors.

Seas of the Pacific Ocean

Bering Sea occupies the northernmost part of the Pacific Ocean. Its area is estimated at 2,268,000 square km., its average depth at 1,400 meters, and its greatest depth at 4,273 meters. It is connected with the Arctic Ocean by the relatively narrow and shallow Bering Strait, 90 km. wide at its narrowest point and 52 meters deep. It is separated from the Pacific Ocean by the arc of the Aleutian Islands with numerous straits between the islands. The deepest, southern part of the sea is over 3,000 meters deep. The Gulf of Anadyr [37] and Olyutorsky and Kresta [36] bays in the northern part have depths of 200 meters.

The climate of the sea is determined by its position between the very cold extremities of the Asiatic and North American continents. In summer the sea is warmed to an insignificant depth (as low as 100 meters) and is free from ice. In winter, however, the northern part is covered for several months by floating ice, the southern limit of which extends from Cape Kronotsky [43] toward the Pribilof Islands. South of this limit the sea never freezes, but along the shores of the USSR it is covered with ice in winter.

The currents in the Bering Sea have been little studied. It is thought that there is a circular current, in a counter-clockwise direction, which at the shores of the USSR goes from north to south and is marked by relatively low temperatures of the water. Between the Komandorskie [42] and neighboring islands, a weak branch of the warm Aleutian Current approaches Soviet shores, under the influence of which the southwestern part of the sea does not freeze.

The Bering Sea is rich in valuable marine animals. It is inhabited by Greenland and Japanese whales, walrus, hair seal, sea lion, and fur seal. In some places, sea otters are found. It is also rich in fish.

The Sea of Okhotsk lies between Kamchatka and the mainland; its area is estimated at 1,527,000 sq. km., its average depth at 840 meters, and its greatest depth at 3,500 meters. It is separated from the Pacific Ocean by the arc of the numerous Kuril Islands [49]; between the islands lie deep straits which connect the sea with the deeper parts of the ocean.

The depth of the sea differs in the northern and southern parts. In the northern part, in Penzhinsk Bay [40], the Gulf of Shelekhov [41], and Nogayevo Bay [44], depths of 200 meters predominate, while in the southern part the depths exceed 2,000–3,000 meters. The Okhotsk Sea, like the Bering Sea, is under the strong influence of the surrounding continental areas with a sharply continental climate, which is apparent in the long period during which the sea is frozen. However, because of the considerable depths and the winds, the southern part of the sea almost never freezes in winter. In summer the sea is free from ice throughout its entire extent. It is known for its prolonged and thick fogs. The surface current moves in a circle, in a counter-clockwise direction. The southern, deep part is under the marked influence of the warm Kamchatka Current. In the Okhotsk Sea, as in no other sea of the USSR, strong tidal movements occur, and in Penzhinsk Bay they attain amplitudes up to 11 meters.

The Okhotsk Sea is very favorable for navigation. It is rich in valuable marine animals. Here, Greenland and Japanese whales, walrus, sea lion, hair seal, and fur seal are found in considerable numbers, and occasionally the sea otter is encountered. The sea is rich in fish also. During the years of the Soviet regime, the transport significance of the Okhotsk Sea has grown considerably.

Of the Sea of Japan, only the small northern part belongs to the USSR. Its greatest depth is 3,743 meters, and it is connected with the Sea of Okhotsk by the narrow, very shallow Tatar Strait [46], 7.5 km. wide at its narrowest part. Except for a very narrow belt of continental shelf, almost the entire sea is characterized by depths of more than 1,000 meters, while in the central part the depths exceed 3,000 meters.

The northwest and north winds, which predominate in winter, blowing from the very cold parts of Eastern Siberia, cool the northern part of the sea with Soviet shores. The open sea in the southern part of Tatar Strait does not freeze, because of the warm Kuroshio Current [52], which branches into the Sea of Japan and washes the eastern shores of Japan. But even near the shores and in the straits along the coast of Sakhalin and along the shore from the mouth of the Amur to Vladivostok, the ice cover in winter is thin and has no appreciable effect on navigation.

Prolonged fogs are characteristic of the Sea of Japan. Fogs are also frequent on the coast of Sakhalin [48], Maritime Kray, and in Vladivostok Bay [53]. The very destructive winds of hurricane type, called typhoons, should also be noted.

The surface current in the Sea of Japan, in general, moves in a counter-clockwise circle. The shores of the USSR from Vladivostok to Olga Bay [51] are sharply indented, rich in bays, and highly favorable for navigation; but in the north, from Olga Bay to De-Kastri (De Castries) Bay [47], there is not a single bay, except Sovetskaya Gavan [SG].

Seas of the Atlantic Ocean

The shores of the southern part of the European portion of the USSR are washed by the Black Sea and the Sea of Azov; those of the northwest by the Baltic Sea (Gulf of Finland) [Fig. 6].

The Black Sea is one of the most important water basins washing the shores of the USSR. This is an inland sea with a maximum depth of 2,243 meters. Egress is through a number of seas and very narrow straits—through the Bosporus into the Sea of Marmara, then through the Dardanelles into the Aegean, and out of the Mediterranean into the Atlantic Ocean by way of Gibraltar, and into the Red Sea by way of the Suez Canal.

The greater part of the Black Sea is deep. The shores are highly diverse in form. From the Rumanian frontier approximately to Yevpatoriya [106 in Fig. 6] on the Crimean Peninsula, shores of estuary type predominate. The estuaries, which are the flooded lower courses of rivers, are favorable for navigation, especially at the mouths of the large rivers. In the south of the Crimea, where mountains approach close to the shore, small and deep bays are very common, as in the Yevpatoriya-Yalta [102] region.

In the Black Sea, two layers of water are observed, entirely different in origin and composition: the upper, with an average depth of approximately 200 meters, and the lower, to the sea bottom. The upper layer of

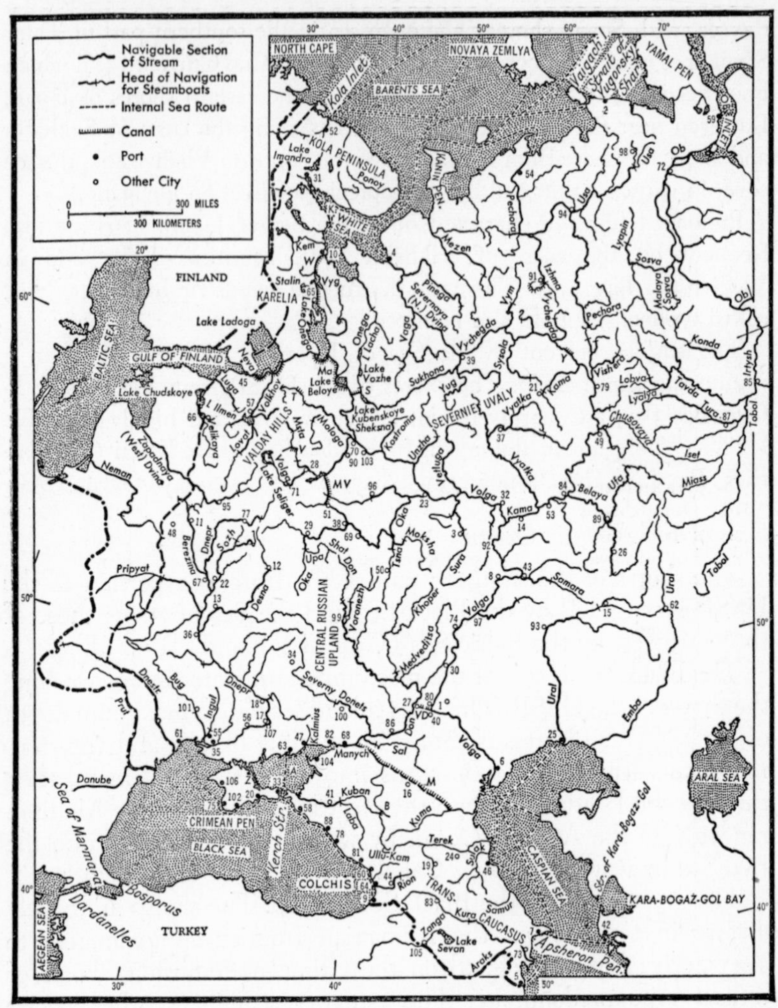

Fig. 6. Water Routes of the European Part of the USSR

KEY TO FIG. 6

1. Akhtuba
2. Amderma
3. Alatyr
4. Archangel
5. Astara
6. Astrakhan
7. Baku
8. Batraki
9. Batumi
10. Belomorsk
11. Borisov
12. Bryansk
13. Chernigov
14 Chistopol
15. Chkalov
16. Divnoye
17. Dneproges
18. Dnepropetrovsk
19. Dzaudzhikau
20. Feodosiya
21. Fosforitnaya
22. Gomel
23. Gorky
24. Grozny
25. Guryev
26. Ishimbay
27. Kalach
28. Kalinin
29. Kaluga
30. Kamyshin
31. Kandalaksha
32. Kazan
33. Kerch
34. Kharkov
35. Kherson
36. Kiev
37. Kirov
38. Kolomna
39. Kotlas
40. Krasnoarmeisk
41. Krasnodar
42. Krasnovodsk
43. Kuibyshev
44. Kutaisi
45. Leningrad
46. Makhach-Kala
47. Mariupol
48. Minsk
49. Molotov
50. Morshansk
51. Moscow
52. Murmansk
53. Naberezhnie Chelny
54. Naryan-Mar
55. Nikolayev
56. Nikopol
57. Novgorod
58. Novorossiisk
59. Novy Port
60. Ochemchiri
61. Odessa
62. Orsk
63. Osipenko
64. Poti
65. Povenets
66. Pskov
67. Rechitsa
68. Rostov
69. Ryazan
70. Rybinsk
71. Rzhev
72. Salekhard
73. Salyany
74. Saratov
75. Sevastopol
77. Smolensk
78. Sochi
79. Solikamsk
80. Stalingrad
81. Sukhumi
82. Taganrog
83. Tbilisi
84. Tikhie Gory
85. Tobolsk
86. Tsimlyanskaya
87. Tyumen
88. Tuapse
89. Ufa
90. Uglich
91. Ukhta
92. Ulyanovsk
93. Uralsk
94. Ust-Usa
95. Vitebsk
96. Vladimir
97. Volsk
98. Vorkuta
99. Voronezh
100. Voroshilovgrad
101. Voznesesnk
102. Yalta
103. Yaroslavl
104. Yeisk
105. Yerevan
106. Yevpatoriya
107. Zaporozhye

A *Sea of Azov*
B *Proposed Nevinnomysky Canal*
K *Kandalaksha Bay*
M *Manych Canal*
Ma *Mariinsk Canal*
MV *Moscow-Volga Canal*
S *Severnaya (N.) Dvina Canal*
T *Tikhvin Canal*
V *Vyshnevolotsk Canal*
VD *Projected Volga-Don Canal*
W *White Sea to Baltic Canal*
Y *Yekaterina Canal*
Z *Sivash Lagoon and Tongue of Arabat*

water is characterized by constant aeration, by the presence of oxygen, and by the development of organic life. The lower layer consists of denser and more saline water from the Mediterranean Sea, which enters the deep basin of the Black Sea with the bottom currents through the Dardanelles and the Bosporus, and is almost devoid of living organisms because of the presence of hydrogen sulphide.

In the relatively shallow part of the sea (between the Danube and the western shore of the Crimea) the temperature of the water in January and February reaches 1.0° to 1.1° below zero Centigrade, and ice forms regularly every year, but attains an insignificant thickness and often is broken up by the action of the wind.

The Black Sea is rich in seaweed, from which iodine is obtained. With respect to transport, the Black Sea occupies first place among the seas which wash the shores of the USSR. Navigation takes place throughout the year. More than ten railroads reach the Black Sea and the Sea of Azov, connecting the largest port cities—Odessa [61], Nikolayev [55], Sevastopol [75], Mariupol [47], Rostov-on-the-Don [68], Novorossiisk [58], and Batumi [9]—with the main economic regions of the country. Through the Black Sea, the Soviet Union maintains trade relations with the capitalist countries of Asia and Europe.

The Sea of Azov [A], connected with the Black Sea by the shallow and narrow Kerch Strait, is a slightly saline body of water, and its greatest depth does not exceed 15 meters. The shores are low, alluvial, and in part dissected by estuaries. There are many spits, of which the longest, the Tongue of Arabat (in the west), divides the shallow Sivash Lagoon [Z] from the sea.

The Sea of Azov is rich in valuable commercial fish—herring, anchovy, pike-perch, bream, and others.

The Baltic Sea washes the shores of our country through the Gulf of Finland. In spite of the small shore line, reaching [in 1939] from the Estonian frontier to the Finnish border, the significance of the Baltic Sea for the USSR is very great. Through this sea the USSR maintains trade connections with the capitalist states of Western Europe and America (by way of the Atlantic Ocean).

Inland Seas of the USSR

The Caspian and Aral seas are the inland seas of the USSR.

Essentially these are not seas, but lakes, the former the largest in the world. They may be called seas because of their origin.

The Caspian Sea is the largest "lake-sea" in the world. Its area is 424,300 sq. km., and its greatest depth is 975 meters.[16] Its extent from north to south is more than 1,200 km., its greatest width is about 560 km., and its narrowest point, between the Apsheron Peninsula and the eastern shore, is slightly more than 200 km. In area, the Caspian is about 6½ times larger than the Aral Sea and 13 times larger than Lake Baikal. A great diversity of natural conditions is associated with its great extent from north to south: in the north, the sea is covered with ice for an average of about two to three months, while in the south it never freezes. On the southern shores evergreen trees grow. As with all lakes which have no outlets, the level of the Caspian undergoes very marked periodic fluctuations. At present, its level is 26 meters below the level of the Black Sea.[17]

From the surface of the Caspian a layer of water over one meter deep evaporates each year on the average. This loss is compensated for by the inflow of water from the rivers which empty into the sea—the Volga, the Emba, the Kuma, the Terek, and others. (The Volga raises the level of the sea an average of 61 centimeters per year, while atmospheric precipitation raises it about 20 centimeters.) The greatest evaporation in the course of the whole year occurs in Kara-Bogaz-Gol Bay, because of the extreme dryness of the climate of the expanses of land which surround it, and hence the level of this unique part of the Caspian on the average is always somewhat lower than that of any other part; it is estimated at about 26.4 meters below sea level. This circumstance is one of the reasons for the constant flow of water from the sea into Kara-Bogaz-Gol Bay through the narrow strait of the same name.

The Caspian is divided into three parts: northern, middle, and southern. The northern Caspian is shallow. The greater part has a depth of less than 100 meters. The low alluvial shores, composed in large part of sand, are difficult for seagoing vessels to approach. Thus, the 12-foot Astrakhan roadstead [6] is located 60 km. from

[16] [Figures given in original corrected to agree with Table 3, p. 44.]

[17] [Since the appearance of the original Russian text, the level of the Caspian has sunk even lower.]

the mouth of the Volga. The average depth of the Caspian in this part is 6 meters. Here the Caspian abounds in shallows and banks, which present considerable obstacles to free navigation by vessels. The middle Caspian is already significantly deeper than the northern part (average depth, 175 meters). The southern Caspian, which is the deepest (average depth, 325 meters), is the part which never freezes; it has sandy, alluvial, little dissected shores.

The average salinity is 12 to 15%, but it varies greatly in different parts of the sea. The least salinity is observed in the northern part; in the middle and southern parts, the salinity of the water increases sharply, reaching its greatest intensity at the east, especially in Kara-Bogaz-Gol Bay. The salinity of the latter is 20%. Because of its geographical position, and the salinity of its waters, which contain Glauber's salt, sodium chloride, and calcium sulphate, Kara-Bogaz-Gol Bay (area 18,346 sq. km., average depth about 10 meters) in geographic literature deservedly bears the name of "the salt bag" of the Caspian.

The Caspian is one of the richest fishing basins, not only in the USSR, but in the whole world. Its waters are inhabited by such valuable fish as various kinds of sturgeon (beluga, *sevryuga, osyotr*), and there are herring, pike-perch, Caspian roach, and others in large numbers.

Through the Caspian Sea transport connections are maintained with the republics of Central Asia and the Trans-Caucasus, and also between the USSR and Iran. The richest oil regions of the Soviet Union border the sea.

The level of the Aral Sea, like that of the Caspian, is subject to marked fluctuation, and on the average is now accepted as 52 meters above sea level. The depth of this sea is not great. Depths of 10 to 20 meters predominate. The greatest depths (to 68 meters) lie along the steep western shore. On the average a layer of water over one meter deep evaporates each year from the surface of the Aral Sea. The loss is compensated for by the inflow from the Amu-Darya and the Syr-Darya [Fig. 5], and also by precipitation, which on the Aral Sea averages 150 millimeters. The Aral Sea freezes chiefly in the northeastern part.

The Aral Sea is rich in commercial fish of various species (a small sturgeon named *ship*, carp, and others).

The seas and oceans which wash the shores of the Soviet Union are assuming an increasingly important role in socialist construction, in the development of fishing and fur trading, and especially in sea and ocean transport. Providing the sea and ocean fleet with all sorts of modern vessels, which is one of the most important tasks of the Third Five-Year Plan, will make possible an even greater increase in the economic significance of its seas in the development of the productive forces of the USSR.

RIVERS

The special features of the hydrographic network of the USSR are determined by the climate, the geological structure, the topography, and the extent of the territory of the Soviet Union.

The interaction of these basic factors differs in character in the various parts of the country, and hence the rivers and lakes in the separate parts of the country differ sharply in character one from another.

The USSR possesses the greatest river systems in the world, which fact is explained first of all by the vast extent of its territory and its compactness. The Ob, the Yenisey, the Lena, the Amur, and the Volga in length and in the area of their basins are among the greatest rivers in the world, being surpassed only by the Mississippi-Missouri river system, the Amazon, the Nile, the Yangtze, and the Congo [Table 2].[18] The rivers of the USSR, except in desert and arid regions, are distinguished also by their volume of water; the Siberian rivers are especially large in volume.

The sources of most of the rivers of the USSR are in plains. The rivers are fed by rain, lake, swamp, spring, and ground water, and also by melting snow. In the central and northern sections of the USSR about a third of the annual precipitation falls in the form of snow. As a result, in spring some rivers spread out for tens of kilometers, widening their valleys and transporting as sediment great masses of eroded material.

Thus, at the confluence of the Mologa and the Sheksna with the Volga [Fig. 6] a surface of slow-moving water from 10 to 13 km. in

[18] [As indicated by Table 2, the Mississippi-Missouri, Nile-Kagera, Amazon, Yangtze, Plata-Parana, and Congo exceed any of these rivers in length and the Amazon, Congo, Mississippi, Plata, and Nile in area drained.]

TABLE 2. LENGTH AND AREA OF THE BASINS OF THE CHIEF RIVERS OF THE USSR AND OF FOREIGN COUNTRIES [19]

[See Fig. 5]

RIVERS	LENGTH (km.)	AREA OF BASIN (in 1,000 sq. km.)
In USSR		
Lena	4,264	2,418
Yenisey and Bey-Kem	3,807	2,707
Amur, Shilka, and Onon	4,354	1,843
Ob and Katun	4,016	2,425
Volga	3,688	1,380
Amu-Darya	2,540	277
Syr-Darya	2,860	219
Kolyma	2,149	644
Ural	2,534	220
Dnepr	2,285	503
Pechora	1,789	327
Severnaya (Northern) Dvina and Sukhona	1,293	411
Don	1,967	422
Kuban and Ullu-Kam	941	51
Foreign		
Mississippi-Missouri	6,793	3,248
Amazon	5,500	7,050
Nile and Kagera	6,500	2,800
Yangtze	5,200	1,175
Congo	4,600	3,690
La Plata and Parana	4,700	3,104
Mackenzie and Peace River	4,046	1,766
Niger	4,160	2,092

width is formed in spring. The Volga at the mouth of the Kama spreads out to 20 km. and more; above Astrakhan [6], it may overflow up to 50 km. and more, and at Sarepta [now Krasnoarmeisk, 40] up to 30 km.;

[19] The data on the length and area of the basins of the chief rivers of the USSR were taken from the explanatory text *Great Soviet World Atlas, Gazetteer of Geographic Names in Vol. I,* which is being prepared for publication by the scientific editing and cartographic section of the Chief Administration of Geodesy and Cartography under the Council of People's Commissars of USSR. [Figures corrected by reference to the source table on pp. 135–138 of the cited work, which was published in 1940. Figures for foreign rivers with lengths of more than 3,000 km. and basins of more than 1 million sq. km. are taken from this source also.]

above Ulyanovsk [92] the Volga in some years overflows up to 20 km. The greatest Siberian rivers—the Ob, the Yenisey, and the Lena—overflow as much as this, or more.

Some rivers of the USSR do not have spring floods in spite of the fact that they are fed by the melting of a considerable snow cover. The Neva, which is distinguished by its volume, is one such river. The floods at Leningrad are caused by strong west winds, which drive the water from the Gulf of Finland.

In spring a merging takes place of the basins of several rivers which flow in opposite directions. At the time of the spring floods the waters of the Don and the Shat unite. The sources of the Volga, the Zapadnaya (Western) Dvina, and the Dnepr are virtually united [Fig. 6]. The Zapadnaya Dvina and the Volga have their source in the lakes of the same waterlogged area. The Dnepr and the Zapadnaya Dvina are joined through a system of lakes which also lie in the same waterlogged divide. Within the Urals the sources of the Kama, the Pechora, and the left tributaries of the Ob converge. The right tributaries of the upper Ob lie very near the system of the upper Yenisey, and are even practically united with this system, through a waterlogged divide, along the river Ket. The most important rivers of the European part of the USSR have their source in one center, radiating out from it in several directions. The region of the Valday Hills, the Severnie Uvaly, and the Central Russian Upland are such centers [Fig. 6]. In the Asiatic part of the USSR all the most important rivers, with the exception of the Amur, flow parallel to one another, from south to north.

For the greater part of their courses, the rivers of the USSR are slow and winding. Often the length of the rivers with all their windings exceeds the direct distance from source to mouth by two or three times or more, which is explained by the character of the topography and of the geological structure of the country.

The sources and upper parts of many rivers which flow through expanses of plains lie close together. This peculiarity of the rivers offers great possibilities of connecting them by canals. The most important canals [Fig. 6] are the Moscow-Volga [MV], White Sea to Baltic [W], Mariinsk [Ma], Vyshnevolotsk [V], Tikhvin [T], and other water systems, and the projected Volga-Don [VD] and other canals.

The peculiarities of the geographical distribution of the rivers and lakes of the USSR offer favorable conditions for connecting by canals the separate river systems and lakes and, in this fashion, creating a single water network for transportation in the Soviet Union.

The majority of the greatest rivers form deltas which are clearly marked in the cases of the Neva, the Severnaya (Northern) Dvina, the Pechora, the Volga, the Lena, the Indigirka, the Kolyma, and the Amur. The rivers which flow into the Black Sea end in estuaries. The flooded lower ends of the Ob and the Yenisey, which empty into the Arctic Ocean through broad mouths invaded by the sea, are called inlets. At low water, the rivers grow considerably shallower than at flood, thus forming shoals and sandbanks. The plains rivers of the USSR do not have significant waterfalls. Several great rivers of the Soviet Union are interrupted by rapids. The Angara and the Srednyaya (Middle) Tunguska, which empty into the Yenisey, are among the rivers with rapids [Fig. 5]. The famous Dnepr rapids are now submerged because of the construction of a mighty dam.

The chief rivers of Siberia [Fig. 5] are the Ob and the Irtysh; the Yenisey with its tributaries, the Verkhnyaya (Upper) Tunguska (Angara), the Srednyaya Tunguska, and the Nizhnyaya (Lower) Tunguska; the Lena with its tributaries, the Aldan and the Vilyuy; the Indigirka; and the Kolyma. The chief natural peculiarity of the rivers of Siberia is their great volume of water. Thus, the Lena River in the width and depth of its stream is one of the most remarkable rivers of the world: at Verkholensk [V in Fig. 5] it has a width of up to 1 km.; at Yakutsk, over 10 km.; at Zhigansk, 10–15 km.; at Bulun, up to 2.5 km.; and closer to its mouth, about 1.5 km. In some places the depths attain 20–25 meters (at Bulun), more than one and one-half times the greatest depth of the Sea of Azov. The delta of the Lena is cut by a number of channels, of which the chief is the Bykovo Channel [28], more than 10 km. wide.

The great volume of water in the Siberian rivers is explained by the fact that almost all the [winter] precipitation enters the rivers in the form of melted snow as a result of rapid and continuous thawing in spring. On the other hand, permanent ground frost impedes the absorption of precipitation into the ground, and increases its run-off into the rivers.

Another very important natural peculiarity of the rivers of Siberia is the fact that they carry from the south a great quantity of heat, and as a result the northern frontiers of the soil and vegetation zones are pushed considerably northward where they cross the rivers.

The Amur River belongs to the basin of the Pacific Ocean and differs from the other rivers of Siberia in a number of essential respects. The floods of the Amur occur in summer during the period of maximum precipitation. It has almost no spring floods, because of the insignificant snow cover in its basin. The summer floods reach large proportions, especially in years when the maximum of the summer rains coincides with the intensive melting of snow in the mountains where many of the tributaries of the Amur have their source.

The chief rivers of Central Asia [Fig. 5]—the Amu-Darya, the Syr-Darya, the Chu, the Ili, the Tedzhen, and the Murgab—have their sources in the mountains and are fed by the melting of glaciers and snows. These rivers flood twice a year—in spring and summer, during the periods of intensive melting of the snows and glaciers. After debouching from the mountains onto the plains, the rivers grow considerably shallower, in part as a result of much evaporation and absorption into the soil, and in part as a consequence of the diversion of their waters for irrigation purposes.

The Amu-Darya is formed by the confluence of two rivers—the Pyandzh and the Vakhsh. The Naryn River begins in the glaciers of the Terskey Ala-Tau, and after merging with the Kara-Darya it is called the Syr-Darya. Both the Amu-Darya and the Syr-Darya empty into the Aral Sea and form deltas of considerable proportions.

The chief rivers of the Caucasus [Fig. 6]—the Kuban, the Terek, the Kuma, the Rion, the Kura, and the Araks—flood twice a year, in spring and summer. The floods in the spring are caused by the melting of snow on the [lower] slopes of the mountains and by rainfall; in summer, chiefly by the melting of glaciers and snow in the mountains. The summer floods reach large proportions, particularly when the thawing of the glaciers coincides with the falling of rain in the mountains. The rivers at these times carry vast quantities of eroded material. The erosive action of the rivers is enormous. To combat it, protective dikes are constructed in some cases; the length of dikes along the Terek amounts to about 450 km.

In winter the rivers of the USSR are icebound for a rather long time. The rivers of Eastern Siberia freeze in the upper sections for six months, from the latter half of October to April, in their central sections for seven to eight months, and in the lower up to nine months. The Amur freezes for six to seven months. The rivers in the north of the European part of the USSR on the average also freeze for six to seven months; the rivers in the central belt of the European part of USSR, for five to six months; and those of the southern part, for three to four months. The rivers of Central Asia on the average freeze for two to four months, with the exception of the Tedzhen and the Murgab, which do not freeze at all. The rivers of the Trans-Caucasus—the Rion, the Kura, and the Araks—also do not freeze.

There is no country in the world so rich in water resources as the USSR. The length of the rivers of the Soviet Union which can serve as excellent waterways for communication and rafting amounts to 350,000 km. The total length of the internal navigable waterways at the end of the Third Five-Year Plan amounted to 115,000 km. In this respect the capitalist countries are far behind the USSR. Thus, the United States has in all 45,000 km. of water routes; France, 17,000; Germany, 14,000; and Italy, 6,000. But in spite of the considerable growth in the utilization of rivers for shipping and timber-floating, the USSR is very far from using its waterways sufficiently. There are still many parts of rivers and even whole river systems that could be used for navigation and rafting.

The Soviet Union is extraordinarily rich in hydraulic energy. Many of the rivers have powerful currents, for example, the Yenisey, the Volga, and the Angara. In wealth of hydraulic energy, the USSR takes first place in the world. According to incomplete and only approximate data, the power of the rivers of the USSR amounts to 280 million kw. of potential hydraulic energy, while the United States has 82.2 million, France, 8.9 million, and Germany, 3.7 million.

The USSR also possesses very rich water resources for irrigation. The arid regions of the country and the regions with insufficient moisture require the irrigation of millions of hectares of land. At the same time, the water resources of the USSR are not sufficiently used for irrigation. Thus, the rivers of Central Asia and the Tran-Caucasus could irrigate an area two and even three times as great as that now irrigated. The Volga-Akhtuba flood plain [1 in Fig. 6] (Stalingrad Oblast and Kalmyk ASSR) offers possibilities for irrigating more than 600,000 hectares.

The greatest problem of water use in the USSR is the Greater Volga—which at one stroke provides the means of creating powerful hydroelectric stations, of irrigating the Trans-Volga, and of increasing navigation. Already two of the greatest installations in the world are being built—two hydroelectric stations in the Kuibyshev area [43] with a total capacity of 3.4 million kw.—which will at the same time solve the problem of irrigating the dry lands of the Trans-Volga and of navigation on the Volga and the Kama.[20]

Another huge problem of water use is the reconstruction of the Dnepr. The utilization of the waters of the Dnepr is not exhausted by the existing construction of the Dneproges [17]. The problem of the Dnepr includes many large-scale works, the most important of which are the building of new hydroelectric stations, the connection of the Dnepr with the Baltic Sea by way of the Zapadnaya (Western) Dvina and the Lovat, and the irrigation of the lands of the lower Dnepr for valuable industrial crops. The Angara-Yenisey problem, the solution of which can give up to 10 million kw. of energy, is of great interest.

The regulation of the Don has great significance for the national economy. Here the first tasks are the construction of the Volga-Don Canal, and the transformation of the Don into a navigable river by building locks in the stretch from the mouth to Voronezh [99] and farther up along its course.

LAKES

The USSR is rich in lakes, especially the Northwest and the West of the European part, where there are several tens of thousands of large and small fresh-water lakes. In these regions are located the large lakes Ladoga and Onega [Fig. 6 and Table 3]. Farther to the south lies the "lake plain" with a multitude of long, shallow, winding lakes, some of them overgrown with vegetation,

[20] [Available Soviet literature does not indicate that construction of this project had begun by 1948.]

* TABLE 3. PRINCIPAL LAKES OF THE SOVIET UNION [21]

(See Figs. 5 and 6)

	AREA (1,000 sq. km.)	MAXIMUM DEPTH (meters)
Caspian Sea	424.3	975
Aral Sea	63.8	68
Baikal	31.5	1,741
Ladoga	18.4	230
Balkhash	17.3	26
Onega	9.9	120
Taimyr	7.0–6.0	—
Issyk-Kul	6.2	702
Khanka	4.4	10
Chudskoye and Pskov	3.6	15
Chany	2.6	10
Ala-Kul	2.3	47
Ilmen	2.2–1.1	10
Zaisan	1.8	8
Sevan	1.4	99
Tengiz	1.2	7
Beloye	1.2	20
Topozero	0.9	56
Selety-Tengiz	0.9	3
Pyasino	0.8	10
Imandra	0.8	67
Segozero	0.8	97
Kulundinskoye	0.6	4
Vygozero	0.5	12
Umbozero	0.5	77
Vozhe	0.44	4
Kara-Kul	0.36	236
Teletskoye	0.23	325
Elton	0.15	1

others in the process of being overgrown as a result of swamp formation. In the lake plain lie a number of large lakes—Pskov [66], Chudskoye, Seliger, Ilmen, Beloye, Vozhe, Kubenskoye, and Lacha. The lakes are sources of many rivers. Some of the lakes are

[21] From *Great Soviet World Atlas, Gazetteer of Geographic Names in Vol. I,* Moscow, 1940, p. 134.

at the same time sources and mouths of rivers—for example, Lakes Onega, Ladoga, Ilmen, and Beloye. The greatest depth of Lake Onega is 124 meters; of Ladoga, 223 meters; and of Imandra, 67 meters.[22]

Many of the lakes are located in the mountains. In the Armenian Highlands of the Trans-Caucasus at an elevation of 1,916 meters is located Lake Sevan (Gokcha) with a depth of 99 meters. The Zanga River flows out of this lake, and empties into the Araks.

In the Pamirs [Fig. 5] lie the high mountain lakes Kara-Kul and Zor-Kul, the source of the Amu-Darya. Remarkable for its recent formation is Sarez Lake in the valley of the Bartang, or Murgab, River. It resulted from the damming of the Bartang valley by a landslide 800 meters high. From the moment of its formation (1911) the lake has been constantly increasing in size: in 1915 the depth was approximately 350 meters; by 1934 it had reached 500 meters, and the length of the lake was 60 km.

The high brackish lake Issyk-Kul is in the mountains of the western Tyan-Shan. On the north and south the lake is bordered by the Kungey Ala-Tau and the Terskey Ala-Tau. The surface of the lake lies at an elevation of 1,583 meters; its greatest depth is 702 meters. At 5 km. from the western end of the lake the Chu River takes its course. Hot springs issue from the slopes of the Terskey Ala-Tau, which in part feed the lake. From this comes the Kirgiz name Issyk-Kul ("hot lake").

The picturesque fresh Teletskoye Lake is in the Altay Mountains. The Biya River flows from it, while higher up the Chulyshman River flows into it. The lake lies at an elevation of about 450 meters; its greatest depth is 325 meters. Baikal—the deepest lake not only in the USSR, but also in the whole world—is outstanding among the mountain lakes. Its greatest depth is 1,741 meters, and the elevation of its surface is 456 meters. Baikal freezes in the beginning of January, and until the middle of May it is covered with a sheet of ice more than one meter thick.

The USSR takes first place in the world in number of mineral lakes and in wealth of different mineral salts.

The mineral lakes of the Soviet Union extend in a belt from Bessa-

[22] [The Gazetteer of the Great Soviet World Atlas referred to above gives the depth of Onega as 120 meters, of Ladoga as 230 meters.]

rabia on the west to the Pacific Ocean on the east, lying in the steppes of the Azov and Black Sea coast, the Caspian Lowland, the semideserts and deserts of Kazakhstan and Central Asia, and the steppes of Western Siberia and Trans-Baikalia. In the expanses of the Central Asiatic deserts the lake belt is represented by tens of thousands of lakes, beginning with the "lake-seas," such as the Caspian Sea, the Aral Sea, Balkhash, and ending with innumerable small temporary salt-water basins. Kara-Bogaz-Gol Bay, the greatest source in the world of mirabilite—decahydrate of sodium sulphate—belongs to this belt of mineral lakes. The quantity of mirabilite deposited annually on the bottom of the bay is about 600 million tons [*sic*].

The USSR is very rich in mineral waters with healing properties. There are many medicinal muds in the USSR. These are the slimy sediments of mineral lakes, which sometimes deposit silt several tens of meters deep on their bottoms. Of late, peat muds also have begun to be more and more widely applied for healing purposes.

The hydromineral resources of the USSR have great economic significance. From the concentrated brines bromium, iodine, potassium, and magnesium salts are obtained; these are raw material for the chemical industry.

SECTION 4. THE CLIMATE OF THE USSR

The climate of the USSR is continental; its continental quality increases as one moves from west to east, where it reaches the greatest extent not only in the USSR, but in all the world (the cold pole is located in Northeast Siberia).

The following conditions have a decisive effect upon the climate of the USSR: (1) the direct and open contact of its territory with the Arctic Ocean; (2) the marked influence of the broad land masses, strongly cooled in winter, which are located in the northeastern part of the USSR between the Arctic and Pacific oceans and contain the so-called cold pole; (3) the presence of the warm Atlantic Current in the western part of the Barents Sea, and the influence of the west winds blowing off the warm Atlantic; and (4) the considerable distance from the sea of the vast expanses of Kazakhstan and Central Asia [23] and the influence of the belt of intracontinental

[23] The inland Caspian and Aral seas located here do not have a decisive influence on the climate of the above arid expanses of the USSR.

deserts of the Northern Hemisphere. [For location and extent of major regions such as Central Asia see Fig. 7, at back of book.]

The first two conditions are responsible for the late arrival of summer and its low temperature in the Far North of the USSR. Results of the third factor are the relatively mild winters and the moderately warm summers with abundant rainfall in the northwestern regions of the European part of the USSR. The desert belt and adjoining regions, removed from the Atlantic and Arctic oceans, are characterized by an extremely dry, almost rainless summer with high temperatures and a severe winter.

Over the wide expanses of the central part of the Arctic Ocean throughout the year, and especially in winter, heavy masses of cold air accumulate which, spreading to the south, in the period of their maximum advance cover considerable expanses of the country all the way to the mountain barriers. There are no natural obstacles to their movement southward except individual low elevations and, in some places, solid forests. In some years the masses of cold air flow along the mountain passes and depressions even into the subtropical regions of the country and produce a sharp fall in the atmospheric temperature.

The cooling is intensified further when, together with the masses of Arctic air, masses of cold air intrude from northeast Siberia (from the cold pole).[24]

In winter there is established at the cold pole an area of high pressure (the area of the Siberian anticyclone), which extends to the southwest and covers extensive areas in Eastern and Western Siberia, and also in Kazakhstan, and, in the form of a belt of high pressure, reaches into the southern half of the European part of the USSR.

At the same time from the area of the Atlantic extratropical maximum south of the Azores a branch of high pressure moves to the northeast, entering into the European part of the USSR approximately at the frontier between the steppe and the forest steppe, and farther east joins the belt of high pressure extending from the area of the Siberian anticyclone.

[24] The cold pole is a broad region in northeast Siberia characterized by high atmospheric pressure and very low temperature in winter. In the valley of the Yana River, at Verkhoyansk, the absolute minimum is −70° C., while in another center, Oimyakon, it is almost −65° C. Such temperatures are the lowest known on earth.

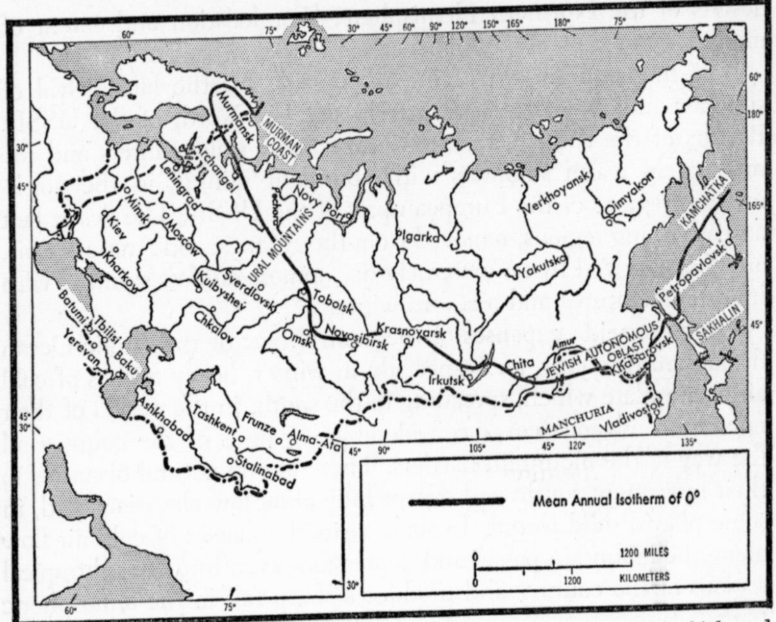

* Fig. 8. Mean Annual Isotherm of 0° Centigrade (32° Fahrenheit) (Adapted from *Climatological Atlas of the Russian Empire,* St. Petersburg, 1900, Plate 14)

This high-pressure belt divides the European part of the USSR into two regions: the northern, with prevailing west and southwest winds, blowing from the warm part of the Atlantic Ocean, and the southern part, with prevailing north and northeast winds, blowing from the above area of high pressure.

In summer as a result of the marked heating of the broad continental expanses of Eurasia, the high-pressure area in northeastern Siberia vanishes and is replaced by an area of low pressure. The high-pressure area over the Atlantic Ocean moves to approximately 10° north of the Azores, and from there in weakened form enters into the southern half of the European part of the USSR. At this time, the influence of the low-pressure area in the deserts in the Central Asiatic part of the USSR has a marked effect upon the movement of the winds.

Because of this the European part of the USSR is under the influence of west and northwest winds, to which, in great measure, it owes its summer rains.

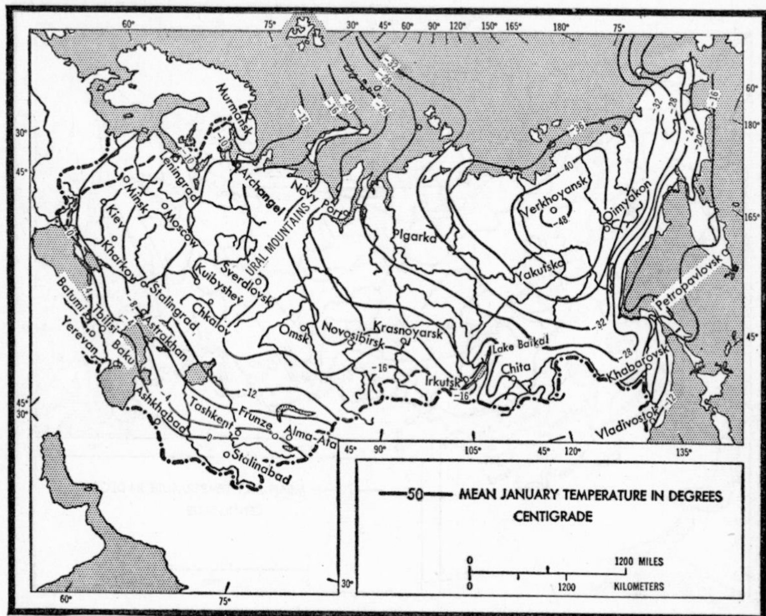

FIG. 9. Mean January Isotherms

The influence of warm Atlantic winds and of west winds on the climate of the USSR is evident most sharply in the average annual and January temperatures. The mean annual isotherms[25] in the USSR proceed from northwest to southeast and keep this direction as far as the limits of the Far East and of northeastern Siberia, where, because of the influence of the Pacific Ocean and its seas, they change to almost the opposite direction, i.e., from southwest to northeast.

The mean annual isotherm of 0° C. runs from the Murman Coast to Archangel, to the sources of the Pechora in the Urals, and thence to Tobolsk [Fig. 8]. From there it passes somewhat to the north of Omsk, Novosibirsk, Krasnoyarsk, and Irkutsk to Chita and thence, across Manchuria, into the Jewish Autonomous Oblast in the Far East, whence it proceeds to the lower Amur, to Sakhalin, and cuts across the southern part of Kamchatka. Thus, the continental

[25] Isotherms are lines on a map connecting places with the same mean temperature.

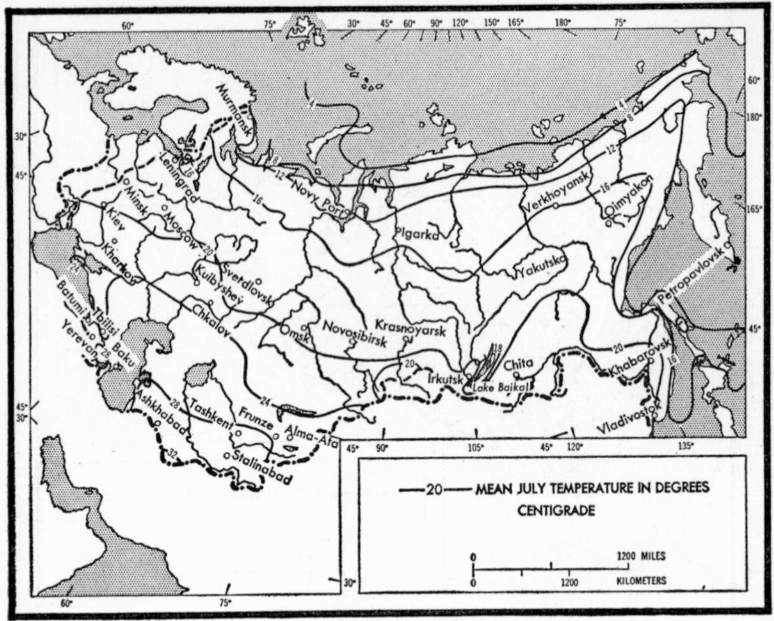

FIG. 10. Mean July Isotherms

nature of the climate of the USSR increases, the farther one goes to the east. The annual means at Leningrad and Chkalov (formerly Orenburg) are identical.

The January isotherms run from northwest to southeast, and in some places along the meridians—i.e., from north to south [Fig. 9]. Their course is almost undisturbed by the Ural Mountains.

For example, Chkalov, at 51° 45′ N. Lat., is colder in January than Archangel, at 64° 32′ [nearly 1,000 miles to the north]. Astrakhan (46° 21′ N. Lat.) is colder than Leningrad (59° 56′). The mean January temperature in Astrakhan is the same as in Murmansk [2,000 miles farther north].

In the southern part of the West Siberian Lowland and in the Central Asiatic part of the USSR the January isotherms run almost in an east-west direction. In Eastern Siberia, the isotherms run in a southeasterly direction; but when they reach Lake Baikal they bend sharply to the north. This is explained by the influence of the lake, which becomes covered with ice only in the middle of January and exercises a warming influence on its coastal regions.

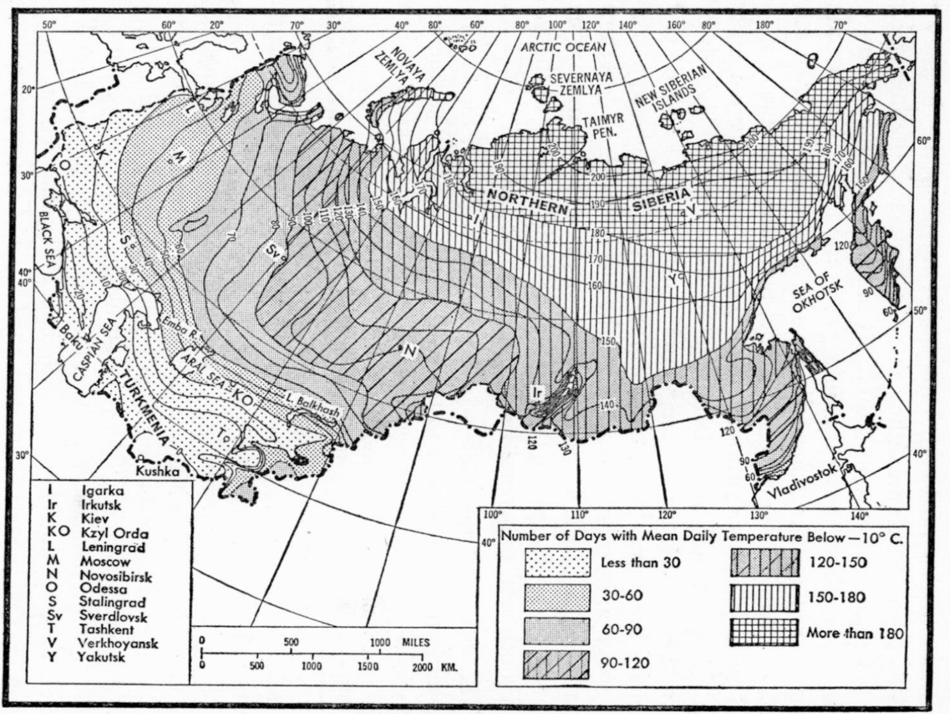

* Fig. 11. Number of Days with Mean Daily Temperature Below −10° Centigrade (14° Fahrenheit) (From *Great Soviet World Atlas*, Vol. I, Plate 106A)

In the region of Verkhoyank and Oimyakon the January isotherms form a circle including the two centers of the lowest January isotherms not only in the USSR but in the whole world.

In the Far East, under the influence of the Pacific Ocean and the bordering mountain ranges, the January isotherms run from southwest to northeast—in general, parallel with the shore line.

The July isotherms run almost in an east-west direction, in both the European and the Asiatic parts of the USSR [Fig. 10]; however, their position in the region of Baikal is opposite that of the January isotherms, because at this time of year Baikal acts as a cooling agent on its coastal areas. In northeastern Siberia and in the Far East, because of the Pacific Ocean, from which the summer monsoons blow at this period, the isotherms bend sharply to the south and southwest, in general following the shore line.

The severity of the winters in the European part of the USSR increases from the northwest to the southeast [Fig. 11]. The number of days with temperature below −10° C. [14° F.] is the same in Leningrad [L], Stalingrad [S], and Kzyl-Orda [KO].

Differences in the severity of the winter in the USSR are very great. Thus, for example, Turkmenia has regions where there are no days with mean daily temperature below −10° C., while in northern Siberia there are more than 200 such days a year.

The increase in the number of days with temperatures above 5° C., 10° C., and 20° C., which are characteristic of the temperature regime in summer, in the main runs from north to south. It is a characteristic fact that on the northern Taimyr Peninsula days with a temperature over 5° C. [41° F.] number ten while at the same time in the south, in Turkmenia, there are three hundred such days. In the same regions the number of days with temperature over 20° C. [68° F.] is respectively zero and one hundred fifty.

The durations of the above temperatures for different regions of the USSR are very characteristic. In northeastern Siberia a mean daily temperature below −10° C. is maintained steadily from the middle of October to the middle of April, while at Moscow temperatures below −10° C. are observed only from January to the middle of February. In the south and west of the European part of the USSR, and also in the regions south of a line from the mouth of the Emba to the Aral Sea and Lake Balkhash, while mean daily temperatures below −10° C. are observed, no definite period with mean daily temperatures below −10° C. can be noted.

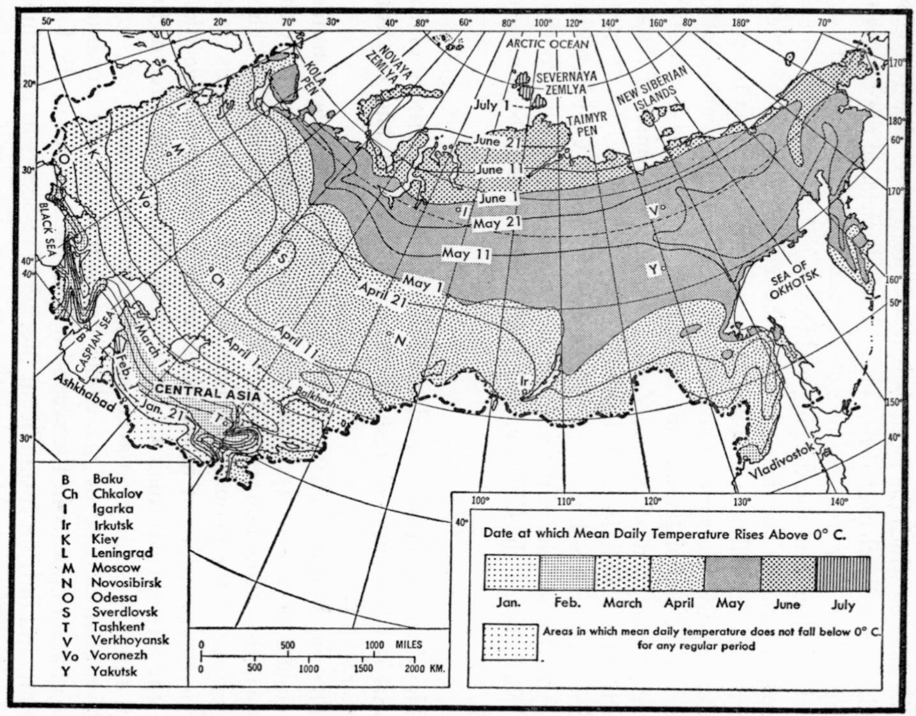

*Fig. 12. Date at Which Mean Daily Temperature Rises Above 0° Centigrade (32° Fahrenheit) (From *Great Soviet World Atlas,* Vol. I, Plate 108V)

The dates on which the mean daily temperature passes above or below 0° C. are equally characteristic. These dates characterize the coming of spring and fall over great expanses of the country; the opening and freezing of the rivers and the thawing and freezing of the soil are also connected with them. The dates on which the temperature passes above or below 0° C. are different in different parts of the USSR: on the plains of Central Asia the spring movement of the temperature above 0° C. occurs at the end of January and in February; on the Kola Peninsula it occurs in May, and on Novaya Zemlya and in the expanses of the Far North of the USSR, in June [Fig. 12].

The dates on which the temperature passes above 20° C., which characterizes the hot part of the year, are maintained steadily only south of the Kiev, Voronezh, Chkalov, and Lake Balkhash line, beginning in July.

The distribution of annual precipitation in the territory of the USSR is exceedingly diverse in quantity, character, and intensity [Fig. 13].

The Far North is characterized by a comparatively low annual precipitation—200 to 350 mm. on the average; however, with the comparatively low temperatures in summer and the thawing of the upper layer of the permanently frozen ground in summer, this quantity is almost sufficient to moisten the soil and sustain vegetation. On the western Murman Coast, because of the Gulf Stream, the total annual precipitation averages 450 mm. and more.

It is characteristic of the whole Far North that the maximum precipitation appears in the second half of the summer in the form of rain, and only an insignificant precipitation occurs in the winter in the form of snow. As a result the snow cover in the Tundra Zone and, in part, in the Taiga Zone in Western and Eastern Siberia is insignificant and, with the exception of the lower Ob and Yenisey, has an average depth of 20 to 40 cm. [Fig. 14]. Along the lower Ob, however, the depth of the snow cover reaches 90 cm. and more.

As one moves to the east along the Arctic Ocean the annual precipitation in the shore belt gradually decreases, and for wide parts of the Yakut ASSR it averages 200 to 300 mm. [Fig. 13]; moreover, the maximum precipitation in Yakutia comes in the second half of the summer—July and August; during the cold period (November to April) there is extraordinarily little precipitation in the form of snow—about 20 to 30 cm. [of snow] a month.

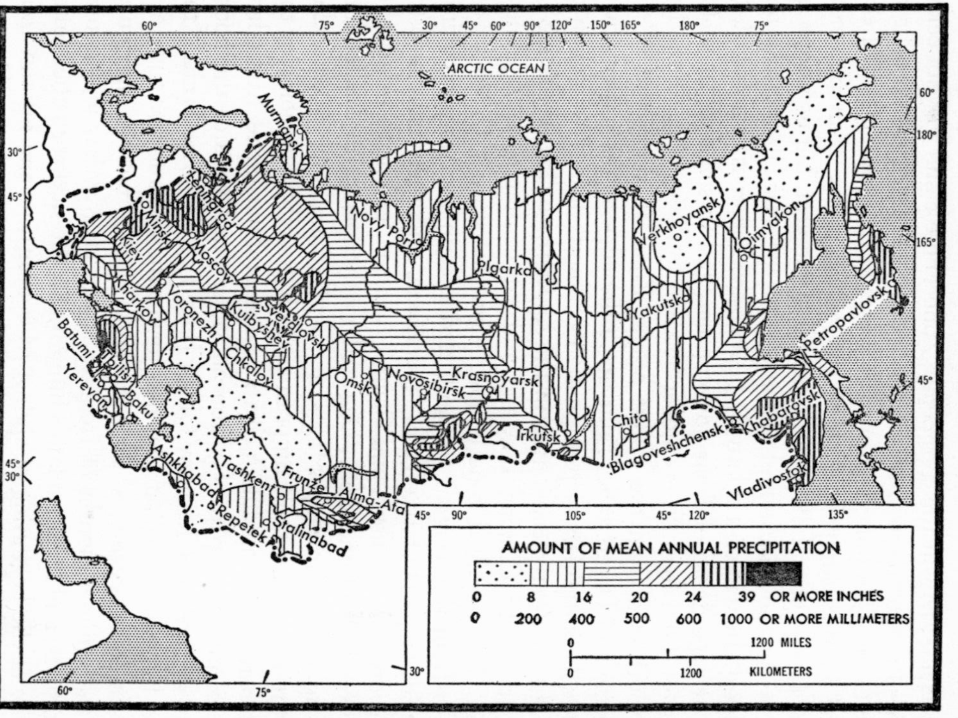

FIG. 13. Mean Annual Precipitation

A wide strip in the Temperate Zone (Forest and Forest Steppe zones) is characterized by an average annual precipitation of from 350 to 400–500 mm.; and in some places in the western half of this zone in the European part of the USSR, more than 600 mm. The precipitation falls in every month of the year, but its maximum occurs in the middle and at the end of the summer—in July and August. In winter a relatively heavy snow cover is established, of an average depth of from 30 to 70 cm. and in some places in the western Ural foothills even over 80 cm.

Southward from the Forest Steppe Zone, in the plains of the Steppe and Desert zones right up to the edge of the mountains, a gradual diminution in precipitation is observed.

The smallest precipitation in the southern section of the USSR occurs in the Caspian Lowland and the central parts of Central Asia. This so-called zone of insufficient moisture stretches in the main from the Yergeni [upland] and encompasses in a semicircle the lower parts of the Terek, the Kuma, and the Volga, and the territory of Kazakhstan and Central Asia, and extends southward to the foothills of the Kopet-Dag and southeastward to the foothills of the Tyan-Shan ranges [Figs. 4 and 7]. In addition, two branches of the zone enter the European part of the USSR, embracing the left bank of the middle Volga approximately as far as Kuibyshev, the southeastern part of Voronezh Oblast, and parts of the northeastern portion of Kharkov Oblast [Fig. 13]. The zone is characterized by annual precipitation not greater than 250 to 300 mm. and in some places even less than 100 mm., by high mean temperatures in the summer months of from 23° to 30° C., by low winter temperatures, and by low relative humidity in the summer period, especially at the beginning of spring. Moreover, in some regions, as in Turkmenia (Repetek), during half the year—from June to November—there is no rain at all.

The central, most arid regions of the zone of insufficient moisture are characterized by an almost rainless summer and a winter with little snow. As a result of the high summer temperatures, evaporation here reaches large proportions, exceeding the precipitation. Such conditions make the balance of moisture negative and insufficient for the growth of vegetation, and hence agriculture in the zone of insufficient moisture is possible only with irrigation, for which ground and especially river water is used.

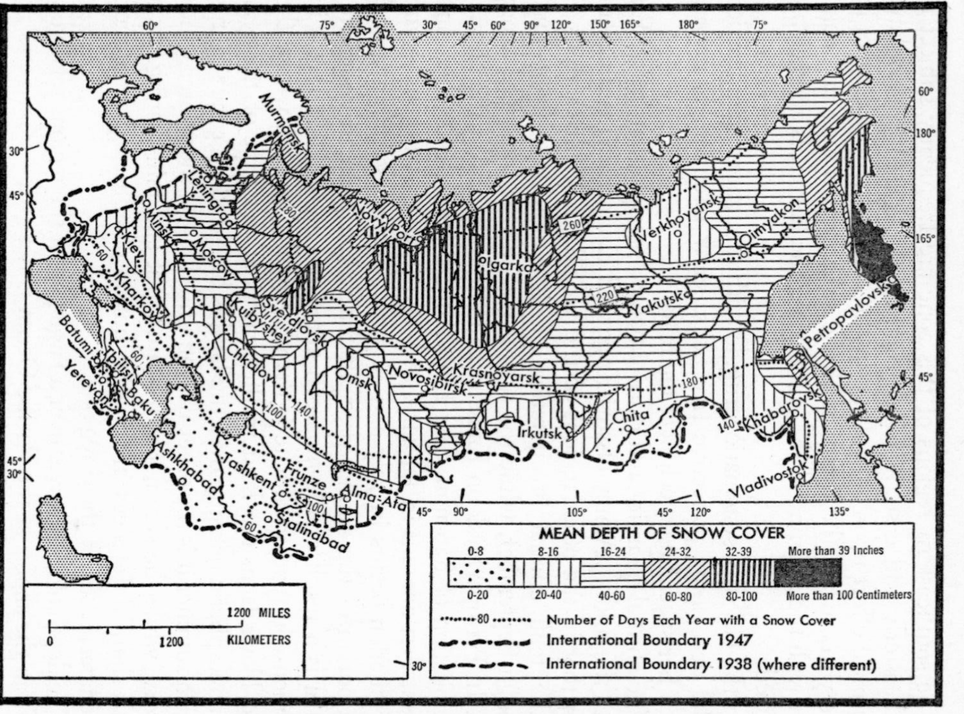

Fig. 14. Depth and Duration of Snow Cover

The southeastern regions of this zone are frequently subject to southeasterly and easterly winds—*sukhoveys*. The sukhoveys have a harmful effect upon agriculture in the arid and semiarid zone. In some years, when the duration of the sukhoveys is long and coincides with the ripening of the grain crops, the harvest is appreciably reduced.

In the USSR a systematic struggle with drought is being carried on by developing protective tree belts, snow retention, irrigation, and other special agrotechnical methods.

The annual quantity and distribution of precipitation in the Far East (the middle Amur, Ussuri Kray, and Kamchatka) is different from that in the other regions of the USSR. In Vladivostok 65% of the total annual precipitation of 570 mm. falls from June through September, while the winter has only 28 mm., i.e., about 5%. In Petropavlovsk on Kamchatka more than half of the annual precipitation of 820 mm. falls from August through October, and the smallest amount in January. In Blagoveshchensk the maximum precipitation occurs in July and August. Such a distinctly seasonal distribution of the annual precipitation in the Far East and Kamchatka is a result of the monsoon climate. The deciding factor in the monsoon type of climate is the change of winds. In winter the wind blows from the land to the sea, as at this time of the year the atmospheric pressure over the land is high and over the sea it is low; in summer it is the other way around. Hence, the winter winds are dry, while the summer winds are moist and rain-bearing. As a result sharp differences in the distribution of annual precipitation are characteristic of these regions.

The depth of snow cover over a large part of the regions relatively far from the shores of the Pacific Ocean is not great—from 10 to 20 cm. on the average—and as one moves west to Trans-Baikalia, less than 10 cm.

Thanks to the monsoons, the Far East (Ussuri Kray, the southern part of Kamchatka, etc.) and the Black Sea coast of Georgia have the largest annual total precipitation in the USSR. In Batumi the largest part of the total annual precipitation of 2,500 mm. falls at the end of the summer in heavy downpours.

At the conclusion of the general characterization of the climate let us consider the distribution of permanent ground frost (*vechnaya merzlota*) in the territory of the USSR.

FIG. 15. Areas of Permanent Ground Frost (Permafrost or *Vechnaya Merzlota*)

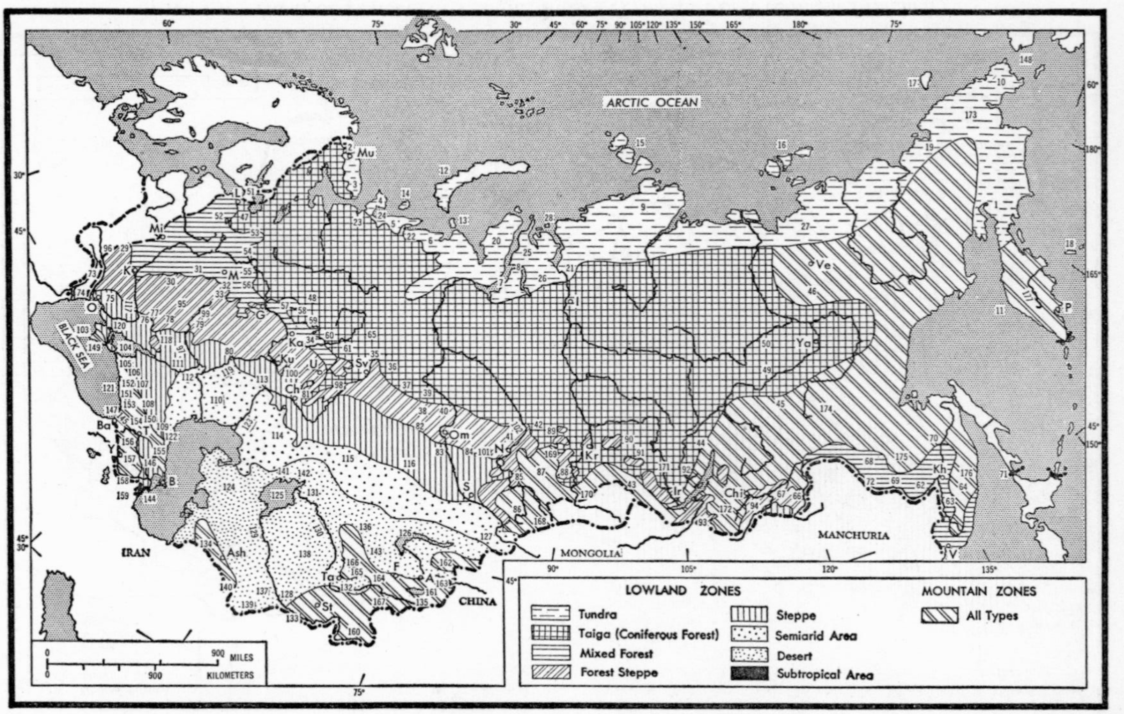

Fig. 16. Natural Zones (after Berg)

KEY TO FIGURE 16

Cities Used for General Orientation (Letters)

A Alma-Ata
Ash Ashkhabad
B Baku
Ba Batumi
Ch Chkalov
Chi Chita
F Frunze
G Gorky
I Igarka
Ir Irkutsk
K Kiev
Ka Kazan
Kh Khabarovsk
Kr Krasnoyarsk
Ku Kuibyshev
L Leningrad
M Moscow
Mi Minsk
Mu Murmansk
N Novosibirsk
O Odessa
Om Omsk
P Petropavlovsk (Kamchatka)
S Semipalatinsk
St Stalinabad
Sv Sverdlovsk
T Tbilisi
Ta Tashkent
U Ufa
V Vladivostok
Ve Verkhoyansk
Y Yerevan
Ya Yakutsk

Other Points Mentioned in Text (Numbers)

Tundra

1. Parapolsky Vale
2. Kola Inlet
3. Ponoy River
4. Kanin Peninsula
5. Malozemelskaya Tundra
6. Bolshezemelskaya Tundra
7. Ob Inlet
8. Taz Inlet
9. Taimyr Peninsula and Tundra
10. Chukotsk Peninsula and Tundra
11. Kamchatka Peninsula
12. Novaya Zemlya
13. Vaigach Island
14. Kolguyev Island
15. Severnaya Zemlya
16. New Siberian Islands
17. Wrangel Island
18. Komandorskie Islands
19. Tundra east of Kolyma River
20. Yamal Peninsula
21. Yenisey River
22. Pechora River
23. Mezen
24. Cheshskaya Bay
25. Gydan Peninsula
26. West Siberian Tundra
27. Yakut Tundra
28. Dickson Island

Forest Zone

29 Zhitomir
30. Karachev
31. Kaluga
32. Oka River
33. Ryazan
34. Balaya, Vyatka, and Kama rivers
35. Tagil River
36. Irbit
37. Tyumen
38. Ishim River
39. Ishim
40. Tara
41. Kolyvan
42. Tomsk
43. Sayany (mts.)
44. Baikal Range
45. Mts. of northern Trans-Baikalia
46. Verkhoyansk Range
47. Leningrad Oblast
48. Kirov Oblast
49 Lena River
50. Vilyuy River
51. Karelian Isthmus
52. Novgorod
53. Tikhvin Canal
54. Bezhetsk
55. Yaroslavl
56. Ivanovo
57. Sanchursk
58. Yaransk
59. Urzhum
60. Sarapul
61. Kungur
62. Amur River
63. Ussuri River
64. Maritime Kray
65. Molotov Oblast
66. Argun River
67. Shilka River
68. Zeya River
69. Bureya River
70. Komsomolsk
71 La Pérouse Strait
72. Blagoveshchensk

Forest Steppe Zone

73. Beletsk Steppe
74. Bessarabia
75. Ingul River
76. Kremenchug
77. Poltava
78. Kharkov
79. Voronezh
80. Saratov
81. Troitsk
82. Petropavlovsk (Kazakhstan)
83. Irtysh River
84. Lake Chany
85. Barnaul
86. Altay Mountains
87. Kuznetsk Area, Kuznetsk Basin
88. Minusinsk Area
89. Achinsk Area
90. Kansk Area
91. Tulun Area
92. Verkholensk Area
93 Selenga Area, Selenga Steppe
94. Nerchinsk Area, Nerchinsk Steppe
95. Kursk (south of which lie the Streletsk and Kazatsk steppes)
96. Podolia
97. Don River
98. Southern Ural Mountains
99. Voronezh River
100. Buzuluk Pine Woods
101. Kulundinsk Steppe
102. Ob River

Steppe Zone

103. Crimean Mountains and Peninsula
104. Sea of Azov
105. Kuban River
106. Krasnodar
107. Labinskaya
108. Pyatigorsk
109. Grozny
110. Caspian Lowland
111. Nizhne-Chirskaya
112. Stalingrad
113. Uralsk
114. Temir
115 Turgay
116. Akmolinsk
117. Dnepr River
118. Severny (N.) Donets River
119. Volga River
120. Askaniya-Nova Steppe Preserve

Semiarid Zone

121. Caucasus or Great Caucasus Mountains
122. Sulak River
123. Ural River
124. Ust-Urt Plateau
125. Aral Sea
126. Lake Balkhash
127. Lake Zaisan

Desert Zone

128. Kerki
129. Amu-Darya (river)
130. Syr-Darya (river)
131. Kazalinsk
132. Khodzhent or Leninabad
133. Termez
134. Kopet-Dag (mts.)
135. Tyan-Shan (mts.)
136. Bedpak-Dala Plateau
137. Kara-Kum (desert)
138. Kyzyl-Kum (desert)
139. Murgab River
140. Tedzhen River
141. Bolshie Barsuki (desert)
142. Malie Barsuki (desert)
143. Muyun-kum desert)

Subtropical Zone

144. Lenkoran Coastal Lowland
145. Rion River
146. Kura River and Shirak, Karayaz, and Shirvan steppes
147. Colchis

Mountain Zone

148. Bering Strait
149. Yaila [highland]
150. Stavropol Upland
151. Laba and Belaya rivers and Caucasus Preserve
152. Maikop
153. Teberda
154. South Osetia
155. Dagestan
156. Armenian Plateau
157 Lake Sevan
158. Araks River
159. Talysh Range
160. Pamir Mountains
161. Issyk-Kul (lake)
162. Dzhungar Ala-Tau (mts.)
163. Zaili Ala-Tau (mts.)
164. Kirgiz Range
165. Chatkal Range
166. Talas Range
167. Fergana Range
168. Chuya Steppe and Kuray Steppe
169. Kuznetsk Ala-Tau (mts.)
170. Us Basin
171. Pre-Baikalia
172. Trans-Baikalia
173. Anadyr Range
174. Stanovoy Range
175. Bureya Range
176 Sikhote-Alin (mts.)
177. Valley of the Kamchatka River

The area of permanent ground frost is approximately 10 million sq. km., which is 47% of the area of the USSR [Fig. 15]. The southern boundary of permanent frost runs approximately somewhat north of the town of Mezen, to Berezovo on the Ob, thence to the mouth of the Nizhnyaya (Lower) Tunguska, where it turns sharply southward along the right bank of the Yenisey and into Mongolia; it again enters the USSR in the region of Blagoveshchensk, whence it proceeds northeastward into northern Kamchatka. The thickness of the permanently frozen ground varies from 1 meter at its southern edge to 400 meters on the shore of the Arctic Ocean. Islands of permanent ground frost are found in the high mountains of the Caucasus and the Pamir.

The significance for the national economy of the study of permanent ground frost is great. No measure should be taken in industry, transport, or agriculture in these regions without allowance for the effect of the permanently frozen ground, as the thawing of the ground leads to appreciable deformation of installations, to waterlogging of the soil, and to the formation of lakes.

SECTION 5. NATURAL ZONES OF THE USSR

Natural zones (regions) are large segments of the earth's surface characterized by certain combinations and interactions of topography, climate, soil and vegetation cover, and fauna, from the point of view of their natural and historic development and the influence of human society in the different stages of its historic development. In the lowlands of the USSR the following natural zones are found from north to south: (1) tundra; (2) temperate forest; (3) forest steppe; (4) steppe; (5) semiarid; (6) desert; and (7) subtropical forest.

In the Caucasus, Tyan-Shan, Altay, and other mountain regions the natural zones have a vertical distribution. The natural zones change with approximately every 500 meters of altitude in the mountain regions, while north and south they change after hundreds of kilometers.

Tundra Zone

The Tundra Zone occupies the Far North of the USSR, extending over a huge expanse along the shores of the Arctic and Pacific oceans as far as the Parapolsky Vale in Kamchatka [1 in Fig. 16; other numbers in this section refer to Fig. 16 also].

The southern border of the Tundra Zone is defined approximately by the following points: the southern end of Kola Inlet [2], the lower course of the Ponoy River [3], Kanin Peninsula [4] to 67° N. Lat., the northern half of the Malozemelskaya [5] and Bolshezemelskaya [6] tundras. Farther on, the border cuts the Ob [7] and the Taz [8] inlets somewhat north of 67° N. Lat. The whole Taimyr Peninsula [9] lies in this zone, and the tundra lies in a strip 100 to 200 km. wide along the Arctic Ocean; it occupies the whole Chukotsk Peninsula [10], and proceeds southward to Kamchatka [11] approximately as far as the Parapolsky Vale, which unites Kamchatka with the mainland. The zone includes both islands of Novaya Zemlya [12], Vaigach Island [13], Kolguyev Island [14], Severnaya Zemlya [15], the New Siberian Islands [16], Wrangel Island [17], and the Komandorskie Islands [18].

The tundra is a wide treeless expanse with moss and lichen vegetation predominant. The Siberian tundras have a very severe, continental climate, while the western (on the Kola and Kanin peninsulas) and the eastern tundras (east of the Kolyma River) [19] have a milder climate, on account of the influence of the Gulf Stream and the Pacific Ocean. The maximum precipitation in the tundra is in summer. The strength of the wind reaches 10 and even 40 meters per second [22 and 90 miles per hour]. Especially strong winds, accompanied in winter by the purga [Arctic snowstorm], occur on the shores of the Yamal Peninsula [20], along the lower Yenisey [21], and in Eastern Siberia. The slight snow cover does not protect the ground from freezing. Permanent ground frost lies at different depths, depending on the soil and the topography. Thus, between the Pechora [22] and Mezen [23] sand is thawed by the end of summer to a depth of 150 cm., clay to a depth of 100 to 125 cm., and peat to a depth of 35 to 40 cm.

As a result of the low atmospheric temperatures, the presence of permanent ground frost, the excessive moisture, and the slight evaporation, decomposition of vegetation proceeds very slowly, which leads to a strong predominance of *glei* processes and to the formation of peat. Hence the bog type of soil formation is characteristic of the Tundra Zone [Fig. 17].

A Alma-Ata
Ash Ashkhabad
B Blagoveshchensk
Ba Baku
Ch Chkalov
D Dudinka
F Frunze
K Kiev
Kh Khabarovsk
L Leningrad
M Moscow
Mi Minsk
Mu Murmansk
O Odessa
P Petropavlovsk
S Stalingrad
Se Semipalatinsk
St Stalinabad
Sv Sverdlovsk
T Tbilisi
Ta Tashkent
Tam Tambov
To Tobolsk
V Vladivostok
Y Yerevan
Glaciers
Red and Yellow Soils
Mountain Meadow and Mountain Tundra Soils
Tundra Soils (except Mountain Tundra)
Mountain Forest Soils (Sierozems of the Crimea and the Caucasus)
Podzols
Peat-Bog Soils
Chernozems and Gray Soils of the Forest-Steppe (Degraded Chernozems)
Mountain Steppe Soils (Chernozems, Chestnut Soils, and Sierozems)
Chestnut Soils
Alluvial and Meadow Soils
Soils of the High Mountain Deserts of the Pamirs
Brown Soils and Sierozems of the Desert Steppes
Solonetz and Solonchak
Sands
0 900 MILES
0 900 KILOMETERS

FIG. 17. Soils

However, the bog type of soil formation in the tundra varies greatly, depending on the topography, the climate, and the vegetation cover, and as a result the soils in the Tundra Zone are extremely diverse. Peaty-bog and peaty-glei soils are found most frequently in low-lying places. Podzolic soils are very widespread in the tundra; they occupy the better drained sandy and sandy loam areas.

It is characteristic of the vegetation cover of the tundra that all the plants are perennial, low, small, dwarfed shrubs. Many remain green in the winter—especially coniferous shrub species, Japanese stone pine in Eastern Siberia, and small shrubs of the cowberry and heather type. In the tundra there are almost no bulb or tuber plants. Herbaceous plants grow in the form of "cushions," and in general appear as sod-forming plants, as, for example, the dryad. In general the tundra is poor in plant species in comparison with the southern zones; the total does not exceed 500. Many people imagine the tundra to be a continuous bog. On the contrary, it includes considerable dry areas, but there are also many bogs; these are lowland, or sedge, bogs. The peat cover in the tundra does not reach a great thickness.

Characteristic representatives of the animal kingdom in the tundra are: the polar bear, the varying hare, the wild and domestic reindeer, the lemming, the arctic fox, the domestic dog, the willow ptarmigan, and the snowy owl. The reindeer is the most important animal in the tundra. It feeds on the moss, lichen, and herbaceous vegetation of the tundra. Without it the mastery by man of wide expanses of the tundra would present great difficulties; it provides a highly nourishing meat, and its skin is used to make clothing, footwear, and tent covering. The reindeer is used also as a draft animal.

The lemming—an animal of the rodent family—appears in the tundra in great numbers during some years.

In spring a multitude of birds fly into the tundra—swans, geese, barnacle geese, and others. In some places they form so-called "bird bazaars." Part of them winter in the tundra. In the southern part some animal species proper to the Forest Zone appear. Here are wolf, bear, fox, and the like.

From west to east the Tundra Zone can be divided into the following types:

(1) The Malozemelskaya [5] and Bolshezemelskaya [6] tundras, predominantly swamps with shrubs and with intensive development of the processes of peat formation—the Malozemelskaya Tundra reaching from Cheshkaya Bay [24] to the lower Pechora [22], and the Bolshezemelskaya [6] from the Pechora to the northern Urals;

(2) The West Siberian Tundra [26], embracing the Yamal Peninsula [20], the region of the Ob-Taz Inlet [7–8], and the Gydan Peninsula [25], and characterized by moist, waterlogged expanses;

(3) The Taimyr Tundra [9], distinguished by a very dry climate and, as a result, by a smaller number of swampy places;

(4) The Yakut Tundra [27], marked by a still drier climate and, as a result, by slight development of the swampy types of tundra; and

(5) The Chukotsk Tundra [10], characterized by a great diversity of topography and, as a result, by very diverse types of tundra, including mountain types.

According to Academician L. I. Prasolov, tundras and forest tundras occupy 14.7% of all the territory of the USSR.[26]

The diverse economic resources of the tundra—the commercially valuable animals, the minerals, and the soils—are now in large measure being recognized, transforming this zone from a neglected outlying part of Tsarist Russia into a rapidly developing region of the Soviet Union.

New cities have grown up with factories and mills. Agriculture also is developing rapidly in the Tundra Zone, having moved already beyond the Arctic Circle. On some islands (Dickson, 76° 30′ N. Lat. [28], vegetables, edible mushrooms, and flowers are cultivated. Experimental stations have developed frost-resistant strains of field and garden crops, which grow successfully in the tundra and yield dependable harvests.

Forest Zone

South of the Tundra Zone, in the region of temperate climate, lies the Forest Zone with severe winters and relatively warm and moist summers.

The southern boundary of the Forest Zone is defined approximately as follows. Somewhat north of 50° N. Lat. the boundary runs along the

[26] L. I. Prasolov, *Soil Geography as a Factor in Agriculture,* publication of the Institute of Experimental Agronomy, 1929.

Zhitomir [29] to Kiev [K] to Karachev [30] to Kaluga [31] line and then along the Oka [32] to Ryazan [33], to Gorky [G] and Kazan [Ka] to the mouth of the Vyatka River [34]; thence it proceeds along the Kama to the mouth of the Belaya River and passes north of Ufa [U], turning sharply south along the southern Urals [98]. Bending around the Urals, it extends along the Tagil [35] to Irbit [36] to Tyumen [37] line, and then along the Ishim River [38], passing somewhat to the south of the town of Ishim [39], to proceed north of Tara [40] and Kolyvan [41], and then south of Tomsk [42], approximately coinciding with the northern frontier of chernozem. In Eastern Siberia the southern edge of the Forest Zone extends to the northern foothills and slopes of the Sayany [43] and to the Baikal Range [44], then along the foothills of the ranges and uplands of northern Trans-Baikalia [45], and around the arc of the Verkhoyansk Range [46] from the west.

The climate, soil and vegetation cover, and fauna of the Forest Zone are highly diverse. The mean temperature of the warmest month is above 10° C. The annual precipitation is about 500 millimeters, but in some regions it rises to 600–700 millimeters. In vegetation this zone is characterized by a predominance of coniferous forests in the north, and of deciduous forests in the south; sphagnum (mossy) bogs are widespread, in some regions of Western Siberia occupying almost the entire interstream areas.

The predominant soils are podzols, in different stages of development. Soils of bog type, chiefly peat soils and bog soils combined with podzolic soils, are important. In some places in the south of this zone, gray podzolized soils of the Forest Steppe Zone are found.

Podzolic soils are very diverse in physical composition. Three main types are distinguished: clay and clay-loam, sandy and sandy-loam, and stony. In certain regions of the European part of the USSR (Leningrad and Kirov oblasts [47 and 48] and others) *rendzinas* are found—soils rich in humus but poorly leached, which have been formed immediately over limestones or marls. They are found in relatively small patches among soils of the podzolic type. In the valley of the middle Lena [49] and its left tributary the Vilyuy [50] solonized soils are common, which in outward appearance resemble leached chernozems.

The area occupied by coniferous and deciduous forests is very large. Forests occupy one-third of all the territory of the USSR, including the mountain regions. The forested area in the USSR equals 610 million hectares, which is 20% of all the forested area in the world. In timber resources the USSR takes first place in the world. The Siberian Taiga alone occupies an area of over 5 million sq. km., an area equal to the territories of all the capitalist countries of Western Europe. No other single state in the world has such a colossal forest area.

The Forest Zone has great economic significance. Timber provides raw material for the paper, wood pulp, and wood-working industries, serves as building material and fuel, and also is an article for export.

The main timber species in this zone are: in the European part of the USSR, spruce, pine, and oak; in the Asiatic part, Siberian spruce, pine, larch, Siberian and Dahurian fir, Siberian and Japanese stone pine; and in the Far East, Yeddo spruce. Birch and aspen also are widespread, but they appear rather as an admixture among the basic species. In the southern part of the Forest Zone broad-leaved species predominate—maple, elm, linden, ash and others.

According to climate and soil and vegetation cover, the Forest Zone is divided into two subzones: (1) the Taiga Subzone, with predominantly coniferous forests of spruce, larch, fir, and Siberian and Japanese stone pine; and (2) the Subzone of Mixed Forests, with predominantly broad-leaved species—oak, elm, maple, and linden. As admixtures in these subzones there appear pine, aspen, birch, alder, and others.

The boundary between the above subzones passes through the following points: the Karelian Isthmus [51], Novgorod [52], the Tikhvin Canal [53], Bezhetsk [54], Yaroslavl [55], Ivanovo [56], Gorky—that is, along the northern edge of the distribution of oak on the watersheds. In the Volga area, approximately at 57° N. Lat., begins the belt of fir, spruce, and oak forests, the northern edge of which runs through Sanchursk [57], south of Yaransk [58], and Urzhum [59], to Sarapul [60] and Kungur [61].

In the Far East the Subzone of Broad-Leaved and Mixed Forests occupies the basin of the middle and part of the lower Amur [62], the basin of the Ussuri River [63], and Maritime Kray [64].

From west to east, the Taiga Subzone divides into three sections. In the western section Norway spruce is the characteristic forest-forming species. In the central section Norway spruce is gradually replaced by Siberian spruce. The West Siberian section is characterized by the following basic forest-forming species: Siberian spruce, Siberian larch, fir, and Siberian stone pine. In some places these species form solid stands, with fir predominating. The Subzone of Mixed Forests is divided into two sections, western and eastern. Oak is the characteristic forest-forming species in the first; in the eastern section, linden becomes predominant.

The spruce forests of the European part of the USSR in certain sectors occupy 60 to 80% of the whole forested area (Molotov Oblast [65]). Pine forests are equally widespread; but, unlike the spruce forests, they extend far southward into the Forest Steppe Zone and, in some places, even into the Steppe Zone. The spruce and pine forests in the Forest Zone are associated with definite soil and topographic conditions.

In the East Siberian Taiga the basic forest-forming species is the Dahurian larch, which in Yakutia forms continuous forests. This larch grows very well in places with permanent ground frost. The wet larch taiga, adapted to sandy-loam and clay-loam soils, is distinguished from the cowberry larch taiga growing on dry and more fertile soils. In addition to larch forests there are forests of pure pine, and of pine with larch and Japanese stone pine.

The brown bear, marten, fox, squirrel, varying hare, and elk are characteristic taiga animals. In Siberia sable and wild reindeer have been preserved.

The capercaillie, hazel grouse, and willow ptarmigan are characteristic birds of the taiga.

The fauna of the Subzone of Mixed Forests is similar in many respects to the fauna of the taiga. In some places in the Subzone of Mixed Forests elk and roebuck are found.

The broad-leaved forests of the Far East really form a special section of the Forest Zone, which because of the peculiarity of its natural conditions may be regarded as a separate natural zone.

It extends eastward in a comparatively narrow strip, beginning at the confluence of the Argun [66] and the Shilka [67], including the middle and lower course of the Zeya [68] and the lower Bureya River [69]. On the north the boundary runs along the parallel of 50° N. Lat. approximately to Komsomolsk-on-Amur [70]; thence it turns sharply to the southeast, including the lowlands of the Amur and its tributary the Ussuri. The coastal strip of Maritime Kray also belongs to this zone approximately to the latitude of La Pérouse Strait [71].

Characteristic features of this zone are: a monsoon climate with maximum precipitation during the warm period (80 to 90% of the total annual precipitation falls from April to November); and a wet summer, but with sufficient warmth (the mean temperature of July is 20° C.). The winter is distinguished by marked dryness and an insignificant snow cover (except in the extreme south).

The soils are alluvial, meadow, and half-bog soils, black, resembling chernozems and not inferior to them in fertility. Typical podzolic soils also are common.

The zone under consideration is noted for rich vegetation, represented by dense forests of Manchurian oak, Asiatic white and Dahurian birch, elm, linden, ash, Amur maple, and euonymus.

Along the Amur, from Blagoveshchensk [72] to the mouth of the Ussuri, expanses of lowland covered with rich herbaceous vegetation are common. A peculiarity of the zone is the coexistence of vegetation indigenous to regions of subtropical climate (Amur wild grape) with vegetation of the Taiga Subzone. This feature is true also in the distribution of fauna. The Ussuri tiger is found along with the sable and squirrel, as well as the deer and roebuck.

The forests of the USSR are rich in valuable fur-bearing animals.

In the Forest Zone there have been organized numerous stations which are busy collecting valuable furs. In order to protect and propagate valuable productive animals, extensive preserves have been created. In the Sayany one such gigantic preserve alone, created for the protection and increase of the precious sable and the very rare and valuable wild reindeer, occupies an area of 1,100,000 hectares. This is the largest preserve in the world. The Sayany preserve contains bear, roebuck, musk deer, and elk in addition to sable and wild reindeer.

In the Forest Zone there are wide expanses of peat bog. According to incomplete data, peat bogs occupy 27.5 million hectares in the European part of the USSR, while in the Asiatic part of the USSR they occupy no less than 100 million hectares. Many power stations run on peat, supplying the Northwestern and Central regions of the European part of the USSR with cheap power [Fig. 7].

Under the conditions of socialist agriculture, wide areas of podzolic soils in the Forest Zone are being transformed into bases for a highly productive grain economy.

Forest Steppe Zone

The Forest Steppe Zone is a transitional section between the Forest and the Steppe zones.

The southern boundary of the Forest Steppe Zone is defined by the following line: the northern edge of the Beletsk Steppe [73] in Bessarabia [74]; the source of the Ingul [75]; Kremenchug [76]; Poltava [77]; somewhat south of Kharkov [78]; Voronezh [79]; Saratov [80]. From Saratov the boundary follows along the Volga to Kuibyshev [Ku], where it turns toward Chkalov [Ch], passing slightly to the north of it. (In the Trans-Ural area it runs from Troitsk [81] to Petropavlovsk [82], crosses the Irtysh [83] at 54° N. Lat., then proceeds to Lake Chany [84], and southeast to Barnaul [85], ending in the foothills of the Altay [86]. Separate islands of forest steppe are found in the Kuznetsk [87], Minusinsk [88], Achinsk [89], Krasnoyarsk [Kr], Kansk [90], Tulun [91], Verkholensk [92], and Irkutsk [Ir] areas, and in Trans-Baikalia (Selenga [93] and Nerchinsk [94] areas.)

In addition to forests there are considerable areas of steppe in this zone. At the north in the main there are meadow forest steppes, while at the south there are mixed herbaceous steppes with great diversity of vegetation, as seen in the Streletsk and Kazatsk steppes south of Kursk [95]. Here, in an area of steppe one meter square, as many as eighty plant species may be counted.

The fauna of the Forest Steppe Zone is a mixture of the animals of the Forest and the Steppe zones.

According to the character of its soil and vegetation cover, the zone is divided into western and eastern forest steppe. The western forest steppe is marked by the occurrence of so-called oak groves, i.e., woods consisting entirely of oak, developed on relatively rich soils, in part on leached and degraded chernozems and in part on sierozems (degraded clay-loams).

In the oak groves, ash, linden, maple, and elm are found as an admixture, and in the west, hornbeam. The undergrowth in large part consists of filbert, which is one of the typical features of the oak groves.

In the Right-Bank Ukraine [that part of the Ukraine west of the Dnepr, 117] there are also hornbeam groves, which consist of oak, ash, and hornbeam. In Podolia [96] beech forests predominate.

East of the Don [97] on solodized and solonized soils there are aspen groves, which have penetrated far into the northern part of the Steppe Zone.

The eastern forest steppe is characterized by birch-aspen groves, called *kolki*, developed in part on solonized soils and in part on leached chernozems. The boundary between the western and the eastern forest steppe is the southern Ural, which is also the eastern limit of the distribution of oak.

Of the coniferous trees, pines also are found in the forest steppe, on sandy and sandy-loam soils. Such are the pine woods of Voronezh Oblast, spread along the left [east] bank of the Voronezh River [99], the Buzuluk pine woods [100] on the right bank of the Samara River, and the pine woods of the Kulundinsk Steppe [101] and of the left [west] bank of the Ob [102]. The annual precipitation in the northern part of the forest steppe reaches 400 to 450 mm., and in the south 300 mm.

The maximum precipitation is in June and July, the minimum in January and February.

In the Forest Steppe Zone podzolic and chernozem types of soil are found in different stages of development. In the northern part gray forest clay loams (degraded clay loams) are found, which are podzolic soils in different stages of podzolization; in the south, leached and degraded chernozems. Among the other soils of the forest steppe, the "solods" are found in low-lying areas. These are soils depleted of humus and conspicuously leached of mineral content.

Steppe Zone

The steppes are wide treeless expanses with a predominantly herbaceous vegetation.

The southern boundary of the Steppe Zone is determined by the shores of the Black Sea (on the Crimean Peninsula [103] it reaches to the foot of the northern slope of the Crimean Mountains) and the Sea of Azov [104], and in the North Caucasus by the lower Kuban River [105]. Farther on, it follows the Krasnodar [106] to Labinskaya [107] to Pyatigorsk [108] to Grozny [109] line. In the Caspian Lowland [110] the boundary conforms with the limits of the distribution of the light-chestnut soils, running along the Grozny to Nizhne–Chirskaya [111] to Stalingrad [112] line and reaching almost as far as Saratov [80]. From there it corresponds approximately to the line of the Saratov-Uralsk [113] railroad. In Western Siberia the boundary of the zone runs along the Temir [114] to Turgay [115] to Akmolinsk [116] to Semipalatinsk [S] line, ending in the foothills of the Altay [86].

Climatically, the Steppe Zone differs from the Forest Steppe Zone in its warmer and relatively dry summer. The annual precipitation ranges between 300 and 350 mm., and in some places it is 200 mm. The maximum rainfall occurs in the first half of the summer. The precipitation falls in the form of heavy downpours. The snow cover is relatively insignificant, and on the average reaches a depth of from 10 to 30 cm. In summer a strongly marked dry period lasts from one to one and one-half months, with low relative humidity, reaching 35 to 46% at one P.M. The southeastern section of the steppes in the European part of the USSR is sometimes subject in summer to the harmful influence of sukhovey winds from the southeast and the south.[27]

As for soil cover, the Steppe Zone is characterized by an extensive development of chernozem and chestnut soils. In the thick chernozems the humus horizon sometimes has a thickness of 80 to 100 cm. or more. The humus content of chernozems amounts to 6 to 10%, and in some places even 15%, as seen in the chernozems of the Trans-Volga area. Of the intrazonal soils,[28] solodized soils are found

[27] The well known climatologist A. A. Kaminsky associates the origin of the sukhovey winds with the descending masses of air in the region of the anticyclone, which lies over these areas.

[28] Soils which nowhere form zones of their own, and which are included in another zone, are called intrazonal soils. The solods or solodized soils of the chernozem zone, for example, are of this sort. Intrazonal soils should be distinguished from azonal soils. "Azonol" refers also to soils which do not form zones of their own, but are found in all soil zones. For example, meadow soils are found in the tundra, podzolic, chernozem, and other soil zones. The same distinction is made in the geography of vegetation.

in the Aleshkovsk sands, along the lower Dnepr [117]; in some places solonized and salinized soils are found, chiefly along the southern edge of the zone in the form of patches within the zone of chestnut soils. In the valleys on the right [west] banks of the large rivers—the Dnepr, Severny (Northern) Donets [118], Don [97], and Volga [119]—there are chernozem sands and sandy loams. In Western Siberia, at the northern edge of the steppes, southern chernozems are found in a narrow strip; the southern part is characterized by chestnut soils.

The chernozems of the Azov-Kuban Plain belong to a special type, called Azov chernozems, whose humus horizon attains a depth of 120 to 150 cm.

From north to south, the Steppe Zone is divided into two subzones—the Northern Meadow Zone and the Southern Feather Grass-Fescue Zone. Mixed herbaceous steppes predominate in the former, feather grass with fescue steppes in the latter.

The following animals are typical of the steppes: the spotted suslik, of the rodent family, which carries to the surface of the ground a large quantity of soil in the form of low mounds; the jerboa; and the hamster. Characteristic birds are the great and little bustard, crane, Calandra lark, duck, heron, and shore birds. The insect pests include the migratory locust, which breeds in the reed thickets along the lower river courses, and the caterpillar of the beet webworm. The wolf, fox, and other large animals are found.

The Steppe Zone together with the Forest Steppe Zone is the granary of the Soviet Union. According to Academician Prasolov, it occupies about 4 million sq. km., or about one-fifth of the area of the USSR. Very few untouched expanses of steppe remain in the USSR. These are in most cases preserves, where for purposes of scientific investigation the authorities are keeping the land in its natural condition.[29] Wide expanses of the steppes have been plowed up, however, because of the fertility of the chernozem soils. No other country in the world has such wide expanses of these soils as the USSR.

The Steppe Zone and in part the Forest Steppe Zone provide the natural conditions for growing valuable industrial crops. Here

[29] The Askaniya-Nova Steppe Preserve [120] is outstanding. It is 50 km. southeast of Kakhovka in the Black Sea steppes and has an area of about 25,000 hectares. [This preserve was established in the 1880's by Count F. E. Faltz-Fein and had an international reputation among zoologists for the cross-breeding of domestic and wild species which was carried on there.]

are found the main areas of sugar beets, sunflowers, hemp, tobacco, and other industrial crops. Moreover, in the years of Soviet power, cotton cultivation and viticulture have been successfully developed in the southern part of the Steppe Zone.

Semiarid Zone

The semiarid areas (semidesert) form a transitional belt from the Steppe Zone to the intracontinental deserts with temperate climate.

Within the USSR, the Caspian Lowland [110] and part of the eastern foothills of the Caucasus [121] as far as the lower Sulak [122] on the south, and the lower course of the Ural River [123] lie in the Semiarid Zone, while beyond the Ural River its area is limited on the south by the northern cliffs of the Ust-Urt [124]. In Central Asia the boundary of the semiarid area proceeds somewhat north of the Aral Sea [125] and Lake Balkhash [126] and south of Lake Zaisan [127], ending at the frontier of the USSR with China.

In climate this zone is distinguished by the following features: (1) a small annual precipitation, which rarely exceeds 250 mm., the maximum coming at the end of May and the beginning of June and a secondary maximum in autumn; (2) relatively high summer temperatures (the July mean is from 24° to 26° C. and in some places higher); (3) low relative humidity, with marked dryness of the air; and (4) a severe winter with frosts of 40° [below zero] and more. Another peculiarity of the climate of the semiarid areas is the rapid rise in the temperature in spring.

The soil cover is very diverse, but light chestnut soils, desert sierozems, and primitive and gypsum-bearing sierozems with a considerable mineral salt content predominate. In depressions, solonized and salinized soils are found. The soils have a low humus content, which is explained by the scanty vegetation and the dry climate. Nevertheless, the soils of the semidesert, as a result of slight leaching, contain enormous quantities of mineral salts—calcium, magnesium, sodium, and potassium—and with artificial irrigation are distinguished by great fertility. The parent rock has a great influence on the nature of the soil cover; the physical composition of the parent rock in the Semiarid Zone gives rise to sandy, sandy-loam, clayey, and stony soils.

A mosaiclike composition is characteristic of the vegetation cover of the semidesert. While in the steppes the vegetation forms a solid cover, in the semidesert it appears in patches, separated by bare soil. Wormwood [sagebrush] steppes are the characteristic type of vegetation in this zone.

According to the character of the vegetation, the Semiarid Zone may be divided into two subzones, northern and southern.

The northern, or wormwood-grassy, semidesert, is marked by the complexity of the vegetation cover. Slight changes in the topography invariably produce alternation of patches bearing vegetation of the steppe type (grasses) with patches of desert vegetation (wormwood and halophytes). In the grassy stretches the grass stand, consisting of fescues, xerophytic feather grasses, and desert wheat grasses, covers not less than 60% of the surface.

The southern, wormwood-halophyte-grassy subzone is marked by an even more sparse vegetation cover, predominantly of white and black wormwood with an admixture of halophytes and grasses. In some places there are scattered tamarisk thickets.

Typical animals in the Semiarid Zone are the white and yellow suslik. Hamsters and jerboas also are common. Among the large animals, the corsac fox is rather widespread. In the deltas and flood plains of the rivers there are many species of birds—swans, geese, and others.

Desert Zone

This zone occupies about one-ninth of the total area of the USSR. It extends southward from the Semiarid Zone, approximately from the line of the northern edge of the Ust-Urt and Lake Balkhash, and extends to the south as far as the foothills of the mountains bordering the Turanian Lowland.

As for climate, the following features are typical of the Desert Zone: (1) an insignificant precipitation—not over 200 mm. per year, and in many places 100 to 150 mm. per year; (2) low temperatures in the winter (below 0° C.) and high mean temperatures in the summer, reaching 26° to 30° C. in July—i.e., 2° C. higher than the mean July temperature in the tropics—and in some places the absolute maxima reach 50° C. [122° F.]; (3) low relative humidity, with evaporation exceeding precipitation in the summer.

Thus, in Kerki [128] (on the right bank of the Amu-Darya [129] in the Turkmen SSR) the evaporation in August is ten times greater than the precipitation. Hence, the constant dryness of the climate, which has a marked effect on the character of the vegetation. The snow cover is insignificant, and lasts a very short time: in Kazalinsk [131], seventy days; in Tashkent [Ta], five days; and in Khodzhent [Leninabad, 132], twenty days. About half of the precipitation comes in spring; precipitation in summer is an exceptionally rare phenomenon.

The desert has very little cloudy weather. The number of clear days per year is large. For example, in Termez [133] there are over two hundred clear days per year. The Desert Zone is sunny country.

As a result of weak leaching, a large quantity of mineral salts is accumulated in the desert soils, and with artificial irrigation they are not inferior to the chernozems in productivity.

The soil cover here is very diverse. Soils of the structural sierozem type predominate. Solonchaks and playas are scattered in large patches. In the loessial deserts typical sierozems are common.

According to the character of the soil cover and vegetation the following types of desert are distinguished: clayey, stony, sandy, and solonchak. For the clayey deserts of the northern variety the characteristic type of vegetation is the wormwood steppe, and for the southern, loessial variety, in a narrow strip along the foothills of the Kopet-Dag [134] and the Tyan-Shan [135], a diverse vegetation consisting of ephemera represented by two basic species—sedge and bluegrass—together with other plants which have a short growing period.

Stony deserts occupy a large area in the plains of the Ust-Urt [124], the Bedpak-Dala [136], and also on the northern shore of Balkhash [126], and other places. They have stony soils, rich in calcium salts; crusty solonetz areas and solonchaks are widespread in low sections. The higher places are occupied by vegetation with white wormwood predominating, while the low places are occupied by the shrubs *biyurgun* [*Anabasis salsa*] and *boyalych* [*Salsola arbuscula*]. The southern stony deserts are separate islands among the other types of desert. The most important sections of stony desert are found among the sandy deserts of the Kara-Kum [137] and Kyzyl-Kum [138]. The total area of these wormwood-halophyte deserts is about 80 thousand sq. km.

Solonchak deserts occupy an area of approximately 120 thousand sq. km., of which 70 thousand are in the northern part and 50 thousand in the southern. This type of desert is associated with the river terraces of the Syr-Darya [130] and the Amu-Darya, and in the south with the terraces of the Murgab [139], the Tedzhen [140] and other rivers, or else with low sections. The salinization of these deserts is mainly by chlorides (chiefly sodium chloride, although soda and sulphates are found in some quantity). The vegetation is poor and monotonous, but with a rich interchange of colorful combinations in the course of the vegetative period. The vegetation consists of halophytes, among which succulents play an important role—i.e., plants for which the stems serve as leaves; shrubs and even trees are also found (black saxaul [*Arthrophytum*]). In the solonchak deserts playas, solonchaks, and saxaul groves are found.

Sandy deserts occupy the largest expanses in the desert zone: the Bolshie [141] and Malie [142] Barsuki, the Muyun-Kum [143], the Balkhash sands [126], and the wide Kara-Kum [137] and Kyzyl-Kum [138]. The Kara-Kum and Kyzyl-Kum alone occupy an area of about 550 thousand sq. km. A considerable diversity of plant species is characteristic of this type of desert, from annual and perennial herbaceous plants to shrubs and even trees.

This diversity of vegetation is explained by the properties of sandy soils.

Sand is distinguished by its permeability to water, which permits the accumulation of moisture. Being weak in capillary action, sand protects the deeper layers from drying, and promotes the condensation of atmospheric water vapor in the soil. In sand at a depth of 140 to 150 cm., there is a layer of permanent moisture and, in addition, there is another "pendent" horizon of moisture, which changes its position according to the season of the year.

Typical herbaceous species in the sandy deserts are the sand sedge, blue grass, wheat grass, and brome, and, among trees, the white and the black saxaul [*Arthrophytum*]. The white saxaul grows on sandy, nonsaline soils; the black saxaul, in salinized sandy and clayey soils, forming pure stands of trees four to six meters tall and even taller. The wood of the saxaul is very hard and strong. It is used as a local fuel. Significant areas of black saxaul are found in the valleys of the Amu-Darya and the Syr-Darya.

The rich soils of this zone, with the warm climate and with planned irrigation, are the base in the Soviet Union for cultivating the best strains of cotton, especially Egyptian.

Under Soviet rule considerable areas of this zone have been covered with a network of irrigation canals, utilized for the production of cotton and other valuable industrial crops. In the deserts and semideserts, rubber-bearing plants have been found and are now being cultivated (tau-sagyz, kok-sagyz, and others); they provide natural rubber for the rubber industry. In this zone, huge reserves of copper, sulphur, coal, and so on have been discovered. On the basis of the natural wealth, great industrial and agricultural regions have grown up, which are starting points for a fundamental transformation of nature in this zone.

Subtropical Zone

The subtropics occupy two discrete regions—the Black Sea coast of the Trans-Caucasus and the Lenkoran Lowland [144] in the eastern Trans-Caucasus. This zone is marked by special climatic conditions, the peculiarity of which appears in the existence of a frost-free period, in the large annual precipitation, and in a richly developed vegetation, represented here by broad-leaved forests of subtropical type. The soils are the red soils and yellow soils of moist subtropical areas. Along the lower Rion [145] there is a small block of bog soils, and in the Lenkoran Lowland a very narrow belt of alluvial soils, extending in a sharp wedge along the shore of the Caspian from the mouth of the Kura [146] to the frontier with Iran.

The vegetation of Colchis [147, the Black Sea region of the Trans-Caucasus] varies according to the topography. Along the shore there are shrubs twined with vines; next there is a belt of bogs, alternating with sections of dense forest of European alder and Caucasian wing nut. In higher places there appear woods of oak, hornbeam, and Caucasian beech. The trees are twined with evergreen vines. Among the evergreen trees are found box and holly.

The vegetation of the Lenkoran Lowland contains a number of species different from those of Colchis. Here are found the chestnut-leaf oak and in the low-lying parts the Persian parrotia, which yields a very hard wood. Evergreen plants here are relatively fewer than in Colchis.

Cultivated plants which have great significance in the agriculture of the Subtropical Zone are the lemon, orange, tea, grape, and eucalyptus. The fauna of Colchis contains few species. In the Lenkoran Lowland there are the jungle cat, the tiger, the porcupine, and the leopard. The characteristic domestic animal is the zebu.

The significance of the Subtropical Zone for the national economy of the USSR is very great.

The Soviet subtropics are the base for highly valuable agricultural and industrial crops. Of these, citrus products, tea, and tobacco occupy a special place. The subtropics, through their natural conditions, offer unlimited possibilities for the acclimatization of a number of industrial crops from the Tropic Zone.

Mountain Zones

With the exception of the Ural Mountains,[30] the Mountain Zones are along the southern and eastern edges of the USSR from the mountain highlands on the shores of the Crimean Peninsula [103] to Bering Strait [148]. Depending on their geographic position, their elevation, and the dissection of the topography, the mountain landscapes are marked by great diversity.

Mountain Crimea

The climatic peculiarities of the northern and southern slopes of the Crimean Mountains differ sharply. The southern slopes have a warm Mediterranean climate with an uneven distribution of precipitation—the greatest in winter and the least in summer, especially in August. The summer is hot, with high evaporation.

The northern slopes of the Crimean Mountains, up to 500 meters, are similar in climate to the steppes, with maximum precipitation in June, July, and the beginning of autumn, and with a minimum in spring and at the end of autumn. The same climatic conditions are characteristic of the southern coast east of Alushta. The precipitation amounts to 300 to 500 mm.

For the surface of the Yaila [Highland, 149], the climate of the Subzone of Deciduous Forests is typical. On the average the precipitation is 500 to 1,000 mm. It is distributed fairly evenly through the year. The snow cover lasts up to sixty days. The southern shore of Mountain Crimea, approximately up to an elevation of 250 to 300 meters, is characterized by Mediterranean vegetation, represented here by a number

[30] In the Ural Mountains two vertical zones are observed, forest and tundra, and in the Southern Ural, steppe and forest, differing little from the same lowland zones, which surround the Urals on the west and east.

of acclimatized species: cypress, laurel, laurel cherry, magnolia, myrtle, acacia, Chinese coir palm, oleander, cork oak, box, Italian stone pine, and many other species of subtropical vegetation. Higher up there are juniper-oak forests, which give way to Crimean pine. Higher still, up to the very summit of the Crimean Mountains, are found beech forests with an admixture of aspen, maple, hornbeam, and euonymus. On the Yaila, there is mountain-meadow vegetation.

The upper parts of the northern slopes of the Crimean Mountains are covered with beech, oak, and hornbeam forests. Lower down the forest steppe begins, changing into steppe.

The wild mammals typical of the Crimea are the fox, badger, and common hare. In the Crimean Preserve, there are red deer.

Mountains of the Caucasus

Nowhere in the USSR do we have such great diversity of geographical regions as in the mountains of the Caucasus. This is explained by the location of the Caucasus Mountains between the Black and Caspian seas, by the marked dissection of the topography, by the height and extent of the Great Caucasus Range, and by the marked dissection of the ranges and highlands of the Trans-Caucasus.

The western part of the range is under the influence of the Black Sea and is marked by a warm and moderate climate; the eastern part is influenced by the desert expanses of Central Asia and has an arid climate. The Caspian Sea exercises no moderating influence.

From north to south as one goes up the slopes of the Great Caucasus the Steppe Zone merges vertically into the Forest Steppe Zone, beginning approximately on the Krasnodar-Pyatigorsk-Grozny line [106–109]. It is characterized by soils of the gray forest clay-loam type, degraded chernozems, and mountain chernozems, with vegetation differing little from that of the Forest Steppe Zone in the plains of the European part of the USSR, which has been discussed. In this zone is the Stavropol Upland [150]. To the east of it, the Forest Steppe Zone narrows markedly. It attains an average elevation of from 500 to 700 meters. The zone of broad-leaved forests lies still higher, represented by thickets of oak and beech. The predominant soils of this upland zone belong to the type of brown forest soils. Above the broad-leaved forests, between 1,700 and 1,900 meters, are found coniferous forests of oriental spruce and Nordmann fir. By imperceptible degrees the spruce-fir zone merges with the wild mountain-meadow vegetation, which extends up to the very snow line. The most noteworthy forests are the spruce-fir and broad-leaved forests along the upper Belaya and Laba rivers [151], where the Caucasus Preserve is located, and the spruce-fir forests in the Maikop region [152].

East of Teberda [153] the coniferous forests of spruce and fir disappear. Here beech forests predominate.

Among the animals which live in the Caucasus foothills are the wild boar, wildcat, deer, and roebuck.

On the southern slope of the Caucasus, facing the Black Sea, the lower vertical soil and vegetation zones are noteworthy for subtropical species. The chief forest-forming species are the oak, beech, and chestnut. In addition, elm, ash, laurel, maple, and box grow here. This zone of broad-leaved forests extends to elevations of approximately 800 to 1,200 meters. In certain places beech and chestnut are found at 1,800 to 2,000 meters.

Farther up, at 1,200 to 1,900 meters, is a fir zone with an admixture of beech and hornbeam and an undergrowth of evergreen shrubs of laurel cherry and holly. At 1,300 to 2,100 meters there is a subalpine zone, represented by forests of pubescent birch with an undergrowth of beech, laurel cherry, and holly. Herbaceous vegetation, used as pasture, is well developed.

In the mountains of the eastern Trans-Caucasus, with their dry climate, the vegetation differs. Thus, in the mountains of South Osetia [154], on the southern slopes, beech, spruce-fir, and pine forests are found; east of South Osetia, fir forests are absent. However, here subalpine and alpine zones are developed, as in the western Trans-Caucasus.

In Dagestan [155], the vegetation of the foothill zone is typical, rising to elevations of 1,000 to 1,200 meters. On the lower levels are thickets of xerophytic shrubs which lose their leaves in winter. The upper levels are covered with dense broad-leaved forests of Iberian oak, Caucasian beech, maple, elm, and hornbeam. The highest summits of Mountain Dagestan proper are covered with xerophytic vegetation. Pine forests occupy an insignificant area and are found mostly on the northern slopes (up to 2,000 meters).

The soil cover of the Armenian Plateau [156] is very diversified. Here are found chernozem soils, south of Lake Sevan [157]. North of Yerevan [Y] are chernozems of medium and low humus content. Mountain-meadow soils are also found, but brown forest soils, associated with igneous rocks, rich in carbonates, predominate. Thus, according to the character of the soil cover, the whole surface of the Armenian Plateau constitutes a rich agricultural area with large harvests of wheat, barley, corn, and other crops.

The dominant type of vegetation of the highlands is basically the mountain grassy steppe. In some places forests of Aleppo pine are found. On the mountain slopes are thin forests of mountain oak and, in some places, juniper forests. The high mountain meadows of Armenia do not have the tall herbage so characteristic of the Great Caucasus range.

North of the Armenian Plateau, along the middle course of the Kura River, lie the Shirak, Karayaz, and Shirvan steppes [146], at elevations of from 400 to 700 meters, with a semiarid type of vegetation. Farther on, along the lower Kura and Araks, they merge into the Kura-Araks Lowland.

On the slopes of the Talysh Range [159], there are no coniferous forests except for yew and juniper; and no alpine vegetation is found on the upper summits.

Mountainous Regions of Central Asia

The northern edge of the Kopet-Dag [134] extends into the USSR. The small brooks and rivers that drain from it lose themselves in the deserts. There are no forests except for the arborescent juniper, which forms continuous thickets. In some places, chiefly in deep valleys, maple, elm, and other species of trees are found.

The mountain regions of the Pamirs [160] and of the Tyan-Shan [135] have a relatively great diversity of their vertical zones, explained by the altitude of the mountain ranges, which reach above the limits of perpetual snow. The climate of the Pamirs and of the Tyan-Shan is also very unusual. The eastern Pamirs are noteworthy for their peculiarly desert character, with an annual precipitation of about 60 mm. The Pamir Ranges, covered with perpetual snow and glaciers, receive a precipitation of about 4,000 mm. a year or more. Together with moist slopes there are found dry basins which receive up to 300 mm. annually, for example, the Issyk-Kul [161] and Iskander-Kul basins. The peculiar climate of the Pamirs and of the Tyan-Shan is explained by two mutually opposing factors: the hot deserts of Central Asia and the winds bringing moisture from the far-off Atlantic. The high mountain regions are subject to considerable fluctuations in temperature. Thus, on the Pamirs, frosts of −45° C. [−49° F.] occur. In summer, in July, the temperature rises above 30° C. These are the chief features of the climate of the Pamirs and of the Tyan-Shan.

The soil cover also is very diverse, represented by regularly changing vertical soil belts of the semidesert and desert type, rising to 600 meters; by chestnut and chernozem soils, up to 800 meters; and by mountain-meadow soils, up to 1,200 meters and higher, on which there predominates a luxuriant tall herbaceous vegetation used as pasture (syrts).

The mountains of Central Asia are a center of distribution for wild fruit trees and shrubs: apples, pears, pistachios, apricots, Persian walnuts, and grapes. The wild fruit trees and shrubs grow in regular forests twined with grapevines.

Forests of spruce and fir do not extend west of 72° E. Long. They are distributed almost exclusively along the shady northern slopes and in gorges. Deciduous species such as aspen, birch, and maple are found here in admixtures.

A very typical species is Schrenk's spruce, a shapely tree up to 50 meters tall and with a diameter at the roots up to 2 meters. It is widespread in the Dzhungarian [162] and Zaili Ala-Tau [163], and also on the Kirgiz Range [164], and is found in some places on the southern slopes of the Chatkal [165], Talas [166], and Fergana [167] ranges. In the mountains of the western Tyan-Shan the only coniferous tree is the juniper, which here forms a narrow belt of forests adapted to the rocky slopes; along the shady slopes and gorges are forests of Persian walnut and maple.

The Altay

The climate of the Altay [86] is diverse. As in the Tyan-Shan, there are dry basins with an annual precipitation of 300 mm., and high steppe plateaus noted for dry summers and cold winters with an insignificant snow cover and with areas of permanent ground frost. The Chuya Steppe [168] and the Ukok Plateau have these climatic features. In the Altay broad-leaved species are absent, except for the Kuznetsk Ala-Tau [169] where lindens grow.

On the slopes of the Altay Ranges vertical zones are clearly marked. The Steppe Zone, which borders the Altay on the northwest, west, and south, rises to elevations of 400 to 700 meters. In wide, open valleys, it extends to elevations over 1,000, while high mountain steppes are found at 1,500 to 1,800 meters (Chuya and Kuray steppes). However, these steppes have vegetation different from that of the foothill steppes. These are dry steppes similar to the steppes of Mongolia, with an admixture of semidesert and desert vegetation (wormwood, halophytes, grasses).

The Forest Zone, which in the foothills alternates with the steppes, reaches to elevations of 2,000 to 2,500 meters. The dominant species are the Siberian larch, and then Siberian stone pine, fir, and spruce; deciduous species (birch, pine [?], and others) are of secondary significance. With more abundant moisture, the northern slopes are richer in forests than the southern slopes, where timber is found in small coppices on shady slopes and in deep gorges.

The area of alpine meadows is at elevations of 2,000 to 3,000 meters, with a luxuriant and rich herbaceous vegetation; higher up, the meadows are replaced by a type of vegetation that resembles the mountain tundra, with lichens and mosses and with waterlogged areas of sheathed cotton sedge.

The typical animals of the Altay are bear, lynx, badger, mountain goat, mountain sheep, sable, northern dhole, deer, and red deer. Reindeer and musk deer are found occasionally. In the steppes, the suslik, Mongolian mole, and bobac are typical. In general in the Altay we observe a mixture of the animals of the Mongolian Steppes and the Eastern Siberian Taiga.

The Sayany

Except for the Minusinsk [88] and Us [170] basins and the foothills, where soils of chernozem and podzolic type are common, taiga predominates on the Sayany, with the Siberian stone pine, fir, spruce, and larch, at elevations of 600 to 1,800 meters. Higher up is the Alpine Zone, which merges into mountain lichen tundra. The fauna is similar to that of the Eastern Siberian Taiga and differs little from that of the Altay.

Pre-Baikalia and Trans-Baikalia

Hot summers with maximum precipitation in July are characteristic of Pre-Baikalia [171] and Trans-Baikalia [172]. About 80 to 90% of the total annual precipitation of 300 mm. comes in the warm period. Lake Baikal has an effect on the winter and summer temperatures of the adjoining lake shores. The mean January temperatures are higher than the February temperatures, and those of July are lower than those of August. Around Baikal a distribution of temperatures is observed exactly like that found in places with a marine climate.

The soil and vegetation cover is diverse and unique, which is explained by the differences in altitude of the mountain ranges and the dissection of the topography. In Trans-Baikalia three vertical soil and vegetation zones are distinguished: steppe, forest, and the vegetation of bald summits (alpine).

It is difficult to make a sharp division between them. Thus, the taiga on the northwestern slopes of the Khamar-Daban extends to the very shores of Baikal. A difference in the boundaries between forest and steppe is found on moving from north to south; in the south the dividing line between Steppe and Forest zones is higher than in the north—i.e., in the north the forest ends at 1,200 meters, while in the south of Trans-Baikalia it ends at 1,700 to 1,900 meters. The Selenga Steppe [93] lies at elevations of from 500 to 1,000 meters, while the Nerchinsk Steppe [94] lies at 600 to 700 meters.

In the northern part of the Trans-Baikal Taiga forests of Dahurian larch predominate; in the southern part, larch and Japanese stone pine. In addition, forests of pine, birch and aspen are found. Higher up lies the area of bald peak vegetation, with a predominance of lichens and herbaceous plants of alpine type, which in the mountains of Trans-Baikalia form dry meadows.

According to the character of the fauna, Pre-Baikalia and a Trans-Baikalia are an area in which taiga and steppe forms mingle—jerboa, bobac, squirrel, bear, sable, suslik, wolf, mountain sheep, roebuck, reindeer, and elk.

Mountainous Regions of Northeastern Siberia

In the mountains of this broad country the Forest and Mountain Tundra Zones are developed. The dominant species of trees are Dahurian larch and Japanese stone pine, which form rich forests. On the slopes of the mountain valleys are forests of Siberian spruce with an admixture of birch and poplar. The high summits are occupied by mountain-tundra vegetation, with lichens predominating. In spots there are areas covered with talus, especially on the Chukotsk Peninsula [10] and in the Anadyr Range [173].

The fauna of northeastern Siberia has been little studied. In the mountain forests squirrel, fox, musk deer, and mountain sheep are found. In the high mountains live steppe rodents, the bobac and the suslik, which hibernate in winter and are found far to the north.

In the mountains of the Far East (the Stanovoy [174] and Bureya [175] ranges and the Sikhote-Alin [176]) the characteristic vegetation is the Korean pine and broad-leaved forest, which grows up to 400 to 500 meters above sea level, and consists of Korean pine, oak, linden, birch, ash, maple, and hornbeam.

On the outskirts and in the glades the forests are twined with vines and wild grape. In the forests there is a thick undergrowth of Manchurian filbert, euonymus, and honeysuckle. Higher up are coniferous forests of Dahurian larch, Yeddo spruce, and some fir. Broad-leaved forests predominate in the mountains along the middle course of the Amur and the Ussuri, and also in the Sikhote-Alin Range. The high mountain regions are occupied by bald peaks and areas of talus, with a predominance of lichens. The large animals in the mountain forests of the Far East include the black Himalyan bear, the Ussuri elk, Japanese deer, sable, musk deer, and goral.

Kamchatka

The vegetation of Kamchatka, except for the valley of the Kamchatka River [177] and the western coast, consists of typical species among which Erman's birch stands out. It covers the slopes up to 600 to 700 meters. In the valley of the Kamchatka are well developed forests of Yeddo spruce and Dahurian larch. Above the belt of Erman's birch lies the shrub zone consisting of Japanese stone pine and alder. Still higher, beginning approximately at 1,000 meters, is the Mountain Tundra Zone. The fauna of Kamchatka is characterized by marked diversity, but it has been little studied.

The large animals include the mountain sheep, bear, fox, and in some places wild reindeer and sable.

SECTION 6. MINERAL DEPOSITS[31]

The distribution of mineral deposits in the earth's crust is not

[31] See Fig. 18, facing p. 89.

haphazard or random. It is directly dependent on the geological structure and on the geological development of the earth.

The formation of mineral deposits took place with varying degrees of intensity in different eras and had different characteristics, depending on the internal and external forces active during the various geological periods. Since these forces manifested themselves in all the periods of the earth's history, we must assume that the formation of mineral deposits took place in all geological periods and is taking place at the present time. However, the activity of these forces was not the same in various geological eras; thus, periods of powerful folding alternated with periods during which the activity of external forces was intensified.

Conditions favorable to the release and rise of various metals from the depths of the earth were created during periods of intensive activity of internal forces accompanied essentially by the phenomena of folding and fracture of the earth's crust. Therefore, ore deposits are located in regions of the USSR which in past geological periods were subject to processes of mountain formation. The folding processes, in turn, were accompanied by the extrusion of magmatic rocks from the depths of the earth, and their crystallizing at some distance below the surface in the form of intrusive rocks or their outpouring onto the surface in the form of extrusive rocks. The magmatic rocks are the source of the main ore deposits, and the eruption or outpouring of magma from the depths of the earth is always connected, to some extent, with orogeny.

Many mineral deposits—iron and manganese ores, and, less frequently, copper, gold, and other ores of heavy and rare metals—are associated with sedimentary rocks, never subjected to metamorphism and orogeny. To this type of deposits belong the manganese ore reserves at Nikopol in the Ukraine, the bog-lake ores of the northern USSR, the cupriferous sandstones of the Volga Region, the gold and platinum alluvial deposits of the Urals and Siberia, the Kerch ore reserves, and other ore beds. However, deposits of this kind are either of secondary origin, having been formed through the weathering of former primary deposits and the shifting of the weathered products to other locations by the action of external forces, or deposited as a result of chemical decomposition and erosion of the earth's crust and the accumulation of mineral resources in the crust or in marine and lacustrine basins.

During periods of intense activity of external forces, accompanied by increased erosion and leveling of the earth's surface, there took place the opening and the redistribution of the primary ore deposits, and the formation of secondary beds, as well as the creation of new mineral deposits—oil, coal, salts, gypsum, etc.

The overwhelming majority of nonmetallic minerals are associated with sedimentary rocks of marine or continental origin.

The mineral resources most important for the development of the national economy of the USSR are oil, coal, oil shales, peat, iron ore, various ores of nonferrous metals, apatite, phosphorite, potassium salts, sodium chloride, gold, platinum, and ores of other rare metals, as well as various construction materials mined from the earth.

Oil

Oil is associated with rocks of organic origin. But a theory exists that oil was formed inorganically. Nowadays, the majority of scholars adhere to the former theory. The advocates of the organic origin of oil hold that the original materials for its formation were the remains of various animals and plants which were subjected to a process of slow decay with no access to oxygen. Conditions favorable to the accumulation of vast masses of organic matter exist at present in the Black and Caspian seas, whose waters at some depth are contaminated with hydrogen sulphide; organisms which get into those waters provide a source for the accumulation of organic matter.

The eastern and northeastern region of the European part of the USSR, within the East Russian Basin, is very rich in oil. The vast territory of the so-called Volga-Ural oil-bearing area is almost in the center of the USSR, and stretches from the Ural Mountains on the east to the right bank of the Volga on the west. The latest investigations indicate that this extensive oil-bearing area extends to the west of the Volga, the Oka-Tsna divide, and the meridian of Gorky [Fig. 18].

The industrial oil regions in this area extend along the eastern slope of the Timan Ridge, in the region of the Ukhta River and the upper reaches of the Izhma River, near the town of Ukhta (formerly Chibyu), as well as in the Krasnokamsk region, near Perm [Molotov]. Oil deposits here are associated with Upper Devonian sediments. Vast accumulations of oil have been discovered in the Syzran and Buguruslan sections of the Middle Volga Region and the Ishimbay and Tuimaza districts of the Bashkir ASSR. Large oil reserves occupy a vast territory here, equal to approximately a million sq. km., and provide the basis for the creation here of a "Second Baku."

As distinguished from the Ukhta and other regions of the northeastern parts of the European USSR, the deposits of oil in the Middle Volga Region and the Bashkir ASSR are associated chiefly with Lower Carboniferous, and, in part, Permian sediments.[32] Oil penetrated into these strata from deeper-lying rocks along faults and joints. Under the peculiar conditions of the ancient topography, the oil was partially subjected to oxidation and formed varieties of asphalt and petroleum asphalt, deposits of which are found here frequently.

Rich deposits of oil are found in a number of places in the southeast portion of the East European Platform, in the region of the Caspian Basin. This so-called Emba oil-bearing area is located principally in western Kazakhstan and encompasses Guryev and Aktyubinsk oblasts. The deposits are associated with salt domes, which occupy comparatively large areas in the Ural and Emba basins. The oil here is of especially high quality. The most important oil deposits in the area are in the Dossor, Makat, Iskine, Koschagil, Baichunas, and some other regions.

Especially important in the Caucasus are the vast oil deposits along the slopes of the Great Caucasus. The principal oil-bearing areas are Baku, Grozny, and Maikop, where a powerful oil industry has grown up. The vast oil reserves of the Caucasus are associated with the sandy sediments of the Tertiary Period. The formation of oil took place under the condition of depression of Upper Tertiary basins, so that they become landlocked and subsequently contaminated with hydrogen sulphide. Analogous conditions may be observed at the present time in the basins of the Black and Caspian seas.

The industrial oil regions of Central Asia are concentrated in the Fergana Valley and the basin of the upper Amu-Darya. Fergana

32 [Since this book was written deeper drilling has penetrated the Devonian in this area and revealed considerably greater oil reserves than had been found previously in the more recent formations.]

oil (Andizhan and Namangan deposits) is associated with steep anticlinical folds of various types and folded strata of the Mesozoic (Jurassic, Cretaceous) and of the Tertiary system. Oil deposits here principally accompany deposits of light-brown shales and limestones.

Southwest of Fergana, a new oil-bearing area has been discovered recently—the Novaya Bukhara [Kagan], near the city of Bukhara, with abundant yields of oil and gas associated with Cretaceous and Tertiary strata.

In the basin of the upper Amu-Darya the industrial oil reserves are in the Khaudak and Uch-Kyzyl regions of the Uzbek SSR. Structurally, the deposits represent a narrow anticlinal fold, composed mainly of Tertiary limestones.

There are two large oil-bearing areas in the Turkmen SSR, the western and the eastern. The former extends eastward from the Caspian Sea to the Bolshoy and Maly Balkhan ranges. Especially important in it is the industrial Nebit-Dag oil-bearing region, which was developed in the course of the Second Five-Year Plan. The eastern area takes in the banks of the Amu-Darya River from the Afghanistan frontier on the south to the Aral Sea on the north, as well as the Kara-Kum sands, the borderland of the eastern Kopet-Dag, and the Paropamiz.

The spacious territory of the West Siberian Lowland, which belongs to the tectonic zone of Hercynian folding, is little explored from the point of view of mineral resources. However, here and in adjacent Eastern Siberia indications of oil have been discovered. Large oil deposits are found on Sakhalin and Kamchatka. Thus, the rich oil deposits of the USSR are associated principally with strata of sedimentary rocks of marine origin of various ages, from Upper Devonian limestones down to the sandy-clayey deposits of the Tertiary Period. In some cases these oil deposits were subjected to the influence of mountain-forming processes. Therefore, some oil deposits are found in the mountainous regions also, such as the headwaters of the Amu-Darya in the Tadzhik SSR.

Coal

Most of the coal was formed during the so-called Carboniferous Period. It came principally from the remains of vegetation, accumulating and slowly decomposing under water. In some cases the accumulation took place in spacious bogs subsequently buried under sandy-clayey deposits. In other cases the remains of vegetation were brought in by river currents and deposited in the estuary and along the coast of the sea or lake into which the river emptied. These plant remains slowly decomposed under water and were buried under accretions of sandy-clayey sediments. The formation of coal in these two manners is taking place even at the present time. Thus, the accumulation of vegetation remains takes place in vast peat bogs. Similar accumulation of river-transported vegetation matter occurs at the estuaries of many of our rivers, such as the Siberian rivers flowing into the Arctic Ocean. However, the coal now being mined came from plants which differed sharply from those of our time. They were arborescent horsetails and ferns which grew in great abundance. Besides the Carboniferous deposits, principally coastal and in part continental, coal deposits are found also in other geologic systems, such as the Jurassic, Cretaceous, and Tertiary, where their formation took place under approximately analogous conditions.

The principal coal deposits in the USSR are in the Donbas, the Kuzbas, Karaganda, Eastern Siberia, and the Far East [Fig. 18].

The Donets Ridge is an ancient eroded range containing an exceptional combination of natural riches. Outstanding among them are the coal reserves of the Donbas (about 90 billion tons), formed along the coast of a former Carboniferous sea from the transported remains of vegetation, buried gradually under the sandy-clayey and clayey deposits.

The Carboniferous sedimentary strata which compose the Moscow Basin abound in lignite and torbanite [a variety of cannel coal]. The reserves there are estimated at 12 billion tons. The distribution of coal in the coal-bearing strata varies a great deal. The most important and the thickest seams are in the middle and lower parts of the coal-bearing series; they attain a thickness of 2 to 3 meters, and occasionally 6 to 10 meters. In contrast to the Donbas, the seams here occur in the form of lenses and pockets, sometimes stretching over considerable areas.

In the European North lie the rich coal deposits of the Pechora Basin. Its total reserves approximate those of the Donbas.

In the Urals, coal beds are found in the Kizel, Bogoslovsky [Ugolny], Yegorshino, Chelyabinsk, and other districts.

In the Caucasus, the Tkvarcheli and Tkvibuli coal deposits of the Georgian SSR contain reserves of approximately 200 million tons.

During the period of the first two Five-Year plans, numerous and relatively large coal deposits were discovered in Central Asia, the total coal reserves of which at present are over 18 billion tons. Among these deposits the richest coal basins are in the Fergana Valley (Sulyukta, Kyzyl-Kiya, Shurab, Kok-Yangak, and others), and in the Naryn and other districts of the Kirgiz SSR. Coal is found also in the Tadzhik SSR and the Turkmen SSR (Tashkutan and Kugitan).

Between the Kuznetsk Ala-Tau (range) and the Salair Range, along the Tom River, lies the Kuznetsk Basin (Kuzbas) containing high-grade coal reserves in excess of 450 billion tons. This is the second most important coal base in the USSR. Kuzbas coal was formed during the Paleozoic and Jurassic eras in lake basins with luxuriant vegetation of the Temperate Zone. The basins subsequently disappeared, having been subjected to marked subsidence as a result of orogenic processes.

The third most important coal base of the USSR, Karaganda, has very rich coal reserves (53 billion tons).

In the Siberian Platform are the coal deposits of the Tungus Basin (440 billion tons), which constitute the vast so-called Tungus coal-bearing area, associated with Permian-Carboniferous deposits in the basin of the Upper, Middle, and Lower Tunguska rivers [Angara, Srednyaya Tunguska, and Nizhnyaya Tunguska].

Especially important are the rich coal deposits of the Irkutsk (Cheremkhovo) Basin (80 billion tons), suitable for metallurgy, gasification, and the extraction of liquid fuels.

Vast reserves of lignite are concentrated in the Lena (203 billion tons) and Chulymo-Yenisey (43 billion tons) basins, and on Taimyr Peninsula. Coal is found also in the Minusinsk (20 billion tons) and Kansk (42 billion tons) basins. The Lena lignite constitutes the vast Lena coal-bearing area, located in the Lena-Vilyuy Lowland and encompassing the basin of the lower Aldan, almost the entire basin of the Vilyuy River, and, farther down, a narrow strip along the valley of the middle and lower Lena. The following Trans-Baikal coal deposits should be mentioned: Bukachacha, Gusinoye Ozero, and Chernovskie Kopi.

Thus, the scarcely explored reserves of the main basins of the

Siberian Platform alone exceed 800 billion tons, which is approximately 50% of the total Soviet reserves.

The Far East, Sakhalin, and Kamchatka also abound in coal deposits. The most important of these are: (1) the reserves along the Bureya River, making up the so-called Bureya Basin (26 billion tons), which occupies large areas on the western slopes of the Bureya Range, (2) the Kivda-Raichikhinsk, (3) the Suchan, and (4) the Saifun [Suifun] coal basins.

Oil Shales

Oil shales are important both as fuel and as raw material for the chemical industry. The most important oil-shale deposits in the USSR are in the southern part of the Timan Ridge, along the Ukhta River, and especially vast deposits lie along the right bank of the Volga, near Ulyanovsk (Undor shales), near Syzran (Kashpir shales), and in the region of the Obshchy Syrt [Fig. 18]. There are also oil-shale deposits in the Gdov region of Leningrad Oblast, associated with Silurian strata.

The shales were formed from the simultaneous deposition of clay and organic silt, subsequently subjected to a long process of decomposition and thus turned into a dark combustible substance permeating the rock. Putrefied silt, or so-called sapropel, is being formed at the present time also on the bottoms of some lakes and calm bays.

Iron and Manganese Ores

Deposits of iron ore of all varieties are associated principally with the different phases of crystallization of magmatic masses at some depth within the earth's crust or on its surface. Some iron-ore deposits are associated also with sedimentary rocks. The formation of such ores took place in enclosed coastal lagoons or in bog-lakes through a process of geochemical accumulation and deposition of ferruginous aggregations at the bottom.

In the ancient continental crystalline shields and platforms we frequently find vast accumulations of iron ore. In most cases it is magnetite or hematite. Thus, in the Kola-Karelia Massif [Baltic Shield] the Yensk iron-ore deposit is found in the Monchetundry district, where reserves amount to 580 million tons with an average iron content of 45% [Fig. 18].

The iron-ore deposits of the Kola-Karelia Massif are associated principally with granite intrusions.

In the Voronezh Block, where the original platform emerges relatively close to the surface, there are accumulations of magnetite known as the Kursk Magnetic Anomaly. Iron-ore deposits occur at 200 to 600 meters below the surface. The known reserves of ferruginous quartzites in the Kursk Magnetic Anomaly are estimated at about 200 billion tons.

The Ukrainian crystalline shield contains enormous reserves of Krivoy Rog iron ore in the form of hematite and ferruginous quartzites, estimated at 51.3 billion tons. These deposits form the basis for Ukrainian metallurgy. Manganese ores occur along the Bug River [Yuzhny (Southern) Bug]; the beds of manganese ores in the Nikopol district, which are of world-wide significance, are especially rich.

The Kerch Peninsula abounds in limonite, which was formed at the bottom of a former shallow bay by the chemical deposition of iron compounds. The Kerch ore reserves are estimated at over 2.7 billion tons.

Ores of sedimentary origin are found in the vicinity of Tula, Lipetsk, in the basin of the Khoper River, and in the Omutninsk Raion of Kirov Oblast. The Tula iron-ore reserves are estimated at 183 million tons, those of Lipetsk at 85 million tons, and of the Khoper at 166 million tons.

The Urals constitute an exceptionally rich depository of all kinds of metals and minerals. The most important of these are the iron-ore deposits of contact origin of Mount Magnitnaya (485 million tons), which were formed as a result of a complex chemical reaction of limestones with intrusive magma. Also important are the iron-ore deposits of analogous origin of Mount Vysokaya and Mount Blagodat. Other very rich iron-ore deposits are the Komarovo-Zigazynsky [K in Fig. 18] (over 100 million tons), Bakal (over 176 million tons), and Alapayevsk. Vast reserves of chromite (about 500 million tons) are located all along the Urals (Sverdlovsk, Khalilovo, and other regions).

Comparatively rich iron-ore deposits have been discovered in many regions of the Caucasus. The most outstanding are the Dashkesan deposit in Azerbaidzhan, the Taman Peninsula, and the Malka deposits on the northern slopes of the Great Caucasus.

Chromite deposits are found also in the Caucasus, in Armenia.

The Chiatura manganese ores are of very great importance.

In Central Kazakhstan there are ferruginous quartzites of the Krivoy Rog type.

Large reserves of iron ore have been discovered recently south of the Kuzbas, in the region of Gornaya Shoriya (in the Altay).

In the Far East large reserves of iron ore are found in the Nikolayevsk-on-Amur district. Ferruginous quartzites have been found in the region of the Little Khingan [Mountains].

High-grade iron ores which make up the so-called Angara-Ilim group have been discovered in the area of the East Siberian Platform, in the vicinity of the coal deposits.

The Angara-Ilim group containing reserves of more than 400 million tons of iron ore is the largest deposit in the Asiatic part of the USSR. The iron ores of this group are associated with the trap intrusions of the East Siberian Platform.

Copper, Polymetallic Ores, and Rare Metals

The numerous deposits of copper, polymetallic ores, and rare metals are also associated with igneous rocks. They were formed in the course of a complex chemical process resulting from the cooling of magma. While losing its temperature, magma affects the adjacent rocks. The surrounding rocks absorb the heat, sometimes even melt, and become transfused with the vapors and hot gases exuded by the magma. As a result of these complex chemical processes, there takes place a precipitation in the magma and the surrounding rocks of masses of various metals and rare elements, chemically related to one another. In this way, copper, lead, silver, tin, zinc, gold, tungsten, and other very important metals are formed.

Such mineral deposits are associated mostly with mountain elevations, in some measure eroded under the influence of external forces. In some cases the deposits are found in the lowlands and are associated with strata of sedimentary rocks, such as the gold and platinum ores of the Urals and Siberia. However, these are of a secondary origin, formed through a process of shifting and deposition in new areas.

The most important deposits of polymetallic ores and rare metals in the USSR are in the mountains of the Urals, Central Asia, the Altay, Kazakhstan, the Caucasus, Trans-Baikalia, and in the area of the Siberian Platform and the Kola-Karelia Massif [Fig. 18].

Copper ores appear in great abundance in the Urals. They extend in great concentration southward from the headwaters of the Tura River to the sources of the Miass River, and encompass the Turyinsky, Krasnouralsk [Kr in Fig. 18], and Karabash [Ka in Fig. 18] groups, the deposits of Degtyarka, Voznensensk, Blyava, and others.

In a number of regions of the Urals are found alluvial deposits of the rare metals, platinum and gold; there are also deposits of titanium, nickel, and vanadium ores, and of tungsten, bismuth, mercury, and lead.

Of particular importance are the nickel ores, which are in the Orsk-Khalilovo and the Ufaley [Uf in Fig. 18] regions of the Urals, in Monchegorsk, Norilsk, and the Aktyubinsk regions.

Of tremendous importance are the Central Asiatic deposits of polymetallic ores and rare metals. Among nonferrous metals, the copper deposit in the Almalyk region, south of Tashkent, is outstanding. Silver, lead, and zinc are found in the Pamir, antimony and mercury in the Alay Range. The complex Kara-Mazar region [KM in Fig. 18] of polymetallic ores, south of Tashkent, is particularly outstanding. In the Kara-Mazar district there are lead, zinc, silver, tin, tungsten, molybdenum, copper, bismuth, and arsenic. A number of large new discoveries of lead and zinc have been made in recent years in Kirgizia (Kurgan and Aktyuz) and in the Dzhungarian Ala-Tau (Tekeli).

To the south of the Kuznetsk Basin in the Altay are very rich deposits of nonferrous metals. Particularly significant in the region are reserves of zinc and lead, which are the bases of the nonferrous metallurgy of Ridder, Zyryanovskoye, and Belousovskoye, together with incidental reserves of copper, silver, tin, gold, and other metals. Besides this, in the Altay is the Chagan-Uzun [Ch in Fig. 18] mercury and molybdenum deposit. The Kalbin Range contains tin, tungsten, and gold.

More than half of all the Union reserves of copper ore are the large deposits in Central Kazakhstan, particularly in the regions of Kounrad, Dzhezkazgan, and Boshchekul. Here also are a number of lead-zinc, tungsten, and gold deposits. In the Kara-Tau Mountains, in the western [southern?] part of Kazakhstan, in the Turlan group of deposits, is the largest lead-zinc region (Achisay).

On the northern slopes of the Caucasus Range, particularly in North Osetia and in Kabardino-Balkaria [N in Fig. 18], are large deposits of polymetallic ores (lead, zinc, and molybdenum).

The Alaverdi and Zangezur silver and copper deposits are well known. Also well known in the Caucasus are a number of deposits of arsenic and gold; and the number of regions known to contain rare metals is increasing. In the Trans-Baikal region are found significant reserves of polymetallic ores (tungsten, zinc, lead, and silver, as well as gold, tin, and arsenic). The Yakut ASSR is rich in tin deposits [at Ege-Khay]. The Maritime Kray (Tetyukhe) also has polymetallic deposits (zinc, lead, and tin).

In the area of the Siberian Platform are numerous deposits of both metallic and nonmetallic minerals. Gold is found here primarily in alluvial form, and its most important deposits are in the Yenisey Range and in the basins of the Lena, Vitim, and Aldan rivers.

Under the Soviet regime deposits of silver-lead and zinc ores have been found in the Nagolny Ridge [X in Fig. 18] in the Donbas. Large mercury deposits are being worked in the region of Nikitovka [Y in Fig. 18] in the Ukraine.

Apatite, Phosphorites, Potassium Salts, Bauxite, and Other Mineral Resources

Apatite (a light green phosphoric mineral used for the manufacture of phosphate fertilizers) is found in the Khibiny [range on the Kola Peninsula] together with nephelite, which also is a very valuable raw material for its aluminum content.

The total apatite reserves of the Khibiny are estimated at two billion tons with a high content of phosphorus oxide. So far this is the only apatite deposit in the USSR and the largest one in the world. It was discovered under the Soviet regime.

Numerous phosphorite deposits are associated with the sedimentary rocks developed in the European and Asiatic areas of the USSR. Outstanding among them are the reserves of the Vyatka-Kama district, the Moscow region, the Chuvash ASSR, the numerous deposits in the Vinnitsa, Orel, Smolensk, Kursk, Voronezh, and other oblasts, and also the Aktyubinsk and the newly discovered Kara-Tau deposits in Kazakhstan.

Of these the deposits of highest quality are the phosphorites of Kara-Tau; and next, those of the Vyatka-Kama district (in Kirov Oblast), largely the clayey type in origin, containing on the average 25% of phosphorous oxide. The Vyatka-Kama phosphorite reserves are estimated at over 850 million tons.

The world's largest deposits of potassium salts are associated with

Permian strata in the Solikamsk region; these are estimated to contain over 18 billion tons of potassium oxide. In addition, new discoveries of potassium salts have been made recently in the Trans-Volga Region; but as yet they have been little investigated or developed.

Bauxites, graphites, sodium chloride, and sulphur play an important part in the national economy of the Soviet Union.

The bauxite deposit in the Tikhvin region of Leningrad Oblast is very important; other rich deposits are north of the town of Serov in the Urals and in the Bashkir ASSR [north of Ufa at Kukshinsk]. Substantial deposits of bauxite are in the Akmolinsk and Turgay regions, with reserves of over two million tons.

Within the Siberian Platform the rich Tatarsk bauxite deposit (approximately 3 million tons), in the lower reaches of the Angara River, is associated with trap intrusions. Bauxite is found also in the Salair Range.

Graphite deposits are in the Ukraine and along the Kureika River in Krasnoyarsk Kray.

The USSR also has numerous deposits of rock salt and cooking salt (sodium chloride). Rich deposits of rock salt are in the Artemovsk region [A in Fig. 18] of the Ukraine, in the Trans-Volga Region (Baskunchak, Elton), at Sol-Iletsk [Iletskaya Zashchita], Pavlodar, Usolye[U] near Solikamsk, near the village of Usolye on the Angara River, and in other regions.

Such is the distribution of the most important mineral resources and their association with the geological structure of the Soviet Union.

The fundamental results of geological research and the changes in the geography of the known mineral resources of the USSR which took place after the Great October Socialist Revolution, are as follows:

In the years of the Soviet regime an area of over seven million sq. km., representing about 35% of the territory of the country, has been covered by geological surveys of various scales. Before the October Revolution the geological maps covered a little over 10% of the country's territory.

During the prerevolutionary period the USSR lagged far behind the United States and other capitalist countries in known mineral resources. At the present time the USSR leads the largest countries of the world in important mineral resources.

Radical shifts in the distribution of mineral raw materials have taken place in the territory of the USSR as compared with Tsarist Russia.

While in the prerevolutionary period the known mineral resources were concentrated in various districts of the European part of the USSR, the Caucasus, and the Urals, during the years of Soviet power they have increased both in the European part, and in the Asiatic part as well, in Siberia, the Far East, Kazakhstan, and Central Asia, all of which once were considered poor in mineral resources.

During the two Stalin Five-Year Plans new oil-bearing regions have been discovered between the Volga and the Urals, in Central Asia, in the Far East, in the North, etc.

New mineral-bearing industrial regions have been discovered in the Kuznetsk, Karaganda, and other basins. This is true also of iron ores and ores of nonferrous and rare metals.

Mineral resources are available in such quantities as to provide fully for the needs of the national economy of the land of socialism.

The progress of geological research in the USSR has upset the pseudoscientific antagonistic theories that Central Asia, Kazakhstan, and the Volga Region are lacking in mineral resources. Widely developed geological investigations in the USSR have dissipated these "theories." Tremendous resources of mineral raw materials have been discovered precisely in the places which the enemies of the people intentionally ignored. The growth of mineral resources is shown in Table 4.

TABLE 4. DYNAMICS OF THE MOST IMPORTANT MINERAL RESOURCES OF THE USSR DISCOVERED AFTER THE OCTOBER REVOLUTION AS COMPARED WITH 1913.

Most Important Mineral Resources	Known Reserves in 1913 (million tons)	Known Reserves as of Jan. 1, 1938 (million tons)
Oil	900	4,679.3 [a]
Coal	230,000	1,654,400
Peat	Data unavailable	150,600
Iron ores	1,648	267,400 [b]
Manganese	168	784.9
Phosphate and apatite	Data unavailable	3,788 [a]
Potassium salts	Data unavailable	18,368

[a] Reserves in categories $A + B + C_1$. [b] Including ferruginous quartzites.

Mineral Resources of the USSR in Comparison with the Resources of Capitalist Countries

Not a single capitalist country possesses such huge mineral resources as the Soviet Union. In resources of oil, iron, manganese, and several other important minerals the Soviet Union occupies first place in the world, even though a great deal is still unknown regarding Soviet mineral resources [Table 5]. Coal reserves of the USSR exceed considerably the known reserves of the capitalist countries of Europe and Asia combined. In some important mineral resources the USSR holds an outstanding place in the world. Thus, the Soviet resources of apatite represent almost 100% of the world's total; those of potassium salts, 85%; of maganese, 53% (categories A + B); of oil, 58.8%, and of peat, 60% of the total world resources.

TABLE 5. POSITION OF THE USSR IN THE WORLD ECONOMY WITH RESPECT TO THE IMPORTANT MINERAL RESOURCES

Important Mineral Deposits	World Reserves (million tons)	% of World Total Found in the USSR	Position of the USSR in the World Economy	Position of the USSR in Europe
Oil	7,965.1	58.8	1	1
Coal	7,916,000	21.0	2	1
Peat	250,600	60.0	1	1
Iron ores	500,400	53.4	1	1
Manganese	2,458	32.0	2 [a]	1
Phosphate and apatite	16,356	23.0	2	1
Potassium salts	21,468	85.0	1	1

[a] In industrial reserves (categories A + B) the USSR occupies first place.

Ahead of the USSR are the United States in coal, and Chile, the United States, and Northern Rhodesia in copper ore.

Thus, in the USSR are tremendous reserves of various mineral deposits, which completely provide for the development of the national economy.

While there have been tremendous achievements in the geological study of the country, it should be pointed out that great problems have yet to be solved. It must be borne in mind that almost half the territory of the Union has not yet been studied and surveyed geologically. Detailed geological studies of the USSR are particularly inadequate. At the beginning of the Third Five-Year Plan only 4.5% of the entire territory was covered by a large-scale survey (1:100,000 and larger), as compared with 0.45% in 1917. During the Third Five-Year Plan the problem which confronts Soviet geology is to bring to an end the lag of geological surveys behind the development of the national economy of the USSR. In addition, a very important problem of the geological research organizations of the USSR is to convert potential reserves to the industrial category. This problem was given its full weight in the decisions of the 18th Party Congress, where emphasis was given to the need to "develop the work of *geological research,* so as to guarantee industrial reserves of raw materials for existing enterprises and those under construction under the Third Five-Year Plan, as well as to create new industrial reserves for future years in all regions of the USSR."

General Conclusions

Thus, the USSR has diverse natural conditions and natural riches such as are possessed by no other country in the world. "From the standpoint of natural wealth, we are completely secure. We have even more than we need." [33] But in order to put these natural riches completely into the service of the working people, in order to create an abundance of all kinds of products, "there must be a government with the desire and the power to direct the utilization of this huge national wealth for the benefit of the people. Do we have such a government? We do." [34]

In Tsarist Russia the same natural conditions existed as in the USSR; but they were poorly utilized in the development of the economy. Tremendous natural riches were pillaged in the interests of the parasitic classes—landowners and capitalists. Many millions of working people were ruined and impoverished, at the same time that great fortunes existed. Fine forested areas were ruthlessly cut down even in regions where they were essential for the conservation of soil, rivers, and lakes. With the cutting down of forests the rivers grew shallow, extreme gullying took place, and the fertile top soil was washed away. The same plundering attitude toward the exploitation of natural riches exists even now in the capitalist coun-

[33] Stalin, *Questions of Leninism,* p. 324.
[34] *Ibid.*

tries among the parasitic classes. Not until the victory of the Great October Socialist Revolution, when the socialist method of production was accepted, did the natural wealth of the USSR enter the service of the people and begin to be exploited efficiently.

Unlike the capitalist countries, the USSR utilizes the national wealth on a strictly scientific and planned basis, taking into account the natural-historical relations of natural phenomena. Only under socialism is it possible to realize in practice the brilliant prediction of Engels that "the living conditions which surround people, and which up to the present time have ruled over them, will come under the power and control of people, who for the first time will become the real and conscious rulers of nature to the extent to which they become rulers of their own social relations."[35]

[35] Engels, *Anti-Dühring,* 1938, p. 232.

II The Distribution of Productive Forces in Tsarist Russia

Principal Characteristics of the Distribution of Productive Forces Under Capitalism

THE principles of distribution of productive forces are linked inseparably with the basic principles of a given system of production. The nature of the distribution of productive forces changes from one system of production of material goods to another, and its principles become different.

The abnormal distribution of productive forces under capitalism stems from the very nature of capitalist economy. Capitalism, especially in its most advanced and final stage—imperialism—by virtue of the anarchy of production and the irregularity of development peculiar to it, is inherently characterized by an extremely inefficient and unequal distribution of productive forces. Capitalism creates a world market and an international division of labor, and breaks down the isolation of the economies of individual countries. But the international division of labor under capitalism is accomplished, not through the cooperation of peoples as equals, but through the oppression and exploitation of the numerous colonial and semicolonial peoples by the bourgeoisie of the imperialist countries. The colonies and semicolonies specialize in the production of agricultural products, receiving ready-made industrial goods from the industrially developed mother countries.

Analyzing the process of the circulation of capital, Marx concludes that together with the advance of capitalist production and the evolution of means of transportation, industry becomes increasingly removed from its sales markets. "If on the one hand," writes Marx, "with the progress of capitalist production, the development of means of transportation and of communication shortens the period of circulation of a given quantity of goods, then, conversely, that same progress and the conditions which result from improving the means of transportation and communication make it necessary to work towards ever more distant markets—in short, towards a world market." [1]

The colonial policy of the imperialist countries retards the development of industry in colonial and semicolonial countries, which are the largest sales markets for industrial output, and which abound in various raw materials. The concentration of industry in a few mother countries, which as a result is intensified, further increases the separation of industry from the sales markets of its output and the sources of its raw material. This results in an increase of unproductive transport of industrial goods and industrial raw materials from one part of the world to another.

More than 70% of the industrial production of the capitalist world is concentrated in the four largest imperialist countries, the United States, England, Germany, and France, which contain not more than 15% of the population of the capitalist world, and only about 8% of the area. At the same time, in the colonial and semicolonial countries, with more than half the population of the world and with an area exceeding by many times that of the imperialist countries listed above, large-scale industry is either completely absent or in an embryonic stage. Under these conditions the colonial and semicolonial countries are forcibly held back by their imperialist masters.

The profits of colonial exploitation oblige the imperialists to develop production in the colonies to some extent; but this development is directed by them along such channels and to such a degree as to be profitable to the ruling classes of the mother country, and to preserve the interests of the colonial monopoly.

In a period of world capitalist depression, when the contradictions of capitalism become especially aggravated, the international division of labor becomes increasingly abnormal, which in turn is reflected in the distribution of the productive forces of the capitalist world.

The unequal and extremely inefficient distribution of productive forces under capitalism comes about not only on the scale of the

[1] Marx, *Capital,* Vol. II, 1938, p. 216.

entire world capitalist economy, but also within the individual capitalist countries.

Any attempts to plan and regulate the distribution of industry, or to plan the economy, in capitalist countries inevitably result in failure because of the anarchy of capitalist production, the violent struggle of monopolies, depressions which shake the capitalist economy to its foundations, etc.

Bourgeois Apologetic Theories of Distribution

The apologists of capitalism try to represent the distribution of productive forces under capitalism as rational, or organized. For this they have created special theories. The most widely held are the so-called location theories, in particular the theory of industrial location of Alfred Weber. The essence of this bourgeois apologetic theory is that capitalist production is distributed according to the principle of lowest costs. In reality, figures used here are not real costs, but capitalist costs, that is, surplus value is excluded from them.

Marxian political economy distinguishes between the capitalist cost of production of goods (*c* plus *v*), and the actual cost (*c* plus *v* plus *m*). "The value of a commodity to a capitalist," writes Marx, "is measured by the expenditure of capital. The actual value of the commodity is measured by the expenditure of labor. For this reason capitalist costs of production of a commodity are quantitatively different from its value or the real cost of its production." [2] Hence, Weber is operating not with real, but only with capitalist costs of production.

The distribution of capitalist industry is subject to the general principles of capitalist production. The rate of profit is the driving force of capitalist production; it also regulates basically the distribution of capitalist industry. The capitalist tries to build a plant or factory in a place where he expects to get the maximum profit. Weber's explanation of the distribution of industry exclusively by capitalist costs of production is wrong to start with, since capitalist costs of production, especially under monopolistic capitalism, do not of themselves determine the rate of profit, which is, in the last analysis, the prime interest of the capitalist. Given small costs of production for particular commodities under monopolistic predominance, a high rate of profit is still not necessarily forthcoming, and *vice versa*. Here a tremendous role is played by monopolistic prices and other factors.

[2] Marx, *Capital*, Vol. III, 1938, p. 26. [*c* = fixed costs, *v* = variable costs or wages, *m* = surplus value.]

As we know, the application of the latest achievements of science and technology diminishes the cost of production per unit of output. But monopolistic prices hold back the application of these achievements under capitalist production.

In this connection, Lenin wrote: "To the extent that monopolistic prices are established, even for a time, the motives for technical, or any other, progress disappear in some measure, and to the same extent, furthermore, it becomes economically possible artificially to hold back technical progress. . . . Of course, the possibility of lowering the costs of production and of increasing profit by means of the introduction of technical improvements operates in favor of change. But the tendency toward stagnation and decay, characteristic of monopoly, continues to operate, and in particular branches of industry, and in particular countries, it holds the upper hand for certain periods of time." [3]

Such methods of monopolistic warfare as dumping and other forms of trade war, especially characteristic of the epoch of imperialism, influence the rate of profit.

In determining the cost of production, Weber completely ignores such an extremely important fact as the diverse levels of productive forces, including the difference in the level of technology in various countries and regions. The cost of production per unit of a commodity depends, to a large degree, also on organizational-technical factors. There is a big difference between the handicraft shop on the one hand and continuous mass production on the other. But Weber completely ignores this fact on the basis that it lacks "geographic preciseness."

According to Weber's theory, the distribution of industry is determined by three factors: (1) transportation, i.e., the aspiration of capital ists to build plants in places with the lowest transportation costs; (2) labor, i.e., the aspiration of capitalists to locate their industrial enterprises in places with the cheapest labor power, and finally (3) agglomeration, i.e., the aspiration of capitalists to build plants and factories in places where other industrial enterprises are concentrated.

According to Weber, capitalist enterprises, on the basis of a strictly mathematical evaluation of all these factors, gravitate toward areas where the costs of production are lowest. Thus, the distribution of capitalist industry, according to Weber, takes place "in an organized manner," "rationally," as though according to a preestablished plan.

If we scrutinize carefully the three factors which, according to Weber,

[3] Lenin, *Works,* Vol. XIX, p. 151.

alone determine the costs of production and, consequently, the distribution of industry, the inconsistency of his entire conception is revealed to an even greater degree.

Weber holds that industry is based on the location of labor power, while he ignores completely the no less important point that labor gravitates to industrial centers. Weber makes the same error in relation to transportation. He considers only the influence of transportation on the distribution of industry, and completely ignores the reverse influence. It is well known that the distribution both of labor power and of transportation is adapted to large-scale industrial production.

"In the centers of contemporary industry—factories, metallurgical works, etc.—workers move away and then return in greater numbers, as a result of which in the last analysis the number employed increases although in constantly declining proportion in comparison with the scale of production." [4]

In another place Marx states that the absolute growth of the population does not determine the distribution of machine output, but rather it is large-scale industry which determines the growth and distribution of the working population. Evidence of this is the colossal stream of immigrants who came at one time to the United States, Canada, etc., when large-scale industry was expanding rapidly in those areas.

Speaking of the fact that a revolution in the techniques of production in one sphere of industry creates conditions which bring about a similar revolution in other spheres, Marx wrote that the means of transportation and communication inherited from the handicraft period soon became insufferable fetters to large-scale industry with its constant transfer of masses of capital and labor from one sphere of production to another, and with its creation of new relations expanding into the world market. For that reason transport gradually became adapted to large-scale industrial methods of production.

As capitalism develops, the distribution of manufacturing becomes increasingly less dependent on the location of sources of raw material. Egyptian and Indian cotton are processed in England, rubber grown in Indonesia is processed in European and American plants, etc. Innumerable examples may be cited to show that as technological progress is made, the distribution of capitalist industry becomes increasingly less dependent on the location of the raw materials. This constantly growing breach between industry and the sources of raw materials is one of

[4] Marx, *Capital*, Vol. I, p. 511.

the characteristic traits of the distribution of productive forces under capitalism.

All this proves without a doubt that Weber's factors of distribution—labor, transportation, etc.—do not in any way reveal the real causes determining the distribution of industrial enterprises under capitalism.

The task of Weber's theory and other location theories is to represent the distribution of capitalist production as "rational" and without contradictions, and their method corresponds to this. The method is one of complete abstraction from complicated reality and in particular from the contradictions of capitalist production which determine its distribution.

Weber's theory is based on a metaphysical method, the separation of the principles of the distribution of production from the principles of the development of production. Actually, the distribution of production is one side of its development. The abstraction which is the basis of Weber's theory is unscientific, since Weber makes abstractions not from secondary but from primary factors such as the productive relationships of capitalism, competition, the pursuit of capitalists after profits, etc.

"As an object of theoretical analysis," writes Weber, "each conceptual economic province is taken in isolation. Thus the economic structure of each province is examined in simplified form, that is, it is conceived as though 'cleansed' of some of those strata which are superimposed during various *historical periods by various social-economic systems.* One problem of theory is the establishment of so-called 'pure' or general laws for this abstract or purely economic organism." [5]

As a result of such abstraction, Weber retains only natural-technical indices for the development of his theories.

Weber's "isolated conceptual economic province" is also an intolerable abstraction since the world market and the international division of labor exert a very strong influence on the distribution of industry in the world capitalist economy.

Weber vainly tries to proceed from the abstract to the concrete. He even treats such categories as "approximation to reality," "industry in the system of national economy," etc., in a vain attempt to approach a "realistic theory." But in the last analysis Weber remains a prisoner of his empty abstractions.

Weber examines the location of a particular plant, or, as he says, "industrial unit," in isolation from the national economy. This enter-

[5] A. Weber, *Theory of Distribution of Industry,* p. 15.

prise Weber isolates from the national economy, which he understands as the simple aggregate of separate industrial units. We are not speaking now of the fact that Weber analyzes the distribution of industry in isolation from agriculture and from other branches of the national economy.

Thus Weber's theory has nothing to do with the true distribution of capitalist industry, for he consciously avoids just those specific capitalist categories which actually condition the distribution of capitalist industry. Weber's theory, like other bourgeois location theories, demonstrates the complete inconsistency of bourgeois science and its inability to give a truly scientific analysis of the distribution of capitalist production.

Despite the clearly metaphysical method of Weber, some of his successors have tried to identify his metaphysical method with the method of Marx. They have asserted that Weber's method resembled Marx's in many ways. In so doing, qualities have been attributed to Weber that he never even dreamed of. The adherents of Weber, enraged, argued that to dispute the general methodological aim of Weber's theory was to dispute the possibility of a scientific statement of the problem of the distribution of industry. They did not understand the method of Marx, since they identified it with the unscientific method of Weber. They did not understand that Marxist abstractions represent actual reality and are not farfetched. Weber's abstractions, on the other hand, are an absolute fantasy, having nothing to do with actual reality.

The enemies of the people used Weber's theory in the struggle against the socialist distribution of productive forces. With Weber's theory as a weapon, they fought against the creation of a second coal-metallurgical base in the East of the USSR, against the industrialization of the national republics, etc.

The basic characteristics of capitalist distribution of productive forces considered above were inherent in Tsarist Russia also, and were aggravated by its economic backwardness.

The Economic Backwardness of Tsarist Russia

Tsarist Russia stood out as one of the most economically retarded countries in the capitalist world. Here, according to Lenin, a modern, capitalist imperialism was interwoven with an especially complex network of precapitalist relationships.

The per capita output of electric power, pig iron, steel, and coal indicates the degree of economic backwardness of Russia as compared with the countries of Western Europe and the United States. In 1913 the per capita output in Russia was:

Electric power: one-fifth of that in Germany, and one-seventeenth of that in the United States.

Pig iron: one-eighth of that in Germany and one-eleventh of that in the United States.

Steel: one-eighth of that in Germany and one-eleventh of that in the United States.

Coal: one-fifteenth of that in Germany and one twenty-sixth of that in the United States.

Despite the rather rapid development of capitalism after the abolition of serfdom and the still more rapid development of large-scale industry in the 1890's, Russia remained an agrarian country, and in the international division of labor was a producer of grain and other agricultural products as well as some types of raw material (wood, oil, furs) for the international market. Thus, of the total value of industrial and agricultural output in 1913 (excluding small-scale production), agriculture represented 57.8%, and industry 42.2%. An equally significant index was the relationship between urban and rural population; in 1912 the agricultural population of Russia constituted more than 86% of the total population of the country.

Tsarist industry was characterized by relatively high concentration. This was connected indissolubly with the growth of monopolistic capital, which by the beginning of the Imperialist War [World War I] had won a predominant position in the most important branches of industry. The concentration of Russian industry on the eve of the October Revolution was far greater than in Germany, England, or even the United States. As Comrade Stalin points out, "54% of all the workers in Russia were employed in enterprises of over 500 workers, whereas in such a highly developed area as North America, a total of only 33% of all the workers were employed in analogous enterprises." [6] Comrade Stalin has pointed out the tremendous importance of this fact in the development of a revolutionary movement, in the preparation and victory of the socialist revolution in the Soviet Union.

However, despite the high degree of concentration, the industry

[6] Stalin, *Questions of Leninism*, p. 38.

of Tsarist Russia lagged far behind the industry of the advanced capitalist countries in its technique and in the productivity of labor. The mechanization of the basic productive processes, especially in the extractive industries was negligible. Thus, the mechanization of coal mining in Russia in 1913 was only 1.7%, whereas in the United States it was more than 50%. While in the English coal industry the average annual output of a worker before the war was 15,000 poods [270 short tons] of coal, and in the United States it was 41,000 poods [740 tons], in Russia it was only 9,000 poods [162 tons].

One of the most important indices of the backwardness of prerevolutionary Russian industry was the complete insignificance of machine construction, chemistry, and other branches of heavy industry. Tsarist Russia imported the bulk of its machinery and chemical products from abroad.

On the eve of the Imperialist War [World War I], Russia produced only a third (in value) of the equipment of its industry, and imported almost two-thirds from abroad.

The Dependence of Russian Capitalism on Western European Capitalism

"A direct consequence of the economic and political backwardness of Russia was the dependence both of Russian capitalism, and of Tsarism itself, on Western-European capitalism.

"This was expressed by the fact that such very important branches of the national economy as coal, oil, electricity, metallurgy, etc., were in the hands of foreign capital, and Tsarist Russia was obliged to import almost all its machinery and equipment from aboard." [7]

Russia itself led a semicolonial existence, although it was at the same time one of the largest imperialist powers. Tsarist Russia contracted loans from foreign capitalists under unfavorable conditions, giving up its natural resources as concessions. Foreign capital was invested chiefly in those regions and branches of the economy which guaranteed the maximum profit, for example, mining, and metal working, in which was invested more than half of all the foreign capital. The Donbas and the Krivoy Rog region, the only coal-metallurgical bases of prerevolutionary Russia, were almost entirely in

[7] *History of the Communist Party of the Soviet Union, Short Course,* Politizdat, 1938, pp. 95–96.

the hands of foreign capital [Fig. 19]. Baku, the main oil base of Russia, was in the same situation. Foreign capital extended its tentacles into the Urals and into Kazakhstan, penetrating even into far-off Yakutia, to the Lena River, where it exploited the gold fields.

Foreign capital derived enormous profits by the merciless exploitation of Russians, Ukrainians, Azerbaidzhanians, and other workers and peasants, and by plundering Russia's natural resources.

The influence of foreign capital went far beyond the extractive and iron-working industries. A whole series of plants in the central districts, including St. Petersburg and Moscow, belonged to foreign firms. But these plants were strictly speaking assembly shops, branches of concerns located abroad. Thus, the Lyuberetsky agricultural machinery plant near Moscow was principally for the assembly of parts imported from aboard. The Podolsk sewing-machine plant (south of Moscow) [5 in Fig. 19] also was composed of assembly shops of the Singer company. In these shops, machines were put together from parts imported from abroad, etc.

The influence of foreign capital was evident also in the dependence of Tsarist Russia on foreign raw materials, which were imported in large quantities. Thus, more than half of the cotton processed in the textile plants of Tsarist Russia was imported.

Many railroads were built by foreign capital in Russia in order to extract various types of raw materials from the country. The streetcar lines in the largest cities of Russia—Moscow and St. Petersburg—were in the hands of a Franco-Belgian syndicate.

Foreign capital also made itself felt in the development of the productive forces of Russia in the sense that the regions in which it predominated developed at the expense of the development of other regions, where foreign capital was represented to a lesser degree.

Concentration of Manufacture in the Old (Central) Industrial Regions

Against this background of general Russian backwardness, the central industrial regions stood out by virtue of a level of industrial development which more nearly approached that of the Western European countries.

The bulk of Russian manufacturing was concentrated in the central industrial regions. This can be explained on the one hand

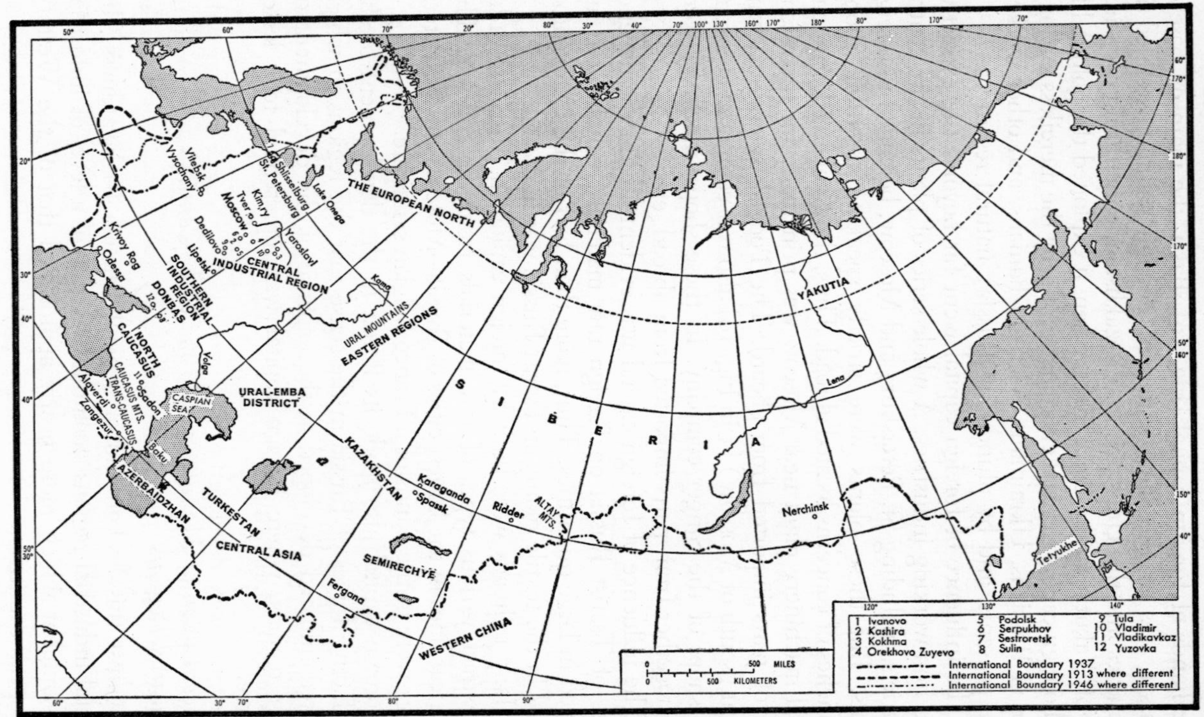

* Fig. 19. Places of Important Economic Development in the Russian Empire (referred to in Chapter II)

by the history of these regions, and on the other by the Tsarist and Russian bourgeois policy of hindering in every way possible the development of manufacturing in other regions.

Lenin distinguishes three principal stages in the development of capitalism in Russian industry, referring primarily to the old industrial regions.

The first stage of this development is small-scale production which grows out of domestic and handicraft industry. The latter is an indispensable part of any barter economy, in which goods are manufactured from wood, flax, hemp, and other local types of raw materials produced by peasant households exclusively for their own needs. The small producer works for a market, but remains a peasant, following the traditional methods of processing raw materials. However, already within this small-scale production, the separation of industry from agriculture begins, although the manufacturer cannot yet be distinguished from the farmer.

On the basis of small-scale output there arises a factory in which already the division of labor is applied on a broad scale; territorial division of labor develops, which is related directly to a general division of labor. Territorial division of labor is expressed in the specialization of different regions in the making of one product, sometimes of one type of product, or even of a particular part of a product.

"A factory," writes Lenin, "not only creates continuous regions, but also introduces specialization within such regions (commodity division of labor). The presence of a raw material in a given locality is by no means a precondition for a factory and is scarcely even a commonplace condition, for a factory is based on rather broad commercial relationships." [8]

Factories were developed to an appreciable extent in Russia as early as the end of the seventeenth and the first quarter of the eighteenth century. At that time, there were more than 200 factories, chiefly in the old industrial regions. Noting this circumstance, Lenin points out that "most typical of Russian capitalist manufacturing is the nonagricultural center." [9] Here were built the first large factories in Russia. Thus, in 1632 near Tula [9 in Fig. 19] (on the Tulitsa River) the foreigner

[8] Lenin, *Works,* Vol. III, p. 335.
[9] *Ibid.*

Vinius built the first metallurgical plant in our country. This operated on local ore and local wood fuel, and up to the latter half of the nineteenth century its power supply was the water power of the Tulitsa River, which operated the mill wheels. Later, in Moscow, the great cloth factory was built—at that time the largest plant manufacturing cloth—and the government sail factory. In Yaroslavl, the great Yaroslavl factory was built; in Kokhma [3 in Fig. 19] (near Ivanovo), a linen factory; in Tula and Sestroretsk [7] (near St. Petersburg), armament plants; etc. Together with large-scale factories, domestic work was widespread. Domestic weaving crafts were particularly widely developed.

After buying up great quantities of thread and warp, the large-scale industrialists manufactured them, partly in large shops, and partly through distribution among small artisans and peasant craftsmen, who, on a piecework basis, wove at home or in small establishments and turned over ready-made cloth to the industrialist. "The small rooms or houses in which the weavers work," as Lenin points out, "are only external departments of a factory." [10]

During this factory period, the separation of industry from agriculture received a great impetus.

The specialist-artisans emerged from the peasantry and no longer practiced agriculture. Industrial villages and towns arose, such as Ivanovo [1] (later the city of Ivanovo-Voznesensk), etc.

During the period of factory production a series of large regions came into existence, each specializing in a particular type of production. This had great significance in the development of a large-scale machine industry, which had begun already in the reform period after 1861.

"A large-scale machine industry could not have developed as quickly in the reform period if it had not been based on a prolonged period of training of the workers by the factory. . . . For this reason, the development of a whole series of large manufacturing regions, specializing in a particular product and turning out many skilled workers, was of great significance." [11]

As an example, Lenin cites the remarkably skilled weavers of Vladimir Guberniya, who played a very important role in the development of a large-scale textile industry in Ivanovo-Voznesensk [1], Orekhovo Zuyevo [4], etc.

[10] Lenin, *Works*, Vol. III, p. 300. [11] *Ibid.*, pp. 333–334.

In addition to Moscow, St. Petersburg, Ivanovo-Voznesensk, etc., the so-called factory villages were centers of capitalist manufacturing. Here were located the distributing centers on which masses of neighboring weavers, working at home, were dependent. Later on, large-scale textile and other factories were formed in these centers.

Thus, in Moscow, Vladimir, and other central guberniyas, the way was paved for the development of a large-scale machine industry, in particular cotton, which drew together skilled cadres of textile workers at the factories.

Important in the development of a large-scale cotton industry in the Central Industrial Region was the fact that in the first stage of development it operated on English thread; and later, on imported cotton which came from America via St. Petersburg.

The cadres of skilled shoemakers which grew up in the period of household manufacturing around the village of Kimry played an important role in the development of the shoe industry in the old industrial regions. Lenin notes that factory production of shoes in St. Petersburg could not have developed so rapidly if skilled workers had not been trained around Kimry.

In addition to the historical conditions, the policy of Tsarism and of the Russian bourgeoisie aided in no small measure in concentrating textile, shoe, and other branches of manufacturing in the old industrial regions. This policy hindered in every way possible the development of manufacturing in other regions, especially in the national regions [12] which produced raw materials for these branches of industry.

Distribution of the Extractive Industry in Tsarist Russia

The extractive industry in Tsarist Russia—coal, oil, and the production of ferrous metals—was concentrated in the southern mining-industrial region (Donbas, Krivoy Rog), and partly in the Urals and the Caucasus.

Up to the last quarter of the nineteenth century the Urals constituted the principal and practically the only base of ferrous metallurgy in Russia. It supplied the country with metal over the course of two centuries. Using serf labor and relying on very rich iron-ore deposits and enormous timber resources, the Ural region in its time supplied not only Russia but also Western Europe with

[12] [A national region is an area occupied by a non-Russian minority group.]

metal. Before the discovery of a method of producing pig iron with mineral fuel, England depended on iron from the Urals and in part from Sweden, because her metallurgy had declined with the destruction of her forests. As early as the first quarter of the nineteenth century, the Urals constituted the world's largest center of metallurgy, and iron was one of the most important articles of Russian export. Even in the 1820's, Russia smelted 1.5 times as much pig iron as France, 4.5 times as much as Prussia, and 3 times as much as Belgium.[13] Almost all of this came from the Urals. The rapid growth of industrial capitalism brought into the limelight a new metallurgical region—the South. Indeed, by the end of the century, the Urals had reached a state of stagnation and even of decline and had been definitely forced into the background by the metallurgy of the South. As to the manner in which they were forced back, the following data [Table 6], cited by V. I. Lenin in his work, *The Development of Capitalism in Russia,*[14] are eloquent.

TABLE 6. [PRODUCTION OF PIG IRON IN THE RUSSIAN EMPIRE, 1867–1902]

	Production of Pig Iron						
	Total		Urals		South		Coal Production (million poods)
Year	(thousand poods)	%	(thousand poods)	%	(thousand poods)	%	
1867	17,028	100	11,084	65.1	56	0.3	26.7
1877	24,579	100	16,157	65.4	1,596	6.5	109.1
1887	37,389	100	23,759	63.3	4,158	11.1	276.8
1897	114,782	100	41,180	35.8	46,349	40.7	683.9
1902	158,618	100	44,775	28.2	84,273	53.1	1,005.21

In subsequent years the lag of the Urals behind the southern mining-industrial region became even greater because of the crisis which descended upon Urals metallurgy in association with the general crisis which enveloped the metallurgy of Russia at the beginning of the present century. Plants closed down, and blast furnaces ceased operations. Thus, of the 126 blast furnaces in the Urals in 1913, 52 were inactive.

What was the cause of this decline in Urals metallurgy? V. I.

[13] Lenin, *Works,* Vol. III, p. 377. [14] *Ibid.*, p. 380.

Lenin gives an exhaustive answer to this question in his work, *The Development of Capitalism in Russia.*

"That very same serfdom," writes Lenin, "which enabled the Urals to rise so high during the period of the initial development of European capitalism, was the cause of the decline of the Urals in the period of the flowering of capitalism."[15] The technical backwardness of the Urals was inseparably linked with the enslaved position and the low wage of the Urals workers. The Urals laborers worked, not only as independent wage earners, but also as "hired-out labor," paid in land, in pasture for livestock, in forests, made available to them by the factory either free or at a reduced price. The Urals factory owners were also large-scale landowners with enormous estates. Since his household, his land, etc., were associated with the factory, the Urals worker was bound to the factory, and the Urals factory owners took advantage of this to intensify exploitation and to lower wages. The wage of a Urals worker was scarcely more than a third of that of a worker in the Donbas. The exploitation of the Urals workers, whose work was indeed strenuous, was so great that travelers visiting the Urals, even at the end of the nineteenth century, pointed out that among the Urals workers there were almost no old men, since they seldom lived to reach old age.

It must be noted also as an essential factor that the Urals factory operators, up to the beginning of the present century, received very profitable government orders, which did not stimulate the introduction of new techniques.

Right up to the October Socialist Revolution there were maintained in the Urals blast furnaces built as early as the eighteenth century, using a cold blast. The stoking of furnaces and other work was done by hand. The technical revolution in ferrous metallurgy which was associated with the conversion to mineral fuel hardly touched the Urals. As the forests around the factories were cut down and burned as fuel, an increasing number of plants were deprived of a local fuel base and were shut down.

An important factor in the technical stagnation and decline of the Urals in the old days was its isolation from central Russia and from other important economic regions of the country. Until the end of the nineteenth century, the Urals were connected with

[15] Lenin, *Works,* Vol. III, p. 377.

central Russia only by river routes—the Kama and its tributaries, leading to the Volga—and freight was floated down these river routes once a year.

This isolation of the Urals from the vital centers of the country was connected indissolubly with the isolation and the barter character of the economy of the Urals. Factory districts, introduced as early as the time of Peter I, when each newly erected plant had added to it an area with a radius of 30 versts, were maintained as the structural form of the barter economy in the Urals up to the twentieth century.

One student of the old Urals, V. D. Belov, describes in the following manner the isolated character of the economy of the factory districts of the Urals:

"There was a time, which I still remember, when the Urals plants on their own large estates produced everything themselves, up to the last nail; even cables and tallow candles for the mines came from the plant shops. They had their own sewing workshop for making footwear for the workers, their own paper mills, and their own pottery works for making inkwells and sandboxes." [16]

The southern mining region presented a totally different picture. The development of the ferrous metallurgy of the South was based on the very rich reserves of coal in the Donbas and the iron ore of the Krivoy Rog.

The development of southern metallurgy is inseparably linked with the railroad construction which developed in the last quarter of the nineteenth century. This construction required an enormous amount of metal for the production of rails, locomotives, and cars. The first large-scale metallurgical plants of the South—the Yuzovka [12 in Fig. 19] and the Sulin [8]—produced rails almost exclusively. Other plants of the South, built in the 1880's and 1890's, also were primarily engaged in the production of rails and other types of metal needed in large quantities for railroad transport. In the 1890's alone, more than 21,000 versts [14,000 miles] of new railroads were built in Russia.

In addition to railroad construction and the development of ferrous metallurgy, there took place an important development of the Donbas, whose deposits of coal were hardly exploited before the extension of the railroad to the South (i.e., before the 1870's).

[16] *The 1909 Crisis in the Urals Mining Plants*, SPB, 1910, p. 27.

As a result of railroad construction, the coal of the Donbas was given an outlet into other regions, principally to metallurgical plants as technological fuel. But the railroads themselves consumed the largest part of Donets coal, more than two-thirds of all the coal mined in the Donbas in the 1870's.

The rapid development of the southern mining-industrial region is linked with the influx of foreign capital which was attracted by the high rate of profit on capital. The rate of profit here exceeded by several times the average percentage return in France, England, and other countries of Europe. A large number of foreign engineers and workers came to the southern mining-industrial region in the 1890's. Even entire plants were brought in from abroad. Thus, the ferrous metallurgy and coal industry of the South were almost completely in the hands of foreign capital. The monopolistic combines "Prodamet," uniting the metallurgical plants of the South, and "Produgol," which controlled the Donbas, in every way possible fought the development of ferrous metallurgy and the coal industry in other regions. By mercilessly exploiting the workers and plundering the iron-ore resources of the Krivoy Rog and the coal deposits of the Donbas, foreign capital extracted enormous profits.

Up to the October Socialist Revolution, the southern mining-industrial region represented the basic and substantially the only coal-metallurgical base of the entire country. In 1913, it accounted for about 74% of the total smelting of pig iron and more than 87% of the total coal production of the country.

The Baku oil region grew up almost simultaneously with the Donbas.

The first large-scale enterprise for oil extraction in the Baku region was organized in the 1870's. The Baku Oil District developed so quickly that as early as 1901 it had outdistanced the United States in the size of its oil yield and accounted for about half of the world's oil output. This was indeed the highest point in the development of the Baku region during the prerevolutionary period, after which oil extraction began to be curtailed.

The city of Baku grew along with the development of the oil industry. In thirty to forty years it became one of the largest cities in Russia. The rapid development of the Baku District is explained first of all by the enormous growth in the demand for oil and oil products within the country. The decided reduction in the price of kerosene resulting from a new method of manufacture increased its consumption for lighting and other everyday needs. Before this, kerosene had been imported from America. The railroads became large consumers of oil; oil by-products—mazut, etc.—were used by factories and plants as fuel. In addition, a large quantity of Baku oil was exported at the close of the past century.

The Baku oil region, like the southern mining-industrial region, was in the hands of foreign capital—the Nobel, Rothschild, and Vishau companies, and other foreign capitalists. Ruthlessly exploiting Baku oil, they retarded in every way possible the development of oil extraction in other regions of the country. Thus, they acquired control of local companies in the Volga Region and forbade geological exploration in those regions.

The Caucasus, in essence, was the country's only oil base: it accounted for about 95% of all Russian oil extraction.

The Mother Country and the Colonies of Tsarist Russia

About half the industry of Tsarist Russia was concentrated in the central industrial regions and some 20% in the Ukraine. In the vast remaining expanses of Russia, industry either had not developed at all, or, at best, was in an embryonic form. Thus less than 10% of all Russian industrial production came from all the eastern regions of the country, with 4.7% in the Urals, 2.4% in Siberia, and 1.8% in Turkestan.

In the reform period after 1861 the central industrial guberniyas specialized increasingly in machine industries, chiefly in textiles, while the southern and other outlying guberniyas specialized in agriculture.

As late as the middle of the last century, a whole series of guberniyas in the southern steppes and in the Trans-Volga were regarded as poorly suited for agriculture because of their climate and insufficient water supply. In the 1860's and 1870's they produced less grain than the central chernozem guberniyas. Before long, however, the chief center of grain production shifted to the steppe and the lower Volga guberniyas. At the same time the production of grain in the central chernozem guberniyas fell, and in the 1880's they yielded precedence to the steppe and lower

Volga guberniyas, which became the principal base of grain production for export and for the domestic market.

"This interesting fact of the vast growth in agricultural production in the region described is explained," writes Lenin, "by the fact that the steppe borderlands in the reform period were *colonies* of central, long-populated European Russia. The abundance of free land attracted an enormous influx of settlers, who quickly expanded the land under cultivation. The widespread development of *commercial* crop growing was possible only because of the close economic ties of these colonies, on the one hand with central Russia, and on the other with European countries importing grain. The growth of industry in central Russia and the development of commercial agriculture in the borderlands were indissolubly connected, reciprocally creating a market for each other. The industrial districts received grain from the South where they sold the products of their factories, supplying the colonies with workers, artisans . . . and the means of production (timber, construction materials, tools, and so on). Due only to this social division of labor, the settlers in the steppe districts were able to occupy themselves exclusively with agriculture, selling large quantities of grain in the domestic and especially in foreign markets."[17]

Russian capitalism, like capitalism in other countries, was not able to exist without seizing new markets and sources of industrial raw materials. Industry, especially the textile industry, developing particularly rapidly in the reform period after 1861, was dissatisfied with the dimensions of the former market and strove to go beyond the limits of the old regions.

Analyzing the conditions of the formation of the domestic market and the significance of the border regions in Tsarist Russia, Lenin wrote:

"By the uneven development characteristic of capitalism, one branch of production surpasses others and strives to go beyond the bounds of the old area of economic relations. Take, for example, the textile industry at the beginning of the reform period. Being rather highly developed with respect to capitalism (manufacturing that was beginning to develop into a factory industry), it seized complete control of the market of central Russia. But the large factories which grew so rapidly no longer were satisfied with the

[17] Lenin, *Works*, Vol. III, p. 194.

former limits of the market; they began to seek further markets, among the new population which had colonized Novorossia, the southeastern Trans-Volga, the North Caucasus, then Siberia, and so on." [18]

The textile manufacturers of Moscow, Ivanovo-Voznesensk, etc., needed not only new markets but also their own sources of raw materials. Up to the 1880's the cotton industry of Tsarist Russia operated exclusively on cotton imported from America. Up to this time cotton growing had not been developed at all in Russia itself. At the same time the rapid growth of the cotton industry during the reform period required an ever-increasing quantity of cotton.

The Civil War in the United States (1861–1865) curtailed drastically the export of cotton, and cotton prices advanced rapidly. Attempts were made to establish cotton-growing bases in the southern regions of European Russia, but they were not successful. Russian textile manufacturers succeeded in establishing their own cotton base only after the conquest of Central Asia (Turkestan), which began in the 1860's. Before this, Tsarist Russia imported from Central Asia homemade cloth and homemade thread, produced there from a local, old type of Asiatic cotton. Having conquered Central Asia, Tsarism quickly converted it into a cotton colony, introducing American cotton through every possible channel. In 1884 Central Asia delivered to Moscow the first eight bales of American cotton. This marked the beginning of the rapid introduction of American cotton into Turkestan.

The following figures indicate how intensively cotton growing spread in Turkestan.

TABLE 7. [AREA SOWN IN AMERICAN COTTON IN TURKESTAN, 1884–1913]

1884	300 dessiatines *
1886	12,000
1890	58,859
1913	Over 500,000

* [A dessiatine is equal to 2.70 acres.]

The development of cotton cultivation in Central Asia was promoted by the construction of railroads, since previously the

[18] Lenin, *Works*, Vol. III, p. 462.

delivery of Central Asiatic cotton to the central guberniyas was extremely difficult.

The transformation of Turkestan into a cotton colony of Tsarist Russia was carried out by every possible means, primarily by force. The increase of cotton growing involved the *dekhkan* economy in a commodity revolution. There was a drop in the local production of cloth; it began to be replaced by manufactured textiles from Moscow, Ivanovo-Voznesensk, etc. Grain crops were supplanted by cotton, and grain was imported from other regions. Turkestan became increasingly a single-crop country. Textile manufacturers established in Central Asia a whole network of purchasing offices and bought cotton from the dekhkan workers at absurdly low prices. In the Trans-Caucasus as in Central Asia, a cotton base was created for the textile factories of the old industrial regions. In this way, Russian capitalism created for itself new markets and new sources of raw materials in the vast borderlands of the Russian empire.

Industrial raw materials were carried thousands of kilometers from Central Asia, Kazakhstan, the Trans-Caucasus, etc., to the Central Industrial Region, and the finished products of this raw material made the return journey, thus increasing the cost of production.

The policies of Tsarism and the Russian bourgeoisie were directed toward retarding the development of industry in the Russian colonies—in Turkestan, the Caucasus, Siberia, Kazakhstan, and so on —toward keeping these areas in the role of appendages, sources of agrarian raw materials for the Central Industrial Region, and toward holding back their independent development. The natural resources and the principal productive strength—the large population of the borderlands—were depleted ruthlessly.

Industrial development in the colonies of Tsarist Russia was permitted only to the extent that it corresponded with the interests of the mother country. Capital (for the most part foreign) penetrating into the colonies of Tsarist Russia was concentrated almost entirely in the extraction of raw material and in the first stages of its manufacture so that it could be conveyed more easily to the Central Region or abroad.

Tsarism and the Russian bourgeoisie, in every way impeding the development of industry in the borderlands of Russia, promoted the concentration of industry in the Central Industrial Region and its isolation from the sources of raw material and fuel. In this, the rate policy of the Tsarist Government played a leading role. As early as the 1890's, when a series of large-scale railroads was constructed, connecting the central guberniyas with the borderlands of Russia, the rate system was revised in such a way as to stimulate the transport of raw materials and fuel into the Central Industrial Region. Thus, for the shipment of cotton from Turkestan to Moscow, Vladimir, and other central guberniyas an extremely low rate was established. A reduced rate also existed for Donets and Urals coal shipped into the central guberniyas and so on. By its rate policy the Tsarist Government protected not only the interests of the manufacturers, but also the interests of the landowners and kulaks of the central guberniyas. Thus, for example, in order to oblige the landowners and kulaks of the central chernozem zone, who feared the competition of cheap Siberian grain, the grain economy of Siberia was held back artificially by the establishment in 1896 of the so-called "Chelyabinsk rate divide." This was a type of customs barrier for Siberian grain going to the central guberniyas and abroad.

The purpose of the "Chelyabinsk rate divide" was to make it impossible for Siberian grain to compete with grain produced by the landowners of the central regions of Russia. For this purpose, the railway rate was drawn up in such a way that west of Chelyabinsk the cost of hauling Siberian grain increased rapidly. As a result, Siberian grain that was brought to the central part of European Russia cost substantially more than that of the landowners of the central chernozem zone. Under the pressure of such a tariff policy, the Siberian kulaks were compelled to limit the development of their grain economy.

These facts testify to the unusually contradictory character of the distribution of productive forces in Tsarist Russia, where the development of certain regions and branches of the economy took place at the expense of others.

Tsarism and the Russian bourgeoisie exploited the national borderlands mercilessly, and in every way impeded their industrial development.

National-Colonial Oppression of the People

"Tsarist Russia was a prison of nationalities. The numerous non-Russian nationalities of Tsarist Russia were completely without rights, perpetually subjected to all sorts of humiliations and outrages. The Tsarist Government taught the Russian people to look upon the native peoples of the national regions as inferior races, officially designated them 'non-Russians,' and taught contempt and hatred toward them. The Tsarist Government consciously inflamed national differences, set one nationality against another, and organized Jewish pogroms and Tatar-Armenian massacres in the Trans-Caucasus.

"In the national regions, Russian officials occupied all or practically all government posts. In institutions and in the courts all business was conducted in the Russian language. It was forbidden to issue newspapers and books in the national languages; in the schools it was forbidden to study in the native languages. The Tsarist Government strove to stifle every manifestation of national culture, and instigated a policy of forceful 'Russification' of the non-Russian nationalities. Tsarism was outstanding as an executioner and torturer of non-Russian peoples." [19]

Lenin and Stalin repeatedly emphasized the military-feudal character of Russian imperialism. Fortifying its domination, "Tsarism deliberately cultivated patriarchal-feudal oppression in the borderlands in order to hold the masses in slavery and ignorance. Tsarism deliberately settled the better corners of the borderlands with colonizing elements in order to drive the natives back into inferior regions and to intensify national differences." [20]

Under the pressure of national-colonial oppression, the native population in many national regions of Tsarist Russia became extinct.

Through its colonial policy, Russian Tsarism destroyed the tribal hearths of the native populations.

Certain Tsarist officials directed the attention of the Tsarist Government to this circumstance. Thus, in his inspection report on the Turkestan region, Palen, senator and an official of the Imperial Court, wrote that with the withdrawal of land for colonization, among the native populations "there appears a dislocation, not only of individual Kirgiz farms and small farm villages and winter camps, but of whole hundreds of such farms." [21]

[19] *History of the Communist Party of the Soviet Union, Short Course*, p. 6.

[20] Stalin, *Marxism and the National-Colonial Question*, p. 61.

[21] *Immigrant Affairs of Turkestan*, 1910, pp. 42–43.

The chief cause of the destruction of native communities appeared to be the fact that the lands which were actually free could be converted to the needs of settlement only after a more or less significant expenditure for irrigation had been made, which required time, work, and capital. Meanwhile, it was much simpler and cheaper to organize tracts for the colonists on land that had already been tilled by the native population. The seizure of native peoples' lands assumed ever greater proportions, as the number of colonists increased and their allotments of land were large, especially among the Cossacks, who were a very privileged group. Thus, according to the law of July 3, 1914, concerning the allotment of land to the Semirechye Cossack army,[22] the size of the land shares of convenient land was set at 30 dessiatines for each Cossack male and 300 for each church.

It is self-evident that the constant threat to the stability of landownership hampered extremely the transition of the native population from a nomadic to a settled economy.

Expelled into the barren sands or the mountains, the native populations of Turkestan died out under the pressure of the twofold oppression. This is recorded even in official Tsarist statistics. Thus, in *The General Summary for the Empire of the Results of the Data of the First General Census of Population,* St. Petersburg, 1905, it is shown that according to a previous enumeration of the Kirgiz (Kara-Kirgiz) people living for the most part in Fergana Oblast, there were about 300,000 people, while according to the census of 1897, there were only 200,000.

Cotton growing and other branches of agriculture in Turkestan were carried on by primitive methods. In the well known, many-volumed work *Russia,* edited by Semenov-Tyan-Shansky, the following characterization is given of the methods of cultivation in Turkestan in the prewar years: [23] "The processes and methods of cultivation and in general of crop culture in Turkestan are generally primitive and in most places are today what they were hundreds of years ago. Improvements in agricultural tools are found chiefly among the Russian settlers, while the mass of native people cultivate their land by means of the ketmen and the omach." [24]

[22] Semirechye (Dzhetysu)—the part of Turkestan in the basin of the Ili River and other rivers of the Lake Balkhash basin.

[23] *Russia,* Vol. XIX, *Turkestan Kray,* SPB, 1913, p. 437.

[24] Ketmen = a manual tool resembling a hoe. Omach = a wooden plow with an iron plowshare, but lacking a moldboard.

In the unbounded expanses of Kazakhstan, from the borders of Western China to the Caspian and the Volga steppes, a primitive nomadic economy predominated. What little industry there was, was represented by a few plants controlled almost entirely by foreign capital: the extraction of nonferrous metals at Ridder (Altay), the small Spassk copper smelting plant in central Kazakhstan, a few tiny coal pits in Karaganda, and primitive oil plants in the Ural-Emba district.

The native population of Kazakhstan was forced into the barren sands. Kazakhstan was the largest producer of meat, wool, and hides for the Central Industrial Region.

In the Trans-Caucasus and the North Caucasus the native population was forced into the mountains, while the land confiscated from them was occupied by colonists and Cossacks. In Azerbaidzhan, in spite of cotton growing and sheep raising, there was no textile industry before the Revolution, except the small Tagiev factory in Baku. Industry in Azerbaidzhan was represented chiefly by the extraction of oil in Baku, in which connection it must be kept in mind that "Baku did not grow from within Azerbaidzhan, but was built from the outside, through the efforts of Nobel, Rothschild, Vishau, and others. As for Azerbaidzhan itself, it appears to be a country of the most backward patriarchal-feudal relations." [25] Thus Comrade Stalin characterizes prerevolutionary Azerbaidzhan.

An even more desolate picture was to be observed in the Russian Far North, where the native population was completely without rights, and Russian and foreign tradesmen exploited them mercilessly, selling goods at triple their cost and buying furs and other products at absurdly low prices. Tsarist officials encouraged these arbitrary dealings. Excessive taxes, straightforward robbery, and the absence of the most elementary medical aid, all led to a systematic dying off of the peoples of the North.

Tsarism and the Russian bourgeoisie oppressed the national borderlands through the local gentry, rich landowners, and clergy, who were allowed appropriate privileges at the expense of the increasingly poor conditions of the native working population. Thus, in a secret note to the Tsar, the Tsar's viceroy in the Caucasus, Voronstov-Dashkov, noted that the whole weight of the financial assessments and the Zemstvo obligations lay on the peasant population, and that this led to a decline

[25] Stalin, *Marxism and the National-Colonial Question*, p. 80.

in agriculture in the Caucasus. He also observed that "the chief concern of the Government in the Caucasus centered almost exclusively in the support of the privileged class, chiefly the Georgian nobility, who had indeed rendered us many services in the conquest of the Caucasus." [26]

In withdrawing land from the native population for colonization, "agreements" and "voluntary" cessions of "surpluses" were used. Local officials brought about these "agreements" and "voluntary" cessions through the agency of the rich landowners. The landowners fulfilled the role of intermediaries for a specific fee and profited from the withdrawal of land for Russian settlement. In this way the Tsarist Government, by carrying out a policy of colonization and Russification, created support for itself in the borderlands not only among the Cossacks and Russian kulak settlers from the central parts, but also among the local gentry, rich landowners, and clergy.

Pointing to the predominance in Tsarist Russia of military and feudal imperialism, Lenin wrote in 1915:

"Nowhere in the world is there such oppression of the majority of the people of a country as in Russia; the Great Russians constitute only 43% of the population, that is, less than half, but all the others, as non-Russians, are without rights." [27]

Colonization of the Borderlands and Economic Stagnation in the Central Guberniyas

Analyzing the interrelations in Tsarist Russia between the mother country and her colonies, Lenin at the same time shows the retarding influence of borderland exploitation on the development of capitalism in the central guberniyas of Russia. Tsarist Russia, possessing vast and conveniently located colonies, was in a particularly advantageous position as compared with the other capitalist countries. This opportunity for the widespread development of capitalism in great measure served as an obstacle to the more rapid development of productive forces in the central, longer-settled part of Russia.

"The growth of capitalism deep in the older, long-populated territory," wrote Lenin, "is retarded by the colonization of the borderlands. The resolution of the contradictions peculiar to capitalism and bred by it is postponed temporarily because of the fact that capitalism can easily expand geographically. For example, the

[26] *Report to His Majesty: Note on the Administration of the Caucasus Regions*, by Adjutant-General Count Vorontsov-Dashkov, 1907.

[27] Lenin, *Works*, Vol. XVIII, p. 198.

simultaneous existence of the most advanced forms of industry together with semimedieval forms of agriculture in itself represents a contradiction. If there had been no place for Russian capitalism to expand beyond the limits of the territory already occupied at the beginning of the reform period following 1861, this contradiction between capitalist heavy industry and the archaic institutions of rural life (attachment of the peasants to the land, and so forth) should have led to a rapid and complete abolition of these institutions, clearing the way for agricultural capitalism in Russia. But the possibility of seeking and finding markets in the colonized borderlands (for the manufacturer), and the possibility of going to new lands (for the peasant), weaken the acuteness of this contradiction and postpone its resolution."[28]

In another place, Lenin writes that "the possibility of oppressing and plundering foreign peoples reinforces economic stagnation, for instead of the development of productive forces the source of income often becomes the semifeudal exploitation of 'foreigners.'"[29]

It is just this which explains the economic stagnation in the central chernozem guberniyas, representing part of the mother country of the Russian empire. Industry was developed here only on a very small scale, while agriculture, burdened with the vestiges of serfdom, degenerated under the exceptionally severe agrarian congestion. This "improverishment" of the central chernozem guberniyas was a heavy burden primarily on the working peasantry.

Tsarist Russia annually exported abroad and converted into vodka hundreds of millions of poods of grain. At the same time, the working people of Russia, particularly of the central guberniyas, were regularly undernourished. This circumstance is noted even in the official documents of the Tsarist Government. Thus, in a work published on the centennial of the Committee of Ministers, it was noted: "Grain is exported at the expense of the subsistence needs of the people, since the amount of the annual grain yield remaining (on the average) per person, after the deduction of grain sent aboard and used for distillation, proves below the standard which is accepted as the minimum for the proper nourishment of the people."[30]

An analogous picture was found also in the production of beet

[28] Lenin, *Works*, Vol. III, p. 465, footnote. [29] *Ibid.*, Vol. XVIII, p. 199.

[30] *Our Railroad Policy According to Data in the Archives of the Committee of Ministers*, Vol. IV, SPB, 1902, p. 327.

sugar. While the working peasants were able to have sugar with their tea once or twice a year, in England pigs were fed with Russian sugar because it was sold there at fabulously low, dumping prices.

Territorial Division of Labor and Interregional Relations

The historically developed territorial division of labor among different areas of the country increasingly unified the national economy. The strengthening of interregional economic ties as a result of transportation development, especially by rail, secured this unity to an even greater degree. The European North supplied the timberless southern guberniyas with timber; in turn, the southern guberniyas provided the North with grain, metals, petroleum, etc. Central Asia supplied the Central Industrial Region with cotton and received from it dress goods and other industrial products. Without Donets coal and Baku oil the central regions could not have existed. And, inversely, the Donbas, the Trans-Caucasus, and other southern regions could not have existed without the industrial products of the Central Industrial Region. Specialization of areas and territorial division of labor among them had great significance in the national economy. The territorial division of labor was expressed first of all in the sharp division of areas into industrial (center) and agrarian (borderlands). Such a division of the areas of Tsarist Russia, as indicated above, unfolded historically and reflected the disparity in distribution of productive forces characteristic of capitalism.

The Imperialist War [World War I] and particularly the resulting disorganization of transportation revealed all the abnormality and inefficiency of the distribution of productive forces in Tsarist Russia. First to be felt was the dependence of the northwestern regions, headed by Petrograd [Leningrad], on English coal, delivery of which was extremely difficult during the war. Petrograd had poor connections with the Donbas, as a result of the poorly developed railroad network of Tsarist Russia. Consequently, the industry and urban economy of the Petrograd area were in large measure paralyzed and suffered from a chronic shortage of coal.

The matter of coal was even more acute in the Urals, in the Volga regions, and in other regions far from the Donbas, which supplied about 90% of all the Russian coal output.

Overloading of rail transport with troop movements and other military traffic and the disorganization of transportation in the years which followed revealed all the gravity of the separation of industry from the sources of raw material, fuel, and the areas of consumption. The textile industry of the Central Industrial Region operated with long interruptions caused by the irregular delivery of cotton from Turkestan. The industry of many other areas suffered from the fact that local fuel and raw materials were poorly developed while their delivery from other areas was difficult.

Particularly painful during this period was the separation of manufacturing from its basic sources of raw material and fuel, delivery of which to the Central Industrial Region from the distant borderlands was very difficult. After having developed over the course of many decades, the territorial division of labor among the various areas of the country was undermined, primarily by the disorganization of transportation, which was the blood stream of the national economy. "The economy of the country disintegrated into a series of more or less *isolated areas*. This nullified the progress in the general division of labor attained through capitalist development and threw Tsarist Russia backward many decades." [31]

[31] *History of the Civil War*, 1935, p. 29.

III Basic Problems in the Distribution of the Productive Forces of the USSR

The Rate and Level of Economic Development of the USSR

DURING the years of Soviet rule the USSR has been converted from a backward agrarian country into a mighty industrial power. The structure of the national economy and the relationship between industry and agriculture have been thoroughly transformed. Whereas before the Revolution agriculture was sharply predominant in the economy of the country, industry at present clearly predominates over agriculture.

In 1913 products of large-scale industry accounted for 42.2% of the total value of the industrial and agricultural output of the country, while in 1937 they accounted for 77.4%. The industrial output of the USSR in 1938 was more than nine times as large as the prewar output. In its rate of industrial growth the USSR has outdistanced all the capitalist countries. The following figures, cited by Comrade Stalin in his report to the 18th Party Congress, testify to this:

TABLE 8. GROWTH OF INDUSTRY IN THE USSR AND IN THE MAIN CAPITALIST COUNTRIES FROM 1913 to 1938 (in per cent)

	1913	1938
USSR	100.0	908.8
United States	100.0	120.0
England	100.0	113.3
Germany	100.0	131.6
France	100.0	93.2

The quantitative growth of industry in the USSR was accompanied by its thorough technological modernization. A whole series of very important branches of industry, unknown in Tsarist Russia, has been created: machine tools, automobiles, tractors, airplanes, motors, synthetic rubber, potassium, apatite, nickel, aluminum, and so on.

The socialist modernization of agriculture, the achievement of complete collectivization, and the liquidation of the kulaks as a class have turned the USSR into a country of socialist agriculture, the largest-scale agriculture in the world. In the place of antiquated implements—primitive plows, ketmens, sickles, and the like—the agriculture of the USSR has received first-class technical equipment. In 1938 it was using 483,500 tractors, 153,500 combines, 195,800 trucks, etc.

As has been pointed out already, the technique of production in Tsarist Russia was at an extremely low level. Most of the work in industry was done by hand, while in agriculture primitive implements reigned.

As a result of the Stalin Five-Year Plans, Soviet industry and agriculture have been outfitted with the most advanced technical equipment. From a country which imported the great bulk of its machines, particularly the more complex ones, the Soviet Union has changed into a country which produces the most complex machines. There are no machines which could not be produced in the USSR. This testifies to the high level of technology which the USSR had reached by the beginning of the Third Five-Year Plan.

"It can be said without exaggeration," said Comrade Stalin at the 18th Party Congress, "that from the point of view of techniques of production, from the point of view of the degree to which industry and agriculture are fully supplied with new technical equipment, our country is the most advanced in comparison with any other country, where old equipment is a drag on production and hinders the introduction of new techniques."[1]

Toward the end of the Second Five-Year Plan the USSR emerged in second place in the world, and in first place in Europe, in volume of output of industry as a whole and of its most important branches.

However, while our country in rate of development of industry and level of techniques of production is the most advanced, it is still behind the most advanced capitalist countries in level of economic development expressed as per capita industrial output. Table 9 shows the level of economic development of the USSR in per capita

[1] Stalin, *Questions of Leninism*, p. 575.

production of the most important categories of industrial output, compared with that of the most developed capitalist countries.

TABLE 9. PER CAPITA PRODUCTION OF THE MAIN CATEGORIES OF INDUSTRIAL OUTPUT, IN THE USSR AND IN CAPITALIST COUNTRIES [a]

CATEGORY	USSR	U.S.A.	GERMANY	ENGLAND	FRANCE	JAPAN
Electric power (kw.h.)	215	1160	735	608	490	421
Pig iron (kg.)	86	292	234	183	189	30
Steel (kg.)	105	397	291	279	188	62
Coal (kg.)	757	3429	3313	5165	1065	643
Cement (kg.)	32	156	173	154	86	60
Cotton cloth (sq. m.)	16	58	–	60	31	57
Woolen cloth (m.)	0.6	2.8	–	7.4	–	–
Leather footwear (pr.)	1	2.6	1.1	2.2	–	–
Paper (kg.)	5	48	42	42	23	8
Sugar (kg.)	14	12	29	8	21	17
Soap (kg.)	3	12	7	11	10	–

[a] USSR for 1937, other countries according to the latest published figures. [A dash indicates "no data."] Figures taken from the report of Comrade Molotov to the 18th Party Congress.

These figures demonstrate that economically the USSR still lags significantly behind the most advanced capitalist countries.

Why, then, does the Soviet Union where production develops at a much higher rate than in capitalist countries, and where the techniques of production stand at an extremely high level, still lag behind the most advanced capitalist countries? "Because," says Comrade Molotov, "our country just a short time ago was terribly backward industrially, and, in view of the great size of the population of the country, had extremely low standards of per capita industrial output. In this short time she could not completely compensate for the time that had been lost previously." [2]

The remarkable results of the [first] two triumphant Five-Year Plans assured the consummation of technological reconstruction and a high level of production technique in industry and agriculture. On the basis of this Comrade Stalin set before the USSR a task of

[2] Molotov, *The Third Five-Year Plan for the Development of the National Economy of the USSR*, p. 15.

world-wide historical significance—during the next ten to fifteen years to overtake and surpass, even in the economic sense, the most advanced capitalist countries of Europe, and the United States.

The solution of this fundamental economic problem of the USSR raises the struggle between the two systems, capitalist and socialist, to a new level. "The question is posed of the development of economic competition between the USSR and the decisive capitalist countries. The question is carried over onto international ground. So much the stronger must be our drive to resolve this new problem honorably." [3]

The Socialist Distribution of Productive Forces and Its Basic Principles

The systematic and efficient distribution of productive forces, as Marx and Engels have written already, is possible only under the conditions of a socialist economy.

Engels wrote: "Only a society which harmoniously combines its productive forces in accordance with a single over-all plan can permit industries to be distributed throughout the country in a way most favorable to their own development and to the preservation and development of the remaining elements of production." [4]

The general remarks of Marx and Engels on the distribution of productive forces were developed by Lenin and Stalin to apply to the conditions of socialist construction in the USSR. Lenin and Stalin developed the theory of the socialist distribution of productive forces as a constituent part of the theory of the building of socialism. They applied it to the conditions of socialist construction in the USSR, which is encircled by capitalism.

The following conditions, developed by Lenin and Stalin, are fundamental to the socialist distribution of productive forces:

The bringing of industry closer to the sources of raw material and to the consuming areas, in order to eliminate uneconomic and excessively long freight haulage; the complex economic development of the principal economic regions of the Union, and the supplying of the principal economic centers of the country as far as possible with local resources; the economic and cultural elevation of the previously backward national republics and oblasts; the most rational (efficient) utilization of the natural conditions and resources of the

[3] *Ibid.*, p. 19.

[4] Engels, *Anti-Dühring*, p. 244.

different parts of the country and of the country as a whole; the elimination of the historically developed antagonisms between town and country; the provision of the USSR with the greatest possible capacity for defense.

The socialist distribution of productive forces played an enormous role in the successful fulfillment of the two Stalin Five-Year Plans and in the technological reconstruction of the national economy. The proper distribution of productive forces is very important in raising the productivity of labor, in the efficient utilization of natural resources, in industrializing the formerly backward national republics, and also in destroying the antagonisms between town and country.

The elimination of unproductive and excessively long freight hauls and of cross hauls is of great significance in increasing the productivity of social labor. This is accomplished by a more uniform distribution of production, and by bringing industry closer to its sources of raw materials, fuel, and consuming areas. As a result, an enormous economy of the means of transportation is achieved, socialist regeneration is accelerated, the rate of turnover of merchandise is increased, the cost of production is lowered, and the productivity of labor increases. It then becomes possible for a socialist society to reduce, relatively, its expenditures for transportation, and consequently to expand the fixed capital of industry and agriculture.

The magnitude of the saving in resources which our economy achieves by bringing industry closer to its sources of raw materials and to regions which consume the finished products can be judged by the Magnitogorsk and Kuznetsk metallurgical combines.

It is well known that these new centers of ferrous metallurgy, created during the years of the Stalin Five-Year Plans, are supplying the Urals, Western and Eastern Siberia, the Far East, Kazakhstan, and the Central Asiatic republics with rails and other rolled products [Fig. 20]. The need of these regions for metal for the construction of new railroads, new cities, factories, mines, and also for defense requirements, increases from year to year. If the Magnitogorsk and Kuznetsk metallurgical combines had not been created, then all these regions of the East would have had to be supplied with rails, pig iron, machines, etc., from the Donbas and Krivoy Rog, thousands of kilometers away. According to the rates prevailing in 1938, the transportation of a ton of pig iron and steel ingots from the Donbas to the southern Urals would cost about 70 rubles, and to Kuznetsk, about 95 rubles. The transportation of rails and of other rolled products would cost almost one and one-half times as much. The freighting of machines would be still more expensive. Thanks to the Magnitogorsk and Kuznetsk metallurgical combines alone, the USSR saves a minimum of 250 million rubles annually on the freighting of metal. The cost of the combines was about three billion rubles. Thus, in ten to twelve years the plants will have paid for themselves by this single economy in transportation.

The new geography of agriculture, the transformation of "consuming" regions into "producing" ones, the development of industrial crops in new regions, etc., promote the reduction of long freight hauls to an enormous degree. But the question is not only one of economizing on the hauling of freight. The liberation of transportation facilities for the national economy, the more efficient use of raw materials, the elevation of the economy of previously backward regions, and so on must be kept in mind. If to all these are added considerations of national defense, then it becomes completely clear why our Party gives principal emphasis in the distribution of new construction to bringing industry closer to sources of raw materials and consuming areas, and to the elimination of inefficient and excessively long freight haulage. The regulation of transport and the elimination of inefficient and excessive haulage provide great opportunities for the development of the economy of the USSR, as Comrade Stalin has repeatedly pointed out.

The socialist distribution of productive forces is inseparably linked with Leninist-Stalinist national policy, and it has, in the past, raised the economic and cultural level of the economically and culturally backward national republics to an unprecedented height.

The proper distribution of productive forces is tremendously important in the solution of the basic economic problem of the USSR.

The solution of the economic problem demands enormous capital investments; it demands the construction of a great number of factories, mills, mines, railroads, etc. The effectiveness of capital investments, the effectiveness of the operation of all these undertakings, will depend in large measure on how they are distributed throughout the immense territory of the Soviet Union. The transport facilities required will depend on where the new enterprises are built.

The rate and direction of the economic development of the principal economic regions of the country has tremendous significance. In order to raise the most important branches of the national economy to the level of the economically more advanced capitalist countries, it is necessary to raise the level of all the economic regions of the country. It is necessary to utilize more fully their natural and labor resources.

In the solution of the basic economic problem, the question of which branches of industry and agriculture must be developed in the principal economic centers and economic regions of the country, and on what scale, is raised with exceptional sharpness.

To the extent of the transition from socialism to communism, the proper distribution of productive forces will become increasingly significant.

SECTION 1. QUESTIONS OF THE DISTRIBUTION OF PRODUCTIVE FORCES IN DIFFERENT STAGES OF SOCIALIST CONSTRUCTION

In the first months after the Great October Socialist Revolution, Lenin and Stalin had already put on the agenda the question of the proper distribution of productive forces. In his *Outline of a Plan of Scientific and Technical Tasks* (April, 1918), Lenin, designating the fundamental set-up of a plan for the reorganization of industry and for the economic improvement of Russia, wrote:

"In this plan must enter:

"The efficient *areal distribution* of industry in Russia from the point of view of bringing it closer to raw materials and of the least possible waste of labor in the movement from the original processing of the raw material, through all the successive stages of the manufacture of the semifinished product, up to the receipt of the finished product.

"From the point of view of the newest large-scale industry, and especially trusts, the efficient merging and concentration of production in a few very large enterprises.

"Provisions assuring to the greatest extent possible that the present Russian Soviet Republic (not including the Ukraine or the German-occupied oblasts) shall be able to supply itself *independently* in *all* the main categories of raw material and industry.

"Special attention to the electrification of industry and transport, and the application of electricity to agriculture. The use of second-rate types of fuel (peat, low-grade coal) for the generation of electric power, with the least expenditure possible in the extraction and transfer of fuel.

"The use of water power and wind power in general, and in particular as applied to agriculture." [5]

In the decree of the Council of People's Commissars of April 12, 1918, dealing with the offer by the Academy of Sciences of its facilities for investigating the natural resources of the country, questions of the proper distribution of industry were given a leading position in its program.

". . . to point out to it [the Academy of Sciences] how especially important and urgent is the task of the systematic solution of the problems of the proper distribution of industry in the country, and of the most efficient utilization of its economic forces." [6]

In the first general plan for the restoration and reconstruction of the national economy—the Goelro Plan—questions of the redistribution of productive forces correlated with the electrification of the country, and of the division of the country into economic districts, occupied one of the central positions.

"It is inconceivable," reads the Goelro Plan, "that the rationalization of our industry will not be accompanied by a significant transfer of industry to the East in order to permit bringing manufacturing industry as close as possible to basic sources of raw material or fuel for general economic reasons. The enormous role of the electrification of entire regions in this process is incontestable, since the availability of cheap and convenient power is the basis for the quickest creation in these regions of the various branches of industry."

In the resolutions of the 10th and 12th Party Congresses, in accord with the reports of Comrade Stalin, the importance of eliminating the economic and cultural backwardness of the nationalities inhabiting the USSR was emphasized, as was the necessity of creating industrial centers in the national republics.

[5] Lenin, *Works*, Vol. XXII, p. 434.

[6] *Ibid.*, p. 621 [erroneously given as p. 597 in original].

A resolution of the 10th Congress (1921) pointed out that the very first problem of the proletarian revolution, in the eastern border regions, "is the systematic elimination of all remnants of national inequality in all branches of public and economic life and, before all else, the systematic propagation of industry in the outlying districts by the transfer of factories to the sources of raw materials (Turkestan, Bashkiria, Kirgizstan, the Caucasus—the textile, woolen, and leather industries, and others)." [7]

The propagation of industry in the national regions is, thus, one of the fundamental methods of realizing the instructions of Lenin on bringing industry closer to its sources of raw materials.

In the years of the Civil War and in the period of transition to peacetime work through the restoration of the national economy, when new construction was still insignificant, no large-scale shifts in the distribution of productive forces took place. But certain very essential measures were taken even then.

The 12th Party Congress (1923) demanded concentration of production in those enterprises which were best equipped technically, and best situated geographically. The Congress rebuffed the traitor Trotsky who proposed "to close such large plants, important to the national defense, as the Putilov [in Leningrad], Bryansk, and others, which, as he maintained, were not yielding profits. The Congress indignantly rejected Trotsky's suggestion." [8]

The Party carefully and with much thought selected and determined the order in which the ruined enterprises were to be restored.

The abnormality of the distribution of productive forces inherited from Tsarist Russia, which was aggravated in the period of the blockade and intervention, demanded tremendous efforts in the restoration of the old industrial regions and the development of productive forces in new regions during the first years of Soviet power. Before all else this was concerned with the partial conversion of the economy of a number of regions, particularly of the old industrial regions, to local fuels.

The extraction of peat, which was insignificant in prerevolutionary Russia, had increased to more than three times its prerevolutionary size by 1923 (5.3 million tons in 1928, as against 1.7 million tons in 1913). Coal mining in the Moscow area had increased almost four times by

[7] Stalin, *Marxism and the National-Colonial Question,* p. 208.

[8] *History of the Communist Party of the Soviet Union, Short Course,* p. 251.

1927–28 as compared with 1913, and in other coal basins exclusive of the Donbas almost twice; in that time the mining of Donets coal increased only 8%, but oil production increased 26.2%.

Particularly important shifts occurred in the power supply of the Leningrad and Moscow industrial regions.

The completion and expansion of the "Elektroperedacha" station (now the Klasson GES) [K] [9] operating on peat, the erection of the Shatura Station [Sh] (which started to function in 1925) also operating on peat, and the Kashira Station (which started to function in 1922) operating on Moscow coal, permitted a significant reduction in the fuel brought in from a distance for the power economy of Moscow and its adjacent regions. The erection of the first hydroelectric station, the Volkhov Station (put into operation in 1926), and of the "Krasny Oktyabr" Electric Power Station operating on peat, were of similar importance to Leningrad. The regional electric power stations of the Moscow and Leningrad areas operated in large measure on local fuels and water power.

Electric power station construction developed even in the districts which had previously been industrially backward. As examples one can point out the Zemo-Avchala Hydroelectric Station (near Tbilisi), Boz-Su (near Tashkent), and Yerevan Station.

The construction of factories and mills was less developed, but even at that time there was emphasis on the redistribution of productive forces, bringing industry closer to the sources of raw material, and on the elimination of the economic backwardness of the outlying regions. In the period of transition to peacetime construction the creation of the textile industry in the Trans-Caucasus (Kirovabad, Leninakan) and Central Asia (Tashkent) was begun. A new paper industry was started (Balakhna, Syas, Kondopoga, etc.). Significant shifts in the distribution of the glass industry were accomplished (the construction of the Dagestanskie Ogni factory in Dagestan, and others), as also in the leather, food, and a number of other branches of industry.

These were the first steps in the realization of a more uniform distribution of industry by bringing it closer to the sources of raw material. In the period of the socialist industrialization of the country the scope of new construction shifted and the principles of the socialist distribution of productive forces were still more clearly manifested.

On the tenth anniversary of the October Socialist Revolution the

[9] [Place names mentioned in this chapter are located on Fig. 20; abbreviations in brackets refer to abbreviations on Fig. 20.]

foundation was laid for the Lenin Dnepr Hydroelectric Station [Dneproges in Fig. 20]. Almost at the same time work began on the giant agricultural machine building plant in Rostov-on-Don, "Rostselmash." The completion of these undertakings, and the beginning of others, already belong to the heroic years of the Stalin Five-Year Plans.

The construction which took place during the first revolutionary decade is important not only in that it was the first step along the road to a new socialist distribution of productive forces, but also in that it accumulated experience, it laid the groundwork for new branches of industry which had not existed in the country previously, and it created a qualified labor force in the national republics and other regions of the nation previously backward industrially. By the same token it provided the conditions for realizing the Stalin Five-Year Plans.

The wide study of the natural resources of the country also had great significance. The Party and the Government had developed for the country a grandiose program for the distribution of productive forces in the First and Second Five-Year Plans.

The decisive shifts in the distribution of the productive forces of the USSR were directed to the East, which even before the revolution was renowned for its enormous natural resources. In this movement to the East the creation of the Ural-Kuznetsk Combine was of decisive significance.

In 1929 the Party and the Government decided to build the Magnitogorsk metallurgical plant; and, during the First Five-Year Plan for the development of the national economy of the USSR, the fundamental objectives in the construction of the Ural-Kuznetsk Combine were designated. "On the axes of the coal of the Kuzbas and the iron ore of the Urals," reads the First Five-Year Plan, "we will create two new centers of basic industry for the Soviet Union in the East—sufficiently powerful and varied to serve as supporting bases, conveniently located for systematic advancement farther east, for the enormous natural resources found there."[10] At this point is raised the question of improving the Siberian Railroad for the delivery of Kuznetsk coal to the Urals.

The decree of the Central Committee of the Communist Party of the Soviet Union of May 15, 1930, concerning the work of the Uralmet [Ural Metallurgical Trust], had already noted that "a

[10] *The Five-Year Plan*, Vol. III, p. 191 [corrected from p. 151 in original].

vitally necessary condition for the quick industrialization of the country is the creation in the East of a second primary coal and metallurgical center, by the utilization of the very rich coal and ore beds of the Urals and Siberia." The 16th Congress, in accord with the report of Comrade Stalin, confirmed this decision.

Approving the decision of the Central Committee of the Communist Party of the Soviet Union to create the Ural-Kuznetsk Combine, the 16th Party Congress at the same time acknowledged the necessity of pressing the development of other branches of industry as well in the eastern regions (the Urals, Siberia, Kazakhstan, the republics of Central Asia), these industries being based on local raw materials (nonferrous metallurgy, the textile industry, food industry, and others).

Thus, the movement to the enormous sources of raw materials and power of the East was predetermined not only in terms of heavy industry, but also in terms of light industry and the food industry.

The decisions of the 17th Party Congress, which promulgated a rounded program for the distribution of productive forces during the Second Five-Year Plan, in accordance with the problem of completing the technical reconstruction of the national economy of the USSR, were very important in the new distribution.

The Struggle with the Enemies of the People for the Socialist Distribution of Productive Forces

The socialist distribution of productive forces is being accomplished under conditions of capitalist encirclement and of struggle with the enemies of the people, who have done considerable damage in this field.

The contemptible enemies of the people—Trotskyists and Bukharinists—have fought against the policy of our Party in the field of the socialist distribution of productive forces. Trotskyists, foaming at the mouth, argued that a uniform distribution of productive forces was conceivable only on a world scale. Within one country, however, it would be impossible. It is not difficult to understand that this is the refrain of the counterrevolutionary theory of the impossibility of building socialism in one country. Rightist capitulationists spoke against constructing the Dneproges, against converting the old industrial regions into a base for industrializing the entire country. To this purpose they argued that Moscow must remain a textile center, and that it was not necessary to construct machine works there.

Counter to the Party line on the more uniform distribution of industry throughout the entire country and opposing this very important task of socialist construction, the saboteurs put forward the point of view of "optimal" regions, according to which industry can be developed in only a few regions of the country. These hostile aims were cloaked beneath Weber's theory of the distribution of industry, and one of the saboteurs wrote that the industrialization of the previously backward regions of the country was not expedient, since it would mean a completely unproductive expenditure of government means and a slowing down of our industrial development. Instead of a uniform distribution of industry, he advocated limiting industrial construction to two or three regions.

The saboteurs were especially persistent in their fight against the creation of a second coal and metallurgical base in the East of the USSR. They argued that the only "optimal" region for the development of ferrous metallurgy was the South. The struggle of the saboteurs against the creation of a second coal-metallurgical base in the East of the USSR was carried on in order to facilitate the contemplated intervention in our country. The Ukrainian coal-metallurgical base, according to the plans of the interventionists, was to have been seized first. Afterward, it seemed to them, the country, deprived of coal and metal, would not be difficult to take.

The saboteurs also carried on a struggle against the introduction of local fuel, with the aim of creating a fuel crisis in the principal economic regions of the country during the time of the intervention.

Making their task the restoration of capitalism in the USSR, the saboteurs defended the necessity of developing predominantly light industry, since the development of heavy industry in the USSR was supposed to be disadvantageous from the point of view of the international division of labor. They defended the necessity of increasing the dependence of the USSR on foreign capital, of the virtual destruction of the monopoly of foreign trade, of the unlimited granting of concessions to foreign capitalists, and so on.

The Party shattered all these hostile purposes and dispersed them completely.

SECTION 2. THE DISTRIBUTION OF PRODUCTIVE FORCES AS A RESULT OF THE TWO STALIN FIVE-YEAR PLANS

The turbulent growth of productive forces in the years of the Stalin Five-Year Plans was accompanied by their redistribution through the territory of the USSR. The new, efficient distribution of productive forces was one of the most important factors in increasing the rate of economic development.

The New Distribution of Raw Material and Fuel Resources

The new geography of raw materials and fuel, which was created in the years of the Stalin Five-Year Plans, had enormous significance for a more uniform distribution of industry throughout the territory of the USSR, for bringing industry closer to the sources of raw materials and the regions of consumption, and for the industrialization of the national republics.

In bringing industry closer to the sources of raw materials and the areas of consumption, not only are the known raw materials taken into consideration but, with the help of geological explorations and the corresponding development of agriculture, the very geography of raw-material and fuel resources is changed.

In the struggle against the building of socialism the enemies of the Soviet people placed a great deal of hope on the limited knowledge of the natural resources of the USSR. At the beginning of the First Five-Year Plan many bourgeois professors, engineers, and simple hack journalists, with an air of erudition, announced orally and in print that the USSR had an organic deficiency of iron ore, coal, oil, and other mineral resources. On this they built their fictions concerning the lack of realism in the policy of the industrialization of the USSR. In their arguments they frequently referred to the experience of Tsarist Russia.

The knowledge of the mineral raw-material base of the country left to us by Tsarist Russia was insignificant. During the First and Second Five-Year Plans, paralleling the powerful industrial construction, geological exploration was developed on a broad front. The need for great expansion of geological explorations, alongside the industrialization of the country, was pointed out by the 16th Party Congress, which declared in its resolution that "the guaranteeing of the development of the national economy impels the necessity of speeding the rate of geological research to such a degree that it will significantly outstrip the rate of development of industry, for the purpose of preparing mineral raw materials well in advance." [11]

In the years of Soviet power geological knowledge of the USSR has been greatly advanced. Geological surveys have covered an enormous territory, more than 7 million sq. km., which is six times greater than the area of Germany, France, and England taken together. And what is particularly important to note is the great impetus given precisely to the detailed geological study of the country.

Geological exploration, developed in the years of the triumphant Five-Year Plans, guaranteed the colossal growth in the known reserves of mineral deposits of our country.

Before the Revolution most regions of our country were considered poor in their resources of raw materials and power. With regard to such regions as Kazakhstan, Siberia, and Central Asia, there even existed a theory of their "lack of prospects."

The geological explorations of the First and Second Five-Year Plans upset these old notions. Kazakhstan changed from a "land without a future" into one of the most important regions of the USSR for coal (Karaganda), phosphates, polymetals (Altay and Kara-Tau), and rare metals (tin and tungsten). And in copper ores Kazakhstan became the richest region of the Union. More than 60% of all the copper-ore reserves of the Union are found within its territory (at Kounrad, Dzhezkazgan, etc.). In the Ural-Emba District the known reserves of oil, phosphorites, and so on are growing rapidly. Thus, there was created in Kazakhstan a very rich raw-material and power base for the development of various branches of industry.

A similar picture is seen in other regions previously considered "without prospects." Even the far Siberian taiga and tundra, where human foot had never stepped before, could not bar the way to Soviet geologists. In the Srednyaya [Middle] Tunguska Basin the enormous Tungus Coal District was discovered. East of the Tungus coal-bearing area, in Yakutia, was found another large coal district. Far beyond the Arctic Circle our geologists uncovered a very rich nickel deposit (Norilsk, Monchetundry); coal beds were discovered on Cape Nordvik; and so on. It is difficult to name a part of the

[11] *16th Party Congress, Stenographic Report,* p. 727 [?].

USSR in which Soviet geologists, with the active support of local organizations and peoples, have not discovered various sources of raw materials and fuel.

In this way a new geography of raw materials and fuel was created for industrial construction, which played an enormous role in the realization of a proper, more uniform distribution of industry throughout the territory of our immense native land.

The Reconstruction of the Old Industrial Regions and the Industrialization of the National Republics

As a result of the Stalin Five-Year Plans radical changes have taken place in the distribution of the productive forces of the USSR. In the old industrial regions, which had acted as the supporting base for the industrialization and technical reconstruction of the economy of the country, together with the textile and other industries which had developed there historically, there were built first-class plants for the manufacture of complex precision machinery, enterprises for electrotechnical production, basic chemical plants, etc. Moscow, Leningrad, and other old industrial centers were turned into gigantic bases through the mastery of new methods of production.

With the support of the old industrial regions, the national republics firmly set forth on the road to industrialization. Hundreds of large-scale industrial enterprises grew up near sources of raw materials and fuel, in which our republics are so rich.

The industry of the national republics is developing at a much higher rate than that of the old industrial regions. Thus, the industrial output of the Union republics increased between 1928 and 1937 as follows:

RSFSR	5.7 times
Ukrainian SSR	5.7
Belorussian SSR	8.5
Azerbaidzhan SSR	4.5
Georgian SSR	12.5
Armenian SSR	almost 12.0
Turkmen SSR	6.5
Uzbek SSR	5.7
Tadzhik SSR	26.0
Kazakh SSR	almost 12.0
Kirgiz SSR	14.0

It should be born in mind at the same time that industry in the national republics is being developed on a high technical level to start with.

The old industrial regions achieved modern technology gradually, passing through definite stages; but in the republics of the Soviet East, where large-scale industry has been created only in the past ten to fifteen years, it was possible to by-pass different stages of technological development in industrial and agricultural production. The aid of the old industrial regions, which equip the national republics with the newest industrial appliances, was a tremendous factor in the process.

The bourgeois theories, according to which nomadic and colonial peoples in general, by virtue of habits centuries old, were supposed not to be able to take up the new technology, were disproved completely by the industrialization of the national republics and the creation of a qualified force of industrial workers, engineers, and technicians from the native population. Hundreds and thousands of remarkable Stakhanovites of the national republics are known to all our country. They are shining models of the mastery of the foremost techniques of industrial and agricultural production.

The creation, through the initiative of Comrade Stalin, of a second coal and metallurgical base in the East of the USSR, the Ural-Kuznetsk Combine, introduced tremendous changes in the distribution of the productive forces in the USSR.

The old "hoary" Urals, as Lenin called them, have been covered with hundreds of new enterprises. In the Urals there arose the gigantic Magnitogorsk Metallurgical Combine, copper smelting combines, the Chelyabinsk tractor factory, the Uralmashzavod [Ural Machine Plant, at Sverdlovsk], the Uralvagonzavod [Ural Railroad-Car Works, at Nizhny Tagil], and other machine-building plants, serving primarily the eastern regions of the USSR. At the same time, chemical and other branches of industry have grown up, and large electric power stations, which the old Urals had never known.

The Kuzbas, with its rich reserves of coking coal and its dozens of large, highly mechanized mines, is turning into a second Donbas. The productive powers of Eastern Siberia, of the Far East, and of the Far North, with their inexhaustible natural resources, are growing.

The industrialization of the national republics and oblasts, the creation of a second coal and metallurgical base in the East of the USSR, and the development of industry in the Volga area and other regions previously backward industrially have led to the point where "the former division of our oblasts into industrial and agrarian has already been eliminated."[12] This is the most striking indication of our success in achieving a more uniform distribution of productive forces in our country. (See Figs. 27 and 28, [p. 201].)

Bringing industry closer to the sources of raw materials and areas of consumption has played a tremendous role in achieving interregional economic coordination by reducing unproductive and excessively long haulage, which is very important in accelerating the rate of socialist construction.

In spite of the enormous progress in the distribution of productive forces, many deficiencies still remain, which are noted in the decisions of the 18th Party Congress, and which must be eliminated in the Third Five-Year Plan.

These persisting deficiencies cause inefficient and unnecessarily long haulage and cross haulage, the elimination of which is one of the most important tasks of the Third Five-Year Plan.

The New Distribution of Fundamental Branches of the National Economy of the USSR

As a result of the Stalin Five-Year Plans not only has the production of metal in the country been increased, but even its geography has been altered significantly. The metallurgical industry of the South has tripled its smelting of pig iron as compared with prewar times. Metallurgy in the Center and the East is developing still more rapidly.

Large centers of ferrous metallurgy have been created: the Magnitogorsk in the Urals and the Kuznetsk Metallurgical Combine in Western Siberia.

Since the creation of the Ural-Kuznetsk Combine the eastern regions of the USSR have been supplied with pig iron, steel, and rolled products mainly from these plants. However, up to now cross hauls of metal from the Ukraine to the Urals and into Siberia, and back, still occur. As a result of harmful specialization, smaller sizes of rolled structural forms are lacking in the East, while larger sizes are lacking in the Ukraine. They have to be hauled from each region to the other for exchange. The elimination of harmful special-

[12] Stalin, *Questions of Leninism,* p. 455.

ization in the rolling mills, with the assurance at the principal metallurgical bases of a supply of rolled products of all the leading types of metal, is one of the most important problems in the development of ferrous metallurgy in the Third Five-Year Plan.

The Stalin Five-Year Plans have introduced radical changes in the distribution of the fuel industry of the USSR. The geography of coal mining has been changed. The thorough reconstruction of the socialist Donbas has tripled the extraction of coal in comparison with prewar times, and in spite of this its relative importance in the total coal output of the country from year to year has been lowered. This is explained by the growth in the eastern USSR of a second Donbas, the Kuznetsk Basin, while in Kazakhstan a third coal base has been created for the country, Karaganda. At the same time coal basins of local importance have been widely developed. Mining in the Moscow Basin has expanded enormously—almost twenty-five times. Coal mining in the Urals has received a great impetus—Kizel, Chelyabinsk, and Yegorshino coal, and others; coal mining in the Irkutsk (Cheremkhovo) Basin, in the Far East (Kivda, Raichikhinsk, Artem, etc.), in Central Asia (Kirgiz coal and others), in the Trans-Caucasus (Tkvarcheli, Tkvibuli), and so on [Fig. 20, facing p. 143].

But together with the great progress in the development and distribution of the coal industry great deficiencies still exist. Saboteurs, working within the Gosplan and other organizations, have hindered in every way possible the use of local coal and other kinds of local fuel, hoping to create a fuel crisis in a number of important regions.

The directive of Comrade Stalin to the 17th Party Congress, on the necessity of developing the mining of local coal as quickly as possible, has not been adequately realized. There is every possibility to develop the coal industry in all regions of the country, so that in the near future the importation of coal to the Urals and other regions will stop.

Significant changes have occurred in the geography of the oil industry of the USSR. Together with the development of the Baku District, the Grozneft [Grozny Oil Trust], Embaneft [Emba Oil Trust], and especially Maikopneft [Maikop Oil Trust], have also been greatly developed. During the years of the Stalin Five-Year Plans oil drilling has been organized in new regions also: at Ishimbay, Krasnokamsk, Chusovskie Gorodki (in the Urals), at Nebit-Dag (in the Turkmen SSR), on Sakhalin, and in other regions. Because of the rapid increase in the number of tractors, automobiles, and other machines which consume motor fuel it is necessary to ship an ever increasing quantity of oil and oil products from Baku to the central, eastern, and northern regions of the USSR, as the need for liquid fuels grows much faster than the oil industry in the new fields. Deliveries of oil and oil products to these areas are made primarily by railroad.

In the years of the Stalin Five-Year Plans brilliant results have been achieved in electrifying the USSR. The Goelro Plan, contemplating the construction within ten to fifteen years of thirty regional electric power stations with an output of 1.5 million kw., was fulfilled and surpassed in the years of the First Five-Year Plan. Thanks to electrification it is now possible to use the rich water-power resources of the country, and also local fuels which are cumbersome to transport (peat, oil shale, coal). This is particularly important for regions which are without large reserves of high-calorie fuels but have a large supply of available water power, peat, oil shale, coal, and so forth. A great many very large electric power stations based on the use of local power resources and by-products of the coal and oil industry (culm, mazut) have been created in different parts of the USSR. The efficiency of these electric power stations is greatly increased by the creation of large electric power supply systems. The creation of such systems permits the fuller utilization of the power of hydroelectric plants by coordinating their output with that of the thermal electric power plants.

Great shifts have taken place in the distribution of machine building in the USSR. Machine building has developed rapidly not only in the old industrial regions, where dozens of first-class machine-building factories have been created, but also in the national republics and in other regions which had had no machine building before the Revolution. Thus, in Tashkent a large agricultural machinery factory has been built; in Ufa, a motor plant; in Izhevsk, a motorcycle plant; and in Gomel, an agricultural machinery factory. Machine building has grown in the Volga Region—in Kuibyshev, Saratov, Stalingrad, etc.

There has been a particularly important development of the machine-building industry in the Urals, where such giant plants as the Chelyabinsk tractor factory, the Uralmashzavod, the Nizhny Tagil Railroad-car Combine, and the Chelyabinsk machine-tool factory have been created. Machine building in the Ukraine also has seen great development—the Kharkov tractor and turbo-generator plants, the Kramatorsk plant for building heavy machinery, the Voroshilovgrad locomotive factory, and so forth. Thus, a new geography of machine building has been developed in the USSR in the period of the Stalin Five-Year Plans.

Alongside the tremendous achievements in this field, very substantial defects still exist. There exists, in the machine-building industry of the USSR, a whole series of unique specialized enterprises whose products are shipped for many thousands of kilometers. Such is the situation in the production of turbines, boilers, and automobile and tractor equipment.

Along with production facilities, the production of consumers' goods has been greatly developed during the years of the Stalin Five-Year Plans. Under the Second Five-Year Plan the production of these goods more than doubled. Even the distribution of their production in the regions of the USSR has been changed. It is true that there are still individual branches of light industry and of the food industry, the distribution of which has a long way to go to overcome the heavy legacy of the past—particularly in the textile field. New textile enterprises have been built in the republics of Central Asia and in the Trans-Caucasus where their raw materials are immediately at hand, and also in Siberia. However, this construction has effected only relatively small changes in the geography of the textile, particularly the cotton, industry. At present the old industrial regions yield about 95% of all cotton cloth produced. The disproportion between the preparing and spinning mills, and between spinning and weaving, has not yet been eliminated in the old industrial regions. Under the Third Five-Year Plan these disproportions should be eliminated by the construction of small spinning mills in these regions.

Greater changes have occurred in the distribution of the food industry, many branches of which have been created almost for the first time. In Tsarist Russia there were no meat combines. Instead there were primitive slaughterhouses, where the butchering of cattle was conducted under unsanitary conditions. Since the inception of the Stalin Five-Year Plans, twenty-four large meat combines have been created in the USSR, including the Mikoyan Meat Combine in Moscow, and the Leningrad Meat Combine, which are models of the most progressive techniques in the industry.

Tsarist Russia had no large-scale bread-baking industry. Maxim Gorky painted the desolate picture of the primitive bakeries which existed in the towns. Now, more than three hundred large mechanized bakeries are at work in different parts of the country.

The fishing industry of the USSR is also being transformed into an advanced branch of the food industry. The Volga-Caspian fishing grounds have been changed beyond recognition as a result of socialist reconstruction. Murmansk has grown into one of the largest fishing centers. Before the Revolution the Barents and White Seas provided an insignificant quantity of fish—not more than 6.1% of the total catch of the country in 1913; but in 1937 they yielded 20.6% of the country's fish. The largest trawling base in the world has been established at Murmansk.

Fishing in the Far East has been tremendously developed. In 1937 its waters provided 25.2% of the total catch of the Union. Dozens of canneries have been built there, and a first-class fishing fleet has been launched. However, the fishing industry is still lagging behind, in spite of enormous possibilities.

Important shifts have occurred in the development and distribution of other branches of the food industry. Sugar-beet factories have been built in Kazakhstan, Kirgizia, Altay Kray, etc. New centers have been developed for flour milling and confectionery.

In the socialist reconstruction of agriculture, and consequently in its distribution, industry has a leading and transforming role. The transfer of industry to the East and the industrialization of formerly backward national republics and other agricultural regions have been accompanied by radical changes in the distribution of agriculture. The creation of new industrial centers in the various regions of the USSR demanded the establishment of agricultural areas around them which would supply the cities with vegetables and dairy products. The development of branches of industry operating on agricultural raw materials—the synthetic rubber, textile, leather, sugar, and canning industries—demands a corresponding development and areal distribution in the cultivation of potatoes, cotton, flax, sugar beets, and so on.

The development of industry in the Ukraine, in the Volga Region, in the North Caucasus, and in the Central Chernozem Region has already reached the point where they cannot export as much agricultural produce as before. From this follows the task which Comrade Stalin set before the 17th Party Congress—to establish in each region its own agricultural base. This refers especially to the old industrial regions and to the entire belt formerly "consuming."

The efficient distribution of agriculture throughout the USSR is of vital importance to the national economy. It assures the best utilization of soil and climatic conditions, the substitution of more profitable crops for less profitable, and also an independent supply of the most important subsistence and industrial crops—products which had previously been imported (cotton, tea, citrus fruits, etc.). Without the proper distribution and specialization of agriculture among the regions, efficient crop rotation, which plays a tremendous role in raising the productivity of the socialist fields, is inconceivable.

The proper distribution of the fundamental agricultural branches and crops assures the further growth of grain production in the primary grain regions, the creation of a self-reliant subsistence base in the central and northern regions, and increase in the output of industrial crops in the primary regions of their production, together with the development of industrial and highly valuable crops in new areas.

It must be remembered also that, because of the creation of local subsistence and raw-material bases in the oblasts previously "consuming," long freight hauls of agricultural products have been reduced.

Having solved the grain problem, the Party has been able to organize the supply of grain to the livestock, sugar-beet, flax, and other regions, assuring specialization in their most valuable and profitable products. Thus our country has been able to assure itself of a supply of cotton and to increase the flax crop, the sugar-beet crop, highly valuable oil and coarse fiber (bast) crops, citrus fruits, etc. This has resulted, first of all, in the growth and change in the structure of the area under cultivation. The increase in the area under cultivation during the years of the Stalin Five-Year Plans has taken place chiefly in the industrial, truck-gardening, and fodder crops, and in wheat growing.

The geographical distribution of the increase in the area under cultivation is very significant. Approximately 30% of the increase has taken place in the northern and central industrial regions, more than 34% in the southern regions, more than 27% in the eastern regions, and approximately 9% in the republics of Central Asia and the Trans-Caucasus. Thus, very large shifts have occurred in the geography of agriculture.

It is particularly important to note the great growth in the cultivated area of the central and northern oblasts, where before the October Socialist Revolution, under the impact of competition from the cheap grain of the steppe belt, the cultivation of wheat was being displaced, and plowed land was being turned into meadow and pasture.

The conversion of agriculture to collective and state farms has assured the rapid growth of the cultivated area in the consuming (central industrial and northern) oblasts by the clearing of shrubs and wooded areas and by the reclamation of so-called abandoned lands.

The central industrial and northern oblasts are successfully creating their own subsistence bases. Particular progress has been achieved in advancing wheat cultivation into the northern and central oblasts of the USSR. On this basis the previously consuming regions are being turned into producing ones. A second wheat base in the East of the USSR is being strengthened and successfully developed. In this way a new geography of grain cultivation has come into being.

"In the past three years," said Comrade Stalin at the 18th Party Congress, "the base of surplus marketable grain has been transferred from the Ukraine, which used to be considered the granary of our country, to the north and east, that is to the RSFSR. It is well known that in the past two or three years the Ukraine has provided about 400 million poods of grain annually, while the RSFSR in these years has provided 1.1 to 1.2 billion poods of surplus marketable grain annually."[13]

The successful solution of the grain problem in turn has guaranteed the successful development of industrial crops.

The rapid increase of industrial crops is combined with their new distribution through the territory of the USSR. Together with the strengthening of the old industrial crop regions, new regions in which these crops previously had not been developed at all, or had

[13] Stalin, *Questions of Leninism*, p. 583.

been developed to an insignificant degree, have been drawn into cultivation.

The New Distribution of Productive Forces and the Destruction of the Antagonisms Between Town and Country

In the years of the First and Second Five-Year Plans great progress was made in overcoming the antagonisms between town and country. The socialist distribution of productive forces played a tremendous role in this.

The antagonism between town and country has an age-long history. It began with the transition from barbarism to civilization and has persisted through the entire history of civilization. The gulf between town and country, the development of antagonism between town and country, as Marx expressed it, sums up the entire economic history of society.

Under capitalism, particularly in its more advanced stages when industry is completely separated from agriculture, the antagonism reaches its greatest depths, condemning the rural populations to the imbecility of village life, while the laboring population of the large towns, as Engels put it, suffocates in its own refuse.

The elimination of the antagonism between town and country is linked inseparably with the new distribution of productive forces, with the socialist reconstruction of agriculture, with the transformation of agricultural labor into a species of industrial labor, and with the transformation of the countenance of the village itself.

The industrialization of the national republics and peasant regions which previously had been backward industrially, and the elimination of the old division of regions into industrial and agrarian, is tremendously important in the final obliteration of the antagonism between town and country.

Some woebegone theorists and enemies of the Soviet people have tried to thrust upon the Party the "theory" of the dying away and self-liquidation of towns as the primary path toward the elimination of the antagonism. They have demanded that the existing large towns be broken up into smaller units, and that Moscow be preserved and maintained only as a museum city.

The Party has exposed these "theories" as inimical to Marxism-Leninism. "We proceed towards the elimination of the antagonisms between town and country," said Comrade Kaganovich, "not on the basis of the liquidation of the towns, but on the basis of their modification, and the socialist alteration of the village and its elevation to the level of the most advanced urban culture." [14]

Urban-rural relations in the USSR have changed radically. Under capitalism the town systematically robs the village. In the eyes of the peasants the town stands out as the focal point of their exploitation.

"Under capitalism the town gave the village that which corrupted it—politically, economically, morally, physically, and so on. Under our system the town of itself is beginning to give the village the direct opposite." [15]

Today Soviet towns are helping the villages to organize a collective economy and to raise their cultural level. The very countenance of the kolkhoz [collective farm] village has been radically changed since it was supplied with the most advanced technology. The kolkhoz village has created its own intelligentsia, schools, and network of cultural institutions. The towns themselves also have changed beyond recognition. Thanks to socialist reconstruction, their slums and filthy cellars, where under Tsarism the workers had been cooped up, have disappeared. The new Moscow is a living example of how sharply the old towns are changing their appearance.

In the years of the Stalin Five-Year Plans new towns have sprung up, with advanced urban culture, near extensive sources of raw materials and fuel. Such are Magnitogorsk, Berezniki, Stalinsk, Kemerovo, Karaganda, and Kirovsk [Fig. 20].

In building new towns we are promoting progressive urban culture in the previously backward national republics, where not long ago there ruled darkness, lack of culture, and actual savagery. The towns created in these regions are extremely important in the transformation of the adjoining village localities.

In the USSR hundreds of towns are springing up also on the basis of large-scale socialist agriculture. Machine tractor stations and large sovkhozes [state farms] are the foundations of the towns in the agricultural regions.

Besides this, the kolkhoz village quickly develops its own industry —machine tractor stations, small electric power stations, repair shops, and enterprises for the processing of agricultural raw materials.

Thus, a consolidation of industry with agriculture is taking place,

[14] From the report on the June plenum of the Central Committee of the Communist Party of the Soviet Union, 1931.

[15] Lenin, *Works*, Vol. XXVII, p. 390.

and on this foundation the agricultural regions are being transformed.

"A characteristic feature of the socialist development of our towns is that on the basis of the expedient distribution of productive forces, of the utilization of natural resources, and of the power and raw-material bases of the entire country, we are proceeding toward the gradual elimination of the antagonisms between town and country. That is, toward the development of modern industry, toward the development of an advanced, urban, socialist culture where none existed before—where there was savagery and age-old darkness." [16]

SECTION 3. THE DISTRIBUTION OF THE PRODUCTIVE FORCES OF THE USSR UNDER THE THIRD FIVE-YEAR PLAN

Proceeding from the remarkable results of the [first] two Stalin Five-Year Plans, the 18th Party Congress approved the new program for the development and distribution of productive forces in the Third Five-Year Plan. In this program of great works, questions of the proper distribution of new enterprises throughout our immense country occupy a central position.

The basic principles of the socialist distribution of productive forces, worked out by Lenin and Stalin—the bringing of industry closer to sources of raw materials and consuming areas, the raising of the economy of the previously backward regions, the complex development of the economy of the different regions—are the basis for the decisions of the 18th Congress on the distribution of new construction.

"The Congress feels," say the resolutions, "that the *distribution of new construction* in the regions of the USSR according to the Third Five-Year Plan must take as its point of departure the bringing of industry closer to sources of raw materials and consuming areas in order to eliminate inefficient and excessively long freight haulage; and also the greatest possible elevation of the regions of the USSR which were economically backward in the past." [17]

[16] L. M. Kaganovich, *For the Socialist Reconstruction of Moscow and the Towns of the USSR*, OGIZ, Moskovsky Rabochy, 1931, p. 68.

[17] *Resolutions of the 18th Congress of the Communist Party of the Soviet Union*, p. 28.

The Complex Development of the Primary Economic Regions and the Elimination of Inefficient Transportation

In the Third Five-Year Plan the socialist distribution of productive forces rises to a new level. It guarantees the complex development of the primary economic regions of the country, the most complete and expedient utilization of local labor, power, and raw-material resources, and the manufacture of a maximum quantity of products locally. "Particularly significant," read the resolutions of the 18th Congress, "is the assurance, in the large-scale industrial regions, of a local supply of fuel and of certain products which are difficult to transport. The dependence of these regions on the importation of bulky cargoes from a distance has increased in proportion to their industrial growth and the rapid increase in their urban population."[18]

The guaranteeing of local fuel, building materials, chemical fertilizers, and abundant supplies of the products of light industry and of the food industry accelerates the development of productive forces in all parts of the country, and is tremendously important for the elimination of unproductive and excessively long freighting. The development of local fuel and building materials, the cement industry in particular, should result in an especially great reduction of long freight hauls, since these items take up approximately 50% of the entire freight transportation of the country.

For the maximum utilization of local coal and other types of fuel, the construction of small and medium thermal electric plants is assuming great importance.

The most important part of the construction program in the sphere of electrification in the Third Five-Year Plan is the assurance of increased electric power by the building of new small and medium electric power stations of 25 thousand kw. and less. The Third Five-Year Plan provides for the erection of 102 regional thermal electric plants of small and medium capacity in the various regions of the USSR. At the same time small local hydroelectric stations must be widely developed.

In the Third Five-Year Plan the building of the greatest electrical installation in the world is being developed, the Kuibyshev Hydroelectric Station, with a total capacity of 3.4 million kw.

[18] *Ibid.*

The creation of a second oil base in the East of the USSR is assuming particular importance. In the region between the Volga and the Urals an enormous oil-bearing area, with great reserves, has been discovered. The Prikamneft [Kama Oil Trust], Syzranneft [Syzran Oil Trust], Buguruslanneft [Buguruslan Oil Trust], Bashneft [Bashkir Oil Trust], and other oil enterprises are already operating there. However, only the first steps have been taken in the development of this rich region. The 18th Party Congress set as one of the most important tasks in the development of the oil industry under the Third Five-Year Plan "the creation of a new oil base in the region between the Volga and the Urals—a 'Second Baku.'"[19]

This will radically change the geography of oil production and decrease the long-distance transfer of oil and oil products.

The projected new construction under the Third Five-Year Plan assures the quicker growth of capital construction in the eastern and far eastern regions, which assures bringing industry into greater proximity to its sources of raw materials and consuming areas. In solving this problem, the elimination of the harmful specialization of rolling mills and the creation of new metallurgical bases in the East of the USSR are of tremendous significance. Together with the further growth of metallurgy in the Urals and in Western Siberia, under the Third Five-Year Plan, new centers of ferrous metallurgy are being created in Eastern Siberia and in the Far East, with a complete cycle of production, in order to provide locally for machine construction and other consumers. Of the twenty blast furnaces which will be built under the Third Five-Year Plan, fifteen will go to the eastern regions. The smelting of pig iron in the eastern regions should rise from 28 to 35% of the national total during the Third Five-Year Plan.

The rate of development of machine building in the Third Five-Year Plan, as a leading element in all of industry, is significantly greater than the general rate of industrial development. Together with the completion of the construction of three heavy machine-tool-building plants, a milling-machine plant in Gorky, and a plant for automatic machine tools in Kiev, the Third Five-Year Plan provides for the construction of new plants for the manufacture of machine tools in various parts of the country. Also, the construction of a new automobile factory in Siberia is being effected, as well as

[19] *Ibid.*, p. 17.

new auto-assembly plants, ball-bearing factories, plants for the fabrication of heavy and medium chemical equipment, etc.

In the decisions of the 18th Congress the task is set forth of increasing the utilization of labor in the USSR by one and one-half to two times in the years of the Third Five-Year Plan. In accordance with this a great program for the construction of enterprises in the food industry and in light industry is developing in different regions of the country.

The goal of new construction is more radically to change the geography of the textile industry, especially the cotton industry, in the direction of moving it closer to its sources of raw materials and areas of consumption.

The Struggle Against Gigantism and the Creation of Duplicate Enterprises

The mania for gigantism and the enthusiasm for planning and constructing industrial giants and complex combines without considering local conditions and economic necessity, which have been condemned by the Party, hinder the efficient distribution of industry and the elimination of unproductive and excessively long freight hauls. The mania for gigantism leads to great delays in construction, to the paralysis of government resources, to difficulties in the mastering of production, and so forth.

"In order to shorten the time spent on construction and to set productive power into action," reads a resolution of the 18th Party Congress, "and also to increase the dispersion of new enterprises in the primary economic regions of the country, the 18th Party Congress demands a decisive *struggle against gigantism* in construction and a wide-scale transition to the construction of medium and small enterprises in all branches of the national economy of the USSR." [20]

In a resolution of this Party Congress the enthusiasm for large electric power stations, to the detriment of small and medium ones, is condemned as wrong and as harmful to the national economy.

In our country to this day there is a whole series of narrowly specialized enterprises which supply all regions of the country with one or another type of product. Moreover, the output of these unique enterprises has to be shipped for many thousands of kilometers, and frequently interruptions occur in the supply of industrial

[20] *Ibid.*, p. 35.

items from such units. From this stems the task set by the 18th Party Congress:

"Under the Third Five-Year Plan, to create in such *economic centers* of the country as the eastern regions, the Urals, and the Volga Region, duplicate enterprises in the ranks of the machine-building, oil-processing, and chemical industries, in order to remove the element of chance in the supply of certain industrial products from unique enterprises." [21]

The creation of duplicate enterprises is of great importance for the further industrialization of such regions as the Volga Region, the Urals, and Western Siberia. It is important for strengthening the country's capacity for defense.

The decision of the 18th Party Congress concerning the provision of proper controls for the fulfillment of the decisions of the Central Committee of the Communist Party of the Soviet Union, and of the Council of People's Commissars of the USSR, regarding the prohibition of the construction of new enterprises in Moscow and Leningrad, and the extension of this ruling to the other large cities of the USSR—Kiev, Kharkov, Rostov-on-Don, Gorky, and Sverdlovsk—has enormous significance for the further dispersion of industry throughout the economic regions of the country.

In accordance with Lenin-Stalinist national policy, the greatest possible improvement of the national republics is taking place. The construction of new plants and factories, electric power stations, railroads, new irrigation systems, and the greatest possible mechanization of agriculture are projected in the republics and oblasts of the USSR; "to assure," reads a resolution of the 18th Congress, "the furthest agricultural and cultural improvement of *the national republics and oblasts* in accordance with the fundamental goals of the distribution of productive forces under the Third Five-Year Plan." [22]

The Creation of Their Own Supply Bases in the Republics, Krays, and Oblasts

Under the Third Five-Year Plan a very great growth of socialist agriculture is in progress. Agricultural production should increase more than one and one-half times (in monetary value). The mean annual harvest of grain should increase from the 5.8 billion poods of the Second Five-Year Plan to 8 billion poods. Great increase in

[21] *Ibid.*, p. 28. [22] *Ibid.*, p. 29.

production should be assured in industrial crops—sugar beets, raw cotton, flax fiber, etc. The problem of livestock raising should be completely solved under the Third Five-Year Plan. The attainment of these goals requires the accomplishment of a whole series of measures, the most important of which are: the completion of the complex mechanization of agriculture; the widespread introduction of advanced agricultural techniques; correct crop rotation with the use of grass-sowing and fallow periods; and the creation of a stable fodder base for livestock raising. At the same time, the great irrigation and drainage projects in the republics of Central Asia (Vakhsh, Murgab oasis) and in the Trans-Caucasus (Colchis) must be completed. The offensive against drought in the southeastern regions of the USSR is developing on a wide front.

The more efficient distribution of socialist agriculture should play a great part in its further development. The 18th Party Congress posed the problem:

"To create around Moscow, Leningrad, Baku, Kharkov, Kiev, the industrial centers of the Donbas, Kuzbas, Gorky, the cities of the Far East, and all other large cities, *potato-vegetable and livestock-raising bases* which will assure these centers of a full supply of vegetables, potatoes, and to a significant degree milk and meat."[23]

The realization of this program not only will improve the supply of food products to the large industrial centers, but also will reduce the necessity for shipping potatoes, vegetables, and meat and dairy products great distances.

The instructions of Comrade Stalin to the 17th Party Congress concerning the necessity of creating their own supply bases in all of the republics, krays, and oblasts of the USSR, in the Third Five-Year Plan, are being put into practice to the fullest extent.

Under the Third Five-Year Plan the development of production in sufficient quantity of such foods as potatoes, vegetables, milk products, and meat products is being assured in each republic and in each kray and oblast. The further flourishing of socialist agriculture and the development of the Stakhanovite movement should assure a great increase in the agricultural production of our country under the Third Five-Year Plan.

The development of the productive forces of our country is taking place under conditions of capitalist encirclement and the growing

[23] *Ibid.*, p. 23.

danger of attack by warmongers. Proceeding from this basis, the Third Five-Year Plan provides for the necessity of building up large-scale government reserves of fuel, electric power, and certain defense production in order to assure the uninterrupted improvement of the economy under any circumstances.

The necessity of providing for the proper distribution of these reserves throughout the enormous territory of our country in order to eliminate unproductive and long-distance shipping, and to assure the primary economic centers of the country a maximum quantity of local resources, is emphasized as strongly as possible in the decisions of the 18th Congress.

The successful fulfillment of the Third Stalin Five-Year Plan will introduce still more grandiose changes in the economic map of our country and will raise it to a new level on the road to the complete triumph of communism.

IV The Population of the USSR and Its Distribution

THE DISTRIBUTION of the population, the decisive productive force of a society, is the most important element in the economic geography of the USSR.

"The revolutionary class itself is the greatest productive force," [1] wrote Marx. *"The primary productive force of all humanity is the worker, the toiler,"* [2] emphasizes Lenin. ". . . Of all the valuable types of capital in the world, the most precious and the most decisive one is the people, the workers," [3] points out Comrade Stalin.

The distribution of population, the greatest of productive forces, can be analyzed only on the basis of the law of population which is peculiar to a given method of production. For there is no abstract, nonhistorical law of population.

Basic Features of the Law of Population Under Capitalism

According to Marx, the law of population under a capitalist society—the law as a result of which the accumulation of capital leads inevitably to relative overpopulation, to unemployment and poverty in town and country—not only determines the changes in the population engaged in production, but also explains its distribution and migration. Moreover, the Marxian law of population accounts also for the destiny of the so-called "natural" increase in the population under capitalism (births, deaths, total increase). What are the basic features of the law of population in a capitalist society?

Relative overpopulation takes place continuously under the influence of the universal law of capital accumulation under capitalism.

[1] Marx, *The Poverty of Philosophy*, Partizdat, 1937, p. 120.
[2] Lenin, *Works*, Vol. XXIV, p. 298.
[3] Stalin, *Questions of Leninism*, p. 491.

The relative overpopulation increases in proportion to the accumulation of capital. This means that unemployment in its visible form grows in the towns, while in the country poor peasants and hired laborers, reduced almost to the position of beggars, increase in numbers. "Capital accumulation constantly produces (in proportion to its intensity and its extent) relatively excessive labor population, i.e., excessive by comparison with the average requirements of capital for its own expansion, and therefore unnecessary and surplus." [4] The industrial reserve army of unemployed looks for jobs, exerts pressure on the labor market, reduces the price of labor force below its real value, makes working conditions worse, and, in short, creates "the background against which the law of labor supply and demand operates." [5]

Assuming various forms—fluid, hidden, or stagnant—the relative overpopulation under capitalism sometimes (in circumstances favorable to capital) partially decreases, sometimes grows in times of crisis, but in all cases remains a permanent feature of capitalism. Relative overpopulation is not only a product of capitalist production, but is also a condition for its existence. It is apparent, therefore, that the more highly developed the capitalist method of production in a given country, the more noticeable the relative overpopulation of that country." [6]

One of the features of the capitalist law of population consists in the peculiar distribution of the labor force and, consequently, of the people. Spontaneous transfers of capital, made in pursuit of the highest profit, cause an equally spontaneous migration of the labor force seeking employment. The towns become increasingly removed from the country. An impassable gulf deepens between them. One branch of industry after another becomes separated from agriculture. The urban industrial population grows at the expense of the rural agricultural population.

"The basis for any elaborate division of labor," writes Marx, "accomplished by means of commodity exchange, lies in the separation of town from country. One might say that the development of this opposition is the essence of the entire course of the economic history of society." [7]

Lenin pointed out that the irregularity of capitalist development

[4] Marx, *Capital*, Vol. I, p. 501.
[5] *Ibid.*, p. 509.
[6] *Ibid.*, Vol. III, p. 213.
[7] *Ibid.*, Vol. I, p. 266.

is a law of the bourgeois regime. This irregularity becomes especially acute during the period of imperialism. The very irregularity of distribution of cities in various countries, or in different regions of the same country, can be explained primarily by the irregularity of capitalist development.

In Russia, for example, one can trace how the precapitalist distribution of population was still quite common during the period of small-scale commodity production and during the period of manufacturing, and how the rural population continued to a considerable extent to be tied down to the land. By taking advantage of the compulsory attachment of the peasant-semiproletarian to his small land allotment, capitalism obtained an exceptionally cheap labor force: "Since the peasant cannot move to the factory, the factory moves to the peasant. The peasant is not completely free . . . to seek the most profitable employer, but the employer knows very well where to find the cheapest worker." [8] Large-scale machine industry completely destroys the patriarchal isolation of the rural population, and brings about a rapid migration of population and its concentration in towns.

The development of capitalist industrialization, intensified impoverishment, and relative overpopulation increase still more the mobility of the labor force and bring about the movement of large masses of workers not only within one country but on an international scale.

"The constant shifting of workers into the category of 'superfluous,'" writes Marx, "necessitates emigration from heavily industrialized countries and leads to the colonization of new lands. . . . A new international division of labor is created, which corresponds to the distribution of the chief centers of machine production and makes some sections of the globe predominantly areas of agricultural production, others predominantly areas of industrial production." [9]

However, this is true only in the early stage of the transformation of capitalism into a world economy. In the last phase of capitalist development, under imperialism, migration of population takes on a different aspect. The largest capitalist countries, such as the United States and France, become the centers of attraction for

[8] Lenin, *Works*, Vol. III, p. 410.

[9] Marx, *Capital*, Vol. I, p. 348.

cheap labor from the colonies. "One of the peculiarities of imperialism," writes Lenin, ". . . is the decreased emigration from imperialist countries and increased immigration (influx of workers and transmigration) into these countries from those which are more backward and have lower wage-scales." [10]

The composition of immigrants also has changed radically during the period of imperialism. While during the second half of the nineteenth century the so-called "old" immigration of the United States was principally from the industrial countries of Europe—England, Germany, France, Holland, Sweden, and Norway—the "new" immigration, of the beginning of the twentieth century, was mainly from the agrarian countries of Eastern and Southern Europe, which supplied largely a cheap, unskilled labor force. Lenin notes especially that in the United States immigrants from Eastern and Southern Europe take jobs with the lowest pay. This cheap, poorly organized labor force is subjected by capital to particularly cruel exploitation.

Industrial relations under capitalism also affect materially the so-called natural increase in the population. The very existence of relative overpopulation creates human material always ready and available for capitalist exploitation and in numbers independent of the limits of natural population increase. However, the exceptionally rapid exhaustion of the labor force creates a demand for quick replacements of the generations of workers. "The contradiction that the natural increase in the labor population does not satisfy the demands for the accumulation of capital, even though at the same time it surpasses them, is a contradiction inherent in the movement of capital itself." [11]

The basic features of the natural increase in population under capitalism are: (a) a shortening of the life span of the labor population; (b) an increased death rate and a relatively high birth rate among workers, which insures a quick replacement of generations; (c) relatively large workers' families; (d) early marriages among workers; and (e) the nature of reproduction among the working class, which is elemental in character, which does not require any expenditures by capital, and which is based upon the workers' instinct for self-preservation.

[10] Lenin, *Works,* Vol. XIX, p. 157.
[11] Marx, *Capital,* Vol. I, p. 511.

The natural increase in the labor population determines to a large extent the dynamics of the total population increase. Under imperialism the natural population increase diminishes. This point is illustrated in Table 10.

Table 10. NATURAL INCREASE OF POPULATION PER THOUSAND [PER ANNUM, IN MAJOR CAPITALIST COUNTRIES]

Country	1908–1913	1928	1934
United States	10.0	7.8	5.7
England	10.9	5.0	3.3
Germany	13.0	7.0	3.5 [a]
France	1.2	1.7	1.0
Italy	12.0	10.4	10.1

[a] For 1933.

Bourgeois demographers prophesy a further diminution of natural population increase in the majority of countries. Capitalism is growing senile. This fact is acknowledged more and more frequently even in the writings of bourgeois ideologists. Bourgeois scholars are trying to give the status of everlasting and compulsory "law" to capitalist phenomena which spring from a constant impoverishment of the working masses. They assert that, as the industrialization of a country grows, the increase in population must inevitably slow down and decrease. The experience of the socialist state shows clearly that all these fictions are false and exposes them graphically. Socialism alone liberates humanity and creates all the conditions necessary for a rapid population increase.

History has demonstrated that the socialist revolution, having destroyed the universal principle of capitalist accumulation, at the same time has limited the operation of the law of population, inherent in capitalism, which is based upon that principle.

Basic Features of the Law of Population Under Socialism

Before our very eyes the new socialist law of population is beginning to take effect in the USSR.

As a result of socialist industrialization, of collectivization, and of the destruction of the kulaks as a class, unemployment in the towns has been eliminated, and the remains of the so-called "agrarian overpopulation" and poverty and pauperism in the country have been eliminated. The causes that brought the natural stream of labor force from the country into the towns have also been destroyed. A planned distribution of the labor force has been established, as has been the organized transfer to towns of agricultural workers, carried out in accordance with special contracts with the kolkhozes. Such a distribution of the labor force is in keeping both with the general plan for economic development and with the increase of labor productivity.

The socialist method of production changes radically the former *distribution of population.* The distribution of the working population changes in accordance with the new, planned distribution of all productive forces.

Bringing industry closer to the sources of raw materials and to the consuming regions, striving for a complex development of the main economic areas of the country, and industrializing the national republics, we have succeeded, in the course of our socialist construction, in altering noticeably the traditional distribution of population. Following a definite plan, the Soviet state is transferring labor forces to the new industrial regions in the East and to the national republics, and is training national cadres of skilled workers and specialists.

This process will proceed even more intensively under the Third Five-Year Plan and during the entire period of transition from socialism to communism.

In *Anti-Dühring,* Engels points out that through the communist society we shall attain a more or less uniform distribution of both productive forces and people.

The socialist law of population affects also the *natural increase of population:*

1. Elimination of exploitation, radical improvement in labor conditions, the raising of material and cultural standards of living, Stalin's intense concern with the human being, confidence in the future—all these factors lead to a considerable lengthening of the workers' life span. This is accompanied by a drastic decrease of mortality in general and of infant mortality in particular.

2. Tremendous improvement in the standard of living is directly connected with an increase in the birth rate. What Engels foresaw even in 1866, when he wrote to Lange that under socialism "humanity would be able to reproduce itself more rapidly than is compatible with present bourgeois society," [12] is now coming to pass.

[12] Marx and Engels, *Letters,* p. 163.

3. With the general growth of population, the number of dependents per worker becomes smaller, both because of the absence of unemployment and because of the constant increase in number of workers engaged in production and in auxiliary branches of work. This process of decreasing the number of dependents is greatly facilitated by the large-scale introduction of women into the labor forces in all branches of socialist production.

4. The natural increase in population ceases to be the private affair of every individual family. The Soviet Government carefully safeguards the health of children and young people. The socialist state develops a wide network of free maternity hospitals, renders tremendous material help to mothers with large families, looks after the social upbringing and education of children, gives legal protection to both children and mothers, etc.

Growth of Population in the USSR

Census data vividly confirm the vast superiority of the socialist economic system over the capitalist.

In 1897 the population of Russia was 106.4 million. In 1913 on the eve of the first Imperialist War, its population (within the present boundaries of the USSR) numbered 139.3 million. The Imperialist War and the Civil War resulted in a considerable decrease in the total population. In 1920, there were only 134.2 million people in the USSR. The population census taken as of December 17, 1926—when the restoration of the national economy had been completed, and the Soviet state entered upon the socialist reconstruction of its economy—showed a vast increment in population, which by that date had reached 147 million. Finally, the population census of January 17, 1939, showed that the population of the USSR had reached 170,467,186.

The population of the Western Ukraine and Western Belorussia, included within the boundaries of the USSR [in late 1939], accounts for [another] 13 million.

From the end of 1926 to the beginning of 1939, the population of the Soviet state gained almost 23.5 million (15.9%). During the same period the population of all the capitalist countries of Europe together increased by slightly more than 32 million, or by only 8.7%. The average annual rate of population increase in the USSR attained 1.23%, while the natural population increase in the United

States during this period was 0.67%; in Great Britain, 0.36%; in Germany, 0.62%; and in France, 0.08%.

The unprecedented improvement in the public welfare results in a constant decrease in mortality, a further rise in the birth rate, and the lengthening of the average life span. These factors are responsible for the high figures for natural increase of population which are characteristic of the Soviet state.

Mortality in the USSR towards the end of the Second Five-Year Plan was 40% lower than in prerevolutionary Russia.

In Tsarist Russia usually 25 to 30% of infants died before reaching the age of one, while during periods of famine infant mortality rose to 40%. Now the situation has changed radically. In Moscow and Leningrad, for example, mortality has decreased more than 2.5 times [by over 60%] since the Revolution; in fact it is lower than in London, Paris, Berlin, and Vienna. But the birth rate is an even more striking index. In 1938 in the cities of Leningrad, Kiev, Kharkhov, and Moscow, average births per thousand were 27.4 to 28.5. During the same year the birth rate in the capitals of the major capitalist countries was less than half as great: 11.5 per thousand in Paris, 13.5 in New York, 13.6 in London, 14.1 in Berlin.

At the present time the Soviet state is a country of truly happy and joyous children. To a large extent this can be explained by the tremendous attention the Government gives to the welfare of children, by the vast assistance given to large families, and by the considerable strengthening of the Soviet family, now the most stable in the world.

According to data for 1926–1927, in the USSR the average life span of men is ten years greater and of women thirteen years greater than during the prewar period.

Particularly rapid is the natural increase of population among the formerly oppressed nationalities. The Soviet socialist regime has created all the necessary conditions for a speedy economic and cultural growth of the peoples of the national republics. Nationalities formerly doomed to extinction and physical extermination have received under the Soviet system all the facilities necessary for fruitful development. The census of 1926 showed that already the rate of natural increase among the formerly backward nationalities surpassed considerably the average birth rate of the USSR as a whole.

Noteworthy are the data pertaining to the natural increase of population in the Union republics during recent years. It is characteristic, for example, that in 1938 the number of births in the RSFSR exceeded the number of deaths by 97.5%; in the Ukrainian SSR, by 159.4%; in the Belorussian SSR, by 266.7%; in the Azerbaidzhan SSR, by 132%; in Georgia, by 234%; in Armenia, by 234.9%; in the Turkmen SSR, by 100.9%; in the Uzbek SSR, by 141.9%; in the Tadzhik SSR, by 118.3%; in the Kazakh SSR, by 137%; and in the Kirgiz SSR, by 139%.

The result of these shifts in natural population increase is the characteristic age structure of the population of the USSR, which is distinguished from all the capitalist countries by its much younger composition.

While in the United States the age group from fifteen to sixty-five accounts for 65% of the population, in Great Britain for 68%, and in Germany for 69%, this same age group in the USSR constitutes approximately 57 to 58% of the total. This means that the Soviet Union has significantly more children than other countries, that our country is younger in population composition. This fact provides unbounded possibilities for further development of the country and considerable population reserves for widespread future employment in industrial production.

Even before the Revolution, when the petty bourgeoisie made attempts to revive the Malthusian theory of the limitations of population increase, Lenin bore down on them with the full force of his authority. He exposed them as ideological spokesmen for the callous and selfish narrow-minded couple who mutter fearfully: "May God help us sustain ourselves somehow. As for children—we can do better without them." Lenin argued that "a class-conscious worker is infinitely remote from such a point of view." [13] Even languishing under capitalist oppression, the workers consider their children to be promoters of the cause for which their fathers fight. In bringing to realization the socialist revolution, the working class is waging and winning a battle not only for its own immediate benefit, but also for the sake of future generations.

The more numerous the army of champions coming to relieve the present generation, the richer will be the life of our socialist motherland.

[13] Lenin, *Works*, Vol. XVI, p. 498.

Class Structure of the Population

The most profound shifts in population changes can be explained fundamentally by changes in production relations. The radical transformation of the class structure in Soviet society is characterized in the following data [Table 11]:

TABLE 11. CHANGES IN THE SOCIAL COMPOSITION OF THE SOVIET POPULATION

	PER CENT OF TOTAL			
	1913	1928	1934	1937
Workers and other wage earners	16.7	17.3	28.1	34.7
Collective farmers and members of artisans' and craftmen's cooperatives	none	2.9	45.9	55.5
Individual farmers (excluding kulaks) and artisans outside the cooperatives	65.1	72.9	22.5	5.6
Bourgeoisie (landowners, upper and lower urban middle classes, merchants, and kulaks)	15.9	4.5	0.1	—
(Of which, kulaks)	(12.3)	(3.7)	(0.09)	(—)
Other population (students, pensioners, army, etc.)	2.3	2.4	3.4	4.2
TOTAL	100.0	100.0	100.0	100.0

Irreconcilable class conflicts divided the population of landlord-capitalist Russia into violently hostile classes. The exploiting classes—landowners, kulaks, upper and lower urban middle classes, and merchants—accounted for 15.9%, or approximately one-sixth, of the total population. The other five-sixths languished under the yoke of unbearable exploitation. Individual farmers, both of poor and of moderate means, and also small-scale artisans and craftsmen, made up two-thirds of the population. In the vast expanse of peasant holdings, 65% of the households were poor, 20% were of moderate means. Against this tremendous mass of proletarian and semiproletarian households, only 15% of the total were kulak establishments. Of the peasant farms, 30% had no horses, 34% had no implements, 15% had no fields under cultivation. The prerevolutionary village suffered cruelly from unemployment, from hidden and stagnant forms of overpopulation. The number of persons deprived of the opportunity to work ran into millions. However, the

Tsarist Government preferred not to organize any labor exchanges and not to take a census of the unemployed; therefore, we have to gauge the actual extent of unemployment by circumstantial data.

Thus, the population census taken in St. Petersburg in 1911, in Moscow in 1912, and in Baku in 1913 revealed that in those cities the number of unemployed constituted 3.2 to 2.5% of the self-supporting population.

A special commission appointed by the Tsarist Government to study the welfare of the rural population was forced to admit that in European Russia there were 23 million "superfluous" peasant-workers.

It can be inferred from passport records that the number of the poor and of the lower strata of the rural middle class who took to the towns in search of employment came to about 10 million annually. The country was but a stepmother to these people. Driven by hunger and privation, great masses were forced to move wherever they could.

Looking for an opportunity to make a living, some people emigrated to other countries, particularly across the ocean to the United States. In spite of the struggle of the Tsarist Government to put an end to emigration, people driven by privation continued to leave the country in ever increasing numbers. While towards the end of the nineteenth century no more than 100,000 emigrated from Russia annually, in 1906–1907 their number rose to 200,000, and in 1913 to almost 300,000. According to the [U.S.] census of 1910 there were 1.7 million Russian immigrants in the United States.

Lenin pointed out that between 1891 and 1900 American capitalism drew 594,000 emigrants from backward Russia, and between 1900 and 1909, 1,410,000. Germany, then on a higher level of capitalist development than Russia, attracted 308,000 Russian workers in 1911 and 1912. Nine-tenths of them were untrained and unskilled laborers and farm workers.

The Tsarist Government strongly encouraged settlement of the borderlands of the country. In particular from 1896 to 1913 over 5 million people moved from the central districts to Siberia.

The settlement of Siberia bore unmistakable traits of police punishment of malcontents. Striving to protect the landowners from revolutionary demonstrations by the peasants, the Government turned colonization into a form of exile. According to the figures announced from the platform of the Duma, 108,000 Siberian settlers died of hunger in the period from 1906 to 1911. Hundreds of thousands of others found no accommodations at all.

All these data demonstrate conclusively how under the conditions of capitalist division of labor, of separation of industry from agriculture, and of class stratification the distribution of population inherent in capitalism came into being, at the price of human sacrifices and general impoverishment.

The socialist reorganization of the Soviet Union has changed radically the class structure of society.

Landowners and kulaks, manufacturers and bankers, merchants and speculators—in short, all the exploiting classes—have been liquidated in the USSR. Only the working class, the peasant class, and the intelligentsia have remained. The nature of these social groups has changed profoundly.

The working class has ceased to be a proletariat in the proper sense of the word.

There is no proletarian class in the USSR, no class of hired workers, for hired labor presupposes the existence of capital at the opposite end of the social structure. The working class still exists as a class, but its social characteristics are different: the working class of the USSR is in full possession of the government power, it is free from exploitation, it has at its disposal the means of production, which have been socialized. Such a working class is a new phenomenon in the history of humanity.

The peasantry in Tsarist Russia was oppressed by exploitation and in complete economic dependence on the capitalist, landowner, kulak, usurer, and speculator. The majority of peasants led a pitiable existence. They were semiproletarians, who, in spite of hard work, could not make both ends meet, and who were unable to keep themselves nourished from one harvest to the next. The position of the Soviet collective farmers is quite different. Having combined their efforts and socialized the means of production, the collective farmers have discovered a new life, free of all exploitation. Such a peasantry the world has never known.

Under capitalism the bulk of the intelligentsia was employed by the landowners and capitalists. In Tsarist Russia education was the privilege of the masters—the nobility and the bourgeoisie. The situation is different in the USSR. Between 80 and 90% of the Soviet intelligentsia are leaders who have emerged from among the ranks of factory workers, peasants, and office employees. The bulk of the new Soviet intelligentsia faithfully serves its people, the workers and peasants; it has tied its own fate completely to that of socialism. There has never been, there will never be, and there *could* never be such an intelligentsia in any capitalist country.

Economic and political conflicts among the workers, peasants, and intelligentsia in the USSR are diminishing and are being obliterated, and the old class distinctions are being destroyed and are disappearing. Thus, the basis for the moral-political unity of the Soviet people has been created, a unity which solidifies the whole country and constitutes a threat to the enemies of socialism.

The Soviet Union is a state of many nationalities. It unites approximately sixty national groups. According to the census of 1926, Russians accounted for 53% of the total population; Ukrainians, 21.2%; Belorussians, 3.2%; Kazakhs, 2.7%; Uzbeks, 2.7%; Tatars, 2%; Jews, 1.8%; Georgians, 1.24%; Turks, 1.16%; Armenians, 1.07%; Mordvians, 0.91%; [14] Germans, 0.84%; Chuvash, 0.76%; Tadzhiks, 0.67%; Poles, 0.53%; Turkmens, 0.52%; Kirgiz, 0.52%; Bashkirs, 0.49%.

Tens of millions of people—almost half the population—formerly suffering under a double form of oppression (class and national) have been truly liberated as a result of the socialist Revolution.

The national borderlands of Russia were regarded as colonies by the Russian military-feudal imperialism. Only after the establishment of Soviet power, only after the elimination of exploitation and national oppression, and only on the basis of mutual friendship and brotherly cooperation of peoples under the system of the Soviet government of workers and peasants, did the former national borderlands find a new life. The rapid growth of the socialist economy and the flourishing of culture, national in form but socialist in content, led to the rapid development of brotherly nations contained in the single Soviet family.

The preliminary data of the 1939 census are characteristic. While the population of the Soviet Union as a whole increased 15.9% in the preceding twelve-year period, during the same time the popula-

[14] [In the original Russian text this figure was given as 1.91%. However, this was clearly a typographical error, since the 1,340,415 Mordvians given by the 1926 census were 0.91% of the total population.]

tion of the Georgian SSR increased 32.3%; the population of the Armenian SSR, 45.4%; of the Uzbek SSR, 37.6%; of the Tadzhik SSR, 43.9%; of the Turkmen SSR, 25.6%; of the Azerbaidzhan SSR, 38.7%; and of the Kirgiz SSR, 45.7%. The population of the autonomous republics increased 23.5% during these years.

The rate of growth of the population in the Karelian ASSR [now Karelo-Finnish SSR] is ten times greater than in Finland. The population increase in the Komi ASSR is thirty times greater than in Estonia [now Estonian SSR].

This tremendous growth in rate of population increase in the national republics is due both to the natural increase of population and to immigration into these republics from other parts of the Soviet Union.

Density of Population and Its Geographical Distribution

Density of population is of tremendous importance in the distribution of productive forces, since the natural resources of a given territory and the products of the labor of its former inhabitants (as embodied in machines, raw materials, and fuels) can be set in motion and used for the common good only upon the application of human labor.

The material life of a society cannot be developed without the presence of a certain number of people.

It would be very erroneous to assert, however, as the bourgeois economists do, that the density of the population is the basic factor in any economic development and that it even determines the changes of economic forms. This point of view is upheld by the bourgeois economist Schmoller, who contends that a density of population of 0.02–0.05 [persons per sq. km.] corresponds to a hunting or fishing economy, and that a density of 0.7–1.8 corresponds to a nomadic pastoral economy, etc. According to this "remarkable" classification, the USSR (with a density of 8) should fall into the category of a transition economy from a nomadic to a settled economy; the United States would belong to the class of extensive, fallow agriculture; and India would be classified among the countries with intensive agriculture and well developed industry. Essentially the same mistake was made by some Soviet economic geographers who maintained that the density of population is an important characteristic of a given phase of economic development.

On that basis the USSR in economic development would be classified among countries lagging far behind not only capitalist Europe, but even China.

In his article "On Dialectical and Historical Materialism," Comrade Stalin points out that population increase either facilitates or deters the development of a society, but that it cannot determine the character of the social structure.

"If population increase were the determining factor in social development, then a greater density of population would necessarily evoke a correspondingly higher type of social system. Actually, however, this does not occur. The density of population in China is four times greater than in the United States. Nevertheless, the United States has reached a higher level of social development than China, for in China semifeudal conditions still prevail, while the United States reached the highest point of capitalist development long ago. The density of population in Belgium is nineteen times greater than in the United States and twenty-six times greater than in the USSR. Yet the United States has attained a higher level of social development than Belgium, while the USSR is a whole historical era in advance of Belgium, for a capitalist system still prevails in Belgium, while the USSR has passed the capitalist stage and has established a socialist system." [15]

In his *Capital*, Marx emphasized that the density of population under feudalism provided one of the initial impulses and was one of the material prerequisites for the transition from the feudal to the capitalist order, but that the development of capitalism itself altered substantially the former distribution of population.

Socialism has inherited from the capitalist system a definite allocation of population, but in turn changes this allocation most decisively.

The distribution of population under socialism is linked with the realization of socialist principles of the distribution of productive forces.

As long as, under capitalism, the areal distribution of productive forces in general and of population in particular is determined in the final analysis by the conditions of the most profitable exploitation of workers, socialism cannot pursue at all the policy of repro-

[15] Stalin, *Questions of Leninism*, pp. 549–550.

ducing the former capitalist geographic division of labor. Eventually, the attainment of planned reallocation of the population of a socialist country should result in a considerably more uniform areal distribution of people over the territory of the country.

Thus far, the population of the USSR is still distributed very unevenly over the various regions. This is a result of the capitalist past. At the beginning of 1939 there were in our country on the average 8 persons per sq. km. In the tundra and taiga belt and in the southern sand deserts of Kazakhstan and the Central Asiatic republics the density of population is less than 1 per sq. km. In the rest of the USSR the average population density is somewhat higher than in the United States.

The census of 1939 shows that two-thirds of the territory of the USSR provided living space for 6% of the population, while 48% of the people were concentrated on 6% of the territory.

In order to understand the great changes in the distribution of population which have occurred in the USSR, it is necessary to know what sort of conditions the Soviet Government inherited in this field.

The abolition of serfdom led to an exodus of population from the agricultural center.

"From the central agricultural belt the population moved into the industrial districts, into the capital cities, into the southern and eastern borderlands of European Russia, settling lands uninhabited till then." [16]

The development of capitalism in Russia resulted in a rapid transfer of population.

The most densely populated provinces in prerevolutionary Russia were the guberniyas where the capital cities were located, the guberniyas of the Industrial Center, and the guberniyas of the Ukraine [Fig. 21]. Thus [by the official estimate of January 1, 1913] Moscow Guberniya had 113.8 persons per square verst; St. Petersburg Guberniya, 76.2; Vladimir Guberniya, 45.8; Nizhny Novgorod Guberniya, 46.0; Yaroslavl Guberniya, 40.1; Tver Guberniya, 39.9; and Smolensk Guberniya, 41.4.[17] In the Agricultural Center and in the Southwest the following guberniyas had the greatest density of population: Podolsk, 106.3 persons per square verst; Kiev, 105.8; Poltava, 85.5; Kursk, 77.5; Ryazan,

[16] Lenin, *Works*, Vol. XI, p. 358.

[17] [Densities of population in 1913 are shown in Fig. 21 and in Appendix *Table A10, p. 520; names and boundaries of the political divisions on that date are shown in Fig. 22 at the back of the book.]

71.4; Kharkov, 70.9; Tula, 68.1; Chernigov, 67.9; Orel, 65.6; and Voronezh, 61.1. In the South the densest population was in the guberniyas of Yekaterinoslav, 58.7; Kherson, 57.9; and Tavrida, 36.9.

In the Trans-Caucasus most thickly populated were the Rion River valley and the central valleys of the Kura River (in Kutais Guberniya there were 55.6 persons per square verst).

The eastern borderlands were thinly populated. While in European Russia the density of population was 22.1 per square verst, in Siberia, it was 0.5, and in Central Asia 2.5 [*cf.* Table A10, p. 520]. In 1913, in Siberia, only Tomsk Guberniya had 4.5 persons per square verst, while in Tobolsk and Irkutsk guberniyas and Trans-Baikal Oblast the density was considerably lower—1.1 to 1.6 per square verst. The Amur, Maritime, Yakut, and Kamchatka oblasts were even more thinly populated. There the density of population was less than 1 inhabitant per square verst.

In Central Asia population was densest in the valley of the Zeravshan River and in Fergana Oblast—about 20 persons per square verst. In the other oblasts the density of population did not exceed 4. In European Russia the most thinly populated were the regions of the Far North.

The distribution of population which the Soviet Government inherited from capitalism had a number of traits peculiar to it which stemmed directly from the class relationships of capitalism.

Being mortally afraid of the growing revolutionary temper of the masses, the Tsarist Government resorted to a fine stroke of policy and in 1906 passed the so-called Stolypin law, designed to make the kulak class a stronghold of Tsarism in the country. This scheme was carried out by forcing the peasants to leave their communes and to settle down as individual farmers. Thus the former system of communal land tenure was destroyed. A single landholding was given to the peasants who left their communes. From 1906 to 1915 over 2 million separate holdings were set up. The Government required the allotment of the best land to the kulak farmers. This process went on, depriving millions of poor peasants of their land. Depending largely on hired help, many farmsteads and holdings took on the character of estates of a sort. Plundering the communal lands, the kulaks bought the meager allotments of the poor on a great scale and for low prices.

Stolypin's reform sharply accentuated the stratification of the peasant class, forced vast numbers of indigent farmers off the land, and made

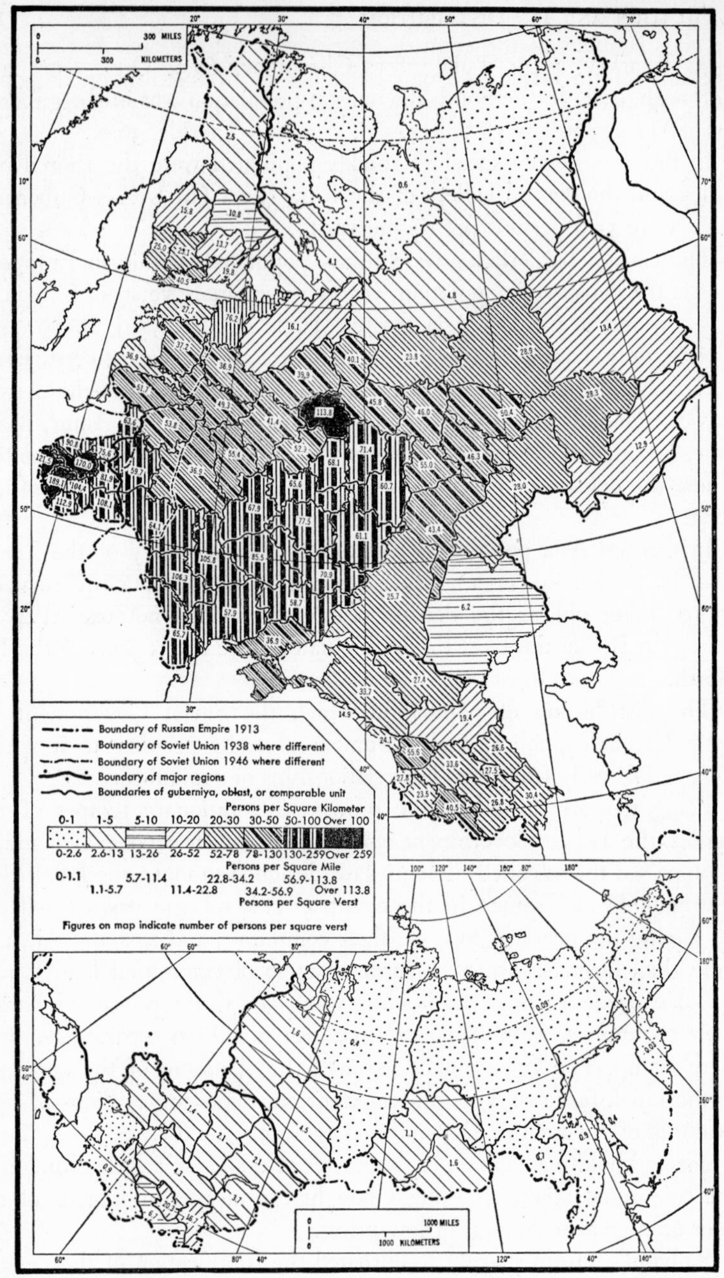

* Fig. 21. Density of Population of the Russian Empire by Administrative Areas, January 1, 1913. (Sources same as *Table A10, pp. 520–522)

the class conflicts in the country more acute than before. At the same time this reform introduced new elements in the distribution of population. In the western guberniyas, especially in Belorussia, villages decreased in size. The population of each inhabited locality was small, but the distance between such localities was also relatively small.

Quite different was the picture in a number of steppe regions, particularly in the areas of Cossack settlements, in the Oblast of the Don [Cossack] Army on the Kuban [6 in Fig. 22 at the back of the book]. There, as a rule, every stanitsa consisted of several thousand farmsteads, but the distance between the settlements was considerably greater. This peculiarity was due to the fact that the Tsarist Government, striving in every way possible to turn the Cossacks into a bulwark against revolution and into a prop for colonial exploitation of the borderlands, settled them in compact masses, in whole army units.

TABLE 12. DENSITY OF POPULATION IN THE UNION REPUBLICS [Cf. Fig. 23]

UNION REPUBLIC	AREA (in 1000 Sq. Km.)	POPULATION 1926 Census (in 1000)	POPULATION 1939 Census (in 1000)	DENSITY PER SQ. KM. 1926 Census	DENSITY PER SQ. KM. 1939 Census
RSFSR	16,510.5	93,458.0	109,278.6	5.66	6.62
Ukrainian SSR [a]	445.3	29,042.9	30,960.2	65.22	69.53
Belorussian SSR [a]	126.8	4,983.2	5,568.0	39.30	43.91
Azerbaidzhan SSR	86.0	2,313.7	3,209.7	26.91	37.32
Georgian SSR	69.6	2,677.2	3,542.3	38.47	50.90
Armenian SSR	30.0	881.4	1,281.6	29.38	42.72
Turkmen SSR	443.6	998.2	1,254.0	2.25	2.83
Uzbek SSR	378.3	4,565.4	6,282.5	12.07	16.61
Tadzhik SSR	143.9	1,032.2	1,485.1	7.17	10.32
Kazakh SSR	2,744.5	6,074.0	6,145.9	2.21	2.24
Kirgiz SSR	196.7	1,001.7	1,459.3	5.09	7.42
USSR	21,175.2	147,027.9	170,467.2	6.94	8.05

[a] Data for the Ukrainian SSR and the Belorussian SSR are given for the territory covered by the census of 1939. The population of the liberated areas of the Western Ukraine (88,000 sq. km.) is 8 million and the density is over 90 per sq. km. The population of Western Belorussia (108,000 sq. km.) is 4,800,000, and the density is 44.4 sq. km.

The census of 1939 already reflects considerable shifts in the distribution of population in the USSR, which are evident particularly in the changes in density of population among the Union republics.

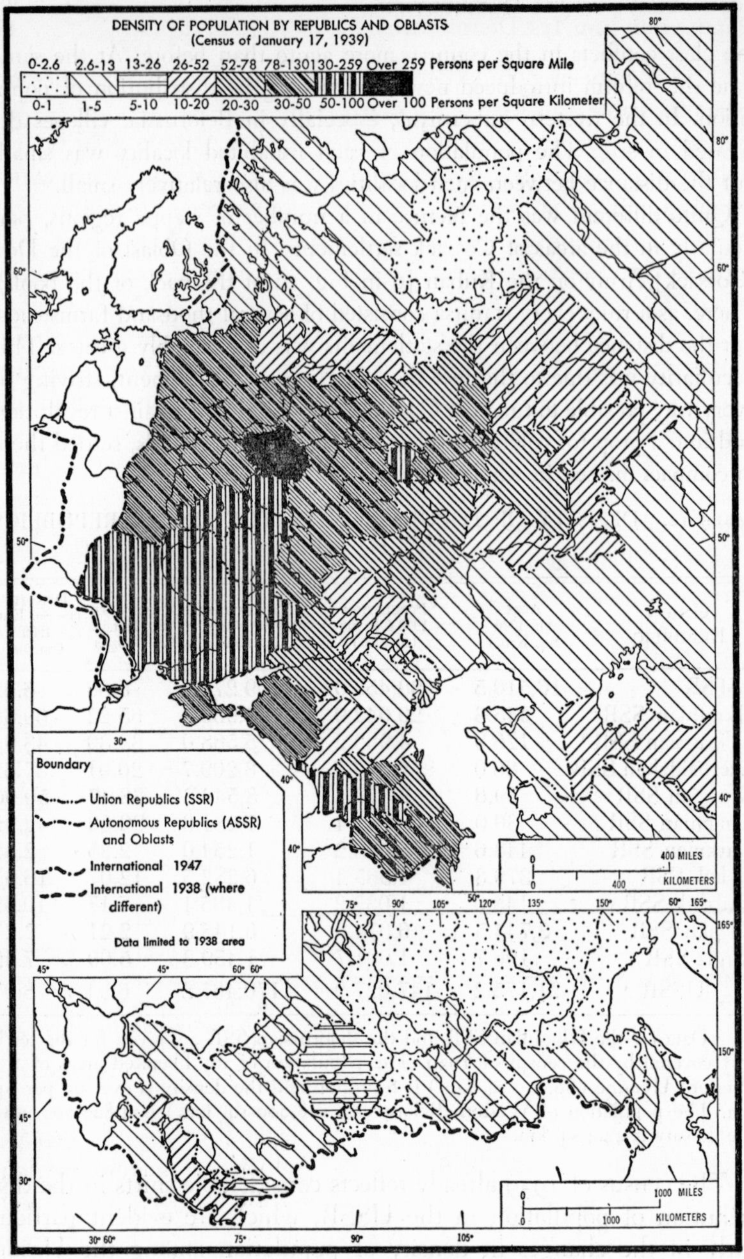

FIG. 23. Density of Population by Administrative Areas, 1939

The density of population of the separate Union republics appears in Table 12.

Stressing the tremendous variation in population density, the above table shows also the very characteristic rapidity with which changes in distribution take place under socialist construction.

The density of population broken down according to the individual oblasts appears in Fig. 23. The data are taken from the census of 1939.

At present Moscow Oblast has the highest density of population —180.5 per sq. km. [Appendix Table A2, p. 507]. Next come the Ukrainian SSR (69.5), the central chernozem oblasts, and the Georgian SSR.

Localities which before the Revolution were among the most thinly populated now have a markedly higher density of population. This applies to Novosibirsk Oblast, the Ural regions, Altay Kray, Vologda Oblast, and a number of others [Appendix Tables A2, A10, A11 and Figs. 21 and 23].

The increase in the density of population in various regions of the USSR can be accounted for by the development of a socialist national economy and, especially, by the rapid growth in these regions of the number of workers and other employees in socialist industry.

As a result of the industrial developments in the East, during the years of the Second Five-Year Plan the number of factory and other workers in the Urals, Siberia, and Kazakhstan increased by 36% to 48%, and in the republics of Central Asia by 59.5%. At the same time, the number of factory and other workers in the old industrial regions (the Central, Northern, and Northwestern regions of the RSFSR as well as the Ukraine) increased by 22.2%.

Urban and Rural Division of Population

Under capitalism, the distribution of population, even as the distribution of production, takes place fundamentally regardless of the people's will.

As pointed out by Marx, the capitalist method of production, by its very nature, constantly decreases the agricultural population in relation to the nonagricultural. The available data show that this process has continued uninterrupted up to the present time. Table 13 demonstrates the point.

TABLE 13. PERCENTAGE OF URBAN POPULATION IN VARIOUS CAPITALIST COUNTRIES [1800–1930]

COUNTRY	1800	1850	1890	1920	1930
England and Wales	21.3	39.5	72.1	78.0	80.0
Germany	—	—	47.0	62.9	67.0
France	9.5	14.4	37.4	46.7	49.0
United States	3.8	12.0	37.7	51.4	56.0
Japan	—	—	—	18.0	23.9
Ireland	7.8	10.1	26.4	33.5	—
Austria	4.4	5.8	32.5	60.2	—
Sweden	3.9	4.7	18.0	30.5	33.0
Denmark	10.9	9.6	32.4	40.6	44.0
Norway	3.3	5.3	22.2	29.6	28.7

As in other countries, the development of capitalism in Russia resulted in a much more rapid growth of urban population than rural. The towns grew, in the main, by continually absorbing emigrants from the country. The concentration of population in large cities went on with particular speed. In his book *Development of Capitalism in Russia*, Lenin gives figures showing that the urban population grew twice as rapidly as the rural. From 1863 to 1897 the rural population increased 48.7%; the urban, 97%.

Lenin notes in this connection that "the tremendous growth of large industrial centers and the formation of a whole series of new centers is one of the most characteristic symptoms of the reform period after 1861." [18]

Particularly rapid was the increase of urban population in the capital and government cities of the Industrial Center. The urban population of the southern guberniyas also grew rapidly. In the cities of the Central-Agricultural, Middle-Volga, and the Ukrainian guberniyas east of the Dnepr, as well as in the Urals, Siberia, the Caucasus, Kazakhstan, and Central Asia, the population increased at a slower rate. This lack of uniformity in the distribution of urban population was due to the fundamental nature of the distribution of capitalist industry and to the deliberate obstruction of the industrial development of the national borderlands.

[18] Lenin, *Works*, Vol. III, p. 437.

A general picture of changes in the urban population of capitalist Russia can be obtained from the following table [Table 14].

TABLE 14. GROWTH OF POPULATION IN TSARIST RUSSIA (WITHIN THE BORDERS OF THE SOVIET UNION AT THE BEGINNING OF 1939) [a]

	Total (in millions)	Urban (in millions)	Rural (in millions)	Percentage Urban
1860	61.7	7.0	54.7	11.3
1870	65.2	8.0	57.2	12.3
1880	78.6	10.2	68.4	12.9
1900	109.6	14.1	95.5	12.8
1910	130.4	18.6	111.8	14.3
1914	139.0	20.4	119.5	14.6

[a] The urban population and its percentage of the total are given in accordance with the Tsarist town census, which understated the actual number of the urban population. V. I. Lenin, analyzing capitalist development in Russia, noted that one-third of all the factory proletariat (152,600 out of 451,000) worked in enterprises located not in towns but in villages with factories and home industries. This is due to the fact that the survivals of feudalism limited the freedom of movement of the impoverished peasant and hampered his separation from the commune.

The total population of Russia more than doubled during the period from 1860 to 1914. During this same period of capitalist development, the urban population was almost tripled. (The actual increase was even somewhat higher, since the Tsarist statisticians understated the real size of the urban population.)

The irreconcilable antagonism between town and country grows continuously under capitalism. The capitalist town drains the country of its best forces, plunders it, and hinders its cultural development. The industrial growth of the town results in the sharp expansion of a goods economy and, consequently, increases the number of functions performed by the town in its capacity as a commodity and transport center. Because of their industrial development, the towns become points of concentration for the principal forces of the proletariat and bourgeoisie, thus acquiring ever increasing political importance. Class conflicts become especially acute in the towns. These elements predetermine the importance of the town as a leading center of proletarian revolution.

The victory of the socialist regime in our country introduced decisive changes both in the distribution of population and in the interrelations between town and country.

During the years of the Civil War the urban population somewhat decreased, particularly in the large industrial centers. This was due, on the one hand, to the fact that approximately 2 million persons who belonged to the former ruling classes fled abroad. On the other hand, a considerable part of the working class was drawn off to the Civil War front. Lastly, in view of the limited opportunities for industrial development, and also the deficiencies in food supply, part of the urban population temporarily moved to the country. According to available data, in 1920 the urban population was 16 million as against 20 million in 1917. The reconstruction of the national economy resulted in a rapid growth of towns, so that by 1926 the urban population considerably exceeded the prewar level (26.3 million, or 17.9% of the total population).

In the years preceding the war, the average annual increase of urban population was about 0.5 million. During the last twelve years that rate has been over 2 million.

The industrialization of the country and the brilliant realization of the two Stalin Five-Year Plans has resulted in an increase of urban population in the USSR during recent years. According to the census of 1939, the urban population of the USSR more than doubled during the twelve-year period, accounting for 55.9 million persons, or 32.8% of the total population at the beginning of 1939 [Appendix Table A1, pp. 504–505].

It took the United States thirty years, Germany forty years, and England seventy years to double their urban population during the period of capitalist development. These figures show clearly that Soviet towns are growing considerably faster than those of the capitalist countries.

The relative increase of urban population by regions of the USSR is reflected in Fig. 24.

The basic factor in the development of Soviet towns is, first of all, the socialist industrialization of the country. The building of new towns and new industrial regions in the Soviet Union proceeds at an unprecedentedly rapid pace. Simultaneously with this process, the old industrial centers also continue to grow.

The industrialization of agriculture, the creation of large sovkhozes [state farms] equipped with the most modern technical devices, the formation of MTS's [machine tractor stations] as economic and political centers of kolkhoz [collective farm] production

Fig. 24. Percentage which Urban Population Constituted of Total Population by Administrative Areas, 1926 and 1939

—all lead to the establishment on these bases of new settlements and of new centers of economic, administrative, and cultural importance.

Where does the urban population come from? During the period from 1926 to 1939, 18.5 million persons moved into the towns from the country. The natural increase of the urban population in those years constituted about 5.3 million. Finally 5.8 million persons were added to the urban population by the conversion of villages into urban communities.

During the period covered by the two Five-Year Plans the number of towns with 50,000 inhabitants or over increased almost 4.5 times. The number of towns with a population of 100,000 or over increased almost 6 times. Ten new towns with a population of more than 100,000, and twenty new towns with a population of more than 50,000 first appeared on the map during the period of the last two Five-Year Plans [cf. Appendix Table A12, p. 527].

Table 15 shows graphically the changes in the rate of urban development in our country during recent years.

TABLE 15. [RATE OF GROWTH OF CITIES IN THE USSR, 1897–1910 AND 1926–1939]

Town	Population (in 1000) 1897	Population (in 1000) 1910	12-Year Increase (in 1000)	Population (in 1000) 1926	Population (in 1000) 1939	12-Year Increase (in 1000)
Moscow	1038.6	1481.2	442.6	2029.4	4137.0	2107.6
Leningrad	1264.9	1861.1	596.2	1690.1	3191.3	1501.2
Kiev	247.7	527.3	279.6	513.6	846.3	332.7
Kharkov	174.0	244.6	70.6	417.3	833.4	416.1
Minsk	90.9	105.5	14.6	131.8	238.8	107.0
Baku	111.9	127.6	15.7	453.3	809.3	356.0
Tbilisi [Tiflis]	159.6	303.2	143.6	294.0	519.2	225.2
Yerevan	29.0	29.0	—	64.6	200.0	135.4
Gorky	90.0	101.5	11.2	222.4	644.1	421.7
Dnepropetrovsk	112.8	211.9	99.1	236.7	500.7	264.0
Stalino	32.0	48.4	16.4	174.2	462.4	288.2
Stalingrad	55.2	100.6	45.4	151.5	445.5	294.0
Sverdlovsk	43.2	70.0	26.8	140.3	425.5	285.2
Novosibirsk	8.4	55.7	47.3	120.1	405.6	285.5
Zaporozhye	16.4	38.2	21.8	55.7	289.2	233.5
Alma-Ata	22.9	36.3	13.4	45.4	230.5	185.1
Frunze	6.6	13.8	7.2	36.6	92.7	56.1

In the Urals alone there are now 3.5 million urban residents. Yet before the Revolution the total urban population there comprised only 681,000 persons. Before the October Revolution there were only five towns in Novosibirsk Oblast. Now there are twenty towns, and the total urban population of that area has increased more than 9 times during the period from 1914 to 1939. A number of entirely new towns have been created there: Stalinsk, Prokopyevsk, Anzhero-Sudzhensk, Leninsk Kuznetsky, Kemerovo [Inset on Fig. 26]. (The growth of towns in the USSR from 1926 to 1939 [and their relative size] are shown in Figs. 25 and 26.)

Socialist Moscow has changed beyond recognition. The Red capital of the Land of the Soviets is one of the most beautiful cities in the world. Before the Revolution Moscow was a textile city. It was not very attractive: it was a unique large village with hundreds of churches, flour stores, dead-end streets, crooked lanes, and torn pavements. Socialist Moscow—the capital of the great Soviet power—is a focus of well developed industry, such as machine building, power, chemicals, light industry, and food. Soviet Moscow is the largest transport center of the country. It is a center in which cadres of workers are trained for the whole USSR. And it is the greatest center of culture, science, and art. The whole country is justly proud of the Moscow subway, the canal connecting Moscow with the Volga, the wonderful new bridges, parks, theaters, and scientific and educational institutions.

The appearance of other industrial centers of the Soviet Union is being changed just as decisively.

"The appearance of our big cities and industrial centers has changed. An inevitable feature of the large bourgeois cities is their slums, the so-called workers' sections on the outskirts of town, which consist of a heap of dark, damp, in most cases cellarlike, dilapidated dwellings, where the poor find shelter, crawling in filth and cursing their fate. The Revolution in the USSR has brought about the disappearance of these slums from our country. They have been replaced by good, light, newly built workers' sections, which in many instances are more attractive than the center of the town."[19]

During the years of the [first] two Stalin Five-Year Plans over 17 billion rubles was invested in urban residential construction,

[19] Stalin, *Questions of Leninism*, p. 457.

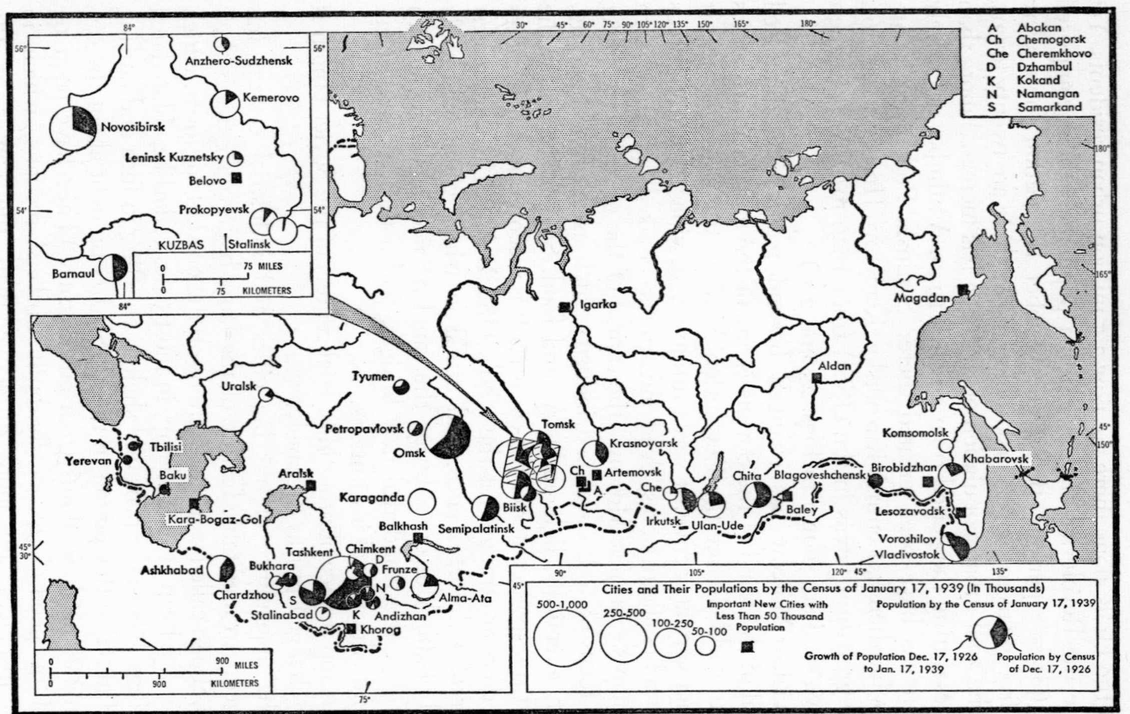

FIG. 26. Population and Growth of Cities in the Asiatic Part of the Soviet Union, 1926–1939

and about 8.5 billion rubles was spent on urban public welfare and on the improvement of the municipal economy.

The triumph of the kolkhoz system in the country and the cultural revolution which has taken place in the village have changed the appearance of the Soviet rural community as well. The natural increase in the rural population was about 18.1 million in the twelve-year period. The migration into the towns of a considerable portion of the rural population and the reorganization of many rural settlements into towns have reduced the farm population. As a result, the total rural population of the USSR, which in 1926 was 120.7 million, dropped to 114.6 million in 1939, a decrease of 5.1%.

The capitalist town subjugated the village and artificially retarded its cultural development. For this reason, in the eyes of the peasants the town was always the focus of their exploitation.

After the victory of the socialist revolution the interrelations between town and country changed radically. The Soviet town supplies the kolkhoz village with means of production, with the best machinery. The Soviet town insures the training of skilled workers for the village. In short, the town introduces genuine culture to the rural community.

The Soviet village today has a tremendous army of rural intelligentsia who have been educated in the city. In 1939, there were in the country 715,300 public-school teachers, about 132,000 physicians and other medical personnel, 107,000 agronomists, about 28,000 surveyors, engineers, and topographers, 92,000 agrotechnicians and zootechnicians, 17,000 veterinarians, etc.

The bonds of economic and cultural fellowship between town and country are growing stronger from day to day. Before our very eyes agricultural labor is becoming a branch of industrial labor. Hundreds of thousands of people are now working on the farms in the capacity of tractor drivers, combine operators, chauffeurs, maintenance men—in short, people who are masters of their machines. Machine tractor stations, repair shops, electric power stations, and a number of other industrial enterprises organized in the kolkhozes testify to the fact that the Soviet village now has its own industry. The imbecility of rural life, of which Marx wrote in his time, has been eliminated once for all.

The Soviet village is fulfilling with enthusiasm the request of Comrade Stalin to release 1.5 million young collective farmers annually for work in our growing industries. This measure helps strengthen the kolkhoz system. In spite of some reduction in the rural population, the total volume of agricultural production has increased sharply. This is graphic evidence that the Soviet village releases some of its labor force to the town without any detriment to its economic development.

Changes in the Distribution of Population in the USSR

The new distribution of population and the development and growth of towns in the USSR are based principally on socialist industrialization of the Soviet Union and on the planned allocation of productive forces under socialism. The general redistribution of the population of the country is related directly to the growth of towns, to the new regional allocation of industry, and to the systematic settlement of sparsely populated regions.

The population is growing at a particularly rapid rate in the eastern regions—the Urals, Siberia, and the Far East. From the end of 1926 to the beginning of 1939 the population of Sverdlovsk Oblast increased 53%; Novosibirsk Oblast, 53%; Irkutsk Oblast, 49%; Chita Oblast, 73%; the Buryat-Mongol ASSR, 39%; Khabarovsk Kray, 136%; and the Maritime Kray, 42%. Altogether, during the past twelve years the population of the Urals, Siberia, and the Far East has increased by 5.9 million (33%). Over 3 million people have moved there from other regions of the country.

During the same years the population of the Uzbek, Tadzhik, Turkmen, and Kirgiz Soviet Socialist Republics has increased by 2.9 million (38%). Approximately 1.7 million people have moved into these republics from other regions of the USSR.

The population of other industrial centers of the country also has grown significantly. Thus, the population of Moscow Oblast has increased 74%; Leningrad Oblast, 44%; Gorky Oblast, 28%; Stalino Oblast (Ukrainian SSR), 91%; Voroshilovgrad Oblast, 37%; and Karaganda Oblast (Kazakh SSR), 25%.

During the same years an intensive industrialization has been carried out in the European North. As a result, the population of Archangel Oblast has increased 25%, and that of Murmansk Oblast has increased nine times.

Along with this population increase in the regions where industry was developing rapidly, there are a number of oblasts in which the population decreased somewhat during the past twelve years, because a part of the inhabitants moved to the industrial centers and especially to the eastern sections of the country. Thus, in comparison with 1926, the 1939 population of Kalinin Oblast dropped 8%; Kursk Oblast, 10%; Ryazan Oblast, 9%; Penza Oblast, 18%; Smolensk Oblast, 11%; Poltava Oblast (Ukrainian SSR), 15%; Vinnitsa Oblast, 7%; Pavlodar Oblast (Kazakh SSR), 32%; and Kustanay Oblast, 23%.[20]

Data on exchanges of population among various republics of the USSR indicate that during the past twelve years there has been a significant transfer of part of the population of the Ukrainian SSR and the Belorussian SSR to the industrial centers (especially those newly developed) of the RSFSR. Skilled workers of the Ukrainian plants and mines have assisted in developing new enterprises and new regions, and have been especially helpful in creating the second coal and metallurgical base in the eastern USSR.

The changes which have taken place during recent years are only the beginning of the new distribution of population which is associated with the victory of socialism. The plans for socialist construction provide for the necessity of a further transfer of part of the rural population into the towns, and of drawing additional labor force not only into industry, but also into agriculture in the eastern regions.

The total number of workers and other employees, which in 1926–1927 was 10.9 million, had risen almost to 28 million in 1938, and continues without interruption to increase from year to year. This very growth of the working class and of our Soviet intelligentsia constitutes the basic factor that determines the movement of population, the formation of new towns, and the flourishing of the socialist economy and culture in all regions of our country.

Settlement of Sparsely Populated Regions

The most important factor in the further redistribution of population should be the systematic resettlement of peasants from the areas where land is scarce, to those where land is abundant but man power is not sufficient. To the latter category belong the Trans-Volga area, Omsk, Chelyabinsk, Novosibirsk, and Chkalov oblasts, Altay Kray, the Far East, and Kazakhstan.

In the decree of the Central Committee of the Communist Party

[20] [Fig. 83 at the back of the book shows location and boundaries of these political units as of 1939.]

of the Soviet Union and the Sovnarkom [Council of People's Commissars] of May 26, 1939, entitled "On Measures for Safeguarding Against the Squandering of Kolkhoz Public Lands," great attention is devoted to the systematic resettlement of collective farmers in the sparsely populated regions. The grandiose plans for the socialist development of productive forces in the East can be realized only if there is a systematic influx of population into these territories. The natural resources of this part of the Soviet Union are indeed incalculable. The infinite wealth contained in the depths of the earth, in the seas, and in the rivers of the Soviet East has remained untouched through the centuries. Only the Soviet regime could set into motion these latent productive forces.

The fabulous resources of the Soviet Far East are difficult to enumerate. Nature provides absolutely everything needed for an all-around complex development of all branches of the economy. The fuel industry, metallurgy, machine building, the production of cement and of all types of construction materials, lumber enterprises, and every kind of light industry and food industry—all can be developed in the Far East on the basis of local raw materials. There is an abundance of fish in the seas and rivers of the Far East, and there are sea animals—the hair seal, Steller's sea lion, northern fur seal, whale, sea otter, walrus, beluga sturgeon, etc.

The All-Union Agricultural Exposition demonstrated the remarkable achievements of the agricultural leaders of the Far East, who have obtained magnificent harvests of all crops. The rich soil of the Far East yields everything—wheat, oats, barley, millet, buckwheat, winter rye, rice, magnificent fruits and vegetables. Only man power is needed to exploit its amazing resources. It is no wonder that the attention of the whole country is riveted on this remarkable territory. The great economic future of this part of the USSR can be realized only if a systematic influx of Soviet people to the Far East can be organized.

The Resettlement Administration organized by the SNK (Sovnarkom) of the USSR now has special offices in the Union republics, the oblasts, and the krays. It is charged with effecting a systematic resettlement of collective farmers in the sparsely populated regions.

A considerable part of the labor force is released for employment in industry or settlement in sparsely populated regions, because of the fact that in the areas where land is scarce the possibilities of making standard homestead allotments to collective farmers are very limited. Another factor is the present bolshevist campaign in all the kolkhozes against loafers who evade participation in the public work, a campaign which also serves to eliminate the artificial labor shortage on the collective farms. These economic conditions make it fully possible to transfer substantial sections of population to the East in accordance with the interests of our socialist motherland.

Change from a Nomadic to a Sedentary Mode of Life

At the same time that it is changing the historical distribution of population, the Soviet Government is also solving with tremendous success the very complicated problem of converting large masses of nomads to a sedentary mode of life. Before the Revolution there were over 2 million nomadic households in the steppes and deserts, in the mountainous regions, and in the tundra. If an average household consisted of 4 to 5 persons, the total number of people who lived under a primitive nomadic economy can be estimated at about 10 million. Nomadic economy was most widespread in Kazakhstan, Central Asia, Azerbaidzhan, the Kalmyk Steppes, Buryat-Mongolia, and among the peoples of the Far North.

The bourgeois-landowning Government of Tsarist Russia expropriated all the best land from the natives. Regarding the lands of Kazakhstan and Central Asia as a reserve for colonization, the Tsarist Government tried in every way possible to drive the nomads into the semideserts and mountains. They were thus deprived of the opportunity to change over to a sedentary life and were doomed economically to a beggardly standard of living and to cultural backwardness. The Tsarist Government deprived the nomadic peoples of good winter grounds, and as a result great numbers of livestock perished from lack of fodder and from emaciation. The suffering was greatest among the indigent masses of nomads, for only the kulaks and rich landowners, taking advantage of the economic ruin of the poor, found the extensive nomadic economy profitable.

In order to overcome the economic and cultural backwardness of the formerly nomadic and seminomadic peoples, the Soviet Government is helping them to settle down on the land. Large-scale socialist industry and powerful, mechanized socialist agriculture are growing day by day in the regions of Kazakhstan, Central Asia, the

Trans-Caucasus, and the Far North. The nomads of yesterday are settling down on the liberated soil, organizing kolkhozes, and acquiring new technical skills. While overcoming the survivals of the patriarchal way of life, the socialist regime is also destroying the whole semifeudal, semicapitalist exploitation of man by man which in both apparent and hidden forms prevailed in these regions. Thus, the former nomads are taking up a new way of life, and in the harmonious family of Soviet peoples are improving their material and cultural well-being.

V The Distribution of Industry in the USSR [1]

Industry in Tsarist Russia

THE INDUSTRY of prerevolutionary Russia, in comparison with that of the largest capitalist countries, was extremely retarded. In 1913 the total Russian industrial output was valued at 11 billion rubles, which represented only 2.6% of world production. Russian output before the Revolution was one-fourteenth that of the United States and one-sixth that of Germany. England produced 4.5 times as much, and France 2.5 times as much.

The most important industries in Russia at that time were light industry and the food industry. These together accounted for approximately 60% of the total output of industry in 1913. All branches of heavy industry combined accounted for slightly over 40% of industrial production. The food industry occupied first place in volume of output, accounting for 26.6% of total industrial production; the textile industry was second, with 21.6% (cotton fabrics, 18.3%). Among the other industries, ferrous metallurgy represented 4.7%; the oil industry, 1.8%; coal, 2.9%; and machine construction, 5.8%.

Many of the most important branches of industry either were completely nonexistent or were in the earliest stages of development. It was through imports that Russia satisfied all her needs in aluminum and rubber, 97.4% of her lead, 92.3% of her zinc, 37% of her chemical fertilizers, 40% of her paper, and almost all her requirements in all basic types of equipment for the metallurgical, electrical, fuel, and chemical industries.

It was not until after the Great October Socialist Revolution, and

[1] [Figs. 27 and 28 portray industrial production by cities for both the European and the Asiatic USSR for 1913 and for about 1935.]

in particular during the Stalin Five-Year Plans, that the true blossoming of the industry of our country took place. The age-old backwardness and the dependence on the advanced capitalist countries were eliminated. By the end of the Second Five-Year Plan, the USSR had become the largest industrial power in the world, having surpassed the foremost capitalist countries on a technical level and in the rates at which production was increasing.

Growth of Industry in the USSR

In 1937 Soviet industry produced goods worth 95.5 billion rubles, which was 13.7% of world industrial output. At that time, Germany accounted for only 11.6% of world output; England, 9.3%;

TABLE 16. POSITION OF THE USSR IN INDUSTRIAL OUTPUT IN THE WORLD [AND IN EUROPE IN 1913 AND 1937]

Branches	1913		1937	
	World	Europe	World	Europe
Gross output of all industry	5	4	2	1
Electric power	15	7	3	2
Coal	6	5	4	3
Oil	2	1	2	1
Peat	1	1	1	1
Iron ore	5	4	2	1
Manganese ore	1	1	1	1
Pig iron, steel, rolled products	5	4	3	2
Copper	7	3	6	1
Aluminum	—	—	3	2
Gold	4	1	2	1
Superphosphate	16	13	3	1
Sulphuric acid	8	6	4	2
General machine construction	4	3	2	1
Agricultural machine construction	5	3	1	1
Combines	—	—	1	1
Tractors	—	—	2	1
Automobiles	—	—	4	3
Trucks	—	—	2	1
Locomotives	No data	No data	1	1
Freight cars	No data	No data	2	1
Cement	6	5	4	3
Beet sugar	2	2	1	1
Shoes	No data	No data	2	1
Fish catch (Maritime)	2	1	2	1

and France, 5.7%. Only the United States, with 41.9% of world industrial output, surpassed the Soviet Union.

The clearest index of Soviet industrial development is the growth of those branches of industry producing goods essential to other production. Under the Soviet regime the output of such industries increased from 5.4 billion rubles in 1913 to 62.1 billion rubles in 1937, or almost 12 times. Steel smelting and coal mining more than quadrupled, oil production increased 3.3 times, and the output of electric power 18 times. Particularly significant was the production of machinery, which increased 28 times.

As a result of this industrial growth, the USSR took first place in the world in many branches of industry which were tremendously important in the technical reconstruction of the national economy and in strengthening the country's defensive capabilities [Table 16].

By the end of the Second Five-Year Plan, Soviet industry emerged in first place in world production of agricultural machines, combines, locomotives, synthetic rubber, and beet sugar, in the mining of manganese ore, and in the extraction of peat. It was second to the United States in total industrial output, in the extraction of oil and iron ore, in the volume of its total machine construction, in the smelting of electric steel, and in the production of trucks, freight cars, tractors, and shoes. It was second to Japan in its fish catch, and second to the Union of South Africa in gold mining. In the output of electric power, coke, pig iron, steel, and rolled products, and in the smelting of aluminum, the USSR occupied third place after the United States and Germany; in the output of superphosphate, it occupied third place after the United States and Japan. In coal output the USSR is still [1939] surpassed by the United States, England, and Germany; in the production of automobiles by the United States, England, Germany, and France; in sulphuric acid output, by the United States, Japan, and Germany; in cement output, by the United States, Germany, England, and Japan; and in copper smelting, by the United States, Chile, Canada, Northern Rhodesia, and the Belgian Congo.

Soviet industry has successfully mastered the production of the most complicated types of products and equipment, which in the past were imported from abroad. By the end of the Second Five-Year Plan, the USSR still imported a substantial part of its tin, lead, natural rubber, tea, jute, and Manila twine. But domestic production provided for all other types of products and equipment necessary to the national economy and the national defense.

Machine construction is especially important in the technical reconstruction of the national economy, the strengthening of the country's defensive capacity, and its technical and economic self-sufficiency. The value of the country's output in machine construction and metal working in 1937 was 27.5 billion rubles. This was 29% of the entire Soviet industrial output, and placed machine construction first among all branches of industry.

Large-scale capital investments and success in establishing a native machine-building industry permitted the USSR to carry out a thorough renovation and reconstruction of all branches of the national economy, especially industry, on the most up-to-date technical foundation. More than 80% of the industrial output of the country comes from new or thoroughly reconstructed enterprises.

The industry of the USSR has in its plants, erected for the most part during the years of the First and Second Stalin Five-Year Plans, the newest and technically most perfect equipment. More than 70% of all industrial power equipment (boilers, turbines, Diesel engines, motors, electric generators) and as much as 80% of all metal-working equipment have been produced and installed since 1929, hence are not more than ten years old. In the United States, on the other hand, 65% of the metal-working equipment and as much as 70% of the power equipment is *more* than ten years old.

The USSR is ahead of all the capitalist European countries and now equals the United States in the electrification of industrial plants.

Thus the USSR is ahead of the foremost capitalist countries in the rate of its industrial development and in the level of its industrial technique. Soviet industry is being developed even more extensively under the Third Stalin Five-Year Plan.

In accordance with the basic economic purpose of the USSR, of the 111.9 billion rubles allocated to capital investment in industry under the Third Five-Year Plan, 93.9 billion will go to developing branches producing means of production and 18 billion to developing branches producing consumers' goods. Thus, more rapid rates of development of the leading branches of industry are assured.

Machine construction, production of electrical energy, ferrous and nonferrous metallurgy, and the chemical industry show especially rapid growth. On the growth of these branches depends the successful solution of the fundamental economic problem of the USSR, which is to overtake and surpass—economically—the main capitalist countries.

Machine construction must assure the future technical equipment of the national economy and the introduction of the newest techniques into all its branches, and must provide the most up-to-date technical equipment for the needs of national defense. Machine construction and metal-working have increased their output 130%. The partial disproportion between the great growth of industry and the inadequate increase in the capacity of electric power stations is being eliminated under the Third Five-Year Plan; to achieve this it is planned to increase the total capacity of electric power stations 110%. This will not only permit an increase in output of electric energy beyond the growth of industry, but also assure the creation of necessary reserves of electric power. The chemical industry and ferrous and nonferrous metallurgy are growing rapidly. The Third Five-Year Plan is the era of chemical products and quality steels.

The output of consumers' goods is being developed on a broad scale. The total output of consumers' goods is scheduled to increase by 70%, while the output of local and cooperative industry is scheduled to increase by 100%.

Changes in the Geography of Industry

The geographic distribution of industry also has changed radically. The industrial development of the USSR has affected not only the old industrial regions, but also, and with particular force, a number of new areas, particularly the eastern regions and the national republics, which possess inexhaustible natural resources. Many new industrial centers and supporting bases of industrialization have arisen throughout the country, even in the most remote regions [see Table 17 and Figs. 27 and 28, facing pp. 200 and 201].

The distribution of industry is undergoing particularly large-scale changes under the Third Five-Year Plan. These changes have been directed towards bringing industry as close as possible to sources of raw materials and to consuming areas, in order to eliminate inefficient and exceedingly long hauls and to attain the further

TABLE 17. GROSS OUTPUT OF LARGE-SCALE INDUSTRY BY REGIONS OF THE USSR FOR 1913 AND 1937

ECONOMIC REGIONS AND REPUBLICS	OUTPUT (million rubles) 1913	1937	COMPARATIVE INCREASE [a]
RSFSR	7,806	65,948 [b]	8.5
European North	201	1,624	8.0
Northwest and Central Regions	5,568	45,343	8.1
Volga Region	687	4,809	7.0
North Caucasus and Crimea	464	4,736	10.2
Urals and Western Siberia	675	7,726	11.5
Eastern Siberia and the Far East	211	2,928	13.9
Ukrainian SSR	2,226	16,152	7.2
Belorussian SSR	119	1,733	15.4
Azerbaidzhan SSR	398	2,297	5.2
Georgian SSR	53	909	17.0
Armenian SSR	17	214	12.6
Turkmen SSR	35	264	7.6
Uzbek SSR	284	1,512	5.4
Tadzhik SSR	1	157	157.0
Kazakh SSR	60	841	14.0
Kirgiz SSR	1.2	139	116.0
Total	11,000	90,166 [b]	8.2

[a] Number of times by which 1937 output exceeded 1913 output.

[b] [Apparently there is an error in the original since the sum of the six entries for regions in the RSFSR is 67,166. The total for the eleven Union republics should be 91,384 if the figures for the six regions within the RSFSR are correct but 90,166 if the total given for the RSFSR is correct.]

development of regions of the USSR which formerly were backward economically.

Within the principal economic regions of the Union the extraction of fuel and the production of cement, chemical fertilizers, glass, and a mass of products of light industry and of the food industry are being organized on a scale designed to provide for the needs of these regions.

Each republic, kray, and oblast must produce in sufficient quantities such widely used food items as dairy produce, meats, confectionery, flour, and beer, and also such articles in general demand as dry goods, products of the sewing industry, bricks, and lime.

In such economic centers as the eastern regions, the Urals, and the

Volga Region, duplicate plants are being built under the Third Five-Year Plan in a number of branches of machine construction, oil refining, and the chemical industry, in order to eliminate the element of chance in the supply of certain industrial products from unique plants.

The Third Five-Year Plan provides also for a more rapid growth in the volume of capital investments and in the construction of new enterprises in the eastern and far eastern regions of the Soviet Union, as well as the development of a complex metallurgical base in these regions.

In addition, a new, large-scale production base of the textile industry is being created in the East, processing cotton grown in Central Asia.

The further industrialization of the national republics and oblasts is taking place, in accordance with the basic aims for the distribution of productive forces under the Third Five-Year Plan.

Such were the basic directives of the 18th Congress of the Communist Party of the Soviet Union concerning the distribution of Soviet industry. Large-scale changes in the geography of all branches of industry have been planned in accordance with these directives.

The struggle against the mania for gigantism in plant construction is especially important in securing a more uniform distribution of production throughout the country.

An intelligent specialization and cooperation among plants within the principal economic regions and centers of industrial concentration must be carried out under the Third Five-Year Plan.

An important consideration in the proper distribution of plants is the collective utilization of raw materials and fuel by combining individual plants on the basis of their successive utilization of the processed raw material and fuel, the utilization of waste products, etc. Such combination of plants must by no means result in the erection of giant plants. A combination of medium and small plants on the basis of collective utilization of raw materials and power makes it possible to bring industry closer to its sources of raw material and fuel and to distribute industry more uniformly throughout the oblasts, krays, and republics.

Such are the basic tasks contemplated by the Third Five-Year Plan in the distribution of Soviet industry.

SECTION 1. POWER ECONOMY OF THE USSR

Power engineering is one of the most important foundations for the development of a modern economy. The power supply of a given country is a clear index of its technical and economic development.

As a result of the First and Second Stalin Five-Year Plans, the USSR, compared with other countries, achieved the greatest increase in motors and power equipment in all branches of the national economy. This played an enormous role in reconstructing the national economy and raising the productivity of labor.

Power Resources of the USSR

The chief sources of power in the present-day economy are coal, oil, gas, water, peat, oil shale, and firewood.

The great progress in geological prospecting, particularly under the First and Second Five-Year Plans, has made the USSR the world's richest country in known reserves of fuel and energy.

Coal reserves of the USSR have increased from 230 billion tons in 1913, to 1,654 billion tons in 1937, an increase of 600%. They now comprise 20% of the world's coal reserves. Only the United States, with total coal reserves of 3,485 billion tons, exceeds the USSR. But in hard-coal reserves the Soviet Union is ahead of the United States and is first in the world.

The known reserves of oil in the USSR reached 4,679 million tons in 1937, comprising 59% of the world reserves, or more than the total oil reserves of all the capitalist countries put together.

In addition to oil, the USSR has a large quantity of natural gas, with total reserves amounting to 985.8 billion cubic meters.

The USSR is outstanding in the wealth of its water-power resources. The water-power reserves of the numerous rivers amount to 280 million kw., approximately equivalent to the power of 500 Dneprogeses, whereas the water-power resources of the United States are 82 million kw.; Canada, 37 million; Japan, 21 million; France, 8.9 million; and Germany, 3.7 million.

Peat, of which the USSR possesses reserves of 150 billion tons, is very important in a number of regions of the USSR. The total peat reserve of all the capitalist countries is 100 billion tons.

The USSR also exceeds all other countries in the size of its forested area, having 610 million hectares.

The USSR occupies third place in the world in its geological reserves of oil shale (55 billion tons). The reserves of oil shale which have been discovered thus far are only a part of the actual oil-shale resources of the Soviet Union, since in this field to date prospecting has been on a very small scale and unsystematic.

Thus, the USSR has taken first place in the world in its reserves of water power, oil, peat, and firewood.

The inexhaustible stores of power resources serve as a reliable natural base for the rapid growth of the power economy of the Soviet Union, and for its complete independence of the capitalist countries in power resources.

The favorable geographic distribution of fuel and power resources and their presence in the basic economic regions of the country constitute a great advantage for the USSR [Table 18].

This distribution of fuel and power resources in the country makes possible the complete fulfillment of the task set by the 18th Party Congress, which was to create, under the Third Five-Year Plan, in each economic region of the country, its own fuel and power base capable of fully supplying the needs of all branches of the economy and of eliminating the existing inefficient fuel hauls.

The fuel and power economy of Tsarist Russia was extremely backward. The low level of fuel extraction kept Russia constantly in the throes of a fuel famine and even made it necessary to import coal from other countries. Firewood played an enormous role in the fuel balance of the country, comprising 23.4% of the fuel used by industrial consumers alone. Such sources of power as oil shale and gas went completely unused, and peat production was insignificant.

The geography of the fuel economy of prewar Russia was exceptionally abnormal. Almost 90% of the total extraction of mineral fuel (coal and oil) was concentrated in the Donbas and in the Caucasus. The enormous fuel and power reserves of the other regions were scarcely touched. One of the reasons for such an abnormal distribution of the fuel economy of the country was the stubborn policy of foreign capital—which had seized Donets coal and Caucasian oil—of preventing the development of fuel extraction in other regions, in order to protect its own monopolistic position.

TABLE 18. DISTRIBUTION OF POWER RESOURCES OF THE USSR BY REGIONS FOR 1937

Regions	Total Comparison Fuel Reserves in Millions of Tons (all types fuel)	Water-Power Reserves (average annual capacity in 1,000 kw.)
RSFSR	1,283,209 [a]	206,903 [b]
European North	42,465	5,337
Northwest Region	5,340	1,139
Industrial Center	6,385	1,077
Central Chernozem Region	168	225
North Caucasus	23,333	12,370
Crimean ASSR	29	—
Volga Region	4,633	7,067
Urals	10,352	4,589
Western Siberia	486,574	24,371
Eastern Siberia	610,023	116,743
Far East	96,500	41,293
Ukrainian SSR	66,650	2,310
Belorussian SSR	1,215	414
Azerbaidzhan SSR	4,275	4,530
Georgian SSR	571	9,661
Armenian SSR	26	1,232
Turkmen SSR	2,938	2,948
Uzbek SSR	3,006	5,793
Tadzhik SSR	1,523	25,890
Kirgiz SSR	7,004	8,585
Kazakh SSR	153,250	11,687
Total	1,523,677 [a]	280,000 [b]

[a] [Apparently there is an error in the original Russian text. The sum of the figures for the eleven regions under the RSFSR is 1,285,802; if these figures are correct the total for the USSR is 1,526,260 instead of 1,523,677.]

[b] [The sum of the figures for the eleven regions under the RSFSR is 214,211. Since no figure is given for the Crimean ASSR, the total for the RSFSR should be slightly larger. The total of the regions in the USSR for which figures are given is 279,953; the obviously rounded figure of 280,000 would allow 47 for the Crimea, but this figure cannot be very accurate.]

Only after the Great October Revolution did it become possible to overcome the backwardness of the country's fuel economy and to subject it to thorough reconstruction.

DISTRIBUTION OF THE COAL INDUSTRY

Before the Revolution (1913) coal production in Russia was 29.1 million tons, for the most part concentrated in the Donets Basin, which alone produced 25.3 million tons, or 87% of the total for all Russia. Aside from the Donbas, coal was mined in insignificant quantities in the Moscow Basin (300 thousand tons), the Urals (1.2 million tons), the Kuzbas (0.8 million tons), Eastern Siberia (0.8 million tons), the Far East (0.4 million tons), and Central Asia (0.14 million tons). The total mined in all other regions was only 0.16 million tons. In Siberia, the Far East, and Central Asia coal was mined almost exclusively for the railroads.

During the years of the Soviet regime coal mining in the USSR has increased 340%, and by 1937 had reached 127.9 million tons.

Despite this huge progress, to date the USSR still occupies only fourth place in world coal production and is still far behind the leading capitalist countries in per capita output of coal. In the USSR in 1937, 757 kg. of coal per capita were mined, while in England 5,165 kg. per capita were mined; in the United States, 3,429 kg.; in Germany, 3,313 kg.; and in France, 1,065 kg.

By the end of the Third Five-Year Plan (1942) it is planned to increase the output of coal in the USSR to 243 million tons, or almost twice as much as was mined in 1937.

Geographic Distribution of Coal Mining by Regions

The geographic distribution of the coal industry of the USSR is basically different from that of prerevolutionary Russia. In addition to the Donbas, a whole series of new large-scale coal bases have been created in the country, as well as a large number of locally important bases in almost all regions of the Soviet Union. Whereas

TABLE 19. COAL OUTPUT BY BASINS, 1913 AND 1937

Basins or Regions	Output (million tons)		
	1913	1937	1937 Index (1913=100)
Donbas	25.29	77.54	303
Kuzbas	0.77	17.81	2,314
Moscow Basin	0.30	7.50	2,500
Ural basins	1.22	8.08	663
Karaganda	—	3.94	—
Basins of Eastern Siberia	0.85	5.81	1,020
Basins of Far East	0.37	4.82	781
Basins of Central Asia	0.14	0.91	507
Basins of Trans-Caucasus	0.05	0.40	800

FIG. 29. Fuel Production, 1938

the output of coal in the Donets Basin has increased threefold, the output of all the other basins has increased fourteenfold.

The Kuznetsk Basin has become the second most important coal base in the Soviet Union, and Karaganda the third.

In the Ukraine, in addition to the mining in the Donbas, mining of lignite has begun west of the Dnepr River. In the Urals, the Kizel, Yegorshino, and Chelyabinsk basins have been greatly developed [Fig. 18, p. 89, and Fig. 29]. In Eastern Siberia, in addition to the Cheremkhovo Basin, which has developed rapidly, coal is being mined in comparatively small quantities in the Bukachacha, Kansk [Irsha], Minusinsk [Chernogorsk], Sangarkhay (near Yakutsk), and other deposits. Coal is mined also in the vicinity of Norilsk and on the Kolyma River [Kolymo-Indigirka Basin in Fig. 18]. In the Far East, in addition to Suchan, the coal beds of Artem, Kivda-Raichikhinsk, Sakhalin, and Kamchatka are being mined.

In the Kazakh SSR, in addition to Karaganda, coal is mined for local needs in the Lenger, Baikonur, and Ber-Chogur deposits. In Central Asia coal mining thus far remains concentrated in the Fergana Valley, chiefly in the coal beds of the Kirgiz SSR [Kok-Yangak and Tashkumyr]. In the Trans-Caucasus coal is being mined in the Tkvarcheli and Tkvibuli beds in the Georgian SSR.

This development of coal bases in new regions has resulted in a relative decrease in the importance of Donets coal in the nation's total coal output from 87% in 1913 to 60.5% in 1937. In many cases it has made possible the creation of local fuel bases for the rapidly developing national economies of the remote regions and of the national republics.

Creation of Local Fuel Bases and Elimination of Long Fuel Hauls

However, in many regions coal mining still lags behind the local economic demands. These regions are compelled to import coal from distant basins, thus increasing the average length of the coal haul on the railroads. Despite the vigorous growth of the Moscow Coal Basin, the Central Industrial Region has been forced to bring in 15 million tons of Donets coal annually. Donets coal in large quantities goes to Leningrad Oblast, Belorussia, and the Volga Region, which do not themselves possess a coal supply.[2] The regions of the

[2] [Regional names are located on Fig. 7, and oblasts on Figs. 40 and 83, at the back of the book.]

European North, in addition to mining and hauling coal from Spitsbergen Island [Svalbard], also import a substantial amount of fuel from the Donbas. Although the coal output of the Ural basins has been increased several times, only half the local demands are met with local coal, and the remainder is imported from the Kuzbas and Karaganda. The Far East, which has increased its coal mining eightfold, still imports hundreds of thousands of tons of coal from the Kuzbas and Cheremkhovo. The regions of Central Asia also import hundreds of thousands of tons of coal from the Kuzbas.

The vigorous development of productive forces in new regions and the lag in the development of their power bases have led to a steady increase in the average length of the railroad coal haul. In 1913 the average length of a coal haul was 485 km.; in 1928 it was 615; in 1932, 662; and in 1937, 709 km. Taking into account the fact that such a discrepancy between the rate of industrial growth in the various regions and the rate of growth of their power bases cannot be tolerated, the 18th Party Congress placed in the category of most important problems the greatest possible development of local fuel bases and the elimination of long, unproductive hauls. This task is related entirely to the development and distribution of the coal industry under the Third Five-Year Plan. With this goal for the development of the coal industry, the Third Five-Year Plan provides for a more rapid rate of growth for local coal bases, as compared with the over-all growth of Soviet coal output and as compared with the rate of development of the chief Soviet coal-producing regions, the Donbas and Kuzbas. Whereas total coal output in the Soviet Union under the Third Five-Year Plan is scheduled to increase an average of 90%, coal mining in the Donbas will increase only 55% and in the Kuzbas only 49%. On the other hand, during the same period the output of the Moscow Basin should increase 270%; of the Urals, 210%; of the Far East, 170%; of Central Asia, 340%; and the Trans-Caucasus, 400%.

The rapid rates at which the new local coal basins are being developed should solve the problem of halting the increase in transportation of Donets coal to the central regions and the European North. In addition to Donets coal, the Volga Region should receive a considerable quantity of coal from the southern Urals (Dombarovka Basin), Karaganda, and Ber-Chogur. The Urals

Region should provide fully for its power needs with its own coal production and limit the importation of Kuznetsk coal to the requirements of fuel for metallurgy. The hauling of Kuznetsk coal to the Far East and to the Central Asiatic republics should cease entirely.

The fulfillment of this program for the development of the coal industry and the production of other types of local fuel will assure the creation of a local fuel base in each economic region of the country and will make it possible to decrease significantly the average length of the coal haul on the railroads.

DISTRIBUTION OF THE OIL INDUSTRY

The Oil Industry of Prerevolutionary Russia

The oil industry appeared in Russia in 1821 in the Baku region. Before the 1870's it was worked only by Russian industrialists, applying the most primitive methods of extraction and of producing kerosene. Until 1869, oil output did not exceed 42,000 tons annually. But even this enabled the Baku industrialists to drive foreign oil from the domestic market and to export some Baku oil.

In the 1870's foreign capital began to take over the industry—first the Nobel Brothers Company, later the French Caspian-Black Sea Society headed by Rothschild, and finally English capital. Oil output began to increase rapidly, reaching 662,000 tons in 1880, 4 million tons in 1890, and, at its highest point in prerevolutionary Russia, 11.5 million tons in 1901. At that time Russia held first place in the world in oil output, accounting for 51% of the total world supply, having surpassed the United States, which extracted only 9 million tons. At the same time the shipment of oil abroad reached its maximum figure of 1,153 thousand tons.

But from 1901 to the Great October Socialist Revolution oil output in Russia declined, never again reaching the 1901 level. In 1913, 9.2 million tons were extracted in Russia, and in 1917, 8.7 million tons. During the same period the output of the United States increased rapidly, reaching 34 million tons in 1913 and 45 million tons in 1917, thus far surpassing Russia. By 1917, Russia was overtaken by Mexico as well. Mexico had begun to produce oil only in 1907 and was already producing more than 8 million tons in 1917.

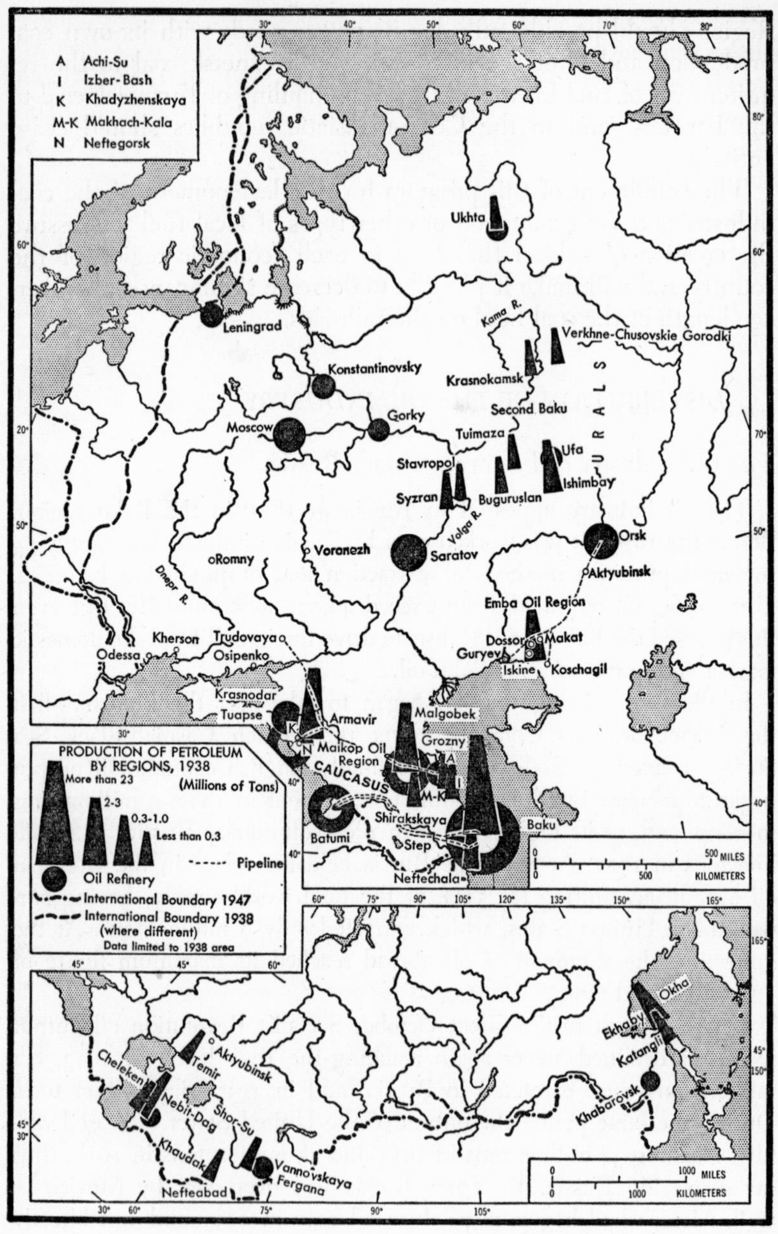

FIG. 30. Petroleum Production, 1938

The geographic distribution of oil extraction in prerevolutionary Russia was marked by its lack of uniformity. In 1913, 97.1% of all the oil output was from the regions of the Caucasus—83% from Baku, 13.1% from Grozny, and approximately 1% from the Maikop region [Fig. 30]. Outside the Caucasus, oil was extracted only in Emba (1.3%) and in Central Asia (1.6%). Thus, almost all oil refining was concentrated in the Caucasus. Foreign capital, retarding the development of the Russian oil industry, hindered in every possible way the development of new oil regions.

Until 1920, oil extraction in the Baku region, which had been seized by English interventionists, was being greatly curtailed. After the liberation of Baku from the interventionists in that year, only 3.8 million tons of oil were extracted, and Russia occupied third place, coming after the United States and Mexico in world production of oil.

Distribution of Oil Extraction in the USSR

From 1921 on, oil extraction increased steadily. It was reconstructed technically and, as a result of increased prospecting, oil reserves grew rapidly in the old, and especially in new, regions. In 1937 the extraction of oil (including gas) in the USSR increased to 30,485 thousand tons, which meant an increase of 230% over 1913, and a 700% increase over 1920. The USSR is now firmly established in second place in world oil output (the United States is first), having surpassed Mexico and Venezuela.

Noticeable changes have taken place in the geography of oil extraction [Table 20].

While the extraction of oil in the Baku region increased 200%, and in the Grozny region 130%, it increased in the Emba more than 300%; in the Turkmen SSR, 250%; and in the Uzbek SSR and the Tadzhik SSR combined and in Krasnodar Kray, 1600%. Oil fields have been opened in new regions as well, including the Bashkir ASSR, Kuibyshev and Perm oblasts, Sakhalin, and the Dagestan ASSR, and the foundations of oil extraction are being laid in the Komi ASSR (Ukhta-Pechora), the Crimean ASSR, and Aktyubinsk Oblast.[3] The Ishimbay region in the Bashkir ASSR has been developed with particular speed; it was opened in 1932, and by 1937

[3] [Names of specific oil-producing localities are indicated in Table 20 footnote a and are located on Fig. 30.]

was already yielding 984,000 tons of oil. As a result of the organization and growth of oil extraction in new regions, the percentage of the total output produced in Baku and Grozny declined from 96.1 in 1913 to 85 in 1937.

However, these changes in the distribution of oil extraction are far from sufficient. Belorussia, the central and northwest regions, and all of Siberia [4] are entirely lacking in local oil. With the rapid economic development of these regions this lack increases the mileage of oil hauls across the country.

The Third Five-Year Plan contemplates further large-scale changes in the geographic distribution of oil extraction. While there is to be a general increase in oil extraction (including gas) of up to 54 million tons, an increase of 77%, oil output in the Baku region is to increase by only 31%, and in Grozny by only 67%. Thus it is the new regions which are to develop most rapidly. Output of oil in the region between the Volga and the Urals is to be increased 7 times, in the Emba region 4 times, in Central Asia 2.5 times, in Sakhalin almost 4 times, in the Dagestan ASSR 5 times, and in Maikopneft 2.8 times. A large oil-producing region, the "Second Baku," is being established between the Volga and the Urals, with an expected output in 1942 of 7 million tons of oil. Outside the Ishimbay region, oil production is increasing rapidly from the Syzran, Buguruslan, Tuimaza, and Kama deposits. Oil extraction is increasing dozens of times in Georgia, the Crimea, and Aktyubinsk Oblast. Oil production in the Komi ASSR (Ukhta deposit) is reaching 400 thousand tons, and new oil fields are being opened in the Ukraine (in the vicinity of the city of Romny) and in Kamchatka. Oil prospecting is being pushed in the region of Lake Baikal and in the Arctic (Nordvik and Ust-Port) [Ust-Yeniseisky Port] [Fig. 18, facing p. 89].

By the end of the Third Five-Year Plan, this rapid development of the new regions should decrease the relative importance of the old oil regions—Baku and Grozny—from 85% to 65%, which will alter radically the existing geography of oil extraction and will assure such regions as the Volga, the Urals, the Far East, the European North, Central Asia, and Kazakhstan of a sufficient quantity of oil of their own production and sharply curtail the unnecessarily long hauls of oil from the Caucasus to all parts of the country.

[4] [Siberia does not include the Soviet Far East.]

TABLE 20. EXTRACTION OF OIL, INCLUDING GAS, BY REGIONS, 1913 AND 1937

Regions [and producing trusts] [a]	Extraction (thousand tons) 1913	Extraction (thousand tons) 1937 [b]	Percentage 1913	Percentage 1937 [b]	1937 index (1913 = 100)
Azerbaidzhan SSR—Azneft	7,669.1	23,227.0	83.0	76.21	303
Chechen-Ingush ASSR—Grozneft	1,208.2	2,825.0	13.1	9.25	234
Krasnodar Kray—Maikopneft	86.8	1,479.0	0.9 [c]	4.80	1,719
Dagestan ASSR—Dagneft	—	174.3	—	0.60	—
Kazakh SSR—Embaneft	117.6	487.4	1.3	1.60	414
Kazakh SSR—Aktyubneft	—	5.8	—	0.02	— [d]
Turkmen SSR	129.5	452.0	1.4	1.50	349 [d]
Uzbek SSR	—	365.0	—	1.20	1,718 (Uzbek and Tadzhik combined)
Tadzhik SSR—	22.9	28.4	0.3	0.09	
Bashkir ASSR	—	983.6	—	3.23	—
Kuibyshev Oblast	—	17.2	—	0.06	—
Perm [Molotov] Oblast	—	23.0	—	0.08	—
Komi ASSR	—	41.7	—	0.13	—
Georgian ASSR	—	8.9	—	0.03	—
Crimean ASSR	—	0.7	—	—	—
Far East—Sakhalinneft	—	356.0	—	1.20	—
Total USSR	9,234.1	30,485.0	100.0	100.00	331

[a] [The main producing centers are as follows: Azerbaidzhan SSR—Baku, Chechen-Ingush ASSR—Grozny, Krasnodar Kray—Maikop, Dagestan ASSR—Makhach-Kala, Embaneft in Kazakh SSR—Dossor, Aktyubneft in Kazakh SSR—Temir, Turkmen SSR—Nebit-Dag, Uzbek SSR—Khaudak, Tadzhik SSR—Nefteabad, Bashkir ASSR—Ishimbay, Kuibyshev Oblast—Syzran, Perm Oblast—Verkhne-Chusovskie-Gorodki, Komi ASSR—Ukhta, and Far East—Okha. See Fig. 30.]

[b] [For 1937 production the figures given for the regions total 30,475.0. Since it is not known where the error lies, it has not been possible to correct minor errors in the figures for percentage of production, 1937.]

[c] [1.0 in the original.]

[d] [The original table gave 349 for Kazakh SSR, Aktyubneft, and 234 for Turkmen SSR, an obvious error.]

Distribution of Oil Refining

The proper distribution of oil refineries throughout the country, as well as of oil extraction, is also of great importance. Oil-refining plants in prerevolutionary Russia were located in the Caucasus, in the Baku, Batumi, and Grozny regions.

As a result of the First and particularly the Second Stalin Five-Year Plan the geography of oil refining has changed radically. A number of powerful plants have been built in towns along the Volga—Saratov, Gorky, and Konstantinovsky near Yaroslavl [Fig. 30]. These plants refine Caucasus oil at points where it is transferred from Volga River transport to the railroads. Oil-refining plants have been built in Tuapse, Odessa, Kherson, and Osipenko —at points where oil was transferred from rail to ship, or from ship to rail [Fig. 30]. A large plant has been erected in Ufa for refining Ishimbay oil, in Orsk for refining Emba oil, and in Khabarovsk for refining Sakhalin oil. Refineries have been built in such large centers as Moscow and Leningrad. Refineries in the Caucasus have been expanded considerably and reconstructed. Plants have been built in Fergana and in the western part of Turkmenia for refining Central Asiatic oil.

Further changes in the geographic distribution of oil refining will take place under the Third Five-Year Plan. A whole group of new plants capable of refining 6 million tons of oil annually will be built in the region of the "Second Baku." New plants will be built and old plants enlarged in all new regions, sufficiently to assure the refining of all the oil extracted in these regions. In the Center, on the Volga, and in the Ukraine, new plants will be erected to refine Caucasus oil.

Transportation of Oil

The proper organization of the transportation of oil and oil products is extraordinarily important. The concentration of oil extraction in the Caucasus and the lag in the development of new oil bases as compared with the development of productive forces in other regions of the USSR have increased the average length of haul for oil products. The average distance which oil was carried by rail in 1913 was 601 km.; in 1928 it was 728; in 1932, 891; and in 1937, 1,228 km.

The measures contemplated by the Third Five-Year Plan for the rapid development of oil bases in new regions at a distance from the Caucasus should curtail sharply the length of haul. But this is still not enough to relieve the burden on rail transport. The rail transport load must be eased significantly by means of a decisive increase in oil transportation by water and by oil pipelines.

The USSR is far behind the United States in the transportation of oil by different means.

In the transportation of oil in the USSR, as compared with the United States, the very insignificant proportion of oil pipelines and the very great proportion of rail hauls is striking [Table 21].

TABLE 21. TRANSPORTATION USED FOR OIL IN USA AND USSR

MEANS	PERCENTAGE	
	United States	USSR
Railroad	2.2	42.7
Water	26.6	45.9 [a]
Oil pipelines	71.2	11.4
	100.0	100.0

[a] Of which, river transport comprises only 11.8%.

At present the USSR has the following oil trunk lines: Baku to Batumi, for the transportation of Baku oil to the Black Sea; Grozny to Makhach-Kala, for the transportation of Grozny oil to the Caspian Sea and thence by sea to the Volga; Grozny to Armavir to Maikop to Tuapse, for the transportation of Grozny and Maikop oil to the Black Sea; Armavir to Trudovaya (Donbas), for the transportation of Grozny oil to the Ukraine and the central regions; Guryev to Orsk, for the transportation of Emba oil to the southern Urals; Sterlitamak [near Ishimbay] to Ufa, for the transportation of Ishimbay oil to the refinery plant in Ufa [Fig. 30]. In addition, there are small oil pipelines of local importance linking individual enterprises with railroad and water transport lines. Prerevolutionary Russia had oil pipelines only from Baku to Batumi and from Grozny to Makhach-Kala. All other existing lines have been built under the Soviets.

Under the Third Five-Year Plan, in accordance with the directives of the 18th Party Congress, a network of new oil pipelines is to be constructed. Of especial importance is the proposed installation of a number of oil pipelines in the "Second Baku" region, from Trudovaya Station to the Dnepr and to Voronezh (and farther into the central region); from the region of the "Second Baku" or Orsk to Western Siberia; and in the Far East.

It is essential also that the transportation of oil by water, especially by way of rivers, be increased in every way possible. Since 1913, while rail transport increased its oil haulage by 300%, and sea transport by 200%, river transport, in spite of the enormous river network of the USSR, increased its oil haulage by only 30%. This would indicate the intolerable backwardness of this form of transportation. There are tremendous unexplored possibilities for transferring oil shipments from the railroads to water transport.

The rapid development of new oil regions, the erection in these regions of refineries, and the installation of a network of new oil pipelines and increased river transport of oil will assure the fulfillment of the directives of the 18th Party Congress concerning the elimination of long hauls.

DISTRIBUTION OF THE GAS INDUSTRY

The creation in the USSR of a large-scale gas industry is one of the most important tasks of the Third Five-Year Plan. The realization of this depends on the broad utilization of the very rich stores of natural gas, and upon the development of gasification of all types of fuel, particularly of underground coal.

The USSR has the world's largest reserves of natural gas, which total 985 billion cubic meters.

Almost all the oil-bearing deposits in the USSR are also gas-bearing. The amount of gas in the oil-gas deposits is approximately 10 to 15% of the amount of oil. The total reserves of gas found in such deposits are estimated at 712 billion cubic meters. The pure or dry natural gases found in many regions of the USSR are estimated at 273 billion cubic meters, or 27% of all the natural gas.

Saboteurs have tried in every possible way to prevent the extraction and utilization of natural gas, which provides the cheapest and most efficient power fuel and is a raw material for the chemical industry. Consequently the development of this branch of industry has been much retarded. In 1937 the USSR extracted only about 2 billion cubic meters of natural gas, whereas in the same year the United States extracted 70 billion cubic meters, created a large network of gas pipelines, and made wide use of natural gas in industry, in municipal economy, and for household needs.

Reserves of natural gas are found in significant quantities in many regions of the USSR. Practically all oil-working regions have oil-and-gas-bearing deposits. Particularly large oil-gas deposits are found in the Azerbaidzhan SSR, in the Maikop region, and in the Emba district. Oil-gases are found also in the Volga-Urals region, in Grozny, and in Central Asia.

The largest oil-gas deposits are found in the Baku region, which in 1937 produced 1.8 billion cubic meters of gas, or 90% of the total Soviet output. Gas is used as a fuel for electric power stations and for municipal and household needs in the city of Baku. In other oil regions gas is not yet produced, but on the Emba and in Grozny the gas which escapes into the air is set afire, forming gigantic flares.

The distribution of pure gas-bearing deposits and the amount of reserves are shown in Table 22.

TABLE 22. RESERVES OF PURE (DRY) GAS BY REGIONS

REGION	TOTAL RESERVES OF GAS million cu. m.
Dagestan ASSR	2,117
Ordzhonikidze Kray	1,344
Krasnodar Kray	7,080
Crimean ASSR	4,876
Ukrainian SSR	2,150
Saratov Oblast	96
Kazakh SSR	183,750
Turkmen SSR	23,400
Kalmyk ASSR	48,544

The deposit in the Dagestan ASSR has been the most thoroughly investigated. Here gas is produced principally for the glass industry.

The gas beds of the Komi ASSR must also be mentioned among the chief gas regions. Here with the introduction of pipelines the rich deposits may be used to supply the industrial regions of the northwestern part of the Urals: Solikamsk, Berezniki, and Perm [Molotov].

There is a large gas region in the Buryat-Mongol ASSR.

The Third Five-Year Plan has set the task of increasing gas extraction by 250%, which necessitates bringing production of natural gas up to 7 billion cubic meters, 2 billion of which must come from pure gas-bearing deposits. In addition to the development of gas in the Baku region, gas production will be organized in all oil regions, especially in the Komi ASSR, Krasnodar Kray, the Dagestan ASSR, and on a somewhat smaller scale in Ordzhonikidze Kray, in the Crimea, the Ukraine, the Kalmyk ASSR, the Turkmen SSR, and the Buryat-Mongol ASSR. Gas prospecting is being increased in the Donbas, along the Yenisey River, and in Kamchatka.

Underground coal gasification is especially important for the power economy of the USSR. Only in the USSR is it being adopted on an industrial scale. The first industrial station for the underground gasification of coal in the Donbas was put into operation as early as 1938. For the first time in history, gas was produced underground for industrial use. In the Moscow Basin an experimental station for the underground gasification of Moscow Basin lignite is under construction. Successful experimentation will make possible the broad development of gasification for industry and for the needs of the Moscow population.

In addition to developing underground gasification of Donets and Moscow coal, the Third Five-Year Plan proposes the creation of a number of stations in the eastern and far eastern regions. An experimental plant for underground gasification of oil shales is also planned. By assuring Leningrad and the Volga Region, which have very rich beds of oil-shales, of a supply of fuel, this would completely change their position with respect to power supply.

Coking and blast-furnace gases are extremely important in the gasification of the country. They will be used as fuel almost entirely by metallurgical plants and by the chemical industry.

As gas production in the USSR increases, the use of the most diversified types of local fuel will become increasingly significant. By this method the USSR extracts more than 10 billion cubic meters of gas, equivalent to more than 2 million tons of comparison fuel. More than 30% of the gas-generating installations are in the Ukraine, approximately 15% in the Center, and 20% in the Urals. This type of gasification should be spread widely and on a large scale throughout the Union.

DISTRIBUTION OF THE PEAT INDUSTRY

Peat is one of the most important types of local fuel. The transportation difficulties necessitate its use predominantly at the point of extraction as a fuel for electric power stations, industrial plants, or other uses. By making it into briquettes, it can be used at short distances from its natural source.

Gasification at the point of extraction and transmission of the gas for rather extended distances through gas pipelines for use as a power fuel or a chemical raw material are particularly important in the utilization of peat.

In Tsarist Russia peat extraction was only slightly developed. During the Imperialist War [World War I], the difficulties of fuel supply forced an exploration of the peat bogs of the central part of Russia. By 1916 only 227,000 hectares of peat bogs had been surveyed and the possibilities of their utilization determined.

Under the Soviets the first important work was done in the study and practical utilization of the huge peat reserves of the country.

The first widespread use of peat began under the first plan for the electrification of Soviet Russia (the Goelro Plan), which provided for the construction of a number of large electric power stations using peat. Among the stations built to use peat were the Shatura and Klasson [Kl] in Moscow Oblast, the Dubrovka and "Krasny Oktyabr" in Leningrad Oblast, the Ivanovo, Yaroslavl, Gorky, and Belorussian [Belges], requiring many millions of tons of peat [Fig. 31, p. 233].

Important work has been done in the discovery and further study of the peat bogs of the Soviet Union. Reserves of peat are now estimated at 150 billion tons, corresponding to 62 billion tons of comparison fuel. The USSR is first in the world in its peat reserves, exceeding the total reserves in all the capitalist countries by 50 billion tons. By the end of the Second Five-Year Plan, 23.8 million tons of peat were extracted annually in the USSR. The distribution of peat resources and the extraction of peat by regions appear In Table A3 (in the Appendix) [p. 510].

The greatest peat reserves are found in the European North and in Western and Eastern Siberia. Here are concentrated 121.5 billion tons of peat, or 84% of the total reserves of the Union. But in these regions the important bogs are in the most water-logged areas, where natural conditions make extraction difficult, and where the peat product is only slightly decomposed. Thus, the extraction in these regions is small, amounting to only 90.6 thousand tons, or 0.4% of the total for the country. Peat is also extracted in small quantities in the southern parts of Vologda, Omsk, and Novosibirsk oblasts.

Peat is most important for the Belorussian SSR, the northwestern part of the Ukrainian SSR, and Leningrad, Kalinin, Moscow, Ivanovo, Yaroslavl, and Gorky oblasts. The development of extraction in these areas will make possible a decrease in the consumption of fuel brought from a distance. In each of these regions, 1.5 to 5 million tons of peat are extracted.

These regions, while containing only about 11.5% of the reserves of the Union, yield more than 80% of the peat production. Peat is particularly important in the fuel balance of the Belorussian SSR and of Ivanovo Oblast.

The Third Five-Year Plan expects to increase peat extraction in the country by more than 100%, with an output of 49 million tons by 1942. The extraction will increase particularly in the Northwestern and Central regions, in Belorussia, in the Volga Region, and in the Urals.

A particularly important problem confronting the Third Five-Year Plan is the elimination of seasonality in the peat industry and the assuring of year-round extraction through artificial dehydration, briquetting, and chemical utilization of peat as a raw material for obtaining gas and tar.

The complex mechanization of all the laborious processes in the peat industry must be completed; and the gap between the mechanization of extraction and the mechanization of dehydration, gathering, and transporting must be eliminated completely.

DISTRIBUTION OF THE EXTRACTION OF OIL SHALE

Oil shale is a low-calorie type of local fuel. The low heat value and high ash content thus far have hindered its wide utilization. In prerevolutionary Russia shale extraction was organized for the first time on a small scale in Estonia, during the Imperialist War [World War I], to supply the industrial plants of the Leningrad region. Shale extraction did not exist in other regions of Russia.

Under the Soviet regime a great many reserves of oil shale have been discovered in various regions of the country. The total geological reserves of oil shale are estimated at 55 billion tons and are distributed among the chief regions as follows [Table 23]:

TABLE 23. RESERVES OF OIL SHALE, BY PRINCIPAL REGIONS (in millions of tons)

Komi ASSR	13,016
Kuibyshev Oblast	4,316
Saratov Oblast and Volga German ASSR	3,940
Chkalov Oblast	3,963
Leningrad Oblast	2,590
Kirov Oblast and Udmurt ASSR	2,283
Kazakh SSR (Kenderlyk)	1,479
Gorky Oblast and Chuvash ASSR	1,232

The shale beds in Leningrad Oblast and in the Volga Region, where there are no coal reserves, are very important. In Leningrad Oblast the shales are concentrated in the famous Gdov bed, where one shaft is already at work, two shafts are being completed, and the foundations of a number of new shafts are being laid [Fig. 18, facing p. 89].

The Volga Region has large reserves of shale in Kirov Oblast, the Chuvash ASSR, Gorky and Kuibyshev oblasts (Kashpir and Ulyanovsk), and particularly in the region of the Obshchy Syrt in Chkalov and Saratov oblasts [Fig. 18]; and extraction of shales is under way in the Chuvash ASSR, in the Kashpir region (near Syzran), and in the Savelyevka district of Saratov Oblast.

The large Kenderlyk shale deposits in the Kazakh SSR may, in the future, have great significance as a fuel base for nonferrous metallurgy in the Altay; but they are not being worked, because of lack of transportation facilities.

The task has been set under the Third Five-Year Plan to increase in every possible way the extraction of shales, especially in regions lacking other fuel resources. It will increase by almost 700%—from 516,000 tons in 1937 to 4 million in 1942. In addition to the development in Gdov [at Slantsy], Kashpir, and Savelyevka [at Rukopol] [Fig. 29], shale extraction will be organized in new regions—Chudovo Region (Leningrad Oblast) [Fig. 18], and in the regions of Ulyanovsk and Ozinki (Saratov Oblast).

The proposed gasification of shales, the distillation of shales into liquid fuel, and the development of methods of using shale ash to produce building materials will be very important steps in the future development of the shale industry.

FIREWOOD RESOURCES: DISTRIBUTION & UTILIZATION

Wood unsuited for more practical uses which can be cut into firewood is used for fuel. Firewood is obtained also from various waste products of the lumber industry, the woodworking industry, and the wood-finishing industry. Firewood serves as an excellent medium-calorie local fuel, but its preparation is extremely laborious. Difficulty of transportation limits significantly the possible utilization of firewood in regions removed from the places where the wood is produced.

The USSR is first in the world both in its reserves of firewood, and in its utilization of firewood. The total reserves in the USSR are estimated at 24.2 billion cubic meters, which corresponds to approximately 10 billion tons of comparison fuel. In 1937, 90.2 million cubic meters of firewood were produced and shipped; in addition, a considerable quantity of firewood was used as fuel at the source, as were various waste-wood products of the woodworking industry. The distribution of reserves of firewood and the shipment of firewood by regions of the USSR appear in Table A4 (in the Appendix) [p. 511].

About three-fourths of the total resources of firewood of the country are concentrated in the regions of Western and Eastern Siberia and in the Far East. As a result of the inaccessibility of a number of these forest regions and the inexpediency of hauling logs to the European part of the USSR, firewood is produced and shipped in only relatively small quantity in the Siberian and Far Eastern regions. While possessing almost three-fourths of all the nation's firewood, they produce and ship only 16.2% of all the firewood produced in the USSR.

The regions of the Center, Northwest, and Volga utilize a particularly large proportion of their firewood reserves. With only 5.4% of all the wood reserves of the Union, they produce and ship annually as much as 42% of all the firewood in the USSR. The Central Industrial Region alone, with only 2% of the nation's wood reserves, produces and ships more than 20% of the total.

The European North and the Urals produce a great deal of firewood. The northern sections produce firewood chiefly for shipment to other regions of the USSR, principally to those of the Center. The Urals use the greater part of their firewood for the Ural charcoal metallurgy.

The Ukraine and Belorussia, which together have only 0.4% of the total reserves of firewood, produce approximately 7% of the total firewood of the Union.

Because of insufficient resources, the republics of Central Asia and the Trans-Caucasus use but very small quantities of firewood. Only the Georgian SSR has relatively large resources (about 300 million cubic meters); and production and utilization of wood here is complicated by the difficulties of the mountainous terrain.

Under the Third Five-Year Plan production of firewood in the USSR is scheduled for an 86% increase, which will bring the total produced and shipped to 160 million cubic meters. An especially great increase is planned for the regions of the European North, the Far East, the Urals, the North Caucasus, Eastern and Western Siberia, and the Volga.

The Central and Northwestern regions will have a considerably smaller increase under the Third Five-Year Plan.

The deliberate development of other types of fuel should aid in decreasing the length of the firewood haul from the Volga regions to the Center, from the northern and central regions to the Ukraine, from Siberia to Central Asia, and from the northern region to the central and northwestern areas.

SECTION 2. ELECTRIFICATION OF THE NATIONAL ECONOMY OF THE USSR AND DISTRIBUTION OF ELECTRIC POWER STATIONS

The discovery of electricity, the solution of the problem of its long-distance transmission over wires, and its subsequent application in all phases of economic life, have altered radically the techniques of production.

The founders of Marxism—Marx and Engels—after learning about the first experiments in transmitting electrical energy over wires, felt that electricity would be of tremendous importance in the future development of human society.

"The recent discovery of Deprez," writes Engels, "that an electric current of very high voltage can, with comparatively little loss of energy, be transmitted over an ordinary telegraph wire for such distances as we have not dared to dream of until now, and that this current can be utilized at the receiving point (the matter is still in its embryonic stages)—this discovery definitely liberates industry from almost all confines imposed by local conditions and also makes possible the harnessing of even the most distant water power. If at the outset it will be useful for towns only, in the end it will become the most powerful lever for overcoming the antagonisms between rural and urban society. It is perfectly clear that, thanks to this discovery, productive forces will grow to such an extent that their management will become increasingly beyond the powers of the bourgeoisie." [5]

Electricity was first used for illumination in the 1870's; in the 1880's it was used for power, and electrified municipal transport appeared. But even by the end of the 1890's electricity was swiftly penetrating into industry. Lenin said concerning this period that the "electrical industry is most typical of the newest technical advances, most typical of capitalism at the end of the nineteenth and the beginning of the twentieth centuries." [6]

Prerevolutionary Russia had a very slightly developed electric-power economy. In 1913 the total capacity of electric power stations in Russia was only 1,098 thousand kw., which produced 1,945 million kw-h of energy. These were small, preponderantly industrial stations, making but slight use of their very limited capacities. They were concentrated for the most part in the principal industrial centers and large cities. The rest of Russia scarcely knew of electricity.

Electrification of the USSR

With the end of the Civil War, Lenin and Stalin immediately faced the necessity for the large-scale electrification of the country.

Large projects for electrification were set forth in the Goelro Plan, approved by the 8th All-Russian Congress of Soviets in 1921.

[5] Marx and Engels, *Works,* Vol. XXVII, p. 289.
[6] Lenin, *Works,* Vol. XIX, p. 124.

The Goelro Plan provided for what was at that time a grandiose program of electrification by building in ten to fifteen years thirty large regional stations with a total capacity of approximately 1.5 million kw., or 1½ times the capacity of all the stations existing in Tsarist Russia.

The plan was based on the necessity of concentrating electricity output in large regional stations using local energy resources (coal waste products, peat, water power, etc.), of unifying the electric power of the stations in a single high-voltage regional network, and of transmitting it for considerable distances. The plan was set up according to regions, having in view the future development of each region as related to the construction of power bases.

It did not require fifteen years to realize the Goelro Plan. Even in 1928, eight years after it was approved, as a result of the construction of a number of stations provided for by the plan, the total capacity of electric power stations had increased by 1,300 thousand kw., and all the stations of the Union produced 6.3 billion kw-h of electric power, or 250% more than prewar Russia.

The First and Second Stalin Five-Year Plans saw a particularly vigorous growth in the electrification of the USSR. By the end of the Second Five-Year Plan the capacity of all the stations had increased to 8,177 thousand kw., with an output of 36.4 billion kw-h of electric power. While the total capacity of the stations increased 7.5 times as compared with 1913, the output of electric power increased more than 18 times. As a result of these advances the USSR became one of the world's largest producers and consumers of electric power. In 1937, it ranked third in the world in the production of electric power, following the United States and Germany. In 1913 Tsarist Russia had ranked fifteenth.

One of the most important characteristics of the electric power economy of the USSR is the ever-increasing importance of the regional stations, whose capacity in 1937 was 65.1% of the total capacity of electric power stations in the USSR, while the capacity of the industrial stations dropped to 25%.

The electric power produced is used chiefly in industry and in municipal economy, very little as yet in transport and especially in agriculture. In 1937 industry consumed 69% of all the electric power produced in the country; municipalities consumed 13.7%; transport, 3.2% (of this only 1.1% for electric traction); and agriculture, only 0.9%.

As a result of the tremendous application of electric power in industry, the USSR has surpassed the United States, England, Germany, and the other capitalist countries in the coefficient of electrification of machinery used in industry.

During recent years the utilization, in industry and for the household needs of the population, of steam and heat wastes from electric power stations has become particularly important. Central heating stations, not in existence before the Revolution, developed only from 1924 on; in 1937 the capacity of central heating stations already exceeded 1.5 million kw.

In 1913, almost all stations in Russia operated on fuel brought from a distance; 60% of the electric power was produced from fuel oil, and almost 40% from Donets and English coal. In 1937 only 19.1% of all electric power was produced from fuel brought from a distance, and 80.9% from local types of fuel and water power.

The construction of electric power stations operating on peat has reached large proportions, already furnishing 18.5% of all electric power. Stations using coal from the Urals and Siberia produce 14.8% of the electric power; those using local culm (anthracite dust), 12.6%; and those using coal from the Moscow Basin, 9.5%. Peat is used to operate such large stations as the Shatura and Klasson [east of Moscow], Dubrovka and "Krasny Oktyabr" [at Leningrad], Gorky, Ivanovo, and Belorussian [Belges] [Fig. 31]; anthracite refuse to operate Shterovka, Zuyevka [Z in Fig. 31], and Shakhty [in the Donbas], Stalingrad, and others; Moscow Basin coal to operate Kashira, Stalinogorsk, and others; [south of Moscow]; Ural coal to operate Chelyabinsk, Berezniki, Kizel, Sredne-Uralsk [near Sverdlovsk], Tagil [Nizhny Tagil], and others. The Siberian and Far Eastern stations operate on local fuel.

Construction of Hydroelectric Stations

There has been great progress in the construction of hydroelectric power stations in the USSR. There were no such stations in prerevolutionary Russia. The beginnings of construction date from the first years of Soviet power with the construction of the Volkhov hydroelectric station [Volkhovges] in Leningrad Oblast. This was followed by the building of the Dneproges, Svir, Nivskaya, Baksan, Gizeldon, Zemo-Avchala [Zages], Rion [Rionges], Dzorages, Kana-

Fig. 31. Electric Generating Stations by Type of Energy Used

ker, Varzob [Varzobges], and a number of other hydroelectric stations [see Fig. 31].

By the end of the Second Five-Year Plan the total output of electric power from hydroelectric stations was approximately 4 billion kw-h, or 12% of the electric power of the Union. This would indicate the inadequate utilization at that time of the country's very rich river power resources. The United States produces 39 billion kw-h, or 40% of its total electric power, from hydroelectric stations; Canada, 23 billion kw-h, or 98% of its total power; France, 7.8 billion kw-h, or 51% of its power; Japan, 16.3 billion kw-h, or 82% of its power; and Germany, 5.7 billion kw-h, or 15.7% of its total electric power. Though the Soviet Union possesses the greatest water-power resources in the world, it lags behind these countries in output of hydroelectric power and especially in its relative importance to the total production of electric power.

The Chief Power Systems of the USSR

One of the most important measures carried out by the Soviet regime in systematizing the utilization of the country's power economy was the interconnection of electric power stations and the formation of large power systems, all the stations of which operate as a single electric network in a given region. This makes possible a more uniform utilization of the stations and a more effective distribution among consumers of the power produced. The chief power systems of the country are Moscow, Leningrad, Gorky-Ivanovo, Dnepr, Donets, Ural, and Kuzbas [Fig. 31].

The Moscow system alone in 1938 produced 3 times as much electric power as prewar Russia; the Leningrad system, 1.5 times as much; the Dnepr system, 1.5 times as much; the Donets system, 2 times as much; the Ural, 1.5 times as much; and the Gorky-Ivanovo system, almost the same amount as prerevolutionary Russia. The Moscow system is the most powerful in the world. It exceeds in output such very large systems in the United States as the Niagara-Hudson and New York Edison (5 billion kw-h) and the Pacific (4 billion kw-h).

The *Moscow power system* equals in capacity all the stations of prewar Russia, and gives three times as much electric power as all the stations of Russia in 1913. It includes such large electric power stations as Kashira, Shatura, Stalinogorsk, Smidovich, Stalinsk TETs[7] No. 11, and the Skhodnya and Ivankovo hydroelectric stations.

The *Leningrad power system* includes the first and second Leningrad GES,[8] the Dubrovka, "Krasny Oktyabr," and the Volkhov, Svir, and Neva hydroelectric stations.

The *Gorky-Ivanovo power system* includes the Gorky GES, Ivanovo TETs, and Ivanovo GES.

The *Dnepr power system* embraces the Dnepr hydroelectric station [Dneproges], Dneprodzerzhinsk, Krivoy Rog, and a number of others.

The *Donets power system* embraces all the stations of the Donbas: Zuyevka, Shterovka, and Severo-Donetskaya. The Kurakhovka station is under construction [Fig. 20].

The *Baku power system,* comprising the power stations of Baku and the oil enterprises, includes the "Kraznaya Zvezda" and Krasin stations [in Baku]. The large Sumgait station is under construction [Fig. 20].

The *Ural power system,* comprising all the main stations of Sverdlovsk, Perm [Molotov], and Chelyabinsk oblasts from Solikamsk [or Berezniki] to Magnitogorsk, includes the Magnitogorsk, Chelyabinsk, Sredne-Uralsk (near Sverdlovsk), Nizhny Tagil, Kizel, Berezniki, and other stations.

The *Kuzbas power system* includes the Kemerovo, Stalinsk, and a number of other stations.

The Moscow, Leningrad, Dnepr, Donets, and Ural power systems, separately, far exceed the power output of such large power networks of Germany as the Rheinisch-Westfälisches Elektrizitätswerk, which produces 2.1 billion kw-h; the Vereinigte Elektrizitätswerke Westfalen, which produces 1.8 billion kw-h; and the Bewag (Berlin), which produces 1.3 billion billion kw-h.

In addition to the very large power systems, the USSR has many new regions and industrial centers where regional stations operate as a unified high-voltage network for each region.

The largest of these are the Azov and Black Sea, the Kharkov, the Stalingrad, the Kiev, the Ordzhonikidze [Dzaudzhikau] (North Osetia and the Chechen-Ingush ASSR) [Gizeldon and Grozny], and the Odessa systems. Large power systems have been created also in the Georgian SSR, the Armenian SSR, and the Uzbek

[7] [TETs = Teploelektricheskytsentral, a central heat and electric power station.]

[8] [GES = Gosudarstvennaya Elektricheskaya Stantsiya (State Electric Station) Bewag = Berliner Elektrizitätswerke A.G.]

SSR. There is also output of electric power on a large scale in Voronezh, Saratov, Kuibyshev, Novosibirsk, Bryansk, and Kazan. An entire group of stations of the regional type has been built to meet the needs of the Far East.

Many small and medium electric power stations supply power and light to the most remote regions of the Soviet Union, formerly totally undeveloped.

Electrification of the USSR Under the Third Five-Year Plan

However, notwithstanding the rapid growth of electric power output, the development of the Soviet national economy and the growth in techniques of production have made such demands on the electrical industry that it has not been able, of late, to maintain an adequate supply.

The Third Five-Year Plan provides for the further rapid development of the electrical industry and the elimination of the lag.

To accomplish this, the Third Five-Year Plan allows an increase of 110% in the capacity of all electric power stations, from 8.1 million kw. in 1937 to 17.2 million kw. in 1942, whereas the total increase in industrial output under the Plan will be only 92%. Such a growth in the capacity of electric power stations will enable the demands of the national economy for electric power to be satisfied and will create reserves of 10 to 15% in the power systems of the USSR.

The Third Five-Year Plan provides for the construction of 102 regional thermal electric plants and an even greater number of industrial and municipal stations. In the construction and distribution of the stations special attention must be given to stations using local types of fuel and to the struggle against overlarge electric power stations. "In the construction of thermal electric stations"—reads the decision of the 18th Party Congress—"emphasis is on small and medium electric power stations of 25,000 kw. and smaller. The promotion of large electric power stations at the expense of small and medium ones is censured as wrong and harmful to the national economy." [9]

The realization of this decision to construct small and medium electric power stations will go far toward achieving even more uni-

[9] *Resolutions of the 18th Congress of the Communist Party of the Soviet Union*, p. 18.

formity in the distribution of the nation's productive forces. Among the many thermal electric stations scheduled for construction and commencement of operations under the Third Five-Year Plan [Fig. 20, p. 143] are the following: Kurakhovka [Ku], Nesvetavevsk, several TETs stations in Moscow and Leningrad, Chelyabinsk TETs, Sumgait, Komsomolsk, Kiev, Karaganda, Nikolayev, Kirov-Cheptsa, Syzran, Orsk, and Krasnodar. Still another TETs, operating on peat, is being built in Ivanovo for the textile industry.

The Third Five-Year Plan gives particular emphasis to the construction of water-power stations. The greatest installation in the world is under way—two Kuibyshev water-power stations with a combined capacity of 3.4 million kw., which is equal to the total capacity of six Dneproges plants. When completed, the Kuibyshev hydroelectric unit will produce up to 15 billion kw-h of electric power [each year], or seven times as much as all the stations of prerevolutionary Russia. The Kuibyshev project in addition to the output of huge amounts of electric power will also solve the problem of irrigating the arid lands of the Trans-Volga, and will alter radically the conditions of navigation along the Volga.

The Third Five-Year Plan will see the completion of construction and the commencement of operations of the Uglich, Rybinsk, Chirchik No. 2, Kanaker, Svir No. 2, Khrami, Niva No. 3, Sukhumi, and a number of other hydroelectric power stations [Fig. 20].

Construction of the following new hydroelectric stations is under way: Kaluga on the Oka River, which will be a part of the Moscow power system; Verkhnekama [Upper Kama] in Perm [Molotov] Oblast, in order to provide power in that oblast, and partly in order to transmit power to the regions of the northern Urals. The Mingechaur hydro station, to be constructed in the Azerbaidzhan SSR, will supply the industry of Baku with electric power and at the same time irrigate hundreds of thousands of hectares of land under cotton cultivation. The Ust-Kamenogorsk station in the Altay will furnish electric power to the Soviet Union's largest center of polymetallic industry. The Gyumush station on the Sevan-Zanga cascade in the Armenian SSR will supply the growing chemical, nonferrous, and other industries of Armenia. The construction of small local hydroelectric power stations is being broadly developed in all regions, especially in the region of the Urals—on the Tura, Ufa, Chusovaya,

Belaya, Miass, and other rivers—and also on the Severny (Northern) Donets [Fig. 6, p. 32].

The construction of small power stations and wind-driven installations in kolkhozes, sovkhozes, and machine tractor stations to meet domestic and production needs is under way on a large scale.

Throughout the Third Five-Year Plan the grid interconnection of electric power stations and the creation of power systems continues. The linking of the Moscow, Ivanovo, Gorky, and Yaroslavl systems into a single power system of the Central Industrial Region will be completed. The Dnepr, Donets, and Rostov systems are also being joined into one unified power system. The Urals, the Kuzbas, the Trans-Caucasus, and other regions are expanding their power systems significantly. In connection with the construction of the Kuibyshev hydroelectric unit, the groundwork will be laid for the creation of a single power system, uniting the electric power stations of the Moscow, Ural, and Volga River systems.

The electrification of the USSR according to the program of the Third Five-Year Plan, will accomplish three main purposes. First, it will furnish all regions with a power base for the rapid development of productive forces. Secondly, it will guarantee a sharp increase in the proportion of electric power produced from local types of fuel and from water power, thus decreasing the present unnecessarily long and inefficient fuel hauls by railroad. And, thirdly, it will provide for all regions and systems the necessary reserves of electric power which will guarantee uninterrupted work for the consumers.

SECTION 3. DISTRIBUTION OF FERROUS METALLURGY

Level and Rate of Development of Ferrous Metallurgy in the USSR

The development of ferrous metallurgy in many respects determines the growth of all industry and of the national economy. The industrialization of the country and the technical reconstruction of all branches of the national economy demanded an extensive development of ferrous metallurgy, since without metal, machine building, the construction of factories, plants, railroads, towns, etc., would be impossible. Under the Stalin Five-Year Plans ferrous metallurgy was greatly developed in the USSR. The output of pig iron reached 14.5 million tons in 1937, compared with 4.2 million tons in 1913. In this period, production of steel increased from 4.2 million tons to 17.7 million tons. But even now the USSR lags noticeably behind the most advanced capitalist countries in per capita output of pig iron. The United States produces 3.4 times as much, Germany 2.7 times as much, and England 2.1 times as much.

The production of quality metal was practically untouched in Tsarist Russia; but under the Soviets the development of a powerful machine-building industry required the establishment of quality metal production. Output of high-grade rolled products grew from 70 thousand tons in 1927–1928 to 2,508 thousand tons in 1937, and is expected to reach 5 million tons by 1942. The output of all rolled products in the period from 1927–1928 to 1942 increased by approximately sixfold, as compared with output of quality rolled products, which during the same period increased seventyfold. In other words, during this period a new branch of ferrous metallurgy —quality metallurgy—had been created.

This development was accompanied by geographic changes in the location of ferrous metallurgy and by the creation of new metallurgical bases, chiefly in the eastern part of the USSR.

The geographic distribution of ferrous metallurgy underwent a number of changes even in prerevolutionary Russia. Metallurgy before Peter the Great—devoted to casting cannon, manufacturing gun barrels, nails, scythes, sickles, locks, etc.—was developed chiefly near the heart of the Moscow state. The largest plants were located near Tula, Kashira, Serpukhov, south of Moscow, and near Lipetsk. [Nos. 9, 2, and 6 in Fig. 19, p. 114]. They operated on local ores—chiefly from Dedilovo and Lipetsk. Another region, far less important than the Moscow region, was on Lake Onega, using Onega ores and also supplying the Moscow center.

The geographic distribution of Russia's ferrous metallurgy shifted abruptly during Peter's time and the principal producing districts were in the Urals until the second half of the nineteenth century. The most important reasons for this geographic transfer were the discovery in the Urals of large beds of high-quality iron ore, the presence of huge wooded areas, and an abundance of rapid streams. All these factors were unusually significant in view of the fact that at that time the only type of metallurgy was based on charcoal, while falling water was the chief source of power. In all these respects the Urals had enormous advantages over the older center south of Moscow.

In the last quarter of the nineteenth century, Russian metallurgy underwent rapid development because of the enormous increase in the demand for metal. The increased demand was the result of the large-scale railroad construction, of the conversion of metallurgy to mineral smelting, of the proximity of Krivoy Rog iron ores to Donets coal, and of the great influx of foreign capital. Consequently a new southern region, the present Ukrainian SSR, became the center of Russian ferrous metallurgy. The output of pig iron in Russia in 1885 was 463 thousand tons, of which 78% came from the Urals and the East, 13.4% from the Center, and 8.6% from the South. In 1913, of the total of 4.2 million tons smelted, only 21.5% came from the Urals and East and about 5% from the Center, while the South, assuming the leading role, produced 73.6%.

As a result of the Stalin Five-Year Plans, in 1937 almost as much pig iron (4.1 million tons) was produced in the East of the Soviet Union as in all Russia before the Revolution [Table 24], while in rolled products the output was even greater than the entire output of prerevolutionary Russia. Metallurgy in the Center also increased, since its powerful machine-building industry created a great demand for metal. While there was an over-all increase in pig-iron output in all regions, the relative importance of different regions changed noticeably.

TABLE 24. SMELTING OF PIG IRON [BY REGIONS, 1913 AND 1937]

Regions	1913 Output (in thousand tons)	1913 %	1937 Output (in thousand tons)	1937 %
South	3,104.9	73.6	9,215.6	63.6
East	901.7	21.5	4,104.5	28.3
Center	209.5	4.9	1,167.3	8.1
Total	4,216.1	100.0	14,487.4	100.0

Conditions for the Location of Ferrous Metallurgy in the USSR

The geographic location of ferrous metallurgy requires, in addition to general favorable conditions, peculiar technical and economic characteristics, which must be considered in the selection of sites for new enterprises. The location of sources of ore deposits and fuel is very important.

Reserves of iron ore in the USSR are extremely large. Compared with the capitalist countries, the total geologic reserves of iron ore in the USSR are characterized by the following figures (see Table 25).

TABLE 25. WORLD RESERVES OF IRON ORE [BY COUNTRY IN 1910 AND 1938 (INCLUDING LOW-GRADE ORE)]

COUNTRIES	1910		1938	
	Million tons	%	Million tons	%
Russia	1,648	1.13	—	—
USSR	—	—	267,305	53.44
United States	73,363	50.34	94,324	18.84
England	39,000	26.75	12,168	2.43
France	3,300[a]	2.26	11,790	2.36
Germany	3,608	2.47	1,548	0.30
Japan	55	0.03	77	0.01
Brazil	5,710	3.91	15,400	3.08
Other countries	19,100	13.11	97,781	19.54
World	145,784	100.00	500,393	100.00

[a] [The figure for France is 3,800 in the original but 3,300 matches the percentage given for France and make the country figures add up to the world total given.]

Table 25 also includes reserves of poor ores, in particular iron-bearing quartzites, to the extent to which their industrial value has been proved experimentally, and in a number of cases they have been considered economically very profitable. Known reserves or rich ores alone in the USSR exceed 11 billion tons and comprise 14% of world reserves, being second only to those in the United States [Table 26].

Iron ores are found in many regions of the Soviet Union.

The data cited indicate that the largest reserves of iron ore are found in the Ukraine, the Crimea, the Urals, Siberia, and the Far East. Ferruginous quartzite reserves are particularly large in Kursk Oblast, with 203.7 billion tons in the region of the Kursk Magnetic Anomaly (KMA), and in the region of the Ukrainian SSR, with

TABLE 26. REGIONS CONTAINING BEDS OF [RICH] IRON ORE [a]

[See Fig. 7 for location and boundaries of regions and Fig. 18 for location of iron-ore deposits.]

Regions	Million Tons	% of Total USSR Reserves
First coal and metallurgical base of the USSR	4,176	36.5
Including: Ukrainian SSR	1,454	12.7
Crimean ASSR	2,722	23.8
Second coal and metallurgical base of the USSR	2,516	22.0
Including: Urals	2,371	20.7
Western Siberia	145	1.3
Eastern Siberia and the Far East	1,153	10.0
Including: Eastern Siberia	966	8.4
Far East	187	1.6
Other regions	3,610	31.5
Including: West and European North	1,597	13.9
Industrial Center and Chernozem Center	1,266	11.0
Volga Region and North Caucasus	327	2.9
Azerbaidzhan SSR	193	1.7
Kazakh SSR	171	1.5
Others	56	0.5
Total	11,455	100.0

[a] The data cited here are given according to large regions; more detailed characteristics of the reserves according to individual oblasts and deposits are given in the regional part of the course [Vol. II, a separate work].

51.3 billion tons in the region of Krivoy Rog [Fig. 18, facing p. 89].

Serving as technological fuel for ferrous metallurgy in the USSR are the following: 1) for charcoal smelting—charcoal produced by incomplete combustion or dry distillation of wood—the heat-giving capacity of charcoal is twice as great as that of wood and reaches 7,000 calories and higher; 2) for coal smelting—coke extracted from coking coals by heating them to a high temperature out of contact with air—around 1.3 to 1.4 tons of coal are needed to produce 1 ton of coke, and the heat-giving capacity of coke is 7,000 to 7,500 calories.

Charcoal metallurgy plants, since they use wood on a large scale (the charcoal extracted is equal to 20 to 24% of the weight of the air-dried logs used), are located where deposits of iron ore are close to large wooded areas. In the USSR the most important region of charcoal metallurgy is the Urals. Charcoal metal accounts for about 7% of all the pig iron produced in the USSR.

Deposits of fuel for coal metallurgy—coking coal—are extremely large in the USSR. The majority of the important coal regions of the Soviet Union supply coking coal [Fig. 29, p. 212]. Thus, in the Donets Basin, coal suitable for coking is about one-fourth of all the coal. In the Kuznetsk Basin, of the total reserves of coal found to a depth of 500 meters, about 50% may be used for coking. Kuznetsk coal is particularly good because of its low sulphur content (0.5 to 0.6%), whereas Donets coke has a much higher sulphur content (1.8 to 2.0%). In the Karaganda Coal Basin many beds yield coking coal.

Before the Revolution, ferrous metallurgy (coal metallurgy) in Russia as in Western Europe was located chiefly in regions of coal, rather than of ore. During the years of Soviet rule a number of ferrous metallurgy plants have been built in regions where iron ore is mined. As the amount of coal required averages 25 to 33% less than the amount of iron ore, the cost of transporting raw material is lower if the plant is built near the iron ore than if it is located in the coal region. In cases where the iron ore and coal regions are far from one another, it is to the national economic interest to build plants near both the coal and iron-ore regions, equalizing railroad transportation in both directions. This involves the delivery of coal and ore according to the so-called "principle of the pendulum." Such a solution of the problem is especially expedient in the USSR because it provides for more uniform distribution of productive forces.

Another characteristic feature of the present-day distribution of ferrous metallurgy in the USSR, as distinguished from the prerevolutionary distribution, is the fact that at present approximately three-fourths of the coke produced is made at metallurgical plants and only one-fourth is produced at mines, whereas before the war coking took place chiefly at the mines and to a lesser extent at metallurgical plants. This change was due to the fact that territorial juxtaposition of coking with ferrous metallurgy makes it possible to utilize the heat of blast-furnace gas for coking, because in a blast furnace the temperature reaches 1,750° C., and coke is produced at a temperature of 750 to 1,050° C. On the other hand, coke gas is now generally used as a raw material in producing various chemical products, such as ammonia, ammonium sulphate, benzol, and naphthalene. Thus, a large metallurgical plant constitutes a large combine in which metallurgy, coking, and various chemical industries are carried on together.

In selecting the site for a metallurgical plant another essential condition is the presence of *fluxes*, which are added to the blast-furnace charge for the best smelting. Limestone is the main type of flux. It is used in making pig iron in a blast furnace and in making steel in an open-hearth furnace. In blast-furnace production, depending on the quality of the ores, the fuel, and the fluxes themselves, the amount of fluxes needed per ton of pig iron varies from 0.5 to 1.0 ton. Because such a large quantity of fluxes is consumed, their source generally must be near the metallurgical plant. Limestones are generally dispersed widely enough throughout the country, but limestones of the quality needed for metallurgy (not containing silicic acid or admixtures of clay, or containing them only in small quantity) are far from universally present. Thus, the presence of large deposits of limestones of the necessary quality may, in many cases, be an essential factor in determining the location of a metallurgical plant.

Finally, in selecting the site of a metallurgical plant, *water supply* is an essential factor, for even where circulating water is used, 15 tons of fresh water are required for each ton of pig iron. The enormous water requirements may be illustrated by the fact that the requirement of circulating water for the Stalin Magnitogorsk Metallurgical Combine exceeds by several times the capacity of the Leningrad water supply system. It is perfectly clear, therefore, that wherever a metallurgical plant is built, there must be large natural or artificial reservoirs close to it and at approximately the same elevation so that there need not be any great expense in pumping.

The problems of socialist distribution of productive forces and the particular conditions of the geographic location of iron ore, coking coal, etc., have necessitated the creation of several metallurgical bases in different regions of the country (see Fig. 32).

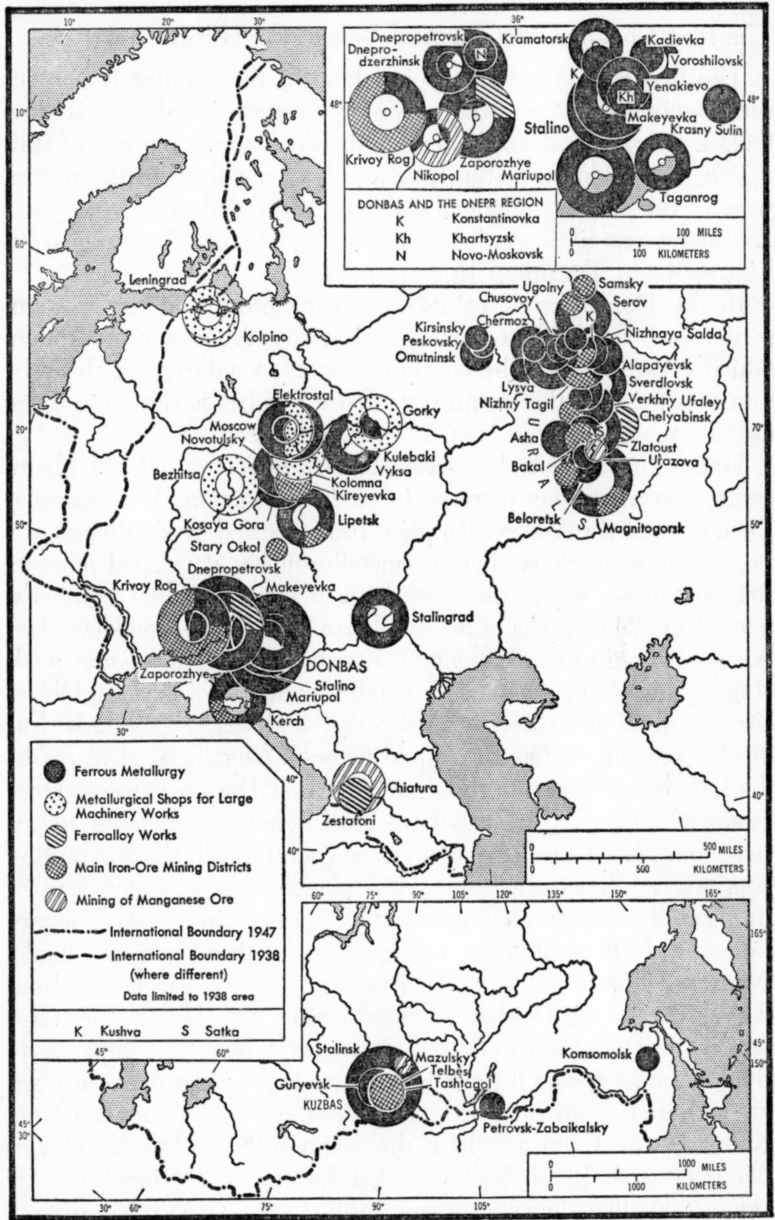

Fig. 32. Ferrous Metallurgy

The First Coal and Metallurgical Base of the USSR

The first coal and metallurgical base of the country is part of the Ukrainian SSR and the adjoining Crimean ASSR and Rostov Oblast. Before the Revolution more than half of the pig iron of this region was produced in the Donbas, about one-third in the region west of the Donbas [along the Dnepr River and at Krivoy Rog], and about one-sixth south of the Donbas [in the Azov region at Mariupol and Taganrog] [Fig. 32 inset].

In the Donbas itself plants were concentrated in the western section, where the best coking coal is found. Another condition which contributed to the concentration of metallurgy in this section was the fact that southwest of the Donbas is the large Yelenovka limestone deposit [Fig. 27D, facing p. 200].

Under the Soviets, large-scale reconstruction of all old plants assures an enormous increase in their production. For example, the output of the Makeyevka plant has increased by six times since prerevolutionary times. Ferrous metallurgy has developed most in Stalino Oblast, where there are large plants in Stalino (formerly Yuzovka), Makeyevka, Ordzhonikidze (formerly Yenakievo [recently restored to its old name]), Konstantinovka, and Kramatorsk [Fig. 32 inset]. The centers of metallurgy of Voroshilovgrad Oblast are Voroshilovsk (formerly Alchevsk), and Sergo (formerly Kadievka [recently restored to its old name]). Metallurgical plants in the Dnepr region and in the Azov group—at Dnepropetrovsk, Dneprodzerzhinsk, Kerch, etc.—have undergone considerable reconstruction. New large-scale plants have been built in the Krivoy Rog area and at Zaporozhye. The new plants have promoted a more uniform distribution of ferrous metallurgy than in prerevolutionary times and have assisted also in the rationalization of railroad hauls. Formerly, a large number of railroad cars, having carried ore from Krivoy Rog to the Donbas, returned empty. In addition, the water supply in Dnepropetrovsk and Zaporozhye oblasts is superior to that in the Donbas. Of great importance is the large Azovstal plant at Mariupol, built on the basis of iron ore to be supplied from Kerch in the Crimea, where the Kamysh-Burunsky Combine is being erected. In an agglomeration factory at Mariupol the extracted dustlike, low-percentage (36%) ore is subjected to concentration and sintering, and at the same time vanadium is extracted. The Azovstal plant, representing a great step forward in the creation of a more uniform distribution of ferrous metallurgy within the first coal and metallurgical base, will be finished by the end of the Third Five-Year Plan. Since it uses Kerch ore and Donets coal, its site was selected at Mariupol, midway between its sources of raw material and fuel.

Development of Ferrous Metallurgy in the Eastern Regions

The most important metallurgical centers in the eastern regions of the Soviet Union are in the Urals, Siberia, and the Far East. In the past, metallurgical plants were located chiefly in the Central Urals, where deposits of iron ore and large forested areas are in close proximity. Before the Revolution, the Urals had an exclusively charcoal metallurgy; the plants were small and very backward. Small plants were also operating in Siberia—at Guryevsk, and at Petrovsk-Zabaikalsky [Fig. 32].

The need to develop ferrous metallurgy in the eastern part of the Soviet Union became apparent shortly after the Great October Socialist Revolution. However, this development was long impeded by saboteurs, in particular by a group in the Ukraine, agents of foreign capitalists who had controlled Ukrainian metallurgy before the Revolution and who expected to regain "their" factories at the points of interventionists' bayonets. Naturally they preferred that the Soviet Union should expand these Ukrainian plants rather than build new plants in other regions. But the plans of the saboteurs were frustrated. On May 15, 1930, a decision of the Central Committee of the Congress of the Communist Party of the Soviet Union was published concerning Uralmet, and soon after that a decision of the 16th Party Congress concerning the Ural-Kuznetsk Combine. The development of ferrous metallurgy in the East proceeded so rapidly that as early as the 17th Congress of the Communist Party of the Soviet Union, Comrade Stalin said: "The foundations of the Ural-Kuznetsk Combine have been laid in the linking of Kuznetsk coking coal with Ural iron ore. We may therefore consider that the new metallurgical base in the East is no longer a dream, but a reality." [10]

The creation of the Ural-Kuznetsk Combine provided for the construction of twin plants, first the Magnitogorsk plant in the

[10] Stalin, *Questions of Leninism*, p. 439.

Urals, and second, the Stalinsk plant in the Kuzbas. Kuznetsk coal is sent by railroad to the Urals, to Magnitogorsk, and ore is sent from Magnitogorsk in the opposite direction.

However, in the future, Magnitogorsk will be supplied increasingly with Karaganda coal, while the metallurgy of Siberia will depend on its own iron ore.

The creation of the Ural-Kuznetsk Combine demanded large-scale railroad construction. A railroad was laid to Magnitogorsk, the railroad in the Kuzbas was straightened, and double tracks were laid on the entire line between the Kuzbas and the Urals.

As a result of this grandiose industrial and transport construction under the Stalin Five-Year Plans, powerful metallurgical bases have been created in the East, in the Urals and in Western Siberia.

Ferrous metallurgy in the Urals. Chelyabinsk Oblast is particularly important in the Urals in the production of pig iron, supplying approximately two-thirds of all the pig iron produced there. Sverdlovsk Oblast supplies approximately one-fourth of the Ural pig iron. In 1937 Perm [Molotov] Oblast supplied 5.7% and the Bashkir ASSR, 3.2% of the Ural pig iron. The dominant role of Chelyabinsk Oblast is due entirely to the Magnitogorsk Metallurgical Combine—that foundation of the Ural-Kuznetsk Combine which has assured the economic advancement of the southern Urals, which before the Revolution were almost wholly undeveloped.

The Magnitogorsk plant is located next to the largest Ural deposit of iron ore—Magnitnaya [Magnetic] Mountain, with reserves of 485 million tons of high-quality iron ore (magnetite with an iron content of 62%, sulphur content of 0.1 to 0.4%, and phosphorus content of 0.035 to 0.04%) [Fig. 18, facing p. 89]. The deep Ural River, on the left bank of which the Magnitogorsk Combine is located, supplies water to the plant. The plant is also guaranteed a supply of limestone, from a deposit 8 km. from the plant. There is manganese in the Bashkir ASSR, approximately 50 km. from Magnitogorsk.

A new large metallurgical plant in the Urals, under construction in Nizhny Tagil, is to be completed under the Third Five-Year Plan. In addition, the Urals have a number of charcoal metallurgical plants which underwent large-scale reconstruction after the October Revolution (see Fig. 33). The largest of the charcoal

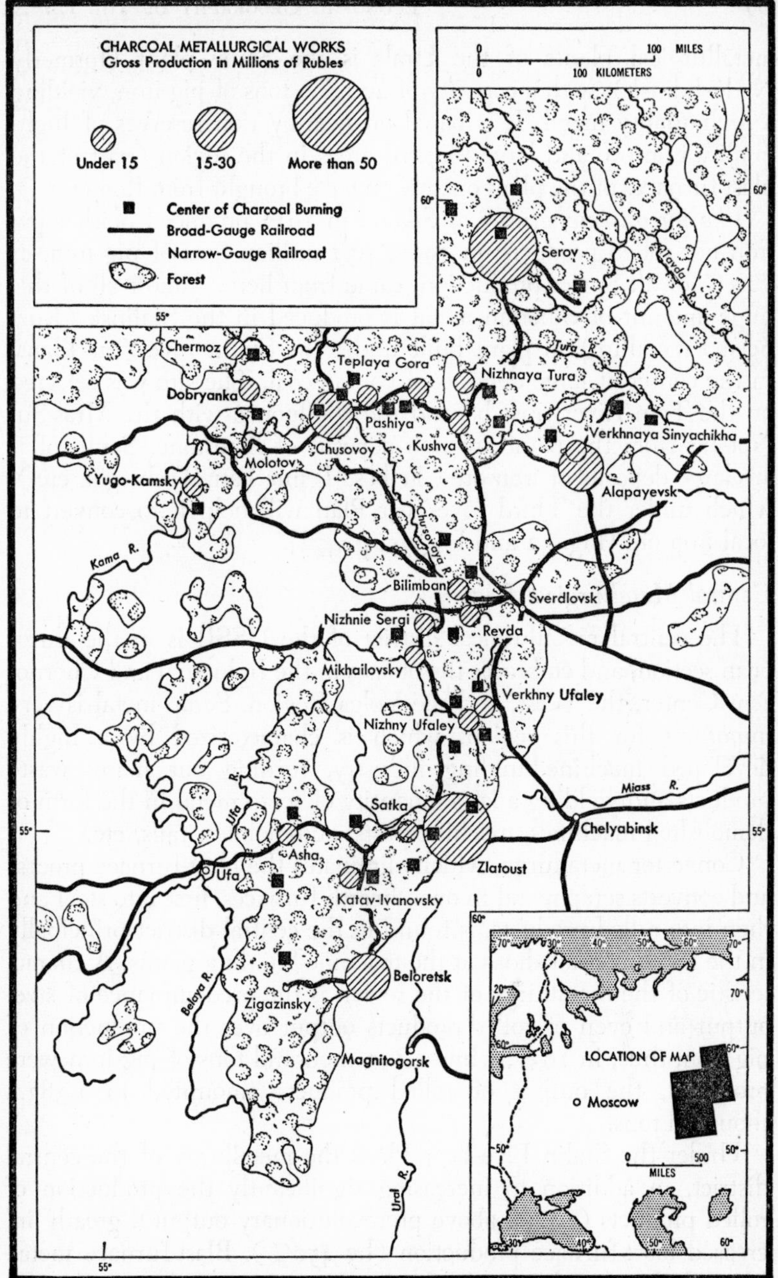

FIG. 33. Charcoal Metallurgy of the Urals

metallurgical plants of the Urals is the Serov plant (formerly Nadezhdinsk), with a capacity of 400,000 tons of pig iron, yielding a high-quality metal. It is based on near-by rich reserves of high-quality iron ore and large forested areas in the region (part of the blast furnaces of the plant operate on coke brought from Kemerovo).

The ferrous metallurgy of Siberia in 1913 produced neither pig iron nor rolled products; in 1937, 1.51 million tons of pig iron, or 10.3% of all Soviet production, came from here. Almost all of this huge amount of Siberian metal is produced in the Stalinsk (Kuznetsk) metallurgical plant built under the Stalin Five-Year Plans, in the center of large deposits of coking coal. The site was selected on the Tom River, just beyond the confluence with the Mras-Su. Not far from the plant are rich deposits of limestone. South of it are large deposits of iron ore (Telbes, Temir-Tau, Tashtagol, etc.), which under the Third Five-Year Plan will help it to convert to local iron ore [Fig. 32 and Fig. 75, p. 472].

Central Metallurgical Region

The central metallurgical district of the USSR is in the European section, and embraces the oblasts in the Industrial and Chernozem Center, the West, and the Volga Region. Scrap metal is very important for this region, which is characterized by a highly developed machine-building industry, turning out many waste products and yielding a large quantity of scrap metal in the form of demolished machines, machine parts, automobiles, rails, etc.

Converter metallurgy, which eliminates the blast-furnace process and converts scrap metal in open-hearth furnaces, first into steel and then into rolled products, is found in the central district principally in the metallurgical shops at the machine-building plants. A characteristic of the metallurgy of the region is the predominance of steel output and even of rolled-products output over the production of pig iron; thus, in 1937, while 1,145 thousand tons of pig iron were produced, the output of rolled products amounted to 1,383.4 thousand tons.

Under the Stalin Five-Year Plans the metallurgy of the central district, in addition to increasing significantly the production of rolled products (240% above prerevolutionary output), greatly increased blast-furnace production (by 450%). Blast-furnace metallurgical plants in the central district are concentrated at two points:

at Tula (the reconstructed Kosaya Gora plant and the newly built Novotulsky plant), and at Lipetsk (the reconstructed "Svobodny Sokol" plant and the newly built Novolipetsky plant). These plants for the most part turn out foundry cast iron. The specialization of the blast-furnace plants of the central district results, first, from the demands of the surrounding oblasts for foundry cast iron (for automobile motors, pipes, radiators, etc.) and, secondly, from the properties of the raw material (containing both silica and aluminum oxide). Metallurgical shops in machine-building plants may be found chiefly at Leningrad, Moscow, Kolomna, Gorky, Ordzhonikidzegrad [Bezhitsa], and Stalingrad [Fig. 32].

Quality Metallurgy

Before the October Socialist Revolution, high-grade steel was produced in small quantities at the Putilov [in Leningrad], Izhorsk, Zlatoust, and several other plants. The development of quality metallurgy in the USSR has proceeded along two lines: first, by the conversion of old plants which manufactured commercial grades to the production of high-grade rolled products and, secondly, by the construction of new plants. The old Ural plants, which operated on charcoal and produced only commercial-grade iron, now produce the more appropriate brands of high-grade metal. Of great importance in the production of high-grade metal is *electric steel,* of which about a million tons were smelted in the USSR in 1937. The production of electric steel requires large quantities of electric power: in smelting one ton of steel using a cold (hard) blast-furnace charge, 700 to 900 kw-h of electric power are required; using a liquid charge (duplex process) the power required amounts to 200 to 300 kw-h. Consequently, the largest electric steel plants are near large sources of electric power. Such plants are the Elektrostal plant, near the largest regional electric power station in the country using peat, the Klasson station in Moscow Oblast, near Noginsk; and the Zaporozhstal plant [at Zaporozhye], which is part of the Dnepr Combine, located near the largest hydroelectric station in the USSR—the Dneproges [Figs. 31 and 32].

Ferroalloys, used to make high-grade steels, are of increasing importance. One of the most important is ferromanganese, an alloy of iron and manganese (75 to 82% manganese), which gives steel an extreme hardness. The production of one ton of ferromanganese requires two tons of manganese ore, 0.25 tons of iron ore, and 3,500 to 4,000 kw-h of electric power, as well as coke or coal, limestone, fluorspar, etc. Consequently, ferromanganese production in the USSR has developed near the chief manganese deposits where a large quantity of cheap electric power is also available. The largest beds of manganese in the Union are at Nikopol in the Ukrainian SSR (reserves of 522 million tons, or 66% of the nation's supply), and at Chiatura in the Georgian SSR (reserves of 175 million tons) [Fig. 32]. However, the Chiatura deposit has been more thoroughly investigated, and its reserves in A and B categories [i.e. proved and probable reserves] exceed the reserves of the Nikopol deposit. In addition, the Chiatura ores have a higher manganese content than the Nikopol ores (52% as compared with 35 to 48% manganese). In the vicinity of these deposits large-scale production of ferromanganese has been established: at Zestafoni in the Georgian SSR, within 35 to 40 km. of the large Rion hydroelectric station [Rionges]; and at Zaporozhye, included in the Dnepr Combine, 70 km. from the Nikopol manganese deposit. In Zaporozhye, in addition, ferrosilicon and a number of other alloys are produced.

The largest center producing ferroalloys is the Chelyabinsk plant.

The ferrosilicon manufactured in this plant is an alloy of iron and silicon which is important in obtaining silicon steel. Silicon steel possesses magnetic and many other properties. To produce ferrosilicon, along with the initial raw material which is quartz (from 1.3 to 3 tons, depending on the silicon content of the ferrosilicon being manufactured), a large amount of electric power is needed (from 6,000 to 17,000 kw-h). Of great importance is the production of ferrochrome, which is needed to obtain acid- and heat-resisting steels for the building of airplanes and automobiles. Along with chromite and a number of other materials (charcoal, quartz, lime, etc.), 4,500 to 7,000 kw-h of electric power are needed for one ton of ferrochrome, depending on the variety of ferrochrome being produced. The ferrotungsten manufactured is used to prepare high-speed steels and a number of other special types of steel. In addition to the concentrate of tungsten ores, coke, lime, etc., about 6,000 kw-h of power are expended to produce one ton of ferrotungsten.

The creation of such a large specialized plant for producing various types of ferroalloys at Chelyabinsk is due, first, to the fact that near by, in Chelyabinsk Oblast, there are deposits of rare metals—tungsten, chromium, etc. Secondly, it is very essential that Chelyabinsk be in a region of well developed metallurgy and machine-building, which require large quantities of ferroalloys. Finally, Chelyabinsk is centrally located in relation to the other metallurgical regions of the Union and is at some distance from the borders. To meet the electric power requirements of the ferroalloy plant, it has a considerable deposit of coal for power (Chelyabinsk Basin), on the basis of which large electric power stations have been built already and more will be built in the future.

Ferrous Metallurgy Under the Third Five-Year Plan

Under the Third Five-Year Plan ferrous metallurgy will develop further. Ten large metallurgical plants are being completed, and the construction of a number of new plants is being begun. In all, the Third Five-Year Plan provides for building twenty blast furnaces, as well as the restoration of three charcoal blast furnaces in the Urals. A large number of sintering plants will be built for the preparation of ores for smelting. In blast-furnace production, the oxygen blast is being widely introduced. Low-alloy steels, principally those of naturally alloyed pig irons from ores of the Khalilovo and other deposits [Fig. 18, p. 89], are produced so far as possible. The production of cast-iron and steel pipes by centrifugal casting is being developed; at all plants in operation laborious processes are being mechanized and automatic production is being widely introduced.

The utilization of scrap metal plays an increasingly large role. As a result, the output of steel is increasing even more than that of pig iron. The following data [in Table 27] testify to this:

TABLE 27. [PRODUCTION OF PIG IRON, STEEL, AND ROLLED PRODUCTS, 1937, AND PLANNED PRODUCTION, 1942]

PRODUCTS	OUTPUT (in millions of tons)		1942 INDEX (1937 = 100)
	1937	1942	
Pig iron	14.5	22.0	152
Steel	17.7	28.0	158
Rolled products, including pipes and forgings from ingots	13.0	21.0	162

Output of rolled products, especially of high-grade rolled products, is growing rapidly. A resolution of the 18th Party Congress, according to a report by Comrade Molotov, states: "The Third Five-Year Plan is the Five-Year Plan of specialized steels. The Congress 1) decrees an increase of 100% in the output of high-grade rolled products, 2) guarantees a sharp increase in the output of special steels, hard alloys, rust-proof steel, acid- and heat-resisting steels, tool steel, precision steel, transformer steel, and also ferroalloys, and 3) plans to develop widely the production of charcoal cast iron from ores free of sulphur and phosphorus." Under the Third Five-Year Plan the smelting in open-hearth furnaces of ball-bearing and other types of high-quality steels must be mastered and developed.

The Third Five-Year Plan is rapidly developing all the metallurgical regions of the Union. The first coal and metallurgical region is completing the construction of a number of huge plants: the Zaporozhstal [at Zaparozhye], Azovstal [at Mariupol], Krivoy Rog, Novo-Moskovsk sheet-metal, and Nikopol pipe plants [Fig. 32].

In the Urals the construction of the Magnitogorsk Combine, the Nizhny Tagil metallurgical plant, and the Novo-Uralsky pipe plant is being completed; in addition, the construction of new metallurgical plants (using Khalilovo and Bakal ores), and of a plant for manufacturing welded pipes, is under way [Fig. 18, facing p. 89].

In Siberia and the Far East the Petrovsk-Zabaikalsky plant and the Amurstalstroy are being completed. In Eastern Siberia a new metallurgical plant and a pipe-rolling plant are under construction. As a result, the importance of the eastern regions in the total smelting of pig iron will increase from 28% to 35%, and a new metallurgical base, with a complete metallurgical cycle for supplying all the local demands of machine building will be created in the Far East.

In the central regions the construction of a pipe-casting plant will be undertaken; in Tula repair shops are being built. In the region of the Kursk Magnetic Anomaly [Fig. 18, facing p. 89], the construction of mines to supply ore for the ferrous metallurgy of the central district will be undertaken, and at the same time preparatory measures will be taken for the construction of a new metallurgical plant.

The Third Five-Year Plan is laying the foundations for *new metallurgical districts in a number of the Union republics.* Thus, through the utilization of scrap and metal waste products, the construction of small repair plants for local needs in the regions of *Central Asia* and the *Trans-Caucasus* is developing. The industrial survey of the Ata-Su and Karsakpay deposits in Kazakhstan is being completed [Fig. 20, facing p. 143].

Metallurgical plants constructed under the Third Five-Year Plan will assist in the realization of one of the most important goals in the distribution of productive forces—namely, the elimination of inefficient and excessively long hauls. This will be achieved by eliminating harmful specialization of rolling mills, as a result of which the shortage of rolled products of certain shapes in such highly developed metallurgical regions as the South and the Urals has led to cross hauls and excessively long hauls of metals. Now at the chief metallurgical bases of the country all the leading types of metal will be rolled.

In the Urals and in Siberia the extraction of manganese ores will be increased to eliminate the need of importing these ores from the South.

SECTION 4. DISTRIBUTION OF NONFERROUS METALLURGY

The nonferrous metals—copper, zinc, lead, aluminum, nickel, and tin—and their alloys, have acquired tremendous importance in the contemporary world economy. Unlike iron and steel, various types of nonferrous metals have valuable properties in addition to solidity and strength. They have a high resistance to oxidation, high fusibility, electric conductivity, plasticity, and are tooled with relative ease.

The utilization of these properties in various combinations has brought a great increase in the use of nonferrous metals and alloys in electrical engineering, in automobile and airplane building, in precision machine construction, in the chemical industry, in the manufacture of high-grade steel, and in light construction. The application is especially important in those branches of industry connected with the production of armaments.

Nonferrous metals are much rarer in the earth's crust than iron, and their content [in ore deposits] is usually slight.

FIG. 34. Nonferrous Metallurgy

Nonferrous Metallurgy in Prerevolutionary Russia

The development of nonferrous metallurgy in prerevolutionary Russia was at an extremely low level. Copper, zinc, and lead were mined in very small quantities. Prerevolutionary Russia produced no nickel, aluminum, or tin, and was entirely dependent on other countries for them.

Under Peter I, Russia began to produce its own copper as well as its own iron. The copper industry was concentrated entirely in the Urals.

In the middle of the eighteenth century, Russia rapidly developed its copper industry and became one of the world's largest producers. Having satisfied its own relatively modest requirements, it became a large exporter of copper. However, towards the 1880's production declined.

The period of industrial advance in Russia in the 1890's brought another rise in the industry. A new copper region appeared in the Caucasus (Alaverdi and Zangezur [Kafan]) and grew rapidly, producing 3,750 tons of copper in 1900, while the Urals produced only 4,000 tons [Fig. 34]. The new region was in the hands of foreign capital.

The period from 1900 to 1914 was characterized by a widespread encroachment on Russia's nonferrous industry by foreign capital. It intrenched itself not only in the Caucasus, but in the Urals as well.

In 1914 the Urals produced 16.3 thousand tons of copper; the Caucasus, 6.9 thousand; Kazakhstan, 5.1 thousand; and Siberia, 0.6 thousand tons. This was the peak of copper smelting in prerevolutionary Russia. Meanwhile, as a result of military needs, the demand far exceeded the supply, and Russia was forced to import copper from other countries.

The smelting of lead, as of copper, began in Russia in 1704, under Peter I, in the Nerchinsk region (Eastern Siberia) [Fig. 19]. Lead was produced here as a by-product of the smelting of silver. Not until the beginning of the nineteenth century did the Nerchinsk plant specialize in lead. But by the end of that century the reserves of acid lead ores had been exhausted, and smelting ceased. The chief obstacle was the fact that the lead ores were found with an admixture of zinc, and no technique for extracting the zinc had yet been developed.

In the Urals and the Altay lead was also smelted in connection with silver smelting, but in very small quantities.

Lead smelted from the Sadon deposit in the North Caucasus (North Osetia) was the most important. In 1898 a lead plant was built at

Vladikavkaz [Dzaudzhikau], and in 1904 Belgian capitalists erected a zinc plant [Fig. 34].

In 1913, the North Caucasus produced 96% of the lead, and the Urals, 3.6%. Zinc smelting in 1913 was concentrated entirely in the North Caucasus.

In the Far East, in the region of Tetyukhe, mining of polymetallic ores was organized. These were not manufactured into metal but were exported as raw material.

At the time of the Imperialist War [World War I], in spite of the increased demand for nonferrous metals, their output fell sharply.

Soviet Russia inherited from Tsarist Russia a completely ruined nonferrous metallurgy, which had to be created anew. In 1923 only 2,000 tons of copper were smelted, 200 tons of zinc, and 300 tons of lead.

Under the First and Second Stalin Five-Year Plans nonferrous metallurgy really flourished. By the end of the Second Five-Year Plan the smelting of copper had increased by 250% over 1913, and the smelting of zinc and lead had increased dozens of times. Large-scale native production of aluminum, nickel, tin, and rare metals was created. The USSR became one of the leading countries of the world in the production of all types of nonferrous and rare metals. More than 85% of the entire production of nonferrous metallurgy comes from new or radically reconstructed plants. During this period a number of new enterprises have been built and many deposits in new regions have been brought under exploitation.

Copper Industry

The chief centers of the copper industry, as formerly, are the Urals, Kazakhstan, and the Trans-Caucasus, the regions with the richest reserves of copper ore [Table 28].

The principal copper region, smelting 84.2% of the total blister copper, is the Urals. The Kazakh SSR occupies second place, and the Armenian SSR third. This distribution of production does not correspond to the distribution of copper reserves in these regions. Kazakhstan, which has the richest reserves of copper in the Union, does not yet occupy a corresponding position in the production of copper.

TABLE 28. RELATIVE IMPORTANCE OF DIFFERENT REGIONS IN RESERVES OF COPPER AND IN SMELTING OF BLISTER COPPER IN 1937

REGIONS	% OF RESERVES	% OF SMELTING
Urals	15.97	84.2
Sverdlovsk Oblast	8.79	59.2
Chelybinsk Oblast	2.04	17.9
Chkalov Oblast	2.14	—
Bashkir ASSR	3.00	7.1
Kazakh SSR	52.34	9.8
Armenian SSR	9.20	6.0
Uzbek SSR	15.04	—
Krasnoyarsk Kray	4.00	—
Other regions	3.45	—
Total area of the USSR	100.00	100.0

The Third Five-Year Plan has set the task of increasing copper smelting by 180%, in considerable measure by introducing production into Kazakhstan and other new regions.

In the Urals the manufacture of copper is concentrated in Sverdlovsk Oblast at the Krasnouralsk, Kirovgrad, Revda, and Pyshma plants; in Chelyabinsk Oblast, at the Karabash and Kyshtym plants; and in the Bashkir ASSR, at the Baimak [Baimak-Takalykovo] plant [Fig. 34]. The Pyshma and Kyshtym plants carry on electrolytic refining of copper.

A new center for copper smelting, Mednogorsk (near Blyava station), has been built in the Orsk-Khalilovo district of Chkalov Oblast.

In the Kazakh SSR until recently copper smelting was limited to two plants completed under the Soviets—the Karsakpay plant and the Irtysh copper plant, which operates on copper waste products from lead production. Copper smelting will increase considerably as a result of the opening of the Balkhash Copper Combine and the expansion of the Irtysh and Karsakpay plants. Under the Third Five-Year Plan there will be constructed on the basis of Dzhezkazgan copper ores [Fig. 18, facing p. 89] the new Dzhezkazgan Copper Combine, equal to the Balkhash plant in copper smelting. In central Kazakhstan, in the Karaganda region, using power from the Karaganda regional electric power station, a copper electrolysis plant is to be built, capable of refining all the copper from the Balkhash and Dzhezkazgan combines and the Karsakpay plant.

In the Armenian SSR the production of copper is concentrated at two points—Alaverdi and Zangezur. In Zangezur the copper ore is mined at the Kafan deposit. The concentrated copper ore goes for refining to the Alaverdi metallurgical plant. At Alaverdi there are ore mines, a concentration works, and a metallurgical plant which smelts copper both from its own ores and from imported Kafan ore. The Pirdaudan copper-molybdenum deposit in Armenia has great possibilities for development [Fig. 18, facing p. 89].

The Uzbek SSR and the Khakass Autonomous Oblast in Krasnoyarsk Kray have large copper reserves. Under the Third Five-Year Plan a new copper combine will be built in the Uzbek SSR using the Almalyk copper deposit [Fig. 18]. In the Khakass Autonomous Oblast careful prospecting will be conducted preparatory to exploitation of the copper deposits.

The Monchegorsk and Norilsk nickel combines are beginning to smelt copper as a by-product [Fig. 34].

Copper smelting is located at points where copper ore is mined because the copper content of the ore is comparatively small, and it would be senseless to haul gangue for long distances. The elimination of inefficient hauls of copper ore is especially important in the Urals, where the dispersion of ore bases demands a radical improvement in the organization of the ore economy.

In the past, the excessive concentration in the central regions of the chief consumers of copper evoked a corresponding concentration of both the refining of scrap copper and the production of copper semimanufactured goods and copper products. Copper refining is chiefly in the regions of Moscow, Leningrad, Kolchugino, and Kiev [Fig. 34]. In connection with the enormous transfer of all branches of the natural economy into the eastern regions, it is urgent to create in the regions of the Volga, the Urals, and Siberia a number of copper-processing plants capable of supplying the demands of the eastern regions for copper products.

Production of Zinc and Lead

Zinc and lead, as a rule, are found together as secondary minerals in polymetallic ores. Other components of polymetallic ores are gold, silver, copper, and rare metals. Sometimes the primary metals—

zinc and lead—are found to be far less valuable than the secondary minerals. The rare metals and sulphur, for example, have great value. One of the principal problems in the distribution of polymetallic ore industries is to assure, so far as possible, the complete extraction of all the component elements at the point where the ore is mined in order to keep together territorially the enterprises extracting the different elements from these ores.

Geographic separation of the various enterprises inevitably leads to a great loss of valuable metals and to inefficient long hauls of concentrates.

Here, as in the copper industry, the relatively low percentage of metal content in the ores and the inefficiency of hauling gangue over great distances require the location of the polymetallic industry in areas which have the raw material resources. In regions which possess no reserves of polymetallic ores but consume large quantities of zinc and lead, it is more expedient to import the finished metal than to import the concentrates and to organize locally the production of zinc and lead.

Large amounts of fuel and electric power are required in the production of zinc, lead, and other metals. Zinc electrolysis requires especially large amounts of electric power. However, it does not follow that it is necessary to locate zinc and lead plants where fuel extraction and electric power production are already concentrated. Reserves of fuel and even of hydroelectric energy are more uniformly distributed throughout the country than nonferrous metals, and it is generally possible to create separate power bases for the polymetallic industries.

The distribution of the nonferrous metals industry must take into special consideration the interests of national defense and must guarantee the establishment of duplicate plants in the production of various nonferrous metals in different parts of the country.

Zinc and lead production is concentrated in the regions listed on page 262 [Table 29]:

The main regions of the polymetallic industry are the Kazakh SSR (Altay and Chimkent), North Osetia, and the Far East. Zinc is produced also in the Ukraine, and in Chelyabinsk and Novosibirsk oblasts [Fig. 34].

The chief region of the lead-zinc industry is the Kazakh SSR, which has 62.2% of the total deposits of lead in the country,

TABLE 29. RELATIVE IMPORTANCE OF DIFFERENT REGIONS IN RESERVES AND SMELTING OF ZINC AND LEAD IN 1937

Regions	Zinc			Lead	
	% of Reserves	% of Extraction	% of Smelting	% of Reserves	% of Smelting
Kazakh SSR	41.90	42.5	—	62.16	74.0
Including:					
East Kazakhstan Oblast	35.20	30.0	—	42.70	25.0
South Kazakhstan and Alma-Ata Oblasts	6.70	12.5	—	19.46	49.0
North Osetian ASSR	6.12	15.5	36.5	6.26	13.5
Sverdlovsk Oblast	15.47	—	—	—	—
Chelyabinsk Oblast	2.84	17.0	26.0	—	—
Bashkir ASSR	1.37	—	—	—	—
Novosibirsk Oblast	11.70	23.5	21.0	1.70	—
Altay Kray	2.42	—	—	2.77	—
Chita Oblast	7.00	—	—	10.20	—
Far East—Maritime Oblast	4.41	11.5	—	5.54	12.5
Tadzhik SSR	1.36	—	—	5.24	—
Kirgiz SSR	—	—	—	4.28	—
Ukrainian SSR	—	—	16.5	—	—
Other regions	5.41	—	—	1.85	—
Total	100.00	100.00[a]	100.00	100.00	100.00

[a] [Since the total of the several percentages in this column comes to 110.0, one or more of them must be in error.]

and 42% of the zinc deposits. The area richest in polymetallic ores is the Altay mountain district in East Kazakhstan Oblast, which has 42.7% of all deposits of lead in the USSR, and 35.2% of the zinc. The development of this very rich region was retarded in every possible way by the saboteurs. In the Altay there is large-scale mining of zinc and lead ore, as well as 25% of the lead smelting of the country. As yet there is no zinc smelting in the Altay, and zinc concentrates are transported from the Altay to distant centers for further processing. This results in the loss of much metal, and inefficiently long hauls. The chief obstacles to production in the Altay have been lack of direct railroad connection with other regions, particularly with the fuel base in the Kuzbas, and inadequate development of an electric power base. The construction of the Rubtsovsk-Ridder railroad line [Fig. 70, p. 442] now gives this connection; and under the Third Five-Year Plan it is planned to install a large hydroelectric station on the Irtysh, near Ust-Kamenogorsk [Fig. 20], which will guarantee cheap hydroelectric power for Altay industry, in particular for zinc electrolysis. This construction has made it possible under the Third Five-Year Plan to arrange for a large expansion here of both zinc and lead production. The new zinc and lead plants will assure the proper complex utilization on the spot of the local polymetallic ores, and will greatly enhance the role of the Altay in the nonferrous metallurgy of the USSR.

The second important center of the polymetallic industry is the Chimkent lead plant, which operates on ores from the Achisay deposit, in the Kara-Tau (mountains) [Fig. 34]. The ores are insufficient to supply the plant; consequently it will use ores also from the recently opened rich lead deposits of the Tekeli area of Alma-Ata Oblast [Fig. 18, facing p. 89]. In addition, the plant is expected to process polymetallic ores from the Aktyuz and Buurdu deposits, in the Kirgiz SSR.

Another large region of polymetallic industry is the North Osetian ASSR. In the area around the town of Ordzhonikidze [Dzaudzhikau] are a number of lead and zinc enterprises, operating in considerable measure on their own ore base, the Sadon deposit [Fig. 34]. By the beginning of the Third Five-Year Plan, North Osetia was producing 13.5% of the nation's lead and 36.5% of the smelted zinc. However, while producing 36.5% of the nation's smelted zinc, North Osetian mines produced only 15.5% of the output of zinc ore; the remaining raw product is imported from distant regions, in particular from the Altay, which necessitates extremely inefficient long hauls. The chief problem here is the creation of a local raw material base in North Osetia to supply the zinc industry, which has developed on a large scale.

In the Far East, a large center of the polymetallic industry has been created in the region of Tetyukhe. Here, as in the Altay, zinc production has not yet been organized, and the zinc concentrates are exported or are shipped across the entire country as far as the Ukraine. The problem in this region is to produce enough zinc locally to cover the growing needs of the Far East.

In the Ukraine, at Konstantinovka, there is a large zinc plant operating exclusively on zinc concentrates brought from the Far East and the Altay. The serious problem here is the creation of a local raw material base by intensified prospecting in the Donets Nagolny Ridge, where the presence of polymetallic minerals has been noted [X in Fig. 18]. At Chelyabinsk there is a zinc plant operating on waste products of the copper-smelting plants of the Urals and on zinc concentrates from the Altay. In Novosibirsk Oblast the newly erected Belovo zinc plant has its own raw-material base in the Salair polymetallic deposits [Fig. 34].

In addition to these bases, there are reserves of zinc and lead in Trans-Baikalia, Altay Kray, and the Tadzhik SSR (Kara-Mazar) [KM in Fig. 18]. The use of these ores will make possible new bases of polymetallic production in the USSR.

Production of Aluminum

The USSR had no aluminum production before the Revolution. Under the Soviet regime a rich deposit of bauxite was explored in the Tikhvin region of Leningrad Oblast [Fig. 18, facing p. 89]. Using Tikhvin bauxite and electric power from the Volkhov hydroelectric power station, the first Volkhov aluminum plant was created under the First Five-Year Plan, producing the first Soviet aluminum in 1933.

Shortly afterwards, the Dnepr aluminum plant was built [at Zaporozhye], operating on hydroelectric power from the Dneproges and on bauxite from Tikhvin.

By the beginning of 1938, the USSR occupied third place in the world in the production of aluminum, following the United States and Germany.

During the course of the Second Five-Year Plan, in addition to the increase in reserves of Tikhvin bauxite to 5.6 million tons, the reach for new deposits of bauxite was highly successful [Fig. 18, facing p. 89]. In the Urals the "Krasnaya Shapochka" deposit of bauxite, near the town of Serov (Nadezhdinsk), with reserves of 8 million tons was discovered on January 1, 1938; in Chelyabinsk Oblast the Sokolov, Pirogov, and other deposits were discovered, with reserves amounting to 8.5 million tons; in the Bashkir ASSR, the Kukshinsk and other deposits; in the Kazakh SSR, the Akmolinsk and Turgay deposits; in the Kuzbas, the Salair deposit; in Eastern Siberia, the Tatar deposit; and in the Kirgiz SSR, the Maili-Su deposit. The Ural deposits are the largest. Here a new, large base for aluminum production has been built in the Kamensk-

Sinarsk [Kamensk-Uralsky] region of Chelyabinsk Oblast [Fig. 34].

The production of aluminum is one of the industries consuming most power. The production of one ton of aluminum requires up to 20,000 kw-h of electric power, but only two tons of aluminum oxide. Consequently the industry must be located near sources of cheap water power or where cheap fuel is available.

Under the Third Five-Year Plan aluminum plants are to be built in the Kuzbas and in Kandalaksha (Kola Peninsula), and construction of two other plants is to be begun [Fig. 20]. The Kandalaksha plant will operate on a new aluminum raw material—nepheline—derived as a waste product in the processing of Khibin apatite. An important prerequisite for the development of aluminum production is the construction of the Kuibyshev and Kama hydroelectric stations; a considerable part of the cheap water power produced will be used for the production of aluminum. Two other regions of potential importance are the area around the city of Serov, where the rich "Krasnaya Shapochka" bauxite deposits are close to the Bogoslovsk [Ugolny] coal deposit [Fig. 18]; and the Bashkir ASSR, where it is planned to work the rich bauxite deposits, utilizing the hydroelectric power of the Belaya River. The region of the Angara River, with its very rich reserves of hydroelectric power, and the Azerbaidzhan SSR are of potential importance in the distant future. In the latter area the reserves of alunite in the Kirovabad region may be used as raw material, while cheap hydroelectric power can be produced on the Kura River [Fig. 18].

Production of Nickel

Nickel in nature is always found in close conjunction with other metals, such as copper, iron, and cobalt. As separation of nickel from the other metals is a very complicated process, it was known only as an undesirable impurity until the nineteenth century.

There was no nickel production in prerevolutionary Russia. During the years of the First and Second Stalin Five-Year Plans very rich deposits have been explored in various regions of the country. The biggest of them are [Fig. 18]: the copper-nickel deposits in the Monchetundry of the Kola Peninsula; the Ufaley [Verkhny Ufaley], Verkhnenevyansk [Verkhne-Neivinsky, west of Rezh, Fig. 34] and the Rezh deposits in the central Urals; the Orsk deposits [at Khalilovo] in the southern Urals; the Kimpersay deposits in Aktyubinsk Oblast of the Kazakh SSR; and the Norilsk deposits in northern Krasnoyarsk Kray [Fig. 18]. By the beginning of the Second Five-Year Plan, the first Soviet nickel plants in the Urals had been completed. These—the Ufaley and Rezh plants—produced in 1934 the first Soviet nickel.

At present, the construction of several large nickel combines, the Severny (Monchegorsk) on the Kola Peninsula, the Norilsk, and the Orsk, is being completed [Fig. 34]. With the opening of these plants the USSR will step into a leading position in the smelting of nickel.

Rare and Precious Metals

Tin mining was nonexistent in prerevolutionary Russia and was organized first under the Soviets. By the beginning of the Second Five-Year Plan tin had been discovered in the USSR only in Trans-Baikalia, in Chita Oblast (Onon, Khapcheranga, and other deposits [Fig. 18]), where it was mined only on a small scale, completely inadequate to satisfy the country's requirements. Despite the efforts of saboteurs to disrupt the creation in the USSR of a native tin industry, the country made tremendous progress under the Second Five-Year Plan in ascertaining the size of its tin resources and in organizing mining on a broad scale. In addition to those of Trans-Baikalia, rich deposits of tin were discovered in the Yakut ASSR, of which the Ege-Khay is the largest in the USSR. Here a combine is being built for mining tin, and detailed prospecting is being conducted for opening up the Delbekinelgekh group of deposits and those of Burgavlin. The northeastern part of Yakutia is becoming the largest tin-mining region.

Before 1936 the Far East had no known reserves of tin. Now large deposits of ore have been discovered and their industrial utilization has begun. The principal tin region is Bolshaya Sinyancha [Fig. 34]. These ores also contain lead, zinc, and silver. Wide-scale industrial explorations are being conducted in the Stalinsk district of the Maritime region and at the Ipatyevsk deposit on the Bureya River.

In the Kazakh SSR there are tin deposits in the region of the Kalbin Range (Altay) and in central Kazakhstan [Fig. 18]. In order to exploit them, the "Kalba-Olovo" industrial trust has been organized.

In the Kirgiz SSR, the Aktyuz and Kurgan deposits are potentially important in the development of the industry. The Urals and the Caucasus are being carefully prospected for tin. The success of the explorations has made possible the complete liberation of the USSR from dependence on the capitalist countries for tin.

The prospecting of the First and Second Five-Year Plans has shown that the USSR is one of the world's richest countries in various rare metals. Sizable deposits of tungsten, molybdenum, antimony, mercury, cobalt, bismuth, and other rare metals have been uncovered and are now being worked. There are deposits of tungsten in the Buryat-Mongol ASSR, Chita Oblast, the Kabardino-Balkar ASSR, Khakass Autonomous Oblast, Western Siberia, the Kazakh SSR, the Georgian SSR, the republics of Central Asia, and Chelyabinsk Oblast.[11] There are deposits of molybdenum in Chita Oblast, the Kabardino-Balkar ASSR, the Buryat-Mongol ASSR, the Altay, and the Armenian SSR. There are deposits of antimony in the Kazakh SSR (Turgay), Krasnoyarsk Kray, Chita Oblast, the Far East, the Uzbek SSR, and the Georgian SSR. Mercury deposits occur in the Oirot Autonomous Oblast [Altay Kray], the Kirgiz SSR, and the Ukrainian SSR.

There are considerable reserves of cobalt in the nickel ores of the Urals, Kazakhstan, and Murmansk Oblast. In the Urals, the Kazakh SSR, the Tadzhik SSR, and the Azerbaidzhan SSR pure cobalt deposits have been discovered. There are reserves of bismuth in the Tadzhik SSR, the Altay, and Chita Oblast.

Many of the deposits enumerated above are now being worked on an industrial scale.

The USSR has the world's largest reserves of *gold*. Gold mining has been increased by many times in the old regions of the Urals, the Lena River, the Yenisey, and Trans-Baikalia; new gold regions—on the Kolyma, and a number of deposits in the Far East—have been discovered and are being exploited on a wide scale; gold mining has increased particularly in the Kazakh SSR (Altay and North Kazakhstan) [Fig. 18]. The USSR is second only to the Union of South Africa in the mining of gold, having already surpassed Australia, Canada, and the United States.

Almost the entire production of *silver* in the USSR is concentrated in the regions of lead smelting (Altay, Chimkent, North

[11] [See map of administrative divisions, 1939, Fig. 83 in the back of the book.]

Osetia, and Tetyukhe), where silver is extracted from polymetallic ores. Mining of platinum is concentrated in the Urals and in the northern part of Krasnoyarsk Kray.

SECTION 5. THE DISTRIBUTION OF THE CONSTRUCTION OF MACHINERY

Before the Revolution, machine building was among the most retarded branches of Russian industry. The value of its output was 6.8% of the value of total industrial output. Railroad and agricultural machine building were further advanced than the others. The development of railroad equipment building was associated with the great period of railroad construction in the final quarter of the last century and the beginning of the present one. Agricultural machine building barely satisfied the requirements of the manorial and kulak farms. Other branches—the production of miscellaneous industrial equipment, power equipment, machine tools, and various types of fine and precision machinery—were either embryonic or completely absent. The machine-building industry of prerevolutionary Russia was owned in large measure by foreign capital.

The Creation of a Powerful Machine-Building Industry in the USSR

Since it is "the basic lever in reconstructing the national economy" (Stalin), machine building has received a tremendous development in the Soviet Union. In 1938 the industry in the USSR was 30.6 times as great as before the war, while during the same period the output of the industry in the United States increased 5.3 times, in England 2.5 times, and in Germany 1.9 times. As a result of the [first] two Stalin Five-Year Plans, the USSR was able to re-equip all of its socialist industry on a new, modern, technical foundation.

At the beginning of the Third Five-Year Plan (1938), machine building accounted for 25.5% of the total gross output of Soviet industry, whereas before the depression of 1929, even in the most advanced capitalist countries, the United States, England, and Germany, it represented 19.7%, 15.3%, and 12.2%, respectively.

The *structure* of the industry has changed considerably. The production of power equipment has grown especially fast, and now comprises 13.4% of the total value of Soviet machine-building output, as compared with 6.3% in prerevolutionary times. The relative importance of production of equipment for various branches of industry has increased; transportation equipment, though characterized by a large absolute increase, has diminished in relative importance. As a whole, the structure of the machine-building industry in the USSR reveals the following picture [Table 30]:

TABLE 30. STRUCTURE OF THE MACHINE-BUILDING INDUSTRY IN THE USSR AT THE END OF THE SECOND FIVE-YEAR PLAN

Branches	Percentage of Value of Output
Power machinery and equipment	13.4
Industrial machinery	15.4
Agricultural machinery	13.4
Machinery for transportation and communication	37.0
Other branches	20.8
Total	100.0

An extremely uneven distribution characterized the Russian machine-building industry before the Revolution. More than 50% of the total output came from the small area of the old industrial regions—Moscow, St. Petersburg, and the adjacent guberniyas. These produced 75% of the power equipment, 50% of the steam engines, and 97% of the electrotechnical equipment. Only agricultural implements were produced in other regions of the country, principally in the Ukraine (in Kherson, Tavrida, and Yekatrinoslav guberniyas),[12] the North Caucasus, and the Chernozem Center.

During the years of the Stalin Five-Year Plans great changes have taken place in the distribution of machine building. Along with the rapid growth of the industry in the old industrial regions, a diversified machine-building industry has been created in the Ukraine, the Urals, and the Volga Region. Separate focal points have been created in the Trans-Caucasus, Central Asia, Western and Eastern Siberia, and the Far East.[13]

[12] [Location of these and other guberniyas as of 1913 is indicated on Fig. 22, at the back of the book].

[13] [Regional names are located on Fig. 7, at the back of the book].

FIG. 35. Production of Power Machinery and Machine Tools

Power Machine Building

One of the basic branches of the machine-building industry is power machinery, which embraces the production of steam boilers, steam engines, steam turbines, hydraulic turbines, steam traction engines, internal combustion engines, Diesel engines, transformers, generators for steam turbines and water turbines, motors, storage batteries, and other prime movers and electric power equipment.

Boiler construction at the end of the Second Five-Year Plan was ten times greater than before the war [World War I]. The production of steam turbines and a number of other machines was created practically anew in the USSR; production in certain branches was increased by more than 50 times (as in the case of transformers) and in some cases even 100 times (as in the case of hydraulic turbines).

In the first years of the Stalin Five-Year Plans the newness of production of most types of power equipment demanded the erection of the new plants in regions where skilled workers, engineering and technical forces, and scientific research organizations (such as special institutes, construction branches, and plant laboratories) were concentrated.

Such a distribution of new plants for building power machinery was most expedient also because the metal requirements for most types of power equipment are relatively small and tend to grow increasingly smaller. Thus, before the war, the weight of an engine (Diesel) was 120 kg. per horsepower, while at present it may be as low as 8 to 18 kg. On the other hand, production of power equipment is being converted increasingly to special types of steel—to high-grade metal.

As a result of these conditions, the initial development of power machine building was chiefly in such industrial centers as Leningrad and Moscow (Fig. 35), where, by 1924–1925, the old plants of most branches of the industry (boiler construction, turbine construction, electrical engineering, etc.) already exceeded or closely approached the prewar production rate. The erection of new power machinery plants in the first years of Soviet rule took place also in the old centers (Elektrokombinat in Moscow) or in the towns close to the old industrial centers (such as the electromechanical plant in Yaroslavl and the Diesel engine plant in Voronezh). But even under

FIG. 36. Production of Industrial Equipment

the First and Second Stalin Five-Year Plans power machine building was developed in other regions as well, particularly in the Urals (Sverdlovsk), the Ukraine (Kharkov), and the Volga Region (Saratov). This process of extensive development of the construction of power machinery in new regions of the country is receiving especial impetus under the Third Stalin Five-Year Plan.

Production of Tools and Machine Tools

Comrade Ordzhonikidze termed the production of machine tools "the core of the machine-building industry." The production of machine tools has increased to thirty-six times its prewar quantity; an output of 53.9 thousand metal-cutting machine tools was achieved in 1938.

The importance of skilled labor and of high-grade metal in both *machine-tool* and power-equipment production has led to the erection of the most important machine-tool plants chiefly in the large industrial centers—Moscow, Leningrad, Gorky, the Urals, and the Ukraine. Among the newly built machine-tool plants, particularly important are the turret-lathe plant in Moscow, the milling-machine plant in Gorky, the heavy-machine-tool plant in Chelyabinsk, the gear-cutting and combination-lathe plant in Sverdlovsk, the automatic-machine-tool plant in Kiev, and the Molotov machine-tool plant in Kharkov.

Tool production before the Revolution had been developed chiefly in the Urals—in Zlatoust and in Miass, where high-quality steel was manufactured from the excellent Bakal ores. After the Revolution, in addition to expanding and reconstructing these and a few other old plants (in Leningrad, Sestroretsk, Moscow, etc.), a number of new tool plants were erected in Moscow (the "Frezer" and "Kalibr" plants), and in such centers of ancient domestic metal crafts as Pavlovo, Vorsma, and Vacha (Gorky Oblast), where large-scale tool plants grew up on the foundation of small shops and artels [Fig. 20, facing p. 143].

Production of Industrial Equipment

The production of industrial equipment in the USSR is distributed chiefly on the basis of regional demand for a particular machine (Fig. 36). Thus, machine-building plants which turn out equipment for the metallurgical and mining industry are located in the principal metallurgical and coal-mining regions. Such a distribution is explained by the large quantities of metal required by this branch of machine building and by the difficulty of transporting its products (rolling mills, equipment for blast furnaces and open-hearth shops, etc.).

The metallurgical equipment industry was created almost entirely under the Stalin Five-Year Plans, when the Kramatorsk heavy-machine-building plant (Ukrainian SSR) and the Uralmashzavod (Sverdlovsk) were built.

Production of mining equipment, particularly for coal mining, is distributed in the main coal regions [Fig. 36]: the Ukraine (Stalino, Gorlovka, Druzhkovka [Dr.], Kharkov, etc.), and Siberia (Novosibirsk, Anzhero-Sudzhensk, and Irkutsk). While the Donbas plants, operating as small workshops, existed before the Revolution and were basically reconstructed under the Stalin Five-Year Plans, the Siberian plants were built entirely after the Revolution.

Since the chemical industry was developed along with the coal and metallurgical industries in these same regions of heavy industry—the Urals, the Ukraine, and Siberia—during the years of the Stalin Five-Year Plans, the chemical machine-building industry also grew up here, in the neighborhood of Sverdlovsk (Uktus), Sumy, etc. Equipment for the gold-mining industry is produced in the Urals (Ufa and Votkinsk), in Eastern Siberia (Irkutsk), and in the Far East (Blagoveshchensk).

The main oil and peat regions contain branches of the machine-building industry which serve these industries. Baku and Grozny are the chief centers producing equipment for the oil industry; Ivanovo and Kalinin are centers for peat machinery. The relatively great distance of these regions from the metal-producing areas is balanced by the relative advantage of shipping metal over shipping ready-made machinery.

There is a close connection between the branches of the light and food industries and the corresponding branches of machine building. Thus, the main textile-machinery plants are found principally in the textile centers—Moscow, Leningrad, Ivanovo, Shuya, and others. Plants producing equipment for the food industry are located in the areas where the food industry is concentrated, particularly in the oblasts of the Chernozem Center (Kursk, Voronezh), in the Ukraine (Kiev, Kharkov, Odessa, Melitopol, etc.), in the

Crimea (Simferopol, Kerch), in the North Caucasus (Taganrog), and in the Trans-Caucasus (Tbilisi), etc.

Construction of Agricultural Machinery

During the period covered by the Stalin Five-Year Plans, the construction of agricultural machinery has received an enormous impetus. Since the Revolution the output of agricultural machinery has increased more than forty times. The production of a whole series of new types of agricultural machines—tractors, combines, machinery for the cultivation of flax, cotton, beets, etc.—has been introduced into the Soviet Union. But it has not been simply a matter of quantitative growth. New agricultural machines essentially signify a technical revolution in agriculture. At the 18th Party Congress, Comrade Andreyev reported that the brothers Oskin (Chkalov Oblast), "working two combines, did the work of 1,637 men, 373 horses, 25 reapers, 25 threshers, 25 winnowers, and 40 sorters; to have done the harvesting by hand, as was the case formerly, 3,323 men would have been required."

At present, tractor construction is the most important aspect of agricultural machine building.

The first tractors were produced in the USSR in 1923. Nevertheless, before the First Five-Year Plan, imports accounted for most of the supply of tractors for agriculture (between 1923 and 1928, 3.8 thousand tractors were produced in the USSR, 29.3 thousand were imported). In this period tractor output was concentrated chiefly in the Kirov plant in Leningrad (at that time called "Krasny Putilovets"), which manufactured 10/20 horsepower tractors.[14] In addition, the Kharkov locomotive works produced the "Kommunar" tractors.

Under the First Five-Year Plan two giant plants of the tractor-building industry—the Dzerzhinsky plant in Stalingrad (1930) and the Ordzhonikidze plant in Kharkov (1931) (Fig. 37)—were put into operation. These originally produced wheel tractors and were subsequently rebuilt for manufacturing caterpillar tractors. They are in the middle of the largest agricultural areas in the country—the Ukraine and the Volga Region—where need for tractors is greatest, and close to the most important coal-mining and metal-

[14] The first figure is the traction power using a hook, the second, using a gear pulley.

FIG. 37. Production of Agricultural Machinery

lurgical base, which supplies raw materials for these plants. Even under the First Five-Year Plan the Soviet industry produced more than 115 thousand tractors, accomplishing V. I. Lenin's program of supplying agriculture with 100 thousand tractors. At the beginning of the Second Five-Year Plan work began on the Chelyabinsk tractor plant, to be greater than the Milwaukee (United States) plant of the International Harvester Company, previously the largest tractor plant in the world. One reason for the selection of the site of the Chelyabinsk plant may be found in its location "at the gates" of the huge agricultural areas of Western Siberia and the southern Urals, regions with a demand for especially powerful tractors, such as the 50/60 horsepower "Stalinets" caterpillar tractors turned out by the Chelyabinsk plant. Another reason is the proximity of the metal of the Ural metallurgical plants. In 1938, the USSR produced 32.2 thousand caterpillar tractors.

The most important grain regions of the country contain the chief centers of combine building: the Ukraine (Zaporozhye), the North Caucasus (Rostov), and the Volga Region (Saratov). In addition, combines are produced to the north in Moscow Oblast (Lyubertsy). The USSR occupies second place in the world in tractor output; in the annual output of combines, it has for many years held first place. In 1938 it produced 22.9 thousand combines.

The production of the essential attachable tractor and of horse-drawn agricultural equipment—plows, harrows, cultivators, seeders, etc.—is carried on also in the chief grain regions of the Union. Under the First Five-Year Plan, a very large new plant producing various agricultural machines was created in Rostov-on-Don. Large centers of agricultural machine building in the Ukraine are Kharkov, Kirovograd, Odessa, Kherson, and Osipenko; and in the RSFSR, Lyubertsy, Orel, Chelyabinsk, and Omsk.

Machines are now in wide use not only for grain cultivation and general agricultural tasks connected with soil cultivation, but also in a number of other branches of agriculture. Here too, production of a particular type of agricultural machinery develops in regions of the greatest development of the branch of agriculture which uses it. Thus, machinery for flax cultivation and potato cultivation is made in the western provinces and in the Industrial Center—Rzhev and Torzhok (Kalinin Oblast), Lyubertsy (Moscow Oblast), and

Fig. 38. Construction of Transport Machinery

Ryazan. Tashkent makes cotton-growing machinery, Gomel makes machinery used in livestock raising, etc.

Construction of Transport Machinery

Construction of transport machinery in the USSR includes that of railroad equipment, automobiles, and ships. *Construction of railroad equipment* has been extensively developed during the years of the Stalin Five-Year Plans. The USSR holds first place in the world in the number of locomotives manufactured, and second in the world and first in Europe in the number of passenger and freight cars.

Since before the Revolution the most important centers of locomotive and railroad-car construction have been concentrated in regions having the heaviest railroad networks (Fig. 38), chiefly in the central industrial guberniyas. This includes the area south of Moscow (the Kolomna locomotive plant [K in Fig. 38] and the Mytishchi railroad-car plant [M]), Gorky (locomotive and railroad-car building at the Sormovo plant), Ordzhonikidzegrad (formerly [and recently renamed] Bezhitsa) (locomotive and railroad-car building), Leningrad, and Kalinin (railroad-car building). In addition, locomotive building has been developed to a small degree in the Ukraine (Kharkov and Voroshilovgrad) and railroad-car building in the Urals (Ust-Katavsky).

Old plants have been expanded and reconstructed under the Stalin Five-Year Plans. New types of engines have been adopted on the railroads—electric locomotives, Diesel locomotives, and steam locomotives with tender-condensers. New types of cars also have been produced—large-capacity freight cars, passenger cars with soft seats, suburban electric-train cars, subway cars, etc. (Mytishchi and Kalinin plants). At the same time, a number of new, large-scale plants have been constructed: the locomotive building plant in Voroshilovgrad, and the railroad-car building plants in the Urals (Nizhny Tagil) and the Ukraine (Dneprodzerzhinsk and Kryukov). The location in the Ukraine and in the Urals of the new plants for building railroad machinery is due to the large metal requirements for locomotive construction and the large wood requirements for railroad-car building. The Ukrainian car-building plants are provided with local metal and receive wood from the regions of the upper Dnepr. The new centers of car construction are in the middle reaches of the river. The Ural plants are supplied locally with both metal and wood.

Maritime shipbuilding was, in the past, located chiefly at Leningrad, Nikolayev, and Sevastopol, and *river shipbuilding* on the middle and lower Volga (at Gorky, Kazan, and Astrakhan). Today the industry is much more broadly dispersed throughout the USSR. The opening of the Northern Sea Route and the expansion of navigation in the Pacific Ocean have resulted in the erection of new plants and a great expansion of the old ones (in Murmansk, Archangel, Vladivostok, and Komsomolsk-on-Amur). River shipbuilding plants have been erected on the upper Volga at Yaroslavl and Rybinsk, on the Dnepr at Kiev, and on the Kama at Perm [Molotov]. In the Asiatic part of the USSR, with the development of navigation along the Ob, Yenisey, and Lena, shipbuilding is developing in Tyumen, Krasnoyarsk, Zhigalovo, etc.

Automobile construction was begun in the USSR as a completely new industry. Before the Revolution, Russia had only small shops (in Moscow, St. Petersburg, and other towns) which assembled single machines, chiefly passenger cars, from imported parts.

During the period of its existence after 1908, the Russian Baltic railroad-car plant in Riga turned out fewer than 50 machines. The automobiles in prerevolutionary Russia, which numbered 8,800 in 1913, consisted entirely of imported machines. During the Imperialist War of 1914 the Tsarist Government hastily purchased 30 thousand automobiles, of which a substantial number were secondhand machines, reconverted junk, sold off by various firms at three times their value.

The production of new automobiles in the USSR began in 1923–1924, when the former AMO (Aktsionernoye Moskovskoye Obshchestvo or Moscow Joint-Stock Company) automobile repair shop turned out 10 machines. During the years of the First Five-Year Plan this shop produced a total of 1.4 thousand machines. A small plant in Yaroslavl which operated during these years provided an additional 200. Thus, before the end of the First Five-Year Plan, the entire output of the automobile industry was 1.6 thousand machines, drawn entirely from two small plants in Moscow and Yaroslavl.

Under the First Stalin Five-Year Plan the large-scale Stalin ZIS automobile plant was erected in Moscow on the site of the former AMO plant. The location was determined by the presence in Moscow of (1) a whole group of machine-building plants allied with automobile building, (2) trained workers, (3) scientific research facilities for the development and perfection of automobile building and of the production of high-grade metals.

The Yaroslavl automobile plant, under the First Five-Year Plan, was reconstructed on a large scale and converted to the manufacture of five-ton trucks and busses. Yaroslavl also became a center for the manufacture of automobile tires; here were erected a rubber-asbestos combine and a synthetic rubber works. During the years of the First Five-Year Plan the Soviet automobile industry produced 57 thousand machines—a 250% increase over the total number of automobiles in existence [in the Union] at the beginning of the First Five-Year Plan.

By the end of the First Five-Year Plan a new, even larger automobile plant named after Molotov had been erected in Gorky. Gorky was selected as the site for the new plant because previously it had been a center specializing in transportation machine building (locomotives, railroad cars, and ships), and consequently had at its disposal a large number of workers skilled in machine building. Another essential condition was its location on the Volga, which made possible cheap delivery of raw materials and semimanufactured goods (from Yaroslavl and from the Urals by way of the Kama and Volga rivers, etc.), as well as the shipment of automobile parts to other points where automobile assembly plants are being erected.

In the course of the Second Five-Year Plan, as a result of the erection of the new Gorky plant and the reconstruction of the Stalin plant in Moscow, the automobile industry multiplied its output by almost 10.

A distinctive feature of the Soviet automobile industry is the great importance of freight-carrying vehicles [trucks] (90%), which results from the demands of the growing freight turnover of the country. The USSR is fourth in the number of freight-carrying motor vehicles, following the United States, England, and France; and in the output of such vehicles it occupies first place in Europe and second place in the world, yielding only to the United States.

Automobile assembly plants are under construction. Already one with a capacity of 40 thousand machines has been put into operation in Rostov-on-Don, and in 1940 construction is to begin on another in Omsk with a capacity of 45 thousand.

There are a number of large-scale allied plants connected with the automobile industry. First in importance is the Kaganovich state bearings plant ("Gospodshipnik") at Moscow, which surpasses both European and American plants in size. A number of such plants have been built in Ivanovo Oblast, which is advantageously placed among three oblasts in which the automobile industry has been developed. Among the allied plants in Ivanovo Oblast are the "Autopribor" plant at Vladimirskoye [V, northwest of Yaroslavl], making precision measuring instruments, oil-controlling instruments, fuel indicators, windshield wipers, etc.; and the plant at Kirzhach [northeast of Moscow], manufacturing automobile accessories such as lamps and headlights.

Machine Building Under the Third Five-Year Plan [15]

The Third Five-Year Plan places particular emphasis on machine building. A resolution of the 18th Party Congress points out the need "to increase the output of the machine-building industry at least 130% by the end of the Third Five-Year Plan, that is, considerably higher than the over-all industrial rise." To overcome the relative lag of power machinery construction behind the rapidly growing requirements of the Soviet national economy, the Third Five-Year Plan provides for the erection and opening of four steam-turbine plants in the regions of Sverdlovsk, Ufa, Novosibirsk, and Kaluga. It also plans to initiate construction of a steam-turbine plant in the vicinity of Kuibyshev. Boiler plants are also under construction (Orsk and others).

The machine-tool industry is developing rapidly. The output of metal-cutting lathes is increasing (up to 70 thousand); the assortment of machine tools is approaching 800 types and sizes; the output of pneumatic, electrical, and other types of skilled tools is increasing. Along with the completion of a milling-machine plant at Gorky and an automatic-machine-tool plant at Kiev, the construction of a number of machine-tool plants of medium capacity for various types of machine tools is under way in new regions, especially in the East.

The Third Five-Year Plan provides for large-scale construction of new plants to produce equipment for ferrous and nonferrous metallurgy and for the chemical, paper, textile, knitting, shoe, and food industries.

[15] [Places mentioned under this heading are located on Fig. 20, p. 143.]

As agricultural development and ferrous metallurgy have increased in the eastern regions, a base for the production of agricultural machines and for assembling and repairing tractors will be created in the East under the Third Five-Year Plan.

New truck plants will be erected in Siberia; a number of new automobile assembly plants at Ryazan, Kremenchug, Irkutsk, Komsomolsk-on-Amur, and Tashkent; a small plant for producing low-powered automobiles at Moscow; and a number of allied automobile plants.

The machine-building industry of the USSR will be more uniformly distributed as a result of construction under the Third Five-Year Plan. Together with further growth of the basic regions where machine building had been developed (the central and western regions and the Ukraine), the industry is developing particularly rapidly in the eastern regions of the Soviet Union—the Urals, the Volga Region, and Siberia, where duplicate plants in a number of branches of machine building will be erected under the Third Five-Year Plan.

SECTION 6. DISTRIBUTION OF THE CHEMICAL INDUSTRY

Before the Revolution the chemical industry played an insignificant role in Russia. In 1913 it provided only 2.8% of the total value of industrial production of the country. The rubber industry, the largest of the branches of the chemical industry, depended entirely on imported rubber; the production of nitric acid also depended on imported raw materials. In prewar years, in spite of a slight general growth of the chemical industry, there was a curtailment of production in certain branches, and the country became increasingly dependent on foreign imports. Thus, while 1,800 tons of sulphur were mined in Russia in 1885, only 6 tons were mined in 1910, and more than 2,060 tons were imported from abroad during the last years before the war. Phosphates are another example. Extraction fell from 26,000 tons in 1900 to 2,500 in 1912, while the quantity imported during the same years grew from 5,200 tons to 48,400.

Introduction of Chemistry into the National Economy of the USSR

In the USSR there is an intensive development of the chemical industry, an introduction of chemistry into the national economy, and an introduction into all branches of the economy of chemical methods of utilizing substances. A number of new branches of the chemical industry have been created: synthetic rubber, synthetic fiber, plastics, electrochemistry, biochemistry, etc. Chemical methods are becoming increasingly widespread in various branches of industry. They are used in the preparation of raw materials for the blast-furnace charge in ferrous and nonferrous metallurgy, in the cracking of mazut and of waste products in the oil-refining industry, in the treatment of wood and the production of cellulose for the paper industry, in the production of "Kotonin" fiber, in the production of tanning agents for the leather industry, in extraction in oil manufacturing, in the hydrogenation of light oils to produce margarine, etc. Consequently, in summing up the results of the First Five-Year Plan, Comrade Stalin said: "We had never had a serious and up-to-date chemical industry. We have it now." [16] In the course of the Second Five-Year Plan the chemical industry increased its output 200%, and in 1938 already accounted for 6.4% of the value of all Soviet industrial output, having increased by 15 times over prewar amounts.

The most important branches of the chemical industry are: (1) the basic chemical industry, making various acids and salts; (2) rubber and synthetic rubbers (accounting for approximately half the production of the whole industry); (3) the aniline-dye and lacquer-paint industries; (4) the production of plastics; and (5) the chemical-pharmaceutical industry.

Basic Chemical Industry

Within the basic chemical industry the chief branches are the production of fertilizers and the production of sulphuric acid.

The most widely used mineral fertilizers are the phosphoric, since without phosphorus the growth of plants is impossible, and each year a huge quantity (2 to 2.5 million tons) of phosphorus pentoxide (P_2O_5) is carried off from the soil. Phosphoric fertilizers represent half of all the artificial fertilizers used in the world, and in the USSR they represent an even greater proportion of the total. They not only increase the size of the harvest, but also improve the quality of the products. Thus, they increase the sugar content of beets, improve the ratio between chaff and grain, and increase the starch content of potatoes.

[16] Stalin, *Questions of Leninism*, p. 373.

The main type of *phosphoric fertilizer* is superphosphate, manufactured by combining finely ground phosphorite with sulphuric acid. Since sulphuric acid is difficult to transport (it is dangerous to move, requires special containers, etc.), superphosphate plants, as a rule, have their own sulphuric acid shops.

The chief raw materials for obtaining phosphoric fertilizers in the USSR are apatites, which are found in the region of Kirovsk in Murmansk Oblast [Fig. 39]. This deposit was unknown before the Revolution. The total reserves here are estimated at 2 billion tons, and the industrial reserves at 431 million tons. These apatites have an average P_2O_5 content of 20 to 30% and are the finest in the world. There are phosphorites in various regions of the European USSR, chiefly in Vinnitsa, Kursk, Orel, and Moscow oblasts, the Chuvash ASSR, Kirov and Chkalov oblasts, and also in Aktyubinsk and South Kazakhstan oblasts of the Kazakh SSR.[17]

The production of superphosphates before the Revolution was dependent to a considerable extent on foreign raw materials imported from the French North African colonies. Consequently, two superphosphate plants in prerevolutionary Russia were located in ports (Odessa and Leningrad). The Vinnitsa plant operated on local rock phosphate; in addition, the Perm [Molotov] plant and the Chernorechensk plant (at Dzerzhinsk in Gorky Oblast) manufactured superphosphates [Fig. 39]. The total production of superphosphates in 1913 was estimated at 63 thousand tons.

In 1938, 1,571 thousand tons of superphosphates were manufactured in the USSR, that is, 25 times more than in prerevolutionary times. As a result of this growth the USSR at the beginning of the Third Five-Year Plan manufactured more superphosphates than Spain, Holland, Belgium, Australia, England, Germany, Italy, and France. In 1913, before the Revolution, Russia had produced far less than any of these countries.

After the Revolution, in addition to the reconstruction of the old superphosphate plants, which were converted entirely to native raw materials (Odessa, Vinnitsa, Chernorechensk, and Perm [Molotov]), a number of new, large plants were built in the USSR. Thus, on the Yegoryevsk deposit of phosphorite [Fig. 18] in Moscow Oblast, there has been erected a large chemical combine (at Voskresensk)

[17] [The location of these political units is indicated on Fig. 40 in the back of the book.]

Fig. 39. Chemical Industry

[Vo in Fig. 39], which produces not only superphosphates, but also dicalcium phosphate dihydrate—a general-purpose phosphoric acid fertilizer, suitable for all plants, and at the same time a good filler for fodder. This is manufactured also by the chemical combine in Aktyubinsk, erected under the Second Five-Year Plan on the basis of Aktyubinsk phosphorites. In Leningrad in place of the former small enterprise operating on imported raw materials, there has been erected the large Neva Chemical Combine, operating on Kirovsk apatites. A large superphosphate plant has been built in the Donbas (Konstantinovka).

The production of *nitrogenous fertilizers* is also very important, since they are essential to agriculture in most regions of the USSR. Nitrogenous fertilizers in the USSR are obtained from coke-oven gas (by a low-temperature method), or from carbon monoxide (by a conversion method). The raw material for both methods is coal (for the first method, coking coal is required), and therefore nitrogenous fertilizer combines are located in the coal regions of the Union or at metallurgical plants where coking takes place. Accordingly, the combines are found in the USSR in the Donbas (Gorlovka, etc. [Fig. 39 inset]), Kuzbas (Kemerovo), Urals (Berezniki, Magnitogorsk), and Central Industrial Region (Stalinogorsk) [Fig. 39].

No *potassium fertilizer* was produced in prerevolutionary Russia. About 80,000 tons of potassium were imported from abroad and used in negligible quantities in the western part of the country—in Leningrad, Kalinin, and Smolensk oblasts, in the Belorussian SSR, and in the northwestern part of the USSR. At the same time, potassium fertilizers are very essential in the regions of podzolic soils. The presence of potassium in the USSR was established in 1925 by prospecting in the region of the city of Solikamsk. These deposits amount to 18.4 billion tons of potassium oxide; the corresponding reserves in capitalist countries (Germany, Spain, France, the United States) amount to 3 billion tons. In the USSR, in addition to the Solikamsk-Berezniki region, traces of potassium have been discovered in the Turkmen SSR and the Kazakh SSR (Lake Inder near the Ural River). A potassium combine has been created in the Solikamsk-Berezniki region. Under the Second Five-Year Plan it was already producing 1.8 million tons of sylvite, containing 15% potassium oxide. The sylvite processed at the concentration plant yields potassium chloride, which in admixture with sylvite produces an agricultural fertilizer. The carnallite also produced here is a valuable raw material in the manufacture of metallic magnesium.

Sulphuric acid is an essential auxiliary material for the production not only of fertilizer, but also of nitric and other acids, of paints, of paper, and is required in petroleum refining. As a result of these varied uses, its production in the USSR has increased considerably over the 1913 level, and has exceeded that of Belgium, Italy, France, and England, all countries which had surpassed Russia before the war.

The most common sulphuric acid raw material in prerevolutionary Russia and in the USSR before the Second Five-Year Plan was pyrite from the Urals. There is pyrite in the Caucasus also, and in the central industrial and chernozem oblasts as an impurity in other rocks. Under the Second Five-Year Plan flotation residues of copper pyrite came into use in the manufacture of sulphuric acid, as well as sulphurous gases in nonferrous metallurgy, thus increasing the role of the Urals in the production of sulphuric acid. Carbonaceous pyrite from the Donbas and the Moscow Basin also came into use in the extraction of sulphuric acid.

The Rubber Industry and the Production of Synthetic Rubber

More than two-thirds of the prerevolutionary Russian rubber industry was devoted to the production of overshoes, and was dependent entirely on imported rubber. For this reason, the largest of the rubber works were located in the ports of St. Petersburg and Riga.

In the USSR, rubber requirements have increased immensely. In 1913, about 13 thousand tons of raw rubber and gutta-percha were imported, while in 1937 the Soviet consumption of rubber was almost 100 thousand tons. This tremendous growth was due primarily to the demands of the automobile industry. For example, the production of inner tubes for automobiles in 1913 amounted to 10,000. By 1937 it had increased to more than 4 million. Furthermore, rubber is widely used in aviation, in electrical engineering, and in the production of many consumers' goods.

In the years following the October Revolution, in addition to the enormous expansion and reconstruction of the old rubber works in Leningrad and Moscow and the development and remodeling of the border plants which had been evacuated to Moscow, a new large rubber-asbestos plant was built in Yaroslavl. The core of this combine is an automobile-tire plant. The location of the plant, and of the whole combine, is related to the presence of the Yaroslavl automobile plant, and also to the proximity of Yaroslavl to other cities with large automobile plants, such as Moscow and Gorky, which also use tires from the Yaroslavl Rubber-Asbestos Combine. The USSR with its great growth in rubber consumption has decreased the amount of imported rubber by increasing domestic production. The creation of a domestic base for producing natural rubber has been undertaken. The area under rubber-bearing plants—*kok-sagyz* [*Taraxacum kok-saghyz*], *tau-sagyz* [*Scorzonera tau-saghys*], guayule [*Parthenium argentatum*], milkweed [*Asclepias*], and so on—is now approximately 25,000 hectares, and rubber gathering as yet plays a small role in the USSR. The growing of natural rubber is scattered principally throughout the south of the Kazakh SSR and the Ukrainian SSR, in the Union republics of Central Asia and the Trans-Caucasus, in the Crimea, and in the watershed between the river Don on one side and the Donets and the upper Oka on the other. The increase in yield of the rubber-bearing plants and the discovery that the euonymus plant, which is widespread throughout the USSR, contains gutta-percha, account for the growing importance of Soviet natural rubber.

At present, synthetic rubber (SK [abbreviation for *sintetichesky kauchuk*]) is of decisive importance as it meets the overwhelming majority of Soviet needs for raw material for the rubber industry. The USSR occupies first place in the world in the production of synthetic rubber.

Synthetic rubber in the USSR is obtained through polymerization of butadiene. The polymerization of butadiene takes place in the presence of metallic sodium, and such rubber is called "sodium butadiene rubber" (SK-B [abbreviation for *sintetichesky kauchuk-butadien*]). Butadiene itself is obtained from common alcohol (ethyl alcohol), which is distilled chiefly from potatoes.

Since the alcohol comprises only a small fraction of the weight of potatoes used, and the weight of the rubber is only about one-third the weight of the alcohol, it is expedient to produce synthetic rubber in potato-growing areas in order to avoid long hauls. Synthetic rubber production in the USSR was begun in 1932. The first large plant was built in Yaroslavl to supply the rubber-asbestos combine with raw material. Other large synthetic rubber works have been built in Voronezh Oblast (Voronezh), Tula Oblast (Yefremov), and the Tatar ASSR (Kazan) [Fig. 39].

Another method of obtaining synthetic rubber uses limestone (an intermediate product is calcium carbide) as the initial raw material. This also requires carbon in the form of coke or anthracite and a large amount of electric power (3 to 3.5 thousand kw-h is required for one ton of carbide).

After being tested at the Leningrad experimental plant, the limestone method of obtaining rubber ("Sovpren") was started industrially at Yerevan in the Armenian SSR. High-quality limestone, of which there is a great quantity near Yerevan in the Dabalynsk region, serves as the raw material for the Yerevan plant. Cheap electric power is obtained locally from the Kanaker hydroelectric power plant.

Production of Paints and Dyes

The production of paints and dyes is represented by the aniline-dye and lacquer-paint industries. The aniline-dye industry produces organic dyeing substances chiefly from coal tar. These artificial organic dyes have greatest application in the textile industry for dyeing fibrous materials, and are used in the dyeing of fats and food substances, in the production of inks, cosmetics, etc. The lacquer-paint industry produces lacquers (varnishes) and paints which serve as a protective covering to protect metals from corrosion and wooden structures from decay.

Before the Revolution there was almost no aniline-dye industry in Russia. Prerevolutionary needs for aniline dyes in Russia were met principally through imports from Germany. The small Tsarist Russian plants for synthetic dyes were almost exclusively branches of German or Swiss dye factories. The lacquer-paint industry was represented by domestic craft enterprises.

With the general increase in production of both lacquer and paint, the lacquer-paint industry at the end of the Second Five-Year Plan exceeded by three times (in weight) the production of the Tsarist aniline-dye [lacquer-paint?] industry. The raw materials for the most widely used oil paints and lacquers are linseed and wood oils, synthetic resin, and rosin. The large-scale lacquer-paint industry is located principally in Yaroslavl, Leningrad, Moscow, and Rostov oblasts, and also in the Ukrainian SSR (Kharkov, Odessa) and the Georgian SSR (Kutaisi); at Kutaisi, near a barite deposit, a lithopone plant has been erected. The manufacture of intermediate products by the aniline-dye industry, using coal as the initial raw material, is concentrated in the Donbas (Rubezhnaya in Voroshilovgrad Oblast), while most of the manufacture of finished dyes takes place in the textile centers—Moscow and Ivanovo oblasts (Kineshma) [Fig. 39].

Production of Plastics

The production of plastics was completely nonexistent in prerevolutionary Russia, but by the end of the Second Five-Year Plan the output was already valued in hundreds of millions of rubles. The chief types manufactured in the USSR are galalith, carbolite, bakelite, and celluloid. Galalith is made from casein, which is obtained from skimmed milk. It is used in the manufacture of some electrical appliances and of buttons, pocket pencils, pens, combs, etc. Carbolite and bakelite are made from phenols, principally carbolic acid, which in turn is obtained through dry distillation of wood and coal. Carbolite is used in machine building (bearings, rollers, some machine parts), in electrical engineering (insulators, measuring instruments), in the production of consumers' goods (buttons, combs, fountain pens). Bakelite is used in the manufacture of electrotechnical appliances, chemical appliances, phonograph records, etc. For celluloid the initial raw material is wood. Its most important use is in the production of cinematographic and photographic film. In addition, it is used in the manufacture of "triplex" shatter-proof glass, toys, combs, etc.

Plastics are still produced chiefly in the old industrial regions, which mastered earlier the methods of applying them, and the output is most widely distributed, particularly in Moscow and Moscow Oblast (Orekhovo-Zuyevo, Kuskovo), Leningrad, Ivanovo Oblast (Vladimir), and Kalinin [Fig. 39].

Chemical-Pharmaceutical Industry

There was practically no large chemical-pharmaceutical industry in Tsarist Russia. Small enterprises were occupied principally with the measuring out and packaging of ready-made imported preparations and various household commodities. The development of a chemical-pharmaceutical industry in the USSR meant that the majority of preparations, formerly manufactured in completely negligible quantities or not at all, were being produced by the end of the Second Five-Year Plan in the hundreds, thousands, and millions of kilograms (for example, aspirin, phenyl salicylate, codeine, and industrial salicylic acid). The principal centers of the chemical-pharmaceutical industry are in Moscow, Leningrad, the Ukrainian SSR (Kharkov, Kiev), the Kazakh SSR (Chimkent), and the Azerbaidzhan SSR (Baku) [Fig. 39].

The Chemical Industry Under the Third Five-Year Plan

Under the Third Five-Year Plan the chemical industry will undergo particularly intensive development. Production will increase by 140%. The Third Five-Year Plan is the age of chemistry. The chemical industry is becoming one of the leading branches of industry, and will completely meet the requirements of the national economy and national defense. New sulphuric acid plants are being constructed, chiefly utilizing the waste gases of nonferrous metallurgy, also, new fertilizer combines, sodium carbonate plants, and synthetic rubber works. Tire-manufacturing plants with rubber-reclamation shops and plants for the production of artificial fibers and plastics are under construction. New branches of organic synthesis (synthetic alcohol, acetic acid, etc.) are being created, utilizing by-products of oil refining, rubber production, coke production and natural gases.

SECTION 7. DISTRIBUTION OF THE WOOD INDUSTRY

Before the Revolution three-fifths of the wood industry consisted of logging and transport (55% logs), and only two-fifths was concerned with the mechanical and chemical processing of wood. Felling, carried on without any view to conservation, was done by hand with axes and two-handed saws. In the rich forest land of the European North the yield from 1 hectare of land in 1913 was only 0.45 cubic meter of wood, and in even richer, remote regions it was only 0.28 to 0.25 cubic meter. But in the less densely forested central region the annual average yield of 1 hectare was from 2.3 to 4.2 cubic meters of wood. This was three times as great as the yearly growth of wood, and as a result, from about 1890 to the First Imperialist War [World War I], of the privately owned forests under forest preserves, over 26 million hectares were cut down and 15 million completely destroyed.

In the USSR soon after the end of the Civil War, a forest code was introduced (August 1, 1923) defining territories of limited wood utilization in the interests of the particular needs of the national economy. In 1931, forest-cultivation zones were created where lumber cutting was prohibited in a strip 1 km. wide on either side of the middle and lower course of the Volga, Don, Dnepr, and Ural rivers. In 1936 the water-conservation zone was expanded to 20 km. on either side of these rivers and along the upper course of the Zapadnaya (Western) Dvina, as well as a zone of 4 to 6 km. along their tributaries. As a result, lumbering is now on a scale which does not interfere with the regimes of the river systems.

Timber Reserves of the USSR

The wood reserves of the USSR are enormous. Forested areas extend over approximately 610 million hectares, or more than 20% of the forested area of the world [Fig. 16, p. 60]. In lumber reserves the USSR occupies first place in the world. Canada, which is second, has only half the forested area of the USSR, and the United States, which is third, has only one-third. The Forest Zone of the USSR is, to an overwhelming extent, taiga with coniferous forests of spruce, larch, fir, and stone pine, and to a much smaller extent, pine. The taiga embraces entire oblasts, krays, and republics of the RSFSR, chiefly between 60° and 70° N. Lat. Both in the European and in the Asiatic parts, as one moves from west to east, the [southern] border of the taiga gradually advances to the south. The northern border extends to 70° only in the Yakut ASSR, while in the remaining territory it generally ends near the Arctic Circle. In Khabarovsk Kray the taiga ends in still lower latitudes, on the northern border of the Koryak National Okrug [No. 31 in Fig. 40 in the back of the book]. In the oblasts, krays, and republics of Siberia, the forest cover reaches 35 to 50%. In the oblasts and republics of the Forest Zone of the European part of the USSR it varies from 30 to 60%.

The remaining forested zone—the Subzone of Mixed Forests, occupying about 12 to 13% of the forest area of the USSR—is located in the European part of the Union and in the Far East in the basin of the middle and lower Amur River. Along the western border of the USSR, this subzone extends from 50° to 60° [N. Lat.], but it decreases in width toward the east and terminates in the Urals (55° to 57° [N. Lat.]). In the subzone, side by side with conifers, there are many soft deciduous species (aspen, alder), and also birch, and to a lesser extent such broad-leaved species as oak. In the Subzone of Mixed Forests—in Kalinin, Moscow, and Smolensk oblasts, the Belorussian SSR, etc.—the forest cover is 20 to 25%.

Logging and Lumber Transport

By 1937 the wood industry had increased its production by almost 4 times over prerevolutionary times. Under the Second Five-Year Plan it surpassed the production of lumber of all the European countries and of the United States. The structure of the wood industry of the USSR had changed also. While logging and lumber transport increased by 100%, the relative importance decreased. They now comprise approximately 40% of the total value of the output of the wood industry, while the mechanical and chemical processing of wood comprises 60%.

During the last years of the Second Five-Year Plan, more than half of the logging and lumber transport took place in the Taiga Zone, chiefly in the regions of the European North, next in the Urals, and lastly in Siberia and the Far East. About 40% of the logging took place in the Subzone of Mixed Forests. Of this, more than half was in the western oblasts of the RSFSR (Leningrad, Kalinin, Smolensk oblasts) and in the Belorussian SSR. As a rule, logging of industrial wood predominates everywhere. Altogether, about two-thirds of the total Soviet wood supply is used for industrial purposes, while about one-third is used for firewood.

The Sawmill and Plywood Industries

The largest branches of the woodworking industry in volume of output are the sawmills and the plywood plants, which account for about one-fourth of the production of the entire wood industry. The distribution of sawmills corresponds, in the main, to the location of logging, except for the unforested areas of the lower Volga and the areas of the Ukraine located along the middle and lower course of the Dnepr. Large quantities of lumber are floated down the Volga to the sawmills of Saratov, Stalingrad, and Astrakhan and down the Dnepr to Kiev, Cherkassy, Kremenchug, Dnepropetrovsk, and Zaporozhye [Fig. 41]. All these sawmill centers are at points of juncture between water and rail transport. The logs are floated downstream to the sawmills and then, in the form of lumber, are carried farther by railroad. Stalingrad is very typical of such strategic points. Here wood arrives by river, is processed at the sawmills in large quantities, and then as lumber is shipped on by railroad. Thus, the sawmills of the unforested areas of the Ukraine and the lower Volga produce almost one-tenth of the total output of the sawmill industry of the USSR.

The oblasts and autonomous republics of the European North [Fig. 41] have a large-scale sawmill industry based completely on local logging. This area produces about one-fifth of all lumber in the USSR, and Archangel Oblast and the Karelian ASSR [Karelo-Finnish SSR] are especially important. Here the largest sawmill centers are concentrated at the mouths of the Severnaya (Northern) Dvina (Archangel), Onega (town of Onega), Mezen (town of Mezen), Kem (town of Kem), and other rivers [Fig. 6, p. 32, and Fig. 41]. In addition, a large number of more or less important sawmill centers are found in cities, workers' settlements, and other populated points along the railroad lines from Vologda [V in Fig. 41] to Archangel (Vologda, Permilovo, Plesetsk, etc.), and from Petrozavodsk to Murmansk (Suna, Belomorsk, Kovda, etc.). The majority of the sawmill centers of the European North and along the shores of the White Sea, particularly Archangel, produce for export.

In the Urals, the most important sawmill areas are in Sverdlovsk and Perm [Molotov] oblasts, where the chief centers of lumber production have grown up at points of juncture of railroads with rivers, such as the Tavda and Lobva in Sverdlovsk Oblast, and the Perm and Chusovaya in Perm [Molotov] Oblast [Fig. 6, p. 32]. In Siberia the main centers of the sawmill industry are concentrated along the Siberian railroad trunk line—Omsk, Novosibirsk [N in Fig. 41], Krasnoyarsk [Kr], Kansk, Irkutsk, Chita, Khabarovsk, Lesozavodsk, etc. Large sawmill centers have arisen also on the principal rivers of Siberia—on the Ob and the lower courses of its tributaries, at Barnaul, Tomsk [T], Mogochino, etc.; and on the

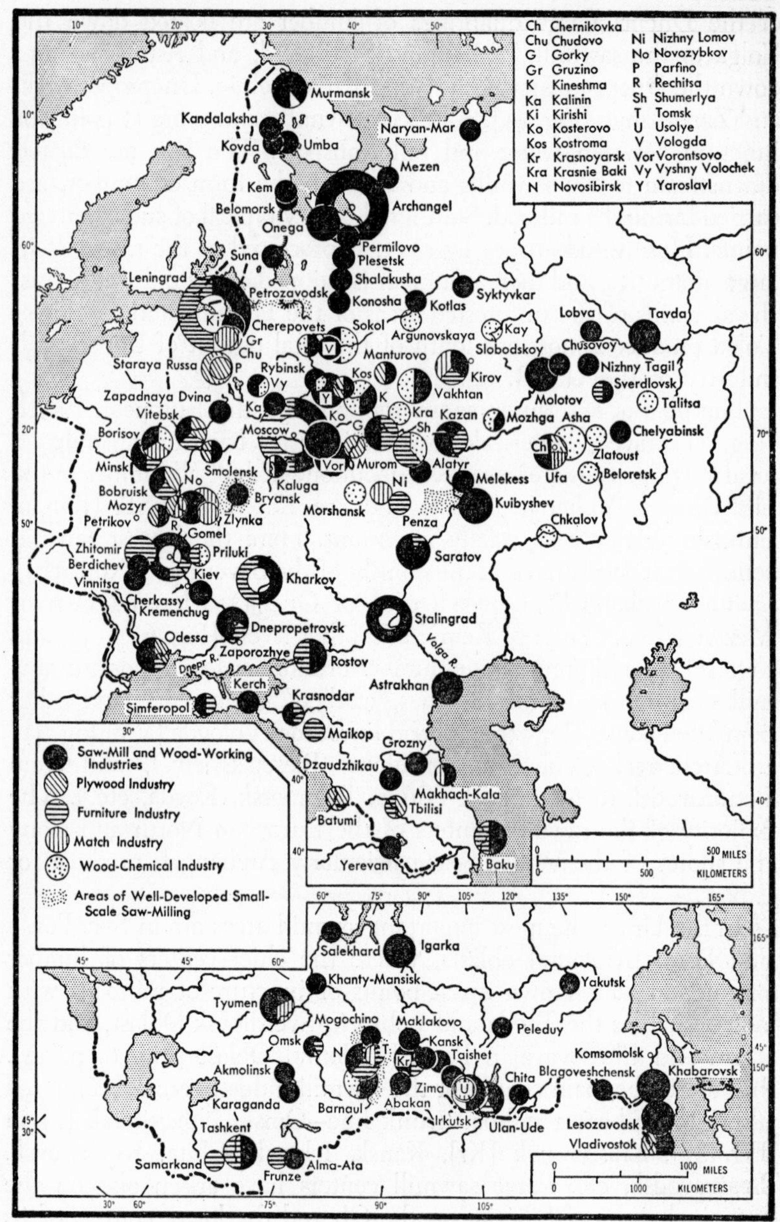

FIG. 41. WOOD INDUSTRY

Yenisey, at Maklakovo and especially Igarka. Lumber from Igarka and other sawmill centers located on the Yenisey and Ob rivers goes largely for foreign export.

The sawmills in the Subzone of Mixed Forests are largely concentrated in the most thickly forested regions of Leningrad and Kalinin oblasts, in Belorussia, in the western part of Orel Oblast, and especially in Kuibyshev Oblast and the region of the Volga republics—Chuvash, Tatar, and Mari [Fig. 40 in the back of the book, Fig. 16, p. 60, and Fig. 41]. Here sawmills have easy access to transportation.

The *plywood* industry is closely linked with the sawmill industry. Plywood is used in cabinet work, in the production of containers, and as a construction material.

A basic raw material for the plywood industry is birch, and to a lesser extent alder. Of the wood used for plywood, 90 to 95% is birch or alder and 5 to 10% is pine. For one cubic meter of birch plywood, 2.2 to 2.4 cubic meters of birch are required. From the technical and economic point of view, therefore, it is expedient to produce plywood in regions where the appropriate species of trees are common. Thus, the plywood industry of the USSR is concentrated principally in the Subzone of Mixed Forests. In Belorussia are found the larger new centers, Bobruisk and Vitebsk, as well as the old centers, Gomel, Mozyr, and Petrikov; in Leningrad and Smolensk oblasts there are centers at Staraya Russa, Parfino, and Smolensk; in Gorky Oblast, at Murom and Manturovo; in the Bashkir ASSR, at Chernikovka (a new center); in Western Siberia, at Tyumen; and in the Caucasus, at Batumi [Fig. 41].

Furniture Industry

Among the branches of the woodworking industry, furniture manufacturing has grown especially rapidly. Before the war [World War I], industrial enterprises produced furniture to a total value of 26 to 28 million rubles. By the beginning of the Third Five-Year Plan furniture production was valued at 900 million rubles, and the furniture industry had been developed in all regions of the country. This development reflects the growth in the material well-being of the population. The inexpediency of transporting furniture for great distances because of its cumbersome bulk has necessitated the wide distribution of the furniture industry.

There are furniture factories in the oblasts of the Industrial Center, in the western regions, in the oblasts of the Chernozem Center, in the Volga Region, in the North Caucasus, and in Western and Eastern Siberia [Fig. 7 and Fig. 41]. At the same time, a large number of centers of the furniture industry have been established in the Ukrainian SSR, the Belorussian SSR, the Union republics of the Trans-Caucasus, and the republics of Central Asia. In the overwhelming majority of cases, the factories in these centers either are completely new or were built on foundations of handicraft furniture factories, which before the Revolution produced the great part of the furniture in the nation.

Paper Industry

The cultural growth of the Soviet Union has placed enormous demands on the paper industry.

Before the Revolution the paper industry of Russia far from satisfied its very limited paper demand with domestic production. It operated from its inception exclusively on rags and was concentrated chiefly in the metropolitan centers of the West, the provinces surrounding them, and the Industrial Center. The use of wood raw material, beginning with the last third of the nineteenth century, did not result in any great changes in the distribution of the industry in prerevolutionary Russia. The main bulk of the paper was manufactured in the western guberniyas (St. Petersburg, Novgorod, Tver, Kaluga, and Mogilev) and in the guberniyas of the Industrial Center (Yaroslavl, Vladimir, and Moscow [Fig. 22, in the back of the book]). Until the October Revolution, the Russian paper industry, notwithstanding the enormous wood resources, continued to produce about 50% of its paper from rags. In addition, cellulose and wood pulp were approximately equally important. The domestic production of wood pulp satisfied only 40% of the needs of the industry, so that the greater part had to be imported. At the same time, pulp wood, the material from which wood pulp and cellulose are produced, was exported abroad in enormous quantities. (During some years, 80 times more pulp wood was exported abroad than was used in the production of wood pulp within the country.)

By the end of the Second Five-Year Plan, the paper industry of the USSR had more than quadrupled its output, having increased from 197 thousand tons in 1913 to 832 thousand tons in 1937. The assortment of paper produced had also changed. Before the Revolution almost two-thirds of the paper produced was of the industrial type, and only slightly more than one-third was of cultural grade. By the end of the Second Five-Year Plan, already more than 50% of all the paper manufactured in the country was of cultural grade, almost half of this being newsprint.

The production of semimanufactured products increased particularly over prerevolutionary times (wood pulp by 7 times and cellulose by 9 times). As a result, the paper industry no longer imported cellulose and wood pulp. At present, combines are under construction in the paper industry which include the production not only of paper but also of wood pulp and cellulose. The production of wood pulp illustrates the advantages which a combine affords.

At the wood-pulp plant in the paper combine, the liquid containing the fiber is concentrated to a 2% solution, so that it may be transferred in liquid state through pipes to the paper factory to be used directly in manufacturing. If the wood-pulp plant were separate, then before the wood pulp was sent to the paper factory, it would have to be reduced to an air-dry condition—a process requiring large amounts of fuel. On the other hand, at the paper factory, power is expended in pulverizing the wood pulp again and part of the wood is completely lost. Inasmuch as the production of paper and semimanufactured goods requires great quantities of electric power (about 325 kw-h for 1 ton of paper, about 250 kw-h for 1 ton of cellulose, and about 1,200 kw-h for 1 ton of wood pulp), and the production of paper and cellulose also requires much steam, a cellulose and paper combine must also include an electric power station, as a rule a TETs, in order to supply the combine with both electric power and steam.

The proportion of cellulose and wood pulp varies in different types of paper: for newsprint, approximately 75% wood pulp and 25% cellulose; for printing and writing paper of the highest quality, cellulose and rags are used, with no wood pulp. At present in the USSR, approximately equal amounts of cellulose and wood pulp are used on the whole. For manufacturing both wood pulp and cellulose, a great deal of wood is needed. Thus, for 1 ton of wood pulp, about 3.5 cubic meters of pulp wood, weighing more than 2 tons, is required. This, of course, necessitates the location of cellulose and paper combines in forested (spruce) regions with favorable conditions for transporting the wood, chiefly by water.

FIG. 42. Paper Industry

In the distribution of paper plants, proximity to timber, the basic raw material, is particularly essential. In the manufacture of cellulose, spruce and fir are used (the sulphite method in which the wood is heated with an aqueous solution of calcium bisulphate), and also pine (the sulphate method, in which sodium sulphate is used). Since the sulphite method is more productive (by 20%)

and is generally more profitable (a lower temperature is required in cooking the cellulose, smaller boiler capacity is needed, etc.), it is now used almost exclusively; it utilizes chiefly spruce. For the production of wood pulp (pulverizing the wood into small fibers, not chemically as in the production of cellulose, but mechanically), spruce is also generally used; of the deciduous trees, aspen and poplar are used.

Finally, in the location of the paper industry, water supply is very important. In spite of the use of circulating water, by which the same water is used repeatedly in production, about 150 thousand cubic meters of water is still required to produce 1 ton of dry wood pulp. Consequently, cellulose and paper combines must be located near suitably large rivers or substantial reservoirs.

The most important of the old paper factories is the group in the western part of the USSR (Fig. 42), in Leningrad Oblast (Leningrad, Dubrovka, and Okulovka), in Kalinin Oblast (Kuvshinovo), in Smolensk Oblast (Kondrovo), and in the Belorussian SSR (Dobrush). Before the Revolution these factories were, for the most part, supplied with cellulose from abroad. Even before the First Five-Year Plan, the large Syasstroy Cellulose and Paper Combine was built to supply them with domestic semimanufactured materials. Cellulose is manufactured at the combine itself only to a small degree, and for the most part is used to supply the paper factories of the Western Region. This combine was erected in the northeastern part of Leningrad Oblast on the Syas River, thus having access to both raw materials and water. The region of the Union which has the second largest paper enterprises remaining from prerevolutionary times is the European part of the Taiga Zone. As a result of reconstruction, large cellulose and paper combines have been built in the city of Sokol (Vologda Oblast) and in the workers' settlement of Novaya Lyalya (Sverdlovsk Oblast). These combines are located amid the enormous spruce areas along the large Sukhona and Lyalya rivers.

The new cellulose and paper combines are especially important. Besides the Syasstroy Cellulose and Paper Combine mentioned above, the large Kondopoga Combine has been built in the Karelian ASSR [Karelo-Finnish SSR] on Lake Onega, in a region of extensive spruce forests; the lumber reaches the combine chiefly by water. The combine manufactures principally newsprint. A still larger cellulose and paper combine, also manufacturing newsprint, has been built in Gorky Oblast, near Balakhna, at Pravdinsk. Wood is floated to this combine from the basin of the Unzha River [Fig. 6, p. 32]. A regional electric power station located in Balakhna serves the combine [Fig. 31, p. 233]. Two large combines have been erected in the Urals in Perm [Molotov] Oblast on the basis of huge reserves of spruce; one at Krasnovishersk on the Vishera River, a tributary of the Kama; the other at Krasnokamsk on the Kama [Fig. 42].

Match Industry

The match industry, which for the manufacture of matchsticks requires soft species of deciduous wood (chiefly aspen), is located almost entirely in the Subzone of Mixed Forests. The largest centers of the match industry are in Leningrad Oblast (Chudovo [Chu in Fig. 41], Gruzino [Gr], etc.), in the Belorussian SSR (Borisov), in Orel Oblast (Novozybkov [No], Zlynka), in Tula Oblast (Kaluga), in Penza Oblast (Nizhny and Verkhny Lomov [Ni]), and in Kirov Oblast (Kirov, Slobodskoy). In Siberia the most important centers of the match industry are in Novosibirsk Oblast (Tomsk [T]) and in the Far East. The production of matches, compared with prewar times, has doubled, and in the total output of matches the USSR surpasses all countries of Europe.

Wood-Chemical Industry

The wood-chemical industry was only slightly developed before the Revolution, notwithstanding the tremendous reserves of raw materials available. Rosin, acetic acid, wood alcohol, and even high-quality turpentine were imported from abroad. In the dry distillation of wood, less than half a million cubic meters of wood were used, of which two-thirds were processed in the handicraft plants of the Urals. In addition, in the Urals about 10 million cubic meters of firewood were used in the manufacture of charcoal without recovery of any acetic acid or wood (methyl) alcohol. In the European North there was an ancient tar-distilling industry, which produced resin and low-quality turpentines.

At present, by dry distillation, from coniferous species of trees turpentine and resin are produced and from deciduous species wood alcohol and sawdust (from which subsequently acetic acid is derived). A very large center of dry distillation of wood is the city of Asha, in Chelyabinsk Oblast, where a plant larger than any other in Europe has been built. But tapping has acquired great importance in the USSR; this involves the exploitation of live trees. The area over which tapping was carried on under the Second Five-Year Plan was about 700 thousand hectares. Oleoresin, drawn from coniferous trees (usually pine) by means of taps and the opening of the resin channels, is used to make rosin and turpentine (1 hectare of wood yields about 100 kg. of oleoresin, from which 70 kg. of rosin and 12 kg. of turpentine are produced).

In addition to the dry distillation of wood and tapping, the USSR has organized the extraction of rosin and turpentine from pulverized pine stumps (stump tar). The largest extraction plant in the USSR is the Vakhtan Plant in Gorky Oblast. The hydrolysis of wood is being developed, making it possible to manufacture alcohol, acetic acid, etc. An experimental hydrolysis plant is operating at Cherepovets in Vologda Oblast.

In addition to the large centers of the wood chemical industry which have been mentioned, there are, in various oblasts, krays, and republics of the Union, many other small enterprises engaged in wood chemistry. They are chiefly in the Urals (in Chelyabinsk and Sverdlovsk oblasts and the Bashkir ASSR) and in the European North (in Archangel and Vologda oblasts).

Wood Industry Under the Third Five-Year Plan

The 18th Party Congress pointed out the need "to terminate the backwardness of the wood industry." [18] Logging must undergo a broad and complex mechanization. It is developing especially rapidly in the Northern and the Northwestern regions of the European part of the Union, in the Urals, and in the Far East. The shipment of wood from Siberia to the European part of the Union is being curtailed.

The output of the sawmill and woodworking industries is increasing in the European North, in Siberia, and in the Far East. The manufacture of paper is increasing by 80%. A number of cellulose and paper combines are being completed, and a number are under construction, in the European North (Kondopoga, Archangel, Solombala, Kotlas, etc.), in the Urals, in the Volga Region (the

[18] *Resolutions of the 18th Party Congress*, p. 20.

Fig. 43. Building Materials

Kama and the Mari), a newsprint factory in the Kirov area, in Siberia and in the Far East (Krasnoyarsk and Komsomolsk combines), and also in other regions. Wood chemistry, hydrolysis of wood, and production of alcohol from sawdust and waste products of the paper industry are being developed in every way.

SECTION 8. DISTRIBUTION OF THE PRODUCTION OF BUILDING MATERIALS

In prerevolutionary Russia the production of building materials was very limited. Brick, lime, alabaster, and other bulk types were produced by small enterprises of the handicraft industry type. The production of cement was chiefly concentrated in the region of Novorossiisk and at Volsk (Volga Region), whence it was shipped to all other parts of the nation [Fig. 43]. There was almost no production of categories like refractory material, pitched roofing paper, or Ruberoid (roof-sheeting material), and only small amounts of asbestos, marble, coating materials, tuff, etc., were produced.

The enormous scale of expansion in all branches of the national economy under the Soviets evoked a great demand for various building materials and resulted in a rapid growth of their production. The manufacture of building materials has become one of the most important branches of the national economy, and upon its further development will depend to a considerable extent the completion of the grandiose projects under way in the Soviet Union.

In order to guarantee the mass output of building materials, many completely mechanized plants have been newly built in a number of regions.

The brick industry is territorially one of the most decentralized. The manufacture, with few exceptions, has been organized to the required extent throughout all regions of the Union. The production of lime in significant quantities has been organized also in almost all oblasts, krays, and republics.

The main bulk of brick and lime production is concentrated in the central regions, in Leningrad Oblast, in the Ukraine, and in Belorussia.

The great growth of capital construction in the eastern regions will demand, under the Third Five-Year Plan, increased construction of new brick and lime works in these regions.

The distribution of alabaster production is somewhat more difficult. The chief regions of production are the Ukrainian SSR, the Industrial Center, the Urals, the Volga Region, Eastern Siberia, the Uzbek SSR, and the Kazakh SSR [Fig. 43]. The Far East, the Belorussian SSR, and many of the krays, oblasts, and autonomous republics produce no alabaster. In most regions of the Union there will have to be more intensive prospecting for raw material and organization of its local production.

The quarrying of chalk is concentrated in a few regions of the Soviet Union. Almost half of the total production is in Kursk Oblast [at Belgorod]. Voronezh Oblast and the Ukrainian SSR account for much of the remainder. Many regions must be supplied with chalk chiefly either from Kursk or from Voronezh.

In 1937, the production of cement was 3.7 times greater than in 1913. Many plants have been built in new areas, basically altering the pattern from that in prerevolutionary Russia.

But these changes clearly are still inadequate. In 1937 about 73% of the cement was produced in the central regions, the Ukraine, the North Caucasus, and the Volga Region. There is still no cement production in the European North, Eastern Siberia, the Turkmen SSR, the Tadzhik SSR, the Kirgiz SSR, or the Kazakh SSR. In the Northwestern Region, cement is produced only at Leningrad (Vorovsky plant) and Chudovo [Fig. 43]. The central oblasts have cement plants in Moscow Oblast (Podolsk, Voskresensk, and Golutvin [Kolomna]), Orel Oblast (Bryansk), Tula Oblast (Kosaya Gora [K] [19]), Voronezh Oblast (Podgornoye and Lipetsk), and Ryazan Oblast (Mikhailov). In the Volga Region production is concentrated almost entirely in Saratov Oblast, in the Volsk group of plants, and to some extent in Kuibyshev Oblast (Sengiley plant). In the North Caucasus cement is produced only in the Novorossiisk group of plants, which yield more than a million tons; in the Urals it is produced in Sverdlovsk Oblast (Bogdanovich station, Nevyansk, Pashiya, Kushva, and Nizhnyaya Salda plants) and Chelyabinsk Oblast (Katav-Ivanovsky plant). In Western Siberia cement is produced only in Novosibirsk Oblast (Yashkino and Chernorechensk [at Iskitim?] plants), and in the Far East only at the Spassk plant in Maritime Kray.

[19] [This letter refers to an abbreviation on Fig. 43, as do other bracketed letters in the following paragraphs.]

In the Ukrainian SSR cement is produced in Amvrosievka [Donetsko-Amvrosievka], Kramatorsk [Kr], Dnepropetrovsk [D], Dneprodzerzhinsk [Dn], Kharkov, and Ordzhonikidze [Yenakievo, Y].

In Azerbaidzhan cement is produced at the Baku and Tauz [misprinted Gauz in original] plants; and in Georgia, at Kaspi station. There is a similar plant in Armenia [at Ararat] in the region of Davalu station.

In Central Asia there is cement production in the Uzbek SSR at the Kuvasay and Khilkovo [Kh] plants. In Belorussia cement is produced at the large Krichev plant.

By the end of the Third Five-Year Plan in 1942 the production of cement will have increased to 11 million tons, twice the 1937 figure. Many medium and small plants will be built in new regions which do not make their own cement. Production will be organized in the Kazakh SSR (at Karaganda, Syas-Tyube, and Novo-Taubinka), the Tadzhik SSR (at Stalinabad), the Turkmen SSR (at Ashkhabad, at the Bezmein deposit), Archangel Oblast, and Eastern Siberia (at Krasnoyarsk and at the Temlyuy deposit in the Buryat-Mongol ASSR) [Fig. 20, p. 143]. New centers for cement production are being created in the Far East (at Londoko, Komsomolsk-on-Amur, and other points), the Urals (at Sterlitamak, Magnitogorsk), and Leningrad Oblast (at Pikalevo and Volkhovo). New, large plants are being completed at Podolsk (Moscow Oblast) and Bryansk.

Cement production is growing especially rapidly in the Far East, the Northwestern Region, and the Urals. All the economic regions of the country will be able to satisfy their requirements through local production, thus eliminating long hauls from the European part of the USSR to the eastern regions and Central Asia.

Highly significant is the development in the USSR of domestic production of refractory materials, essential in the technological processes of ferrous and nonferrous metallurgy, machine building, the chemical industry, and power production. Before the Revolution, they were imported in large measure from abroad. At present the USSR meets all its own needs through domestic production. In 1937, 1,780 thousand tons of refractory-brick products were manufactured, as compared with 572 thousand in 1913. The production is located in the principal metallurgical and machine-building centers of the Soviet Union, where the demand is greatest. The Ukraine provides 48.2% of the refractory products; the Urals, 13.1%; the Center, 20%; the Northwest, 13.7%. All other regions combined provide only 5%. Dinas-brick manufacture is a new industry, and in 1937 amounted to 594 thousand tons, almost entirely in the Ukraine (74%) and the Urals (20.4%). In 1937, the Urals produced 92 thousand tons of magnesite and chrome brick, and 184 thousand tons of magnesite metallic powder—the total production of these in the Soviet Union.

The production of new roofing materials—pitched roofing paper and Ruberoid (roof-sheeting material)—has been developed considerably.

The production and extraction of new building materials have increased. These include artificial stone, tuffs, coquina, pressboard made of reeds, marble, and granite.

The 18th Party Congress set as one of the chief tasks the overall development of all types of building materials in all economic regions of the country, and the development of brick and lime in all oblasts, krays, and republics until the domestic production satisfies local demands completely.

SECTION 9. DISTRIBUTION OF LIGHT INDUSTRY

During the years of the [first] two Stalin Five-Year Plans, the most important branch of industry producing consumers' goods—the textile industry—increased its output 180%, whereas during the same period (1928–1937) the United States, England, Canada, and Japan increased their output only 3 to 50%. Other countries did not even maintain the 1928 level. Poland and Belgium, in particular, curtailed their production by one-fifth, and France by more than one-third.

The total output of consumers' goods in the Soviet Union was valued at 40.3 billion rubles in 1937. Somewhat more than one-third of this was from various branches of the food industry, about one-third from light industry, and somewhat less than one-third from industrial cooperatives manufacturing products of the food and light industry.

Textile production comprises more than half of light industry; sewing and leather and shoe production, approximately one-sixth;

and knitted fabrics, glass and china, and other branches, the remaining portion.

The Cotton Textile Industry of Tsarist Russia

Before the Revolution the textile industry was the predominant branch of industry both in the number of workers employed and in the value of output. Cotton was especially important, accounting for about 73% of the textile output. Almost the entire manufacture of cotton fabrics was concentrated in the central guberniyas—Vladimir, Moscow, St. Petersburg, Yaroslavl, Kostroma, and Tver [Fig. 22, at the back of the book, and Fig. 27, p. 200]. The raw material for this industry was imported from Central Asia and Azerbaidzhan, a distance of 3,000 to 4,000 km., and also from abroad.

The central guberniyas supplied the entire country with cotton goods.

After the first cotton factories had been built by foreign capital at St. Petersburg [Leningrad] and Shlisselburg [Petrokrepost], the manufacture of cotton print developed extensively in Moscow, Vladimir, Yaroslavl, and other guberniyas between the Oka and the upper Volga [Fig. 19, p. 114]. In these guberniyas the tenant system prevailed, guaranteeing large reserves of "hired" labor; and the linen industry, particularly the printed linen cloth industry, prepared a skilled labor supply for the subsequent cotton manufacture. These conditions were long important in determining the concentration of cotton printing in the area. Later, weaving mills were added to the cotton-printing factories, and spinning was also developed in the same area.

Thus, by a series of historical developments, the great cotton textile region of the country was created: the present Moscow Oblast, with such centers [Fig. 44B] as Moscow, Orekhovo-Zuyevo, Glukhovo, Pavlovsky Posad, and Serpukhov; Ivanovo Oblast, with centers at Ivanovo, Shuya, Vichuga, Kineshma, Sereda, etc.; Leningrad Oblast, with centers at Leningrad and Shlisselburg [Petrokrepost] [Fig. 44A]; and Kalinin Oblast, with centers at Kalinin, Vyshny Volochek, etc.

Since fiber derived from cotton-ginning plants weighs approximately one-half that of unginned raw cotton, the cotton manufacturers of the central guberniyas of European Russia preferred to import from Central Asia and the Trans-Caucasus cotton which had

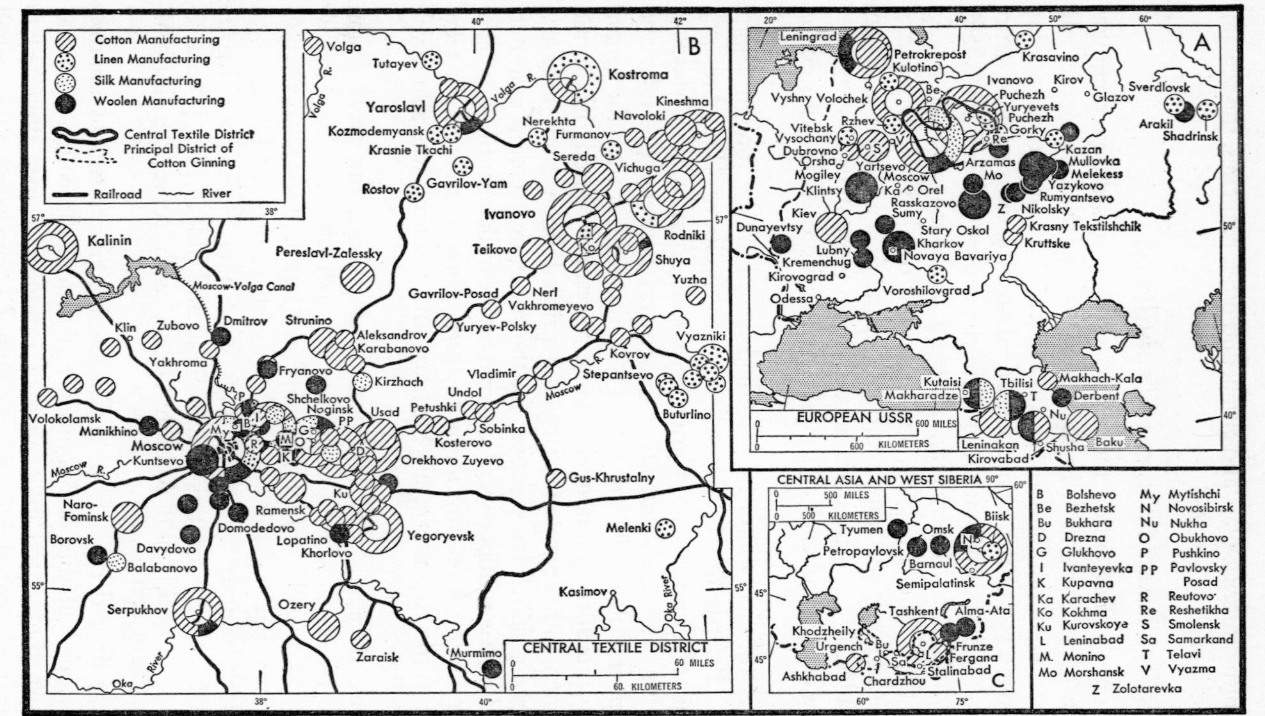

FIG. 44. Textile Industry (A, European USSR. B, Central Textile District of the European USSR. C, Central Asia and West Siberia)

been processed already, with the first stage of manufacture effected at the source.

The Cotton Industry of the USSR

After the October Revolution the cotton industry made a number of important strides. Before it the Russian industry had been very backward technically.

As a result of the Stalin Five-Year Plans the situation has changed radically. A domestic textile machine-building industry has been created. The production of the majority of textile machines has been mastered. In the history of the capitalist countries there has been no instance of the creation of a domestic textile machine-building industry in such a short space of time. As a result of the Stakhanovite movement, the textile workers have learned to operate a large number of machines. In the factories of Tsarist Russia one female weaver handled 1 to 2 machines. In England and the United States one man handles at most 8 to 10 ordinary weaving machines. In the USSR in 1938 many weavers were handling 20 machines. With automatic weaving machines, one weaver can handle as many as 210, 216, or 284 machines.

The progress of the cotton industry in solving the problem of raw material has also been great. Before the Revolution, about 45% of the cotton used was imported from abroad. Now the USSR, instead of importing, is exporting cotton. The needs of its own textile industry are completely satisfied. This was accomplished by developing cotton growing both in the old regions of Central Asia and Azerbaidzhan and in new regions in the Ukraine, the North Caucasus, the Crimea, Kazakhstan, and other areas where conditions for the cultivation of cotton are satisfactory. In addition to the types of cotton formerly grown, Egyptian cotton is also being picked in large quantities.

However, in spite of this progress, the industry is still far from adequate to supply the demands of the country. As was indicated at the 18th Party Congress, enemies of the people in the management of the textile industry have sabotaged the program of the Second Five-Year Plan for that industry, so that it has not been fulfilled. They have held back artificially the development of the industry in the USSR, have created a disproportion between spinning and weaving, have tried to wreck equipment by failing to keep it in repair, have squandered the resources supplied to the industry, and have created a breach between the raw-material resources and the industry itself. The great efforts made under the direction of the Party and the Government to eliminate the consequences of sabotage have improved conditions in the textile industry.

The cotton industry has made great progress in new regions. In summing up the accomplishments of the First Five-Year Plan, Comrade Stalin said: "We used to have only one single base for the textile industry—the northern part of our country. We have succeeded in arranging that, in a short time, we shall have two new bases of the textile industry—in Central Asia and in Western Siberia." [20] As a result of the Stalin Five-Year Plans large centers of the cotton industry [Fig. 44C] have been established in the USSR in Central Asia (Tashkent, Fergana, Ashkhabad) and also in Western Siberia (Barnaul), where a mixed combine has been erected. New cotton factories have been built in the Trans-Caucasus, where before the Revolution almost no cotton was manufactured; in the Azerbaidzhan SSR at Kirovabad; and in the Armenian SSR at Leninakan [Fig. 44A].

In the old cotton manufacturing regions, in addition to the reconstruction of old enterprises to eliminate the discontinuity between separate shops, spinning factories have been built in Moscow Oblast (Kurovskoye [Ku in Fig. 44B] and Ivanteyevka [I]) and Ivanovo Oblast (Ivanovo, Undol, Vladimir, Vichuga, etc.).

The Flax [Linen] Industry

The flax industry is one of the oldest in the country. In Tsarist Russia large quantities of flax had always been gathered, and a great deal exported to the countries of Europe and Asia. Lenin included in the "domestic flax-growing region," nineteen guberniyas outside the chernozem area, that is, the present western oblasts and the northern part of Belorussia, the oblasts of the Industrial Center, the southern part of the oblasts of the European North, and the northwestern part of the Urals. Flax was processed where it was gathered, either with the aid of the "Pskov brake" or, in the overwhelming majority of cases, by hand, which consumed a great deal of time and labor, principally of women.

From the western part of the belt, that is, the present Leningrad,

[20] Stalin, *Questions of Leninism*, p. 374.

Kalinin, and Smolensk oblasts, a great deal of flax was exported abroad. In spite of this, Tsarist Russia, with its characteristic backwardness, imported fine linen fabrics from abroad. In the western part of the flax belt there were linen-spinning factories only in the territory of the present Vitebsk Oblast—at Vitebsk and in the vicinity of Vysochany. The linen industry was located for the most part in the present Yaroslavl Oblast at Kostroma, Gavrilov, Tutayev, and Rostov; in Ivanovo Oblast at Vyazniki, Yakovlevsk (near the town of Sereda), Vichuga, etc.; in Vologda Oblast at the Krasavino factory ([just northeast of] Veliky-Ustyug); in Gorky Oblast at the Molotov factory (in Kanavino, a former suburb now part of the city of Gorky); and there were other smaller factories [Fig. 44]. The flax grown in the eastern part of the belt was processed chiefly by small handicraft industries. A few factory centers (mostly small enterprises) were concentrated on the Volga, particularly in Kazan and Melekess, and also in Kirov, Sverdlovsk, and Shadrinsk.

In order to grow flax the following natural conditions are required: (1) uniform heat and moisture during the growing period; (2) relatively cool climate—the sum of the [daily] temperatures during the vegetative period must not exceed 2,200° C. and must not fall below 1,400° C.; and (3) predominantly clayey soils. A considerably larger part of the USSR than the old flax-growing regions satisfies these requirements. Consequently the area under flax was doubled after the Revolution. As a result, the raw-material base for the industry has been broadened significantly. However, in the development of flax cultivation there are still some big shortcomings. The national economy requires high-count flax. The count of the flax, however, is still extremely low; the yield is also low. The location of the industry has changed substantially (Fig. 44). In addition to the new enterprises in the old regions of the flax industry—the weaving factory already built in Vyazniki and the flax combine in Kostroma, as well as the flax combines under construction in Vologda Oblast (at Krasavino and at Vologda itself)—new centers of the flax industry are being created under the Stalin Five-Year Plans, chiefly in the Western Region, with flax of higher quality that in the past was almost exclusively exported. A flax combine has been built at Smolensk and a carding factory at Vyazma; in the Belorussian SSR (Orsha) a carding factory and a combine have been built, and in Kalinin Oblast combines are being built in the most important flax-growing regions (Bezhetsk and Rzhev). The industry is also developing in the eastern part of the flax-growing belt. A combine is being built in the Udmurt SSR (Glazov). Thus the industry is dispersing throughout the entire flax-growing region, and its distribution is becoming more and more uniform.

The Hemp-Jute Industry

The hemp-jute industry, operating on hemp, jute, and in part on flax, manufactures ropes, sail, net, etc., for water transport and fishing; sacks, tarpaulins, etc., for agriculture and other branches of the national economy; fire hose for fire-fighting; etc.

The chief hemp growing regions of the USSR are somewhat south of the flax belt, because hemp requires more heat. These are the southern regions of the flax-growing oblasts—Smolensk, Moscow, and Gorky—and the southern part of the Belorussian SSR and the western regions of the Ukrainian SSR.[21] The oblasts of the Chernozem Center—Orel, Kursk, and Ryazan—are especially important. Another important type of raw material, jute, is not cultivated to any extent in the USSR; a feasible substitute is *kenaf* hemp [*Hibiscus cannabinus*], which is cultivated in the USSR. The demand for jute is still met in considerable measure by import from abroad, but imported jute is being increasingly displaced by kenaf, of which the crops in the USSR are increasing rapidly.

The largest industrial enterprises of the hemp-jute industry in prerevolutionary Russia were located in those ports on the Black and Baltic seas, Odessa and Leningrad, through which came the most important raw material, jute. In addition, a number of centers were located near large industrial towns—in Moscow Oblast (Pushkino), Leningrad Oblast (Kulotino), Gorky Oblast (Reshetikha), and Kharkov Oblast (Novaya Bavariya). A group of enterprises in the hemp-jute industry were in operation in the oblasts of the Chernozem Center—Orel Oblast (Klintsy), Ryazan Oblast (Kasimov), and Kursk Oblast (Stary Oskol). A number of less important centers existed in Belorussia and in Smolensk Oblast.

During the years of the Soviet regime, a number of new centers of the hemp-jute industry have been created. With the development of navigation and fishing on the northern seas, hemp-jute enterprises have arisen in Murmansk Oblast (Murmansk, etc.) and

[21] [Administrative divisions are shown on Fig. 83 in back of the book.]

Archangel Oblast (Archangel). The hemp-jute industry has been developed further in Orel Oblast (Karachev, Orel). Finally, in the Ukraine a new center of the hemp-jute industry has arisen at Kirovograd.

The Wool Industry

The wool industry in what is now the USSR was represented before the Revolution by fine cloth factories at Leningrad; by worsted and fine cloth factories in Moscow Oblast (Moscow, Pavlovsky Posad, Kuntsevo, Fryanovo, etc.) and Orel Oblast (Klintsy); and finally by coarse cloth factories in Tambov Oblast (Rasskazovo and Morshansk), Penza Oblast (Nikolsky hamlet, Zolotarevka), and Kuibyshev Oblast (Yazykovo, Rumyantsevo). The worsted and fine cloth factories operated, for the most part, on imported raw material (wool and yarn). Imported yarn comprised about 40% of the total wool consumed in Russia. The introduction of new types of raw material and the use of waste products of the flax, leather, sheepskin coat, and other industries have enabled the USSR to discontinue importing wool. However, raw material still remains one of the most important problems of the Soviet wool industry, and upon its solution depends the future development of the wool industry.

New construction in the wool industry has been directed chiefly toward bringing the factories closer to the raw-material regions (Fig. 44). Thus, a number of cloth factories have been built in the Ukraine (Kharkov and Kremenchug), the Georgian SSR (Kutaisi and Tbilisi), and the Kazakh SSR (Semipalatinsk). In the old region of the wool industry—Leningrad—a special factory has been built to make industrial cloth for the paper industry, thus enabling the USSR to discontinue importing such cloth.

The Silk Industry

The silk industry before the Revolution imported 80% of its raw silk (while at the same time the raw materials—cocoons—were exported). Three-fourths of the industry was owned by foreign capital. It was located entirely in the central part of Russia—nine-tenths of it in Moscow Oblast (Moscow, Pavlovsky Posad, Shchelkovo, Bolshevo, etc.) and Ivanovo Oblast (Kirzhach). In addition to the factory silk industry in the central region, there existed a well developed handicraft silk industry in the Pavlovsky Posad and Kirzhach districts.

The USSR discontinued the import of raw silk and the export of cocoons, having strongly developed its own production of raw silk at the old silk-reeling factories and having constructed a number of new silk-reeling factories in new raw-material areas. Among the old centers of silk-reeling, the largest are Azerbaidzhan (Nukha, Shusha) and Uzbekistan (Fergana). New silk-reeling factories have been built in the Georgian SSR (Telavi, Khoni, and Ozurgety [Makharadze]), the Turkmen SSR (Ashkhabad and Chardzhou), the Tadzhik SSR (Leninabad and Stalinabad), the Kirgiz SSR (Osh), and the Uzbek SSR (Samarkand, Bukhara, and Margelan) [Fig. 28B, p. 201 and Fig. 44C]. The newly built silk-reeling factories are large, especially that at Margelan, which is larger than any in Europe.

In addition to the development of the silk-reeling industry, the manufacturing industry has grown since the Revolution. It is particularly essential that it is developing in new regions, near the sources of raw material, whereas in the past the manufacture of silk was separated from the source of raw material. A number of new plants have been erected in the Georgian SSR (Tbilisi, Kutaisi, and Makharadze) and the Azerbaidzhan SSR (Nukha).

The Soviet industry does not operate on natural silk alone, which supplies only about 35% of the total raw material consumed. Artificial silk, a very new branch of the industry, has existed only about half a century. In prerevolutionary Russia there was only one small factory in Mytishchi, near Moscow, which belonged to an English capitalist. Under the Soviet regime a number of factories have been built where artificial silk is produced—at Klin in Moscow Oblast, at Mogilev in the Belorussian SSR, and at Leningrad. As a result of all these steps, the silk industry has increased its production by 125% over 1913, more than any other branch of the textile industry.

The Sewing and Knitting Industries

Sewing and knitting are new branches of manufacturing. Before the Revolution they existed chiefly in the form of handicraft production in small workshops. The system of distributing work to be done at home or at the home of the customer was widely practiced.

FIG. 45. Clothing Industry (Sewing and Knitting)

A small number of more or less important sewing and knitting factories existed in Leningrad and Moscow. In addition, knitting enterprises existed in a number of centers in Moscow Oblast (Pushkino, Lobnya) and in the Ukrainian SSR (Kharkov), while there were some sewing enterprises in the Tatar ASSR (Kazan) [Fig. 45].

After the Revolution large sewing and knitting factories were erected. Their output exceeds the output of prerevolutionary factories in the knitting industry by more than 50 times, and in the sewing industry by almost 150 times. Thus, these branches of the industry are essentially completely new. The chief raw material for the knitting industry is cotton thread and for the sewing industry cotton and woolen fabrics. In addition to expanding the enterprises which existed in the old centers—Moscow, Leningrad, and Kharkov—new sewing and knitting factories have been set up in the large cities of the Ukrainian SSR (Kiev, Odessa) and the Belorussian SSR (Vitebsk). Furthermore, sewing factories have been built, with only a few exceptions, in all oblast and republic centers (Fig. 45): in the Central Industrial Region (Yaroslavl, Ivanovo, and Gorky), in the Urals (Sverdlovsk, Perm [Molotov], and Chkalov), in the Volga Region (Kuibyshev and Stalingrad), in the South (Rostov-on-Don and Simferopol), in Western and Eastern Siberia (Novosibirsk and Irkutsk), in the Ukrainian SSR (Dnepropetrovsk, Vinnitsa, Stalino, Mariupol, etc.), in the Belorussian SSR (Minsk, Gomel, etc.), in the Union republics of the Trans-Caucasus (Baku, Kirovabad, Tbilisi, Batumi, and Yerevan), in the Union republics of Central Asia (Tashkent and Bukhara), and in many other places. Moscow Oblast (Kosino and Zagorsk) and the Ukrainian SSR (Poltava) have also become centers of the knitting industry.

The Leather and Shoe Industry

Before the Revolution, the leather and shoe industry existed largely in the form of small shops and handicraft industries.

The raw material came, for the most part, from Siberia, Kazakhstan, Central Asia, and the Caucasus. There was a shortage of the heavy leather used in making soles, and a large quantity had to be imported from abroad. The smaller skins were exported abroad. In return, chrome leather, manufactured from Russian skins, was imported, chiefly from Germany. Tanning of hides was done principally by the old-fashioned pouring method (pouring ground bark over the hides in pits which were then filled with water). Tanning extracts, used in small amounts, were entirely imported.

Fairly large plants which manufactured sole leather with imported tanning materials were located for the most part in ports—Leningrad, Taganrog, and Odessa; there were small plants also in Moscow. Uppers from small skins (chrome) were not manufactured at all in Russia, and uppers from the skins of cattle (welts and inner soles) were semimanufactured; Russian leather—finished leather for the uppers of boots, for leather bags, etc.—was manufactured at small plants in Kalinin (Ostashkov), Kirov (Kirov), Orel (Yelets and Bolkhov), and other oblasts [Fig. 46]. There were shoe factories at Leningrad and Moscow, and in Ryazan and Kirov oblasts. Siberia had no enterprises of any size for the production either of shoes or of leather. The chief centers of the leather and shoe crafts were in Kalinin (Kimry), Gorky (Bogorodskoye), and Kirov (Slobodskoy) oblasts.

After the Revolution, the manufacture of leather substitutes was organized, particularly of rubber soles. These are now made in plants at Leningrad, Moscow, Yaroslavl (part of the Yaroslavl Rubber-Asbestos Combine), Ivanovo, etc.

The USSR no longer imports tanning materials, having developed its own tanning-extract industry. It uses both vegetable raw material—found chiefly in the Volga Region in Saratov Oblast (Volsk), Kuibyshev Oblast (Melekess), the Chuvash ASSR (Shumerlya), and in other regions of the Union—and wastes of the paper industry (sulphite-pulp lyes) and the coke by-product industry (Donbas). The USSR, instead of importing chrome leather, has set up its own production of chrome uppers in plants at Leningrad, Ostashkov, Moscow, and Kirov. Big construction is under way in the shoe industry. In addition to the reconstruction and enormous expansion of the old enterprises in Leningrad and Moscow, a whole series of factories have been erected (Fig. 46) in the Urals (Sverdlovsk, Sarapul), in Siberia (Novosibirsk, Krasnoyarsk, Stalinsk), in the South (Rostov-on-Don), in the Union republics of the Trans-Caucasus and Central Asia (Tbilisi, Tashkent), in the Ukrainian SSR (Kiev, Odessa), and in the Belorussian SSR (Minsk, Gomel, Vitebsk). Finally, in the East of the USSR where sheep are raised,

FIG. 46. Leather Tanning and Shoe Industries

a number of sheepskin and fur-coat plants have been built at Novosibirsk, Alma-Ata, Chita, etc.

The Glass and Pottery Industries

The enormous construction projects throughout the entire country, the great demand of the population, and the difficulty of transporting glass and pottery over long distances make it imperative that these industries be established widely through the country. However, inasmuch as the most suitable raw materials—quartz sand (60% of the raw material used for glass and 30 to 35% of that used for pottery) and kaolin (35% of the raw material for pottery)—are concentrated in several special regions, it is in these regions, for the most part, that the chief glass and pottery industries are located. The most important of the regions is the western section of the country where reserves of quartz sand and kaolin are found (Fig. 47): Leningrad, Vologda, Kalinin, Smolensk, and Orel oblasts (the former Maltsevskaya group of plants [north of Bryansk]), the Belorussian SSR, and the Ukrainian SSR (particularly Kamenets-Podolsk and Zhitomir oblasts).[22] Centers of well developed glass and pottery industries have been established also in the central district, which has particularly good raw material resources—clays of different types and quartz sand—in Moscow Oblast (Likino and Dulevo [L in Fig. 47]), and Ivanovo Oblast (Gus-Khrustalny [inset in Fig. 47]). As these branches of industry have a tremendous fuel requirement (in glass furnaces the temperature reaches 1,450° C.), the Stalin Five-Year Plans have created large glass plants where cheap fuel is abundant, and where at the same time other construction has a great demand for the products, as in the Donbas (Konstantinovka) and the Dagestan ASSR ("Dagestanskie Ogni").

The "Dag-Ogni" plant uses natural combustible gas for fuel and at the same time is well supplied with local quartz sand; it receives sulphate by sea from Kara-Bogaz-Gol. In the Asiatic part of the USSR, glass and china plants are found at Tomsk and Krasnoyarsk, in Irkutsk Oblast (Mishelevka), and at Ulan-Ude. Plants manufacturing bottle glass are typical in regions where there are sources of mineral water—at Mineralnie-Vody in the North Caucasus, and at Borzhomi in the Georgian SSR.

[22] [These political divisions are indicated on Fig. 83 in the back of the book.]

Light Industry Under the Third Five-Year Plan

The development of light industry under the Third Five-Year Plan is linked primarily with the full utilization of the raw-material resources of the country, with the technical perfection of equipment, and with increasing the assortment and improving the quality of output.

The most important branch of light industry, cotton, is undergoing especially large-scale new construction. In the oblasts of the Industrial Center, small spinning factories are being built in order to eliminate the disproportion between spinning and weaving. But the cotton industry is being developed most intensively in the raw-material regions—in Central Asia and the Trans-Caucasus, as well as in Western Siberia, where communication with Central Asia is good: the second section of the Tashkent Cotton Combine, the Leninakan spinning factory, and the cotton factories in Novosibirsk, the Kuzbas, and Barnaul are being put into operation. The wool industry is being supplemented by new cloth combines at Kiev and Semipalatinsk. Also a number of new, small flax combines, and a number of silk, knitted goods, and stocking plants are being built. The leather and shoe industry is to have a new plant at Kalinin for manufacturing rubber soles, and a plant at Kazan for making artificial leather. Small enterprises for producing glass containers are also under construction.

SECTION 10. DISTRIBUTION OF THE FOOD INDUSTRY

"In old Russia there was no real food industry, except for vodka, sugar, and tobacco. . . . These were excise industries, which provided an enormous revenue for the treasury, and their development was supported by the Tsarist Government for fiscal reasons. . . . But even these favored branches of industry were poorly developed, and their technology was on a very low level." [23]

In recent years dozens of excellent new enterprises have been created, according to the latest American and European technology. These include factories which are examples of the finest technology in the world. As for the factories which existed before the Revolu-

[23] A. Mikoyan, *The Food Industry of the Soviet Union*, p. 89.

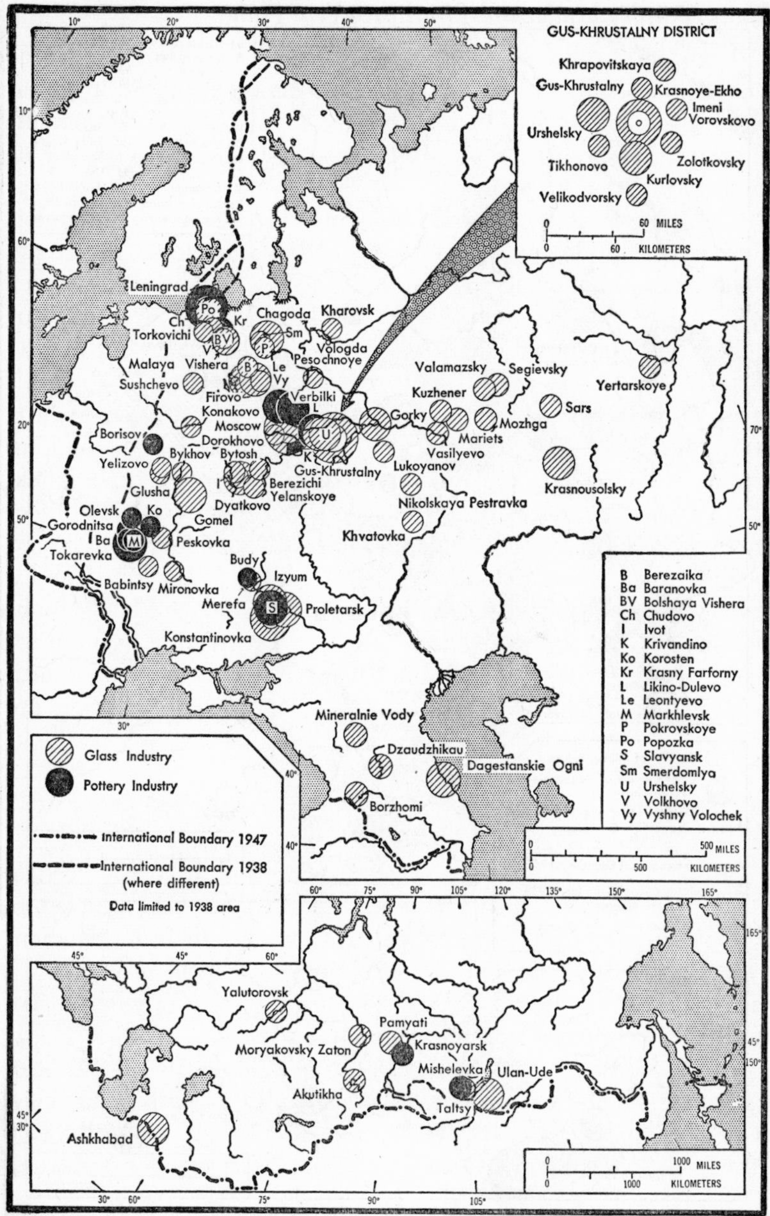

Fig. 47. Glass and Pottery Industries

FIG. 48. Flour and Vegetable-Oil Industries

tion and are still in operation, "we must say that many of them are old frames with new techniques, with new contents." [24]

The food industry is a large one, most uniformly distributed throughout the country. The enterprises engaged in it comprise more than one-fifth of the industrial enterprises in the USSR. Every republic, kray, or oblast has dozens of large food enterprises.

Among the most important branches of the industry are milling and groats, bread baking, and confectionery. Next in importance is the meat and fish industry, including canning. Third place falls to the dairy industry and to the production of animal and vegetable fats; fourth to the sugar industry; and fifth to distilling and wine making. The rest of the various branches of the food industry account for approximately 10% of food production.

Milling and Groats Industry

The most important branch of the food industry is the milling and groats industry, which produces flour and groats. These account for 40% of the food budget. Before the Revolution more than 95% of the enterprises in the milling and groats industry were windmills and water mills. There were only somewhat more than 2 thousand mechanized enterprises, which processed less than 10 million tons of grain.

The large commercial mills, worn out during the Imperialist War and the Civil War, were subjected to thorough reconstruction during the years of the Stalin Five-Year Plans. In very large part processed grain is used for flour; only about 7% for groats. Of all the manufactured flour more than two-thirds now comes from wheat.

Large-scale milling has been developed in the most important grain regions (Fig. 48): the Ukrainian SSR; the Crimean ASSR; the oblasts and krays of the North Caucasus; the Chernozem Center; the Volga Region (particularly the middle Volga); the Tatar ASSR; the Bashkir ASSR; Chelyabinsk, Omsk, and Novosibirsk oblasts; and also Altay, Khabarovsk, and Maritime krays.[25] As a rule, the largest commercial mills are at railroad junctions, to which grain from the surrounding grain regions is transported.

A number of milling centers are in the oblasts of the upper Volga,

[24] *Ibid.*, p. 57.

[25] [See Fig. 7 and Fig. 83 in the back of the book for the location of these regional and administrative areas.]

where grain is not cultivated extensively: at Kalinin, Rybinsk, Yaroslavl, Kineshma, and Gorky. Milling in these cities is founded on the processing of grain which comes by way of the Volga, while part of the flour is used locally and in the adjacent regions, and part is sent by railroad to other cities. Baku and Tashkent also are large centers of commercial milling developed on grain brought from a distance. Baku supplies the greater portion of the Trans-Caucasus with flour from grain of the North Caucasus and the Ukraine, which is shipped by railroad, and of the Volga Region, which is shipped by way of the Caspian Sea. Tashkent is the center of flour distribution for the republics of Central Asia; most of the grain received here for milling comes from Kazakhstan and the Volga Region. The changes in the location of the flour-milling industry from prerevolutionary times are especially substantial in the national republics and the eastern regions, where in the years of the Soviet regime sixty first-class flour-milling and groats enterprises have been built.

Bread Baking

There was no large-scale industrial automatic bread baking before the Revolution.

The manufacture of bakery products in prerevolutionary Russia has been vividly described by M. Gorky in his remarkable story "Twenty-six Men and a Girl": "From day to day, amid flour dust and amid dirt dragged in by our feet from the outside, in dense, redolent closeness, we twisted dough and made pretzels, moistening them with our sweat, and we hated our work with a sharp hatred; we never ate what came from our own hands, preferring black bread to pretzels."

The supplanting of homemade bread with factory-made bread has proceeded throughout the years of the Stalin Five-Year Plans. More and more, not only home baking, but also production by small bakeries is being supplanted, inasmuch as by hand an experienced baker can bake only 14 to 15 poods of bread, whereas at a mechanized bread factory one worker can produce as much as 140 poods—approximately ten times as much.

At present bread factories are widespread throughout all the oblasts, krays, and republics. Aside from Moscow and Leningrad, where there are dozens of bread factories, a large number of other cities also have several bread factories each. These include not only the republic and oblast centers [Fig. 48], such as Kiev, Kharkov, Odessa, Dnepropetrovsk [Dn], Rostov-on-Don, Gorky, Ufa, Novosibirsk, Tashkent, Ashkhabad, Baku, and Tbilisi, and not only the large industrial centers, such as Magnitogorsk, Berezniki, and Ordzhonikidzegrad [Bezhitsa], but also many cities representing medium industrial centers, such as Noginsk, Pavlovsky-Posad, Vyshny-Volochek, and Astrakhan. There is usually a minimum of one bread factory in each industrial town and in the larger workers' settlements.

Finally, we should note the presence of bread factories at large railroad junctions, where, in order to supply a large number of passengers, especially transients, it was necessary to create large bread factories, as at Znamenka, Tikhoretsk, Ruzayevka, and Bologoye.

Confectionery and Macaroni Industries

The confectionery industry by 1938 had increased 14.7 times over prerevolutionary times. The factories which existed before the Revolution were thoroughly reconstructed. For example, the Moscow factory, "Krasny Oktyabr" (formerly Einem), produced 7 thousand tons in 1913, while its output in 1937 was 59.3 thousand tons. Another Moscow factory, Babayeva (formerly Abrikosova), in 1913 produced 3.7 thousand tons, while in 1937 its output was 49.7 thousand tons. These two factories alone in 1937 produced 50% more than the entire confectionery industry of prerevolutionary Russia. While in the past the industry was located almost entirely in the largest industrial centers, Moscow, Leningrad, and Kharkov, during the years of the Stalin Five-Year Plans many enterprises have been constructed in other cities. Thus, factories have been built in Gorky, Voronezh, Ufa, Kazan, Minsk, Gomel, Baku, Tbilisi, Tashkent, and Ashkhabad.

The macaroni industry is completely new in the USSR. The small macaroni factories which existed before the Revolution in Leningrad and Moscow have been rebuilt and expanded. Dozens of new macaroni factories have been built. Macaroni is produced from hard varieties of wheat (rich in albumins, with a vitreous grain), which grow chiefly in the North Caucasus and the Ukraine. The macaroni industry thus is located to a large extent in the North

FIG. 49. Meat, Fish, and Dairy Industries

Caucasus [Fig. 48] at Krasnodar, Maikop, Armavir, Novorossiisk, Taganrog [T], and Rostov-on-Don; and in the Ukraine at Odessa, Nikolayev [N], Kherson, Osipenko [O], Vinnitsa, Zhitomir, etc. There are a number of macaroni centers on the Volga—at Astrakhan, Saratov, and Kuibyshev. Macaroni industries have been established also at a number of centers in the national republics—Ufa, Kazan, Baku, Tbilisi, Yerevan, etc. In order to eliminate excessively long hauls, production of macaroni has been undertaken in the eastern regions as well.

The Meat Industry

The meat industry of prerevolutionary Russia was characterized by small enterprises with unsanitary conditions and complete absence of mechanization. The primitive slaughterhouse was, as a rule, only a wooden shed. Under the Soviet regime, production has been expanded to a large-scale industry. The principal type of enterprise has become the meat combine, which completely processes meat carcasses to give a wide assortment, not only of foods (meat, sausage, smoke-cured products, canned meats, and fats), but also of industrial products (industrial fat, meat and bone fodders, and fertilizers, hides, bristles, glue, etc.) and special products (pepsin, adrenalin, catgut). In the meat combines, artificial refrigeration is widely used. The combines have at their disposal complex power and subsidiary establishments, which manufacture steam and electric power, supply hot, warm, and cold water, and remove waste water.

At the present time meat combines are widespread throughout the entire Union (Fig. 49). In addition to the huge meat combines at Moscow and Leningrad, there are many large meat combines at other centers as well—Bryansk, Baku, Leninakan, Semipalatinsk, and others. There are many centers of the industry in the republics and oblasts in which livestock raising is well developed, as in the Kazakh SSR, the Ukrainian SSR, the Far East, Siberia, the Urals, and the North Caucasus.

The Fish Industry

In prerevolutionary Russia the fish industry was a home industry. Fish were processed in primitive handicraft fashion. Old Russia imported 4 million centners of fish annually from abroad

During the years of the Stalin Five-Year Plans the fish industry increased from 7.5 million centners in 1927 to 14.9 million centners in 1938. The USSR occupies second place in the world in its fish catch, having outstripped Norway, England, and the United States; only Japan now has a greater catch. The industry is now technically well equipped, having 6.7 thousand motor vessels, about 100 trawlers, a number of large ship-repair plants, dockyards for building wooden ships, radio stations, and airplanes, which conduct surveys of the fish shoals. Besides the large state industry, sixty motor fishing stations (MRS) have been created under the Second Five-Year Plan.

Before the Revolution, about two-thirds of the fish were caught in the Caspian Sea, 10.5% in the Far East, 6.1% in the European North, and about 18% in all other seas and lakes. The present location of the fishing industry is radically changed (Fig. 49). The catch in the Barents Sea has increased by almost 200%, now providing 20.6% of the total catch of the entire USSR. The catch in the Far Eastern basin, which now provides 25.2% of the total fish of the USSR, has increased by 150%. The catch in the Caspian Sea is relatively less important than it was and now occupies second place, after the Far Eastern region, providing 23% of the total fish catch of the USSR. The Caspian Sea is extremely rich in fish, as conditions for breeding are unusually favorable in the deltas of the Volga, Kura, Ural, and Emba rivers [Fig. 6, p. 32]. In the Caspian Sea many sturgeon of several types are caught (the common sturgeon, *sevryuga* sturgeon, and *beluga* sturgeon); also large quantities of Caspian roach, pike perch, pike, bream, catfish, gray mullet, and others. Most of the rivers to which the fish from the cold Okhotsk Sea go to spawn are in the western part of Kamchatka. Here, therefore, are concentrated many centers of the fishing industry. In the southern part of Khabarovsk Kray fishing for the most part is in the Tatar Strait, at the mouth of the Amur, and in southwestern Sakhalin Oblast [Fig. 5, p. 24]. In Maritime Kray, where fishing is carried on along the entire coast, the industry is concentrated especially in the Bay of Peter the Great.

In the Pacific Ocean fishing is developed on the shores of Kamchatka and on the shores of Maritime Kray. The waters of Kamchatka are among the richest spawning grounds in the world for anadromous salmon (those that live in the sea and enter the rivers to spawn), and the Pacific chum and pink salmon predominate. In addition to the salmonids, there are also herring, flatfish, navaga, cod, smelt, mackerel, and others.

The rapid development in the Barents Sea is due to the unusual wealth of fish in the sea. The fish caught are chiefly cod, haddock, navaga, and herring. Trawling is highly developed. Murmansk is the center of the industry.

Fishing in the Sea of Azov is relatively important, particularly on the shores of Rostov Oblast and Krasnodar Kray. On the Ukrainian shores the catch is small. The fish caught are predominantly pike-perch, bream, herring, and *taran* (a species of carp).

In the Black Sea fishing is negligible. In the coastal strip the development of animal life is hindered by the great fluctuations in temperature and salinity, while at a depth of 150 to 200 meters there are no fish because of the presence of hydrogen sulphide.

Of the fishing areas on the Black Sea, the south shore of the Crimea, the region of Odessa, and the region of Novorossiisk are of some importance.

In addition to changes in fishing methods, there have also been decisive changes in the processing. While the production of salted fish has decreased, that of fresh-frozen, smoked, and canned fish has increased. The preparation of culinary products has been organized.

The Canning Industry

The canning industry is new in the world as a whole. In prerevolutionary Russia canning was of a household and semihousehold nature, producing 90 million jars of food per year. In 1937 the total output exceeded a billion jars. New plants have been built. The productive capacity of many of them exceeds the total prewar output (the Stalin plant in Kherson, the Mikoyan plant in Krasnodar Kray, etc.).

Almost 60% of the canned products are fruits, vegetables, and tomatoes; 18% are meats; about 17%, fish; and 5%, milk. The distribution of the industry is determined first of all by proximity to raw materials, inasmuch as it is impossible to transport perishable foods long distances for canning. Proximity to sources of containers—tin cans and glass jars and bottles—is also important. In selecting a spot for a plant, a readily available supply of water and fuel, in large quantities, is also essential.

* FIG. 50. Centers of Canning and of Artels

Plants for canning fruits and vegetables are for the most part in the southern part of the USSR. Thus, in the RSFSR the chief regions of production of canned fruits and vegetables are the North Caucasus (Rostov Oblast, Krasnodar Kray, Adygeya, North Osetia, the Chechen-Ingush ASSR [now mainly Grozny Oblast], and Dagestan) and the Crimea (Simferopol, Kerch, Balaklava, and Feodosiya).[26] In the Ukrainian SSR the chief centers of the industry are in the southwestern part (the Moldavian ASSR [now SSR], Odessa, and Kherson). A number of large centers of the industry are in the Union republics of the Trans-Caucasus (Yerevan in Armenia, Gori and Kutaisi in Georgia, Lenkoran and Khachmas in Azerbaidzhan) and in Central Asia (Leninabad and Kanibadam in the Tadzhik SSR and Kaunchi in the Uzbek SSR). Meat and fish canneries are located near large meat combines and in the chief fishing regions [Fig. 49].

The production of canned milk is a completely new branch of industry. It was begun only in 1932. Comrade Mikoyan, speaking of the canning industry, said, "Our border regions, whence milk cannot be brought, and where there is more milk than can be disposed of (for example, in Kazakhstan, Siberia, and Bashkiria)—here is a base for the production of condensed milk."

The Milk Industry and the Production of Animal and Vegetable Fats

Before the Revolution, the rudiments of the industrial processing of milk were to be found in only three cities—Moscow, St. Petersburg, and Odessa, where annually, on the whole, 25 thousand tons of milk were processed. In the USSR a huge *milk* industry has arisen. In 1937, it processed 420 thousand tons of milk. The production of whole milk and lactic acid products has been developed in most of the large cities in all regions of the Union. The production of whole milk has been developed particularly vigorously in the oblasts of the West and of the Industrial Center, characterized by a great abundance of dairy cattle. The most important regions of butter production are in the European part of the Soviet North (especially Vologda Oblast), while in the Asiatic part of the USSR,

[26] [Fig. 7 and Fig. 83 in the back of the book give regional and administrative names. Fig. 50 indicates the location of towns mentioned in this paragraph.]

Omsk and Novosibirsk oblasts (Fig. 49) are butter-producing regions.

The *vegetable oil* industry is one of the few branches of the food industry which were rather highly developed before the Revolution. However, the enterprises remaining from former times needed large-scale reconstruction. The raw-material supply was scant. This inadequacy of raw material for the oil industry is still a problem.

Very important in the oil industry of the USSR is the manufacture of sunflower [seed] oil, which comprises 55 to 60% of the total vegetable-oil output. Some 20 to 25% of the total output is cottonseed oil, 10 to 12% linseed oil, and about 5 to 8% other oils. The principal regions which manufacture sunflower oil have large sunflower crops. These are the oblasts and krays of the North Caucasus, the Chernozem Center, and the Ukraine. The regions which manufacture cottonseed oil are the chief cotton republics of Central Asia and the Trans-Caucasus (the Uzbek SSR, Tadzhik SSR, Turkmen SSR, and Azerbaidzhan SSR). The regions which produce linseed oil are the chief oblasts of the flax-growing belt in the European part of the Union (Smolensk, Kalinin, Leningrad, and Yaroslavl oblasts) and in Western Siberia (Novosibirsk Oblast and Altay Kray).

Under the Soviets new methods of extracting oil have been mastered. Especially powerful oil-extracting factories for processing sunflower seeds have been built in the North Caucasus (Krasnodar and Kropotkin) [Fig. 48], in the Chernozem Center (Alekseyevka [Al] in Voronezh Oblast), and in the Far East (Voroshilov-Ussuri-isky). The first plant in the world for extracting oil from cotton seeds was built at Katta-Kurgan [Ka in Fig. 48] in the Uzbek SSR.

The Sugar Industry

Sugar is another branch of the food industry which was developed in prerevolutionary Russia. However, the dumping of sugar abroad, particularly in England, created high prices on the domestic market. As a result, in Tsarist Russia the poor peasant class and most of the middle peasant class were unable to buy sugar.

In the years of the Stalin Five-Year Plans the sugar industry was technically re-equipped and the production was increased significantly. In 1938, 2.5 times as much sugar was produced as in 1913. By 1935 the USSR had gained first place in the production of beet

FIG. 51. Sugar Industry

sugar. Formerly half of the sugar-beet factories were located at a distance from the railroads. Now the factory railroad network has been increased by three times, and the sugar industry is fully provided with good transportation for raw material, fuel, and accessory materials, and for the shipment of the manufactured sugar. Hauling the beets from the fields, pumping out the refuse, and filtration are being widely mechanized. The average working time of the sugar-beet factories is being increased, as is the sugar content of the beets (in 1912–1913, 14.8%; during the years of the Five-Year Plans, an average of 16.7%). The beet pulp (residue) is now widely used for cattle fodder.

The distribution of the sugar industry has changed considerably during the years of the Stalin Five-Year Plans (Fig. 51). Climatic and soil conditions make possible the production of sugar beets with an even higher sugar content in many oblasts, krays, and republics to the east of the old sugar-beet region. In the years of the Stalin Five-Year Plans, in addition to sugar-beet factories previously existing in the oblasts of the Ukraine and the Chernozem Center (Vinnitsa, Kamenets-Podolsk, Kiev, Chernigov, Sumy, Poltava, Kursk), new factories have been built in Voronezh Oblast, Kirgizia, Kazakhstan, the North Caucasus, Georgia, the Volga Region, Western Siberia, and the Far East.

The Distilling Industry and Wine Making

Formerly alcohol was used exclusively in the manufacture of spirituous liquors. Today it has acquired great importance in the chemical industry and in the national economy as a whole. It is used in the manufacture of rubber. A large quantity is used also in cosmetics (eau de Cologne, perfume). Alcohol has increasing importance in aviation and automobile transport, in the form of absolute alcohol. The quantity used for vodka is half as much as in prerevolutionary times. At present in the USSR alcohol is manufactured chiefly from potatoes. Corresponding to the potato belts, the chief distilling regions are the Belorussian SSR, the western part of the Ukrainian SSR, Smolensk, Kalinin and Leningrad oblasts, and the oblasts of the Industrial Center and the Chernozem Center. Wine making, as well as viticulture, has developed chiefly in the Union republics of the Trans-Caucasus—especially the Georgian SSR—and also in the North Caucasus, the Crimea, and the Union republics of Central Asia.

The Food Industry Under the Third Five-Year Plan

The more than 50% increase in the demands of the workers under the Third Five-Year Plan, corresponding to the increased income of laborers, peasants, and white-collar workers, necessitates a marked increase in the food industry. The building of new bread factories and confectionery factories is under way. The processing of animal products is growing especially rapidly. A number of meat combines are being completed and put into operation [Fig. 49]: in the Industrial Center (Ivanovo), the Volga Region (Kuibyshev, Engels), the North Caucasus (Nalchik), the Urals (Sverdlovsk and Orsk), Siberia and the Far East (Irkutsk, Ulan-Ude, Khabarovsk), the Ukraine (Dnepropetrovsk, Voroshilovgrad), and the Union republics of Central Asia (Ashkhabad, Stalinabad). A large number of meat combines of average capacity are under construction also in various regions of the country.

Under the Third Five-Year Plan the backwardness of the fish industry is being resolutely overcome. The catch is increasing significantly in all basins, and especially in Murmansk and the Far East. For some time provisions have been made to increase the rate of development of the Kamchatka, Okhotsk, and Ayan regions. Shipyards are under construction at Murmansk, Nikolayevsk-on-Amur, and Petropavlovsk-on-Kamchatka. The processing of fish is increasing. Many fish combines and refrigerators are under construction in various regions of the USSR—on the Caspian Sea (Mangistan), on the Sea of Azov (Akhtari), on Lake Balkhash, in Kara-Kalpakia (Muinak) [Aral Sea], and in the Far East (Komsomolsk-on-Amur, Khabarovsk, Sovetskaya Gavan, Petropavlovsk-on-Kamchatka, etc.). A combine in Moscow is being completed. In every way possible, the fish economy is being developed, on the basis of locally important water bodies (rivers, lakes, and ponds).

Under the Third Five-Year Plan the sugar industry is undergoing further development, both in the old regions of the Ukraine (Kiev and Vinnitsa oblasts) and the oblasts of the Chernozem Center (Kursk and especially Voronezh oblast), and in new areas: Kazakhstan, Kirgizia, and Armenia. Construction of a number of new factories—alcohol, butter, condensed milk, various canned goods, etc.—is under way.

SECTION 11. DISTRIBUTION OF LOCAL AND COOPERATIVE INDUSTRY

Local and cooperative industry are called upon to use easily available raw materials and waste products of large-scale industry to satisfy local needs for consumers' goods, fuel, building materials, etc. During the Soviet regime they have been highly developed and play an important role in satisfying the needs of the population for various consumers' goods. They produce almost 18% of all the industrial output of the Union. The chief branches of local industry, since the transfer of the light and food industries to the corresponding people's commissariats in the republics, are metal working, which produces 40% of the total output of local industry; chemicals, 17% (of which plastics account for 12%); building materials, and glass and pottery, 12% each; school supplies, 7%; printing, 5%; musical supplies, 3%; and fuel, 1%.

The distribution of local industry is still somewhat uneven. The central regions and Leningrad Oblast produce 53% and the Ukraine 20% of the total output, while the Urals, Siberia, and the Far East produce only 5% in all, the republics of Central Asia and Kazakhstan 2.2%, the republics of the Trans-Caucasus 3.2%, and the regions of the European North 0.3%. Local industry is well developed in Belorussia, the Volga Region, and the North Caucasus.

Local industry under the Third Five-Year Plan is scheduled to increase its output by 100%. Special attention is given to increasing the output of metal commodities, chemical plastic products, high-quality toys, dry goods, sewing articles, furniture, local types of fuel, and building materials from local types of raw material.

The most important problem is the need for a basic change in geographic distribution, to guarantee first of all the economic development of local industry in regions formerly backward.

Handicraft cooperatives have as many as 60,000 workmen's associations (artels), in which more than one million cooperative craft workers are employed.

The cooperative industry plays an enormous role in supplying the population with consumers' goods. Industrial cooperatives produce over 20% of all the consumers' goods manufactured in the entire country (excluding foods). Industrial cooperatives produce 35% of all the furniture manufactured in the country, 50% of the knitted outer garments, 35% of the felt boots, 42% of the metal consumers' goods, 65% of the metal beds, 33% of the sewing articles, 15% of the knitted underwear, and 80% of the dry goods. High-priced and artistic rugs, embroideries, lace goods, scissors, primus stoves, many types of wooden and metal dishware, children's toys, and musical instruments are manufactured almost entirely in the workmen's associations of industrial cooperatives.

Like local industry, handicraft cooperation is distinguished by excessive concentration in the Central Industrial Region and very slight development in remote regions of the Union [Fig. 50]. The Central and Northwestern regions provide 48% of the total output of cooperative industry, and the Ukraine 21.4%, while the Urals, Siberia, and the Far East provide only about 7%. Dry goods, children's toys, wooden furniture, household necessities, dishware, primus stoves, primus burners, phonographs, radio receivers, and domestic electrical appliances are produced almost exclusively in the regions of Leningrad and Moscow. The production of knives and forks, small metal tools, wooden spoons, and technical chains for fishing and timber rafting is almost wholly in the confines of Gorky Oblast. Such a distribution leads to inefficient long hauls of cumbersome articles, such as carts, sleighs, wheels, light wooden materials, wooden and iron containers, and metal utensils, needlessly burdening the railroad system.

By the end of the Second Five-Year Plan general shops had become the most widespread type of handicraft cooperative. Some handicraft centers were remodeled, grew considerably in size and strength, and became famous throughout the USSR and in some cases even throughout the world. In Gorky Oblast the Pavlovo-Vacha handicraft region, manufacturing knives, locks, and metal tools, has developed rapidly, having more than 100 workmen's associations with mechanized shops, and the Semenovsky handicraft region, manufacturing more than 100 million wooden spoons annually, have acquired fame. The Zaovrazhye region, which supplies the whole Union with technical chains for timber rafting and for the fish industry, is also famous. In Moscow and Leningrad, large industrial artels have been created for the production of electrotechnical items. Here large artels making knitted goods are concentrated. The lace artels in Vologda and Yelets are well known; the artels in Zvenigorod, producing musical instruments; the Zagorsk artels, manufacturing 100 million rubles' worth of children's toys annually; the Kimry boot artels in Kalinin Oblast; and the Tula artels for manufacturing hardware and locks [Fig. 50]. The artels of the Ukraine, Belorussia, Archangel Oblast, and the Mordovian, Mari, and Chuvash republics are noted for their embroideries, and the Tula, Saratov, and Borovichi craftsmen for their accordions.[27]

[27] [Location of oblasts and republics is indicated on Fig. 83 in the back of the book.]

The village of Kabugi (in Dagestan) is famous as the oldest center for jewelry, and Kholmogory and Tobolsk are famous for their bone carvers. The artistic artels of Palekha and Mstera (Ivanovo Oblast) are world-famous. In the Volga German Republic, and in the region of Baltser [misprinted Beltser in the original and now called Krasnoarmeisk], etc., there are very large centers for the production of high-quality homemade striped cotton cloth. Chkalov Oblast is well known for the production of down kerchiefs. The largest centers of carpet production in the Union are concentrated in the Turkmen, Azerbaidzhan, Georgian, Armenian, and Dagestan republics. The Mary [Merv] region in Turkmenia is the largest center in the Union for carpet production, providing about half of the total output of carpets in the Soviet Union.

Industrial cooperation under the Third Five-Year Plan is receiving further development and is increasing its total output by more than 100%. Industrial cooperatives, now mostly in the large cities and in the central districts, must be decentralized in so far as possible throughout the whole country and developed in the small oblast, kray, and republic centers.

The Third Five-Year Plan has begun the mass technical reconstruction of the handicraft industry by creating shops with mechanized production processes.

A wide network of various types of repair shops is being created in order to meet fully the needs of the population.

VI Distribution of Agriculture in the USSR

SECTION 1. GEOGRAPHY OF AGRICULTURE BEFORE THE REVOLUTION[1]

Backwardness of Agriculture

IN prerevolutionary Russia, modern techniques were absent in agriculture. The principal tools on the peasant farms of Tsarist Russia were crude wooden plows and harrows. According to the census of 1910, on the peasant farms there were 10.0 million wooden plows, 4.2 million iron plows, and 17.7 million wooden harrows.

In most regions until the Revolution the three-field system prevailed (fallow, winter grain, and summer grain), although it had long since been abolished in the leading countries of Western Europe and had been replaced by the multiple-crop system with great emphasis on fodder and industrial crops. The existence of communal land use with periodic reapportionments of land and the practice of dividing peasant fields by strips of land belonging to different owners precluded introducing crop rotation. Chemical fertilizers were used in altogether negligible quantities and only on the manorial estates. The small number of livestock (most peasant farms were without cows, or had only one cow) meant that manure also entered the soil in insufficient quantity. Productivity was low. The average grain yield was 6 to 7 centners per hectare [9 to 11 bushels per acre]. Poor harvests and starvation were common among the peasants.

The chief reasons for the extreme backwardness of the agricultural

[1] [Fig. 22 indicates the location of the guberniyas and other prerevolutionary political units mentioned in this section, and Fig. 7 locates regional names. Both figures are in the back of the book.]

economy of Russia were landlord oppression and the survivals of serfdom. Through an analysis of the statistics of land ownership in 1905 in Tsarist Russia, Lenin showed that 30 thousand of the biggest landowners had about 70 million dessiatines of land. An equal amount of land was in the hands of 10 million peasant farmers. Half of the peasantry owned no more than 1 or 2 dessiatines each [2.7 to 5.4 acres]. The peasants were compelled to rent land from the landlords under very unfavorable conditions, frequently under a share-cropping system—that is, they turned over to the landlords half of their harvest as rent. The hiring-out system was very widespread. Under it the peasant paid his rent by cultivating a certain part of the landlord's property without remuneration, using his own cattle and implements.

Class Stratification in the Rural Communities

After the abolition of serfdom, the development of capitalism in Russia was rapid both in the town and in the country, notwithstanding survivals of serfdom. The peasant economy was drawn increasingly into commercial relationships, and the marketability of agricultural products increased. Class stratification of the peasantry took place. Most of the middle peasants [serednyaks] were ruined; they joined the ranks of the poor and of the farm laborers, creating an agricultural proletarian class of hired workers with land allotments. Only a minority went into the ranks of the kulaks.

Before the Revolution, among the peasant holdings 65% were those of poor peasants [bednyaks], 20% of middle peasants, and 15% of kulaks. Of the peasant farmsteads 30% had no horses. The poorest peasants sowed small plots, turned over the rest of their land for rent to the kulaks, and then themselves worked for wages. Before the Revolution, every year about 2 million poor peasants of the central guberniyas went to the North Caucasus and the Ukraine, working as hired laborers for kulaks and landlords. A still larger number went to the cities to work for wages. The poor peasant paid large fees to the kulak for the temporary use of his horse and plow. The rural bourgeoisie exploited the poor and middle peasants, lending them money and seeds under very unfavorable terms. The kulaks, comprising 15% of the peasant farm owners, claimed half of the peasant crops; they grew rich, profiting from the work of hired laborers and day laborers.

The stratification of the peasantry increased after the issuing in 1906 of the Stolypin agricultural law. This gave each peasant the right to separate himself from the commune, and to sell his share of the communal land. The kulaks took over the farmsteads, buying land from the poor peasants at low prices. The kulak class grew strong by depriving the poor peasants of land and ruining them.

The class structure of the agricultural economy of Russia is illustrated clearly by the figures for the distribution of gross and commercial output of grain according to classes. Thus, of the total gross output of grain, 12% was produced by landlords, 38% by kulaks, and 50% by poor and middle peasants. Of the commercial output of grain, 21.6% was in the hands of landlords, 50% in the hands of kulaks, and only 28.4% in the hands of poor and middle peasants.

Thus, the chief producers of commercial grain were the landlord and kulak farmsteads. The great majority of holdings—those of the poor and middle peasants combined—produced only half of the gross output of grain and approximately one-fourth of the commercial output. The marketability of grain was higher on the manorial estates (47% of the total output). On the holdings of the middle and poor peasants the marketability of grain was very low (14.7% of the total output).

A large part of the commercial grain went abroad. Before the Imperialist War, Russia exported more than 500 million poods of grain annually [300 million bushels]. Grain and other agricultural products were exported at the cost of malnutrition of millions of poor peasants in the country, who lived in a state of semistarvation.

Peculiarities in the Development of Capitalism According to Regions

The development of capitalism in the agricultural economy took place unevenly in the various regions of Russia. According to level and rate of development of capitalism, there were three groups of agricultural regions: (1) the southern and eastern chernozem steppe guberniyas, (2) the central chernozem guberniyas, and (3) the nonchernozem guberniyas—central, northwestern, and northern.

In the *steppe guberniyas* of the southern and eastern borderlands of European Russia (the southern Ukraine, the North Caucasus, the Trans-Volga, and Siberia), where serfdom never existed, there were no such survivals of serfdom in the form of hired-out labor as in the manorial central chernozem belt. The development of capitalist agriculture consequently was more rapid than in other regions of

Russia. Large kulak farms were of greater relative importance than in other guberniyas. The abundance of land favored the growth of large capitalist farms based on hired labor. On the manorial estates of the southern and southeastern guberniyas the capitalist system of agriculture prevailed. Here the land was worked by hired agricultural workers.

The steppe borderlands, the chief regions of grain cultivation, attracted many seasonal workers from the central guberniyas. The guberniyas of Bessarabia, Kherson, Tavrida, Yekaterinoslav, Samara, Saratov (southern part), Orenburg, Don Oblast, and the North Caucasus were the chief regions of influx of hired agricultural workers. At the same time, in the steppe guberniyas agricultural machines were widely used, such as iron plows, reapers, and threshers, enabling the large capitalist farms to increase the land under cultivation and to reduce the cost of grain production. The application of machinery forced out the hired workers, increased the agricultural labor reserve, and thus resulted in lower wages; the rate of work increased and the exploitation of agricultural laborers was intensified.

The *central chernozem guberniyas*—Kazan, Simbirsk, Penza, Tambov, Ryazan, Tula, Orel, Kursk, Voronezh, Kharkov, Poltava, and Chernigov—were outstanding for the least development of capitalism. Here large manorial estates, based on a system of hired labor and share-crop economy, were most numerous, and here also the survivals of serfdom were most prominent. In the central chernozem guberniyas the cruel exploitation by the landlords led to the impoverishment and ruin of the peasant masses. Prerevolutionary literature called these guberniyas "the impoverishing center." As a consequence of the shortage of arable land and the cruel exploitation by the landlords, the great majority of the peasants were half starved. Their own grain was enough to last half a year only. They consumed, on the average, one-half pound of sugar per person per year. As a result of chronic malnutrition and unsanitary living conditions, mortality was very high.

The central chernozem guberniyas were the chief region of agricultural emigration. The poor peasants who had been ruined, who had land allotments too small to provide enough food, migrated in masses to the South, to the less populated outskirts which were open for settlement in regions where there was a high demand for hired labor. The workers with land allotments represented a concealed labor reserve, which reached huge proportions in prerevolutionary times and pushed the level of wages down, both in the country and in the city.

In the *non-chernozem industrial guberniyas* (St. Petersburg, Moscow, Yaroslavl, Nizhny Novgorod, etc.), hiring-out was less developed than in the central chernozem guberniyas.

The development of industrial capitalism was evident in the agriculture of these regions. The proximity to industrial centers promoted the development of market relations and the growth of commercial dairy production and truck farming based on hired labor. A large part of the poorer peasants went to the city to work for wages, and the proletarization of the peasantry here progressed rapidly.

Specialization of Agricultural Regions

As Russia developed a commercial agricultural economy, certain regions came to specialize in particular market products. "The very isolation of various agricultural regions was one of the most characteristic traits of agriculture in Russia in the reform period after 1861."[2] In the last half of the nineteenth century certain regions came to specialize in grain cultivation, flax growing, dairy production, sugar-beet cultivation, cotton growing, etc. In the specialization of agricultural regions the development of the social division of labor appeared.

The region of *grain cultivation* included the southern and eastern margins of European Russia. In the 1860's and 1870's the chief regions of grain production were the central chernozem guberniyas; but in the 1880's the steppe borderlands became most important. The abundance of free land attracted many settlers, and the area under cultivation expanded rapidly.

Grain cultivation in the borderlands was developed through the expansion of the tilled area. This resulted in an unbalanced grain economy. According to the agricultural census of 1917, Samara Guberniya had 97.1% of its cultivated area in grain crops; Orenburg Guberniya, 97.3%; Ufa Guberniya, 94.2%; Don Oblast, 91.6%; and Saratov Guberniya, 93%. The most important grain crop was wheat.

[2] Lenin, *Works*, Vol. III, p. 191.

The steppe chernozem guberniyas of the South and the Trans-Volga supplied grain to the central industrial districts of Russia. They also exported a large quantity of grain to foreign markets. The southern and southeastern regions were the most important wheat-export areas.

At the end of the nineteenth century, the production of grain increased significantly in the Trans-Urals and Siberia, where there were also great expanses of land suitable for the cultivation of wheat and other grain crops. However, development of grain cultivation in these regions was hindered by their distance from markets and by the disadvantageous railroad rates. The Tsarist Government, to protect the manorial economy of the central chernozem guberniyas from the competition of cheap Siberian grain, had established higher rates for the transfer of grain by railroad from the Urals to the center of Russia (the so-called "Chelyabinsk divide").

In Siberia the production of butter had become highly developed. Before the Revolution it was the chief butter-exporting region, exporting to the markets of Western Europe (chiefly England). Dairying was widespread. Poor breeds of Siberian cattle, coarse fodder (hay and straw), cold sheds, and lack of any care for the cattle were the chief traits of dairying in Siberia before the Revolution. Commercial butter production was for the most part in the hands of large-scale kulak farmers.

On the steppe margins of Russia large-scale capitalist farms developed rapidly, based on the use of agricultural machinery and hired labor.

In the non-chernozem zone agricultural specialization proceeded along the lines of dairy farming, truck farming, and flax growing. This was promoted by the proximity of industrial centers which served as a market for milk and vegetables. Thus, *dairying, truck farming,* and *potato growing* developed into major commercial branches of agriculture in the central and northwestern industrial guberniyas, especially around cities. Also, the increased cultivation of potatoes in a number of regions was connected with the development of starch manufacturing.

The well-to-do and kulak farmers bred high-production cattle and developed hotbed and hothouse truck farming. In the northern districts (Vologda Guberniya) the production of butter for export was developed.

In the central and northwestern non-chernozem guberniyas (Pskov, Tver, Yaroslavl, Moscow, etc.) flax-growing regions were distinguished. Flax cultivation in these regions expanded with the increase in demand for flax fiber in the foreign markets and also with the growing domestic flax industry. As it expanded, the rural population became more stratified. "Capital ruined masses of small landowners, lowered the quality of the flax, depleted the soil, led to the lease of land plots, and in the long run increased the number of seasonal workers." [3]

With the development of dairying and flax growing in the central and northwestern non-chernozem guberniyas, fodder crops were introduced. According to the census of 1917, fodder crops occupied 15.9% of the area under cultivation in Moscow Guberniya; 10.1% in Smolensk Guberniya; 11.1% in Tver Guberniya; and 13.5% in Petrograd Guberniya. The percentage of the area in industrial crops reached 22.2 in Smolensk Guberniya, 17.7 in Tver Guberniya, and 14.1 in Yaroslavl Guberniya. Potatoes were a very important crop in these guberniyas.

While in the steppe margins capitalist agriculture was developed by expanding the sown areas, in the non-chernozem belt it took the form of an intensification of agriculture: an increase in the number of livestock per unit of area and an expansion of the area under intensive crops (flax, potatoes, vegetables, etc.).

In the central chernozem guberniyas, the growth in the marketability of agricultural products was connected with the development of distilling, which demanded an increase in *potato* production. The spread of potato cultivation for distilling took place on the manorial estates and well-to-do peasant farms.

The chief regions for production of *beets* were the southwestern guberniyas (Kiev, Volyn, etc.) and to some extent the southern part of the central chernozem guberniyas (Kursk, Kharkov). Sugar-beet cultivation was chiefly on the manorial estates, where sugar factories were located. The expansion of beet cultivation increased the demand for labor power, transforming the mass of the peasantry in the sugar-beet regions into an agricultural proletariat.

Turkestan (the territory of the present republics of Central Asia) specialized increasingly in *cotton*. This was the result of an increase in the demand for cotton from the developing textile industry of

[3] Lenin, *Works*, Vol. III, p. 216.

Moscow, Ivanovo, etc. Oppressive forms of exploitation—"hiring-out," usury, etc.—were widespread here. The development of cotton growing was accompanied by the ruin of the great mass of peasants, and the enrichment of the kulak classes (rich landowners).

The increase in the demand for meat in the central industrial districts promoted the development of commercial livestock raising in Kazakhstan (sheep and cattle) and the drawing of the nomad peasant economy of Kazakhstan into market relationships. However, here the marketability of the peasant farm products remained less than in other regions.

The specialization of Russian agriculture assumed different forms in different regions. Those enumerated above cover only the chief types of commercial agricultural regions in prerevolutionary Russia.

Specialization and Increase in the Marketability of Agricultural Products

The specialization of agriculture according to regions reflected the process of disintegration of the natural economy, and the subjugation of agriculture to the market (domestic and foreign). The development of market relationships depended on the growth of social division of labor. "That process of specialization which distinguishes one type of manufacturing process from another and creates an increasing number of branches of industry, appears also in agriculture, creating specialized agricultural regions (and systems of agricultural economy), bringing about exchange not only of agricultural and industrial products, but also of various types of agricultural products." [4]

The development of industry during the reform period following 1861 led to an increase in the demand for agricultural products—for articles of food for the growing urban population and for raw materials for industry—leading to an exchange of products between agriculture and industry. The growth in railroad construction, bringing agricultural producers closer to the market (domestic and foreign), promoted the specialization of agricultural regions.

The specialization of agricultural regions meant the exchange of various agricultural products. While the natural peasant economy produced all products necessary to itself the peasant found it more profitable, with the development of the market, to expand his pro-

[4] Lenin, *Works*, Vol. III, p. 16.

duction of one or another commercial agricultural product, making it the chief product of his farm and adapting all other phases of agriculture to this product. Thus, in the flax-growing regions the peasant expanded the area in flax, meeting his demand for bread in large measure through purchased grain.

The growth of a commercial economy was fundamental to the development of capitalism. By bringing about an exchange among the various agricultural regions, the development of commercial agriculture promoted the creation of a domestic market for capitalism. By drawing the peasant economy into market relationships, agricultural specialization hastened the disintegration of the peasantry, with the growth of an agricultural bourgeoisie on the one hand, and of an agricultural proletariat and semiproletariat on the other hand.

SECTION 2. GENERAL CHARACTERISTICS OF AGRICULTURE IN THE USSR

USSR—the Nation Having the Most Highly Mechanized Agriculture

By the construction of kolkhozes [collective farms] and sovkhozes [state farms] the USSR has changed from a nation of small peasant farms to a nation of socialist agriculture on the largest scale in the world. Instead of 23.7 million individual poor and middle peasant holdings, there were in 1938 242.4 thousand kolkhozes with an average cultivated area of 484.6 hectares. The average farm in the United States has 20.2 hectares [49.9 acres]; in France, 5.7 hectares; and in Germany, 3.5 hectares.

On July 1, 1938, 93.5% of the peasant farms had been collectivized, and the total cultivated area included was 99.3% of the former peasant farms.

Collectivization eliminated small strips and broken plots and made possible the use of tractors and agricultural machines and advanced agricultural techniques. Thanks to the kolkhozes, rural poverty has disappeared and conditions have been created conducive to a comfortable and cultural life for all the working peasants.

Under the First Five-Year Plan a huge network of large highly mechanized sovkhozes, or state farms, was created. The sovkhozes, through their new techniques and with the aid of the surrounding peasants, were of tremendous importance in converting the working peasantry to collectivization. They are a very important source of commercial agricultural production.

In 1938 the USSR had 3,961 sovkhozes with an average cultivated area of 2,691 hectares. They were distributed according to type of product (by leading branches) as follows: grain, 478; meat and dairy, 769; swine breeding, 659; sheep breeding, 204; horse breeding, 119; poultry breeding, 102; other livestock, 62; fruit and vegetables, 474; market-gardening [around the larger cities], 723; and industrial crops and other types, 371.

The level of mechanization of agriculture on the sovkhozes is very high. In 1937 the percentage of work done by tractor on the sovkhozes was: tilling, 97%; planting grain, 98%; and harvesting grain, 95%. In 1937 the grain sovkhozes produced an average of 344.4 centners of grain per worker. This testifies to the high productivity of labor on the sovkhozes.

The Government, through machine tractor stations (MTS), has supplied the kolkhozes with modern technical equipment. In 1938 there were 6,358 machine tractor stations which served 93.3% of the cultivated area of the kolkhozes.

Agricultural reconstruction in the USSR on the basis of modern techniques has, for the most part, been completed. In 1938 three-fourths of the arable land was worked by tractors, and the agricultural economy of the USSR was using 483.5 thousand tractors with a capacity of 9,256.2 thousand horsepower; 153.8 thousand combines; 195.8 thousand trucks; and hundreds of thousands of different agricultural machines—tractor-drawn grain drills, threshing machines, flax-swingling machines, beet diggers, etc. In the introduction of modern techniques, the agriculture of the USSR occupies first place in the world. In the large capitalist countries of Western Europe—England, France, Germany, and Italy—tractors total only 20,000 to 30,000 and there are only a few dozen combines. Even in the United States, which has the largest number of tractors, only 13.4% of the total number of farms have tractors. The greater size of the farms in the USSR permits a more effective utilization of tractors and machines. The average annual output of each tractor in the USSR exceeds by several times the output of a tractor in the United States.

"Our agriculture is, consequently, not only a larger, more mechanized, and therefore more commercial agriculture, but is also more thoroughly equipped with modern techniques than the agriculture of any other country."[5]

The mechanization of agriculture has resulted in an enormous growth in the productivity of labor.

By way of illustration we may cite the following: In order to harvest and thresh by hand one hectare of grain, the work of three men for five days is required. In order to harvest by horse-drawn machines and thresh by hand one hectare of grain the work of three men for three days is required. With a combine, however, three men (tractor operator, combine operator, and his assistant) can usually harvest one hectare in an hour. The labor productivity of the Stakhanovite combine-operators, who harvest 30 to 40 hectares per day, is especially high. In addition to increasing the productivity of labor, the tractor at the same time provides for the cultivation of the soil (deep plowing, etc.) and decreases the time consumed in sowing and other farm work, thus playing an enormous role in increasing the harvest yield. The combine helps to get the harvest in on time and without loss.

The mechanization of agriculture releases labor for industry from the kolkhozes.

Increase in Cultivated Acreage

Large-scale mechanized socialist agriculture guaranteed a rapid increase in agricultural production. During the years of the Stalin Five-Year Plans the cultivated acreage has expanded greatly. The area under cultivation in the USSR in 1938 was 136.9 million hectares, as compared with 105 million in 1913. Thus, the cultivated area in the USSR in 1938 had increased by 31.9 million hectares since prewar [World War I] times.

The expansion of cultivation required the utilization of large areas of virgin land. Before the Revolution the small peasants with their primitive tools were not equipped to work new land or abandoned land. United in kolkhozes and armed with tractors and other machines, they were able to plow large areas of virgin land and thus rapidly increase the cultivated area. The sovkhozes were very important in the utilization of new land and the expansion of the cultivated area.

Cultivation expanded chiefly in the southern and eastern regions

[5] Stalin, *Questions of Leninism*, p. 582.

(the Ukrainian SSR, the North Caucasus, the Crimea, the Volga Region, the Urals, Siberia, the Kazakh SSR), and also in the regions of the Industrial Center.

Cultivated areas in industrial, vegetable, and fodder crops have grown particularly rapidly. The proportions of the cultivated area devoted to different crops in the USSR at present differs significantly from prewar times [Table 31].

TABLE 31. PERCENTAGE OF THE CULTIVATED AREA IN THE MAJOR CROP GROUPS

TYPE	1913	1938
Grains	89.9	74.8
Industrial crops	4.3	8.0
Vegetables, melons, and potatoes	3.6	6.9
Fodder crops	2.2	10.3

As compared with the prewar period, there has been an increase in the relative importance of intensively cultivated crops, such as industrial crops, vegetables, and fodder, which require a greater expenditure of labor per hectare and yield a greater income per hectare. In spite of the increase in area under grain crops their relative importance has diminished, and the increased importance of the other crops means that agriculture in the USSR has become more skilled and productive. Of the fodder crops, the herb fodders have increased especially. This has been very important in introducing proper crop rotation and developing animal husbandry.

Increase in Agricultural Output

In 1937, 74.4% of the value of the gross agricultural output of the USSR was contributed by crops and 25.6% by livestock.

Through socialization of agriculture, productivity has increased. The quantity of chemical fertilizers used and the proportion of selected seeds have increased significantly. The quality of soil cultivation in the kolkhozes improves with each year. The achievements of the leading kolkhozes and the agricultural Stakhanovites in increasing the yield have been especially great. The Stakhanovite detachments in the kolkhozes are producing 500 to 1,000 centners of sugar beets, 40 to 70 centners of grain, and 50 to 100 centners of cotton per hectare. Such unprecedented harvests are the result of the growth of labor forces which have mastered agricultural techniques, and of the application of the science of agronomy and Stakhanovite methods.

The agricultural output has increased significantly over prewar times. In 1937 the grain harvest amounted to 7,344 million poods, or a gross increase of 2,500 million over the grain harvest in 1913. In 1937, 25.8 million centners of raw unginned cotton were gathered, as compared with 7.4 million in 1913. The gross yield of flax fiber in 1937 was 5.7 million centners, as compared with 3.3 million in 1913. The gross yield of sugar beets increased from 109 million centners in 1913 to 218.6 million in 1937.

The output of livestock also has increased. The value of the gross output of agriculture and livestock production increased from 12.6 billion rubles in 1913 to 20.1 billion in 1937 (in terms of 1926–1927 prices).

Not only the gross output, but also the commercial output of agriculture has increased. The commercial sales of produce from individual peasant farms was low. In 1926–1927 the peasantry sold grain equaling only 11.2% of the gross yield. The sale of grain produced on the kolkhozes and sovkhozes in 1938 was equal to 40% of the gross yield. The sale of milk increased from 15% in 1927 to 31% in 1937.

The high marketability of sovkhoz and kolkhoz produce was a vital factor in the rapid solution of the grain problem, that of supplying an enormous country with commercial grain.

With each year the income of the kolkhozes increases, and with it the prosperity of the kolkhoz farmers.

The All-Union Agricultural Exposition which opened in Moscow in August, 1939, was a demonstration of the flowering of socialist agriculture in the USSR. The numerous exhibits in striking pavilions gave a clear picture of the achievements of the leading kolkhozes, machine tractor stations, and sovkhozes. The pavilions of the national republics showed graphically the improvement of agriculture in the regions formerly backward. The All-Union Agricultural Exposition displayed some remarkable examples which are standards for all Soviet agriculture to meet.

Agriculture Under the Third Five-Year Plan

The 18th Party Congress set as the goal an increase of 52% in agricultural output under the Third Five-Year Plan. This is to be achieved in the first place through increasing the yield of the fields and the productivity of livestock. The gross yield of grain is to reach 8 billion poods, with an average yield of 13 centners [per hectare]. The gross yield of industrial crops is scheduled to make important strides. Livestock is scheduled to increase as follows: horses, 35%; cattle, 40%; pigs, 100%; and sheep and goats, 110%. The Third Five-Year Plan aims to introduce proper crop rotation into the kolkhozes and sovkhozes, to make wide application of advanced agricultural techniques, to increase the use of chemical fertilizer, and to provide high-quality and improved seed. All these measures will assure a great increase in productivity under the Third Five-Year Plan.

The 18th Party Congress in its decisions set forth the problem of completing, under the Third Five-Year Plan, the complex mechanization of agricultural work. Under the Second Five-Year Plan the mechanization of the chief types of agricultural work reached a high level. In 1937 plowing was 71% mechanized; grain threshing, 94%; digging of sugar beets, about 80%; and grain harvesting by combines, 39.8%; in the southern and southeastern grain regions, grain harvesting by combines was more than 60% mechanized. Nevertheless at the end of the Second Five-Year Plan some agricultural processes were only slightly mechanized—for example, the harvesting of flax and maize. The mechanization of cotton harvesting was in a rudimentary state. Under the Third Five-Year Plan these processes, too, will be broadly mechanized. At the same time the mechanization of soil cultivation and combine harvesting will receive further development. Special attention will be directed to the mechanization of laborious processes in livestock raising.

By the end of the Second Five-Year Plan the mechanization of agriculture in kolkhozes had reached the highest level in the southern and eastern grain regions. In the chernozem regions the level of mechanization was considerably lower. Under the Third Five-Year Plan these differences between regions will be significantly reduced.

The planting of high-quality seeds is of tremendous importance in raising the yield of the harvest. Recently, in accordance with a resolution of the Party and Government, a broad network of selection stations and seed-culture farms has been created; these develop and propagate high-yield qualities of grains and of industrial crops. A large Government quality-testing network has been created also, which tests the effectiveness of various types of seeds under the different conditions of the various regions. Under the Third Five-Year Plan planting of grain and other crops must be carried on exclusively with high-quality and improved seeds of both select and local varieties.

The growth of agricultural production under the Third Five-Year Plan is an important step along the road to the achievement of the abundance of products needed to make the transition from socialism to communism, and thus along the road to solving the principal economic problem of the USSR, which is to equal and surpass economically the most advanced capitalist countries of Europe and the United States.

SECTION 3. THE BASES OF SPECIALIZATION AND DISTRIBUTION OF SOCIALIST AGRICULTURE

The Chief Prerequisites of the Proper Distribution of Agriculture in the USSR

At the 16th Party Congress, Comrade Stalin raised the problem of the proper distribution of the chief branches of agriculture in the USSR, and of the specialization of the regions by agricultural crops and branches, and noted the advantages of large-scale socialist agriculture for agricultural specialization. "Of course," said Comrade Stalin, "under a small peasant economy any serious introduction of specialization is impossible. It is impossible since small-scale farming, as an unstable economy deprived of essential reserves, is compelled to cultivate all varieties of crops, in order to make it possible, in case some crops fail, to turn to others." [6]

The conversion of the small peasant economy to a large-scale collective economy and the organization of sovkhozes have created unusually favorable conditions for the proper distribution of agriculture and its various branches. In accomplishing this task, put forward by Comrade Stalin in 1930, great progress has been made. The area in grain crops has been increased in the eastern and non-chernozem regions; wheat has spread northward; new cotton and sugar-beet regions have been created; and new industrial crops have been introduced. Large-scale specialized enterprises have been

[6] Stalin, *Questions of Leninism*, 10th ed., p. 400.

created—grain sovkhozes, livestock sovkhozes, etc. All this characterizes the enormous shifts which have taken place in the specialization and distribution of agriculture in the USSR.

Socialization of industry is the leading factor in the specialization and distribution of agriculture. This is due to the fact that industry supplies agriculture with the means of production—tractors, agricultural machinery, and chemical fertilizers—which make possible the expansion of agricultural production. At the same time the development of industry demands an increase in the production of agricultural raw materials and food products. It leads to the founding of new towns and the expansion of old ones, and demands the creation of a vegetable and livestock base to supply the industrial centers. The growth of the food industry (beet sugar, canning, meat and dairy, etc.) requires a corresponding distribution of the raw-material base. The development of transportation influences to an enormous degree the specialization of agricultural regions.

The specialization of Soviet agriculture differs radically from the specialization of agricultural regions in prerevolutionary Russia.

Under capitalism the specialization was a result of a social distribution of labor basically influenced by the market. The relation of the costs of production and of market prices for agricultural products and the attempt to secure maximum profits were the factors determining the distribution of crops in particular regions of commercial agriculture in prerevolutionary Russia. Private ownership of land had a great influence on the distribution of agricultural crops in a capitalist society, since the rental fees were a heavy burden on the agricultural producer.

In the USSR the agricultural specialization of various crops and branches in different regions is the result of public socialist division of labor among various regions according to a national economic plan. Only under a socialist economic system, where "the development of production is subject, not to the principle of competition and the guarantee of capital profit, but to the principle of planned management and a systematic elevation of the material and cultural welfare of the workers," [7] is the proper distribution of agricultural crops and branches possible in conformity with the interests of the entire national economy.

[7] Stalin, *Questions of Leninism*, 10th ed., p. 397.

Problems in the Distribution of Agriculture

Under planned specialization and distribution of socialist agriculture, the Party and the Government face the following initial problems: (1) to satisfy the needs of industry for agricultural raw materials and of the population for food products, and to create an abundance of agricultural products throughout the country; (2) to combine crops on the basis of proper crop rotation, guaranteeing an increase in the fertility of the soil and in productivity; (3) to curtail long hauls of agricultural products; (4) to strengthen the defense of the country and guarantee her independence of capitalist countries; and (5) to utilize to the best advantage the natural conditions—soil, climate, etc.—in developing particular crops and branches of agriculture.

One of the methods of increasing agricultural production under the Five-Year Plans has been to further specialization of agriculture and to expand certain crops into new regions. The extension of cotton planting in the old cotton regions and the creation of new cotton regions have enabled the Soviets to become independent of imported cotton. The introduction of new crops—rubber-bearing plants, new bast fibers, etc.—has enabled the USSR to eliminate these imports. The creation of potato, vegetable, and livestock-raising bases in the vicinity of the industrial centers has made possible the elimination of inefficient excessively long hauls for agricultural products.

Specialization and Combination of Agricultural Crops and Branches

The most important criterion of the proper distribution of agriculture is the growth in the productivity of labor. In agriculture increased labor productivity is linked closely with the efficient utilization of the land. For systematic regeneration and improvement of soil fertility and increase of productivity, proper crop rotation or alternation of agricultural crops is necessary.

The specialization of different farms and regions in the USSR cannot develop on a one-crop basis, that is, by the planting of any single crop. Crop rotation requires the combination of a whole series of crops, of which certain ones are most important.

Neither can agricultural specialization develop on the basis of any one branch, for example, soil cultivation. Efficient agricultural management requires the combination of soil cultivation with animal husbandry. Livestock consume fodder crops, the so-called waste products of field culture (straw, chaff, etc.), and meadow and pasture growth. On the other hand, animal husbandry provides organic fertilizer for the fields. The development of other branches of agriculture, such as truck farming and gardening, is also of great importance for national consumption and for increasing the earning capacity of the economy. Consequently, proper agricultural specialization requires the efficient combination of various branches of agriculture—field crops, animal husbandry, vegetable growing, etc. Also, crop rotation must include the planting of fodder crops.

The combination of various crops and branches in agricultural enterprises is dependent also upon their seasonal labor requirements. Proper agricultural specialization requires a combination of agricultural crops and branches which will promote a steadier utilization of labor resources and a greater stability of the labor force in the kolkhozes and sovkhozes. For example, if only spring (summer) grain is planted, there is almost no work between the sowing and the harvest. On the other hand, if summer and winter crops are combined, the period between the sowing and harvesting of the summer crops is occupied by plowing and cultivation of the fallows for winter planting, and the harvest period is thus extended.

The introduction under the Third Five-Year Plan of proper crop rotation in the kolkhozes and sovkhozes, with the practice of planting herb fodder crops, guarantees an increase in the fertility of the soil and in the productivity of the fields (perennial herbs—clover, alfalfa, and others—enrich the soil with nitrogen and improve the soil structure), and creates a stable fodder supply for the growing animal husbandry branches.

The Party and Government have recommended that each kolkhoz have at least two animal husbandry farms. In the grain sovkhozes animal husbandry is being introduced, while in the animal husbandry sovkhozes, besides the principal branch, auxiliary branches of animal husbandry are being introduced. These measures are creating conditions favorable to the combination of branches in the kolkhozes and sovkhozes.

Under capitalism the constant fluctuation of prices leads farmers to sow certain crops in conformity with market conditions, and not with the requirements of proper crop rotation. Capitalist agriculture provides innumerable examples of the plundering of natural soil wealth and the lowering of soil fertility as a result of the pursuit of profits. In the steppe margins of prerevolutionary Russia, an extensive unbalanced grain economy (grain crops constituted 92 to 97% of the total cultivated area) was based on exploitive utilization of the natural fertility of the chernozem lands. Here farmers planted wheat crop after wheat crop on the same field over successive years until the soil was depleted, after which they abandoned this section of land and moved to another.

The same exploitive utilization of natural soil riches is found in the United States, where, as the result of single-crop systems and the absence of proper crop rotation, the soil has lost much of its initial fertility.

In capitalist society agricultural specialization is accompanied by the depletion not only of the soil but also of the labor force. The single-crop system, under capitalist conditions—as on a rubber plantation in the Tropical Zone of South Asia, on the islands of the Malay Archipelago, in South Africa, or on a coffee plantation in Brazil—is based on the cruel exploitation of agricultural workers and on peasant poverty. The cultivation of very laborious crops by hand and difficult labor for miserable pay typify the exploitive utilization of labor power under capitalism.

The record of kolkhoz and sovkhoz production testifies that only under a socialist system is agricultural specialization and distribution based on an efficient utilization of the soil, on widespread use of agricultural machines, and on advanced agricultural technique.

The enemies of the people, the Trotskyite and Bukharinite saboteurs, having made their way into agrarian agencies, tried in every way possible to hamper the introduction of proper crop rotation. They made rotation confused, and tried to carry out excessive agricultural specialization. In a number of regions they succeeded in carrying out such a highly saturated planting of the leading crops (flax, cotton, etc.) that disruption of rotation and decreased productivity resulted.

At the 17th Party Congress, Comrade Stalin pointed to the necessity of eliminating excessive agricultural specialization and introducing rotation. The fulfillment of the Party and Government directives covering the introduction of proper crop rotation into all kolkhozes and sovkhozes is a prerequisite to the complete elimination of the aftereffects of sabotage in the field of specialization and distribution of agriculture.

Efficient Utilization of Natural Conditions

Increasing the productivity of agricultural labor and securing high crop yields depend to a large extent on the efficient utilization of natural conditions—soil, climate, etc. In this connection, it is very important to take into account the natural conditions of the different regions of the Union, in order to attain proper distribution of agriculture.

A distinguishing trait of socialist agriculture is not passive adaptation to natural conditions, but radical modification of these very conditions. For example, the magnificent irrigation works of the Trans-Volga region, together with the construction of the Kuibyshev hydroelectric unit; the irrigation installations in Central Asia, the Trans-Caucasus, and other regions; and the development of new strains of seeds, all make it possible to alter essentially the geography of crop production. The work of the Soviet scientists—Michurin, Lysenko, Tsitsin, and their fellow workers—opens broad prospects in altering the natural characteristics of agricultural plants.

The numerous new strains of fruits and berries developed by Michurin, the great worker in transforming nature, make possible the extension of horticulture into almost all corners of the immense Union.

The cotton plant is heat-loving. This fact limits to a great degree the areas in which it can be cultivated. The Academician Lysenko is conducting experiments on a modification of the plant that will require less heat and will permit a significant increase in the area of cotton cultivation.

The method he proposes of planting potatoes in summer in the South will make it possible within a short time to provide the southern and southeastern steppe regions with a local supply of potatoes.

At the All-Union Agricultural Exposition new plants were exhibited, such as perennial wheat, and also new strains of seeds developed by scientific institutions and kolkhoz experimenters.

The work of selection stations and of scientific research institutions on the development of cold-resistant, drought-resistant, and disease-resistant types of grain and industrial crops opens prospects for essential changes in the distribution of agricultural crops.

As an example of the Bolshevist struggle to overcome unfavorable natural conditions which affect the distribution of agricultural crops, one may note the decree of the Council of People's Commissars of the USSR and the Central Committee of the Communist Party of the Soviet Union concerning the expansion of winter planting in the eastern regions, where, up to the present time, winter wheat has been insignificant. The Party and Government at the beginning of 1939 set before the Narkomzem [People's Commissariat of Agriculture] of the USSR and the V. I. Lenin All-Union Academy of Agricultural Sciences the task of developing in two to three years a frost-resistant strain of winter wheat to be grown in the open snowless Steppe Zone, and of producing in three to five years for the Taiga Zone and the northern Forest Steppe Zone a high-yield strain of winter wheat biologically adapted to the severe weather of Siberia. This will make it possible to broaden significantly the acreage of winter wheat in the eastern regions of the USSR.

Many bourgeois scientists affirm that the distribution of agriculture is determined exclusively by natural conditions. Certainly natural conditions have a tremendous influence on distribution; but to attribute the leading role to natural factors is incorrect. In the USSR great changes in the distribution of agricultural crops have taken place since prewar times, although the climatic and soil conditions of the different regions have not changed. This fact shows graphically that the system of social relationships and the level of development of productive forces are decisive factors in determining the distribution of agriculture.

The Complex Development of Agriculture in the Chief Economic Regions

Capitalism is characterized by the unequal distribution of agriculture in different countries and in different regions within each country. "By its very nature, capitalism in agriculture (just as in industry) cannot develop uniformly: it pushes one branch of agriculture forward in one place (in one country, in one region, on one farm), another branch in another place, etc." [8]

Under a socialist economy, where the development of agricultural

[8] Lenin, *Works,* Vol. III, p. 240.

production proceeds according to an over-all plan, founded on a consideration of the interests of the total national economy, and not subject to the capricious requirements of the market and elemental fluctuations of market prices, as under capitalism, all conditions are present which favor technical progress and the development of all the most important branches of agriculture—field-crop cultivation, animal husbandry, vegetable growing, gardening—in the principal economic regions.

The combination of crops and agricultural branches in the kolkhozes and sovkhozes has nothing in common with the universalism of the small peasant economy. The presence of various crops and agricultural branches on the small peasant farm reflected the emphasis on subsistence in this economy, which attempted to provide itself with all necessary food products. Under this system, agriculture in all its branches was conducted on the basis of backward techniques. The combination of crops was not brought into harmony with the requirements of crop rotation.

On the kolkhozes and sovkhozes all branches of agriculture are conducted on a large scale and have tremendous potentialities for development through application of advanced techniques.

The combination of agricultural crops in socialist agriculture is based on the introduction of proper crop rotation and on an efficient combination of branches.

The unequal development of capitalism in prerevolutionary Russia was manifested in the division into industrial and agrarian regions, consuming and producing regions. In the USSR such a division has already been overcome. In his report to the 17th Party Congress, Comrade Stalin said: "We no longer have exclusively agrarian oblasts to supply industrial oblasts with grain, meat, and vegetables, just as we no longer have exclusively industrial oblasts which depend for all essential products on other oblasts. The development indicates that all oblasts are becoming more or less industrial and will become increasingly so. This means that the Ukraine, the North Caucasus, the Central Chernozem Region, and other former agrarian regions can no longer release to the industrial centers as many products as they did formerly, since they must feed their own cities and their own workers, of which the number will increase. But from this we can see that each oblast must establish its own agricultural base, in order to produce its own vegetables, potatoes, butter, milk, and to some extent its own grain and meat, if it expects to avoid a critical food situation." [9]

The 18th Party Congress set forth the problem of the complex development of agriculture in the chief economic regions of the Union. Each republic and oblast must develop all branches of agriculture—field-crop cultivation, vegetable raising, and animal husbandry; it must produce potatoes, vegetables, and dairy and meat products in sufficient quantities. The efficient combination of agricultural branches in coordination with the food, dairy and meat, and light industries is one of the most important tasks of agriculture.

SECTION 4. DISTRIBUTION OF AGRARIAN RESOURCES AND THE GEOGRAPHY OF AGRICULTURE IN THE USSR

The USSR, covering one-sixth of the world's land surface, possesses tremendous agrarian resources, greater than any capitalist country. The entire territory of the USSR occupies 2,115,400,000 hectares. Distribution according to types of [agricultural] land is seen in the following chart [Fig. 32]:

TABLE 32. [POTENTIAL LAND UTILIZATION, JANUARY 1, 1935]

Type of Land	Area (millions of hectares)	Area % of total
Plowland	223.9	10.6
Meadow	53.3	2.5
Pasture, including commons	344.1	16.3
Brush	9.9	0.5
Swamp	107.0	5.1
Total area of the USSR	2,115.4	100.0

About 30% of the territory of the USSR is agricultural land (plowland, meadow, and commons and other pasture). The greater part of the land area of the country is covered with forests, swamps, deserts, and mountains. A considerable part of the unsuitable land—swamps, deserts, etc.—can be converted by reclamation (drainage, irrigation) into land suitable for agricultural production.

Of the agricultural land, 370.8 million hectares are located in

[9] Stalin, *Questions of Leninism*, p. 455.

kolkhozes. This is assigned to the kolkhozes free of charge and in perpetuity. The area of the sovkhozes is 51 million hectares.

The degree of utilization of arable land varies in different regions. The most highly tilled areas are in the Central Chernozem Region, the Ukrainian SSR, and the Volga Region [Fig. 52]. The percentage of the agrarian resources under the plow and in truck gardens is 76 in Kursk Oblast, 71.6 in Voronezh Oblast, and 69.1 in the Ukrainian SSR. Land cultivation in the southern oblasts of the Ukrainian SSR is especially intensive. Seventy-eight percent of the agricultural land is under cultivation in Dnepropetrovsk Oblast, 77.4% in Odessa Oblast, and 73.7% in Vinnitsa Oblast. A large percentage of the land in the Volga Region also is under the plow. Tilled land is 62.7% of all the land in Kuibyshev Oblast, 67.2% in Saratov Oblast, and 73.2% in the Volga German Republic. The Central Industrial Region and the North Caucasus have a smaller percentage of tilled land. In Moscow Oblast tilled land is 47.6% of the total agricultural area; in Smolensk Oblast, 42.1%; and in the North Caucasus, about 50%. Least utilized are the agrarian reserves in the regions of the European North, the Northwestern Region, and other regions of the non-chernozem belt, and also in the eastern regions. Thus, the percentage of the agrarian area under cultivation is 12.5 in Leningrad Oblast, 24.9 in Ivanovo Oblast, 15.1 in the Kazakh SSR, and 16.9 in Western Siberia. In the non-chernozem belt there are large areas of virgin soil covered with brush. When these areas are cleared, extensive arable areas will be available for grain and other crops. Reclamation (draining of swamps, etc.) also may increase significantly the reserves of arable land here. In the eastern regions—the Trans-Urals, Siberia, and the Far East—there are enormous reserves of land for plowing, which may be utilized without any great outlay. Under the Third Five-Year Plan the sown areas in the eastern regions will be greatly increased. The large-scale migration of kolkhoz workers from the central regions, the Ukrainian SSR, and other places to Siberia and the Far East will make possible the utilization of great areas of virgin land in the eastern regions.

The most intensive planting is found in the chernozem zone in the European part of the USSR. Here arable lands are in the highest proportion and agricultural reserves are utilized to a maximum degree.

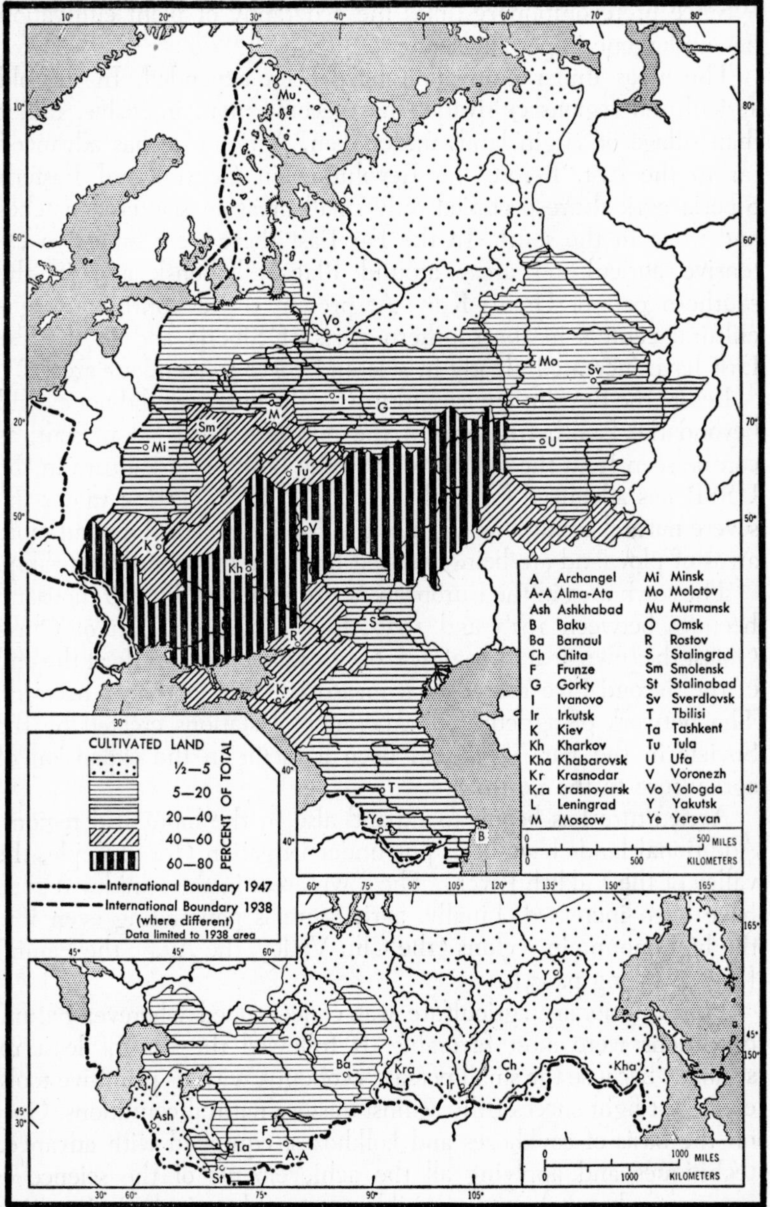

Fig. 52. Percentage of Total Land Cultivated

Since prerevolutionary times the geography of plant cultivation has undergone important changes.

The areas under cultivation have been expanded. In the old agricultural regions cultivation has become more intensive, rather than tillage of virgin lands undertaken. Agriculture has advanced far to the east. Before the Revolution in Central and Eastern Siberia agriculture occupied only small areas in scattered patches and these in the south. In the Far East there were only two extensive agricultural areas—around Blagoveshchensk and in the southern part of Ussuri Kray. At present the discontinuous agricultural centers in the southern parts of Siberia and in the Far East have increased greatly in size and cover tremendous areas.

Before the Revolution, agriculture for the most part did not extend beyond the [southern] limit of the northern taiga. At present, as can be seen from the map [Fig. 53], the limit of agriculture in the USSR has advanced far to the north and is developing under the severe natural conditions north of the Arctic Circle. More and more areas of plowland are being wrested from the taiga and the swamp.

The sown area in the European North increased by 400 thousand hectares between 1913 and 1937. In the northern part of Omsk Oblast the sown area in 1928 was only 544 hectares, while at the end of the Second Five-Year Plan it measured close to 10,000 hectares. The network of agricultural experimental stations created by the Soviets in the Far North has been a factor in the expansion of agriculture to the north.

Agriculture has begun to expand also in the more arid regions. Additional lands have been put under irrigation (for example, the valley of the Vakhsh River). The sown areas in the semidesert zone have been increased. Finally, agriculture is penetrating even into the high-mountain regions (the Chu Valley, the Altay, the Pamir) [Fig. 4, facing p. 13].

Prerevolutionary agriculture was concentrated wherever natural conditions were most favorable. It followed the line of least resistance, because the small peasant economy, with its primitive tools, could not fight successfully against austere natural conditions. Only on the basis of sovkhozes and kolkhozes, equipped with advanced techniques and applying all the achievements of the science of agronomy, has it become possible to extend agriculture into new regions and to overcome unfavorable natural conditions.

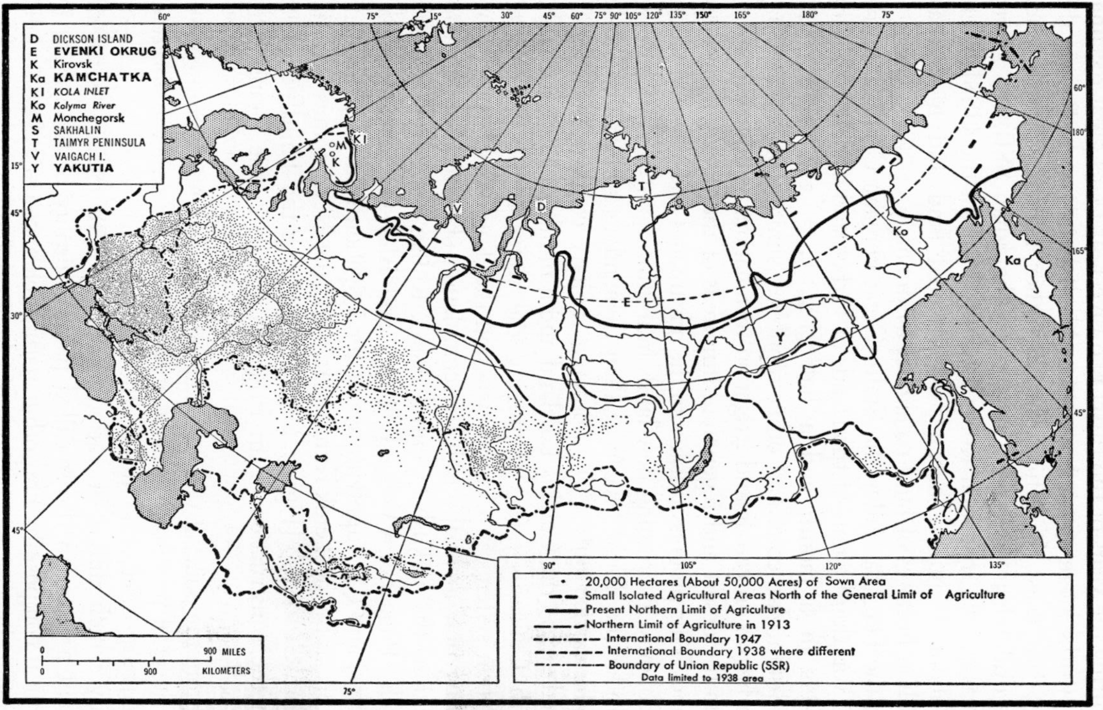

Fig. 53. Area Sown in All Crops

During the years of the [first] two Five-Year Plans great reclamation works were carried out; in the Belorussian SSR, on the Black Sea coast (Colchis), and in other regions, swamp lands were drained; in Central Asia, the Azerbaidzhan SSR, the North Caucasus, etc., irrigation works were installed. In the USSR there are about 6 million hectares of irrigated land and more than 3 million hectares of land reclaimed by drainage.

In the Fergana Valley the Stalin Great Fergana Canal, 270 km. long, was dug by tens of thousands of Uzbek and Tadzhik kolkhoz workers in a month and a half [Fig. 5, p. 24]. In Kirgizia, Kazkhstan, Armenia, and other republics, similar construction has been begun on canals and irrigation installations. The canals bring life to the desert and regenerate hundreds of thousands of hectares of land. This progress testifies to the advantages of a planned socialist economy in bringing new lands into utilization.

Under the Third Five-Year Plan tremendous reclamation works will be carried out: (1) improving sanitary conditions in waterlogged areas (the Colchis Lowland and a number of regions in the North Caucasus); (2) improving the water supply of existing irrigation systems in Central Asia and the Trans-Caucasus; (3) irrigating new areas through the completion of systems under construction—the Vakhsh (Central Asia), Kuban (North Caucasus), Engels, Pugachev (Volga Region), and Aley (Western Siberia) systems; and (4) supplying water for irrigation to arid agricultural regions, as by the Terek-Kuma system and the Nevinnomysky Canal (North Caucasus) [Figs. 5, 6, and 20]. Under the Third Five-Year Plan the construction of an irrigation system in the Trans-Volga will be begun.

"From the point of view of economic fertility," Marx pointed out, "the level of productivity of labor, in the present case the ability of agriculture directly to utilize the natural fertility of the soil—an ability which differs at various levels of development—is as important a factor in the so-called natural fertility of the soil as its chemical composition and other natural characteristics." [10] Socialist economy, by reclamation, use of chemical fertilizers, proper crop rotation, and advanced techniques, offers broad possibilities for increasing the economic fertility of the soil, for deriving rich harvests, and for increasing the productivity of agricultural labor.

[10] Marx, *Capital*, Vol. III, p. 574.

The rich harvests obtained by the leading socialist agricultural workers testify clearly to this.

SECTION 5. AREAL DISTRIBUTION OF GRAIN CROPS

Grain production is the most important branch of agriculture. The development of all other branches of agricultural production depends on that of the grain economy. To increase the production of industrial crops and livestock, people engaged in these branches must be provided with grain. The creation of a reliable fodder base for the livestock industry largely depends on the development of grain crops (oats, barley, maize, etc.).

The full magnitude of the grain problem made itself apparent during the period when the country was being industrialized. Although agriculture as a whole exceeded its prewar level in 1927, total grain output at that time reached only 91% of its prewar level, while the commercial production of grain was only 37% of its prewar level. The grain economy in such a state could not satisfy the demand which had increased concurrently with the industrialization of the country and the rise in urban population. At the root of the lag in grain production was the small surplus provided by the small individual peasant farms. Small farms with their backward techniques were unable to expand grain production rapidly. The only escape from this position was to create large-scale socialist agricultural production able to use modern techniques and to increase to a high level the surplus of agricultural produce available for sale.

Under the leadership of the Bolshevist Party the collectivizing of the peasant economy was achieved. At the same time a great network of large grain sovkhozes was created. In 1938 the area sown in grain on individual farms formed only 0.6% of the total area in grain crops; nearly all grain crops now are concentrated on sovkhozes and kolkhozes.

The socialist reconstruction of agriculture insured the rapid development of grain production. During the years of the First Five-Year Plan the area sown in grain expanded by 7.5 million hectares. The grain problem was already solved under the First Five-Year Plan, and this created favorable conditions for the specialization of agriculture.

The country's grain requirements are increasing. This is due to the following factors: (1) the industrialization of the country and the growth of the urban population; (2) the increasing prosperity of the kolkhoz peasantry and the resulting increase in grain consumption in the village itself; (3) the expansion in production of industrial crops; (4) the development of animal husbandry; (5) the rapid population increase in the USSR. In 1935 Comrade Stalin set the goal of raising the annual grain production in the ensuing three or four years to 7 or 8 billion poods [1.1 to 1.3 billion centners, or approximately 5 billion bushels]. In 1937 the country harvested 7,340 million poods of grain; the task set by Comrade Stalin was essentially accomplished. The Third Five-Year Plan projects an increase in annual grain production to 8 billion poods.

The area sown in grain crops in the USSR totaled 104.4 million hectares [258 million acres] in 1937, exceeding the prewar level by 10 million hectares. (It was 94.4 million hectares in 1913.) The biggest increase occurred in the eastern regions (the Urals, Siberia, the Kazakh SSR). The increase in grain sowings falls essentially to the most valuable grain crop—wheat. The productivity of grain crops has also increased considerably in comparison with the prewar period. As a result of the increases in area and yield the total grain harvest has risen. Total production of grains was slightly over 4 billion poods annually in prewar years. The average annual gross yield during the years of the Second Five-Year Plan was 5.5 billion poods. At the same time the commercial production of grain crops has increased. In 1938 socialist agriculture produced 1 billion poods more of commercial grain than had been produced before the war.

In sown area, first place among grain crops in the USSR is held by wheat; second place by rye; third by oats; fourth by barley; fifth by millet; sixth by maize; seventh by buckwheat; and eighth by rice.

The USSR is first in the world in the area and production of wheat, rye, oats, and barley.

The largest quantity of grain is produced in the chernozem zone, chiefly in the southern and eastern regions. The southern regions (the Ukrainian SSR, the North Caucasus, and the Crimea) account for 27.2% of the total area sown in grain crops, while the eastern regions (the Volga Region, the Urals, Siberia, and the Kazakh SSR) account for 38% [Fig. 54].

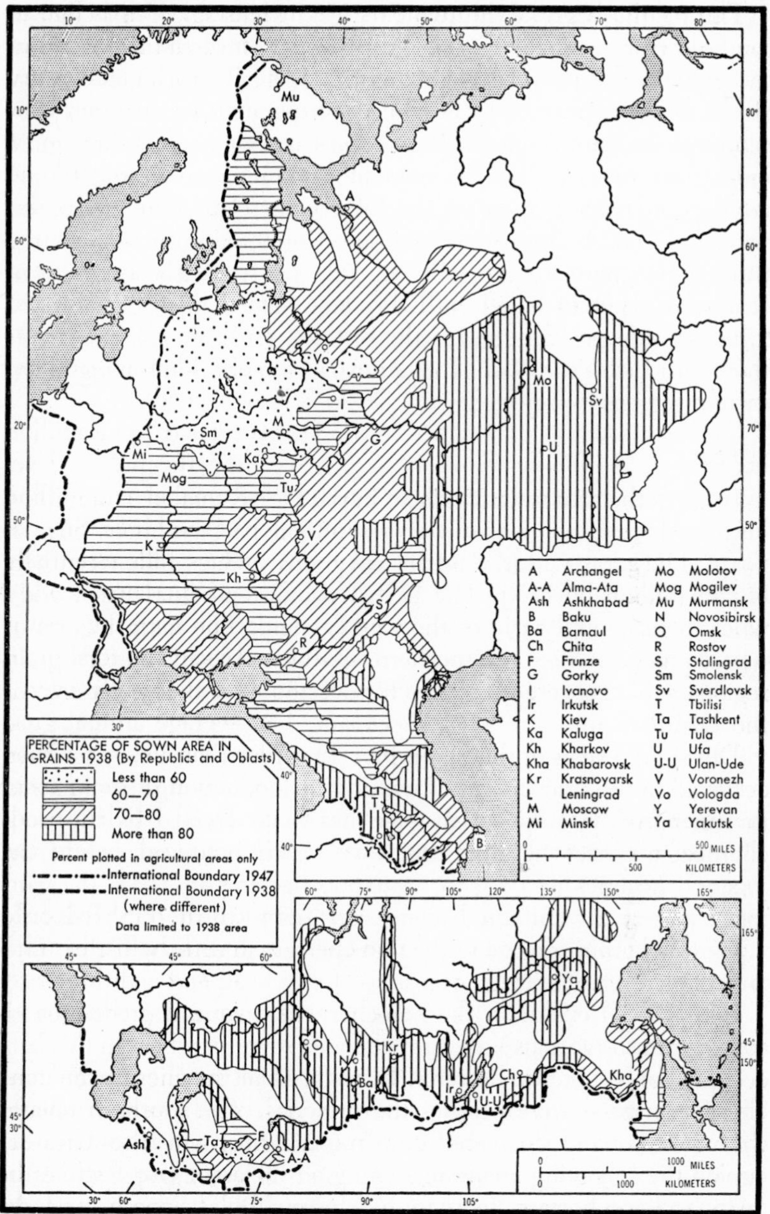

Fig. 54. Percentage Which Grains Constituted of Total Sown Area, 1938

During the years of the two Five-Year Plans important changes first took place in the location of grain crops. The area that was sown in grain in the eastern regions of the RSFSR (the Trans-Volga, the Trans-Urals, and Siberia) was expanded tremendously by plowing up virgin lands. There was a big increase in grain crops, chiefly wheat, in the non-chernozem region of the former consuming belt. The main area of commercial grain production was transferred from the Ukraine, formerly regarded as the country's granary, to the RSFSR. In 1936–1938 the quantity of [commercial] grain stored in the Ukraine totaled approximately 400 million poods annually; and in the RSFSR, 1.1 to 1.2 billion. Under the Third Five-Year Plan a further expansion of grain sowing in the eastern regions is projected.

Wheat

In 1937 the area sown in wheat in the USSR totaled 41.4 million hectares [102 million acres], or 10 million hectares more than in 1913. The total wheat yield in 1937 was 468.6 million centners [1,720 million bushels]. The USSR contains 28% of the world's wheat acreage and 31% of the world's yield. The main regions of wheat production are the southern, southeastern, and eastern grain regions, which together account for over 80% of the wheat area of the USSR.

During the years of the Stalin Five-Year Plans some changes have occurred in the distribution of wheat growing. Sowings have moved to the north. A new wheat base has been created in the non-chernozem zone, where the area sown in wheat has increased from 344,900 hectares in 1928 to 2,730,000 hectares in 1937; the gain totals almost 2.5 million hectares. In 1913 wheat occupied only 1.7% of all grain acreage in the non-chernozem zone, while in 1938 it occupied 13.9% [Fig. 55].

Before the Revolution the non-chernozem zone was the area of coarse grains (rye, oats). In 1913 the area sown in wheat in this belt occupied only 321,100 hectares. In 1937 wheat sowings in the non-chernozem zone were 9 times the prewar level. In certain oblasts the wheat sowings increased even more. Thus, wheat sowings occupied the following areas: in Leningrad Oblast, 2,900 hectares in 1913, 178,300 hectares in 1937; in Moscow Oblast, 500 hectares in 1913, 139,000 hectares in 1937.

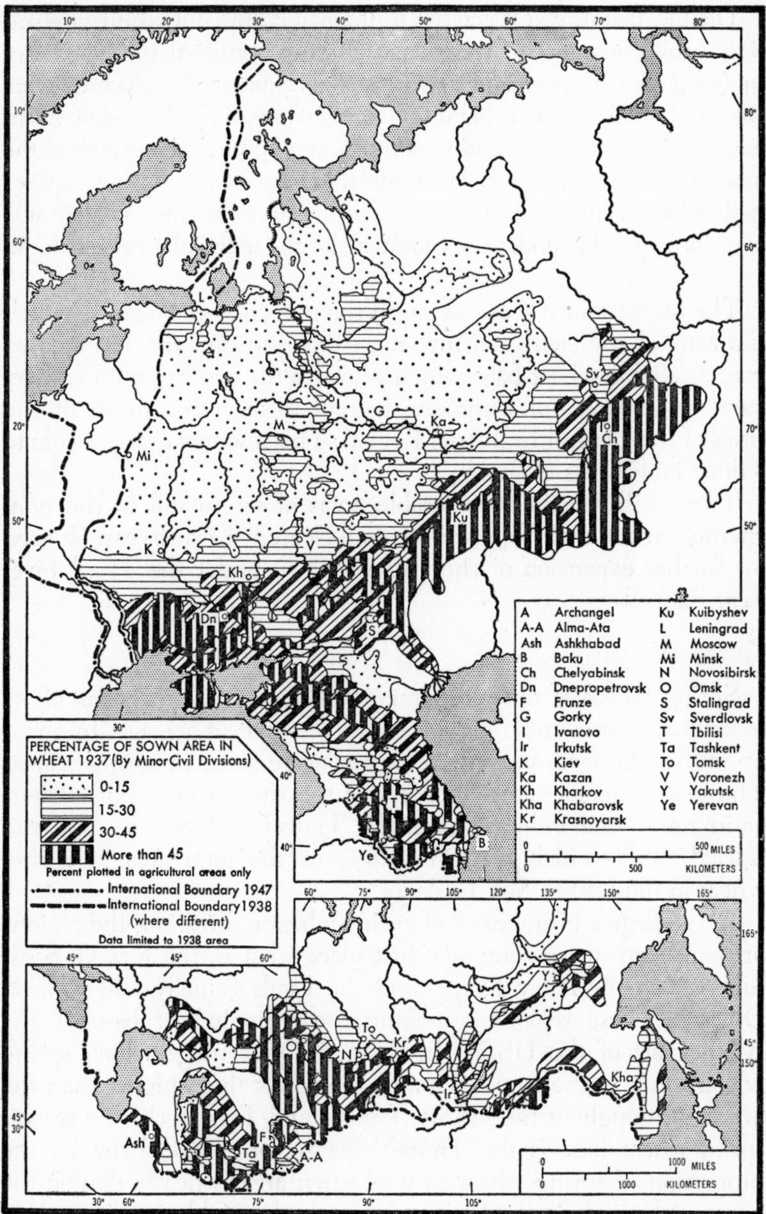

Fig. 55. Percentage Which Wheat Constituted of Total Sown Area, 1937

The increase in wheat acreage in the non-chernozem zone is a result of the collectivization of the village. Having combined into kolkhozes equipped with tractors and agricultural machinery, the peasants were able to plow virgin soil, using it for sowing wheat. The plowing of virgin soil, which involves the clearing of brush, was beyond the capacity of the small peasant farm. Wheat sowing in the non-chernozem zone requires application of the most modern agricultural techniques, which was likewise impossible under the conditions of the individual peasant farm.

The increase in wheat sowing in the non-chernozem zone, which is a zone of sufficient moisture not subject to drought, has created here a reliable wheat base which provides the country with supplementary resources of commercial grain to meet the needs of the cities of the Central Industrial Region. This also makes it possible to reduce long hauls of grain.

There still remain considerable areas of virgin soil in the non-chernozem zone which, once they are cleared of brush, can be used for further expansion of the area in wheat under the Third Five-Year Plan.

Spring Wheat

Spring wheat is the most important grain crop in terms of its sown area. It accounts for 65% of the total wheat acreage. In 1937, 27 million hectares [67 million acres] were sown in spring wheat. The main regions of production are the eastern and southeastern grain zones—the Volga Region, the Trans-Urals, Siberia, and the Kazakh SSR—which contain 72.8% of the total area in spring wheat in the USSR. See Table 33.

In the degree of intensity of spring-wheat cultivation, the regions of the eastern grain zone take first place—that is, the Kazakh SSR, Siberia (chiefly Altay Kray), and the Urals (chiefly Chelyabinsk Oblast). These regions constitute the spring-wheat base of the Asiatic part of the USSR. In them the percentage which spring wheat forms of the total sown area is 2 to 2.5 times higher than the average throughout the USSR [Fig. 55 and Table 33]. The second spring-wheat base is the Trans-Volga region. Here, likewise, the proportion of spring wheat to total sown area is nearly double the average throughout the Union. In Kuibyshev Oblast spring wheat is concentrated primarily east of the Volga.

TABLE 33. AREA SOWN IN SPRING WHEAT IN 1937 [BY REGIONS]

[Location and boundaries of these regions are shown in Fig. 7.]

Regions	Total Sowings (in thousand hectares)	% of USSR Area in Spring Wheat	% of Crop Area of Region
RSFSR	21,199.4	78.4	22.7
European North	159.1	0.6	9.6
Northwestern	295.0	1.1	4.8
Central Industrial	605.7	2.2	6.1
Central Chernozem	1,114.4	4.1	8.8
Upper Volga	974.7	3.6	11.0
Middle and Lower Volga	5,061.2	18.7	37.5
North Caucasus and Crimea	1,157.0	4.3	8.5
Urals	5,185.9	19.2	40.2
Western Siberia	4,947.0	18.3	50.7
Eastern Siberia	1,378.9	5.1	39.7
Far East	320.5	1.2	37.0
Ukrainian SSR	1,161.6	4.3	4.6
Belorussian SSR	158.7	0.6	4.5
Trans-Caucasian republics	226.4	0.8	8.9
Central Asiatic republics	1,184.2	4.4	24.3
Kazakh SSR	3,127.0[a]	11.5	53.6
USSR	27,057.3	100.0	20.0

[a] [The figure, 3,427.0 in the original has been corrected to 3,127.0 which agrees with the percentage of USSR figure given for the Kazakh SSR and makes the figures of total sowings add correctly to the total given for the USSR.]

Before 1933, plantings of spring wheat in the non-chernozem zone were small in extent. At present there has been established here a large area in spring wheat (more than 1,500,000 hectares in 1937). In spring-wheat sowings the Belorussian SSR and Gorky Oblast hold first place among the non-chernozem oblasts. Important areas in excess of 100,000 hectares are found in Vologda, Smolensk, Kirov, Yaroslavl, and other oblasts. In Gorky and Kirov oblasts spring wheat has spread far to the northeast. In the course of the Second Five-Year Plan spring wheat sowings came to occupy large areas in the northern and northeastern regions of the Tatar ASSR.

There used to be a "white-spot theory," to the effect that the northern chernozem belt and Kuibyshev Oblast east of the Volga were not suited for spring wheat. Actually, the fundamental reason for the limited spread of spring wheat in these regions was that the advanced agricultural techniques required here for cultivating the crop were not within the reach of the small peasant farm. The most advanced kolkhozes have disproved in practice the "white-spot theory" by getting large harvests of spring wheat in this zone.

The average yield of spring wheat in the USSR in 1937 was 10 centners per hectare [15 bushels per acre].[11] The leading kolkhozes and farm crews obtain very high yields—20 to 30 centners and more per hectare. In Altay Kray the Yefremov detachments (named after their initiator, Comrade Yefremov) gather 50 and more centners per hectare.

The vast territory comprising the regions of spring-wheat cultivation is distinguished by its great variety of natural conditions. The yield fluctuates noticeably between different regions. It depends in large measure on the supply of moisture, particularly during the period of flowering and earing.

The highest yields from spring-wheat sowings are obtained in Siberia, the Trans-Urals, and also the northern non-chernozem region, where precipitation is adequate.

The yield of spring wheat is lower in the southeastern regions, where precipitation is insufficient and the grain often suffers from drought and dry winds. The Party and Government have set the task of overcoming drought and obtaining dependable harvests in the drought-ridden regions of the southeastern USSR. The introduction of proper crop rotation, deep plowing, vernalization of seed, the completion of spring sowing within a short period, the sowing of drought-resistant strains of seed, the use of fertilizer, snow retention, the planting of shelter belts, the irrigation of sowings—such are the measures laid out by the decree of the SNK [Council of People's Commissars] of the USSR and the TsK VKP(b) [Central Committee of the All-Union Communist Party] in 1938, for assuring dependable harvests in the arid regions of the southeastern USSR.

The irrigation of grain sowings should completely conquer drought. During recent years the kolkhozes by their own efforts have created small irrigation systems based on local runoff; by the end of the Second Five-Year Plan these had covered a considerable area. The construction of the Kuibyshev hydro station will make it possible to irrigate for wheat enormous areas of land in the Trans-Volga. Irrigation, together with the application of modern agri-

[11] [Soviet figures on crop yields are not comparable with U. S. figures; see footnote to Appendix II, p. 534.]

cultural techniques, will assure large dependable harvests in the Volga Region and will increase the importance of this zone in the wheat production of the country.

Winter Wheat

The area sown in winter wheat in the USSR in 1937 was 14.3 million hectares [35.3 million acres], or 10.6% of the total sown area of the USSR and 35% of the total area sown in wheat. During the years of the [first] two Five-Year Plans sowings of winter wheat increased in far greater degree than the sowings of spring wheat. Sowings of winter wheat doubled their prewar level, rising from 7.3 million hectares in 1913 to 14.3 million hectares in 1937, while spring-wheat sowings increased by only 12%. The increase in winter-wheat plantings took place mainly in the southern steppe regions.

The share of individual regions in the production of winter wheat is shown in Table 34.

TABLE 34. AREA SOWN IN WINTER WHEAT IN 1937 [BY REGIONS]
[Location and boundaries of these regions are shown in Fig. 7.]

Regions	Total Sowings (in thousand hectares)	% of USSR Area in Winter Wheat	% of Crop Area of Region
RSFSR	6,105.3	41.9[a]	6.5
European North	18.2	0.1	1.1
Northwestern	214.0	1.5	3.5
Central Industrial	592.5	4.1	5.9
Central Chernozem	993.1	6.8	7.9
Upper Volga	58.5	0.4	0.7
Middle and Lower Volga	161.3	1.1	1.2
North Caucasus and Crimea	4,038.4	27.7	29.6
Urals	10.9	0.1	0.1
Western Siberia	18.3	0.1	0.2
Eastern Siberia	0.1	—	—
Far East	—	—	—
Ukrainian SSR	6,618.1	45.3	26.3
Belorussian SSR	92.6	0.6	2.6
Trans-Caucasian republics	803.0	5.5	31.6
Central Asiatic republics	804.1	5.5	16.5
Kazakh SSR	181.4	1.2	3.1
USSR	14,604.5	100.0	10.8

[a] [The figure 41.8 is given in the original.]

The main winter-wheat regions are found in the southern grain zone of the Union—the Ukrainian SSR, the North Caucasus, and the Crimean ASSR. The southern zone contains over 70% of the total area sown in winter wheat in the USSR.

The ratio of winter wheat to the total sown area in these regions is 2.5 to 3 times higher than the average for the USSR as a whole [Table 34]. There are important areas in the Central Chernozem Region, the non-chernozem belt, the Trans-Caucasus (predominantly the Azerbaidzhan SSR), and Central Asia (predominantly the Uzbek SSR). The highest percentage of winter wheat is found in the Crimea and in Odessa and Nikolayev oblasts (44.1 to 48.6% of the sown area). Next come Dnepropetrovsk Oblast and Ordzhonikidze and Krasnodar krays (36 to 39% of the total sown area).

The years of the Stalin Five-Year Plans have been marked by great changes in the distribution of winter wheat. The sowings of this crop have expanded tremendously in the southern regions at the expense of a reduction in spring wheat. The area sown in winter wheat in the southern zone of the USSR increased from 4,200,000 hectares in 1928 to 10,656,000 in 1937. The sowings of spring wheat in that zone diminished during the same period from 4,956,000 hectares to 2,318,000. As a result, the ratio of winter- to spring-wheat sowings in the southern region has changed sharply. Thus, in 1913 winter wheat occupied only 28.4% of the total area sown in wheat in the Ukraine, while in 1937 it already occupied 85% of all wheat sowings.

The expansion of winter-wheat sowings in the southern grain zone and the displacement of spring wheat is explained first by the fact that winter wheat here gives a higher and more dependable harvest. In the second place, winter wheat can be sown on fallow land, which promotes the clearing of weeds from the fields. In 1937 the average yield of winter wheat in the USSR was 13.7 centners per hectare [20.4 bushels per acre], as against 10 centners for spring wheat [15 bushels per acre]. The leading regions and kolkhozes obtained a considerably higher yield than the average for the USSR.

The leading sovkhozes, kolkhozes, and farm crews get 30 and more centners per hectare. At the kolkhoz named after the 17th Party Congress of the Shcherbinsk region of Krasnodar Kray, brigade member Comrade Kostenko in 1937 harvested 75 centners of winter wheat per hectare from a 70-hectare area.

During the years of the Five-Year Plans winter-wheat sowings have expanded appreciably in the southeastern regions as well. In the Volga Region they increased by almost 250,000 hectares. Winter wheat has penetrated into new regions. In 1937, 101,800 hectares in South Kazakhstan Oblast were sown in winter wheat, and 68,000 hectares in Alma-Ata Oblast.[12] The winter-wheat area there before the First Five-Year Plan was limited to several thousand hectares. The Party and Government have set the task of further and more significant expansion of winter-wheat sowings in the arid regions of the Southeast, at the expense of a reduction in spring grains. The expansion of winter-wheat sowings will promote dependable harvests in the arid regions of the southeastern USSR.

The task of expanding winter sowings (winter wheat and winter rye) has likewise been set for the eastern regions, with the purpose of improving agricultural techniques (winter crops are sown on fertilized fallows) and of achieving a more even distribution of labor power expended in grain production. At present, winter sowings in the eastern regions occupy an insignificant area. The percentage of winter grains to all grains sown in the area in 1937 was 2.8 in Altay Kray, 13.6 in Krasnoyarsk Kray, 13.1 in Omsk Oblast, and 16.8 in Novosibirsk Oblast. The role of winter grains in a number of oblasts in Siberia is growing; but in most regions spring grains occupy nearly the entire area.

The one-sided predominance of spring crops in the eastern regions puts an excessive strain on labor during the spring sowing and the harvesting. The substitution of winter sowings for some of the spring sowings will permit the elimination of the excessive strain on labor during the harvesting and sowing periods and will promote a more even expenditure of labor power in the course of the summer. The short growing period (number of days from germination to ripening) and the severe winters with little snow cover have interfered with the expansion of winter sowings in a number of eastern regions. To the end of extending winter sowings into the eastern regions, scientific agricultural institutions are working on the development

[12] [For location of political units see Fig. 83 at the back of the book.]

of special winter-resistant strains of winter wheat and rye biologically adapted to conditions in Siberia.

Winter Rye

Winter rye is the most important grain crop after wheat. In 1937 the area sown in rye in the USSR attained almost 23 million hectares [57 million acres], which is 16.9% of the entire sown area of the USSR. The USSR contains 50% of the total rye area of the world. Sowings of spring rye are not extensive; in 1937 they totaled only 360,000 hectares in the USSR.

Rye is less exacting than wheat in climate and soil; hence it has a wide distribution, from the tundra on the north to the southern regions (see Table 35).

TABLE 35. AREA SOWN IN WINTER RYE IN 1937 [BY REGIONS]

[Location and boundaries of these regions are shown in Fig. 7.]

REGIONS	TOTAL SOWINGS (in thousand hectares)	% OF USSR AREA IN WINTER RYE	% OF CROP AREA OF REGION
RSFSR	18,365.6	80.1	19.7
European North	387.0	1.7	19.7
Northwestern	1,278.5	5.6	20.6
Central Industrial	2,375.8	10.4	23.8
Central Chernozem	3,394.7	14.8	26.9
Upper Volga	3,054.2	13.2	34.5
Middle and Lower Volga	3,290.4	14.4	24.4
North Caucasus and Crimea	690.0	3.0	5.1
Urals	2,626.0	11.5	20.4
Western Siberia	857.3	3.7	8.8
Eastern Siberia	400.5	1.7	11.5
Far East	11.2	0.1	1.3
Ukrainian SSR	3,323.8	14.5	13.2
Belorussian SSR	998.4	4.4	28.4
Trans-Caucasian republics	18.6	0.1	0.1
Central Asiatic republics	1.4	—	—
Kazakh SSR	217.0	0.9	3.7
USSR	22,924.8	100.0	16.9

The main base of winter-rye production is in the non-chernozem zone, the Central Chernozem Region, and the Volga Region. These regions together account for about 65% of all rye sowings in the

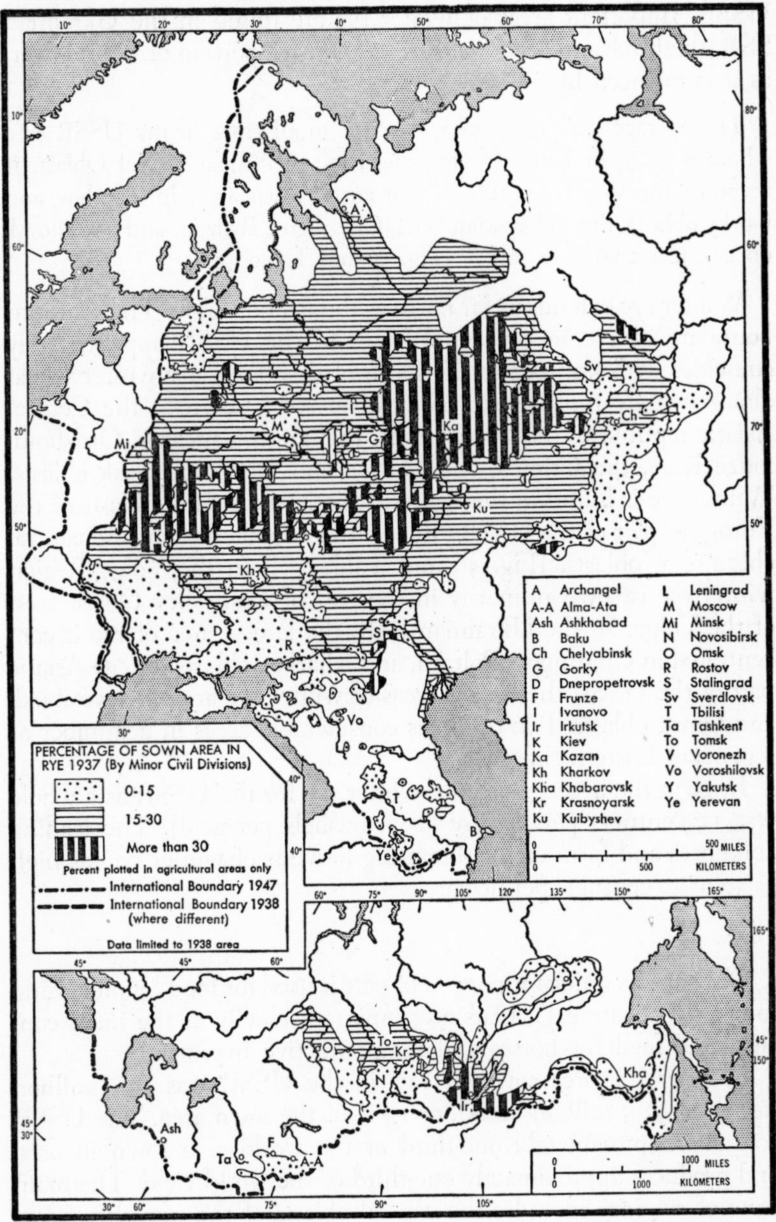

Fig. 56. Percentage Which Rye Constituted of Total Sown Area, 1937

USSR. Important areas of winter rye are found in the Ukrainian SSR, the Urals, and Siberia. But here the proportion of rye is lower, as it is replaced by wheat.

The average percentage of winter rye to all crops in the USSR as a whole is 16.9; in Kirov Oblast, the Tatar ASSR, and Orel Oblast, it accounts for 36.2% to 31% of the entire sown area; in Tambov and Gorky oblasts, the Belorussian SSR, Chernigov, Ryazan, and Sverdlovsk oblasts, it is 29.6% to 26.1% [Fig. 56 and Table 35].

Winter rye extends as far north as the Arctic Circle. The southern boundary of rye in the central part of the USSR approximately coincides with 50° N.; to the south of this boundary winter wheat almost wholly replaces rye. Almost no rye is sown in the Central Asiatic republics, the Kazakh SSR, the Trans-Caucasus, Ordzhonikidze Kray, the Crimea, and Odessa and Dnepropetrovsk oblasts. Winter rye is found in the highest ratio in the central oblasts of the European part of the USSR—the central non-chernozem and central chernozem oblasts. [Fig. 56 and Table 35]. In the Volga Region winter rye is sown primarily in the part of Kuibyshev Oblast west of the Volga. In the Ukrainian SSR, the largest area of rye is concentrated in Chernigov, Poltava, and Kharkov oblasts. In the Asiatic part of the USSR the largest areas of winter rye are in Novosibirsk and Omsk oblasts. Rye occupies considerable areas in a number of regions of Eastern Siberia.

In 1937 the average yield of winter rye for the USSR as a whole was 13 centners per hectare [20.8 bushels per acre]. The leading kolkhozes and farm crews obtain big harvests of winter rye, as high as 30 to 40 centners per hectare.

Oats

Only an insignificant portion of oats is used for food by processing into groats (oatmeal). Oats are important chiefly as the main concentrated feed for horses and for productive livestock.

In 1937 the area sown in oats in the USSR was 17.6 million hectares [43.5 million acres], or 13% of the sown area. The USSR contains approximately one-third of the world area sown in oats, and produces approximately one-third of the world yield. The main zone of sowings includes the central oblasts of the non-chernozem and chernozem regions, the Urals, and Western Siberia [Fig. 57].

FIG. 57. Percentage Which Oats Constituted of Total Sown Area, 1937

The non-chernozem region of the European part of the USSR contains 24.3% of the area in oats; the Volga Region, 17.8%; the Urals, 12.9%; and Siberia, 17.4% [Appendix Table A5]. These regions together have more than three-fourths of all the oat sowings. Oats occupy the largest proportion of the sown area in the Upper Volga Region (23.0%), the European North (24.8%), the Central Industrial Region (22.0%), Western Siberia (21.9%), and the Urals (17.6%). Oat sowings hold an insignificant place in the southern regions (4.3% of all sowings in the North Caucasus and the Crimea, 6.4% in the Ukrainian SSR). Oats withstand reduced temperatures rather well. Thus they can be sown far into the North (in the Yakut ASSR, etc.).

While the average percentage of oats in the sown area is 13 for the USSR as a whole, it is 30.6 to 27.7 in Krasnoyarsk Kray and Kirov and Sverdlovsk oblasts, and 26.9 to 20.7 in Novosibirsk, Gorky, Tula, Omsk, and Smolensk oblasts. In the Ukraine, Chernigov and Kiev oblasts rank first with their areas in oats. (See Table A5 in the Appendix for further details on the regional distribution of oats.)

The oat crop requires considerable rainfall. In arid regions it suffers from lack of moisture. Its growing period is longer than that of barley. The distribution in the northern and central zones of the European part of the USSR and in the eastern regions depends primarily on its natural requirements and on the distribution of horses. Oat sowings in the southern and southeastern regions are comparatively small: barley replaces oats here.

The average yield of oats in the USSR as a whole in 1937 was 12.4 centners per hectare [34.6 bushels per acre]. The average yield during the years of the Second Five-Year Plan reached its highest level in Siberia, the Urals, and the Central Industrial Region. The leading kolkhozes harvest as many as 25 to 30 centners per hectare.

Spring Barley

Barley is a very valuable concentrated fodder for livestock, especially for horses and hogs. Certain strains are cultivated for the brewing industry. Some kinds of barley are used for food, chiefly in the Far North of the USSR, where it ripens better than other grain crops. Pearl barley is made from barley.

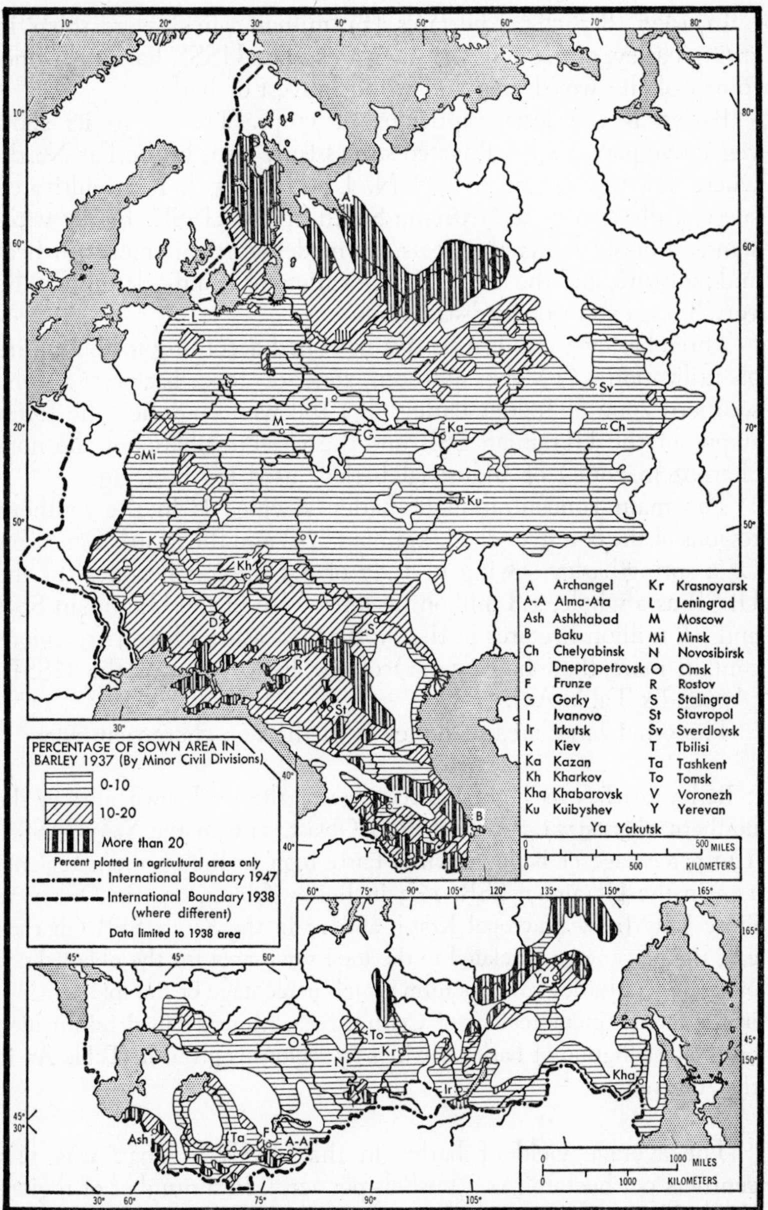

FIG. 58. Percentage Which Barley Constituted of Total Sown Area, 1937

In 1937, 8,565,800 hectares [21 million acres] were sown in spring barley, or 6.3% of the sown area. The USSR has nearly one-fourth of the world area and world harvest of barley.

Barley is the least capricious of crops. Thanks to its short vegetative period it is cultivated successfully even in the Far North, where sowings extend to 70° N. Lat. [Fig. 58]. It is cultivated successfully also in the extreme South of the USSR. Barley withstands drought better than oats. Its moderate requirements in heat and moisture, and the existence of a variety of strains, determine the very broad extent of its distribution.

Three barley zones can be distinguished according to the nature of utilization: (1) the northern zone of food barley; (2) the southern zone of fodder barley; (3) the western zone (the forest steppe of the Ukrainian SSR and the western oblasts of the non-chernozem zone) of industrial barley, used for brewing.

The main concentration of barley sowings is in the southern regions of the country—the Ukrainian SSR and the North Caucasus. Of a spring-barley sowing in 1937 of 8.5 million hectares for the USSR as a whole, 2.8 million hectares were in the Ukrainian SSR and 1.8 million hectares in the North Caucasus. These two regions contain more than half (54%) of the barley area of the USSR. [Appendix Table A5].

The other large area of barley is in the non-chernozem zone.

Barley reaches its highest percentage of the total sown area in the northern oblasts: 21.5 in Archangel Oblast, 21.6 in the Yakut ASSR. The percentage of barley sown is fairly high in the southern regions: 11.3 in the Ukrainian SSR, 16.3 in Rostov Oblast, 13.9 in Ordzhonikidze Kray [now Stavropol Kray], and 17 in the Kirgiz SSR (in each case the percentage is related to the total sown area for the oblast, kray, or republic). Barley sowings form a high percentage of the total sowings in the mountainous regions of Central Asia. More detailed information on the distribution of barley sowings by regions is given in Table A5 in the Appendix.

The average yield of barley in the USSR in 1937 was 11.5 centners per hectare [21.4 bushels per acre]. In a number of regions the yield attained 19 centners and more, and leading kolkhozes and farm crews obtained 30 centners and more per hectare. The record barley harvest of 119 centners from one hectare was obtained on the Stalin Kolkhoz (Yakut ASSR).

Winter barley does not occupy a large area—625,000 hectares (in 1937). It is cultivated primarily in the Trans-Caucasus, the North Caucasus, and the Crimea. Winter barley withstands the winter less well than winter wheat, and therefore is concentrated in regions of mild winters.

Millet (Proso Millet)

Millet is a very valuable meal crop. In 1937, 4,405,000 hectares [10.9 million acres] in the USSR were sown in millet, compared with 3,500,000 hectares in 1913. The biggest areas of millet are concentrated in the Kazakh SSR, in the Middle and Lower Volga, in the Central Chernozem Region, the Urals, and the Ukrainian SSR. In 1937 millet sowings totaled 819,400 hectares in the Kazakh SSR (18.6% of all sowings of millet in the Union); 845,800 hectares in the Middle and Lower Volga (19.2%); and 669,900 hectares in the Central Chernozem Region (15.2% of the entire area sown in millet.) (See Table A5 in the Appendix.)

Millet is characterized by its great resistance to drought. Therefore sowing of this crop is especially important for the southeastern regions.

The decree of the Council of People's Commissars of the USSR and the Central Committee of the Communist Party of the Soviet Union on measures for assuring dependable harvests in the arid regions of the southeastern USSR laid out a whole series of measures for raising the yield of millet in this zone (sowing graded seed in wide rows, organization of special detachments, etc.). The leading kolkhozes obtained as many as 25 to 30 centners of millet per hectare.

Maize

In the USSR maize (corn) is sown chiefly as a fodder crop. Harvested in an unripe state, it is a very important ensilage crop in the chernozem zone. The grain serves for the production of starch, alcohol, and corn syrup; it is used also in oil manufacturing, canning, etc. In a number of regions maize is used for food as well. There are numerous strains of maize differing in the length of growing period. Maize is a crop which requires heat; the minimum total of daily temperatures over 10° [Centigrade] which it requires is 2,300 to 4,000°, depending on the strain; this is approximately twice the minimum total of [daily] temperatures required for oats or spring wheat.

Maize resists drought relatively well. In 1937, 2,820,000 hectares [7.0 million acres] were sown in maize in the USSR, or 2% of the sown area (in 1913, it was 1,300,000 hectares). Maize sowings are chiefly in the South, in the North Caucasus, and in the Ukrainian SSR [Fig. 59]. The Ukraine sowed 1,024,000 hectares in 1937 (primarily in the southern oblasts). In the North Caucasus sowings in 1937 occupied 1,220,000 hectares. These two regions together contained over three-fourths of the total maize area of the Union [Appendix Table A5].

Maize sowings occupy considerable space in the Georgian SSR—400,700 hectares in 1937. The Georgian SSR has a very large part of its sown area in maize—40%.

Since the prerevolutionary period the boundary of maize cultivation within the steppe zone has moved significantly to the northeast. Small sowings are found even in Chkalov Oblast.

The North Caucasus has the highest proportion of maize sowing: in the Chechen-Ingush ASSR, it is 42% of the sown area; in North Osetia, it is 45.9% of the sown area.

The most favorable conditions for maize include a long frost-free season with high temperatures in summer. Georgia has the longest frost-free period—277 days a year. In the south of the Ukrainian SSR and in the North Caucasus the climatic conditions are likewise favorable.

Maize is moving into new regions. In recent years centers have been created in Stalingrad, Voronezh, Kursk, and South Kazakhstan oblasts. The development of frost-resistant strains will make it possible to extend the crop northward from the present zone.

The movement of maize to the north and east is important for raising the yield of grains in these regions, because maize, as a deeply plowed crop, promotes clearing the fields of weeds.

Maize (the grain) is an important concentrated fodder for hogs and cattle. The strengthening of the fodder base for livestock raising in large measure depends on the spread of its production.

The average yield of maize in the USSR as a whole in 1937 was around 14 centners per hectare [22 bushels per acre]. With proper

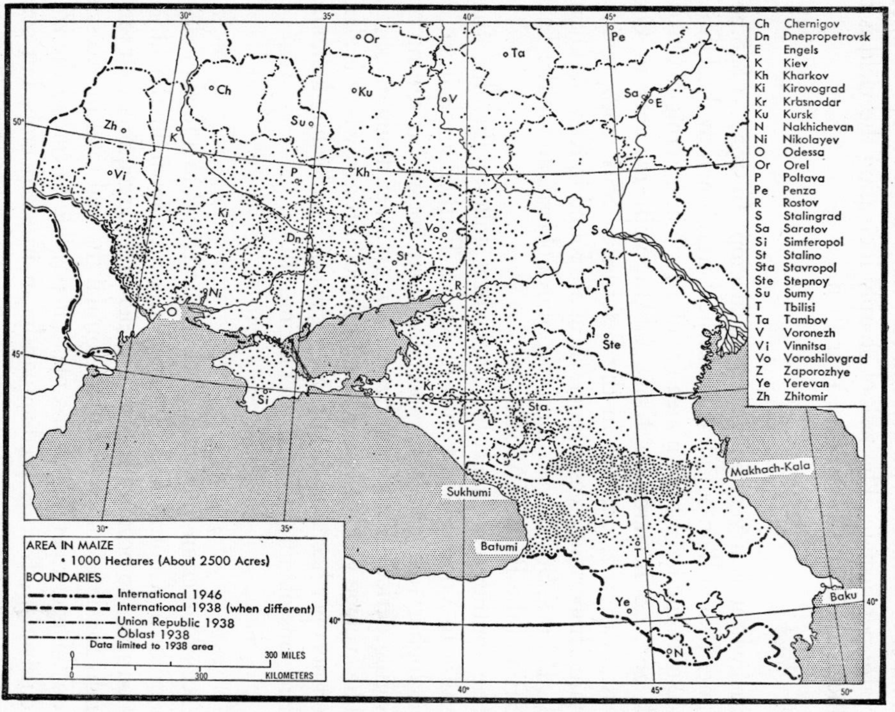

FIG. 59. Area in Maize (Corn)

cultivation it gives yields of as many as 40 to 50 centners per hectare. A number of Stakhanovite detachments have obtained 100 centners of maize per hectare. The task of sharply increasing the yield is to be faced under the Third Five-Year Plan.

Buckwheat

Buckwheat is a very important meal crop. In 1937, 1,848,000 hectares [4.6 million acres] of buckwheat were sown in the USSR. It occupies the largest sown area (as of 1937) in Chernigov Oblast, with 207,000 hectares; in Kursk Oblast, with 131,000; in Orel Oblast, with 162,100; and in the Belorussian SSR, with 137,900 hectares. Important areas in buckwheat are found in Kiev, Zhitomir, Tula, Poltava, Sverdlovsk, and Novosibirsk oblasts, and in the Tatar ASSR and the Bashkir ASSR.

The southern boundary of buckwheat follows the line from Vinnitsa to Voronezh to Penza to Kazan. Farther south it suffers from higher temperatures, especially from hot winds during the flowering period. In the Southeast it suffers from drought.

The average yield of buckwheat in the USSR as a whole is about 7 centners per hectare [15 bushels per acre]. The leading kolkhozes and regions obtain harvests several times this.

Rice

Rice occupies an important place in the USSR as a food product, especially in Central Asia. In 1937 the area sown in the USSR totaled 156,000 hectares [0.4 million acres]. Rice requires four to six months for development, with an annual thermal total in excess of 2,500°. Faster-ripening strains make it possible to extend the zone of cultivation. Rice is predominantly an irrigated crop, but some strains can be grown without irrigation. The chief zones where rice is grown are Central Asia (primarily the Uzbek SSR), the Trans-Caucasus (primarily Azerbaidzhan), and the Kazakh SSR, which together hold 86.2% of the area in rice. During the years of the two Five-Year Plans rice sowing was extended to the North Caucasus (Krasnodar Kray) and the Far East. It has penetrated also into the Ukraine.

The average yield of rice in the USSR as a whole is 21 centners per hectare [41.6 bushels per acre], while the leading kolkhozes obtain as many as 40 to 50 centners per hectare.

Legumes

Legumes occupied 2,981,000 hectares [7.4 million acres] in 1937, an increase of 1,200,000 hectares over 1913.

The seed legumes (peas, beans, lentils) are valuable food crops because of their high protein content. Some legumes (vetch, lupine, etc.) are cultivated for fodder. Leguminous crops also have great agronomic importance: they absorb nitrogen from the air, enriching the soil and increasing the yield of crops which succeed them.

Peas take up two-thirds of the total area sown in legumes. Lentils and beans follow. Peas are less demanding as to heat than other seed legumes; hence the chief zone of their distribution is the non-chernozem oblasts, the Tatar ASSR, and the Urals. Lentils cannot withstand early autumn frosts, and so, in spite of their short growing period, they cannot extend as far to the north as peas and are chiefly in the central zone. Sowings of beans are primarily in the southern regions.

SECTION 6. DISTRIBUTION OF INDUSTRIAL CROPS

The significance of industrial crops lies in the fact that they furnish raw material for a whole series of branches of the light and food industries. The sown area of all industrial crops in the country has increased from 4.5 million hectares in 1913 to 11.2 million hectares [27.7 million acres] in 1937, that is, two and a half times. At the same time the geography of industrial-crop sowings has altered greatly. Kolkhozes and sovkhozes have begun to sow new industrial crops which were completely unknown in Tsarist Russia or were sown in insignificant amounts—new bast crops (kenaf, southern hemp, and others), soy bean, castor plant, peanut, rubber-bearing plants, medicinal plants, and essential-oil plants.

Cotton

The area sown in cotton in the USSR has expanded from 688,000 hectares in 1913 to 2,091,800 hectares [5.2 million acres] in 1937. The total yield of raw unginned cotton has grown from 7.4 million centners in 1913 to 25.8 million in 1937.[13] The USSR has moved

[13] [In the United States about 35% of the weight of raw cotton is lint cotton, and about 65% cottonseed. The 1937 production of lint cotton in the USSR was reported as 3.7 million bales (U. S. Dept. of Agriculture, *Agricultural Statistics, 1941*, p. 121).]

into third place in the world (after the United States and British India) in cotton production. It produces one-tenth of the world's cotton.

Cotton has unusually high temperature requirements. The annual total of daily temperatures in excess of 10° C. required for growing cotton is fixed at 3,500 to 5,000°, depending on the strain. Cotton also needs a large number of cloudless days. In this respect, Central Asia offers very favorable conditions. The annual total heat in the cotton regions of Central Asia is lower than in Egypt, but the number of cloudless days here is higher. Copious rains harm the cotton plant. In the arid republics of Central Asia cultivation of the cotton plant is possible only with irrigation. The loessial soils of Central Asia (sierozems, or gray soils) meet the requirements of the cotton plant; but they are poor in nitrogen and therefore require large quantities of nitrogen fertilizers.

Before the Revolution, cotton sowings were concentrated in Central Asia and partly in the Trans-Caucasus [Fig. 60 and Table 36]. During the years of the Stalin Five-Year Plans enormous changes have occurred in the location of cotton in the USSR.

TABLE 36. AREA SOWN IN COTTON [IN 1913 AND 1937, BY REPUBLICS] [cf. Appendix Table A6]

Republics	1913		1937		% of Cotton Yield in 1937
	Thousand Hectares	% of USSR total	Thousand Hectares	% of USSR total	
RSFSR	—	—	284.1	13.6	4.7
Ukrainian SSR	—	—	223.9	10.7	4.5
Azerbaidzhan SSR	103.2	15.0	192.6	9.2	8.1
Armenian SSR	15.3	2.2	18.0	0.9	0.8
Turkmen SSR	69.4	10.1	155.2	7.4	7.2
Uzbek SSR	423.5	61.6	927.0	44.3	59.2
Tadzhik SSR	26.7	3.9	111.5	5.3	6.9
Kazakh SSR	20.8	3.0	111.3	5.3	4.8
Kirgiz SSR	21.6	3.1	64.1	3.1	3.7
Georgian SSR	7.5	1.1	4.1	0.2	0.1
USSR	688.0	100.0	2,091.8	100.0	100.0

The main cotton base of the Union is in the republics of Central Asia (the Uzbek SSR, Tadzhik SSR, and Turkmen SSR), where 57.2% of the cotton sowing is concentrated, and the largest part is

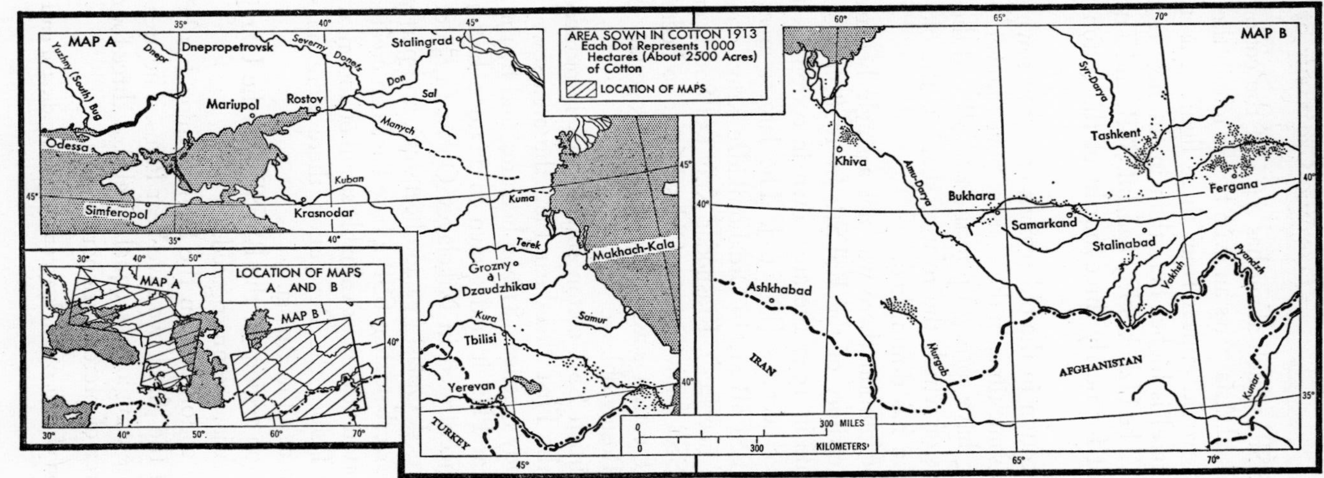

Fig. 60. Area in Cotton, 1913

in the Uzbek SSR, which alone has 44% of the cotton sowing of the USSR. Central Asia plays an even bigger role in the production of cotton [than would appear from these figures], as the yield of cotton [per hectare] is higher here than in the new regions of unirrigated cotton. The Uzbek SSR, Tadzhik SSR, and Turkmen SSR together account for nearly three-fourths of the cotton production of the country.

The area in cotton in the old regions of cotton sowing has been doubled. At the same time, in the years of Soviet power, new regions of cotton sowing have sprung up in the RSFSR and the Ukrainian SSR, as a result of which the relative share of the old regions in cotton production has diminished.

Before the Revolution there was not a single hectare of cotton grown on the territory of the RSFSR; in 1928, 111,000 hectares were sown, while in 1937 the area sown in cotton in the RSFSR reached 284,000 hectares [Fig. 61]. The largest areas of cotton sowings in the RSFSR are in Ordzhonikidze Kray [now Stavropol Kray] (128,200 hectares), Krasnodar Kray (51,800 hectares), and the Crimean ASSR [now Crimea Oblast] (50,000 hectares).[14] Important areas of cotton sowing are in the Dagestan ASSR, and Stalingrad and Rostov oblasts.

In the Ukrainian SSR cotton sowing was introduced in 1930; by the end of the First Five-Year Plan the area sown in that republic had already reached 181,000 hectares, and by the end of the Second Five-Year Plan it had grown to 223,900 hectares. Cotton sowings are concentrated in Nikolayev Oblast (145,000 hectares) and Dnepropetrovsk Oblast (74,400 hectares), and partly in Odessa Oblast. In the Azerbaidzhan SSR a base has been created for growing Egyptian cotton—the most valuable strain of cotton, which yields a longer fiber. Before the Revolution there were no sowings of Egyptian cotton at all in Russia.

The new cotton regions of the RSFSR and the Ukrainian SSR, unlike Central Asia, are unirrigated.

Thus, a new cotton base in the Soviet Union has been created in the course of the [first] two Five-Year Plans. The area of planted cotton in the new regions is equal to almost three-fourths of the whole cotton area of prerevolutionary Russia.

[14] [The location of each ASSR, kray, and oblast is indicated on Fig. 83 in the back of the book.]

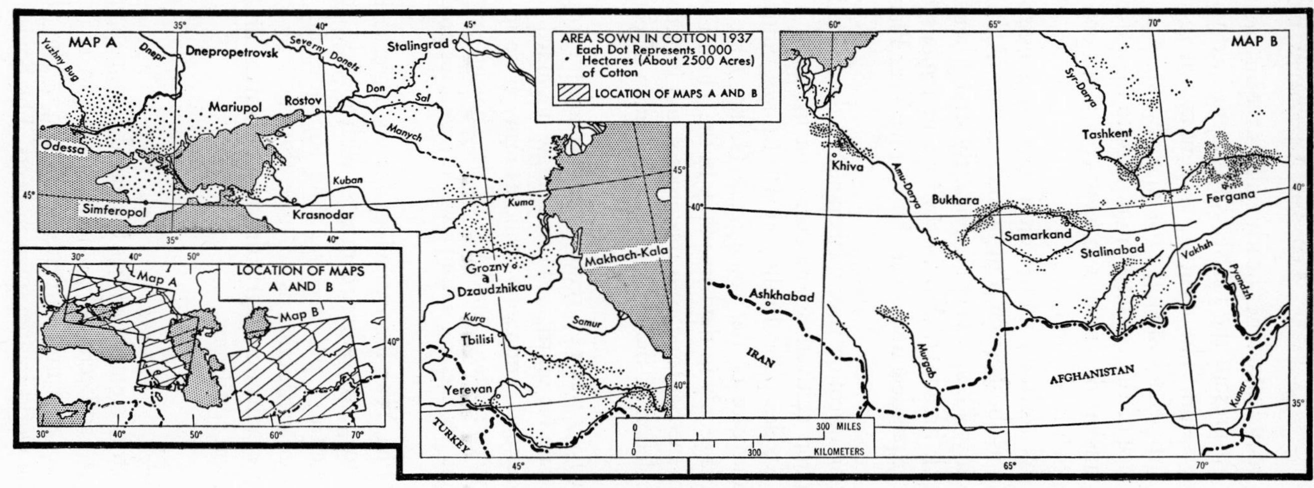

FIG. 61. Area in Cotton, 1937

Prerevolutionary Russia met nearly half its requirements with imported cotton. At present the USSR is fully provided with domestically produced cotton. The creation of new cotton regions, which contain one-fourth of all sowings, has played a big role in assuring the independence of the Soviet Union in cotton requirements.

Further expansion of sowings in new cotton regions is planned under the Third Five-Year Plan.

To restore soil fertility, proper crop rotation is essential, which requires alfalfa as the best crop to precede cotton. Alfalfa, while it raises the cotton yield, also very significantly strengthens the fodder base in livestock breeding. Alfalfa sowings in regions of irrigated cotton will be expanded under the Third Five-Year Plan.

The cultivation of cotton is very laborious. In the individual peasant economy all cotton cultivation was carried on by hand. The soil was worked with a wooden plow. In the cotton kolkhozes, cultivation of the soil, sowing, and care of the young crop (hilling) are mechanized. Mechanization lags only in the harvesting. In the Third Five-Year Plan the task is set of mechanizing even this process, and its accomplishment will mean completion of the complex mechanization of cotton production.

The yield in 1937 was 14.8 centners per hectare for irrigated cotton and 4.6 per hectare for unirrigated cotton (raw unginned cotton). The leading kolkhozes and farm crews obtain as many as 30 to 40 centners of cotton per hectare. Many Stakhanovite detachments have harvested over 100 centners per hectare, setting a world record for productivity.

The Third Five-Year Plan provides for an increase in the raw-cotton harvest to 32.9 million centners, with a yield for irrigated cotton of 19 centners per hectare. The fundamental method of increasing cotton production is to raise the yield by proper crop rotation, the most advanced agricultural techniques, and the application of chemical fertilizers.

Sugar Beets

The area sown in sugar beets has increased from 648,700 hectares in 1913 to 1,193,000 hectares [3.0 million acres] in 1937. The gross yield of beets was 218 million centners in 1937. The USSR holds first place in the world in area sown in beets. The Soviet Union has

35.4% of the world's sown area of sugar beets and 26.5% of its production (1937).

The tremendous growth in sugar-beet sowings is a result of the creation of large-scale mechanized agriculture. At present beet production has reached a high level of mechanization. Not only is soil cultivation mechanized, but also weeding and harvesting, which formerly were performed by hand. In 1937, 79.7% of the sugar-beet sowings were harvested with beet-lifting machines pulled by tractors.

Sugar beets require the following climatic conditions: an annual total of daily temperatures not below 2,200°, and a growing period of 160 to 170 days. The number of sunny days, especially during the second half of summer, has an important effect on the sugar content of the beets. Beets require adequate rainfall. Irrigation considerably increases the yield. In the USSR sugar beets are mostly a crop of the chernozem zone. They respond well to fertilizers. The distribution of sowings appears in the following figures [Table 37]:

TABLE 37. AREA SOWN IN SUGAR BEETS [1913, 1928, AND 1937, BY REPUBLICS] [cf. Appendix Table A6]

Republics	1913		1928		1937	
	Thousand hectares	%	Thousand hectares	%	Thousand hectares	%
RSFSR	115.1	17.74	120.6	15.66	343.7	28.81
Ukrainian SSR	533.6	82.26	649.1	84.34	816.7	68.44
Kazakh SSR	—	—	—	—	13.0	1.08
Kirgiz SSR	—	—	—	—	13.4	1.12
Georgian SSR	—	—	—	—	5.8	0.48
Armenian SSR	—	—	—	—	0.8	0.07
USSR	648.7	100.00	769.7	100.00	1,193.4	100.00

During the years of the [first] two Five-Year Plans sugar-beet sowings in the old regions of production (the Ukrainian SSR, Kursk and Voronezh oblasts, etc.) were expanded one and one-half times; new regions of beet sowing were created (see Table A6 in the Appendix).

Before the Revolution 82% of the sugar-beet sowings were in the Ukraine, while the remainder were in the Central Chernozem Region. In 1937 the share of the Ukrainian SSR was only 68%.

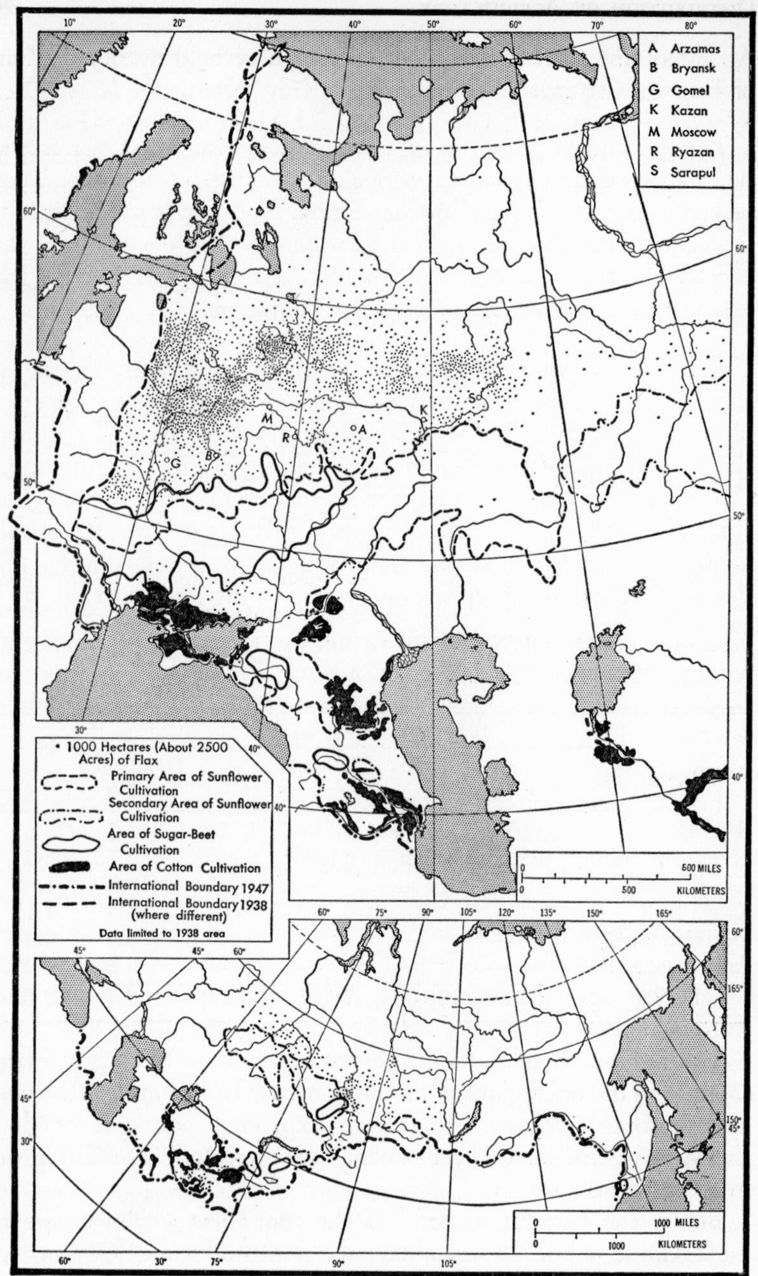

Fig. 62. Industrial Crops

An important place in the production is now held by new regions of beet sowing in the USSR: Altay Kray; Krasnodar Kray; Orel, Saratov, Ryazan, and Tula oblasts; and Maritime Kray [Fig. 62].

Important centers of sugar-beet production have been created in the Kazakh SSR, the Kirgiz SSR, and the Georgian SSR. In yield of beets the new regions of beet sowing do not fall below the old regions and occasionally even exceed them.

The cultivation of sugar beets has spread far beyond the boundaries of the original beet zone, which until recently was still limited to the sector between 47° and 54° N. Lat.

The definitive penetration of sugar beets to the east began only at the end of the First Five-Year Plan. In 1937 the area sown in the Volga Region, Siberia, the Kirgiz SSR, Kazakhstan, and the Far East had already reached 65,000 hectares. New sugar factories have been built in these regions. Over a short period a new base of sugar-beet sowing has been created in the East.

The distribution of beet-sugar production that had developed in Tsarist Russia involved the transportation of sugar over thousands of kilometers to the regions of its consumption. This burdened railroad transport and raised the cost of sugar. The new distribution of sugar beets is solving successfully the problem of bringing beet sowing and the sugar industry closer to the regions of sugar consumption.

Further penetration of sugar beets into the eastern regions will take place under the Third Five-Year Plan.

The location of sugar beets in the vicinity of sugar factories is related to the level of transportation techniques and to the expense of moving beets from their production site to the place where they are processed. Before the Revolution two-thirds of the harvest was brought by wagon from the fields to the sugar factories, while one-third, from greater distances, was delivered by railroads. During recent years sowings have increased near railroad stations. At the same time motor transport has begun to play a big role in the beet regions.

The intensity of sugar-beet sowings is determined by the requirements of crop rotation. The best crops to precede sugar beets are winter wheat sown on fertilized fallow, and herbage [fodder crops].

The average yield of sugar beets in the USSR as a whole was 183 centners per hectare in 1937 [7.4 tons per acre]. The Stakhanovites of the beet fields obtain as many as 500 to 1,000 centners of beets per hectare.

The Third Five-Year Plan has projected an increase in sugar-beet yield to 282 million centners, with an average yield of 235 centners per hectare. A rise in yield is the fundamental way of increasing the harvest. The introduction of proper crop rotation, painstaking care of sowings, and the use of advanced agricultural techniques and of chemical fertilizers will guarantee an increase in the yield of sugar beets.

Fiber Flax

Flax is a very important fiber crop. Linseed is used for the manufacture of oil. The waste products of linseed-oil manufacturing, oil cakes, provide a very valuable fodder for livestock.

In 1937 fiber flax occupied 2,125,500 hectares [5.2 million acres] in the USSR; this is double the prewar level. The USSR holds first place in world flax sowing. The USSR share of the world's flax area is over 20%.

Flax production is mechanized to a large extent on the kolkhozes and sovkhozes. Soil cultivation and sowing are carried on largely with tractors. Flax swingling machines are used in the kolkhoz fields, but the harvesting is still insufficiently mechanized. Factories have been built to process much of the flax produced. Mechanization of the harvesting will be intensified under the Third Five-Year Plan.

Fiber flax is a crop which does not require much heat. It is satisfied with a short summer of 85 to 90 days. Flax sprouts can withstand 4° of frost [down to 25° F.]. The minimum annual total of daily temperatures above 10° [50° F.] must be 1,200° for fiber flax (compared to 3,500° for cotton and 2,200° for sugar beets). The moderate heat requirements of flax promote the wide distribution of this crop throughout the country. Flax sowings extend to 62° N. Lat.

Fiber flax is very exacting as to moisture and for that reason is concentrated in the northern part of the USSR (see Table A6 in the Appendix).

The principal areas of fiber flax are in the non-chernozem zone. The main flax-raising oblasts (1937) are: Kalinin (354,600 hectares), Smolensk (292,000), the Belorussian SSR (255,000), Leningrad (171,000), Kirov (152,000), Yaroslavl (147,000), and Vologda (96,000) [Fig. 62]. These oblasts contain about three-fourths of the area sown in fiber flax in the USSR. The southern boundary of the large-scale distribution of fiber flax coincides approximately with the northern boundary of chernozems. The northern flax-growing regions have the highest yield and the best quality of fiber flax. The southern boundary of flax grown for spinning at present passes approximately along the line from Gomel to Bryansk to Ryazan to Arzamas to Kazan to Sarapul [Fig. 62].

Improper distribution of flax was one of the methods used by saboteurs who made their way into agrarian agencies. In some regions it was cultivated excessively, which led to a breakdown in crop rotation and to difficulties with the labor force, so that part of the crop was unharvested. In other regions flax was a completely insignificant crop, and as such it did not receive due attention. The enemies of the people likewise disrupted the measures of the Party and Government for increasing the yield of flax.

On April 3, 1938, a decree was issued by the Council of People's Commissars of the USSR "on measures for increasing the yield and improving the quality of the fiber and seeds of fiber flax," which presented a program to improve flax growing.

The principal measures for increasing the yield are as follows: introduction of proper crop rotation in flax-growing regions (the best crop to precede flax is clover), planting of selected flax seed, and introduction of sufficient fertilizer into the soil. Using all these methods, Stakhanovite detachments in the flax-growing kolkhozes have obtained as many as 6 to 10 centners of flax fiber per hectare, which is two or three times the average yield in the Union.

The clover-hay area in the flax-sowing oblasts has increased from 744,000 hectares in 1913 to 4,208,000 hectares today. This creates favorable conditions for raising the flax yield.

Under the Third Five-Year Plan the total yield of flax fiber will be increased to 8.5 million centners, with an average yield of 4.6 centners per hectare.

Fiber-flax sowings are being increased in the eastern regions (Urals, Siberia). Special attention is being paid to the development of flax growing in the area of Perm [Molotov] and Sarapul. In this region climatic conditions are favorable to the production of flax fiber of high quality.

Hemp

Northern hemp (central-Russian) is cultivated primarily for its fiber, and also for its seed as a by-product. Hemp fiber is used for making cables and coarse sacking. Ropes, bags, and nets are made of hemp. Hempseed oil is used as food. It is used also for making paints and drying oil. Oil cake, obtained in processing hempseed into oil, is a valuable and nutritious fodder for livestock.

In hemp area the USSR holds first place in the world. The area sown in northern hemp in the USSR totaled 429,800 hectares in 1937. The largest areas growing northern hemp are in Kursk and Orel oblasts, the Ukrainian SSR (principally Chernigov Oblast), the Mordovian ASSR, the Belorussian SSR, Tambov and Novosibirsk oblasts, and Altay Kray. Hemp areas are predominantly south of the regions where fiber flax is grown, because hemp requires considerably higher temperature totals than flax. The growing period of hemp is also considerably longer than that of flax.

New Bast Crops

Among the new bast crops are southern hemp, kenaf [*Hibiscus cannabinus*], Chinese bellflower [*Abutilon*], and ramie. These crops make it possible for the hemp-jute industry to free itself from the importation of raw materials.

Southern hemp differs from northern in having a longer stem and a higher yield of fiber. It requires more heat. Sowings reached 150,000 hectares in 1937, primarily in Krasnodar Kray and in the south of the Ukrainian SSR (Dnepropetrovsk Oblast, etc.). The introduction of southern hemp has made possible a new hemp-jute industry in the South, closer to the regions of consumption. At present, it is moving northward. Sown in regions of central-Russian hemp [i.e., northern hemp], southern hemp does not ripen into seed, but has a fiber yield two or three times higher than the fiber yields of local strains of hemp.

The area of *kenaf hemp* exceeds 30,000 hectares. Sowings are chiefly in the North Caucasus (primarily in Krasnodar Kray) and the Uzbek SSR. The *Chinese bellflower* is sown (6,900 hectares in 1937) in the Belorussian SSR, the North Caucasus, the Central Chernozem Region, and the Uzbek SSR. *Ramie* (Chinese nettle) is a perennial fiber plant requiring a hot moist climate. It is grown in Georgia and has possibilities of expansion in the southern regions of the Union.

Oil Crops

The special oil crops include the sunflower, the castor plant, mustard, false flax [*Camelina sativa*], rape, and sesame. The seeds of the fiber crops—flax, hemp, cotton—are used also for manufacturing oil. In the all-Union total of vegetable-oil production, fiber crops play a large role. Essential-oil crops, which are cultivated to obtain essential oils, also belong to the group of special oil crops.

Together with edible oils, industrial oils are prepared from the seeds of the majority of oil crops. The waste products of vegetable-oil manufacture, oil cakes, are used largely as a concentrated fodder for livestock.

The total yield of the oil crops has increased from 21 million centners in 1913 to 51 million in 1937.

Sunflower

Sunflower sowings have expanded greatly: in 1937 they totaled 3,250,300 hectares [8.0 million acres], as against 968,700 hectares in 1913. The sunflower yields seeds from which oil is manufactured. Sunflower oil is the most important of the vegetable oils. The seeds are used as a food and as a raw material for margarine, glycerine, etc. The plant is heat-loving and drought-resistant. A crop requiring thorough cultivation, sunflowers promote the clearing of weeds and therefore are part of the crop-rotation scheme of the southern grain regions and the southeastern regions. A considerable portion of the crop is grown for ensilage.

The chief zone of cultivation includes the following oblasts: Saratov (west of the Volga), Kuibyshev, Stalingrad, Chkalov, Voronezh (south and southeast), and Rostov; and Krasnodar and Ordzhonikidze [Stavropol] krays [Fig. 62]. There is a large concentration of sunflower sowings in the Ukrainian SSR, primarily in the southern oblasts.

The sunflower yield averages 6.4 centners [per hectare] for the USSR as a whole. The leading kolkhozes get a yield two or three times higher.

Bushy [Seed] Flax

Bushy flax is the oil-producing variety of flax, and is cultivated for its seeds. Oil pressed from its seeds is used for industrial purposes, and also for food. The by-product oil cake is a highly valuable fodder, especially for cattle.

The area sown in bushy flax totaled 333,700 hectares in 1937. The chief zone is in the southern regions, as distinct from the zone of fiber flax, which is found in the northern regions.

Bushy flax, with its better developed root system, withstands insufficient moisture more easily than fiber flax. It also has a longer growing period. This explains the location of bushy flax in the more arid southern regions.

The largest areas of bushy flax are in the Ukrainian SSR (chiefly the Donets and Dnepropetrovsk areas), Central Asia, and Stalingrad Oblast.

Castor Plant

Castor oil, which is used in medicine and as an industrial oil, is made out of the seeds of the castor plant. Before the Revolution the plant was sown in insignificant amounts. In 1937 it occupied 238,000 hectares in the USSR.

The castor plant requires a great deal of heat and moisture. The chief regions of its distribution are Krasnodar Kray, Ordzhonikidze Kray [Stavropol Kray], and the southern part of the Ukrainian SSR (Dnepropetrovsk, Nikolayev, and Odessa oblasts).

Mustard

Mustard oil, made from the seeds of the mustard plant, is used for food, and also in the canning industry. Before the Revolution mustard was sown in insignificant quantities. In 1937 the sowings totaled 333,700 hectares in the USSR, about half of them (159,400 hectares) being in Stalingrad Oblast.

Important areas in mustard are found in the Volga German Republic [now principally in Saratov Oblast], in the Volga Region, Rostov Oblast, Kazakhstan, Saratov Oblast, the Ukrainian SSR, and the Kalmyk ASSR [now principally in Astrakhan Oblast]. The mustard plant withstands drought readily.

Soybean

The soybean is a new crop. It has highly diverse uses in the food industry. Edible and industrial oils, flour, milk products, and other products are made from its seeds. Unripened soybeans are suitable for canning. The young plants serve as fodder for livestock. Before the Revolution sowings were insignificant. In 1937, 173,000 hectares were sown in the USSR. The soybean requires much heat—an annual total of daily temperatures not less than 2,500°. The chief regions of its distribution are the Far East (about half of all sowings), the southern part of the Ukrainian SSR, and Krasnodar Kray.

False Flax [Camelina sativa]

An oil [cameline oil] which has industrial uses is made from false-flax seeds. Its sown area (1937) is 97,000 hectares. More than half of all sowings are in Western Siberia. Important sowings are in Eastern Siberia, the Ukrainian SSR, and the Kazakh SSR.

Rape

Rape is significant as fodder. An oil is prepared from its seeds, which is used in making margarine and also soap. Winter rape covers the largest area. It cannot withstand severe winters or spring frosts, and requires a fertile soil.

In 1937, 52,500 hectares of rape were sown, almost wholly in the Ukrainian SSR (primarily in Vinnitsa, Kamenets-Podolsk, and Kiev oblasts).

Perilla

Perilla is a new oil crop. Before the First Five-Year Plan perilla sowings had no industrial significance. In 1937 they totaled 16,000 hectares. Its chief regions of distribution are the Far East, Krasnodar Kray, and the Ukrainian SSR. Perilla oil is of industrial importance, being used in the lacquer-paint industry.

Peanuts

The peanut is a leguminous plant, from the seeds of which a high-grade edible oil is made. It is heat-loving, and requires a frostless period of five to six months; an excess of moisture is harmful.

It is sown in the North Caucasus, the south of the Ukrainian SSR, the Trans-Caucasus, and Central Asia. Peanut sowings in the USSR totaled 13,600 hectares in 1937 and 22,000 hectares in 1938.

Sesame

The seeds of the sesame are used for halvah [a Near Eastern confection, made of nuts, sugar, and oil]. In 1937, 45,400 hectares were sown, primarily in Central Asia. Before the Revolution sesame was imported. The growing of sesame has freed the USSR from the need to import it.

Safflower [Carthamus tinctorius]

Safflower oil is used for industrial purposes in the preparation of drying oil. The area sown in safflower in the USSR in 1937 totaled 35,500 hectares. Half its sowings (18,000 hectares) are in the Kazakh SSR (primarily in South Kazakhstan Oblast). The rest of its sown area is in Kuibyshev and Orenburg [Chkalov] oblasts, the Uzbek SSR, the Tadzhik SSR, the Kirgiz SSR, and the Ukrainian SSR.

Tung

Tung is a subtropical tree, from the fruit of which the very valuable tung oil is obtained for use in industry. Considerable tung-tree plantations have been laid out in the Subtropical Zone of the USSR.

Essential-Oil Crops

The essential-oil crops include coriander, mint, and anise. In area, coriander holds first place. The essential oils are used in winemaking, the perfume industry, etc. The production of such valuable oils as rose, geranium, and others, which were imported from abroad before the Revolution, has been developed as a new industry in the USSR.

Before the Revolution the area in essential-oil plants totaled about 7,000 hectares. In 1937 it already had reached 173,000 hectares. New essential-oil crops (lavender, Kazanlik rose) have been introduced into the USSR.

Of the total area in essential-oil plants, 132,600 hectares are in the RSFSR—in the Central Chernozem Region, the Volga Region, and the North Caucasus.

Voronezh Oblast has the biggest centers of essential-oil plants; next come Krasnodar Kray, Kursk Oblast, Ordzhonikidze [Stavropol] Kray, and the Ukrainian SSR.

The *medicinal crops* include the German camomile and sage. They are in the southern half of the European part of the USSR. The area under medicinal crops exceeds 5,000 hectares (as against 60 hectares in 1913).

Tobaccos

Tobacco requires a warm climate and a frostless period of five or six months; it cannot withstand frosts of more than 3° [down to

27° F.]. In 1913, tobacco sowings occupied 29,500 hectares; in 1937 they already had attained 97,000 hectares, of which 44,000 were in the RSFSR (primarily in Krasnodar Kray and the Crimean ASSR [Oblast]), 21,000 in the Georgian SSR (primarily in the Abkhaz ASSR), and 13,000 in the Ukrainian SSR (Moldavian ASSR [now SSR], Chernigov, Kamenets-Podolsk, and other oblasts). Important sowings are found in the Azerbaidzhan SSR, the Kazakh SSR, and the Kirgiz SSR.

During the years of Soviet power commercial tobacco raising has been introduced into new regions (Stalingrad Oblast, the Kazakh SSR, and the Kirgiz SSR).

Different sorts of makhorka [an inferior variety of tobacco] growing in the USSR require different climatic conditions. The area in makhorka has increased from 33,000 hectares in 1913 to 107,000 in 1937, of which 65,500 are in the RSFSR (primarily in Ryazan, Tambov, Voronezh, and Saratov oblasts) and 37,000 are in the Ukrainian SSR (primarily in Chernigov and Poltava oblasts). The biggest concentration of makhorka sowings is in Chernigov Oblast; it accounts for one-fifth of all the makhorka sowings in the country.

Chicory

Chicory is cultivated for the coffee industry. The roots are cut into pieces and dried, roasted, and used in ground form as an admixture with natural coffee. Chicory is used also as a raw material in distilling. It has a wide zone of distribution but does not withstand drought well. In 1937 the area sown reached 29,300 hectares, including 24,100 in the RSFSR and 4,300 in the Ukrainian SSR. The largest centers of chicory growing are in Yaroslavl Oblast, the Tatar ASSR, and Orel Oblast.

Rubber-Bearing Plants

Rubber-bearing plants are a new industrial crop. Before the Revolution the requirements of the rubber industry in Russia were met exclusively by the importation of raw materials. At the beginning of the First Five-Year Plan work was begun on the creation in the USSR of its own natural-rubber base. Numerous scientific expeditions took up the search for appropriate plants among the wild flora. These searches were crowned with success. The rubber-bearing plants tau-sagyz [*Scorzonera tau-saghyz*] and kok-sagyz [*Taraxacum kok-saghyz*] were discovered in the Kazakh SSR, and a third rubber-bearing plant of the same type—krym-sagyz [*Taraxacum megalorrhizon*]—was found in the Crimean ASSR [Oblast]. The great work performed by the scientific research institutions in domesticating the wild plants has already produced results. Rubber-bearing plants are entering production and are being mastered by kolkhozes and sovkhozes. Kok-sagyz is the most widely distributed. First sown in 1932, it occupied an area of more than 25,000 hectares in 1938.

Kok-sagyz has the following requirements: high soil fertility and normal soil moisture. The best crops to precede it are perennial herbs (clover, alfalfa), clear and manured fallows, and hemp. It requires large quantities of fertilizer. Research institutions are working on the development of new strains of kok-sagyz which will have larger roots with a greater rubber content.

The work of experimental stations has established the fact that tau-sagyz grows best following alfalfa, and that it requires generous amounts of fertilizer. Its roots contain much more rubber than those of kok-sagyz.

A whole series of experiments has demonstrated the feasibility of growing krym-sagyz on the irrigated lands of Central Asia. There it winters well.

Along with the introduction of new rubber-bearing plants, work is being done on the acclimatization in the USSR of guayule [*Parthenium argentatum*]—a rubber-bearing plant long cultivated in Mexico and the United States. Soviet experimental stations have developed a new strain of guayule which contains more rubber than the American strain. The plant requires much heat. It is cultivated in the Azerbaidzhan SSR.

The sowings of rubber-bearing plants are concentrated in the Belorussian SSR, Tula, Ryazan, and Kursk oblasts, and the Kazakh SSR. The problem of producing natural rubber must be solved under the Third Five-Year Plan.

Tea

Tea is a subtropical crop. High atmospheric humidity, an even and abundant rainfall in summer, and high temperatures are required by this crop. The minimum annual total of daily temperatures required is 3,000°. In 1913 sowings of tea totaled only 900 hectares, while in 1937 they already occupied 45,000. The chief tea region is Georgia (Abkhaz ASSR). Recently tea has been penetrating into new regions (Azerbaidzhan, Krasnodar Kray). Under the Third Five-Year Plan the tea plantation area will be expanded considerably, to new regions.

SECTION 7. DISTRIBUTION OF VEGETABLE, MELON, AND POTATO CROPS

Vegetables are extremely important, containing vitamins necessary to man. Potatoes are significant both as food and as fodder; they serve also as a raw material for the starch and syrup industry and the distilling industry. A waste product of potato processing (called distillery wash) is used as a livestock fodder. There are three main kinds of potatoes: eating, fodder, and industrial. Numerous strains exist, which differ in their natural requirements.

The area sown in vegetables has increased from 487,000 hectares in 1913 to 1,376,000 hectares [3.4 million acres] in 1937; the melon area has increased from 264,800 hectares in 1913 to 739,000 in 1937. Cabbage and cucumbers are the most important among the vegetable crops. In recent years the proportion of tomatoes, lettuce, and other vegetables notable for high vitamin content has increased considerably. A distinction is made between vegetable cultivation in the open (garden and field sowings) and on enclosed soil (sowings under glass and in hothouses).

Large-scale vegetable growing on the kolkhozes and sovkhozes makes possible the widespread use of seeders, planting and transplanting machines, potato diggers, etc., in the cultivation of vegetables. There are about five hundred vegetable and potato machine tractor stations. Sovkhozes specializing in vegetables have been created, chiefly in the RSFSR and the Ukrainian SSR.

An extremely important problem is the elimination of seasonality in vegetable growing and the provision of a year-around supply of vegetables for the population. This is being achieved, first, by combining late vegetables with early ones, and, secondly, by developing hothouse cultivation, which makes it possible to grow vegetables in winter.

Potatoes are concentrated in the non-chernozem oblasts, which include about 40% of the potato area of the country. Next come the Ukrainian SSR, which has 20% of all potato sowings, and the Central Chernozem Region (with 13%) (see Table A7 in the Appendix).

Potatoes occupy the largest percentages of the sown area in the Belorussian SSR (18%), Moscow Oblast (17%), Ivanovo Oblast (12.7%), Leningrad Oblast (12.1%), and Gorky Oblast (11.2%) [Fig. 63]. Large areas of potato sowing are found in the Ukraine (chiefly in the forest steppe). Many of the potatoes in the Central Chernozem Region are cultivated as a raw material for distilleries. About three-fourths of the total area sown in potatoes is in the non-chernozem zone, the Ukraine, and the Central Chernozem Region, taken together. Large areas of potato sowings are in the Urals and in Siberia. The rest of the USSR, with an enormous territory and population, contains only a small proportion of potato sowings. Especially noteworthy for the insignificant size of their potato sowings are the southern and southeastern steppe regions and the republics of Central Asia and the Trans-Caucasus.

The Ukrainian SSR holds first place in vegetables; here are concentrated one-third of the vegetable sowings in the country; the non-chernozem zone comes second, with approximately one-fourth of the vegetable sowings. The North Caucasus and the Crimea hold third place, and the Central Chernozem Region holds fourth. The Ukrainian SSR, the Central Chernozem Region, the North Caucasus, and the non-chernozem regions together contain three-fourths of all the sowings of vegetables in the USSR (see Table A7 in the Appendix).

Great changes in the distribution of vegetables and potatoes will occur under the Third Five-Year Plan. Potato and vegetable sowings will expand in regions where they have occupied small areas up to now, that is, in the southeastern and southern regions; vegetable and potato bases are being created in the vicinity of industrial centers. Sowings of vegetables and potatoes are being expanded considerably in the Urals, Siberia, and the Far East. This will make it possible to eliminate the hauling of potatoes and vegetables over great distances.

Vegetable zones are being created in the vicinity of large cities. Near Moscow, Kiev, and Odessa vegetables will be cultivated on irrigated fields where drainage water and runoff will be utilized to obtain high yields.

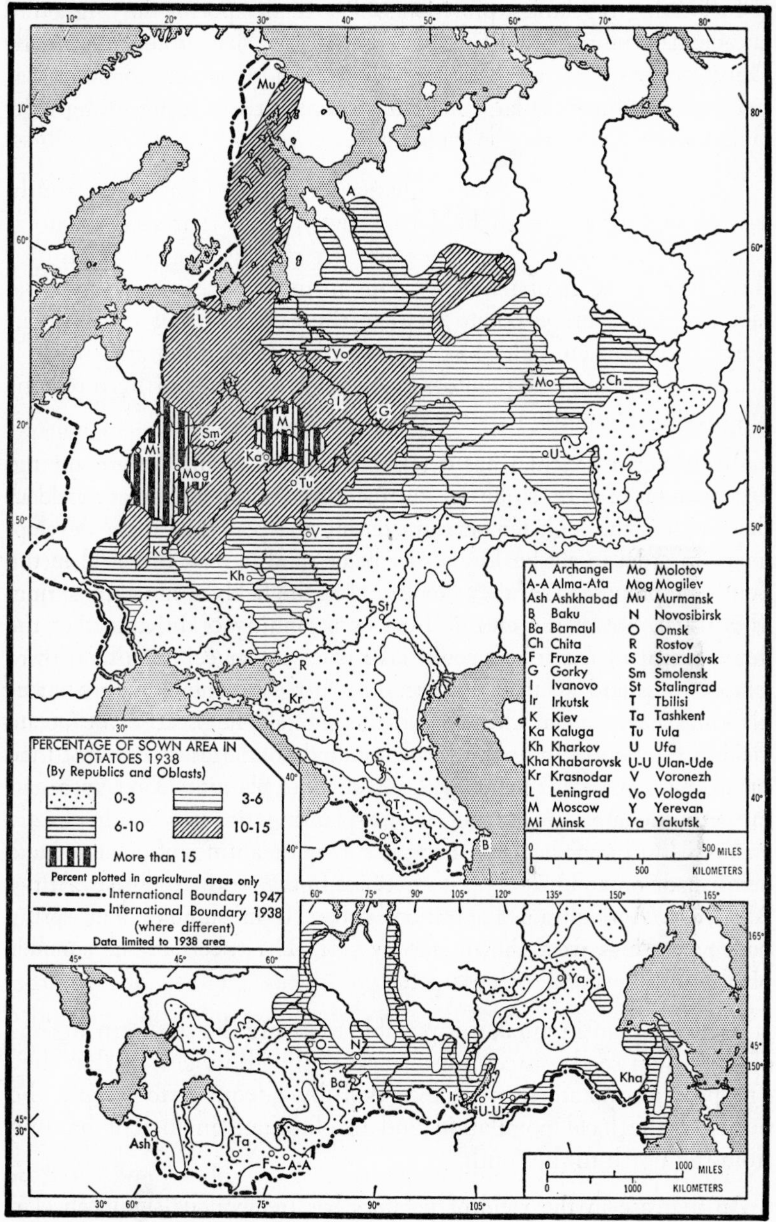

FIG. 63. Percentage Which Potatoes Constituted of Total Sown Area, 1938

In locating vegetables, provision will be made also for the creation of an adequate raw-material base for enterprises which process vegetables. During recent years a whole series of fruit-and-vegetable combines has been created; these are large mechanized enterprises for processing vegetables (canning, making vegetable juices).

The expansion of potato sowings in the southern and southeastern regions has been held back by the fact that seed potatoes, which were brought from the northern regions, degenerated after three or four years of planting. This in great measure explains the fact that the average potato yield in the South is half the yield in the non-chernozem belt. The degeneration of seed potatoes made it necessary to bring seed potatoes every year from the northern regions in order to renew the potato seed.

Academician Lysenko has determined that the chief reason for the degeneration of early strains of potatoes and for the low potato yield in the South is the high temperature during the period of tuber development. In order to get healthy seed potatoes and to raise the yield in the South, he proposed that they be planted in the fields not in early spring, as is usual, but at the end of June or beginning of July, so that the development of the tubers could take place under conditions of lower temperatures and greater moisture. The first experiments with summer plantings have shown already that this method helps raise the potato yield in the South. In 1935 several hundred kolkhozes for the first time carried out mass experiments with the summer planting of potatoes, and in 1936 the area of summer potato plantings in the South already amounted to 17,000 hectares. In 1938 summer plantings of potatoes were being made on an area of 54,000 hectares in the southern oblasts. At the All-Union Agricultural Exposition, tubers from summer and spring potato plantings were shown side by side. The tubers of the summer plantings were several times larger.

Summer planting makes it possible to assure the southern regions of their own seed source and to raise the potato yield, so that they can produce potatoes in quantities fully adequate to supply the needs of the local population and to eliminate inefficient hauling from the north to the south.

An increase in the yield of potatoes has tremendous significance in assuring the industrial regions of a sufficient local supply. The average yield still remains low (100 to 120 centners in the non-chernozem belt and 45 to 55 centners in the southern and southeastern oblasts). By using the most modern agricultural techniques, the leading regions and kolkhozes obtain a potato yield considerably higher than the average yield for the Union as a whole. Many leading kolkhozes harvest 200 and more centners of potatoes per hectare. This shows how great are the possibilities of raising the potato yield. The yield of vegetables also can be increased considerably.

In 1937, in the USSR as a whole, 739,400 hectares [1.8 million acres] were sown in melon plants (watermelon, muskmelon, etc.); this included 409,000 hectares in the RSFSR (the chief regions being the North Caucasus and the Volga Region), 121,000 in the Ukrainian SSR (primarily in the southern oblasts), 40,500 in the Kazakh SSR, 60,000 in Central Asia, and 18,000 in the Trans-Caucasus.

During the years of the Five-Year Plans, vegetable growing has greatly developed in the Far North. In the northern regions of Archangel Oblast the yield of potatoes and vegetables attains a level of 500 centners per hectare. High yields of potatoes and various vegetables are harvested on the shores of Kola Bay in Murmansk Oblast, at 70° N. Lat. At the All-Union Agricultural Exposition the experiment of the Arctic sovkhoz "Industriya" (located near Kirovsk) was exhibited [Fig. 53, p. 367]. With a short summer, given a frostless period of eighty days, this sovkhoz obtained an average potato yield of 124.6 centners per hectare from an area of 102 hectares. Vegetables are cultivated in the open in Kamchatka, Sakhalin, Kolyma, in Taimyr and Evenki okrugs, in the northern regions of the Yakut ASSR, and in other regions which before the Revolution knew neither vegetables nor potatoes [Fig. 53]. In the Far North the sowing of vegetables in the open has increased from 540 hectares in 1926 to 6,194 in 1938; potato sowings have increased from 1,510 hectares to 25,643.

Hothouse production plays an important role in the penetration of vegetable growing into the Far North. Before the Revolution there was not a single hothouse in the Far North. At present vegetables are cultivated in hothouses in a number of regions where they cannot be sown in the open. Enormous hothouses which operate on solar heat provide the workers of Kirovsk and Monchegorsk, of Vaigach Island, Dickson Island, etc., as early as August with tomatoes and other vegetables requiring much heat. In the regions of the Far North vegetables are especially important for protecting the inhabitants from scurvy.

Under the Third Five-Year Plan, in connection with industrial construction and population increase in the Far North, vegetable growing there will be even more widely developed.

SECTION 8. DISTRIBUTION OF ORCHARDS AND VINEYARDS

Fruit growing and viticulture are among the most important branches of agriculture with rich prospects of development. Fruits are a valuable food product, containing vitamins. They have an important place in Soviet export trade. The orchards of the USSR account for approximately one-tenth of the total orchard area of the world.

The fruit, berry, and grape plantings in the USSR as a whole in 1937 amounted to 1,508,600 hectares [3.7 million acres] of orchards, 216,600 hectares of vineyards, and 44,000 hectares of berry patches. In recent years orchards have been laid out over large areas in the kolkhozes and sovkhozes.

The area of orchards in the USSR has doubled since the prewar period.

Fruit Growing

The chief regions of well developed fruit growing are the Ukrainian SSR, the North Caucasus, the Crimea, the Central Industrial Region, the Central Chernozem Region, and the Trans-Caucasus. Over three-fourths of the fruit growing is in these regions. Fruit growing is well developed also in the Volga Region, the Belorussian SSR, the Central Asiatic republics, and South Kazakhstan (see Table A7 in the Appendix). The most valuable citrus orchards (oranges, lemons, tangerines) are on the Black Sea shores of the Caucasus; their area increases yearly, and from 160 hectares in 1913 it became 10,100 hectares in 1938.

Michurin, the great expert in transforming nature, obtained a whole series of new strains of fruits and berries by crossing cultivated fruits with wild ones and northern varieties with southern ones; the new strains have the desirable properties of the southern strains and at the same time are hardier (better able to withstand winter) and better adapted to the climatic conditions of the central regions of the European part of the USSR. This makes it possible to cultivate southern fruits in the middle zone of the USSR. The Michurin strains are most widely distributed in the kolkhozes and sovkhozes of the central and northern oblasts of the European part of the USSR.

At the All-Union Agricultural Exposition, fruit trees which spread along the ground bearing fruit attracted general attention.

In Siberia the horticulturist and scientist Kizyurin developed fruit trees which spread along the ground and, as a result of their inclined form, withstand the cold better. This creates the conditions necessary for the development of fruit growing in the severe climate of Siberia and the Urals and thousands of hectares of orchards have been laid out in recent years where formerly no orchards existed.

The propagation of Michurin strains, the penetration of orchards to the north and east, and the creation of raw-material bases in the vicinity of processing enterprises are among the most important problems of the Third Five-Year Plan in fruit growing.

Viticulture

There were 216,000 hectares of vineyards in the USSR at the beginning of the Third Five-Year Plan; of these 165,000 hectares were old enough to bear fruit.

Some of the grapes are consumed as table grapes, some are processed into wine and juice, and, finally, some are preserved by sun drying (currants, raisins). Factories for the production of Soviet champagne have been created on the basis of grapes from a number of large sovkhozes.

The chief regions of viticulture are the North Caucasus, the Ukrainian SSR (primarily the Moldavian ASSR [now SSR] and Odessa Oblast), the Crimean ASSR [Oblast], the Trans-Caucasus, and Central Asia. Important vineyard centers are found in Dnepropetrovsk, Nikolayev, and Vinnitsa oblasts. Of the total area in vineyards, the North Caucasus and the Crimea have 17.1%; the Ukrainian SSR, 28.2%; the Trans-Caucasus, 38.1%; and Central Asia, 15.7%. In these regions a network of specialized sovkhozes has been created. There are many specialized kolkhozes, where viticulture is the main branch of agriculture, in the Crimean ASSR, the North Caucasus, and the Trans-Caucasus. Viticulture is an extremely important subsidiary branch of production in the kolkhozes of numerous grain and cotton regions where vineyards are found.

The large size of the sovkhozes and kolkhozes permits the mechanization of a number of processes in viticulture which formerly were carried out by hand: planting, cultivation between the rows of the vineyards by means of tractors.

Michurin cultivated a northern strain of grape, adapted to severe climates far to the north of the present zone of viticulture. In the Michurin orchard (Voronezh Oblast) grapes have been growing for many years and yielding a good harvest. The introduction of Michurin strains opens up great opportunities for the development of viticulture in the middle zone of the USSR.

The decree issued on July 29, 1936, by the Council of People's Commissars of the USSR and the Central Committee of the Communist Party of the Soviet Union on the development of viticulture presented a detailed program for the improvement of this branch. The area of vineyards will be considerably expanded under the Third Five-Year Plan, and new plantings of champagne grapes will be included in the program.

SECTION 9. DISTRIBUTION OF ANIMAL HUSBANDRY

Development of Animal Husbandry

Next to the cultivation of the soil, animal husbandry is the most important branch of agriculture. The USSR holds third place in the world in the number of cattle, and second place in the number of hogs and sheep.

Livestock are divided into draft animals and productive livestock. Draft animals include horses, draft oxen, and camels; productive stock include beef and dairy cattle, hogs, and sheep. Horses, which are an extremely important source of traction power, at the same time are tremendously important to the national defense. Productive livestock furnish meat, milk, fats, and raw materials including hides and wool for a number of branches of light industry.

During the years of the Five-Year Plans a large collectivized livestock industry has been created. At present there are more than 1,900 sovkhozes for animal husbandry and more than 400,000 kolkhozes producing for the market.

During the years of collectivization livestock numbers decreased in the USSR as a result of kulak sabotage. At the 17th Party Congress, Comrade Stalin, after noting the decline of the herds, pointed out that raising the level of animal husbandry was a problem of first importance, and that the entire Party, as well as all workers, whether belonging to the Party or not, should be concerned with animal husbandry.

The measures taken by the Party and the Government made certain a change in the development of animal husbandry. From 1934 on, the number of livestock in the country began to increase rapidly. During the period from 1934 to 1938, cattle in the USSR increased 52%; sheep and goats, 82%, and hogs, 123%. Such enormous rates of increase reflect the advantages of large-scale socialist agriculture.

The head of livestock in the USSR compared to the prerevolutionary level is as follows [Table 38]:

Table 38. [HEAD OF LIVESTOCK BY TYPES IN 1916, 1934, AND 1938 (IN MILLIONS)]

	1916	1934	1938	1938 Index (1916 = 100)
Horses	35.8	15.7	17.5	48.9
Cattle	60.6	42.4	63.2	104.3
Sheep	121.2	51.9	102.5	84.6
Hogs	20.9	17.4	30.6	146.4

The head of cattle and of hogs already exceeds the level in 1916. By the end of the Second Five-Year Plan the shortage of cows on the kolkhozes had been basically overcome.

The USSR inherited from Tsarist Russia an animal husbandry of low productivity. Through collectivization and the establishment of sovkhozes, conditions have been created for transforming animal husbandry into a leading and highly productive branch of agriculture. Warm livestock shelters have been built in the sovkhozes and kolkhozes. The zootechnical attention and care of livestock have improved. Great work has been carried out in the improvement of livestock breeds. In 1938 crossbreeding had reached 90% of the cows, 86% of the sheep, and nearly the entire breeding-sow population on the livestock farms of the kolkhozes.

The productivity of livestock has risen considerably. Thus, the average annual milk yield per cow did not exceed 800 kg. before the Revolution. In 1938 the annual milk yield was 1,788 kg. on the meat and dairv sovkhozes of the People's Commissariats for Sovkhozes, and 1,100 kg. on the kolkhozes. The leading farms obtain 3,000 kg. and more of milk per cow annually. Cadres have been developed on kolkhozes and sovkhozes, which have mastered animal husbandry and have attained great success in raising its productivity. Thousands of leaders in animal husbandry participated in the All-Union Agricultural Exposition. The exposition showed animals raised on kolkhozes, including record-holding cows with an annual milk yield in excess of 8,000 liters, pedigreed hogs with a live weight of over 350 kg., and valuable thoroughbred horses and sheep.

Sovkhozes for animal husbandry and kolkhozes producing for the market are the chief medium in raising the level of animal husbandry.

The decree issued on July 8, 1939, by the Central Committee of the Communist Party of the Soviet Union and by the Council of People's Commissars of the USSR presented a detailed program for the development of publicly operated animal husbandry on the kolkhozes. Each kolkhoz must have at least two livestock farms. The minimum sizes of farms are established for various regions. In regions with large haying centers, detachments for mechanized haying have been created at the machine tractor stations.

Chief Regions of Animal Husbandry

Animal husbandry is a component branch of agriculture in all regions of the country, but the degree of specialization in that branch differs in various regions. It can be divided into the following main groups of regions, according to its relative importance in the agriculture of the USSR.

The first group includes the agricultural regions of grains and industrial crops, where animal husbandry is a secondary branch.

The second group includes the agricultural regions with well developed animal husbandry. To this group belong a whole series of agricultural regions in Kazakhstan, the Polesye region of the Belorussian SSR and the Ukrainian SSR, the regions of the Barabinsk Steppe and the Altay regions of Western Siberia, the Ishim and Tobol districts of Omsk Oblast, the mountainous part of Bashkiria, the mountainous regions of the Altay, the eastern regions of Eastern Siberia, a number of regions in the Far East, and a number of northern regions in the European part of the USSR (in Vologda and Archangel oblasts).[15]

The third group of regions includes those of settled and semi-nomadic animal husbandry, where agriculture has little significance and animal husbandry plays the decisive role in the economy. To this group belong the livestock-raising regions of Kazakhstan, Turkmenia, Tadzhikistan, Kara-Kalpakia, Kirgizia, Oirotia, Khakassia, a number of regions in Irkutsk Oblast, the Buryat-Mongol ASSR, the Kalmyk ASSR [now largely Astrakhan Oblast], and the mountainous regions of the Trans-Caucasus and of the North Caucasus.

The fourth group comprises regions of nomadic livestock raising, where agriculture has practically no significance, while animal husbandry is the universal form of production (some regions of the Buryat-Mongol ASSR, the Kazakh SSR, etc.).

Reindeer breeding is the chief branch of agriculture in the Far North [Fig. 65, p. 422]. The lichens which grow in the tundra serve as fodder for the deer, but are not suited for other types of livestock. Reindeer provide food products (meat) and material for clothing (fur) and are used for transportation. By the end of the Second Five-Year Plan there were 1,800,000 in the USSR. In Western and Eastern Siberia and in the Far East deer breeding for young horns is being developed; the young horns of the deer are used in Oriental medicine.

The specialization of a number of regions in the field of animal husbandry as the principal branch of agriculture is determined chiefly by the nature of agrarian resources.

Livestock-breeding regions are regions where arable land amounts to an insignificant proportion of the land area, but which are rich in pastures and meadows. For example, in South Kazakhstan plowland occupies only 4% of the land area, while pastures occupy 55%. Approximately the same situation is found in the mountainous areas and other regions where animal husbandry is the main branch of agriculture.

Distribution of Livestock by Regions

The following figures [Table 39] indicate the geographical distribution of livestock; they show the relative share of the different regions in the number of livestock of the USSR.

[15] [Political units are located on Fig. 83 in the back of the book.]

TABLE 39. DISTRIBUTION OF LIVESTOCK BY REGIONS (PER CENT OF TOTAL USSR, JANUARY 1, 1938)

[Location and boundaries of these regions are indicated in Fig. 7.]

REGIONS	HORSES	CATTLE	COWS	HOGS	SHEEP AND GOATS
RSFSR	65.9	62.0	66.0	56.6	63.0
European North	2.8	2.4	2.9	0.8	1.2
Northwestern Region	7.0	5.4	7.2	7.3	4.7
Central Industrial Region	8.2	6.2	8.5	7.3	6.6
Central Chernozem Region	8.0	6.1	7.0	8.8	5.0
Upper Volga Region	6.4	4.4	5.4	4.7	5.4
Middle and Lower Volga Region	3.9	5.8	5.1	4.0	7.5
North Caucasus and Crimea	6.7	8.9	7.3	8.3	12.3
Urals	8.0	8.3	8.7	5.3	8.1
Western Siberia	8.0	9.0	8.6	6.0	7.8
Eastern Siberia	6.1	4.9	4.6	3.0	4.3
Far East	0.8	0.6	0.7	1.1	0.1
Ukrainian SSR	18.1	15.2	15.2	30.1	5.0
Belorussian SSR	3.9	3.7	4.5	7.6	1.6
Trans-Caucasian republics	2.6	7.8	5.6	3.5	8.4
Central Asiatic republics	5.6	5.2	3.9	0.8	14.1
Kazakh SSR	3.9	6.1	4.8	1.4	7.9
USSR	100.0	100.0	100.0	100.0	100.0

In number of horses the non-chernozem zone of the European part of the USSR holds first place, one-fourth of the horses being concentrated here; the Ukraine holds second place: the eastern regions of the country (the Urals, Siberia, Kazakhstan, and the Far East), which together contain one-fourth of the horses [Fig. 64], are third.

The major part of the cattle is concentrated in the non-chernozem oblasts, the Ukraine, and the eastern regions [Fig. 65]. In these three zones together are found over 50% of the total number of cattle. The distribution of cows is similar.

In the non-chernozem oblasts, and also in the Urals and Western Siberia, livestock raising is primarily for dairy purposes. Dairying is concentrated in the vicinity of industrial centers and supplies the

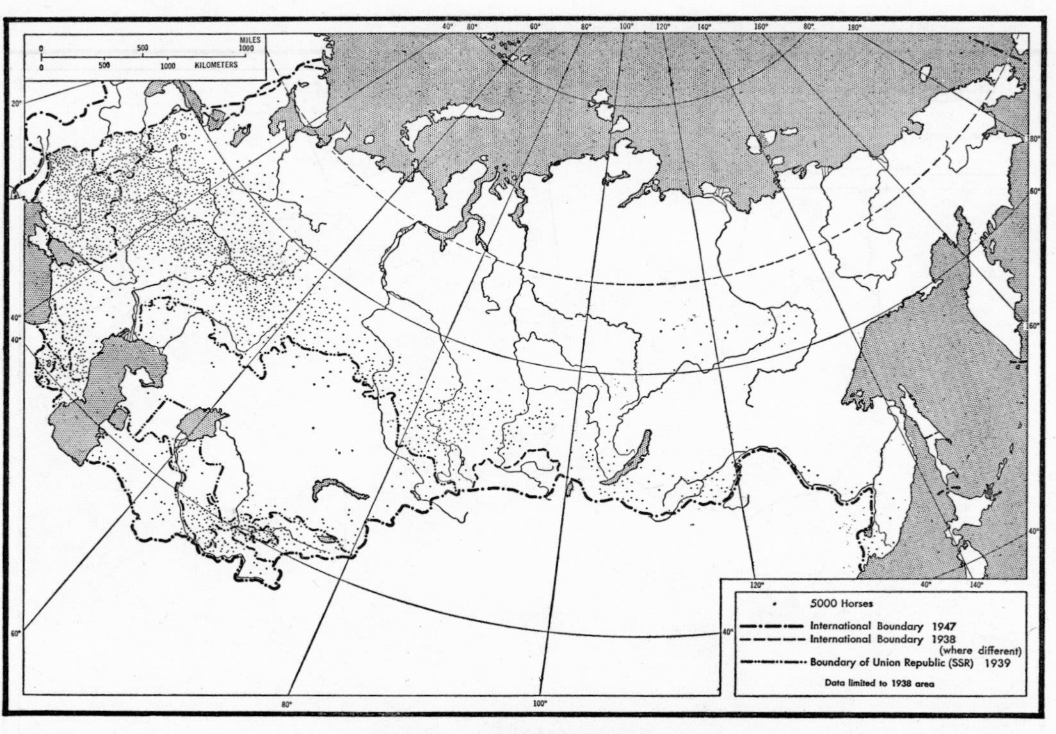

FIG. 64. Number of Horses

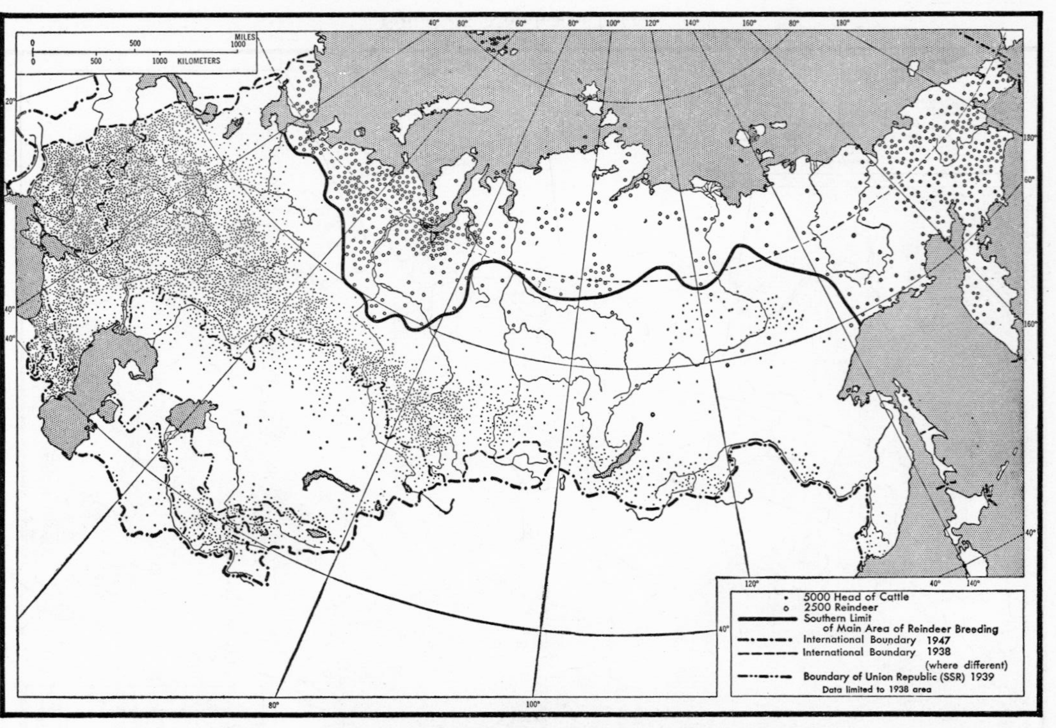

Fig. 65. Number of Cattle and Reindeer

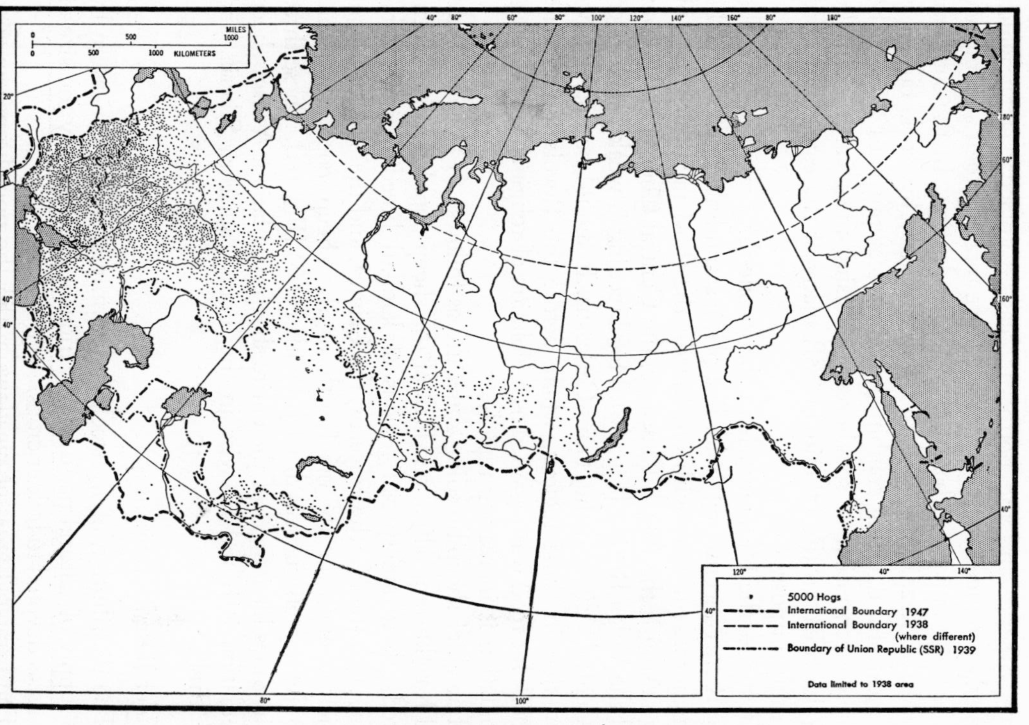

Fig. 66. Number of Hogs

cities with whole milk. In regions farther removed from large cities the major part of the milk is processed into butter and cheese. The Urals, Siberia, and the northern oblasts (Vologda, etc.), which formerly produced butter for export, have retained their significance as the most important base for butter production. In the southern steppes of Kazakhstan and the Lower Volga, livestock raising is for meat and dairying combined, or for meat purposes alone. The main concentration of sovkhozes for raising meat cattle is in the Kazakh SSR. In the Ukrainian SSR many of the cattle are raised for draft purposes (oxen).

In swine, the Ukraine, where almost one-third of all those in the USSR are concentrated, holds first place; second place belongs to the non-chernozem zone with one-fourth; the third important zone of hog raising is the North Caucasus, the Central Chernozem Region and the Volga Region [Fig. 66]. Hog breeding is weakly developed in Central Asia and the Trans-Caucasus. It should be noted, however, that in these regions, where before the Revolution the use of pork for food was regarded as a violation of religious law, the hog population is increasing rapidly.

The chief sheep-breeding zones are as follows: (1) Central Asia and Kazakhstan, where one-fifth of the sheep population is concentrated (there are special regions of karakul breeding in Central Asia); (2) the North Caucasus, the Crimea, and the Volga Region, which contain nearly one-fourth of the sheep population; and (3) the non-chernozem districts (with 17%) [Fig. 67]. These three main zones have 60% of the entire sheep population. A large sheep population is found likewise in the Trans-Caucasus, Siberia, and the Urals.

Fodder Base by Regions

The distribution of livestock is determined in large measure by the supply of natural pastures in various regions and by the size of the areas devoted to fodder crops.

The principal areas of meadows are in the non-chernozem zone (24.4% of the entire meadowland of the USSR), Siberia and the Urals (32.2%), and the Kazakh SSR (17.1%). These regions contain about three-fourths of the haying area of the USSR. Within the non-chernozem zone, the Northwestern Region and Northern Region [European North] (see Table A8 in the Appendix) are

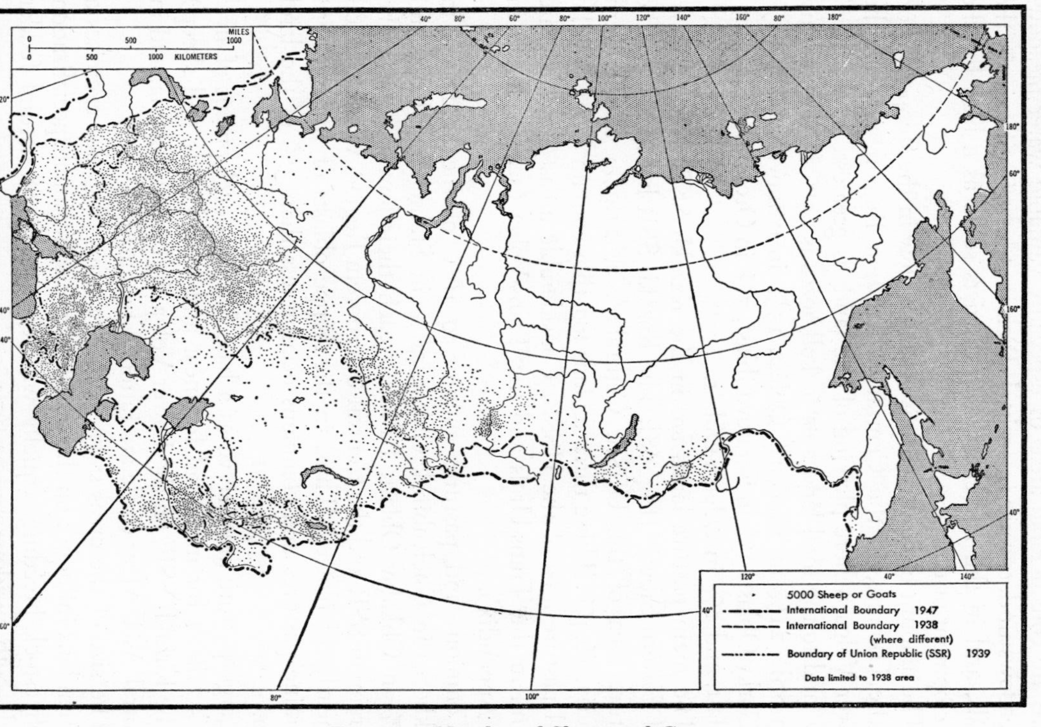

Fig. 67. Number of Sheep and Goats

especially rich in meadows [Fig. 68]. In the non-chernozem zone there are considerable areas of especially valuable water meadows [meadows under water in spring]. Rich meadows in Siberia, in the Urals, and in the non-chernozem districts serve as a base for the development of dairying.

The amount of land in hay is especially low in the steppe portion of the Ukraine, in the Central Chernozem Region, and on the Lower Volga, where plowing of the lands is greatest. The ratio of hay land to the total land area in kolkhozes is 25% in the Belorussian SSR, 21% in Smolensk Oblast, 15% in Ivanovo Oblast, 12% in Gorky Oblast, 3% in Saratov Oblast, 5% in Orenburg [Chkalov] Oblast, and 1% in Odessa Oblast.

The main pasture lands are in the Kazakh SSR, Central Asia, and Eastern Siberia [Fig. 68]. The Kazakh SSR has 44.3% of the pasture area of the USSR; Central Asia, 21.9%; and Eastern Siberia, 16.4%. These three regions together contain 82.6% of the total pasture area of the USSR. Considerable areas of pasture are found in the Trans-Urals and the Trans-Volga (see Table A8 in the Appendix).

Commons and pastures amount to 16% of the land area in kolkhozes in Chelyabinsk Oblast, 36% in Stalingrad Oblast, and 24% in Chkalov Oblast. Pastures reach their lowest ratio in the Ukrainian SSR and the Central Chernozem Region, where the soil is nearly all plowed. Thus, in the steppe oblasts of the southern Ukraine pastures and commons occupy less than 3% of the land area.

Large pasture areas serve as a base for the development of livestock raising for meat and for meat and wool (cattle and sheep) in the Kazakh SSR, on the Lower Volga, in Eastern Siberia, and in Central Asia. Meat cattle are fattened by grazing.

The size of the areas sown in fodder crops [Fig. 69] exercises a tremendous influence on the distribution and regional specialization of livestock breeding, equally with the supply of natural fodder lands, both meadows and pastures.

Fodder crops include: edible root crops (fodder beets, fodder carrots, etc.), ensilage (sunflower, maize, etc.), and annual and perennial herbs. The proportion of fodder crops and their composition depend in large measure on the crop rotation customary in one region or another.

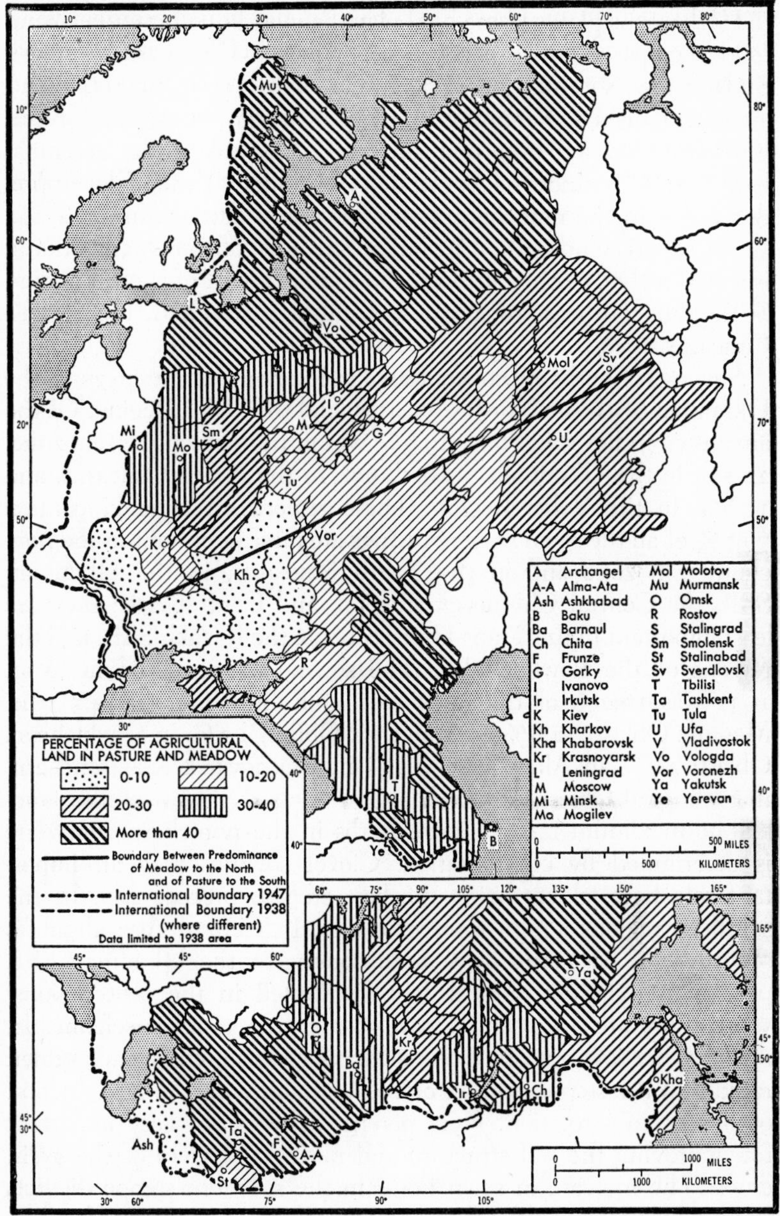

Fig. 68. Percentage Which Pasture and Meadows Constitute of Total Agricultural Land

Herbaceous plants [tame hay] play the most important role among fodder crops. Annual herbs (vetch, *mogar* [Hungarian millet], Sudan grass, sorghum) and perennial herbs (clover, alfalfa, etc.) are distinguished. Perennial herbs can be mowed for hay several years in succession from one sowing. Of the area under perennial herbs, 61% is under clover and 33% under alfalfa. Clover predominates in the non-chernozem and central chernozem areas, the Urals, Siberia, and in the Ukrainian SSR west of the Dnepr. Alfalfa is sown in the North Caucasus, the southern part of the Ukrainian SSR, the southeastern regions, Central Asia, and the Trans-Caucasus.

Sowings of herbs are concentrated in the non-chernozem zone, the Ukrainian SSR, the North Caucasus, and the Volga Region. Of the area sown in herbs in 1937, 29.6% was in the non-chernozem zone, 22.7% in the Ukrainian SSR, 13.6% in the North Caucasus, and 10.8% in the Volga Region. These regions all together contain 76.7% of all the sown herbs. Sowings are most important in the non-chernozem zone and in the North Caucasus, in the Ukrainian SSR, the Central Chernozem Region, and Central Asia; they are least important in the Trans-Urals, Siberia, the Kazakh SSR, and the regions of the Lower Volga. The sowing of perennial herbs in 1937 was 16.2% of the sown area in Kalinin Oblast; 14.5% in Moscow Oblast; 12.8% in Smolensk Oblast; 1.1% in Chelyabinsk Oblast; 2.1% in Altay Kray; 1.2% in Krasnoyarsk Kray; and 2% in Stalingrad Oblast [Fig. 69].

The maximum ratio of sown herbs in the non-chernozem zone is determined by crop rotation. Clover sowings play an important role here, clover being the best crop to precede flax. In the southern regions alfalfa replaces clover. In Central Asia alfalfa is sown as the best crop to precede cotton. In the Ukrainian SSR perennial herbs are most widely distributed in the beet regions, where they are an essential part of the crop rotation scheme. In recent years sowings of perennial herbs (alfalfa, etc.) have grown rapidly in the steppe portion of the Ukraine with the introduction of proper crop rotation. Here perennial herbs are very important for improving the soil structure and raising the yield of the grain crops. The increase in sown herbs in the southern steppe districts is determined also by the necessity of strengthening the fodder base for animal husbandry. By the sowing of herbs it is possible to make up for the shortage of natural meadows and pastures here.

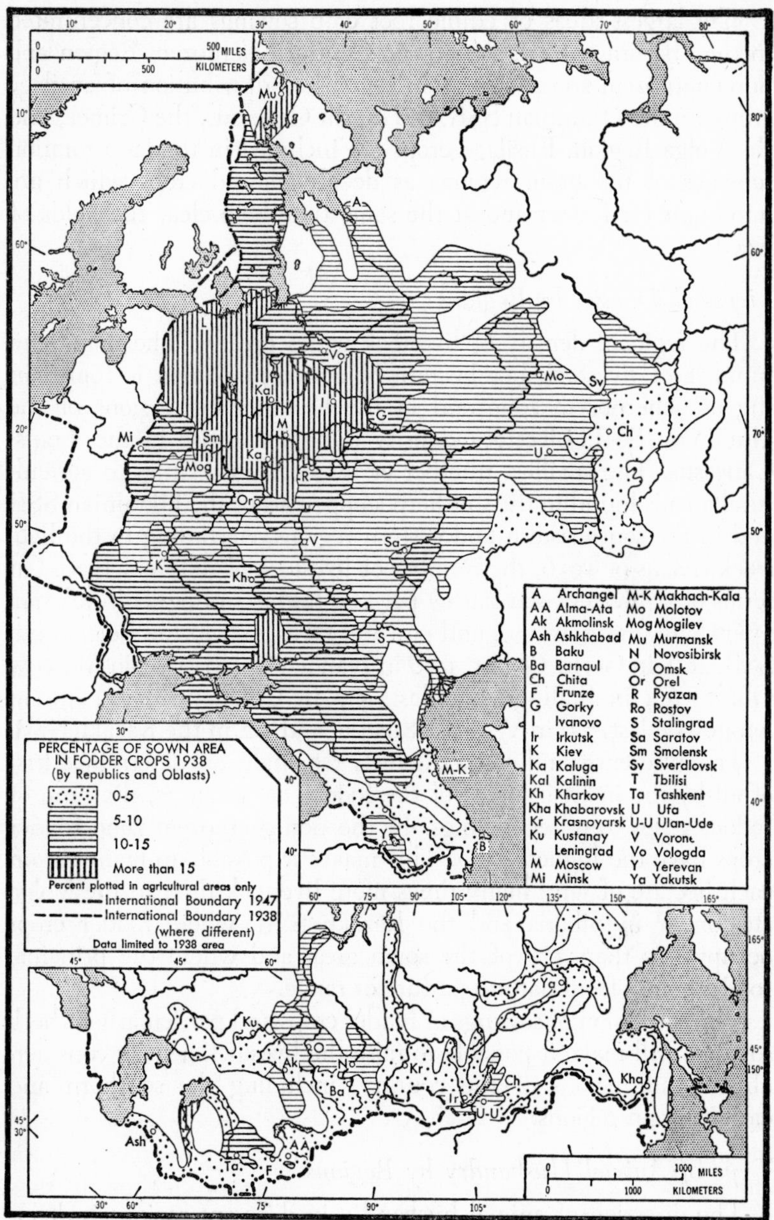

FIG. 69. Percentage Which Fodder Crops Constituted of Total Sown Area, 1938

The largest areas of edible root crop sowings are concentrated in the Ukrainian SSR, and in the Central Chernozem Region and non-chernozem zone. The main regions of distribution of ensilage crops are the Ukrainian SSR, the North Caucasus, the Crimea, and the Volga Region. Ensilage crops are included in the crop rotation schemes of the grain regions as deeply plowed crops which are important for fodder and at the same time help clear the fields of weeds.

Livestock Density by Regions

The regional density of livestock varies greatly. The maximum number of livestock per hectare of agricultural area is found in the non-chernozem zone and in the beet-growing regions of the Ukrainian SSR. Livestock density is high likewise in the Trans-Caucasus. The smallest number of livestock in relation to agricultural area is found in the southern steppe part of the Ukrainian SSR and in the southeastern and eastern regions. According to the livestock census of 1936, the number of livestock of different types (in terms of equivalence to cattle) per 100 hectares of agricultural area (plowland, meadowland, and pastures) was 22.4 in the Belorussian SSR, 20.1 in Gorky Oblast, 17.0 in Ivanovo Oblast, 16.2 in Moscow Oblast, 6.4 in Stalingrad Oblast, 5.7 in Chkalov Oblast, 4.9 in Saratov Oblast, 7.7 in Western Siberia, and 1.2 in the Kazakh SSR.

The differences in livestock density regionally are determined first of all by the intensity level of the fodder base, that is, the ratio of fodder crops to other sowings. In the non-chernozem zone fodder crops have the highest ratio. This makes it possible to maintain on each hectare of land many times more livestock than in the Volga Region or in Siberia and the Kazakh SSR, where fodder crops occupy less than 5% of the sown area, and where the principal fodder comes from natural pasture or range.

The expansion of sowings of fodder crops and particularly of herb sowings will make it possible to raise the livestock density considerably in all regions of the country, including the southern and eastern grain regions.

Type of Animal Husbandry by Regions

The direction of animal husbandry in different regions is determined by the distribution of industrial centers and of enterprises for processing the products (butter factories, meat combines), and by fodder conditions. The demand on the part of the urban population, and the presence of considerable meadowlands together with clover sowing, explain the development of dairying in the non-chernozem districts of the European portion of the USSR. In the Ukraine and the North Caucasus the base for the raising of cattle is the fodder obtained from agriculture—sown herbs, ensilage, waste products of field cultivation, and waste products of the food industry, including beet-sugar production (beet pulp), flour milling (siftings), vegetable-oil manufacture (oil cakes).

Pulp obtained from the processing of beets at sugar factories is an important fodder for cattle in beet-growing regions. Sugar factories likewise fatten cattle which are sent here for this purpose from the southern steppe regions of the USSR. Rich meadowlands and pastures, together with the waste products of grain culture, furnish a base for butter production in the Trans-Urals and Siberia. The development of the raising of meat cattle on the range in the Kazakh SSR and the Lower Volga Region has been determined by the presence of extensive pastures.

The Third Five-Year Plan provides for an expansion of dairying in zones of industrial centers, as well as the development of dairying and meat-and-dairy stock raising in the eastern and southeastern regions, with a maximum utilization of the natural fodder base in turning meat cattle out on the range to graze.

Hog breeding is most developed in the Belorussian SSR, the central and western oblasts of the non-chernozem zone, the Central Chernozem Region, the Ukrainian SSR, the North Caucasus, and the Volga Region. In the non-chernozem and central chernozem areas hog breeding is based on potato crops. In the Ukrainian SSR, the North Caucasus, and the Volga Region it is based on grain and the waste products of the food industry. Hog-breeding farms near large cities use garbage as fodder.

Enormous areas in pasture, which can be used most effectively by sheep, explain the development of sheep raising in the Kazakh SSR and Central Asia. The mountain pastures of the Trans-Caucasus and Central Asia can be utilized only by sheep, and so in the mountain regions sheep raising is the main branch of animal husbandry. Sheep raising here is the source not only of meat and wool, but also of dairy products (*brinza*).[16] There are considerable areas of pasture for sheep in the arid steppes of the Lower Volga

[16] [A Caucasian cheese made from ewe's milk.]

and in a number of regions of the North Caucasus, where sheep raising has been extensively developed.

In regions of the most developed animal husbandry at a distance from industrial centers, meat combines have been established which slaughter livestock and process the products on the site—in the Kazakh SSR, the Volga German Republic [now largely in Saratov Oblast], etc. Large meat combines exist in Moscow, Leningrad, and other very important centers.

The distribution and specialization of animal husbandry in the USSR is planned in such a way as to insure the complete and efficient utilization of fodder resources, including meadows, pastures, sown fodder crops, and the waste products of soil cultivation. Before the Revolution animal husbandry was very weakly developed in the southeastern and southern grain regions and essentially was of a consumer type. During the years of the Five-Year Plans the raising of livestock for the market, which permits fuller utilization of the waste products of grain production and of fodder-producing lands, has been developed in these regions on kolkhozes and sovkhozes.

In contrast to the unbalanced extensive grain economy of the southern regions before the Revolution, socialist agriculture here is founded on the introduction of proper crop rotation, which means the expansion of sowings of fodder crops; this furnishes great opportunities for the development of animal husbandry.

Under the Third Five-Year Plan the increase in the livestock population will be more rapid in the southeastern and eastern regions, where the density is lower than in other regions.

In recent years animal husbandry has been developing rapidly on the grain sovkhozes, so that the excessive specialization observed in the early years of establishing grain sovkhozes is being eliminated. In the livestock sovkhozes secondary branches are being developed together with the main branch of animal husbandry. For instance, dairying is being developed on hog-breeding sovkhozes, sheep breeding on dairy sovkhozes, and so on.

Collectivized animal husbandry on the kolkhozes is being built likewise on the basis of the combination of diverse branches. The Council of People's Commissars of the USSR and the Central Committee of the Communist Party of the Soviet Union, in their decree on measures for the development of collectivized animal husbandry on kolkhozes, recognized that it would be expedient for each kolkhoz to have three farms—or at very least two farms, one for cattle and the other for hog breeding or sheep raising.

The combination of different branches of animal husbandry on the sovkhozes and kolkhozes offers great advantages for the more complete utilization of fodder resources. For example, if the farm has only hogs, the waste products of soil cultivation (straw, chaff), of hay mowing, and, to a considerable degree, of pasturing remain unused. But the combination of hogs with cattle permits the complete utilization of the waste products of soil cultivation and of the fodder lands. Such a combination is expedient also because milk is required for raising young pigs. In combining cattle with sheep, some coarse fodders which cattle eat with reluctance can be fed very effectively to the sheep. Pastures unsuitable for the pasturage of dairy herds frequently can be used for sheep. Sheep can forage for themselves on pastures which have been trampled by cattle.

Poultry Raising

Poultry raising is one of the short-term branches of animal husbandry, providing various products including eggs, meat, down, and feathers. During the years of the Five-Year Plans a large network of incubator poultry-raising stations and poultry kolkhozes for the market has been created, as well as a number of large poultry sovkhozes. The incubator poultry-raising stations, equipped with large incubators for the industrial hatching of chicks, play a large role in the development of poultry raising in the country. By the beginning of the Third Five-Year Plan, incubator stations in the USSR numbered 532, and there were 23,000 poultry kolkhozes.

Before the Revolution, on the peasant farms unpedigreed poultry was bred almost exclusively. On the basis of poultry sovkhozes, incubator stations, and poultry kolkhozes, the quality of poultry is improving rapidly and its productivity is increasing.

Poultry raising is most developed in the North Caucasus (Ordzhonikidze [now Stavropol] Kray, Krasnodar Kray, and Rostov Oblast), the Central Chernozem Region (Voronezh, Kursk), and the Crimean ASSR.

Apiculture

Apiculture is a branch of agriculture which has some extremely important products—namely, honey and wax; it is very important also in raising crop yields, as bees pollinate agricultural plants. Most of the bees are found in commercial kolkhoz apiaries. The chief regions of apiculture are the Far East, the North Caucasus, Voronezh and Kursk oblasts, the Bashkir ASSR, the Tatar ASSR, and Western Siberia. Bee keeping is widespread also in the non-chernozem zone.

Sericulture

Sericulture is the breeding of the mulberry silkworm for its cocoons, which yield natural silk. The chief regions of sericulture are Central Asia and the Trans-Caucasus. In recent years it has penetrated into new regions, far to the north. At present cocoons are gathered in the Ukraine, the North Caucasus, the Crimea, and Kursk and Voronezh oblasts. The Uzbek SSR holds the lead in sericulture: it provides half of the cocoon crop of the country.

Hunting

The most valuable commercial product of hunting is fur. The USSR occupies an important place in the world export of furs.

Hunting and the fur industry form the chief branch of economic production in the regions of the Far North. The fur industry has been developed considerably in Eastern Siberia and the Far East. The acclimatization of fur-bearing animals is being carried on in the USSR. In 1927 the muskrat was brought into the USSR from the United States. It multiplied rapidly and at present has populated the shores of water bodies in the north of the European part of the USSR and of Siberia. In the southern regions of the USSR the coypu (a South American rodent) has been acclimatized. The regions inhabited by domestic species of fur-bearing animals are being expanded. In the Forest Steppe Zone of Western Siberia the common hare, which formerly did not dwell there, is multiplying successfully. The raccoon-dog, which formerly inhabited only the southern zone of the Far East, has been settled in many regions of the Union.

In the northern portion of the European part of the USSR, in Siberia, and in the Far East, animal-breeding farms have been created for cultivating the more valuable fur-bearing animals. On the animal-breeding farms of the sovkhozes and kolkhozes, silver foxes, raccoon-dog, blue arctic foxes, sables, and other valuable animals are bred in cages.

In Tsarist Russia the most valuable resources of commercial hunting were exploited ruthlessly. As a result, by the time of the Great October Revolution the sable, beaver, and a number of other valuable animals were on the verge of extinction. After the October Revolution a network of government game preserves was created for the purpose of protecting fur-bearing animals and developing the fur trade; territories were set off on which hunting was prohibited. Conditions were created for an orderly and efficient utilization of commercial-hunting fauna.

Animal Husbandry Under the Third Five-Year Plan

The Third Five-Year Plan has scheduled an increase in livestock numbers and in the marketable output of animal husbandry products in quantities fully sufficient to provide a solution of the animal husbandry problem in the USSR. The Plan pays particular attention to the development and strengthening of kolkhozes producing for the market. The chief problem of the Third Five-Year Plan will be to raise the productivity of animal husbandry by improving the breeds of livestock, by strengthening the fodder base, and by improving livestock care. Under the Third Five-Year Plan the mechanization of laborious processes in animal husbandry will be expanded on the sovkhozes and kolkhozes.

Leading sovkhozes and kolkhozes have attained high milk yields, a large wool clip, etc. Many Stakhanovite milkmaids obtain on the average 4,000 liters and more of milk per cow each year. These achievements are the result of breeding pedigreed stock, of good feeding, and of painstaking care. The achievements of the leaders in animal husbandry show what large reserves are available for raising the productivity of stock.

The creation of a reliable fodder base is the most important condition for the development of animal husbandry. During the years of the Five-Year Plans the area sown in fodder crops has been expanded greatly. In 1938, 14 million hectares [35 million acres] (as compared to 2 million hectares in 1913) were under fodder crops in the USSR as a whole. The mowing area of perennial herbs increased from 1,449,000 hectares in 1913 to 8,230,000 in 1938. Under the Third Five-Year Plan a further expansion will take place in the production of fodders. An increase in grain production to 8 billion poods and the introduction of proper crop rotation, including sown herbs, will insure the strengthening of the fodder base under the Third Five-Year Plan. Sowings of perennial herbs will increase greatly under the Third Five-Year Plan; they are tremendously important for raising the yield of the fields, and at the same time they are a very important source of fodder supply for animal husbandry. Of special significance is the sowing of herbs in regions which are poor in natural hay.

The Third Five-Year Plan has set the task of creating bases of animal husbandry in the vicinity of large cities, especially dairying bases, as fresh milk cannot be hauled great distances. Each oblast and republic must develop it to the end of having sufficient amounts of animal husbandry products.

All this creates conditions which favor the development of animal husbandry in all regions on the basis of the maximum utilization of fodder resources and in order to reduce sharply the hauling over long distances of its products.

VII Distribution of Transport in the USSR

SECTION 1. BASIC TYPES OF TRANSPORT IN THE USSR

SOCIALIST transport is the circulatory system of the Soviet economic organism. As a conveyer of passengers and freight (raw materials, fuel, industrial products, and foodstuffs) it connects the various republics, oblasts, and krays, and connects the different branches of industry and agriculture with the points at which the goods are consumed.

In the USSR, as distinguished from the capitalist countries, the various types of transport do not compete or struggle against one another, but cooperate among themselves. They are closely joined in a single transportation network.

The basis of the unity of the socialist transportation network is that the railroads, steamship navigation, and automobile and air transport belong to a single master—the socialist government. They are the possession of the government, the property of all the people. The public means of transport of the kolkhozes and cooperatives are also socialist property. On this basis there is established a close connection between the various types of transport and their manifold development in accordance with the unified plan of the national economy.

The transport of the USSR has played a tremendous role in the historic advances of socialist construction. It has provided for the development of new industrial construction, the creation of new industrial centers, and the elimination of the economic and cultural backwardness of the national republics. It has strengthened the bonds between industry and agriculture, it has promoted the socialist transformation and improvement of agriculture, and the elimination of the ancient antagonism between town and country. With the development of a network of communication routes and with the improvement in the level of its operation, there has been a decisive improvement in the transportation service of the vast oblasts and republics of the USSR, with their tremendous natural resources; this improvement has had a tremendous effect on the rapid rise in their productive strength.

Transport, and railroad transport first of all, plays an exceptionally large role in the defense of the country. The more Soviet transport develops and the better it operates, the stronger is Soviet economic power, and together with it the power of the glorious Red Army.

The chief mode of transport in the USSR and the one having foremost significance in the life of the whole country is the railroad.

The USSR is a great railroad power. Comrade Stalin in his speech at the reception of the railroad workers in the Kremlin on July 30, 1935, spoke of the decisive importance of railroad transport for the existence and development of a country with such enormous territorial dimensions as the Soviet Union. He said: "The USSR, as a country, would be impossible without first-class railroad transport to bind its numerous oblasts and regions into one unified whole. In this lies the great significance of railroad transportation to the USSR." [1]

In the vast continuous territory of our immense country, then, it is the railroads that can supply in the best fashion reliable transport in all directions, and unite the hundreds and thousands of large and small towns and villages, the mineral deposits, the forest areas, and the seas. The railroads built under the Soviets have created reliable communication between the central area and the coal deposits of the Kuzbas and Karaganda, the oil beds of Emba and Bashkiria, the ore resources of the Urals and Kazakhstan, the forest areas of the North, the fertile fields of Siberia, and the rich Soviet Far East. In the future the railroads will penetrate new districts and make it possible to utilize new natural resources.

Railroad transport has a number of big advantages. The greater part of the surface of the USSR offers no serious obstacles to construction, and lines can be laid almost everywhere. Railroads provide transfer of goods on a mass scale at low cost. With good organization of traffic railroads should operate as precisely as clocks, carry

[1] *Pravda*, Aug. 2, 1935.

freight quickly, regularly, and without interruption, regardless of climatic conditions. They should provide also complete continuity of transport service for the whole national economy of the USSR.

On a level with the railroads as a major type of mass transport are the waterways.

The USSR has an enormous network of water communication routes, surpassing the railroads in length. On the principal water routes it is possible to provide an even greater transfer of goods on a mass scale at low cost, by virtue of the considerably greater capacity of a water vessel (barges in comparison with railroad cars), and the greater load power of the motive agent (tugboats in comparison with locomotives).[2]

One disadvantage of water transport is that the period of navigation is interrupted for four to five months each year by freezing. Furthermore, it is limited to the natural direction of rivers, distribution of lakes, etc. This drawback is being corrected by the Bolshevists with the construction of canals and dams, among which are such magnificent creations of human genius as the White Sea to Baltic and the Moscow-Volga [W and MV in Fig. 6, p. 32] canals, and the dams on the Dnepr and the Volga (at Kuibyshev [43 in Fig. 6], Rybinsk [70], and Uglich [90]). The task set by the 17th Party Congress is being accomplished: "The creation of a unified water system in the European part of the USSR, linking the White, Baltic, Black, and Caspian seas [Fig. 6]."

Sea transport is the chief means of foreign trade for the USSR. Its low cost makes it very advantageous for domestic communication as well. Grand and petty cabotage considerably exceed foreign overseas traffic.[3] The Northern Sea Route [24 in Fig. 5, p. 24], which joins the European USSR with the Far East and lies along the coast of the USSR, is exceptionally important to the USSR.

Motor transport accomplishes the hauling of freight to stations and wharves and the conveyance of freight arriving by rail and water. It also carries local freight traffic: in the city, for industry, trade, and the municipal economy; in the country, for sovkhozes,

[2] Thus, on the Volga the tugboat *Stepan Razin*, with 1.5 thousand horsepower, tows loads up to 40 thousand tons, which is equivalent to 1,600 oil tank cars. The maximum load of oil barges on the Volga is 12 thousand tons.

[3] "Cabotage" is the name for sea communication between various ports of the same country. Petty cabotage is traffic between ports on the same sea; grand cabotage, traffic between ports on different seas.

kolkhozes, and cooperatives, and between villages. In localities poorly provided with other types of transport, motor transport operates on the main highways which branch off from the railroads. During recent years motor transport has begun to acquire independent arterial significance in the central oblasts of the country as well. The rapid development of motor transport and of motor hauling has made necessary the creation of People's Commissariats of Motor Transport in all the Union republics. These organizations should improve significantly the motor transport service of the national economy of the USSR.

With each year, there has been a steady increase in air transport, which gives speedy conveyance of passengers, mail, and freight. It provides rapid communication with remote points, and in some localities, especially in the East and in Central Asia, where other modes of communication are generally insufficiently developed, it is the chief means of transportation.

SECTION 2. DEVELOPMENT OF TRANSPORT IN RUSSIA BEFORE THE REVOLUTION

Prerevolutionary railroad transport reflected all the contradictions of capitalism in Russia, and was an instrument for exploiting the inhabitants. The distribution of railways was extremely uneven. It reflected the uneven distribution of industry, its concentration in a few districts (while all the rest of Russia was agrarian), and the general economic backwardness of the country. At the time when there were 1.8 to 2.2 km. of railroad per 100 sq. km. of territory in the central and southern industrial guberniyas, there was 1 km. per 100 sq. km. in the Volga Region, 0.3 to 0.35 km. in Central Asia, and only 0.05 to 0.1 km. in the territory of present-day Kazakhstan, Siberia, and the Far East. All Asiatic Russia had only 15% of the railway network, that is, less than the comparatively small territory of the Polish and Baltic guberniyas.

Development of the Railroad Network

Tsarist Russia lagged far behind other capitalist countries in the development of a railway network, although the first railroad—the Tsarskoselskaya (from St. Petersburg to Tsarskoye Selo [now Pushkin] [Fig. 73, p. 463]—was laid down as early as 1837, only two to five years later than the first in France, Germany, and Austria. The serfdom prevailing in Russia, which hampered development of a domestic market and capitalistic production, sharply retarded rail construction in the ensuing quarter-century. Only after its abolition, with the accelerated growth of capitalism and the creation of large-scale industry, was rail construction extensive.

As Lenin points out: "There were two periods of tremendous expansion in the development of Russian railroad construction: the late 1860's (and early 1870's) and the second half of the 1890's." [4] Between 1868 and 1874 the length of the network increased by more than 13 thousand km., and between 1891 and 1900 by more than 22 thousand km. A considerable increase in the construction of new railway lines was noted also before the First Imperialist War [World War I] and during that war. These periods of expansion were characterized by a tremendous sweep of speculation, plundering of small investors, embezzlement, bribery, and large-scale bankruptcies.

In examining the historical evolution of the Russian railway network, one can distinguish several groups of lines.

Trunk lines radiating from Moscow and St. Petersburg formed the framework of the network. They brought raw materials, fuel, and foodstuffs for these cities, with their developing industry. Uniting Moscow and St. Petersburg with the Urals, the Volga Region, and the western border districts, these railway lines broadened the market for industrial products [Fig. 70]. Among them were the St. Petersburg-Moscow line (1843–1851), which for those days was a large-scale and technically advanced installation; the St. Petersburg-Warsaw line (1862); and a number of railroads radiating from Moscow: to Nizhny [Nizhny Novgorod, now Gorky] (1862), Ryazan and Kozlov [now Michurinsk] (1862–1864), Kursk (1868), Minsk and Warsaw (1871), and Yaroslavl and Vologda (1870–1872). Later, in the 1890's and early 1900's, lines were laid from Moscow to Bryansk (1899), Pavelets [65 in Fig. 70] (1900), and Vindava [now Ventspils, 95] (1904) [Fig. 70].

The railroads from Moscow to Kursk and Ryazan were soon extended southward to Rostov (1869–1870). The Kursk line was extended in 1874 as far as Sevastopol. These lines passed through the Donbas and promoted the development of the coal industry. New

[4] Lenin, *Works*, Vol. III, p. 433.

FIG. 70. Railroad Lines (Railroad lines built during World War II are based on a map by Theodore Shabad in *The American Review on the Soviet Union*, Vol. 8, No. 2, March, 1947, pp. 40–41.)

railway lines and branches were soon undertaken in the Donbas [Fig. 72, p. 459]. The laying in 1884 of the Yekaterinoslav (now Dnepropetrovsk) railroad, connecting the Donbas with Krivoy Rog and giving a powerful impetus to the development of metallurgy, had especially great significance for the industrial rise of the South. Construction in these districts was continued in subsequent years. In the 1890's the following important lines were built as outlets for the Donbas: Kharkov-Balashov, Yelets-Valuiki, and Likhaya-Tsaritsyn [now Stalingrad] [Fig. 70]. In the 1900's the Lgov-Liman-Likhaya line and a number of smaller branches were constructed. The Donbas had the densest railway net in Russia.

The other metallurgical district, the Urals, was poorly supplied with railroads. The Ural metallurgy line from Perm [now Molotov] through Chusovoy to Yekaterinburg [now Sverdlovsk], which was built in 1878, had no connection with the rest of the network, and was joined with it only in 1896, when the first link in the Trans-Siberian trunk line, the Samara [now Kuibyshev] to Ufa to Chelyabinsk line, was laid in the southern Urals. Although several other lines were laid in the Urals later (Perm-Kungur-Yekaterinburg, Tyumen-Omsk, and others), nevertheless the Urals network remained sparse.

Almost simultaneously with the construction of the main trunk lines in the central and southern districts, which transported grain, wood, coal, and other freight to internal markets, construction began on a number of railroads to serve the grain export trade. The first of these connected Riga with Tsaritsyn by way of Orel (1871), passing through the grain-producing guberniyas of the Chernozem Center and the Lower Volga Region [Fig. 70]. A second, the Libava-Romensk, joined the port of Libava [Libau, Lepaya] with the guberniyas of the Ukraine, while a third, extending from Kiev to the border, furnished an outlet for southern grain through the German ports of Königsberg and Danzig. Several lines were built to link the grain-growing districts with ports on the Black Sea. These include the railways from the steppe belt of the Ukraine to Odessa (1864–1872), Nikolayev (1873), and Novorossiisk, as well as the above-mentioned railways to Rostov by way of Kursk and Ryazan, and to Sevastopol. Later other lines of importance to the grain trade were built. Those in the Central Chernozem Region and the Volga Region and within the present Ukrainian boundaries included the Kursk-

Kiev, the Kiev-Poltava, Kursk-Voronezh, Saratov-Kozlov [Michurinsk], Syzran-Vyazma, Dankov-Smolensk, Ruzayevka-Batraki, and Chasovnya-Bugulma. Characteristically, all these have a latitudinal direction. The grain-trade railway lines served first the interests of the landlords, kulaks, and grain merchants. While their construction promoted grain exports and grain trade, at the same time it promoted the development of capitalism in rural Russia, the stratification of the peasantry, and increased the antagonism between town and country.

After the framework of the railroad net of the central and southern regions had been more or less established, railroads began to be laid in the border lands. They helped in the exploitation of these Tsarist colonies and the enslavement of their peoples. The Trans-Caucasus road from Tbilisi to Poti, Batumi, and Baku was finished by 1883 [Fig. 70]; its junction with the main network was accomplished only in 1900, however, after construction of the Beslan to Petrovsk-Port [Makhach-Kala] to Baladzhary line, which was much needed by the Baku oil industry. In connection with the Tsarist inroads in Central Asia, a Trans-Caspian railway was built in the 1880's, running at first as far as Samarkand (1888), and later Tashkent (1899); its junction with the main system was accomplished in 1906 with the building of the Orenburg [Chkalov]-Tashkent line, which gave the textile mills of the central guberniyas direct access to the cotton of Central Asia. With the extension of the railroads to Central Asia, cotton growing began to develop significantly, the market for products of the Industrial Center expanded, and the exploitation of the peoples of Central Asia increased. As Lenin wrote, "The Trans-Caspian road 'opened' Central Asia for capital." [5]

In the 1890's work was begun from both the west and the east on the longest railroad in the world—the Siberian trunk line. Between 1891 and 1897 the line was laid from Vladivostok to Khabarovsk, and between 1892 and 1899, from Chelyabinsk to Irkutsk, with an extension as far as Baikal and beyond to the Chinese border [Fig. 70]. By 1903, Russia had completed the Chinese Eastern line, and by 1905 had established rail communication between European Russia and the Far East (with ferry passage across Lake Baikal). The whole line traversing through Russian territory was

[5] Lenin, *Works*, Vol. IV, p. 165.

not opened, however, until 1916, when the sector from Chita to Khabarovsk was completed. The building of this trunk line, which was undertaken in connection with the Tsarist plans for encroachment in the Far East, gave an impetus to the capitalistic development of Siberia, promoted the more intensive exploitation and plundering of the local peoples, and opened new markets for Russian industry. In the 1900's and during the First Imperialist War [World War I], branches of the Siberian trunk line were built to Slavgorod, Semipalatinsk, and Kemerovo.

Several new railroads were built in the northern part of European Russia. Among these were the timber line from Vologda to Archangel (1898, converted to broad gauge in 1916), and the Perm-Vyatka [Kirov]-Kotlas line (1899). Although the latter was to serve originally as a link in the railroad-water route (together with the Severnaya [Northern] Dvina) for the export of grain from Siberia, it proved too long and expensive for this purpose and became important chiefly in hauling timber. Later a line was constructed in the northern guberniyas from Obukhovo [near St. Petersburg, Fig. 73, p. 463] through Vyatka [Kirov], joining St. Petersburg with the Urals (1906) [Fig. 70]. Finally, during the war, the Murmansk road was built, upon which the Tsarist Government depended for establishing convenient communication with the Allies under blockade conditions by way of the ice-free port of Murmansk. The completion of the Murmansk line and its reconstruction were accomplished under the Soviet regime.

In a whole series of districts—in the North, the Trans-Caucasus, Central Asia, and Siberia—the Tsarist regime laid only single railway lines, which were needed for the enslavement and exploitation of these border lands, the colonies of Tsarist Russia.

In the interest of military strategy, many railroads were built also in Poland and the Baltic regions. The density of the railroad network in these localities was comparatively high, promoting their economic development and intensifying the competition between their industries and those of the guberniyas in the interior.

Technical Equipment of Railroad Transport

The length of railroads in 1913 within the [1939] boundaries of the USSR was 58.5 thousand km.; 70.5 thousand km. lay within the old boundaries. The density of the network averaged 0.3 km.

per 100 sq. km. of territory, as compared with about 12 km. in England and Germany. The length of line per 10,000 inhabitants was 4.2 km., one-third to one-fourth that in the foremost capitalist countries. The Russian railroads were poorly supplied with locomotives and cars. For 100 km. of track in Russia there were 29 locomotives, as compared with 61 in England and 50 in Germany; 31 passenger cars, as against 140 in England and 110 in Germany; and 696 freight cars, as compared with 2,122 in England and 1,175 in Germany. The rolling stock was much inferior to that in England and Germany. Especially striking was the contrast with the United States. Although the conditions of operation for railroads were similar in many respects in Russia and in the United States (for example, in the great size of the territory to be served, the protracted length of hauls, and their mass scale), Russian locomotives were much less powerful, Russian cars had a smaller load capacity, and both cars and locomotives showed marked deterioration. Russian railroads were poorly built: their grade was difficult even in the level areas, the rails were light, the signaling and control devices were out of date, and mechanization [of loading and unloading] was absent. Technical transport facilities were poorly utilized and proper exploitation was absent. The network was not uniform: different railroads, built by different entrepreneurs, were variously constructed and had different types of rolling stock, fixed plants, etc. Freight traffic was carried on without any kind of schedule. On the important through routes, crossing districts served by different railroads, there was no single weight norm, nor could there be any.

Hauls

Railway freight traffic, which constituted 132.4 million tons of freight consignments in 1913, was characterized by sharp seasonal variation, and by a series of crosshauls and roundabout, unnecessarily long, and otherwise inefficient transfers.

Before the Revolution the movement of export grain to the Baltic ports, i.e., from the southeast to the northwest, was characteristic of the geography of freight transport. The flow of grain to the Black Sea ports for export was also great. The shipment of grain from Siberia to the west was hindered by the so-called "Chelyabinsk rate divide," which had the object of protecting the landowners, kulaks, and grain merchants of European Russia from the competition of cheap Siberian grain. The entire northwestern belt of Russia, including St. Petersburg, was supplied with coal from abroad. Lumber was exported primarily from the central and western guberniyas. While the central forests were being rapidly cut down, the enormous forest areas of the North and East remained almost untouched. Finally, freight movements in the border areas were negligible as a result of the extremely low level of development of their productive forces.

The uneven and insufficient development of the railroads, their technical backwardness, the poor utilization of transport facilities, the rudimentary evolution of freight transfers, and the sharp fluctuations in their volume according to the year and the month led to continuous difficulties in transportation, interruptions in the movement of Donets coal and of grain on the southern and southeastern railroads, and bottlenecks in the outlets from Siberia, Central Asia, the Trans-Volga, and the Caucasus.

The weakness of railroad transport in Tsarist Russia made itself clearly felt at the time of the Imperialist War of 1914–1918. On many basic trunk lines, which were forced to carry unaccustomed loads, enormous piles of freight accumulated. Millions of tons of coal, lumber, metal, and grain remained unmoved, paralyzing the work of industry, intensifying the famine in the country, and diminishing the supply of consumers' goods to the people. The continuous deterioration of the railway transport system and the decline in the level of its operation aggravated the general disorder.

Water Transport

The railroads of Tsarist Russia were in competition with water transport. With the aid of discriminatory rates and other measures, they impeded and undermined navigation on the rivers, and thus aggravated the backwardness of river transport. A considerable part of the navigable rivers was not exploited. River routes measured in all only about 60 thousand km. The work of transforming into navigable rivers those which were not navigable or were suitable only for rafting was carried forward only in exceptional cases. On the majority of rivers, conditions for navigation were not improved. The Volga abounded in shallows and sandbanks, the Dnepr was split into two parts by rapids, and the Don was unnavigable throughout most of its course [Fig. 6, p. 32]. Only 36 thousand km. of waterways were equipped with illuminated markers permitting 24-hour navigation. Telegraph or telephone communications between river ports were lacking. The network of artificial waterways was wholly insignificant: there were only 894 km. of canals and 1,320 km. of rivers with locks (of which 7.5 km. of canals and 151.5 km. of rivers with locks were in Asiatic Russia), or several times less than in England, France, or the United States.

The river fleet was on the whole low-powered and obsolete. Self-propelled vessels (passenger and freight-and-passenger steamers, tugs, etc.) were sharply differentiated in type and in construction of engines and boilers. The vessels that were not self-propelled (barges, etc.) were almost exclusively wooden; only on the Volga was there a small number of iron barges for oil transport.

The volume of freight hauled by waterway in 1913 totaled only 48.2 million tons (including rafting), as against 132.4 million tons on the railroads. Most freight hauls (up to 70%) were in the Volga Basin, including the Volga-Baltic route. The other basins lagged sharply behind the Volga: the Dnepr accounted for 11% and the Severnaya (Northern) Dvina for 8% of the freight hauled. The percentage of freight turnover on the mighty water arteries of Siberia was very insignificant: on the Ob, 3%; on the Amur, 2%.

The role of Russia in sea transport was completely negligible. In 1914 its share in world maritime tonnage was about 1.5%. Sea transport was handled for the most part by foreign ships—92.4% of the exports and 86% of the imports. While nearly half the exports (grain and oil) passed through Black Sea ports, three-fourths of the imports (coal and machinery) passed through Baltic ports. Russian ports were poorly equipped, causing considerable delay to vessels and excessive freight charges. This lessened the ability of Russian grain and other exports to compete in the world market.

Road Transport

Road transport was at an exceptionally low level in Tsarist Russia. Paved roads were much less common than in England, France, or Germany. In addition, many of the existing highways were built in the border districts for military purposes. The others were ordinary dirt roads, and became completely impassable during periods of thaw and of rains. Losses caused by the lack of roads were estimated at hundreds of millions of rubles each year.

SECTION 3. RAILROAD TRANSPORT OF THE USSR

After the great October Socialist Revolution, the peoples of the USSR achieved enormous success in restoring and developing their national economy—they established socialism in the USSR. Transport was reorganized from its very foundations, becoming one of the most important branches of the national economy of the great and powerful socialist state.

Traffic

The railway transport of the USSR has undergone tremendous development. Freight hauled in 1937 was 517 million tons, almost four times as much as in 1913. Because of the industrialization of the country, traffic in industrial freight has increased particularly: coal traffic has increased 4.5 times; iron ore, 4 times; ferrous metals, 5.5 times; machinery, 7 times; and the principal building materials, more than 6 times. Traffic in agricultural products has also increased greatly, at the same time that it has decreased somewhat in relative importance. Thus, grain traffic in 1937 was twice as high as in 1913; sugar traffic more than doubled; beet traffic increased 3.5 times; and cotton traffic, 3 times. Such an increase in the transportation of agricultural products was made possible only by collectivization, the social reorganization of agriculture, and the increased marketability of agricultural produce. Passenger traffic has increased extraordinarily; in 1937, 1,143 million passengers were carried, 6.5 times as many as in 1913. The above figures reflect the growth in material and cultural levels and the increased prosperity of the population of the USSR.

With the increase in traffic, its geography also has altered greatly. The industrialization of the country, the collectivization of agriculture, the development of industry in formerly backward regions, and the discontinuation of fuel imports, all have led to an expansion, in comparison with the prewar years, of the region consuming Donets coal, and an increase of its movement from the Donbas to the Industrial Center, Leningrad, and the Volga Region. Shipment of coal from local basins also has developed. The interchange of coal and iron ore between the Donbas and the Krivoy Rog region has increased. The northward shipment of oil, the shipment of industrial products from Moscow, Leningrad, etc., are increasing.

Fundamental changes in the geography of freight movements have taken place in connection with the industrial development of the eastern regions—the Urals, Siberia, Kazakhstan, and Central Asia. The creation of a second coal and metallurgical base led to a rapid increase in shipments of coal, iron ore, metals, and other cargoes on the eastern railroads. Deliveries of oil products and industrial products have increased. Shipments of lumber are increasing from the northern and eastern regions. The flow of Siberian and Kazakhstan grain has increased. All these changes have occurred and are occurring in accordance with changes in the distribution of industry and agriculture.

On the Soviet railroads there are still numerous inefficient crosshauls and excessively long hauls. Many of them are a result of sabotage by the enemies of the people. The 18th Party Congress paid serious attention to the necessity of ending such inefficient hauls, and its resolution for the Third Five-Year Plan pointed out: "The most important problem of transport is the achievement of a well regulated planning of freight movement for the purpose of minimizing in every way possible long railway hauls, of eliminating crosshauls and inefficient hauls . . ." Of great significance in the elimination of such inefficient hauls is the relocation of productive forces, bringing industries closer to the sources of raw materials and regions of consumption, and the expansion in all regions of production of bulky foodstuffs. As a result of the projected expansion in the utilization of local coal deposits near Moscow, in the Urals, the Ukraine, the Caucasus, and other places, imports of coal from distant coal basins such as the Donbas, Kuzbas, and Karaganda will decrease relatively. The creation of a new oil base, the "Second Baku," between the Volga and the Urals, will permit a considerable decrease in oil hauls to the Urals, Siberia, and the central regions. Also a large part of the oil traffic will be transferred from the railroads to water transport and to pipe lines. The metallurgical plants must eliminate the existing harmful specialization of rolling mills, which leads to long hauls and crosshauls of metal, and must insure the rolling of all of the leading grades of metal in the principal metallurgical bases of the country. The creation in the eastern regions of duplicate plants in a number of branches of machine building, the chemical industry, and oil refining, to supplement existing unique plants, the products of which are now carried over tremendous distances throughout the country, will greatly affect the reduction of long hauls. Excessively long and inefficient hauls of lumber from Eastern Siberia to the European USSR and from the European USSR to Central Asia must stop. At the same time, the shipment of lumber must increase from North European USSR to the central regions and the South, and from Siberia to Central Asia. As a result of the construction of a number of new cement plants of medium and small capacity in the Urals, Siberia, the Far East, Kazakhstan, and Central Asia, imports of cement from European USSR into the eastern regions and republics of Central Asia will cease. Finally, with the growth of agricultural production in consuming areas the long hauls of grain, vegetables, and meat should be considerably curtailed, while interregional traffic in potatoes should stop entirely.

The following are the chief routes of freight traffic in the USSR: from the Donbas to Krivoy Rog, from the Donbas and the North Caucasus to Moscow and Leningrad, from the Donbas to the Volga Region, from Murmansk to Leningrad, from Archangel to Moscow, from Leningrad to the Urals, from Moscow to the Urals, from Moscow to Central Asia, from the Urals to the Kuzbas, from Siberia to the Far East, and from Siberia to Central Asia.

These routes, along which a considerable part of the total traffic is concentrated, are served by the best equipped railroad trunk lines.

Reconstruction of Railroad Transport

As a result of the reconstruction which has been carried out, the technical aspect of Soviet railroad transport has changed beyond recognition since the great Socialist Revolution, and especially during the years of the Stalin Five-Year Plans. The former technical backwardness of transportation has disappeared. From year to year the percentage of low-power locomotives of the "O," "Shch," and "N" types (axle loadings of 12.5 to 16 tons), and low-capacity freight cars (15 to 16.5 tons) is decreasing; the weight of trains has increased considerably, as have line capacities. The reconstruction has insured an enormous increase in the capacity of transport, as well as its technical improvement; it has been converted to operate with frequent and heavy trains traveling at high speed.

The number of locomotives is being increased by thousands of new powerful locomotives of the "IS," "FD," and "SO" types (axle loadings of 18 to 20 tons).[6] The introduction of powerful locomotives has permitted considerably faster and heavier trains, and at the same time an increase in the line capacities of the major trunk lines. The widespread introduction of locomotives with steam condensers, which was started on the initiative of L. M. Kaganovich, is of tremendous importance. Railroad transport is being electrified (by 1938, some 1,600 km. of track) along with electrification of the country as a whole. Electrification is particularly advantageous for railroads with difficult mountain grades, heavy traffic, or where electricity is available at low cost. Railroad cars, also, have been considerably reconstructed and increased in number. Between 1934 and 1938, over 100,000 four-axle freight cars alone, with a load capacity of as much as 50 to 60 tons, were produced. Locomotive and car repair facilities have been increased; a number of repair plants and 216 car-servicing points have been constructed.

The reconstruction of track permits the introduction of high-power, heavy locomotives and an increase in speed. With the aid of 54 track repair stations, built on the initiative of L. M. Kaganovich, approximately 5,000 km. of old tracks have been reconstructed, and approximately 100,000 km. of track have undergone heavy and medium repair. As much as 38% of the entire network of tracks has been relaid with type "II-a" rails, weighing 38.5 kilograms or more per running meter. The line capacities of a number of lines have increased considerably as a result of the installation of automatic blocking (in 1938 there were 5,500 km. so equipped). More than thirty mechanized hump classification yards have been built, making it possible to double the rate of sorting cars and making up trains. Over 10,000 switches are being converted to centralized operation, and the entire network is being equipped with dispatching and other types of communication.

[6] ["IS" stands for Iosif (Joseph) Stalin, "FD" for Felix Dzerzhinsky, one-time head of the Cheka; and "SO" for Sergei Ordzhonikidze, at the time of his death, Commissar of Heavy Industry. All three of these locomotives resemble recent American types. The "IS" is a passenger locomotive of 2-8-4 wheel arrangement, the "FD" a freight locomotive of 2-10-2 wheel arrangement, while the "SO," a freight locomotive which was brought out before the "FD" type, has a 2-10-0 arrangement. It is significant that the new postwar "Pobyeda" (Victory) type—a freight locomotive of 2-10-2 arrangement—has a lower axel-loading (16–17 tons); this reflects the setback which the war caused to the program of replacing light rails with rails heavy enough for the "IS," "FD," and "SO" locomotives.]

New Railroad Construction

Along with the reconstruction of the existing networks, widespread new railway construction has taken place. Track has increased from 58,500 km. in 1913 to 85,000 km. in 1937. Under the Soviets a number of large new trunk lines, branch lines, and spurs have been built. New construction has been particularly extensive in the eastern regions with their rapid development.

A powerful transportation artery has been created between the Urals and the Kuzbas. In the Urals [Fig. 74, p. 470] the Troitsk-Orsk line (398 km.), with a branch to Magnitogorsk, and the Sverdlovsk-Kurgan line (358 km.) have been constructed; and in the Kuzbas [Fig. 75, p. 472] new lines have been built from Kolchugino [Leninsk-Kuznetsky] to Stalinsk (181 km.), from Stalinsk to Mundybash, and from Novosibirsk to Proyektnaya [south of Leninsk-Kuznetsky] (295 km.). The existing Siberian trunk line has been double-tracked from Omsk to Chelyabinsk and Magnitogorsk, and from Ufa to Chelyabinsk [Fig. 70]; the grades have been moderated and heavy rails laid.

A number of new railway lines have been built in Kazakhstan [Fig. 70]. Among these are the Turkestan-Siberian trunk line (1,442 km.), which furnishes a direct outlet for Siberian grain and lumber to Central Asia; the Petropavlovsk-Karaganda line (717 km), which unites Karaganda, the third most important coal base of the USSR, with the rest of the railway system; the Karaganda-Balkhash line (487 km.), with a branch to Dzhezkazgan, and the Rubtsovsk-Ridder line (335 km.), which are very important to the development of nonferrous metallurgy; and the Guryev-Kandagach line (518 km.), which leads to the Emba oil region.

In the Far East the line from Volochayevka to Komsomolsk (a new city and an industrial center) has been built [Fig. 70], and the Baikal-Amur trunk line is under construction.

To increase communication between the east and west the following new lines have been put into operation [Fig. 70]: Moscow-Kazan-Sverdlovsk (Derbyshki-Sverdlovsk, 885 km.); Gorky-Kotelnich (380 km.), with a bridge over the Volga; and Uralsk-Iletsk (264 km.), which, together with the Saratov bridge, furnishes a new outlet into Central Asia.

Outlets from the Donbas have been considerably increased by: (1) the construction of the powerful double-track Moscow-Donbas trunk line, with heavy rails and a moderate grade; (2) the construction of the new Orsha-Unecha-Vorozhba (253 km.) and Bryansk-Vyazma (234 km.) lines for traffic to Leningrad; and (3) the laying of a second track on the Kharkov-Bryansk and Valuiki-Balashov-Penza-Syzran lines. The last is the outlet to the Volga Region.

Among other important newly built trunk lines is the Kharkov-Nizhnedneprovsk-Kherson line (518 km.), which furnishes a direct outlet from the Dnepropetrovsk industrial region to Kharkov and to the Black Sea. In the Ukraine, Belorussia, the Northwest, and other regions of the country, many lines and branches have been built to shorten distances and relieve traffic congestion.

Improvement in Operation of Railroad Transport

The tremendous growth in railroad traffic has been attained not only by means of its technical re-equipment, but also through the fundamental reorganization and decisive improvement in the quality of its operation. For several years, beginning with 1930, railroad transport functioned poorly. In March of 1935, L. M. Kaganovich was appointed People's Commissar for Transportation, and under his guidance Comrade Stalin's instructions began to be fulfilled to the effect "that transport should function with precision, accuracy, and as punctually as a good clock in its services as a conveyer." [7]

Comrade Kaganovich, in Bolshevist fashion, organized and united the masses of railroad workers to achieve higher levels of operation, improved discipline, the elimination of various limitations and of sabotage and its consequences. The Stakhonov-Krivonosov movement developed widely. Able young workers devoted to the Party of Lenin and Stalin began to move forward. Eminent locomotive engineers such as Krivonosov, Ognev, Bogdanov, Babaitsev, and Troitskaya, and eminent dispatchers such as Zakorko and Kutafin, were appointed to the high posts of railroad chiefs. A whole system of carefully thought out measures was instituted for the fundamental reorganization of all branches of the railroad economy, for the introduction of graphic methods in every operational section, and for the use of proper technological processes and the application of new technical standards. New rules of technical operation were devel-

[7] *Pravda,* Aug. 2, 1935.

oped which would reflect the best and foremost contributions of science and experience. Bolshevist methods of checking the execution of orders and decrees, and concreteness and workability of supervision have been of tremendous importance.

Physical and Geographic Conditions of Operation of Railroad Transport

The physical and geographic conditions of operation of the railway network are generally favorable, considering the extent of the network and the tremendous territory of the USSR, with considerable variations in different parts of the country. The major part of the country is an enormous plain, with but a small territory intersected by high mountain ranges. This facilitates the construction of main trunk lines with moderate grades. For the most part, the railroads either are level or have low grades of up to 0.5% (that is, 5 meters per km.). The remaining grades range chiefly from 0.5% to 1%. Only a very small part of the network has steeper grades, from 1% to 2.5% and greater. Most of the straight sections of the network have an easy grade; this is true of over three-fourths of all lines. The curves as a rule have a radius of over 500 meters, and the proportion of lines with sharper curves is even smaller than that of lines with steep grades.

The majority of the main trunk lines which traverse the European part of the USSR have moderate grades. The grades are somewhat steeper only in those places where the railroad crosses the low Central Russian Upland, the Volga Heights, and the Donets Ridge [Fig. 4, facing p. 13]. On some of the trunk lines work has been done under the Soviet Government to reduce the grades.

On the railroad running north from Leningrad to Murmansk, the grades, formerly steep and protracted, have been moderated considerably under Soviet rule.

There are steep grades also in the Caucasian and Ural mountains, which border the East-European Plain on the south and east. In its central portion, the Caucasus presents considerable difficulties for railroad construction. The existing lines by-pass the main range on the east or cross the low northwestern part of the range by means of a tunnel. Long tunnels are found also in mountainous sections of the Trans-Caucasian Railroad. The Ural Range is low and is easily surmounted by railroads; the mountain sections are found chiefly

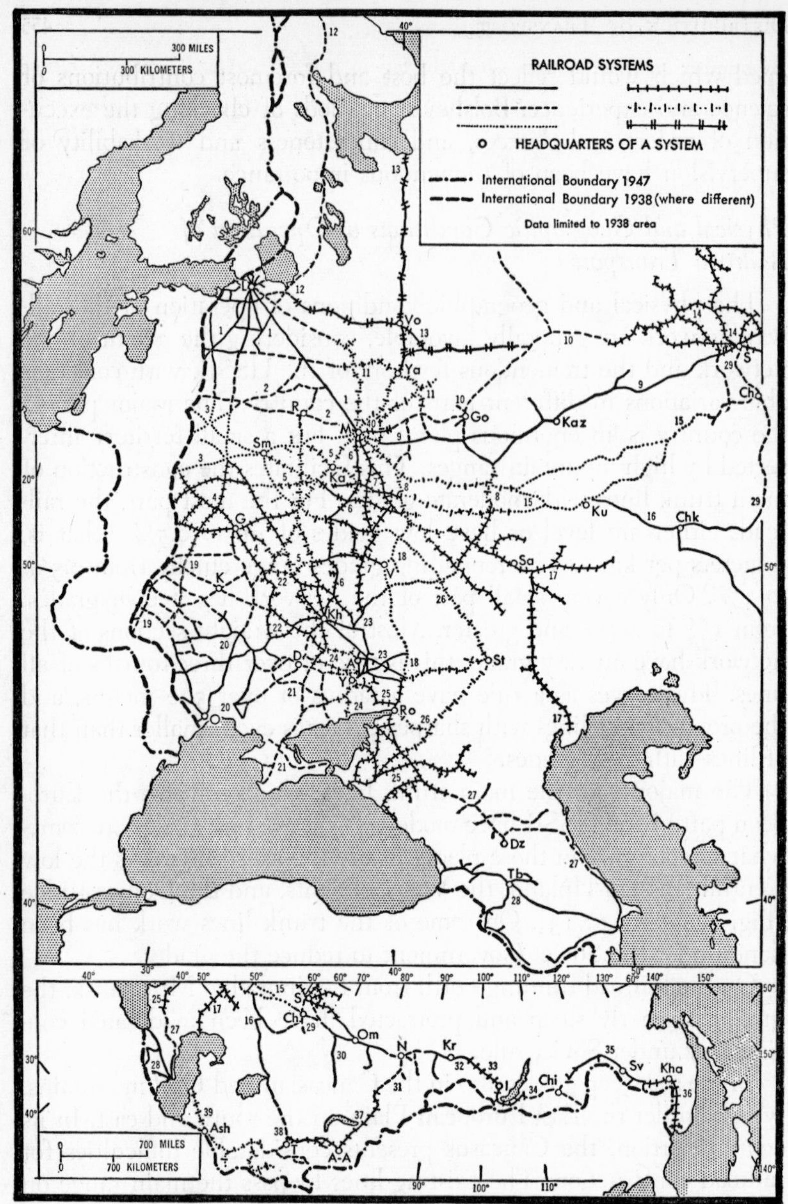

* FIG. 71. Railroad Systems of the USSR, 1937 (Source: Scheme of Railroad and Water Communications, USSR, 1937, scale 1:2,500,000 with insets including Eastern Asia at 1:6,200,000. [Moscow: Transkartografiya, 1937] 4 sheets.)

KEY TO FIG. 71

By number (railroad systems—headquarters in parenthesis) and by letter (cities)

No.	Railroad system	Headquarters
1.	October	(Leningrad)
2.	Kalinin	(Rzhev)
3.	Western	(Smolensk)
4.	Belorussian	(Gomel)
5.	Moscow-Kiev	(Kaluga)
6.	F. E. Dzerzhinsky	(Moscow)
7.	Moscow-Donbas	(Voronezh)
8.	Lenin	(Moscow)
9.	Kazan	(Kazan)
10.	Gorky	(Gorky)
11.	Yaroslavl	(Yaroslavl)
12.	Kirov	(Leningrad)
13.	Northern	(Vologda)
14.	L. M. Kaganovich	(Sverdlovsk)
15.	V. V. Kuibyshev	(Kuibyshev)
16.	Orenburg	(Orenburg, now Chkalov)
17.	Ryazan-Uralsk	(Saratov)
18.	Southeastern	(Voronezh)
19.	Southwestern	(Kiev)
20.	Odessa	(Odessa)
21.	Stalin	(Dnepropetrovsk)
22.	Southern	(Kharkov)
23.	North Donets	(Artemovsk)
24.	South Donets	(Yasinovataya)
25.	K. E. Voroshilov	(Rostov)
26.	Stalingrad	(Stalingrad)
27.	Ordzhonikidze	(Ordzhonikidze, now Dzaudzhikau)
28.	Trans-Caucasus	(Tbilisi)
29.	South Urals	(Chelyabinsk)
30.	Omsk	(Omsk)
31.	Tomsk	(Novosibirsk)
32.	Krasnoyarsk	(Krasnoyarsk)
33.	East Siberian	(Irkutsk)
34.	V. M. Molotov	(Chita)
35.	Amur	(Svobodny)
36.	Far Eastern	(Khabarovsk)
37.	Turkestan-Siberia (Turk-Sib)	(Alma-Ata)
38.	Tashkent	(Tashkent)
39.	Ashkhabad	(Ashkhhabad)
40.	Moscow Belt	(Moscow)

Letter	City
A	Artemovsk
AA	Alma-Ata
Ash	Ashkhabad
Ch	Chelyabinsk
Chi	Chita
Chk	Chkalov (Orenburg
D	Dnepropetrovsk
Dz	Dzaudzhikau (Ordzhonikidze)
G	Gomel
Go	Gorky
I	Irkutsk
K	Kiev
Ka	Kaluga
Kaz	Kazan
Kh	Kharkov
Kha	Khabarovsk
Kr	Krasnoyarsk
Ku	Kuibyshev
L	Leningrad
M	Moscow
N	Novosibirsk
O	Odessa
Om	Omsk
R	Rzhev
Ro	Rostov
S	Sverdlovsk
Sa	Saratov
Sm	Smolensk
St	Stalingrad
Sv	Svobodny
T	Tashkent
Tb	Tbilisi
V	Voronezh
Vo	Vologda
Y	Yasinovataya
Ya	Yaroslavl

on the Middle Ural lines, between Perm [Molotov] and Sverdlovsk, and on some lines in the southern Urals.

Beyond the Urals to the east and south lies another plain, which gradually passes over into elevations and mountains. Grades are very slight on the western part of the Siberian trunk line, between the Urals and the Kuzbas, and between the Urals and the Volga. The eastern end of the Siberian trunk line, however, which passes over mountain ranges, has rather difficult grades and tunnels.

The railroads which cross Central Asia and connect it with the European part of the USSR have a level profile and a relative absence of curves over most of their extent. Steep elevations are found chiefly on branches from the main trunk line, which cross the spurs of the Tyan-Shan and Pamir-Alay.

There are certain difficulties of operation in arid regions, in the sands of Central Asia, and in localities with scant precipitation and ground water. Water-supply difficulties are encountered in the steppes of the North Caucasus on the Stalingrad-Tikhoretsk line and the Salsk-Bataisk line [Fig. 70]. In Eastern Siberia and the Far East, pockets of permanent ground frost must be taken seriously into account; they cause trouble with the water supply and make any sort of construction difficult. The water-supply difficulties may be overcome either by building water conduits and artesian wells, or by introducing locomotives with steam condensers or other types of traction which do not require water, such as electric or Diesel locomotives.

In winter, low temperatures and snow may affect railroad communication, particularly in the northern and eastern regions. However, railroads can prevent interruptions by certain measures, such as installing snow fences or planting trees along their lines, timely removal of snow from the tracks, and heating stations, water tanks, and locomotive cabs.

In 1939 there were forty-three railroad systems in the network, serving different regions and transportation routes [Fig. 71]. Let us examine the chief routes of the network.

Routes of the First Coal and Metallurgical Base

The railways of the southern coal and metallurgical base serve the Donbas and the Dnepr region, and connect Donets coal with Krivoy Rog iron ore [Fig. 72].

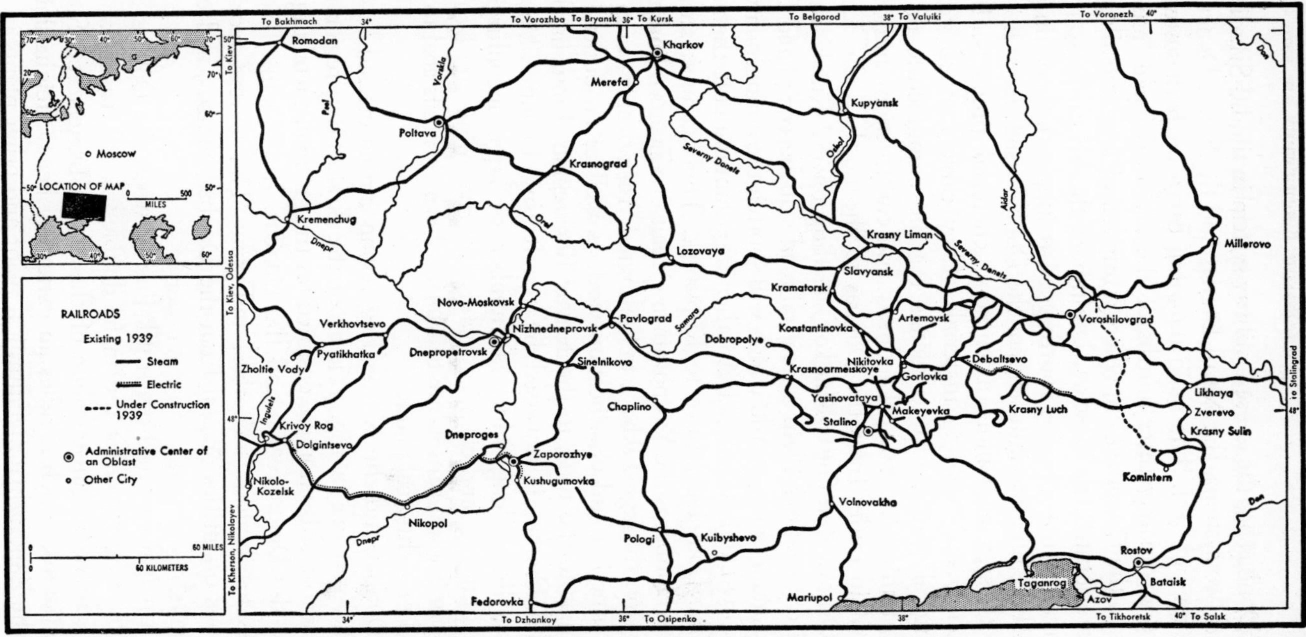

Fig. 72. Railroads of the First Coal and Metallurgical Base (Donbas-Krivoy Rog Area of the Ukraine)

The Donbas has the densest railway system in the USSR, divided between two systems, the North Donets and the South Donets [23 and 24 on Fig. 71]. The main outgoing cargo on both systems is coal. Approximately three-fourths of the coal is shipped from the Donbas to the Dnepr region, where a number of large metallurgical plants are located, to Moscow, Leningrad, the Volga Region, and other areas. The remaining fourth goes to supply the metallurgical and machine-building industries of the Donbas itself. In addition to coal, both systems handle machinery, chemical products, fluxes [limestone], and building materials. They carry iron ore to the metallurgical plants, ferrous metals for the manufacture of machinery, lumber for the coal industry and construction, and grain.

The main outlet from the Donbas to the north is the Krasny Liman-Osnova line (near Kharkov) leading toward Kursk. Under the Third Five-Year Plan, a new railroad will be completed from Krasny Liman to Kupyansk, which will shorten the connection with the Moscow-Donbas Railroad. Another important outlet to the north is the line from Debaltsevo to Kupyansk. The east-west railroad across the Donbas is the Yasinovataya-Debaltsevo-Zverevo line, with an extension through Likhaya to Stalingrad. Yasinovataya is an important junction and classification yard, as well as an outlet from the Donbas to the west, to the Krivoy Rog region. From north to south the Donbas is traversed by the Krasny Liman-Nikitovka-Taganrog line, along which a number of large metallurgical, machine-building, and chemical plants and coal mines are located. South from Stalino runs a line to Mariupol which hauls coal to the Mariupol metallurgical plant.

The Donbas and the Krivoy Rog region are connected by the Stalin Railroad [21 in Fig. 71]. From the Krivoy Rog region the Stalin Railroad ships iron ore destined for the group of metallurgical plants in the Dnepr region and the Donbas. It also ships ferrous metals, fluxes, building materials, and grain. The railroad receives tremendous quantities of coal from the Donbas, lumber, and consumers' goods.

The principal coal and ore trunk line between the Donbas and the Krivoy Rog region is the main double-tracked Yasinovataya-Dnepropetrovsk-Dolgintsevo line of the South Donets and Stalin railroad systems, which handles an extremely heavy freight traffic. Ore for the Zaporozhye metallurgical plant and other plants in the

Donbas is carried on another line, the Dolgintsevo-Zaporozhye-Pologi-Volnovakha line. The Sinelnikovo-Dzhankoy-Sevastopol trunk line leads to the Crimea [Figs. 70 and 71].

The Donbas and Krivoy Rog trunk lines are among the mightiest in the USSR. They have heavy track construction, automatic blocking in some sectors, and well developed stations. The Dolgintsevo-Zaporozhye line is electrified. The other trunk lines use "FD" locomotives.

Donbas-Moscow-Leningrad Route

The southern coal and metallurgical base is connected with Moscow by three double-tracked trunk lines [Fig. 70]. The main coal traffic is concentrated increasingly on the Moscow-Donbas trunk line [7 in Fig. 71], built under the Soviet regime. Besides carrying freight from the Donbas, this railroad also serves the Moscow coal basin.

To the east of the Moscow-Donbas trunk line lies another, the Ryazan route, which carries to the north mainly Donbas coal, and also through freight from the Caucasus—oil and grain. One sector of this route is part of the Southeastern Railroad; another is part of the Lenin Railroad [Fig. 71]. Both these railroads serve a number of industrial enterprises including the large machine-building plants around Moscow. But their main function is to carry through freight. Michurinsk is an important junction on the Lenin Railroad; from Michurinsk a line branches to Saratov [Fig. 70].

The greater part of the freight movement from the south to Moscow is handled by the Kursk route, which is part of the Southern and Dzerzhinsky railroad systems [Fig. 71].

The industrial city of Kharkov, one of the largest railroad junctions of the USSR, is on the Southern Railroad [22 in Fig. 71]. It receives primarily coal, iron, and steel, and ships machinery. This junction performs large classification operations for eight routes, most of which are also part of the Southern Railroad [Fig. 71]. Many passenger trains pass through Kharkov. The greater part of the Kursk route constitutes the main trunk line of the Dzerzhinsky Railroad [6 in Fig. 71]. Approximately half of the freight movement on this railroad is coal, while in a smaller measure it carries metals, metal products, building materials, oil from the Caucasus, and grain from the South. It is one of the most important passenger carriers.

All three of the routes connecting the Donbas with Moscow are well equipped technically and have large line capacities. They use "FD" locomotives.

The Donbas is connected with Leningrad primarily by the Kharkov-Bryansk-Vitebsk route, over the Moscow-Kiev, Western, Kalinin, and October railroad systems [Figs. 70 and 71]. This route carries coal, metals, and grain. Part of the freight is diverted at Bryansk, which is an important machine-building center, as well as an important railroad junction at which six railroad lines converge—among them the new Bryansk-Vyazma line (built during the years of the Stalin Five-Year Plans), through which part of the freight movement is transferred to the main trunk line of the October Railroad (at Likhoslavl). The Vorozhba-Unecha-Orsha line, built under the Soviet regime, is another auxiliary route from the Donbas to Leningrad. From Orsha to Leningrad, in addition to coal, metals, and grain, oil products (from Odessa) are transported.

Lumber from the northern oblasts, as well as from Smolensk Oblast and Belorussia, is carried south to the Donbas on all the main railroads connecting the Donbas with Moscow and Leningrad. In addition to lumber, manufactured products from Leningrad and Moscow are carried south.

The Moscow railroad junction [Fig. 73], with eleven converging railway lines and with a number of connecting lines and stations, is the greatest in the USSR. The tremendous volume of traffic at this junction is accounted for by the fact that Moscow is the capital and the political, economic, and cultural center of the USSR, containing a number of large industrial enterprises. It holds first place in the country in passenger traffic. In addition to the connections between railway lines within the city, the Belt Line links the railways which converge on Moscow; this accomplishes the transfer of freight trains from one railroad to another, as well as loading and unloading. An extensive improvement is under way to increase the capacity of this junction. Main sections which have the heaviest traffic have been supplied with supplementary tracks and equipped with automatic blocking. Mechanized humps have been built in the largest stations. The lines from Moscow to Aleksandrov, Podolsk, Zheleznodorozhny, and Ramenskoye have been electrified [Fig. 73]. Further electrification is planned, as well as the removal of large freight terminals beyond the city limits and partial relocation

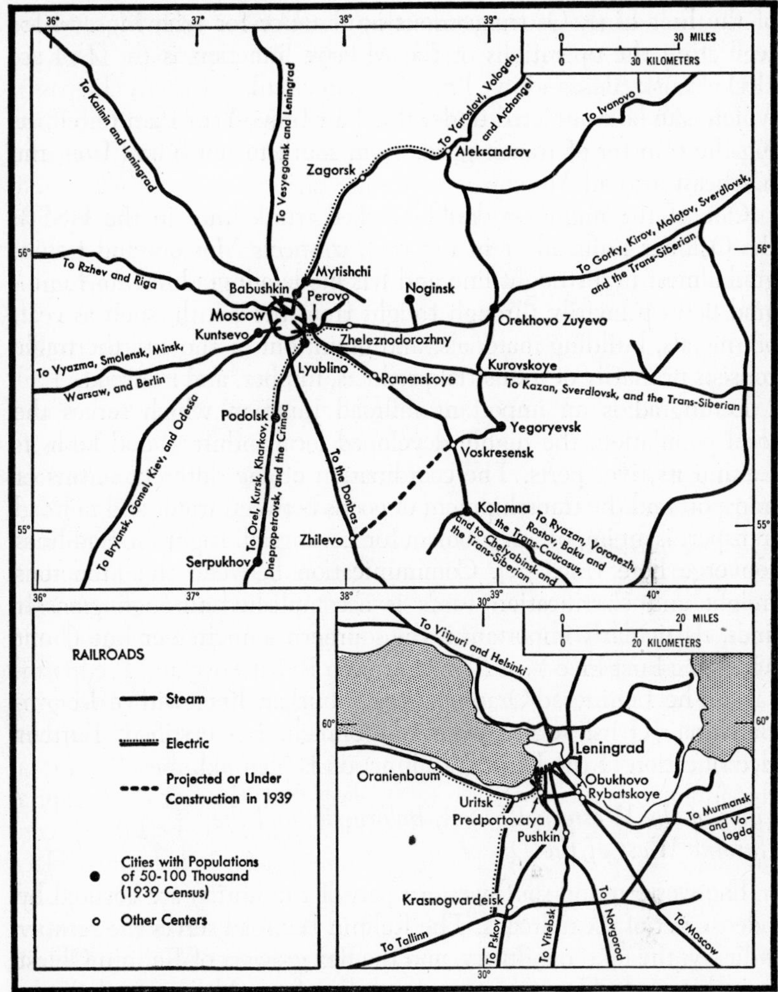

* Fig. 73. Railroads in the Vicinity of Moscow and Leningrad (Moscow adapted from *Great Soviet World Atlas,* Vol. II, Plates 16–17. Leningrad adapted from the International Map of the World, 1:1,000,000, sheets north O35, O36, P35, and P36.)

of the Belt Line. Of tremendous importance for relieving and for regulating the operations of the Moscow junction is the Zhilevo-Voskresensk-Aleksandrov line (a semicircular eastern by-pass), which is to be completed under the Third Five-Year Plan for effecting the transfer of transit goods from south to north and from the northeast around Moscow.

One of the mightiest double-tracked trunk lines in the USSR, the October Railroad [1 in Fig. 71], connects Moscow and Leningrad almost in a straight line and has moderate grades. Into Leningrad flows primarily through freight from the South, such as coal, oil, metals, building materials, and grain; out of the city the traffic consists primarily of industrial products, lumber, and firewood.

Leningrad is an important railroad junction which serves the local population, the highly developed local industry, and both its sea and its river ports. The coordination of the different means of transport and the transshipment of goods between water and railroad transport is an important problem for Leningrad. Eight railroad lines converge here [Fig. 73]. Communication between the numerous freight and classification yards is accomplished through transfer lines. Particularly important is the southern semicircular line (built under the First Five-Year Plan) between Rybatskoye and Predportovaya. The Leningrad-Oranienbaum suburban line, with a Ligovo-Gatchina [Uritsk-Krasnogvardeisk] branch, is electrified. Further electrification of the Leningrad junction is planned.

Lines of the Western RSFSR, Belorussia, and the Ukraine West of the Dnepr

The western and southwestern part of the Union are covered by a dense net of six railroads. The Kalinin Railroad serves the lumber industry, the textile industry, and the flax growers of Kalinin Oblast [2 in Fig. 71]. The important trunk line from Moscow to Sebezh, leading to the western border, is a part of the Kalinin Railroad [Fig. 70]. The Western Railroad [3 in Fig. 71], which connects Moscow with Minsk and the western boundary, is a first-class trunk line; its branches serve Smolensk Oblast and Belorussia. The network of the Belorussian Railroad [4 in Fig. 71] connects all the major industrial centers of Belorussia with its lumber, paper, match, food, and machine-building enterprises, and with its well developed agricultural areas. Important lines of this railroad run from Gomel, which is a large junction, to Bryansk, Minsk, and Bakhmach, and from Zhlobin to Orsha and other points. The Moscow-Kiev Railroad [5 in Fig. 71] connects Moscow with Kiev (as far as Nezhin) and serves the industrial centers of Bryansk and Kaluga, which ship much coal, metals, and building materials. In the fall the southern lines carry large quantities of beets for the sugar factories. The Kharkov-Bryansk-Vitebsk-Leningrad route consists of parts of the Moscow-Kiev, Western, Kalinin, and October railroads [Figs. 70 and 71]. The Southwestern Railroad [19 in Fig. 71] operates in a well developed agricultural region; it has a dense network of branch lines and tracks leading to sugar refineries to which it delivers beets. It serves Kiev, the capital of the Ukrainian SSR, a large industrial city and an important junction of four railroad routes. The Odessa Railroad [20 in Fig. 71] crosses the southwestern part of the Ukraine, with its highly developed grain production, flour mills, distilleries, and sugar industry; it leads to the ports of Odessa, Nikolayev, and Kherson. Odessa forwards by rail the oil which it receives by sea, and receives coal for its own industries, lumber, and grain brought in by water.

The railroads of the southwest operate in collaboration with the Dnepr River traffic.

Northern Lines

The northern oblasts are served by the Kirov and Northern railroads and also by the northeastern lines of the Gorky Railroad [Figs. 70 and 71].

The Kirov Railroad [12 in Fig. 71] passes through Karelia and Murmansk Oblast to the ice-free port of Murmansk; it carries apatite, nepheline, lumber, building materials, and fish. A difficult grade on the one hand and the availability of hydroelectric power at low cost on the other have combined to make the electrification of this line profitable. The Kandalaksha-Apatity-Murmansk section and the branch to Kirovsk are electrified [Fig. 70].

The Northern Railroad [13 in Fig. 71] handles mainly lumber which goes to Moscow and Leningrad, and also through freight from the Urals. It is an important passenger line, since over it pass the Trans-Siberian express trains.

Under the Third Five-Year Plan the new Soroka [Belomorsk] to Plesetsk line will be built, which will connect the Northern and

Kirov railroads [Fig. 70]. This will permit the development of large new forest areas which are now far from railroad and river routes.[8]

The Kotlas line of the Gorky Railroad also is significant for lumber traffic.

Under the Third Five-Year Plan a tremendous new trunk line, the Ukhta-Pechorskaya line, will be constructed northeast from Kotlas [Fig. 70]. It will pass through the oil region of Ukhta (Chibyu) to the high-grade coal deposits of Vorkuta and the fine coal deposits of Intinsk, across the richest forest areas of the country, and a branch line will run from Kotlas to Velsk (Konosha). The new trunk line will insure the further growth of productive forces in the North and the creation there of a large-scale local fuel base to supply industry, the railroads, and the maritime fleet. Forest exploitation, the sawmill industry, the wood-chemical industry, and the paper industry will be greatly developed and will export in large quantities to the central regions.

To increase the capacity of lines connecting Moscow and Leningrad with the North, the most important northern trunk lines—the Kirov and the Danilov-Archangel lines—will be double-tracked.

Lines of the Volga Region

The railroads of the Volga Region are closely connected with the Volga River traffic, reloading cargo from the river fleet and carrying it to Moscow, Leningrad, the Donbas, the Caucasus, the Urals, and Siberia.

The lines from Moscow to Rybinsk, Yaroslavl, Kostroma, Kineshma, and Vesyegonsk are part of the Yaroslavl Railroad [11 in Fig. 71]. Its main freight consists of oil and salt (taken on at the Volga ports of Rybinsk and Yaroslavl), textiles (Ivanovo), and mineral building materials. The main double-tracked trunk line to Yaroslavl also carries a large number of passengers, particularly suburban.

The main double-tracked trunk line of the Gorky Railroad [10 in Fig. 71] connects Moscow with the important industrial center and river port of Gorky, passing through the Vladimir textile region. At Gorky oil and grain are transferred from the river fleet to the

[8] [This connection was opened early in World War II and permitted the continued movement of lend-lease freight from Murmansk after the Kirov Railroad was cut south of Belomorsk.]

railroad. The northeastern lines of the railroad penetrate the lumber regions of Gorky and Kirov oblasts. The significance of the Gorky junction increased greatly after the construction of the bridge across the Volga, providing a direct outlet from the Kotelnich line to Moscow.

The line crossing the Volga at Kazan is part of the single-track Kazan Railroad [9 in Fig. 71] which connects Moscow with Sverdlovsk and is of great transit importance. This railroad passes through several national republics—the Tatar, Chuvash, Mari, and Udmurt—with their tremendous lumber resources and diverse industrial enterprises [Fig. 40 in the back of the book]. The main freight is lumber, metals, machines, and building materials.

The Kuibyshev Railroad [15 in Fig. 71] serves the area between the Urals and the Volga, where under the Third Five-Year Plan a large new oil base, the "Second Baku," is being developed, and construction of the gigantic Kuibyshev hydroelectric project is in full swing.[9] While at present it is substantially a transit railroad, the new developments will greatly increase freight handling. It connects the central regions with the Urals, Siberia, and Central Asia, crossing the Volga at Ulyanovsk and Batraki; the line through Batraki is double-tracked. At Batraki and Kuibyshev oil and grain cargoes are transshipped from the Volga.

An important line from the Donbas extends to the Kuibyshev Railroad from the southwest, from Kupyansk through Valuiki and Balashov to Penza [Fig. 70]. Most of this line is part of the Penza Railroad. Its freight turnover has grown considerably since the industrialization of the Volga Region. It carries coal and metals from the Donbas, oil from the Caucasus, and loads much grain. Because of the increase in traffic, the line has been double-tracked throughout its entire length.

The Lower Volga Region is traversed by two railroad systems, the Ryazan-Uralsk and the Stalingrad.

The Ryazan-Uralsk Railroad [17 in Fig. 71] serves the metalworking and light industries of Saratov, the salt mines of Baskunchak and Elton, the cement plants of Volsk, and the fish-canning industry of Astrakhan. At the large river port of Saratov, oil products and lumber are transshipped to the railroad. Its importance has in-

[9] [Available Soviet literature does not indicate that construction of this project had been started by 1948.]

creased significantly with the construction of the Saratov bridge across the Volga, and of the new Uralsk-Iletsk line, which provides a connection with the Orenburg [Chkalov] Railroad from the Donbas and the central regions, by-passing the overburdened Batraki-Kinel section of the Kuibyshev Railroad. Under the Third Five-Year Plan, the new line from Kizlyar to Astrakhan, and then the Bezenchuk-Pugachev line, will be completed, after which oil products from the Caucasus will go east by way of the Astrakhan-Urbakh route of the Ryazan-Uralsk Railroad, as yet little used for freight.

The Stalingrad Railroad [26 in Fig. 71] depends upon the large railroad junction and river port of Stalingrad, an industrial center, from which lines lead to Moscow, the Donbas, and Novorossiisk. This railroad receives coal and metal from the Donbas, and agricultural products; it ships tractors and transships oil, lumber, and grain from the Volga.

Lines of the Caucasus

Throughout the North Caucasus the Voroshilov and Ordzhonikidze railroads [25 and 27 in Fig. 71] perform highly varied economic services. North of Rostov coal is loaded; at Rostov, agricultural machinery; at Taganrog and Sulin [Krasny Sulin], metals; at Novorossiisk, cement; and at Grozny, oil products. A tremendous quantity of grain and grain products is received from the rich agricultural regions of Krasnodar Kray and Ordzhonikidze Kray [now Stavropol Kray]. Lines lead to the seaports of Rostov, Novorossiisk, Tuapse, and Makhach-Kala, and to the Black Sea and mineral-water resorts.

The Trans-Caucasian Railroad [28 in Fig. 71] serves three flourishing republics—Georgia, Armenia, and Azerbaidzhan. Its main cargo is oil going from Baku to Batumi. Paralleling the railroad there are oil pipe lines. Among other outstanding cargoes are manganese ore from the Chiatura branch, copper ore and copper from the Alaverdi and Kafan regions, and coal from Tkvibuli and Tkvarcheli [Fig. 70]. The difficult grade on the main trunk line has necessitated electrification of part of the line, beginning at the most difficult section, Suram Pass [Fig. 70]. By 1938, the entire Tbilisi-Samtredia section was electrically operated, and the electrification of the Borzhomi branch is under way.

Lines of the Second Coal and Metallurgical Base

Before the Revolution, the railroads of the East served colonial exploitation, and had an insignificant freight turnover. Having secured for the eastern regions a higher level of development, created large industrial centers, and assured the development of socialist agriculture, the Soviet Rule transformed the railroads of the East into powerful transport arteries. On the principal lines in the Urals, Siberia, and Kazakhstan, by the end of the Second Five-Year Plan, the volume of freight turnover was tens of times greater than in 1913.

The three trunk lines which cross the Volga lead from Moscow to the Urals by way of Kirov-Perm [Molotov], Kazan-Sverdlovsk, and Syzran-Chelyabinsk [Fig. 70]. For the Third Five-Year Plan and the years following it, a new outlet to Magnitogorsk is contemplated. Work has begun already on the Kazan-Bugulma line (Fig. 70], which will serve the Tatar ASSR and connect the Kazan and Kuibyshev railroads. Next on the schedule is the construction of the Ufa-Magnitogorsk and Gorky-Kazan lines. In addition, the existing Moscow-Perm-Sverdlovsk-Omsk line will be double-tracked.

Three systems make up the Urals network: the Perm, Kaganovich, and South Urals. [The Perm and Kaganovich railroads earlier had been one system, the Kaganovich (14 in Fig. 71).]

The Perm Railroad, which serves Perm [Molotov] Oblast, carries Kizel coal, lumber products, metal, and chemical raw materials and products from Solikamsk and Berezniki, and oil from Chusovskie Gorodki and Perm (transshipped from the Kama River). The Perm Railroad is single-tracked; its technical equipment has been improved substantially during recent years. The Kizel-Chusovoy-Goroblagodatskaya-Sverdlovsk line (the Goroblagodatskaya-Sverdlovsk section is part of the L. M. Kaganovich Railroad), which has a difficult grade and carries heavy traffic, has been electrified [Fig. 74]. Facilities at the junction points of Perm, Chusovoy, and Goroblagodatskaya have been expanded.

The L. M. Kaganovich Railroad [14 in Fig. 71], which serves Sverdlovsk Oblast, carries ores, metals, machinery, lumber, and grain. It is also single-tracked, but is well equipped technically. Sverdlovsk, an important industrial center and the junction of seven

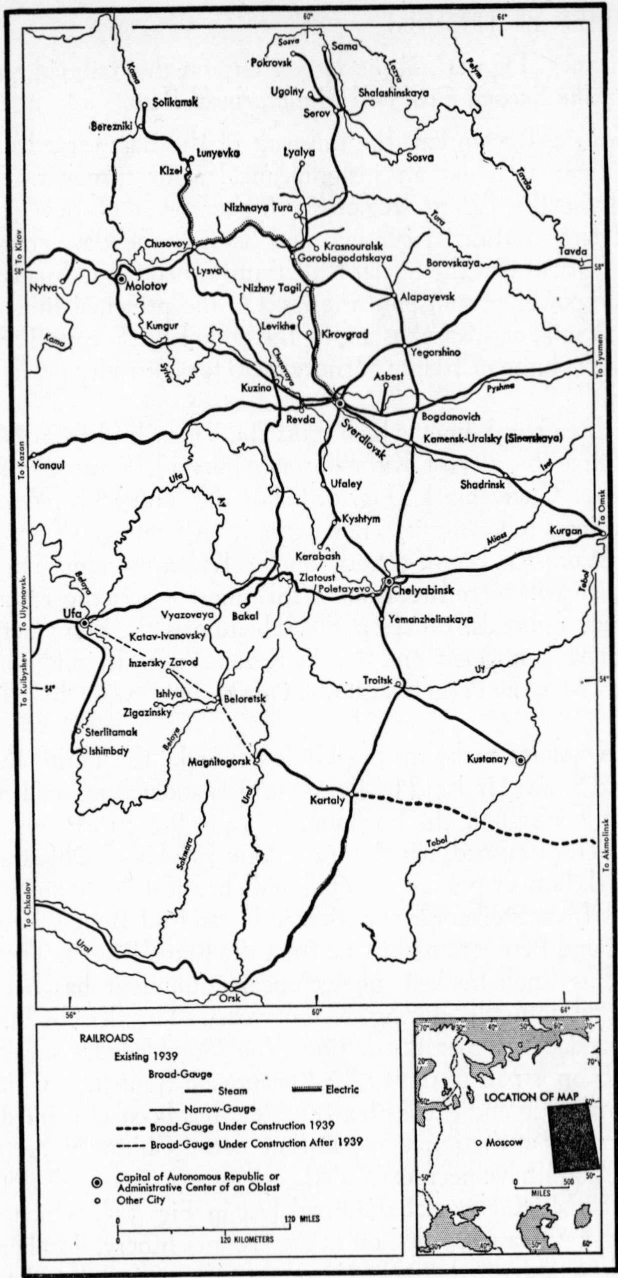

FIG. 74. Railroads of the Urals

railroad lines [Fig. 74], is the largest city on this railroad. A large transit traffic passes through the city, and considerable quantities of freight originate there.

The South Urals Railroad [29 in Fig. 71] serves the large plants, among the most important in the country, in Magnitogorsk and Chelyabinsk. This railroad originates ore, coal (from Chelyabinsk), ferrous metals, and also mineral building materials and grain. It delivers Kuznetsk and Chelyabinsk coal and mineral building materials. It is well equipped technically, with its main lines double-tracked. The Yemanzhelinskaya-Chelyabinsk line was built to bypass the station of Poletayevo [Fig. 74]. Chelyabinsk has become an important junction of four lines. The Troitsk-Orsk line, which was built under the First Five-Year Plan (its southern part belongs to the Orenburg Railroad), is an important outlet to the north from the southern Urals. A new line between Sinarskaya [Kamenetsk-Uralsky] and Chelyabinsk is under construction; it will have easier grades than the old Sverdlovsk-Chelyabinsk line. The railroads and the Kama River fleet jointly provide the transportation for the Urals.

From the Urals there are three railway routes to Siberia: from Sverdlovsk through Tyumen and through Kurgan, and from Chelyabinsk through Kurgan [Fig. 70]. All three feed into the world's greatest railroad line—the Trans-Siberian trunk line, which is double-tracked throughout and measures 9,332 km. from Moscow to Vladivostok and 7,514 km. from Sverdlovsk to Vladivostok.

The western part of the trunk line (operated by the Omsk and Tomsk railroads [30 and 31 in Fig. 71]) is the transport artery of the country's second coal and metallurgical base. It supplies Kuznetsk coal to the Ural metallurgical plants, and Ural ores to the metallurgy of the Kuzbas. The development of this second coal and metallurgical base necessitated considerable new railroad construction in the Urals and Siberia, and reconstruction of the entire route. The Troitsk-Orsk (with the branch from Kartaly to Magnitogorsk [Fig. 74]) and Sverdlovsk-Kurgan lines were built in the Urals, and the Novosibirsk-Leninsk (Proyektnaya) [Fig. 75] and Novokuznetsk [Stalinsk]-Mundybash lines in Siberia. Between the Urals and the Kuzbas the entire route has been made into a double-tracked trunk line, with easy grades, heavy rails, and tremendous line capacity.

The Omsk Railroad carries primarily transit traffic. Most of the

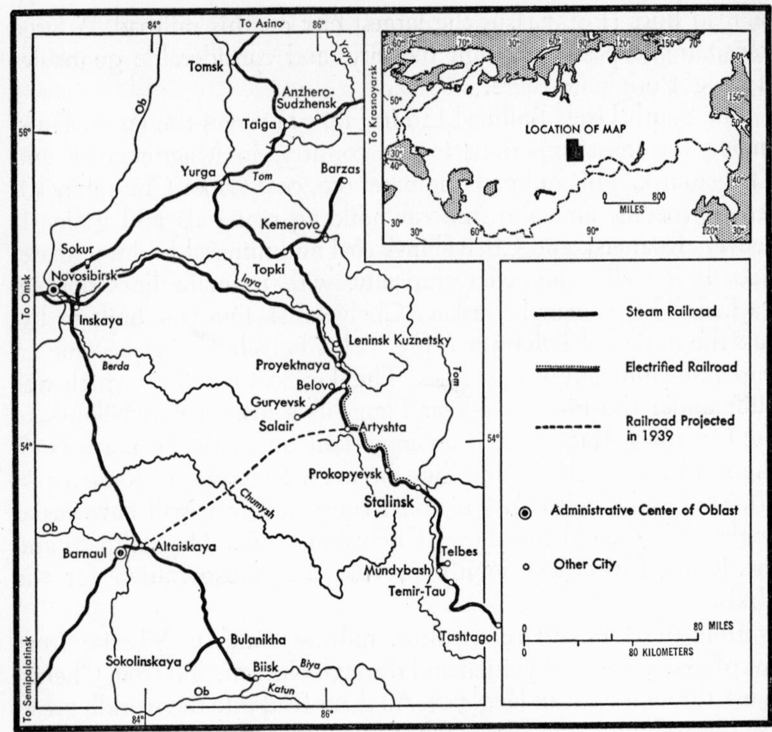

FIG. 75. Railroads of the Kuzbas

freight it originates is coal from the Karaganda line; it also originates much grain on its main line and on the Karaganda and Pavlodar secondary lines [Fig. 70]. The traffic on the Tomsk Railroad is more complex. It serves the metallurgical, coal, and chemical industries of the Kuzbas, the large industrial center of Novosibirsk, the nonferrous metallurgy of the Altay, and the lumber and grain regions of Siberia. This railroad originates primarily coal, but also ore, metals, grain, and lumber. Its main lines have been reconstructed substantially, the track structure has been reinforced, new stations have been built, and the Belovo-Stalinsk line has been electrified [Fig. 75].

The Third Five-Year Plan contemplates the construction of a new large South Siberian trunk line. First to be completed will be the Akmolinsk-Kartaly [Fig. 70] and Barnaul-Artyshta [Fig. 75] lines, its western and eastern sections. The former will permit a considerable increase in the supply of Karaganda coal to Magnitogorsk in place of coal from the Kuzbas, and will reduce the haul by almost half. The latter will shorten the haul of Kuznetsk coal to the Turksib. The middle section of the trunk line, next on the program for construction, will permit a wide development of the coal, copper ore, and salt deposits which are available along the new line. The greater part of the trunk line will be in Kazakhstan territory. The whole line will be of tremendous importance for through shipments. In the future it is planned to extend this line eastward to connect with the Baikal-Amur trunk line which is under construction.

Lines of Eastern Siberia and the Far East

The eastern part of the Siberian trunk line, between Novosibirsk and Vladivostok, is four times as long as the western part. It includes the Krasnoyarsk, East Siberian, V. M. Molotov, Amur, Far Eastern, and Maritime railroads [Fig. 71]. Freight traffic consists mainly of transit goods going to the Far East, Yakutia, and the gold-bearing regions, as well as a large amount of local cargo. Coal from Anzhero-Sudzhensk is shipped west and partly east, and lumber from the Yenisey is shipped west. From Cheremkhovo, coal is shipped approximately as far as Chita. Lumber is hauled from the Amur at Khabarovsk to Vladivostok; and coal is hauled from the Suchan branch. The following are the most important branches from the main trunk line: on the Krasnoyarsk Railroad, the Achinsk-Abakan branch (deep into Khakassia); on the East Siberian Railroad, the Ulan-Ude to Naushki (Kyakhta) branch, built in 1938; on the Molotov Railroad, the Karymskaya-Otpor branch, which leads to the Manchurian border, and the Bukachacha branch, which leads to an important coal deposit; on the Amur Railroad, the Kuibyshevka-Blagoveshchensk branch and the Zavitaya-Raichikhinsk (coal) branch; on the Far Eastern Railroad, the newly built line to Komsomolsk-on-Amur; and on the Maritime Railroad, the above-mentioned Suchan branch [Figs. 70 and 71]. The technical equipment on the eastern railroads has been improved during recent years. Railroad transport plays a tremendous role in the development of the productive forces of Eastern Siberia and the Far East, as well as in the national defense. The railroads operate in conjunction with the large river routes—the Yenisey, Lena, and Amur—and with the motor highways.

Lines of Kazakhstan

Kazakhstan is a part of the Soviet Union in which new railroad construction has received particularly extensive development, a fact which has contributed in large measure to the advances in socialist construction in the Kazakh SSR. Under the First Five-Year Plan, eastern Kazakhstan was traversed by the Turkestan-Siberian Railroad [37 in Fig. 71], insuring deliveries into Central Asia of grain and lumber from Siberia. The increased grain supply in turn promoted the significant development of cotton growing in Central Asia. The trunk line also provided the means of delivering cotton to Siberia, where cotton mills have been established. The laying of the Turk-Sib brought about the development of industry and agriculture, and an increase in the exchange of commodities in all parts of Kazakhstan which lie near the railroad. In northeastern Kazakhstan a railroad has been built from Rubtsovsk to Ridder, the center of nonferrous metallurgy [Fig. 70].

Of great industrial importance is the new Borovoye-Akmolinsk-Karaganda line, which leads to Karaganda, the important industrial center of Kazakhstan and the nation's third coal-mining base. This line has been extended farther south, as far as Lake Balkhash, to supply coal and provide means of shipping the finished products of the Balkhash Copper Combine [Fig. 70]. In 1936 construction was begun on the Neldy-Dzhezkazgan branch from the main line, to connect Karaganda with Dzhezkazgan, another center of nonferrous metals.

Western Kazakhstan is traversed by the Orenburg Railroad [16 in Fig. 71], which carries into Central Asia lumber, metals, and other industrial products from the central regions and the Donbas. In the reverse direction it carries cotton, fruits, and wine. Part of the cargo, chiefly cotton and fish, is brought to the railroad over the Aral Sea. With the construction of the Uralsk-Iletsk line and the Saratov bridge across the Volga, the Orenburg Railroad gained a second outlet to the central districts (in addition to the Kinel-Batraki line) [Fig. 70].

The Guryev-Kandagach lateral line, which is being completed, will connect the Orenburg Railroad with the Emba oil region, previously lacking convenient transportation. Under the Third Five-Year Plan, this line will be continued as far as Orsk. In addition to the railroad, a large oil pipe line was opened from Emba to Orsk in 1936.

Lines of Central Asia

Two railroad systems, the Tashkent and the Ashkhabad, traverse the Central Asian republics, the cotton-growing base of the country. The Tashkent Railroad [38 in Fig. 71] ships cotton, fruits, and vegetables, and also carries articles of local consumption—coal from local basins and grain. The Ashkhabad Railroad [39 in Fig. 71] ships cotton from the regions drained by the Amu-Darya and its tributaries, and oil from Krasnovodsk where it is delivered by sea.

Because of the scarcity of water on parts of the Ashkhabad Railroad it is advantageous to use locomotives with steam condensers, and Diesel locomotives.

Communication between Central Asia and other regions of the country is maintained by three railroads: the Orenburg, the Ashkhabad (to Krasnovodsk and thence by sea), and the Turkestan-Siberian.

SECTION 4. RIVER TRANSPORT

The USSR has a ramified network of river routes, measuring as much as 350,000 km. (rafting routes included). In length of rivers, it occupies first place in the world.

The flat relief of the country is favorable to riverways, just as it is to railways. The sources of the largest rivers in the European USSR are not more than 300 meters above sea level. Since their length is great, the average gradient of the river beds is small. The slow and smooth current is favorable for navigation, but promotes the deposition of solid particles which are carried by the river, and the formation of shoals. The rivers of the Asiatic USSR—the Ob, the Yenisey, the Lena, and the Amur—are among the largest in the world [Fig. 5, p. 24 and Table 2, p. 38]. Thanks to the abundance of water in large rivers, their slow current does not lead to the formation of shoals and sandbanks, as in the rivers of the European USSR, especially the Volga.

The disadvantageous feature of river transport is the freezing of the water in winter, which interrupts navigation. The rivers of the European USSR are navigable six to eight months of the year; the rivers of the Asiatic USSR, which empty into the Arctic Ocean and the Sea of Okhotsk, five to seven months.

Possessing tremendous freight capacity, river traffic is very important in the transport system of the USSR. Sabotage by enemies of the people and laxity and weak discipline among some of the workers in river and sea transport have caused these sectors to lag. Every measure has been taken by the Government to eliminate this backwardness.

River Traffic

The volume of freight hauled in 1937 by the river fleet of the People's Commissariat of Waterways (under power, not including rafting) was 66.9 million tons, while the freight turnover was 33 billion ton-kilometers. By comparison with 1913 the volume of river traffic had slightly more than doubled, while during the same period the railroads had increased the amount of freight hauled by almost four times. The share of river transport in the total freight turnover on railroads and internal waterways had, in 1937, reached only 9.8% of the tonnage hauled and 8.6% of the ton-kilometers. The average length of haul per ton of river freight had dropped to 491 km. in 1937 from 770 km. in 1913; railroads, on the other hand, had experienced an increase from 496 to 688 km. during the same period. These figures testify to the poor performance of river transport, to its backwardness, and to the shifting onto the railroads of freight which should have been handled on the rivers.

The chief river cargoes are lumber—which comprises more than half the traffic by raft and by vessel—petroleum products, mineral building materials, and grain. During recent years other cargoes have begun to increase—coal, metals, and chemicals; but they still comprise only a small part of the total tonnage.

The rivers of the Volga Basin carry the largest part of the traffic—in 1937, 45% of the total [Fig. 6, p. 32]. The riverways of the Northwest account for 15.3% of the total; the northern rivers, 17.5%; the Dnepr, Don, Kuban, and Kura, 10%; and the rivers of Siberia and Central Asia, 12.2%. During recent years, the increase in freight turnover on the waterways has been especially rapid in the Urals, Siberia, the North, and Central Asia, in relation to the rapid rise in the productive forces of these regions.

Development of the River Network

New river routes are now being exploited, and traffic is growing on the Pechora, Khatanga, Indigirka, Kolyma, Selenga, Ili, Amu-Darya, and other rivers, which were not utilized for navigation under the Tsarist regime [Fig. 5, p. 24]. Navigation has begun on a number of small rivers and has proved especially effective in regions poorly equipped with railway and highway facilities. Small rivers are used by kolkhozes as a low-cost means of transporting grain and other agricultural products to the railroads.

The construction of new water communication routes is of tremendous importance: the Dnepr dam, which created a continuous waterway along the Dnepr River, the Stalin White Sea to Baltic Canal, and the Moscow-Volga Canal have been completed [Fig. 6]. Dams are being built on the Volga and the Kama, and construction of a Volga-Don Canal is planned for the future. These enormous hydrotechnical works provide for the unification of Soviet waterways into one single system, and permit a sizable increase in river traffic among the regions of the USSR.

Reconstruction of River Transport

The construction of new waterways is complemented by projects to improve the navigability of existing routes. The major riverways of the European USSR and the large rivers of the Asiatic USSR—the Volga, Kama, Oka, Severnaya (Northern) Dvina, Dnepr, and Don, the Ob, Irtysh, and Tobol—have been furnished throughout their navigable length with day and night (illuminated) warning markers. The length of river routes with daytime installations was 80.8 thousand km. in 1937, while 60.6 thousand km. (more than double the length in 1913) had illuminated installations for night traffic, permitting safe navigation around the clock. Dredges serve a considerable part of the river system, making it possible to increase the depth somewhat where there are sandbanks: on the middle course of the Volga, from 180 to 190 cm.; on the lower Volga, from 215 to 230 cm.; on the lower Kama, from 135 to 145 cm.; on the Oka, from 90 to 105 cm.; etc.

The river fleet, which suffered severe damage at the time of the Civil War and the Intervention, has been considerably restored and enlarged. As a result of the development of the river shipbuilding industry, the river fleet has increased each year during the period of the Stalin Five-Year Plans. New vessels have appeared: mighty 1,200-hp. steamers, Diesel motor tugs, self-propelled Diesel motor barges, oil-tanker barges with load capacities up to 12,000 tons, small passenger ships, dredges, and other vessels. A flotilla of passenger vessels has been built for the Moscow-Volga Canal. In the period of the Third Five-Year Plan the fleet is to be enlarged further with new vessels, standardized in order to do away with the existing variations in size.

The Volga River and the Volga Basin

The chief water artery of the European USSR is the Volga (measuring 3,688 km.) and its tributaries. The largest of these are the Kama (2,009 km.) and the Oka (1,520 km.). The total length of navigable waterways in the Volga Basin measures 17.6 thousand km.; 42.6 thousand km. can be used for rafting.

The freight turnover of steamship lines on the Volga alone constitutes nearly one-third of the total for all rivers.

The Volga is important for carrying Caucasus oil, which is transferred to the railroad system at major centers of the Volga Region (Stalingrad, Saratov, Gorky, Rybinsk for shipment to Moscow and Leningrad; Kuibyshev and Batraki for shipment to the east) [Fig. 6, p. 32]. Upriver also go grain from the Lower and Middle Volga Region to the central districts, and salt from the Lower Volga. In smaller quantities go metals from the Kama, fish from the lower Volga, coal by way of Stalingrad, cement from Volsk, and cotton by way of Astrakhan. Downriver, the chief cargo is lumber from the Kama and the northern tributaries of the Volga, to supply the Donbas, the North Caucasus, and the Trans-Caucasus.

Not nearly enough use is made of the Volga for hauling freight. Millions of tons which could be shipped conveniently on the river are carried entirely by railroad. But even shipments which do move along the Volga could travel much farther by water than they do. Thus, most of the oil moving from the Caucasus to the central region is transferred to the railroad at Stalingrad and Saratov, instead of continuing on to Gorky and Rybinsk, from which the railway trip to Moscow and Leningrad is comparatively short. Lumber cargoes for the Trans-Caucasus are transferred to the railroad at Stalingrad, instead of proceeding by water all the way to Baku.

Passenger movement on the Volga constitutes about one-third of that on all river routes. The volume of passenger traffic, however, is small and cannot compare with that on the railroads.

During recent years a series of reconstruction measures have been carried out on the Volga. By dredging, the normal depth has been increased. In order to improve the approaches to Kuibyshev, Saratov, and Stalingrad, large-scale regulatory operations involving the use of stone have been conducted. Shore installations are being reconstructed. Mechanized mooring facilities and passenger terminals have been constructed at Gorky, Stalingrad, and Astrakhan. Mechanical loading and unloading devices have been installed at Kazan, Kuibyshev, and Saratov.

Of the freight carried on tributaries of the Volga, most goes by way of the Kama, the Oka, and the Sheksna.

Downstream on the Kama pass lumber and ferrous metals from the Urals (the latter almost entirely from Perm [Molotov]), and grain from Chistopol and Chelny [Naberezhnie Chelny]. Oil and cement for Perm and salt for Tikhie Gory move upstream on the Kama from the Volga. The mooring points at Perm and Solikamsk are mechanically equipped.

Cargoes moving up the Sheksna are chiefly lumber and oil and some grain and salt. Their destination, over the long Mariinsk system, is Leningrad. Large quantities of lumber and mineral building materials from the Svir River and Lake Onega join this stream of freight [Fig. 77, p. 483]. Leningrad, a major seaport, is also a river port. Under the Third Five-Year Plan much reconstruction work is being carried out there in order to connect river transport with sea and railroad transport.

The Oka connects the Volga with Moscow. The present depth of the Oka is not great, so that the possibility of developing freight movement is limited. Construction materials, oil, and grain are hauled upstream on the Oka. The wharves at Moscow and Ryazan are equipped with mechanical moorings. The Third Five-Year Plan contemplates beginning construction of the Kaluga hydroelectric station with a dam. Dams on the Oka will increase the depth of the river and make its shallow tributaries navigable.

The water route from Moscow to the Volga by way of the Oka, with its low water level, could not satisfy the needs of the capital city of the Soviet Union. The construction of the Moscow-Volga Canal during the years 1933–1937 provided a complete solution to the problems of both water communication and water supply to the people and industries of Moscow.

The Moscow-Volga Canal [Fig. 76] is among the great creations of human genius. In the scale of its operations and in its economic significance it stands beside the largest canals of the world—the Suez and the Panama. It is 128 km. long, 5.5 meters deep, and can accommodate barges with a load capacity of 22,000 tons—twice the size of the largest Volga barges. Vessels proceeding through the canal are raised by locks from the Volga to the water divide and then lowered into the Moscow River. Pumping stations lift water from the Volga to the divide, from which point it flows into the Moscow River. There are eight locks in the canal. The route extends from the Volga above the Ivankovo dam (124 meters above sea level), through the water divide between the sixth and seventh locks (162 meters), to the Karamyshevskaya dam on the Moscow River (126 meters) and the Pererva dam (120 meters). The differences in water level at various points along the canal are utilized by hydroelectric stations.

With the aid of the large dams on the canal several reservoirs have been created. The largest of these—the Volga Reservoir, or so-called Moscow Sea—has an area of 327 sq. km.; this is more than a third the size of Lake Ilmen.

The Moscow-Volga Canal connects Moscow with the entire Volga Basin, and through the Mariinsk system (under reconstruction) and the White Sea to Baltic Canal, with Leningrad, the Karelian ASSR, and Murmansk and Archangel oblasts. Moscow is being transformed into a major river port.

Following the construction of the Moscow-Volga Canal, the reconstruction of the upper Volga was begun [Fig. 77]. In order to secure the passage of large Volga vessels into the canal, two large hydro installations are being built at Uglich and Rybinsk on the upper Volga (above Rybinsk). The one at Uglich includes a dam, a hydroelectric station, and a lock. At Rybinsk, two dams are being built, across the Volga and the Sheksna. A hydroelectric station is being constructed at the Sheksna dam.

The two dams will permit a significant increase in the water level throughout the upper reaches of the river.

The Rybinsk Reservoir will also be the beginning of the Volga-Baltic water route (Mariinsk system), which proceeds along the

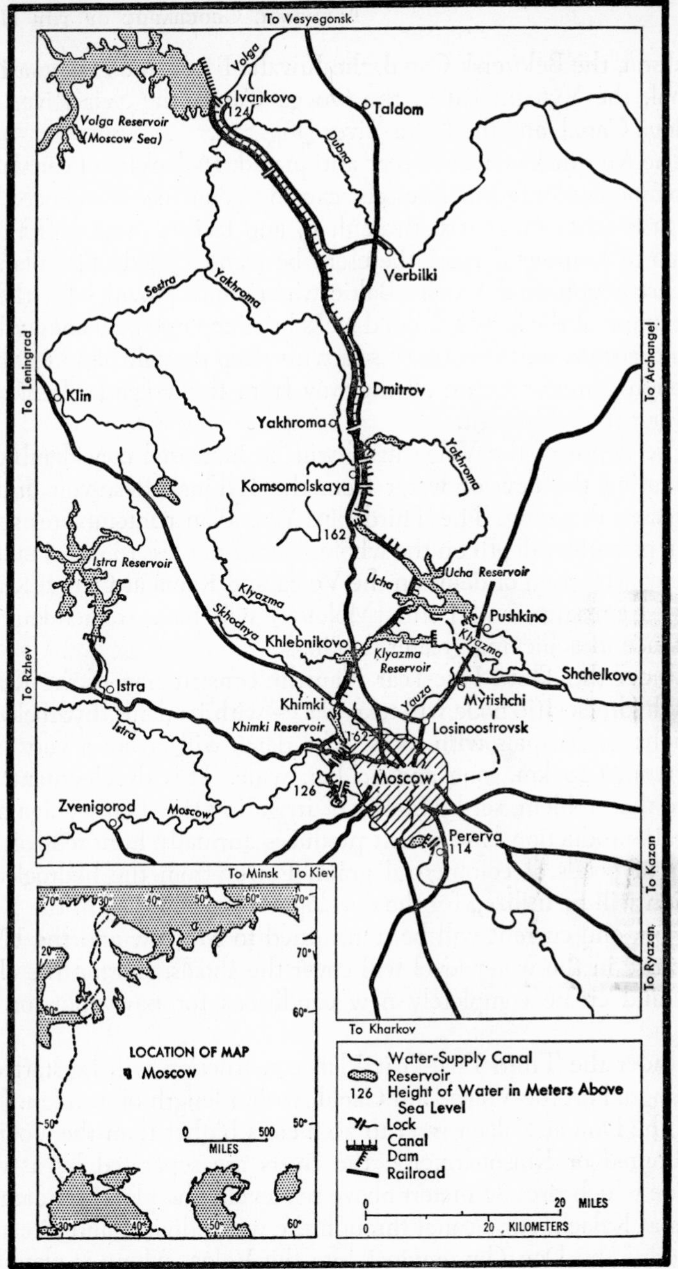

Fig. 76. The Moscow-Volga Canal

Sheksna, the Belozersk Canal, the Kovzha River, the Novomariinsk Canal, the Vytegra River, the Onega Canal, the Svir River, the Ladoga Canal, and the Neva River [Fig. 77].

The Mariinsk system is very antiquated. Its locks and canals can accommodate only small vessels, causing great inconvenience. The Volga barges cannot pass through it, and freight moving from the Volga to Leningrad must therefore be transshipped. The planned reconstruction of the Volga-Baltic water route provides for the replacement of the forty small old locks by nine large new ones, which would accommodate large vessels with deep draught, and establish through communication all the way from the Volga to Leningrad without transshipment.

The depth of the Volga itself will be increased considerably by regulating the flow of water from the Rybinsk Reservoir and by increased dredging. The Third Five-Year Plan contemplates securing a prevailing depth on the whole river of not less than 2.6 meters. The construction of dams on the Volga and Kama at Gorky, Kuibyshev, Kamyshin, and Perm [Molotov] will have tremendous importance in achieving greater depth.

Under the Third Five-Year Plan the construction of the Kuibyshev hydroelectric node will take place—with its dams, hydroelectric stations, and canals with locks. The dams will create a very large reservoir, 600 km. long and 20 km. wide. This development will solve the problem, set by Stalin, of irrigating the Trans-Volga area, a grain-production base which produces annually hundreds of millions of poods of commercial grain. Power from the hydroelectric station will be utilized for the development of industry in the Volga Region, and current will be transmitted to Moscow and the Urals. The rise in the water level will cover the shoals, shorten the channel, and create completely new conditions for navigation on the Volga.

Under the Third Five-Year Plan construction will be started at Stalingrad on the Volga-Don Canal, with a length of 100 km. [Fig. 6]. The Don at Kalach is 33 to 39 meters higher than the Volga at Stalingrad or Krasnoarmeisk; the rivers are separated by a water divide which rises 80 meters above sea level. The plan is to dam the Don at Kalach, cut a canal through the water divide, and direct the water of the Don (by gravity) into the Volga, where it would increase the flow into the Caspian Sea. Donets coal will move north-

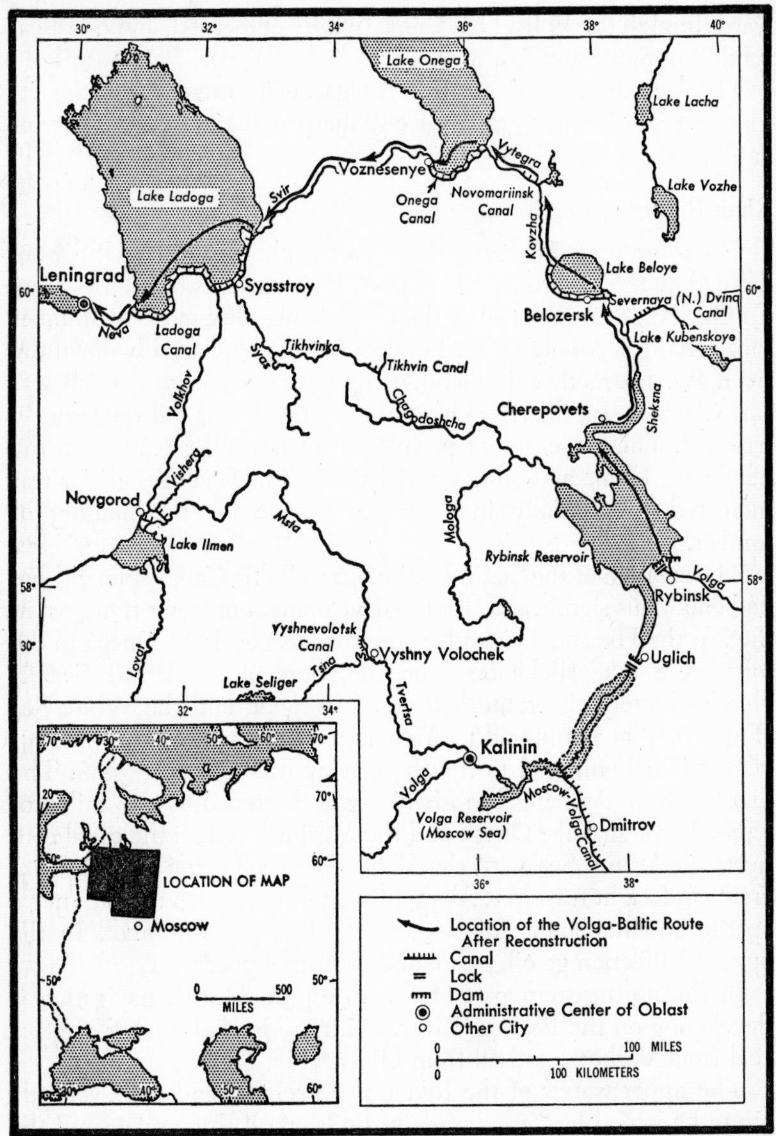

Fig. 77. The Volga-Baltic Water Route

ward through the Volga-Don Canal, while lumber, oil, and chemical goods will move southward.

The reconstruction of the Volga will increase vastly its transport significance and secure a sharp reduction in the cost of hauling.

River Routes of the North

The forest areas of the northern part of the European USSR are drained by the Severnaya [Northern] Dvina and its tributaries [Fig. 6]. On the Severnaya Dvina the chief commodity moved is lumber for Archangel. Saboteurs used to float lumber haphazardly down the river. By this method tremendous quantities were lost, much was carried out to sea, the river channel was obstructed, and vessels were wrecked. The Government prohibited uncontrolled floating on the Severnaya Dvina and other arterial rivers. The fleet of tugboats was increased substantially in order to provide for the hauling of lumber.

The creation of the Stalin White Sea to Baltic Canal [Fig. 78] has had enormous significance for the development of water transport in the North. The canal extends from Povenets on Lake Onega to the town of Soroka [Belomorsk] on the shore of the White Sea. It greatly shortens the route between Leningrad and the White Sea [Fig. 5]: from Leningrad to Archangel by 2,170 nautical miles, or 76%; from Leningrad to Spitsbergen by 920 miles, or 33%. The distance from Archangel to Hamburg is shortened by 406 miles, or 23%. Through Lake Onega and the Mariinsk system the canal connects the White Sea with the Volga Basin, allowing a marked increase in freight turnover. Along the canal from north to south move apatite and nepheline, diabase, marble, fish, and lumber. In the opposite direction go oil, grain, and industrial goods.

In the northeastern part of the European USSR, navigation is developing on the Pechora River. On it are hauled lumber cargoes, coal from Vorkuta, and oil from Ukhta [Fig. 6].

The upper waters of the Kama, the Pechora, and the Vychegda are to be joined by means of dams built on all three rivers and the creation of a large reservoir on the water divide [Fig. 6]. The projected construction of a dam on the upper Kama (at Solikamsk) under the Third Five-Year Plan is of great importance in this connection.

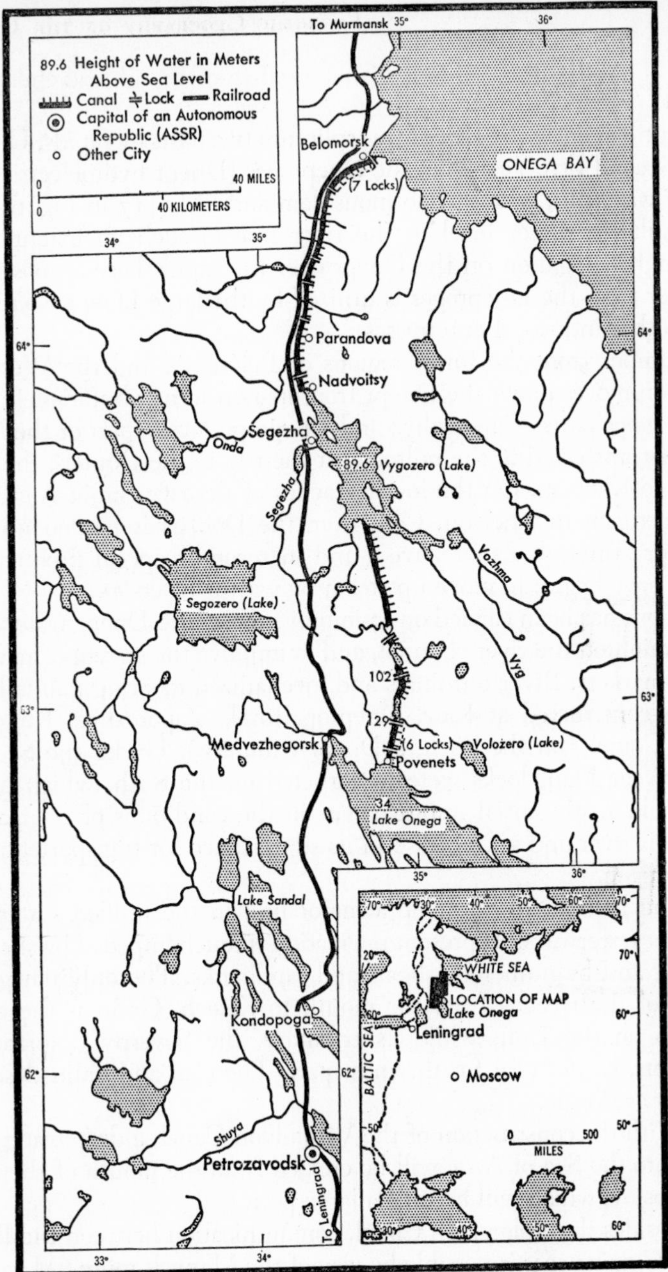

Fig. 78. The Stalin White Sea to Baltic Canal

Dnepr and Don Basins

Until recently the Dnepr was split into two parts by rapids. Under the Second Five-Year Plan the Dneproges [Dnepr hydroelectric station] was built, with its enormous dam and locks [17 in Fig. 6]. As a result the water level in the river rose to such an extent that through navigation on the Dnepr over the rapids became possible. Power from the Dneproges is utilized by the large Dnepr Combine and other industrial enterprises.

Lumber from the forest regions of Belorussia and the Western Region moves down the Dnepr from its northern tributaries. In the big Dnepr ports—Zaporozhye and Dnepropetrovsk—part of the lumber is transferred to the railroad for the trip to the Donbas; the rest goes to Kherson. On the lower reaches of the river grain is carried downstream to Kherson. Coal from the Donbas is hauled up the Dnepr (through Zaporozhye), and in recent years oil products as well have begun to move upstream by way of Kherson.

Work has been carried on to improve the entire Dnepr waterway, to straighten the river channel, and to improve the system of navigation markers. River terminals and mechanized mooring points have been constructed at Kiev, Dnepropetrovsk, Zaporozhye, Kherson, and Gomel (on the Sozh, a Dnepr tributary). Under the Second Five-Year Plan, locks were constructed on the Sozh, which made possible a substantial improvement in the conditions of navigation on this river and an increase in its significance for transportation in Belorussia.

The Don should become a major link in the unified system of Soviet waterways. At present navigation is much impeded by shallow water and by numerous shoals and sandbanks. The only navigable part of the river is from the mouth to Kalach. Grain is the chief cargo on the Don, while its tributary, the Severny (Northern) Donets, carries coal for the most part. The coal and grain descend as far as Rostov.

With the construction of the Volga-Don Canal, a deep-water outlet into the Sea of Azov will be created from the mouth of the Don at Rostov, which will become a large port.

Besides the Volga-Don Canal, communication between the Black and Caspian seas is possible by way of the Manych route (M in Fig. 6.]. Under the Second Five-Year Plan work was carried on in its western sector—from the Don along the Western Manych to the village of Divnoye. Two dams have been built which have raised the water level in the Western Manych. In the future, plans call for the construction of a canal through the Kalmyk Steppe to the Caspian Sea. The water supply for this canal will come from the Kuban and Terek rivers through special feeder channels.

River Routes of Siberia and the Far East

The chief rivers of Siberia and the Far East—the Ob and Irtysh, the Yenisey, and the Lena—flow northward [Fig. 5]. In their upper courses they cross the Trans-Siberian Railway, while their estuaries open onto the Northern Sea Route. As yet, however, they are little utilized for through traffic over their entire length.

The Ob and Irtysh constitute one of the longest river routes in the world, measuring 5,206 km. The Ob is navigable from the junction of the Biya and the Katun, while the Irtysh is navigable throughout its course within the USSR. The chief freight traffic on these rivers is lumber, which moves upstream to Novosibirsk and Omsk, and downstream on the lower course of the Ob to Novy Port. Grain moves downstream along the Irtysh to Semipalatinsk and Omsk, and downstream along the Ob to Novosibirsk and beyond, to supply the Far North. Other outstanding cargoes are oil, which is transferred from the railroad to the waterway (for the most part at Omsk), Kuznetsk coal, and salt.

The Yenisey is navigable for a distance of 3,157 km. from its mouth almost to the border of China. Lumber is the chief cargo. It is carried downstream with the current to Igarka, where sawmills are located and transfer to seagoing vessels takes place. Traffic to Igarka and below includes also a number of other cargoes to supply the Far North—metals and metal products, grain, vegetables, livestock, and kerosene.

Communication with the Yakut ASSR is maintained on the Lena. Since the railroad does not reach the river, freight must be hauled overland to it. Until recently freight was hauled to Kachug and Zhigalovo on the upper waters of the river, to which steamers could not navigate. It then had to be floated on small rowing-barges to Kirensk (beyond which it could be moved under power). This complicated the traffic movement and increased the expense of hauls. Recently the new Angara-Lena highway was built to Ust-Kut, from which freight can move in barges and steamships. Freight turnover on the Lena is increasing rapidly. Large-tonnage cargoes move downstream with the current to supply the Far North, while furs and gold move upstream.

With the development of navigation on the Northern Sea Route, imports are beginning to reach Yakutsk from the north through the mouth of the Lena.

In recent years the Kolyma River and the lower courses of the Khatanga, Indigirka, and other northern rivers have begun to be used for transport.

In the Far East, navigation is developing vigorously on the Amur. On the banks of this river and a number of its tributaries are the largest settlements in the Far East, on which its great transportation significance depends. Lumber rafts move along the Amur, as well as building materials, grain, salt, oil products, and coal.

River Routes of Central Asia and Southern Kazakhstan

In the Aral Basin, the Amu-Darya in conjunction with the Aral Sea, and the Ili River in conjunction with Lake Balkhash, are important transportation routes. The great Syr-Darya, which is paralleled by a railroad, is used chiefly for irrigation.

The Amu-Darya is distinguished by a very rapid current, numerous sandbanks, and a shifting channel, all of which make navigation very difficult. It is maintained with the aid of small native boats, which have begun to be replaced in recent years by motor vessels. The Amu-Darya and the Aral Sea have especially great significance for the Kara-Kalpak ASSR, which has no railroads and is cut off from the south and east by the sands of the Kara-Kum and Kyzyl-Kum [Figs. 4 and 83].

From the station at Chardzhou on the Ashkhabad Railroad oil, lumber, grain, textiles, and other goods are carried to Kara-Kalpakia. Cotton and fish move out of Kara-Kalpakia over the Amu-Darya, the Aral Sea, and the Orenburg Railroad.

Navigation on Lake Balkhash has developed in conjunction with the construction of the Balkhash Copper-smelting Combine. The Ili River handles foreign trade with Sinkiang by way of Kuldzha.

SECTION 5. MARITIME TRANSPORT

The advantages of water transport are even more apparent in maritime than in river transport. The considerably greater capacity of maritime vessels, the complete absence of expenses for maintaining routes (sometimes fairly big in the case of river transport), and the relatively low requirements in labor force and capital investment (per unit of work) result in a much lower level of transit cost. Sea traffic has proved profitable over considerable distances. In addition, a big advantage of maritime transport is that a number of large Soviet seaports do not freeze in winter, and as a result communication can be maintained by sea the year around.

Freight Turnover of Maritime Transport

More than two-thirds of the maritime traffic is carried by ships of the Soviet merchant fleet. In 1937 they carried 29.4 million tons and achieved a turnover of 37 million [billion?] ton-kilometers.

The structure of maritime traffic has altered sharply. The international trade in coal has changed from an import to an export traffic. The import of metals, manufactured articles, and machines during the years of the First Five-Year Plan increased rapidly as the country underwent industrialization, but eventually began to decline with the completion of this phase under the Second Five-Year Plan and to give way to export of machines and metals. The importation of chemicals has stopped almost completely; under the Second Five-Year Plan chemical products began to be exported. Considerable exports of apatite and potassium salts are beginning to appear. The biggest exports by weight are oil and lumber, but even here the nature of the export traffic has altered. Timber, for example, formerly went out almost unprocessed, while now it leaves largely as lumber. The export of grain has decreased significantly.

Oil, coal, building materials, salt, and grain are transported in coastwise navigation.

Maritime Fleet

Construction of the maritime fleet, which underwent a fivefold reduction during the years of the Intervention and the Civil War, developed vigorously beginning with the First Five-Year Plan. At the beginning of the Third Five-Year Plan the load capacity of the maritime fleet had substantially surpassed the prewar level, and was more than three times the 1929 level. An increasingly large proportion of the fleet consists of refrigerator ships, timber carriers, oil tankers, etc., constructed according to the last word in shipbuilding technique. The proportion of Diesel motor ships, which already constitute almost half the fleet, is increasing.

The task of all workers in maritime transport is the struggle to complete the reorganization of the fleet, to raise the level of performance, to eliminate the aftereffects of sabotage, and to increase the productivity of labor through a broad development of the Stakhanovite movement.

Principal Sea Routes

Let us examine the principal sea routes of the USSR. The ports of the White and Barents seas handle about 10% of the freight turnover of all Soviet seaports [Fig. 5]. Outgoing cargoes are chiefly timber, and to a lesser extent grain, apatite, and other freight. Incoming cargoes consist primarily of Spitsbergen [Svalbard] coal and fish. The chief port on the White Sea is Archangel, located at the delta of the Severnaya (Northern) Dvina. The ice-free port of Murmansk, which developed under the Soviet regime, is on the Barents Sea. It has great economic significance, especially in winter, when the Leningrad port is frozen. Both Archangel and Murmansk have been expanded and reconstructed considerably under the Stalin Five-Year Plans. New mooring points and warehouses have been built, and mechanized equipment has been installed. A new port is being built on the Pechora (Naryan-Mar). Through this port move timber and coal as well as supplies for the region adjoining the Pechora.

Through the Baltic Sea stretches the shortest route to the major maritime trading centers of Europe. The share of that sea in the freight turnover of Soviet seaports is 5%. As the most important route for foreign imports into the USSR, it carries half of all the goods entering the country from abroad by sea. Timber and, to a lesser extent, grain are the principal exports through the Baltic. Among the cargoes moving from one Soviet sea to another (in grand cabotage), oil from the Black Sea is especially prominent. All Soviet freight turnover on the Baltic Sea passes through the port of Leningrad, which plays an especially important role in the development of Soviet maritime transport.

Leningrad is linked with the most important industrial centers of the USSR by a network of railroads and river routes. The port of Leningrad has undergone considerable reconstruction. The depth of the sea channel leading from the Gulf of Finland has been increased. A mechanized deep-water harbor for timber export has been built; the transshipment of grain has been mechanized; new refrigerators, elevators, and warehouses have been built; and numerous cranes and other equipment have been installed. After its reconstruction, the Leningrad port had advanced to the level of the finest ports in the world in degree of mechanization and in equipment. It has a large auxiliary and technical fleet. With the aid of icebreakers the navigation season is being lengthened considerably.

The Black Sea holds second place in volume of freight turnover, accounting for more than a fourth of the total. Its outgoing cargoes include oil, grain, manganese, timber, cement, coal, metals, machines, and chemicals. Ships operating between Black Sea ports (in petty cabotage) transport oil cargoes from the Caucasus to Odessa, Nikolayev, and Sevastopol; grain from Odessa, Nikolayev, Kherson, and Novorossiisk; and cement from Novorossiisk [Fig. 6]. Oil and cement are transported in grand cabotage, from the Black Sea to Leningrad and the Far East.

The Black Sea ports are ice-free. Two of them, Kherson and Nikolayev, situated at the Dnepr-Bug estuary, are covered with ice in winter; but the coating is not thick, and navigation can be maintained the year around with the aid of icebreakers. (In warm winters these are not needed.) During the years of the Stalin Five-Year Plans the ports have received new technical equipment. Refrigerators have been built at Kherson and Odessa, and grain elevators at Nikolayev and Kherson. At Tuapse, Odessa, and Kherson (which have become points for transshipment of Caucasus oil), new berths have been equipped for handling oil cargoes. At Novorossiisk the elevator has been reconstructed, installations for cement loading have been improved, a berth for timber shipments has been constructed, and a refrigerator has been installed. All these ports have received a number of mechanical devices: grain-loading gear, conveyers, and cranes. The port of Batumi, which exports oil, and the port of Poti, which exports manganese, have both been reconstructed. The port of Ochemchiri has been built for the shipment of coal. A new port is being built at Sochi.

The Sea of Azov, which is shallow and freezes for more than three months in winter, has a small freight turnover (7 to 8% of the total for all seaports). Prior to the war, grain was the chief export;

now coal outranks it. Over the Sea of Azov moves coal for the Kerch metallurgical plant, and Chiatura ore for the Mariupol plant. Construction of a new mechanized port has been completed on the Sea of Azov at the Mariupol metallurgical plant at the mouth of the Kalmius River. At Mariupol, coal is loaded for export abroad and to Kerch, while ore is unloaded. Rostov should become a major seaport. A deep-water approach from the sea is needed there.

The Caspian Sea occupies first place in maritime freight turnover, accounting for about half of the USSR total. More than four-fifths of the hauls are coastal shipments of oil from Baku to Astrakhan for further shipment up the Volga or to Makhach-Kala, where it is transferred to the Makhach-Kala to Grozny pipe line. The port of Makhach-Kala is being reconstructed.

Freight turnover on the Pacific Ocean comprises 5 or 6% of the USSR total. The traffic consists of coal, oil cake, salt, and fish; cargoes of Sakhalin oil are increasing every year. Most of the freight passes through the first-class port of Vladivostok, which is kept open all year around, in winter by the use of icebreakers. A new port, Nogayevo, has been built on the Okhotsk Sea.

The Northern Sea Route

The Northern Sea Route is of tremendous importance to the country. It has created for the first time a through route along Soviet shores between the European USSR and the Far East, and has provided a reliable and cheap sea outlet for the basins of the Ob, Yenisey, Lena, and Kolyma, which have enormous natural resources.

The route from the Barents Sea to the Kara Sea varies with ice conditions:[10] it passes either through one of the straits between the seas—Matochkin Shar [11], the Kara Gate [10], or Yugorsky Shar [15]—or around [the north end of] Novaya Zemlya and past Cape Zhelaniya [13]. It proceeds across either the southern or the northern part of the Kara Sea to Severnaya Zemlya [23], through Vilkitsky Strait [25], and past Cape Chelyuskin [26] into the Laptev Sea. It then continues on past the New Siberian Islands [29] in the East Siberian Sea, through De Long Strait [32] into the Chukotsk Sea, and past Cape Dezhnev [34] into the Pacific Ocean.

Navigation conditions of the Arctic Ocean are difficult. The

[10] [Number references in the description of the Northern Sea Route refer to locations on Fig. 5, p. 24.]

period of navigation is short, lasting seventy to one hundred and twenty days (usually from July to October); during the rest of the year the ice cover makes it impossible. The ice conditions in different sectors of the route are dissimilar. The Barents and Kara seas, which are protected on the north by islands, have a longer ice-free period than the Laptev Sea, and especially than the East Siberian and Chukotsk seas. The latter are open to the heavy Arctic ice pack, which accumulates over many years, driven down by the north winds.

In the western part of the Northern Sea Route, annual Kara expeditions have been instituted under the Soviet regime. These make possible cheap exportation of timber from Siberia by way of the Ob and the Yenisey. For the transfer of timber from river ships to seagoing vessels, Novy Port was created on the Ob, and Ust-Yeniseisky Port [U] on the Yenisey. Subsequently Igarka, 700 km. from the mouth of the Yenisey, was selected as the chief base for the Kara expeditions. Igarka has important advantages over both Novy Port and Ust-Yeniseisky Port. It is fully accessible to seagoing ships and at the same time allows safe passage for rafts and river vessels. The town of Igarka, with a population of 20,000, is one of the cultural and industrial centers of the Far North. With the development of navigation on the Northern Sea Route, other important centers are also growing on the banks of the Yenisey and the shores of the Kara Sea. At Ust-Yeniseisky Port a fish-canning factory has been built, while the mining of coal and the production of nonferrous metals is developing at Norilsk [No]. On Dickson Island [16], with its convenient port for seagoing vessels, a large radio broadcasting and receiving unit and a geophysical observatory, have been created to coordinate the work of a number of polar stations; on the shore of the Kara Sea, an important mineral raw material, fluorspar, is mined at the port of Amderma [A].

The eastern sector of the Northern Sea Route has begun to be utilized for direct shipment of freight from the west to the mouths of the Lena, Kolyma, and other rivers, replacing the former voyage around the whole of Europe and Asia to Vladivostok and then to the Far North. The direct route greatly speeds and cheapens transportation. In its eastern sector there are several convenient ports and bases for seagoing vessels: Tiksi, at the mouth of the Lena; Ambarchik, at the mouth of the Kolyma; Providenia Bay [35], on the Chukotsk

Peninsula. In this part of the route also the extraction of mineral resources is being mastered—of salt and oil at Nordvik and at Kozhevnikov Bay, and of coal at Ugolnaya Bay [38] and Khatanga Inlet [27]. This coal, like that of the other coal-mining bases of the North, is of tremendous importance for navigation, assuring the supply of maritime vessels with local fuel.

Navigation on the Northern Sea Route is increasing every year. In 1932–1934 the *Sibiryakov, Chelyuskin,* and *Litke* made their first through voyages. During the period of the Second Five-Year Plan more than twenty vessels made the trip through the entire route. Each year hundreds of thousands of tons of freight are hauled; the total for the six-year period 1933–1938 was 1,188 thousand tons.

Navigation has been developing also on the northern rivers. Under the Soviet regime exploitation has begun of such large rivers as the Kolyma, Pyasina, Indigirka, Olenek, Yana, and Anabar. The river traffic of the Glavsevmorput [Chief Administration of the Northern Sea Route] constituted about 200 thousand tons in 1937, as compared with 57.3 thousand tons in 1933.

For the full utilization of the Northern Sea Route further development is necessary in setting up ports and lighthouses; in the careful study of the conditions of navigation and ice movement; in supplying the route with icebreakers, airplanes (that irreplaceable medium for ice observation), and air bases; and finally in the training of an experienced working force. The dense net of polar radio stations is playing an enormous role.

The 18th Party Congress gave as a directive "by the end of the Third Five-Year Plan to turn the Northern Sea Route into a normally functioning water artery, furnishing systematic communication with the Far East."

SECTION 6. HIGHWAY TRANSPORT

Motor Vehicles

Motor transport in the USSR was created under the Soviet power. Prior to the war [World War I] there were about 9 thousand motor vehicles in Russia. Toward the beginning of the First Five-Year Plan there were 19 thousand, almost all of foreign make. During the years of the Stalin Five-Year Plans, however, a powerful motor vehicle industry was created. The construction of the Stalin Automobile Plant in Moscow, the Molotov Automobile Plant in Gorky, and the reconstruction of the plant in Yaroslavl made possible a wide development of motor vehicle production. At the beginning of 1938 the number of motor vehicles was about 760 thousand; by the end of the Third Five-Year Plan it will have reached 1,700 thousands.

Soviet plants produce the 1½-ton GAZ truck, the 3-ton ZIS truck, the 5-ton YaG, and the M-1 and ZIS-101 passenger cars. New types of trucks, passenger cars, busses, and small vehicles have been constructed. Output is increasing in gas-generator vehicles, which operate on locally available wood fuel instead of gasoline hauled from a distance.

In Tsarist Russia almost all the motor vehicles, insignificant in number, were concentrated in the large cities of St. Petersburg and Moscow. In other parts of the country, especially in the East, the motor vehicles could be totaled in one-digit numbers. Today Soviet motor vehicles are distributed differently. They are directed to industrial establishments, new construction projects, kolkhozes, machine tractor stations, and other divisions of farm construction in outlying areas.

The introduction of the automobile has been of tremendous importance in the industrialization of the country and in the socialist transformation of agriculture.

Truck transportation is increasing rapidly. In 1932 it amounted to 113 million tons; in 1937, to 800 million. The 18th Party Congress gave the order to increase truck transportation 4.6 times by the end of the Third Five-Year Plan. The most important task of the People's Commissariats of Motor Transport, which have been created in the Union republics, is the improvement in the utilization of available vehicles and the development of motor freight transfer.

Roads and Road Construction

The increasing role of the motor vehicle has created an especially urgent need for the construction of good roads and the improvement of those already existing.

During the years of the Stalin Five-Year Plans, many new roads have been built. In 1913 there were no graded dirt roads at all; by 1928 these measured 1–1.5 thousand km., and by 1938, 330.9 thousand km. In 1913 there were 23.5 thousand km. of hard-surfaced roads; in 1928, 31.3 thousand km.; and in 1938, 87.5 thousand km. In 1938 there were 936.4 thousand km. of natural dirt roads.

The tremendous network of dirt roads may be divided into those of significance at the oblast or raion level, and subsidiary roads of lesser importance. These roads serve as approaches to stations and wharves, lead to factories, sovkhozes, and machine tractor stations, and, in general, carry out the function of collecting goods in the agricultural districts. The poor condition of many such roads, the decline in passableness during the spring and fall, and the high cost of haulage on them constitute a serious obstacle to the development of local production and result in tremendous yearly losses to the national economy. The improvement of local roads is very important for developing agriculture, increasing the exchange of commodities, and raising the level of local industrial production. The People's Commissariats of Motor Transport must expedite in every way possible the construction of new roads and the improvement of those already existing.

In pace with the increasing use of motor vehicles in the USSR, the length of motor transport hauls will increase continuously, and the proportion of through traffic in both passengers and freight will rise correspondingly. Even with the growth of through service, however, the most intensive freight traffic, just as at present, will be concentrated on short sectors of the suburban road systems of large cities. The nearer to a large city, the greater the traffic density.

The largest road center is Moscow, from which highways radiate in many directions [Fig. 79].

Through Moscow passes the important arterial highway Leningrad-Moscow-Kharkov-Rostov-Ordzhonikidze [Dzaudzhikau]-Tbilisi. This highway is being reconstructed and adapted for heavy traffic by the construction of improved surfaces in a number of sectors. Two first-class, wide, asphalt-concrete arterial highways are being built from Moscow to Minsk and Kiev. These will be adapted for rapid motor traffic, with hotels, filling stations, and repair shops. An important highway leads to Gorky, with its automobile factory. The road from Gorky to the Urals will be rebuilt and transformed into a major motor highway. Shorter roads out of Moscow include the Yaroslavl, Ryazan, and Dmitrov highways.

Many new paved and improved dirt roads have been built in the Ukraine in recent years—in the Donbas, the Dnepropetrovsk area,

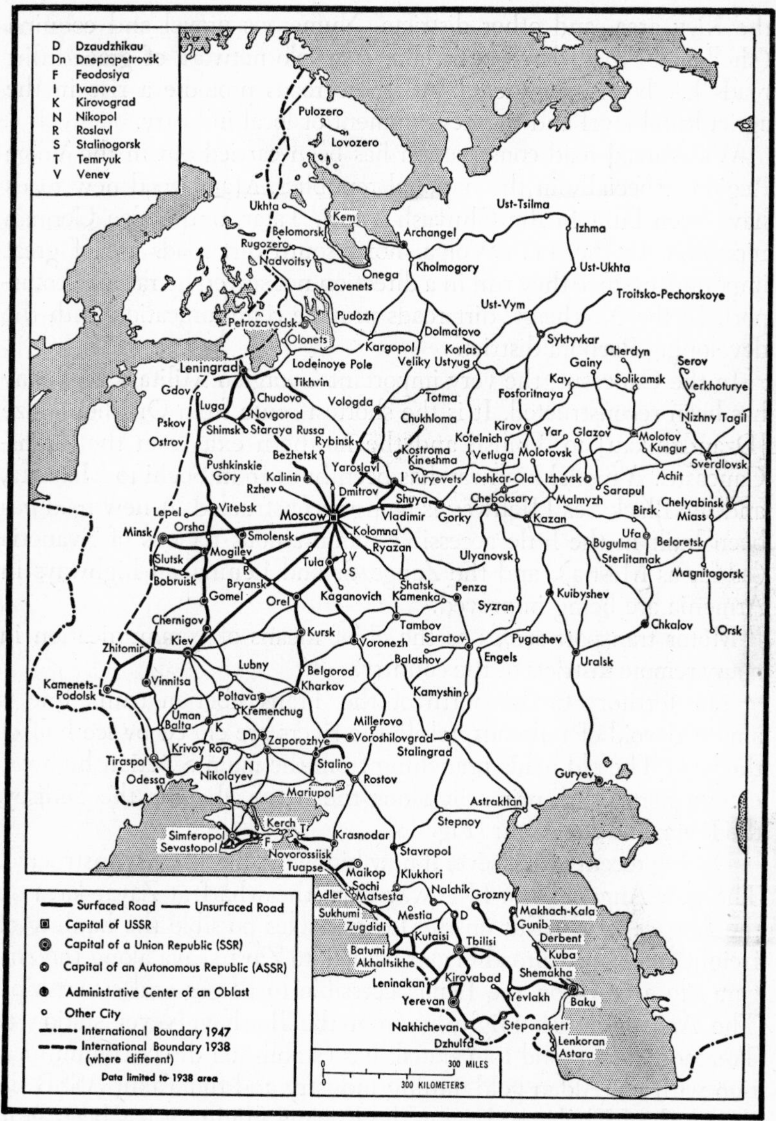

FIG. 79. Automobile Routes of the European Part of the USSR

the Kiev area, and other districts. Numerous gravel and coquina (shell-rock) roads have been laid. A whole network of graded dirt roads has been constructed. All these roads promote a rise in the agricultural level and the development of local industry.

Widespread road construction has been carried out in the Volga Region, especially in the national republics. Many good new roads have been built in the Chuvash, Mari, Tatar, and Volga German republics. In the Trans-Volga, north-south dirt roads are of great importance, since they run in a direction not served by railroad transport. In the Northeast, dirt roads provide communication with the developing Pechora district.

In the Caucasus, the very important Georgian Military Highway has been reconstructed. It is the shortest route from Ordzhonikidze [Dzaudzhikau] to Tbilisi, and the northern exit from the Trans-Caucasus. A model highway has been built from Sochi to Matsesta, and the Black Sea Highway is being reconstructed. A new road has been built in the little accessible mountainous regions of Svanetia (as far as Mestia), and the Zangezur and Leninakan highways in Armenia are being improved.

Motor transport serves as the chief means of communication in many remote districts of the country.

The territory to the north of the Trans-Siberian trunk line is almost devoid of railroads, while the rivers are closed by ice half of the year. The old roads branching from the main Siberian highway extend northward, primarily along the Irtysh, the Ob, the Yenisey, the Lena, and the Amur [Fig. 80].

During recent years, several new highways have been constructed. The new Angara-Lena Highway from the wharf at Zayarskaya on the Angara to Ust-Kut on the Lena, makes possible the hauling of freight from the railroad (from Irkutsk to Zayarskaya along the Angara) to a point on the Lena accessible to barges and steamships. The Amur-Yakutsk Highway from the Bolshoy Never station to Tommot and beyond to Yakutsk has established direct communication with the Aldan gold-mining industry and the Yakut ASSR. In the north of Khabarovsk Kray the Kolyma Highway has been built for Magadan (Nogayevo) to the Kolyma River. In Maritime Kray the Khabarovsk-Vladivostok Highway has been constructed.

A number of new roads have been built and are being built to the borders of Mongolia, Tannu-Tuva, and China (Sinkiang). In

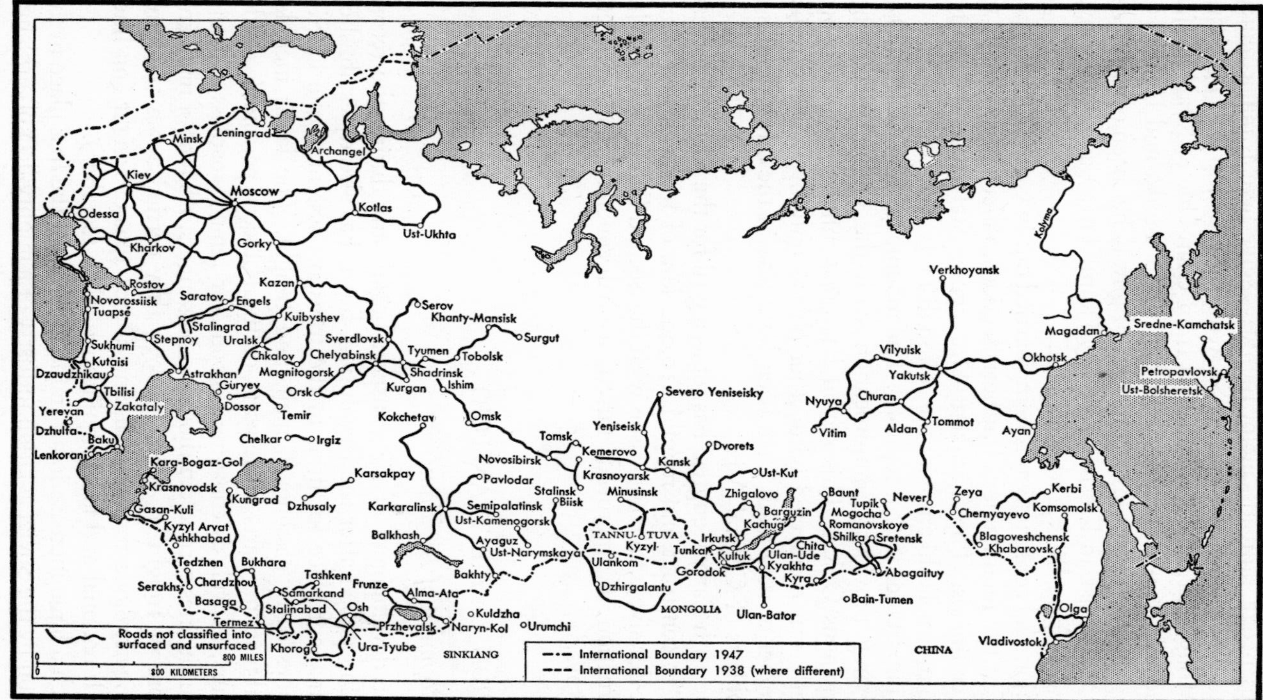

FIG. 80. Automobile Routes of the Asiatic Part of the USSR

the absence of railroads, motor highways serve here as major routes for the foreign trade of the USSR with these countries. Highways into Mongolia from the north lead from Ulan-Ude to Kyakhta and beyond to Ulan-Bator; and from Kultuk to Tunka and beyond to Dzhirgalantu (Ulyasutay). The Usa Highway has been constructed from Minusinsk to Krasny [Kyzyl] (Tannu-Tuva) and the Chuya Highway, from Biisk into Mongolia.

Major road construction is being carried out in Central Asia, especially in the mountainous southern sections, where it is difficult to build railroads. The Tashkent–Ura-Tyube–Stalinabad Highway, which unites Tashkent with the cotton districts of Tadzhikistan, is of great importance to that republic. The mountain highway from Osh to Khorog provides communication with the Gorno-Badakhshan Autonomous Oblast. This region has great mineral resources, but formerly was connected with other oblasts only by winding trails. A number of new roads have been built also in the other republics and oblasts of Central Asia.

The 18th Party Congress has set as a goal for the Third Five-Year Plan "to construct and rebuild 210,000 km. of roadway and to increase decisively, in comparison with the Second Five-Year Plan, the construction of improved, tarred, asphalt-concrete, and concrete highways."

SECTION 7. AIR TRANSPORT

Development of Air Transport

The development of air transport began only during the reconstruction period after the Revolution, but it has already established a permanent place for itself in the transport system of the USSR. Air lines carry passengers, mail, and freight. The latter includes crucial machine parts, spare parts, cultural objects, perishable goods, and furs, as well as consumers' goods for remote roadless districts. While air lines carried 0.2 thousand passengers, 1.8 tons of mail, and 0.1 tons of freight in 1923, in 1937 they carried 203.2 thousand passengers, 8,960 tons of mail, and 36,400 tons of freight (on lines of both national and local significance taken together).

Such a large increase in air traffic was due in the first place to the creation by the Soviet aviation industry of a mighty fleet of airplanes.

At the beginning of the Second Five-Year Plan the nine-seat passenger plane PC-9, the six-passenger K-5 and Stal-3, the three-passenger P-5 mail plane, the six-passenger flying boat MP-1, and others were operating on the air lines. At the beginning of the Third Five-Year Plan, the air fleet began to be enlarged by a series of fast planes of new types—the twenty-one-passenger PS-84, the twelve-passenger PS-89, the ten-passenger PS-35, the G-2 cargo plane (with a working load of 3.4 tons), and others.

The Air-Line Network

The length of air lines also has increased considerably: in 1928 it measured only 9.5 thousand km., but by 1938 it had reached 106.1 thousand km. (including lines of local significance and lines of the Chief Administration of the Northern Sea Route).

The geographic distribution of the network is determined on the one hand by the necessity of establishing rapid communication between Moscow and the republics, krays, and oblasts of the USSR, and on the other by the problems of serving remote localities with poorly developed communication systems.

The Moscow-Vladivostok arterial air line passes across the entire USSR [Fig. 81]. After continuous through traffic has been established on it, it will become the most important aerial artery of the USSR. Its importance is increased by branch lines to Magnitogorsk, Kolpashov (for shipping fur), Kemerovo, Yakutsk, Komsomolsk, and Sakhalin. At present, traffic is densest on the Moscow-Sverdlovsk sector.

Another very important arterial air line leads south from Moscow to Kharkov-Rostov-Baku-Tbilisi. This trunk route links Moscow with the Ukraine, the North Caucasus, and the republics of the Trans-Caucasus, and supports considerable traffic, especially in its northern section.

Major lines lead from Moscow to Tashkent by way of Kuibyshev-Aktyubinsk-Dzhusaly, and to Alma-Ata by way of Sverdlovsk and the new industrial centers of Kazakhstan—Karaganda and Balkhash. Other lines lead from Moscow to Leningrad (for transporting the matrices of the central newspapers), Minsk, the Donbas, the Crimea, Stalingrad, and Astrakhan. The Moscow-Astrakhan line was extended in 1939 by way of Baku to Ashkhabad, offering an enormous saving in time over the former route by way of Tashkent.

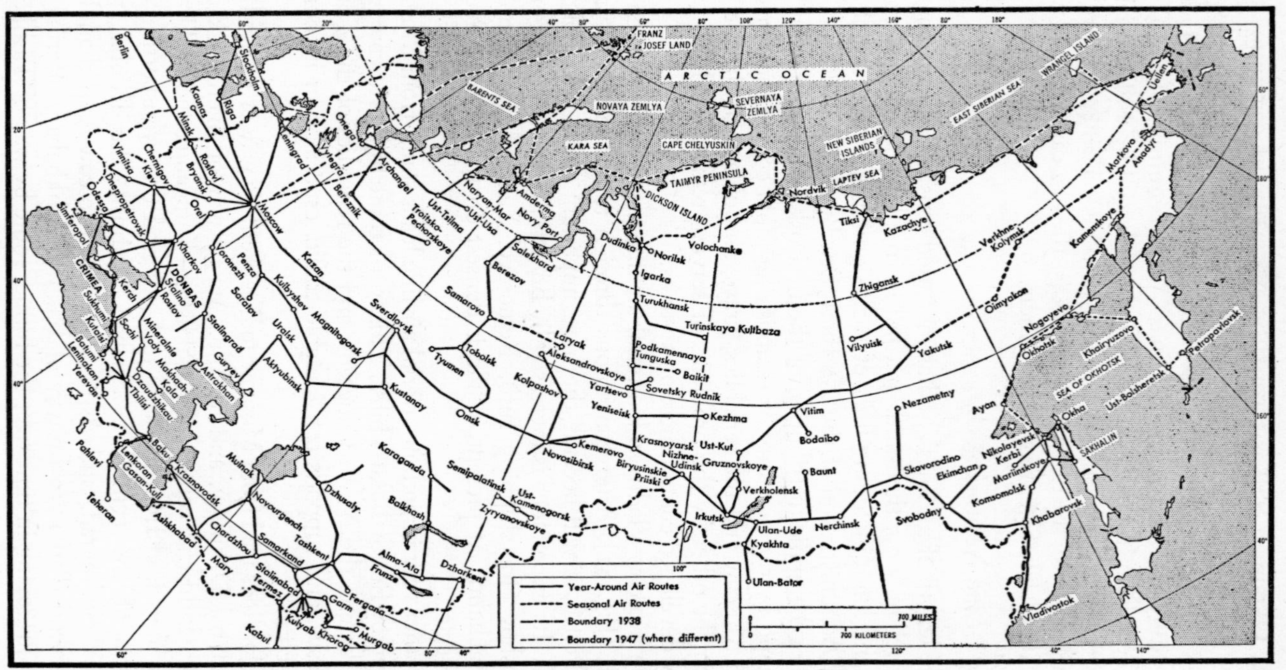

* Fig. 81. Air Routes, 1937 (Adapted from *Great Soviet World Atlas*, Vol. I, Plate 165)

The Ukrainian SSR is covered by a dense aerial communication network, linked with the southern trunk line. This includes the following lines: Kiev-Kharkov, Kiev-Rostov, Kharkov-Odessa, and Kiev-Simferopol.

In the Trans-Caucasus there are lines running from Tbilisi to Yerevan, from Tbilisi to Kutaisi and Sukhumi, from Yerevan to Leninakan, and from Baku to Lenkoran.

Air lines have especially great significance where other types of transport are weakly developed. Here airplanes not only offer a huge saving in time compared with the trip over poor wagon roads, but frequently supply the only means of mechanical transport.

In Archangel Oblast an airplane can fly from Archangel to Naryan-Mar in five hours, but the same trip takes twelve to fifteen days by road. In Krasnoyarsk Kray an airplane makes the trip from Krasnoyarsk to Igarka in ten hours, instead of more than four days by steamer. An airplane flies from Irkutsk to Yakutsk in twenty-five flying hours, while the trip by overland transport sometimes takes weeks. In the Far East, the airplane makes possible much faster communication with Sakhalin and the coast of the Sea of Okhotsk.

Air transport has developed considerably in Central Asia, where it serves the relatively inaccessible mountain districts. The following lines stand out: Tashkent-Frunze, Stalinabad-Kulyab, Stalinabad-Garm, Samarkand-Termez, and Chardzhou-Muinak. In South Kazakhstan there are lines which carry considerable freight traffic.

Side by side with the development of lines of national significance, the great work of creating lines of local significance has been carried on and is still in progress. These lines must provide communication between raion, oblast, and kray centers and industrial points, sovkhozes, and kolkhozes.

Air transport is rather important in furnishing communication between the USSR and other states. Among the international lines are the following: Moscow-Berlin, Moscow-Kaunas, Baku-Pahlevi-Teheran, Tashkent-Kabul, and Ulan-Ude—Ulan-Bator.

The 18th Party Congress has set as a task for the Third Five-Year Plan "to raise the level of technical equipment of the aerial trunk lines, expanding and improving the ground installations."

Heroic Soviet fliers are laying new air routes. There is exceptional significance in the flight to the North Pole of a whole squadron of heavy planes, carrying the four daring Heroes of the Soviet Union,

Papanin, Krenkel, Shirshov, and Fedorov, and in the equipping of the "North Pole" station. Heroes of the Soviet Union Chkalov and Gromov flew across the North Pole to the United States, and Gromov with his companions broke the world record for straight-line distance flight. Heroes of the Soviet Union Kokkinaki and Bryadinsky and three women, Heroes of the Soviet Union Grizodubova, Osipenko, and Raskova, flew in twenty-four hours in standard-make planes from Moscow to the Far East. In the spring of 1939, Kokkinaki and Gordienko flew in twenty-four hours from Moscow to America across the Atlantic Ocean. All these historic flights, marking an epoch in the development of air transport, demonstrate the heroism and the eminent skill and culture of Soviet pilots, the Stalinite falcons of our country. They are ready, if it becomes necessary, to transfer from civilian to military planes and destroy the enemy, wherever he may be.

Appendix I STATISTICAL TABLES

TABLE A1. [URBAN, RURAL, AND TOTAL] POPULATION OF THE USSR [BY REPUBLICS] ACCORDING TO THE CENSUSES OF 1926 AND 1939

Union Republics	1926		
	Urban	Rural	Total
RSFSR	16,785,189	76,672,807	93,457,996
Ukrainian SSR	5,373,553	23,669,381	29,042,934
Belorussian SSR	847,830[a]	4,135,410	4,983,240
Azerbaidzhan SSR	649,557	1,664,187	2,313,744
Georgian SSR	594,221	2,083,012	2,677,233
Armenian SSR	167,098	714,192	881,290
Turkmen SSR	136,982	861,172	998,154
Uzbek SSR	1,012,274	3,553,158	4,565,432
Tadzhik SSR	106,003	926,213	1,032,216
Kazakh SSR	519,074	5,554,905	6,073,979
Kirgiz SSR	122,333	879,364	1,001,697
USSR	26,314,114	120,713,801	147,027,915

[a] [848,830 in original, obviously a misprint.]

TABLE A1. *CONTINUED*

Union Republics	1939 Urban	1939 Rural	1939 Total	1939 Index (1926 = 100) Urban	Rural	Total
RSFSR	36,658,008	72,620,606	109,278,614	218.4	94.7	116.9
Ukrainian SSR	11,195,620	19,764,601	30,960,221	208.3	83.5	106.6
Belorussian SSR	1,372,522	4,195,454	5,567,976	161.9	101.5	111.7
Azerbaidzhan SSR	1,160,723	2,049,004	3,209,727	178.7	123.1	138.7
Georgian SSR	1,066,560	2,475,729	3,542,289	179.5	118.9	132.3
Armenian SSR	366,416	915,183	1,281,599	219 3	128.1	145.4
Turkmen SSR	416,376	837,609	1,253,985	304.0	97.3	125.6
Uzbek SSR	1,445,064	4,837,382	6,282,446	142.8	136.1	137.6
Tadzhik SSR	251,882	1,233,209	1,485,091	237.6	133.1	143.9
Kazakh SSR	1,706,150	4,439,787	6,145,937	328.7	79.9	101.2
Kirgiz SSR	270,587	1,188,714	1,459,301	221.2	135.2	145.7
USSR	55,909,908	114,557,278	170,467,186	212.5	94.9	115.9

TABLE A2. [TOTAL POPULATION AND] DENSITY OF POPULATION IN THE USSR [BY OBLASTS AND REPUBLICS] (ACCORDING TO THE CENSUS OF 1939) [a]

[See Fig. 23, p. 186 and Fig. 83 at the back of the book.]

Republics, Krays, Oblasts	Population	Area (Thousand sq. km.)	Density per Sq. Km.
USSR	170,467,186	21,175.2 [b]	8.05
RSFSR	109,278,614	16,510.5 [b]	6.61
Altay Kray	2,520,084	294.0	8.57
Archangel Oblast	1,199,178	652.0	1.84
Bashkir ASSR	3,144,713	140.5	22.38
Buryat-Mongol ASSR	542,170	331.4	1.64
Vologda Oblast	1,662,258	150.0	11.08
Voronezh Oblast	3,551,009	76.7	46.30
Gorky Oblast	3,876,274	89.2	43.46
Dagestan ASSR	930,527	34.0	27.37
Ivanovo Oblast	2,650,383	63.4	41.80
Irkutsk Oblast	1,286,696	922.4	1.39
Kabardino-Balkar ASSR	359,236	12.3	29.20
Kalinin Oblast	3,211,439	106.4	30.18
Kalmyk ASSR	220,723	74.2	2.97
Karelian ASSR	469,145	136.4	3.44
Kirov Oblast	2,226,109	105.5	21.10
Komi ASSR	318,969	374.9	0.85
Krasnodar Kray	3,172,885	81.5	38.93
Krasnoyarsk Kray	1,940,002	2,143.8	0.90
Crimean ASSR	1,126,824	26.0	43.34
Kuibyshev Oblast	2,767,562	96.2 [c]	28.77 [c]
Kursk Oblast	3,196,814	55.7	57.39 [d]
Leningrad Oblast	6,435,076	143.7	44.78
Mari ASSR	579,466 [e]	23.3	24.87
Mordovian ASSR	1,188,598	25.5	46.61
Moscow Oblast	8,918,389	49.4	180.53
Murmansk Oblast	291,188	138.9	2.10
Volga-German ASSR	605,542	28.2	21.47
Novosibirsk Oblast	4,022,671	611.0	6.58
Omsk Oblast	2,366,603	1,440.5	1.64
Ordzhonikidze Kray	1,949,340	101.5	19.20
Orel Oblast	3,482,388	64.4	54.07
Penza Oblast	1,708,656	— [c]	—
Perm [Molotov] Oblast	2,082,166	190.2	10.95

TABLE A2. *CONTINUED*

Republics, Krays, Oblasts	Population	Area (Thousand sq. km.)	Density per Sq. Km.
Maritime Kray	907,220	206.6 [f]	4.39
Rostov Oblast	2,894,038	100.7	28.74
Ryazan Oblast	2,265,873	49.4	45.87
Saratov Oblast	1,798,805	89.6 [c]	20.08 [c]
Sverdlovsk Oblast	2,512,175	189.9	13.23
North Osetian ASSR	328,885	6.2	53.05
Smolensk Oblast	2,690,779	72.2	37.27
Stalingrad Oblast	2,289,049	135.4	16.91
Tambov Oblast	1,882,139	49.9 [c]	37.72 [c]
Tatar ASSR	2,919,423	67.1	43.51
Tula Oblast	2,049,950	31.9	64.26
Udmurt ASSR	1,220,007	38.9	31.36
Khabarovsk Kray	1,430,875	2,572.0 [f]	0.56
Chelyabinsk Oblast	2,802,949	163.5	17.14
Chechen-Ingush ASSR	697,408	15.7	44.42
Chita Oblast	1,159,478	720.0	1.61
Chkalov Oblast	1,677,013	123.8	13.55
Chuvash ASSR	1,077,614	17.9	60.20
Yaroslavl Oblast	2,271,307	63.1	36.00 [g]
Yakut ASSR	400,544	3,030.9	0.13
Ukrainian SSR	30,960,221	445.3	69.53
Belorussian SSR	5,567,976	126.8	43.91
Azerbaidzhan SSR	3,209,727	86.0	37.32
Georgian SSR	3,542,289	69.6	50.90
Armenian SSR	1,281,599	30.0	42.72
Turkmen SSR	1,253,985	443.0	2.83
Uzbek SSR	6,282,446	378.3	16.61
Tadzhik SSR	1,485,091	143.9	10.32
Kazakh SSR	6,145,937	2,744.5	2.24
Kirgiz SSR	1,459,301	196.7	7.42
Autonomous Oblasts [h]			
Adygey (Krasnodar)	241,773 [f]	3.9 [f]	61.99
Cherkess (Ordzhonikidze)	92,534 [f]	3.3 [f]	28.04
Jewish (Khabarovsk)	108,419 [f]	36.8 [f]	2.95
Karachayev (Ordzhonikidze)	149,925 [f]	9.9 [f]	15.14
Khakass (Krasnoyarsk)	270,655 [f]	49.9 [f]	5.42
Oirot [Gorno-Altay] (Altay)	161,431 [f]	93.1 [f]	1.73

[a] The population and area of the Western Ukraine and Western Belorussia are not included. [The order in this table is the same as in the original; in the RSFSR it follows the Russian alphabetical order. For total population of similar units in 1897 and 1926 see Tables A9 and A11; for densities of population in 1913 and 1926 see Tables A10 and A11.]

[b] [The area obtained by adding the figures for the 11 Union republics is 21,174.6 thousand sq. km.; the area obtained by adding the units in the RSFSR is 16,527.8 thousand sq. km.]

[c] [Penza Oblast was formed February 2, 1939, out of parts of Tambov, Kuibyshev, and Saratov oblasts; although the census was taken on January 17, 1939, the population for Penza Oblast was reported separately. Since the areas given for Tambov, Kuibyshev, and Saratov oblasts include the portions transferred to Penza Oblast but the population figures for these oblasts exclude Penza Oblast, it is obvious that the density figures for these oblasts are much too low.]

[d] [21.49 in original, an obvious error.]

[e] [Corrected from 576,466 in original.]

[f] [From *Great Soviet World Atlas, Gazetteer to Vol. I,* Table 13, p. 175–180.]

[g] [35.40 in original.]

[h] [The population and area of each autonomous oblast is included in the above figures for the kray indicated in parenthesis.]

TABLE A3. DISTRIBUTION OF RESERVES AND EXTRACTION OF PEAT BY REGIONS [1937]

REGIONS	RESERVES (in million tons) JAN. 1, 1937	EXTRACTION IN 1937 (thousand tons)
Total for USSR	145,304 [a]	23,821.8
RSFSR	139,997 [b]	19,859.9 [c]
European North	30,935	82.2
Leningrad Oblast	6,928	3,026.2
Kalinin Oblast	1,840	1,473.8
Smolensk and Orel oblasts	620	1,082.3
Moscow, Tula, and Ryazan oblasts	600	5,790.1
Ivanovo and Yaroslavl oblasts	1,472	3,708.4
Kursk, Voronezh, and Tambov oblasts and Mordovian ASSR	151	1,114.2
Kirov Oblast, Tatar and Udmurt ASSR	1,130	156.8
Gorky Oblast	825	1,921.0
Kuibyshev Oblast	70	329.9
Saratov and Stalingrad oblasts and Volga German ASSR	7	34.3
Sverdlovsk Oblast	3,600	959.1
Chelyabinsk Oblast	650	64.1
Bashkir ASSR and Chkalov Oblast	139	119.1
Omsk Oblast	39,375	2.4
Novosibirsk Oblast	37,500	6.0
Eastern Siberia	13,777	—
Far East	375	—
Ukrainian SSR	2,637	1,507.0
Belorussian SSR	2,670	2,445.3
Armenian SSR	— [d]	2.8
Uzbek SSR	— [d]	1.3
Kirgiz SSR	— [d]	5.5

[a] On Jan. 1, 1939, the total peat reserves in the USSR were determined as 150 billion tons.

[b] [The figure for the regions of the RSFSR fall 3 short of equalling the total given.]

[c] [The figures for the regions of the RSFSR exceed the total given by 10.0.]

[d] Data not available [not included in total].

TABLE A4. DISTRIBUTION OF RESERVES OF WOOD FUEL AND SHIPMENT OF FIREWOOD IN 1937 BY REGIONS OF THE USSR [a]

Regions	Reserves of Wood Fuel		Shipment of Firewood in 1937	
	Million Cubic Meters	% of USSR Total	Million Cubic Meters	% of USSR Total
RSFSR	23,736.9 [b]	98.01 [c]	82.52	91.49
European North	2,739.0	11.30	11.59	12.85
Northwestern Region	373.2	1.54	10.00	11.09
Central Region	510.9	2.11	18.25	20.23
Volga Region	437.6	1.80	9.20	10.19
North Caucasus and Crimea	230.1	0.95	1.20	1.33
Urals	1,674.4	6.90	13.88	15.39
Western Siberia	2,141.9	8.84	3.92	4.35
Eastern Siberia	11,865.5	49.03	6.58	7.30
Far East	3,764.5	15.54	4.12	4.57
Miscellaneous	—	—	3.78	4.19
Ukrainian SSR	50.0	0.20	2.69	2.98
Belorussian SSR	56.6	0.23	3.44	3.81
Republics of the Trans-Caucasus	291.2	1.20	0.60	0.67
Republics of Central Asia	56.4	0.23	0.21	0.23
Kazakh SSR	34.3	0.13	0.74	0.82
Total for USSR	24,225.4	100.00	90.20	100.00

[a] [For location and boundaries of the regions see Fig. 7.]
[b] [The total of the regions given in the RSFSR is 23,737.1.]
[c] [Not in original; sum of figures for regions in RSFSR.]

TABLE A5. DISTRIBUTION OF GRAIN CULTIVATION (1937) [BY REGIONS] [a]

Regions	Millet: Sown Area (thousand hectares)	Millet: % of USSR	Millet: % of Sown Area	Oats: Sown Area (thousand hectares)	Oats: % of USSR	Oats: % of Sown Area
USSR	4,404.7	100.0	3.3	17,633.3	100.0	13.0
RSFSR	3,059.9	69.5	3.3	14,959.0	84.8	16.0
European North	—	—	—	412.9	2.3	24.8
Northwestern Region	0.6	—	—	1,220.3	6.9	19.7
Central Industrial Region	265.6	6.1	2.7	2,191.2	12.4	22.0
Central Chernozem Region	669.9	15.2	5.3	1,815.8	10.3	14.4
Upper Volga	258.5	5.9	2.9	2,035.2	11.6	23.0
Middle and Lower Volga	845.8	19.2	6.3	1,093.9	6.2	8.1
North Caucasus and Crimea	300.4	6.8	2.2	591.1	3.4	4.3
Urals	536.4	12.2	4.2	2,269.8	12.9	17.6
Western Siberia	163.6	3.7	1.7	2,134.7	12.1	21.9
Eastern Siberia	8.4	0.2	0.2	943.4	5.3	2.7
Far East	10.7	0.2	1.2	250.7	1.4	29.0
Ukrainian SSR	439.8	10.0	1.8	1,610.7	9.1	6.4
Belorussian SSR	14.0	0.3	0.4	468.8	2.7	13.3
Republics of the Trans-Caucasus	27.9	0.6	1.1	22.0	0.1	0.1
Republics of Central Asia	43.7	1.0	0.9	85.4	0.5	1.7
Kazakh SSR	819.4	18.6	14.1	487.4	2.8	8.4

[a] [For spring wheat, winter wheat, and winter rye see Tables 33, 34, and 35 on pp. 375, 377, and 380 respectively. For locations and boundaries of the regions see Fig. 7.]

TABLE A5. *CONTINUED*

Regions	Barley			Maize		
	Sown Area (thousand hectares)	% of USSR	% of Sown Area	Sown Area (thousand hectares)	% of USSR	% of Sown Area
USSR	8,565.8	100.0	6.3	2,820.0	100.0	2.1
RSFSR	4,423.3	51.6	4.7	1,313.4	46.6	1.4
European North	237.7	2.8	14.3	—	—	—
Northwestern Region	289.5	3.4	4.7	—	—	—
Central Industrial Region	113.3	1.3 [a]	1.1	—	—	—
Central Chernozem Region	436.7	5.1	3.5	66.4	2.4	0.7
Upper Volga	268.5	3.2	3.0	—	—	—
Middle and Lower Volga	545.9	6.4	4.0	16.0	0.6	0.1
North Caucasus and Crimea	1,793.1	20.9	13.2	1,220.0	43.3	8.9
Urals	367.6	4.3	2.9	—	—	—
Western Siberia	204.6	2.4	2.1	—	—	—
Eastern Siberia	158.1	1.8	4.6	—	—	—
Far East	8.3	0.1	1.0	8.2	0.3	0.9
Ukrainian SSR	2,830.9	33.1	11.3	1,024.3	36.3	4.1
Belorussian SSR	277.0	3.2	7.9	—	—	—
Republics of the Trans-Caucasus	233.6	2.7	9.2	410.4	14.6	16.2
Republics of Central Asia	509.5	5.9	10.4	54.1	1.9	1.1
Kazakh SSR	291.5	3.4	5.0	17.8	0.6	0.3

[a] [11.3 in the original Russian text, obviously an error.]

TABLE A6. DISTRIBUTION OF INDUSTRIAL CROPS (1937) [BY REGIONS] [a]

Regions	Sugar Beets (For Factories)		Egyptian and American Cotton		Fiber Flax	
	Sown Area (thousand hectares)	% of USSR	Sown Area (thousand hectares)	% of USSR	Sown Area (thousand hectares)	% of USSR
USSR	1,193.4	100.00	2,091.8	100.0	2,125.5	100.00
RSFSR	343.7	28.81	284.1	13.6	1,756.7	82.64
European North	—	—	—	—	127.3	5.99
Northwestern Region	—	—	—	—	817.4	38.46
Central Industrial Region	8.9	0.75	—	—	340.5	16.02
Central Chernozem Region	276.5	23.17	0.1	0.005	45.9	2.16
Upper Volga	—	—	—	—	260.5	12.25
Middle and Lower Volga	7.4	0.62	21.6	1.0	—	—
North Caucasus and Crimea	18.2	1.52	262.4	12.5	—	—
Urals	1.5	0.13	—	—	42.3	1.99
Western Siberia	26.7	2.24	—	—	107.4	5.05
Eastern Siberia	—	—	—	—	14.7	0.69
Far East	4.5	0.38	—	—	0.7	0.03
Ukrainian SSR	816.7	68.44	223.9	10.7	113.4	5.34
Belorussian SSR	—	—	—	—	255.1	12.00
Republics of the Trans-Caucasus	6.6	0.55	214.7	10.3	—	—
Republics of Central Asia	13.4	1.12	1,257.8	60.2	—	—
Kazakh SSR	13.0	1.08	111.3	5.3	0.3	0.02

[a] [For location and boundaries of the regions see Fig. 7.]

TABLE A7. DISTRIBUTION OF POTATOES, VEGETABLES, AND ORCHARDS (1937) [BY REGIONS] [a]

Regions	Potatoes			Vegetables		Orchards	
	Sown Area (thousand hectares)	% of USSR	% of Sown Area	Sown Area (thousand hectares)	% of USSR	Sown Area (thousand hectares)	% of USSR
USSR	6,865.1	100.0	5.1	1,376.0 [b]	100.0	1,248.1	100.0
RSFSR	4,730.4	68.9	5.1	826.5	60.0	584.5	46.9
European North	117.8	1.7	7.1	13.9	1.0	0.7	0.1
Northwestern Region	683.4	10.0	11.0	86.8	6.3	42.1	3.4
Central Industrial Region	1,197.2	17.4	12.0	157.1	11.4	116.0	9.3
Central Chernozem Region	891.2	13.0	7.1	122.8	8.9	154.2	12.3
Upper Volga	501.7	7.3	5.7	52.5	3.8	33.8	2.7
Middle and Lower Volga	259.9	3.8	1.9	63.2	4.6	63.3	5.1
North Caucasus and Crimea	189.1	2.8	1.4	163.1	11.9	162.4	13.0
Urals	374.6	5.4	2.9	73.9	5.4	8.3	0.7
Western Siberia	329.7	4.8	3.4	48.6	3.5	2.0	0.2
Eastern Siberia	120.4	1.7	3.5	22.4	1.6	0.4	0.03
Far East	65.4	1.0	7.6	22.2	1.6	1.2	0.1
Ukrainian SSR	1,337.7	19.5	5.3	437.4	31.8	415.9	33.3
Belorussian SSR	631.1	9.2	18.0	38.5	2.8	66.3	5.3
Republics of the Trans-Caucasus	49.4	0.7	1.9	32.9	2.4	102.5	8.2
Republics of Central Asia	33.2	0.5	0.7	24.0	1.8	62.2	5.0
Kazakh SSR	83.3	1.2	1.4	16.5	1.2	16.7	1.3

[a] [For location and boundaries of the regions see Fig. 7.]

[b] [The sum of the figures given is 1,375.8.]

TABLE A8. DISTRIBUTION OF AGRICULTURAL LAND (1935) [BY REGIONS IN PER CENT OF TOTAL FOR USSR][a]

REGIONS	PLOWLAND AND MARKET GARDENS	MEADOW	COMMONS INCLUDING PASTURE
USSR	100.0	100.0	100.0
RSFSR	61.2	71.6	31.2
European North	0.7	4.1	0.6
Northwestern Region	4.1	10.7	0.8
Central Industrial Region	5.3	5.6	0.4
Central Chernozem Region	6.1	1.4	0.3
Upper Volga	4.3	2.8	0.3
Middle and Lower Volga	10.2	3.9	3.7
North Caucasus and Crimea	7.6	5.6	2.5
Urals	9.9	8.9	2.0
Western Siberia	8.7	13.7	3.0
Eastern Siberia	3.3	9.6	16.4
Far East	1.0	5.3	1.2
Ukrainian SSR	13.3	3.6	0.6
Belorussian SSR	1.8	3.8	0.2
Republics of the Trans-Caucasus	1.7	0.9	1.8
Republics of Central Asia	4.0	3.0	21.9
Kazakh SSR	18.0	17.1	44.3

[a] [For location and boundaries of the regions see Fig. 7.]

* TABLE A9. POPULATION OF THE RUSSIAN EMPIRE BY GUBERNIYAS AND OBLASTS, 1897

(The number preceding the name of the division indicates location on Fig. 22.)

DIVISION	POPULATION JAN. 28, 1897 [a]
Russian Empire	125,640,021 [b]
I. European Russia	93,442,864
1. Archangel G [c]	346,536
2. Astrakhan G	1,003,542
3. Bessarabia G	1,935,412
4. Chernigov G	2,297,854
5. Courland G (Kurland)	674,034
6. Don O	2,564,238
7. Estonia G (Estland)	412,716
8. Grodno G	1,603,409
9. Kaluga G	1,132,843
10. Kazan G	2,170,665
11. Kharkov G	2,492,316
12. Kherson G	2,733,612
13. Kiev G	3,559,229
14. Kostroma G	1,387,015
15. Kovno G	1,544,564
16. Kursk G	2,371,012
17. Livonia G (Lifland)	1,299,365
18. Minsk G	2,147,621
19. Mogilev G	1,686,764
20. Moscow G	2,430,581
21. Nizhny Novgorod G	1,584,774
22. Novgorod G	1,367,022
23. Olonets G	364,156
24. Orel G	2,033,798
25. Orenburg G	1,600,145
26. Penza G	1,470,474
27. Perm G	2,994,302
28. Podolsk G	3,018,299
29. Poltava G	2,778,151
30. Pskov G	1,122,317
31. Ryazan G	1,802,196
32. St. Petersburg G	2,112,033
33. Samara G	2,751,336
34. Saratov G	2,405,829
35. Simbirsk G	1,527,848
36. Smolensk G	1,525,279
37. Tambov G	2,684,030

* TABLE A9. *CONTINUED*

Division	Population Jan. 28, 1897 [a]
38. Tavrida G	1,447,790
39. Tula G	1,419,456
40. Tver G	1,769,135
41. Ufa G	2,196,642
42. Vilna G	1,591,207
43. Vitebsk G	1,489,246
44. Vladimir G	1,515,691
45. Volyn G	2,989,482
46. Vologda G	1,341,785
47. Voronezh G	2,531,253
48. Vyatka G	3,030,831
49. Yaroslavl G	1,071,355
50. Yekaterinoslav G	2,113,674
II. Vistula Provinces (Poland)	9,402,253
51. Kalish (Kalisz) G	840,597
52. Keltsy (Kielce) G	761,995
53. Lomzha (Łomża) G	579,592
54. Lyublin (Lublin) G	1,160,662
55. Petrokov (Piotrków) G	1,403,901
56. Plotsk (Płock) G	553,633
57. Radom G	814,947
58. Sedlets (Siedlce) G	772,146
59. Suvalki (Suwałki) G	582,913
60. Warsaw (Varshava, Warszawa) G	1,931,867
III. Grand Duchy of Finland	2,600,033
61. Åbo-Björneborg (Turku-Pori) G	432,129
62. Kuopio G	307,048
63. Nyland (Uusimaa) G	277,872
64. S:t Michel (Mikkeli) G	186,954
65. Tavastehus (Häme) G	286,025
66. Uleåborg (Oulu) G	268,718
67. Vasa (Vaasa) G	446,967
68. Viborg (Viipuri) G	394,320
IV. Caucasia	9,289,364
69. Baku G	826,716
71. Black Sea G	57,478
72. Dagestan O	571,154
73. Erivan G	829,556
74. Kars O	290,654

* TABLE A9. *CONTINUED*

Division	Population Jan. 28, 1897 [a]
75. Kuban O	1,918,881
76, 70, & 78. Kutais G	1,058,241
77. Stavropol G	873,301
79. Terek O	933,936
80 & 82. Tiflis G	1,051,032
81. Yelizavetpol G	878,415
V. Siberia	5,758,822
83. Amur O	120,306
84. Irkutsk G	514,267
85 & 87. Kamchatka O	28,113
86. Maritime (Primorskaya) O	223,336
88. Tobolsk G	1,433,043
89. Tomsk G	1,927,679
90. Trans-Baikal (Zabaikalskaya) O	672,037
91. Yakut O	269,880
92. Yenisey G	570,161
VI. Central Asia	7,746,718
93. Akmolinsk O	682,608
94. Fergana O	1,572,214
95. Samarkand O	860,021
96. Semipalatinsk O	684,590
97. Semirechensk O	987,863
98. Syr-Darya O	1,478,398
99. Trans-Caspian (Zakaspiiskaya) O	382,487
100. Turgay O	453,416
101. Uralsk O	645,121
VII. Dependencies in Central Asia	2,050,000
102. Bukhara Khanate	1,250,000
103. Khiva Khanate	800,000

[a] Population figures are for the actual population present on the day of the census, Jan. 28 (Feb. 9), 1897, except in the cases of Finland (end of 1897) and Bukhara and Khiva (estimates).

[b] Excluding Finland (III) and Bukhara and Khiva (VII). Including these areas the population was 130,290,054.

[c] Abbreviations: G, Guberniya; O, Oblast.

Sources: *First General Census of Population of the Russian Empire, 1897, General Summary for the Entire Empire,* Vol. I (St. Petersburg, 1905), Table 1, pp. 8–11 (in Russian and French). *Statistical Yearbook of Finland,* 1915 (Helsingfors, 1916), pp. 10–11 (for Finland) (in Finnish and French). *Statesman's Year-Book* 1902 (London: Macmillan, 1902), pp. 1034–1035 (for Bukhara and Khiva).

* TABLE A10. DENSITY OF POPULATION IN THE RUSSIAN EMPIRE, JAN. 1, 1913 [a]

(See Fig. 21, p. 184)

(The numbers preceding the name of the division indicate location on Fig. 22 at the back of the book.)

Division	Persons per Square Verst
Russian Empire (except Finland)	8.9
I. European Russia	29.3
1. Archangel G [b]	0.6
2. Astrakhan G	6.2
3. Bessarabia G	65.7
4. Chernigov	67.9
5. Courland G (Kurland)	31.9
6. Don O	25.7
7. Estonia G (Estland)	27.7
8. Grodno G	59.7
9. Kaluga G	52.9
10. Kazan G	50.4
11. Kharkov G	70.9
12. Kherson G	57.9
13. Kiev G	105.8
14. Kostroma G	23.8
15. Kovno G	51.7
16. Kursk G	77.5
17. Livonia G (Lifland)	37.2
18. Minsk G	36.9
19. Mogilev G	55.4
20. Moscow G	113.8
21. Nizhny Novgorod G	46.0
22. Novgorod G	16.1
23. Olonets G	4.1
24. Orel G	65.6
25. Orenburg G	12.9
26. Penza G	55.0
27. Perm G	13.4
28. Podolsk G	106.3
29. Poltava G	85.5
30. Pskov G	36.9
31. Ryazan G	71.4
32. St. Petersburg G	76.2
33. Samara G	28.0
34. Saratov G	43.4
35. Simbirsk G	46.3

* table a10. *CONTINUED*

	Division	Persons per Square Verst
	36. Smolensk G	41.4
	37. Tambov G	60.7
	38. Tavrida G	36.9
	39. Tula G	68.1
	40. Tver G	39.9
	41. Ufa G	28.3
	42. Vilna G	53.8
	43. Vitebsk G	49.3
	44. Vladimir G	45.8
	45. Volyn G	64.1
	46. Vologda G	4.8
	47. Voronezh G	61.1
	48. Vyatka G	28.9
	49. Yaroslavl G	40.1
	50. Yekaterinoslav G	58.7
II.	Vistula Provinces (Poland)	114.7
	51. Kalish (Kalisz) G	121.5
	52. Keltsy (Kielce) G	112.9
	53. Lomzha (Łomża) G	75.6
	54. Lyublin (Lublin) G	108.1
	55. Petrokov (Piotrków) G	189.1
	56. Plotsk (Płock) G	90.8
	57. Radom G	104.4
	58. Sedlets (Siedlce) G	81.9
	59. Suvalki (Suwałki) G	63.6
	60. Warsaw (Varshava, Warszawa) G	170.0
III.	Grand Duchy of Finland	11.0
	61. Åbo-Björneborg (Turku-Pori) G	25.0
	62. Kuopio G	10.8
	63. Nyland (Uusimaa) G	40.6
	64. S:t Michel (Mikkeli) G	13.8
	65. Tavastehus (Häme) G	23.1
	66. Uleåborg (Oulu) G	2.5
	67. Vasa (Vaasa) G	15.7
	68. Viborg (Viipuri) G	19.8
IV.	Caucasia	29.8
	69. Baku G	30.4
	70. Batum O	27.8
	71. Black Sea G	14.9

* TABLE A10. *CONTINUED*

Division	Persons per Square Verst
72. Dagestan O	26.6
73. Erivan G	40.5
74. Kars O	23.5
75. Kuban O	33.7
76. Kutais G	55.6
77. Stavropol G	27.4
78. Sukhum-Kale Ok	24.1
79. Terek O	19.4
80. Tiflis G	33.6
81. Yelizavetpol G	26.8
82. Zakataly Ok	27.5
V. Siberia	0.8
83. Amur O	0.7
84. Irkutsk G	1.1
85. Kamchatka O	0.03
86. Maritime (Primorskaya) O	0.9
87. Sakhalin	0.4
88. Tobolsk G	1.6
89. Tomsk G	4.5
90. Trans-Baikal (Zabaikalskaya) O	1.6
91. Yakut O	0.09
92. Yenisey G	0.4
VI. Central Asia	3.3
93. Akmolinsk O	2.1
94. Fergana O	16.7
95. Samarkand O	20.3
96. Semipalatinsk O	2.1
97. Semirechensk O	3.7
98. Syr-Darya O	4.3
99. Trans-Caspian (Zakaspiiskaya) O	0.9
100. Turgay O	1.4
101. Uralsk O	2.5

[a] In persons per square verst. One person per square verst equals 2.27 persons per square mile, or 0.88 per square kilometer.

[b] Abbreviations: G. Guberniya; O. Oblast; Ok. Okrug.

Sources: Russia—Association of Industry and Commerce, *Statistical Annual, 1913*, by V. I. Shary (St. Petersburg, 1913), Table 1, col. 4, pp. 5–6 (in Russian and French). Finland—Central Statistical Bureau, *Statistical Yearbook for Finland, 1915* (Helsingfors, 1916), Table 3, p. 4 (in Finnish and French).

* Table A11. POPULATION AND DENSITY OF POPULATION OF THE USSR BY GUBERNIYAS AND OBLASTS BY THE CENSUS OF DEC. 17, 1926

(Numbers and letters preceding names indicate locations on Fig. 82)

Division or Region	Population	Persons per Sq. Km.
USSR	147,027,915	6.9
1. Belorussian SSR [a]	4,983,240	39.3
2. Ukrainian SSR	29,018,187	64.3
a. Forest Subregion	2,957,881	54.4
b. Dnepr Prairie Right Bank	8,997,757	87.6
c. Dnepr Prairie Left Bank	7,066,909	74.4
d. Steppe Subregion	5,568,233	45.9
Including:		
1. Moldavian ASSR	572,339	69.1
e. Dnepr Industrial Subregion	2,391,155	50.9
f. Mining-Industrial Subregion	2,036,252	65.3
RSFSR (Numbers 3–21)	100,891,244	5.1
3. Northeastern Region	2,368,440	2.1
a. Archangel (Arkangelsk) G	429,184	1.0
b. Vologda G	1,053,832	9.4
c. Severnaya Dvina G	678,110	6.5
d. Komi AO	207,314	0.5
4. Leningrad-Karelia Region	6,659,711	13.1
a. Karelian ASSR	269,734	1.8
b. Leningrad G	2,792,129	42.2
c. Murmansk G	23,006	0.2
d. Novgorod G	1,050,604	20.3
e. Pskov G	1,788,418	34.6
f. Cherepovets G	735,820	11.7
5. Western Region	4,299,150	43.6
a. Bryansk G	2,006,438	48.3
b. Smolensk G	2,292,712	40.1
6. Central Industrial Region	19,314,024	45.8
a. Vladimir G	1,321,140	40.0
b. Ivanovo-Voznesensk G	1,195,804	35.7
c. Kaluga G	1,151,591	44.5

* TABLE A11. *CONTINUED*

Division or Region	Population	Persons per Sq. Km.
d. Kostroma G	811,619	24.1
e. Moscow G	4,570,836	102.6
f. Nizhny Novgorod G	2,743,344	33.7
g. Tver G	2,242,350	35.4
h. Yaroslavl G	1,343,163	38.6
i. Ryazan G	2,428,914	52.4
j. Tula G	1,505,263	59.1
7. Central Chernozem (Black Soil) Region	10,825,830	57.5
a. Voronezh G	3,308,023	49.4
b. Kursk G	2,906,360	66.6
c. Orel G	1,884,533	61.3
d. Tambov G	2,726,914	58.3
8. Vyatka Region	3,463,197	21.5
a. Votyak AO	756,264	24.9
b. Vyatka G	2,224,832	20.5
c. Mari AO	482,101	21.5
9. Ural Region	6,786,339	3.9
a. Pre-Ural Subregion	1,888,007	17.3
b. Mining-Industrial Subregion	1,500,478	6.6
c. Trans-Ural Subregion	3,205,691	12.3
d. Tobolsk Subregion	192,163	0.2
10. Bashkir ASSR	2,665,836	17.6
11. Middle Volga Region	10,268,168	30.3
a. Orenburg G	773,254	11.4
b. Penza G	2,208,780	47.7
c. Samara G	2,413,403	22.9
d. Tatar ASSR	2,594,032	38.6
e. Ulyanovsk G	1,384,220	40.6
f. Chuvash ASSR	894,479	48.9
12. Lower Volga Region	5,529,516	17.1
a. Astrakhan G	510,386	15.8
b. Kalmyk AO	141,594	1.9
c. Volga German ASSR	571,754	21.4
d. Saratov G	2,897,363	31.8
e. Stalingrad G	1,408,419	14.2

* TABLE A11. *CONTINUED*

Division or Region	Population	Persons per Sq. Km.
13. Crimean ASSR	713,823	27.6
14. North Caucasus Kray	8,363,491	28.5
a. Azov Subregion	1,400,664	45.4
b. Donets-Stavropol Subregion	2,757,930	20.2
c. Kuban-Black Sea Subregion	3,151,533	37.3
Including:		
1. Adygey AO	113,481	37.5
d. Mountain Subregion	1,053,364	25.3
Including:		
1. Cherkess AO	36,996	26.4
2. Karachayev AO	64,613	7.9
3. Kabardino-Balkar AO	204,006	17.7
4. North Osetian AO	152,435	24.7
5. Ingush AO	75,133	23.3
6. Chechen AO	309,860	33.1
15. Dagestan ASSR	788,098	14.5
16. Siberian Kray	8,687,939	2.1
a. Southwest Subregion	5,240,321	9.1
Including:		
1. Oirot AO	99,667	1.1
b. Northeast Subregion	3,447,618	1.0
17. Buryat-Mongol ASSR	491,236	1.3
18. Yakut ASSR	289,085	0.07
19. Far Eastern Kray	1,881,351	0.7
a. Trans-Baikal Subregion	590,101	2.2
b. Amur Subregion	446,175	1.1
c. Maritime Subregion	798,258	0.9
d. Sakhalin Subregion	11,859	0.3
e. Kamchatka Subregion	34,958	0.03
20. Kazakh ASSR	6,503,006	2.2
a. Akmolinsk G	1,211,552	2.4
b. Aktyubinsk G	468,882	1.1
c. Dzhetysuy G	887,845	3.1
d. Semipalatinsk G	1,310,186	2.4

*TABLE A11. *CONTINUED*

Division or Region	Population	Persons per Sq. Km.
e. Syr-Darya G	1,157,088	2.7
f. Uralsk G	638,021	2.4
g. Adayev G	135,555	0.5
h. Kustanay G	389,336	3.8
i. Kara-Kalpak AO	304,541	2.5
21. Kirgiz ASSR	993,004	5.1
22. Uzbek SSR (with Tadzhik ASSR)	5,272,801	16.9
a. Without Tadzhik ASSR	4,445,634	28.3
b. Tadzhik ASSR	827,167	5.4
23. Turkmen SSR	1,000,914	2.2
24. Transcaucasian SFSR	5,861,529	31.7
a. Azerbaidzhan SSR	2,314,571	26.9
Including:		
1. Nagoro-Karabakh AO	125,300	30.1
2. Nakhichevan ASSR	104,956	19.6
b. Armenian SSR	880,464	29.4
c. Georgian SSR	2,666,494	38.5
Including:		
1. Abkhaz SSR	201,016	24.8
2. Adzhar ASSR	131,957	51.2
3. South Osetian AO	87,375	23.6

[a] Abbreviations: SSR. Soviet Socialist Republic; ASSR. Autonomous Soviet Socialist Republic; G. Guberniya; O. Oblast; AO. Autonomous Oblast; SFSR. Soviet Federated Socialist Republic.

Source: Frank Lorimer, *The Population of the Soviet Union: History and Prospects* (Geneva: League of Nations, 1946), Table 26, pp. 67–70, with additions and corrections from USSR, Central Statistical Bureau, Census Section, *All-Union Census of Population, 1926* (Moscow, 1928–1929), Part I, Vols. 4–8 and 11–13, maps at end of each vol., and Vols. 9 and 11, Table 1, cols. 6 and 16.

* TABLE A12. POPULATION OF MAJOR CITIES IN THE USSR BY THE CENSUSES OF 1897, 1926, AND 1939 AND PERCENTAGE INCREASE 1926–1939[a]

(See Figs. 25 and 26, p. 194)

CITY	POPULATION			INCREASE 1926–1939
	Jan. 28, 1897	Dec. 17, 1926	Jan. 17, 1939	
1. Moscow (Moskva)	988,614	2,029,425	4,137,018	103.9%
2. Leningrad (Petrograd, St. Petersburg)	1,267,023	1,690,065	3,191,304	88.8
3. Kiev	247,432	513,637	846,293	64.8
4. Kharkov	174,846	417,342	833,432	99.7
5. Baku	112,253	453,333	809,347	78.5
6. Gorky (Nizhny Novgorod)	95,124	222,356	644,116	189.7
7. Odessa	405,041	420,862	604,223	43.6
8. Tashkent	156,414	323,613	585,005	80.8
9. Tbilisi (Tiflis)	160,645	294,044	519,175	76.6
10. Rostov-on-Don	119,889	308,103	510,253	65.6
11. Dnepropetrovsk (Yekaterinoslav)	121,216	236,717	500.662	111.5
12. Stalino (Yuzovka)		174,230	462,395	165.4
13. Stalingrad (Tsaritsyn)	55,967	151,490	445,476	194.1
14. Sverdlovsk (Yekaterinburg)	55,488	140,300	425,544	203.3
15. Novosibirsk (Novo-Nikolayevsk)		120,128	405,589	237.6
16. Kazan	131,508	179,023	401,665	124.4
17. Kuibyshev (Samara)	91,672	175,636	390,267	122.2
18. Saratov	137,109	219,547	375,860	71.2
19. Voronezh	84,146	121,612	326,836	168.7
20. Yaroslavl	70,610	114,277	298,065	160.8
21. Zaporozhye (Aleksandrovsk)		55,744	289,188	418.8
22. Ivanovo (Ivanovo-Voznesensk)	53,949	111,460	285,069	155.8
23. Archangel (Arkhangelsk)		76,774	281,091	266.1
24. Omsk	37,470	161,684	280,716	73.6
25. Chelyabinsk		59,307	273,127	360.5
26. Tula	111,048	155,005	272,403	75.7
27. Molotov (Perm)	45,403	119,776	255,196	113.1
28. Astrakhan	112,880	184,301	253,655	37.6
29. Ufa	49,961	98,537	245,863	149.5

[a] Figures for 1897 shown only for cities with more than 25,000 population in that year; these figures differ slightly from those given in Table 15.

* TABLE A12. *CONTINUED*

City	Population			Increase 1926–1939
	Jan. 28, 1897	Dec. 17, 1926	Jan. 17, 1939	
30. Irkutsk	51,434	108,129	243,380	125.1%
31. Makeyevka		79,421	240,145	202.4
32. Minsk	91,494	131,803	238,772	81.2
33. Alma-Ata (Verny)		45,395	230,528	407.8
34. Mariupol	31,772	63,920	222,427	248.0
35. Kalinin (Tver)	53,477	108,413	216,131	99.4
36. Voroshilovgrad (Lugansk)		71,765	213,007	196.8
37. Vladivostok	28,896	107,980	206,432	91.2
38. Krasnodar (Yekaterinodar)	65,697	161,843	203,946	26.0
39. Yerevan (Erivan)	29,033	64,613	200,031	209.6
40. Khabarovsk		52,045	199,364	283.1
41. Krivoy Rog		38,228	197,621	417.0
42. Krasnoyarsk	26,600	72,261	189,999	162.9
43. Taganrog	51,965	86,444	188,808	118.4
44. Izhevsk		63,211	175,740	178.0
45. Chkalov (Orenburg)	72,740	123,283	172,925	40.3
46. Grozny		97,087	172,468	77.6
47. Stalinsk (Kuznetsk)		3,894	169,538	4253.8
48. Vitebsk	65,871	98,857	167,424	69.4
49. Nikolayev	92,060	104,909	167,108	59.3
50. Karaganda		—	165,937	—
51. Nizhny Tagil		38,820	159,864	311.8
52. Penza	61,851	91,924	157,145	71.0
53. Smolensk	46,889	78,520	156,677	99.5
54. Shakhty (Shakhtaya)		41,043	155,081	277.9
55. Barnaul	29,408	73,858	148,129	100.6
56. Dneprodzerzhinsk (Kamenskoye)		34,150	147,829	332.9
57. Magnitogorsk		—	145,870	—
58. Gomel	33,846	86,409	144,169	66.8
59. Kirov (Vyatka)		62,097	143,181	130.6
60. Simferopol	48,821	87,213	142,678	63.6
61. Tomsk	52,430	92,274	141,215	53.0
62. Rybinsk	25,223	55,546	139,011	150.3
63. Samarkand	54,900	105,206	134,346	27.7
64. Kemerovo (Shcheglovsk)		21,726	132,978	512.1
65. Poltava	53,060	91,984	130,305	41.7
66. Ulan-Ude (Verkhne-Udinsk)		28,918	129,417	347.5
67. Dzaudzhikau (Ordzhonikidze, Vladikavkaz)	43,843	78,346	127,172	62.3
68. Ashkhabad (Poltoratsk)		51,593	126,580	145.3

* TABLE A12. *CONTINUED*

City	Population			Increase 1926–1939
	Jan. 28, 1897	Dec. 17, 1926	Jan. 17, 1939	
69. Tambov	48,134	72,256	121,285	67.9%
70. Kostroma	41,268	73,732	121,205	64.4
71. Kursk	52,896	82,440	119,972	45.5
72. Murmansk		8,777	117,054	1233.6
73. Sevastopol	50,710	74,551	111,946	50.2
74. Orel	69,858	75,968	110,567	45.5
75. Semipalatinsk	26,353	56,871	109,779	93.0
76. Gorlovka		23,125	108,693	370.0
77. Prokopyevsk		10,717	107,227	900.5
78. Kerch	28,982	35,690	104,471	192.7
79. Dzerzhinsk (Rastyapino)		8,910	103,415	1060.7
80. Chita		61,526	102,555	66.7
81. Ulyanovsk (Simbirsk)	43,298	70,130	102,106	45.6
82. Kirovograd (Yelizavetgrad, Zinovievsk, Kirovo)	61,841	66,467	100,331	50.9
83. Mogilev	43,106	50,222	99,440	98.0
84. Orekhovo-Zuyevo		62,841	99,329	58.1
85. Zlatoust		48,219	99,272	105.9
86. Kirovabad (Yelizavetpol)	33,090	57,393	98,743	72.1
87. Kherson	69,219	58,801	97,186	65.3
88. Ryazan	44,552	50,919	95,358	87.3
89. Novorossiisk		67,941	95,280	40.2
90. Vologda	27,822	57,976	95,194	64.2
91. Zhitomir	65,452	76,678	95,090	24.0
92. Konstantinovka		25,303	95,087	275.8
93. Kramatorsk		12,348	93,350	656.0
94. Vinnitsa	28,995	57,990	92,868	60.1
95. Frunze		36,610	92,659	153.1
96. Petropavlovsk (in Kazakh SSR)		47,361	91,678	93.6
97. Serpukhov		55,891	90,766	62.4
98. Kremenchug	58,648	58,832	89,553	52.2
99. Kaluga	49,728	51,565	89,484	73.5
100. Yenakievo (Ordzhonikidze)		24,329	88,246	262.7
101. Bryansk		45,962	87,473	90.3
102. Makhach-Kala		33,552	86,847	158.8
103. Stavropol (Voroshilovsk)	41,621	58,640	85,100	45.1
104. Kokand	82,054	69,324	84,665	22.1
105. Bobruisk	35,177	51,296	84,107	64.0
106. Andizhan	46,680	73,465	83,691	13.9

* TABLE A12. *CONTINUED*

City	Population			Increase 1926–1939
	Jan. 28, 1897	Dec. 17, 1926	Jan. 17, 1939	
107. Armavir		74,523	83,677	12.3%
108. Stalinabad		5,607	82,540	1372.1
109. Bezhitsa (Ordzhonikidzegrad)		36,040	82,331	128.4
110. Leninsk-Kuznetsky		19,645	81,980	317.3
111. Kutaisi (Kutais)	32,492	48,196	81,479	69.0
112. Novocherkassk	52,005	62,274	81,286	30.5
113. Noginsk		38,494	81,024	110.5
114. Biisk		45,561	80,190	76.0
115. Perovo		23,711	77,727	227.8
116. Syzran	32,377	50,293	77,679	54.5
117. Namangan	61,906	73,640	77,351	5.0
118. Stalinogorsk		—	76,207	—
119. Melitopol		25,289	75,735	199.5
120. Slavyansk		28,771	75,542	162.6
121. Tyumen	29,588	50,340	75,537	50.1
122. Kineshma		34,110	75,378	121.0
123. Kolomna		30,767	75,139	144.2
124. Chimkent		21,018	74,185	253.0
125. Engels		34,345	73,279	113.4
126. Podolsk		19,793	72,422	265.9
127. Anzhero-Sudzhensk		30,199	71,079	135.4
128. Batumi (Batum)	28,512	48,474	70,807	46.1
129. Komsomolsk		—	70,746	—
130. Voroshilov (Nikolsk-Ussuriisky, Voroshilov-Ussuriisky)		35,344	70,628	99.8
131. Losinoostrovsk		15,624	70,480	351.1
132. Michurinsk (Kozlov)	40,347	49,853	70,202	40.8
133. Petrozavodsk		27,105	69,728	157.3
134. Kadievka (Sergo)		17,224	68,360	296.9
135. Leninakan (Aleksandropol)	32,018	42,313	67,707	60.0
136. Chernigov	27,006	35,234	67,356	91.2
137. Maikop	34,191	53,033	67,302	26.9
138. Kovrov		26,584	67,163	152.6
139. Vladimir	28,315	39,654	66,761	68.4
140. Lipetsk		21,439	66,625	210.8
141. Berdichev	53,728	55,613	66,306	19.2
142. Uralsk	36,597	36,352	66,201	82.1
143. Cheremkhovo		14,485	65,907	355.0
144. Orsk		13,581	65,799	384.5

* TABLE A12. *CONTINUED*

City	Population			Increase 1926–1939
	Jan. 28, 1897	Dec. 17, 1926	Jan. 17, 1939	
145. Serov (Nadezhdinsk)		33,345	64,719	94.1%
146. Lyublino		8,391	64,332	666.7
147. Sumy	27,575	44,213	63,883	44.5
148. Vyshny-Volochek		32,022	63,642	98.7
149. Berezniki		16,138	63,575	293.9
150. Pyatigorsk		40,674	62,875	54.6
151. Dzhambul		24,761	62,723	153.3
152. Kuntsevo		9,978	60,963	511.0
153. Mytishchi		17,054	60,111	252.5
154. Pskov	30,424	43,226	59,898	38.6
155. Blagoveshchensk	32,834	52,638[b]	58,761	11.5[b]
156. Chapayevsk		13,529	57,995	328.7
157. Shuya		34,475	57,950	68.1
158. Nikopol		14,214	57,841	306.9
159. Yegoryevsk		29,674	56,340	89.9
160. Artemovsk		37,780	55,165	46.0
161. Volsk	27,039	35,272	55,053	56.1
162. Voroshilovsk		16,040	54,794	241.6
163. Chardzhou		13,950	54,739	292.4
164. Rzhev		32,810	54,081	64.8
165. Kurgan		27,996	53,224	90.1
166. Borisoglebsk		39,788	52,055	30.8
167. Cherkassy	29,619	39,511	51,693	30.8
168. Osipenko (Berdyansk)	27,279	26,408	51,664	95.6
169. Kislovodsk		25,913	51,289	97.9
170. Lysva		27,279	51,192	87.7
171. Kamensk-Uralsky (Kamensk, Sinarskaya)		5,367	50,897	848.3
172. Yelets	37,455	43,239	50,888	17.7
173. Krasny Luch		12,425	50,829	309.1
174. Bukhara	75,000[c]	46,778	50,382	7.7

[b] Unofficial.

[c] Estimate.

Sources: For 1939 and 1926, *Planned Economy*, 1939, No. 6, pp. 14–17 (in Russian); and for 1897, *The Statesman's Year Book, 1902* (London: Macmillan, 1902), p. 986.

* TABLE A13. TEMPERATURE REQUIREMENTS OF CERTAIN CROPS IN DEGREE DAYS

(Annual sum of daily temperatures in degrees centigrade above 10° C.)

CROP	DEGREE DAYS	CROP	DEGREE DAYS
Cotton	3,500–5,000	Corn (maize)	2,300–4,000
Tea	3,000	Sugar beet	2,200
Rice	2,500	Flax	1,200
Soybean	2,500		

Tabulated from the text.

*TABLE A14. DATES OF PARTY CONGRESSES OF THE COMMUNIST PARTY (OF THE SOVIET UNION)

NUMBER	YEAR	NUMBER	YEAR
1	1898	10	1921
2	1903	11	1922
3	1905	12	1923
4	1906	13	1924
5	1907	14	1925
6	1917	15	1927
7	1918	16	1930
8	1919	17	1934
9	1920	18	1939

* *Appendix II* TABLE OF EQUIVALENTS

A. *Length*

1 verst = 0.6629 mi. or 1.067 km.
1 kilometer = 0.62137 mi.
meter = 39.37 in. or 3.28 ft.
centimeter = 0.3937 in.
millimeter = 0.03937 in.
nautical mile = 6,080 ft., or 1.15 statute mi., or 1.853 km.

B. *Area*

1 dessiatine (desyatina, desiatin, deciatine) = 2.70 acres or 1.09 hectares
1 hectare = 2.471 acres
1 sq. verst = 1.14 sq. km. or 0.4394 sq. mi.
1 sq. kilometer = 0.3861 sq. mi. or 247.1 acres, or 100 hectares.

C. *Weight*

1 pood = 16.38 kg., 0.1638 centner, 36.113 lb., or 0.6 bu. (of wheat)
1 kilogram = 2.2046 lb.
1 centner = 100 kg. or 220.46 lb.,
or 3.67 bu. wheat or potatoes
3.94 bu. rye or corn (maize)
4.59 bu. barley or millet
4.90 bu. rice
5.25 bu. buckwheat
6.89 bu. oats

D. *Crop Yield and Population Density Ratio* [a]

1 centner per hectare = 89.22 lb. per acre
or 1.49 bu. wheat or potatoes per acre
1.60 bu. rye or corn (maize) per acre
1.86 bu. barley or millet per acre
1.98 bu. rice per acre
2.12 bu. buckwheat per acre
2.79 bu. oats per acre
0.0405 metric ton sugar beets per acre
1 person per sq. verst = 0.88 per sq. km. and 2.27 per sq. mi.
1 person per sq. kilometer = 2.59 per sq. mi.

E. *Value*

1 ruble = 51.5 cents (gold ruble preceding World War I), later devalued to an official rate of 20 cents but with widely fluctuating value on the nonofficial market.

F. *Temperature*

To convert degrees Centigrade to degrees Fahrenheit, multiply by 1.8 and add 32.

Degrees Centigrade	Degrees Fahrenheit	Degrees Centigrade	Degrees Fahrenheit
100	212	10	50
90	194	0	32
80	176	–10	14
70	158	–20	–4
60	140	–30	–22
50	122	–40	–40
40	104	–50	–58
30	86	–60	–76
20	68	–70	–94

G. *Time*

The Gregorian (New Style) Calendar was adopted Feb. 14, 1918, at which time it was dated 13 days later than the Julian (Old Style) Calendar; i.e., Feb. 14 New Style was Feb. 1 Old Style. The New Style Calendar was dated later than the Old Style as follows: 1582–1699, 10 days; 1700–1799, 11 days; 1800–1899, 12 days; 1900–1918, 13 days.

[a] The United States Department of Agriculture estimates that Soviet crop yield figures should be revised downward 10–20% to make them comparable with U. S. figures. Soviet figures on crop yields apparently apply to crops in the fields and do not take adequate account of harvesting losses.

* *Appendix III* LIST OF ABBREVIATIONS AND SIGNS

A category A; proved resources of mineral deposits
AMO (Aktsionernoye Moskovskoye Obshchestvo) Moscow Joint-Stock Company
AO (Avtonomnaya Oblast) Autonomous Oblast
ASSR (Avtonomnaya Sovetskaya Sotsialisticheskaya Respublika) Autonomous Soviet Socialist Republic
B category B; probable (apparent) reserves of mineral deposits
C category C; possible reserves of mineral deposits
c (Latin *constans*) fixed costs
cm. centimeters
FD (Felix Dzerzhinsky) a type of locomotive
G Guberniya
GAZ (Gorkovsky Avtomobilny Zavod) Gorky Automobile Factory
GES or -ges (gosudarstvennaya elektricheskaya stantsiya) state electric power station
Glavsevmorput (Glavnoye Upravlenie Severnogo Morskogo Puti) Chief Administration of the Northern Sea Route
GOELRO or Goelro (Gosudarstvennaya Komissiya po Elektrofikatsii Respubliki) State Commission on the Electrification of the Republic
Gosplan (Gosudarstvennaya Planovaya Komissiya) State Planning Committee
h. hectare
IS (Iosif Stalin) a type of locomotive
kg. kilogram
km. kilometers
KMA (Kurskaya Magnitnaya Anomaliya) Kursk Magnetic Anomaly
kw. kilowatt (of electricity)
kw-h. kilowatt-hour
L. lake
m. meters

m (German *Mehrwert*) surplus value
mm. millimeters
Mt., Mts. mountain, mountains
MRS motorized fishing station
MTS (Mashino-traktornaya stantsiya) machine tractor station
NOk (natsionalny okrug) national okrug
O Oblast
OGIZ (Obyedinenie Gosudarstvennykh Izdatelstv) State Publishing House
Ok Okrug
R. River
RSFSR (Rossiiskaya Sovetskaya Federativnaya Sotsialisticheskaya Respublika) The Russian Soviet Federated Socialist Republic, the largest of the 16 constituent republics of the USSR
Sevmorput (Severny Morskoy Put) Northern Sea Route
SK (sintetichesky kauchuk) synthetic rubber
SK–B (sintetichesky kauchuk-butadien) butadiene rubber
SNK (Sovnarkom, or Sovet Narodnykh Komissarov) Council of People's Commissars, composed of the heads of the government departments and corresponding roughly to the Cabinet in American government.
SO (Sergei Ordzhonikidze) a type of locomotive
SPB St. Petersburg
sq. km. square kilometers
SSR (Sovetskaya Sotsialisticheskaya Respublika) Soviet Socialist Republic, or Union Republic
stroy (stroika) dam, building, construction
TETs (teploelektrotsentral) district heat and electric power station
TsK VKP(b) (Tsentralny komitet vsesoyuznoy kommunisticheskoy partii-bolshevikov) The Central Committee of the Communist Party of the Soviet Union
USSR (SSSR, Soyuz Sovetskikh Sotsialisticheskikh Respublik) Union of Soviet Socialist Republics
v (Latin *variabilis*) variable costs or wages
VKP(b) (Vsesoyuznaya kommunisticheskaya partiya–bolshevikov) Communist Party of the Soviet Union
ZIS (Zavod imeni Stalina) Stalin auto factory in Moscow
ZSFSR (Zakavkazskaya Sovetskaya Federativnaya Sotsialisticheskaya Respublika) Trans-Caucasian Soviet Federated Socialist Republic, a

former Union republic now split into Armenian SSR, Georgian SSR, and Azerbaidzhan SSR

* An asterisk marks tables, maps, or indexes not found in the original Russian edition but compiled especially for the American edition.

[ ] Brackets enclose footnotes or references not in the original Russian edition but added by the editor of the American edition.

* *Appendix IV* TRANSLITERATION TABLE

The A.C.L.S. (American Council of Learned Societies) Transliteration Scheme is used throughout this text and series. It is nonreversible but slightly more readable than the reversible B.G.N. or L.C. schemes.

The B.G.N. (United States Board on Geographical Names) 1944 scheme is the official guide for the treatment of place names by United States governmental agencies. See U. S. Board on Geographical Names, "Directions for the Treatment of Geographical Names in the Union of Soviet Socialist Republics," (Special Publication No. 12) (Washington, U.S. Board on Geographical Names, revised Nov. 1, 1944), Appendix A, Table for Transliteration of Russian Geographical Names.

The L.C. (Library of Congress) scheme is here indicated because it is the system commonly used by libraries for listing of Russian titles in card catalogues and elsewhere. See *Style Manual of the Government Printing Office* (Washington: Government Printing Office, 1939), pp. 271–272.

RUSSIAN	A.C.L.S.	B.G.N.	L.C.
Single Letters			
А а	a	a	a
Б б	b	b	b
В в	v	v	v
Г г	g (v)[1]	g	g
Д д	d	d	d
Е е	e (ye)[2]	e, ye [3]	e
Е ё	e(yo, o)[4]	ё, yё	ё
Ж ж	zh	zh	zh

[1] v in genitive ending -evo, ovo.

[2] ye initially and after ь, ъ, and all vowels except and ы and и.

[3] ye initially and after ь, ъ, and all vowels.

[4] Standard A.C.L.S. system calls for yo, except o after ж and ш, but in place names in this book ё has been transliterated uniformly as e.

RUSSIAN	A.C.L.S.	B.G.N.	L.C.
Single Letters			
З з	z	z	z
И и	i [5]	i	i
Й й	y (i) [6]	y	ĭ
К к	k	k	k
Л л	l	l	l
М м	m	m	m
Н н	n	n	n
О о	o	o	o
П п	p	p	p
Р р	r	r	r
С с	s	s	s
Т т	t	t	t
У у	u	u	u
Ф ф	f	f	f
Х х	kh	kh	kh
Ц ц	ts	ts	t͡s
Ч ч	ch	ch	ch
Ш ш	sh	sh	sh
Щ щ	shch	shch	shch
ъ	(omit)	"	"
Ы ы	y	y	y
ь	(omit)	'	'
Э э	e	e	ė
Ю ю	yu	yu	i͡u
Я я	ya	ya	i͡a
Combination			
ий	y	iy	iĭ
ый	y	yy	yĭ
ые	ie	yye	ye
ие	ie	iye	ie
ыю	iu	yyu	yi͡u
ыя	ia	yya	yi͡a

[5] yi after ь

[6] y if terminal, i if medial.

* *Appendix V* GLOSSARY OF RUSSIAN TERMS

The stressed syllable is indicated.

A. Words considered to be fully Anglicized with a specific technical meaning, therefore not translated in this book but used as English words not italicized and forming the plural with *s* or *es*.

artél—workmen's cooperative, particularly for handicraft production.

bednyák—poor (poorest) peasant

brýnza (brinza) (Rumanian)—cheese made from ewe's milk in Crimea, Bessarabia, and the Balkans

chernozém—black earth, a zonal, very fertile soil of excellent structure and high humus content developed on temperate grasslands; characterized by dark brown to black surface horizon grading into lighter soil and finally into a layer of lime accumulation.

chinki—escarpments on edges of the Ust-Urt Plateau

dekhkán (Persian)—peasant in Uzbekistan and Turkmenistan.

Dúma—the Russian parliament (1905–1917)

glei (gley)—a soil condition in which the iron oxides are reduced from ferric to ferrous oxides as a result of the lack of oxygen due to poor drainage and which gives the soil a distinctive bluish-gray color.

gubérniya—province or government, specifically the principal administrative territorial division both in Tsarist Russian and in the early period of the USSR; now replaced by the oblast.

ketmen—a manual tool resembling a hoe, used in Central Asia.

kolkhóz (kollektivnoye khozyaistvo)—collective farm

kolki—birch-aspen groves in forest steppe

kray (krai)—region, territory, specifically a principal territorial administrative division of a Union republic coordinate with an oblast but distinguished by its inclusion of special units such as autonomous oblasts or national okrugs.

kulák—peasant capitalist; wealthy farmer.

makhórka—an inferior, cheap kind of tobacco.

óblast—region, province, specifically the principal administrative territorial division of the Union republics, corresponding to the Tsarist guberniya.

ókrug—district, canton, specifically an administrative territorial unit smaller than an oblast, sometimes with a special type of government as a national okrug.

omach—a wooden plow with an iron plowshare but lacking a mouldboard, used in Central Asia.

podzól—a zonal acid soil developed under coniferous or mixed forest, characterized by an organic mat and a very thin organic-mineral layer above a gray leached layer which rests on dark-brown horizon of accumulation.

polésye (polesie)—wooded district, particularly a low-lying poorly drained one; this name has been given to the extensive area of this type west of Minsk.

purgá (Finnish)—Arctic snowstorm or blizzard, characterized by low temperatures, high winds, and whirling snow, and found particularly in the tundra.

raión (rayon)—area or district, specifically the administrative subdivision of an oblast, kray, autonomous oblast, or national okrug, and composed of villages and towns; also (particularly in planning literature) a larger economic region comprising several oblasts; also a city district or ward.

rendzína (Polish)—an intrazonal dark-colored soil derived from highly calcareous materials, very sticky when wet, hence the name (rendzina is the Polish word for rubber).

serednyák—peasant of average means.

sierozém (serozem)—a zonal gray desert soil with a brownish-gray surface horizon that grades through lighter colored material into a layer of carbonate accumulation and frequently into a hardpan layer.

sólod (soloth)—an intrazonal acid soil formed in subhumid and arid regions formed, it is generally believed, by the leaching (solodization) of solonetz soils; characterized by a surface layer of brown friable soil above a gray leached horizon which rests on a very heavy, compact, dark-colored horizon.

solonchák—a salt marsh, or specifically an intrazonal saline soil formed predominantly in arid regions, in poorly drained low-lying spots

solonétz (solonets)—an intrazonal alkaline soil found in arid regions, (sometimes called "white alkali" soil in the U.S.).

particularly in poorly drained low-lying spots, characterized by a columnar structure with hard aggregates with some soluble salts and a high alkaline reaction (sometimes called "black alkali" soils in the U.S.).

sovkhóz (sovetskoye khozyaistvo)—state farm

Stakhánovite—workman with an output much above average, usually used in the phrase "Stakhanovite movement," a government-sponsored movement to increase labor productivity. Named after Aleksey Stakhanov, a Donets coal miner, who increased his daily output of coal by concentrating on one job and rationalizing his distribution of work.

stanítsa—a Cossack village or commune.

steppe (step)—temperate grassland or prairie.

sukhovéy—a hot, dry easterly or southeasterly wind of Central Asia.

syrt (Turkish)—a high mountain pasture, alp.

taigá (Yakut)—the northern coniferous forest which occupies most of the northern part of the USSR.

túndra (Finnish)—treeless plain in Arctic region north of the taiga. The vegetation consists of low-lying lichens and mosses.

Zémstvo—a former local governmental assembly (originally elected), which apportioned state taxation and had power to provide certain local services

B. Russian generic terms for geographic features, not considered to have a specific technical meaning, translated into English equivalents in this volume. It should be noted, however, that the U.S. Board on Geographical Names and the National Geographic Society consider them as integral parts of place names and therefore leave them in Russian.

basséin—basin.

búkhta—bay.

dol—vale, valley

gorá—mountain, mount, peak.

gryadá—ridge, often a long sinuous ridge formed by a terminal moraine.

gubá—bay, gulf, inlet.

khrebét—mountain range.

kotlovína—basin, broad open valley.

kryázh—mountain range.

massív, massif—a block of resistant rocks forming the worn-down stump of an ancient land mass (French).

móre—sea.
mys—cape.
nagórye—highlands, upland.
nizína—lowland.
nízmennost—lowland, plain.
okeán—ocean.
óstrov—island.
ózero—lake.
pereshéyek—isthmus.
perevál—pass.
pik—peak.
plató—plateau, tableland.
ploskogórye—plateau, upland, tableland.
poberézhye—coast, shore, littoral.
poluóstrov—peninsula.
prolív—strait.
protók—channel, canal.
ravnína—plain.
techénie—current (in sea or ocean).
vozvýshennost—upland, hill country, hills, heights.
vpádina—depression, basin.
zalív—gulf, bay.

C. Words neither Anglicized nor translated but left as in the original as part of a place name. These are mostly non-Russian words carried into Russian as components of place names.
belki—snowcapped peak (in Altay Mountains).
dag—mountains.
dárya—river (in Central Asia).
gol—lake.
kul—lake.
kum—sands (in desert).
shan—mountains.
sópka—a more or less isolated hill or peak of conical shape; in Kamchatka refers to a volcano, either active or inactive.
tau—mountain.
yailá—alp; high relatively level treeless mountain area in Crimea used for pasturing sheep.
zemlyá—land.

* *Appendix VI* BOUNDARY CHANGES, 1939–1945

The boundaries described in the text are those of late 1939 after the occupation of Poland by Germany in the west and by the Soviet Union in the east. Since Sept. 1, 1939, the following changes have been made:

* TABLE 1. AREAS ADDED TO THE SOVIET UNION, 1939–1945

(See Figs. 1 and 2, pp. 3 and 5)

	Area Sq. Km.	Prewar Population
1. From Finland		
a. Karelia (Kuolayarvi & Rybachy [a])	35,100	450,000
b. Pechenga (Petsamo [b])	10,480	4,330
2. From Baltic States		
a. Estonia (all)[a]	47,549	1,122,000
b. Latvia (all)[a]	65,791	1,951,000
c. Lithuania (all)[a]	52,822	2,442,000
3. From Germany		
a. From East Prussia (Kaliningrad, or Königsberg)[c]	11,000	1,075,000
b. Memel [c]	2,840	154,000
4. From Poland		
Eastern Poland (incl. Vilnius)[ab]	186,000	12,130,000
5. From Czechoslovakia		
Sub-Carpathian Ruthenia [b]	12,620	798,310
6. From Rumania		
Northern Bukovina [a]	6,000	500,000
Bessarabia [a]	44,400	3,200,000
7. From Tannu Tuva (all)[b]	150,000	70,000
8. From Japan		
a. Southern Sakhalin (Karafuto)[b]	36,090	415,000
b. Kuril Islands (Chishimo-retto)[b]	10,000	4,400
Total (rounded)	670,000	24,300,000

Sources:

[a] *Statistical Yearbook of the League of Nations 1941–42* (Geneva: League of Nations, 1943), pp. 17, 20.

[b] Theodore Shabad, "Political-Administrative Divisions of the USSR, 1945," *Geographical Review,* Vol. XXXVI, No. 2, Apr., 1946, p. 305.

[c] Population calculated from final 1939 census figures for Germany and 1940 census for Memel as given in *Wirtschaft und Statistik,* Vol. XX, 1940, No. 17, Sonderbeilage, p. 3, and Vol. XXI, 1941, No. 16, p. 536. Area calculated from *Statistik des Deutschen Reichs,* Vol. 451, p. 100.

The dates of these transfers and the treaties or agreements covering them are given below under numbers corresponding to those in Table I. Fig. 2 shows the location of the territories in question, except for those in Asia, shown on Fig. 1.

(1a) Karelia, or the Karelian Isthmus, the western and northern shores of Lake Ladoga, territory near the town of Kuolayarvi, and part of the Peninsula of Rybachy and Sredni were transferred by Finland under the Treaty of Mar. 12, 1940, confirmed by the Armistice of Sept. 19, 1944. (For text of treaty see *American Quarterly on the Soviet Union,* Vol. II, No. 4, Apr., 1940, pp. 58–60.) On Mar. 31, 1940, together with the territory of Karelian ASSR, already part of the Soviet Union, much of this area became the Karelo-Finnish SSR, the 12th Union Republic.

(1b) Pechenga (Petsamo) was ceded by Finland under the Armistice of Sept. 19, 1944. (The text of the Armistice is found in *American Review on the Soviet Union,* Vol. VI, No. 2, Feb., 1945, pp. 66–70.)

(2) The three Baltic States of Estonia, Latvia, and Lithuania granted Soviet military rights Sept. 29 to Oct. 10, 1939, and were incorporated into the Soviet Union as the 14th, 15th, and 16th Union republics August 3–6, 1940. (See *American Quarterly on the Soviet Union,* Vol. II, No. 4, Apr., 1940, pp. 71–72 and Vol. III, Nos. 2–3, Nov. 1940, pp. 101–104, 114–117.)

(3) Part of East Prussia was transferred from Germany to the Soviet Union by the Potsdam Declaration of the Big Three Conference in Berlin, July–Aug., 1945. (For text see *New York Times,* Aug. 3, 1945, p. 8, col. 6.) This area lies north of a line extending from a point on the eastern shore of the Bay of Danzig eastward north of Braunsberg and Goldnap to the meeting point of the former frontiers of Lithuania, the Polish Republic, and East Prussia.

(4) The boundary between Poland and the Soviet Union was altered by the Treaty of Aug. 16, 1945. This modified the boundary which had been set on Sept. 28, 1939, between Eastern Poland occupied by the USSR and Western Poland occupied by Germany. (For the text of the treaty and a map see *American Review on the Soviet Union,* Vol. VII, No. 2, Feb., 1946, pp. 62–63.) By this treaty the Przemyśl area in the south and the Białystok-Suwałki areas in the north passed back to Poland; these areas had about 14,200 sq. km. and 850,000 inhabitants.

(5) Sub-Carpathian Ruthenia, or Transcarpathian Ukraine, was ceded by Czechoslovakia under Treaty of June 29, 1945. (For text of the Treaty see *Ibid.,* Vol. VII, No. 1, Nov., 1945, pp. 64–65.) This area previously had been occupied by Hungary on the collapse of Czechoslovakia under German pressure.

(6) Bessarabia and Northern Bukovina were ceded by Rumania on June 28, 1940. (For text of the TASS communiqué on the transfer see the *New York Times,* June 29, 1940, p. 8, cols. 5–7.) Much of Bessarabia was included in the Moldavian SSR created as the 13th Union Republic on Aug. 2, 1940. This boundary was confirmed by the Armistice terms for Rumania of Sept. 12, 1944.) (The text of these terms is given in *American Review on the Soviet Union,* Vol. VI, No. 2, Feb., 1945, pp. 62–65.)

(7) The Tannu Tuva People's Republic on Aug. 17, 1944, requested admission into the Soviet Union and on Oct. 11, 1944, its request was approved and it

became an integral part of the Soviet Union as the Tuva Autonomous Oblast. (See *Ibid.*, Vol. VIII, No. 2, Mar., 1947, p. 85, and the *New York Times*, Oct. 30, 1945, p. 5, col. 4.)

(8) On the surrender of Japan the southern half of the island of Sakhalin and the Kuril Islands were occupied by the Soviet Union in accordance with the Yalta Agreement of Feb. 11, 1945. (For text see *American Review on the Soviet Union*, Vol. VII, No. 3, May, 1946, p. 81.)

(9) Extraterritorial rights have been obtained in Finland and China. (a) The Peninsula of Porkkalla-Udd, southwest of Helsinki, was leased as a naval base by the terms of the Finnish Armistice of Sept. 19, 1944. (Text in *Ibid.*, Vol. VI, No. 2, Feb., 1945, pp. 68–70.) At this time the Soviet Union renounced the rights to Hangö, which had been obtained by the Treaty of Mar. 12, 1940.

(b) Under the Chinese-Soviet Treaty of Aug. 14, 1945, and in accord with the Yalta Agreement of Feb. 11, 1945, Port Arthur became a joint Soviet-Chinese naval base (defense of which was entrusted to the USSR) and Port Dalny (Dairen) became a free port with a section of piers and warehouses leased to the Soviet Union and with provision for the appointment of a Soviet citizen as Chief of the Port. (For text of these two treaties see *Ibid.*, Vol. VII, No. 1, Nov., 1945, pp. 70–71.)

KEY TO FIGURE 82

1. Belorussian Soviet Socialist Republic
2. Ukrainian Soviet Socialist Republic
   - a. Forest Subregion
   - b Dnepr Prairie Right Bank
   - c. Dnepr Prairie Left Bank
   - d. Steppe Subregion
     Including:
     1. Moldavian ASSR
   - e. Dnepr Industrial Subregion
   - f. Mining-Industrial Subregion

RUSSIAN SOVIET FEDERATED SOCIALIST REPUBLIC (Numbers 3–21)

3. Northeastern Region
   - a. Archangel G
   - b. Vologda G
   - c. Severnaya Dvina G
   - d. Komi AO
4. Leningrad-Karelia Region
   - a. Karelian ASSR
   - b. Leningrad G
   - c. Murmansk G
   - d. Novgorod G
   - e. Pskov G
   - f. Cherepovets G
5. Western Region
   - a. Bryansk G
   - b. Smolensk G
6. Central Industrial Region
   - a. Vladimir G
   - b. Ivanovo-Voznesensk G
   - c. Kaluga G
   - d. Kostroma G
   - e. Moscow G
   - f. Nizhny Novgorod G
   - g. Tver G
   - h. Yaroslavl G
   - i. Ryazan G
   - j. Tula G
7. Central Chernozem (Black Soil) Region
   - a. Voronezh G
   - b. Kursk G
   - c. Orel G
   - d. Tambov G
8. Vyatka Region
   - a. Votyak AO
   - b. Vyatka G
   - c. Mari AO
9. Ural Region
   - a. Pre-Ural Subregion
   - b. Mining-Industrial Subregion
   - c. Trans-Ural Subregion
   - d. Tobolsk Subregion
10. Bashkir ASSR
11. Middle Volga Region
    - a. Orenburg G
    - b. Penza G
    - c. Samara G
    - d. Tatar ASSR
    - e. Ulyanovsk G
    - f. Chuvash ASSR
12. Lower Volga Region
    - a. Astrakhan G
    - b. Kalmyk AO
    - c. Volga German ASSR
    - d. Saratov G
    - e. Stalingrad G
13. Crimean ASSR
14. North Caucasus Kray
    - a. Azov Subregion
    - b. Donets-Stavropol Subregion
    - c. Kuban-Black Sea Subregion
      Including:
      1. Adygey AO
    - d. Mountain Subregion
      Including:
      1. Cherkess AO
      2. Karachayev AO
      3. Kabardino-Balkar AO
      4. North Osetian AO
      5. Ingush AO
      6. Chechen AO
15. Dagestan ASSR
16. Siberian Kray
    - a. Southwest Subregion
      Including:
      1. Oirot AO
    - b. Northeast Subregion
17. Buryat-Mongol ASSR
18. Yakut ASSR
19. Far Eastern Kray
    - a. Trans-Baikal Subregion
    - b. Amur Subregion
    - c. Maritime Subregion
    - d. Sakhalin Subregion
    - e. Kamchatka Subregion
20. Kazakh ASSR
    - a. Akmolinsk G
    - b. Aktyubinsk G
    - c. Dzhetysuy G
    - d. Semipalatinsk G
    - e. Syr-Darya G
    - f. Uralsk G
    - g. Adayev G
    - h. Kustanay G
    - i. Kara-Kalpak AO
21. Kirgiz ASSR

22. Uzbek Soviet Socialist Republic (with Tadzhik ASSR)
    - a. Without Tadzhik ASSR
    - b. Tadzhik ASSR
23. Turkmen Soviet Socialist Republic
24. Transcaucasian Soviet Federated Socialist Republic
    - a. Azerbaidzhan Soviet Socialist Republic
      Including:
      1. Nagorno-Karabakh AO
      2. Nakhichevan ASSR
    - b. Armenian Soviet Socialist Republic
    - c. Georgian Soviet Socialist Republic
      Including:
      1. Abkhaz SSR
      2. Adzhar ASSR
      3. South Osetian AO

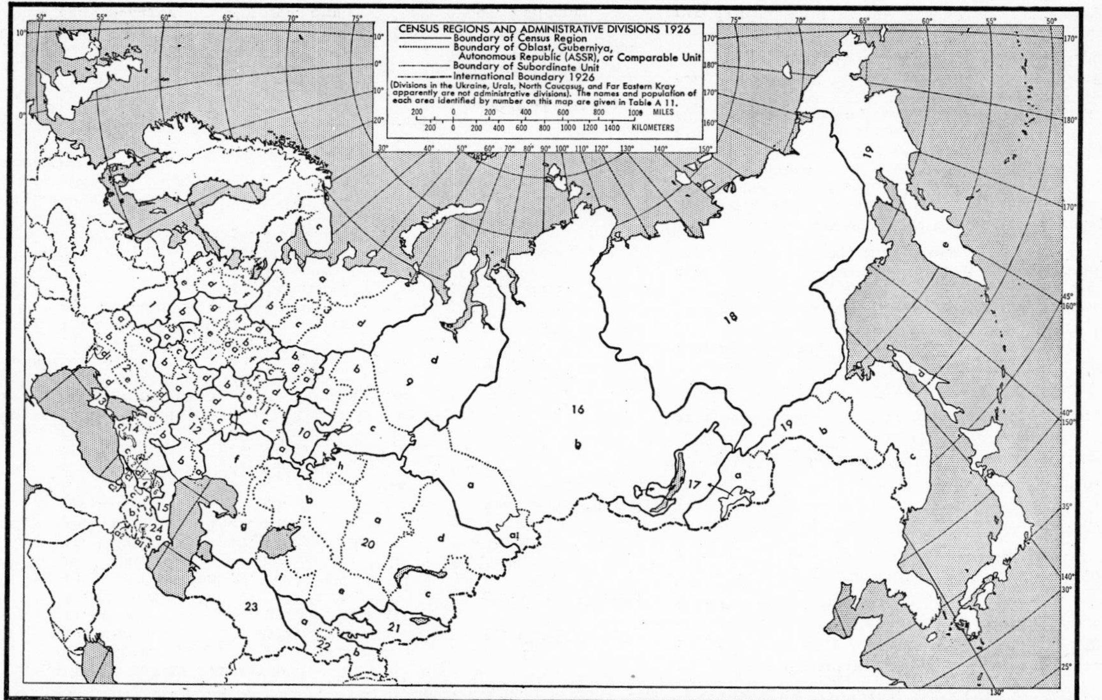

* Fig. 82. Census Regions and Administrative Divisions, 1926 (Adapted from Frank Lorimer, *The Population of the Soviet Union: History and Prospects*, Plate IV, and USSR, Central Statistical Bureau, Census Section, *All-Union Census of Population*, 1926 [Moscow, 1928–1929], maps at ends of vols. 4–8 and 11–13.)

KEY TO FIGURE 83

Source: *Great Soviet World Atlas,* Vol. II, plates 9–10.

Note: The 11 divisions created out of the area added to the USSR between September 1, 1939, and December 5, 1939, are indicated by an x. Names given are those in use in 1939.

Abbreviations: O, Oblast. AO, Autonomous Oblast. NOk, National Okrug.

I. Russian Soviet Federated Socialist Republic

ASSR

1. Bashkir
2. Buryat-Mongol
3. Chechen-Ingush
4. Chuvash
5. Crimean
6. Dagestan
7. Kabardino-Balkar
8. Kalmyk
9. Karelian
10. Komi
11. Mari
12. Mordovian
13. North Osetian
14. Tatar
15. Udmurt
16. Volga German
17. Yakut

Krays

18. Altay
    19. Oirot AO
20. Khabarovsk (areas administered directly by Kray are indicated by number 20; areas administered by subordinate units are numbered 21–27)
    21. Jewish AO
    22. Amur O
    23. Kamchatka O
        24. Chukot NOk
    25. Koryak NOk
    26. Lower Amur O
    27. Sakhalin O
28. Krasnodar
    29. Adygey AO
30. Krasnoyarsk
    31. Khakass AO
    32. Taimyr NOk
    33. Evenki NOk
34. Maritime (Primorsky)
    35. Ussuri O
36. Ordzhonikidze
    37. Karachayev AO
    38. Cherkess AO

Oblasts

39. Archangel
    40. Nenets NOk
41. Chelyabinsk
42. Chita
    43. Aginsk Buryat-Mongol NOk
44. Chkalov
45. Gorky
46. Irkutsk
    47. Ust-Orda Buryat-Mongol NOk
48. Ivanovo
49. Kalinin
50. Kirov
51. Kuibyshev
52. Kursk
53. Leningrad
54. Moscow
55. Murmansk
56. Novosibirsk
57. Omsk
    58. Ostyak-Vogul NOk
    59. Yamalo-Nenets NOk
60. Orel
61. Penza
62. Perm
    63. Komi-Permyak NOk
64. Rostov
65. Ryazan
66. Saratov
67. Smolensk
68. Stalingrad
69. Sverdlovsk
70. Tambov
71. Tula
72. Vologda
73. Voronezh
74. Yaroslavl

II. Ukrainian Soviet Socialist Republic

ASSR

75. Moldavian

Oblasts

76. Chernigov
77. Dnepropetrovsk
78. Drogobych (x)
79. Kamenets-Podolsk
80. Kharkov
81. Kiev
82. Kirovograd
83. Lvov (x)
84. Nikolayev
85. Odessa
86. Poltava
87. Rovno (x)
88. Stalino
89. Stanislav (x)
90. Sumy
91. Tarnopol (x)
92. Vinnitsa
93. Volyn (x)
94. Voroshilovgrad
95. Zaporozhye
96. Zhitomir

III. Belorussian Soviet Socialist Republic

Oblasts

97. Baranovichi (x)
98. Belostok (x)
99. Brest (x)
100. Gomel
101. Minsk
102. Mogilev
103. Pinsk (x)
104. Polesye
105. Vileika (x)
106. Vitebsk

IV. Georgian Soviet Socialist Republic

107. Georgian SSR (not divided into oblasts)
108. Abkhaz ASSR
109. Adzhar ASSR
110. South Osetian AO

V. Armenian Soviet Socialist Republic

111. Armenian SSR (not divided into oblasts)

VI. Azerbaidzhan Soviet Socialist Republic

112. Azerbaidzhan (not divided into oblasts)
113. Nakhichevan ASSR
114. Nagorno-Karabakh AO

VII. Turkmen Soviet Socialist Republic

Oblasts

115. Ashkhabad
116. Chardzhou
117. Krasnovodsk
118. Mary
119. Tashauz

VIII. Uzbek Soviet Socialist Republic

ASSR

120. Kara-Kalpak

Oblasts

121. Bukhara
122. Fergana
123. Khorezm
124. Samarkand
125. Tashkent

IX. Tadzhik Soviet Socialist Republic

Oblasts

126. Garm
127. Kulyab
128. Leninabad
129. Stalinabad

AO

130. Gorno-Badakshan

X. Kazakh Soviet Socialist Republic

Oblasts

131. Akmolinsk
132. Aktyubinsk
133. Alma-Ata
134. Dzhambul
135. East Kazakhstan
136. Guryev
137. Karaganda
138. Kustanay
139. Kzyl-Orda
140. North Kazakhstan
141. Pavlodar
142. Semipalatinsk
143. South Kazakhstan
144. West Kazakhstan

XI. Kirgiz Soviet Socialist Republic

Oblasts

145. Dzhalal-Abad
146. Frunze
147. Issyk-Kul
148. Osh
149. Tyan-Shan

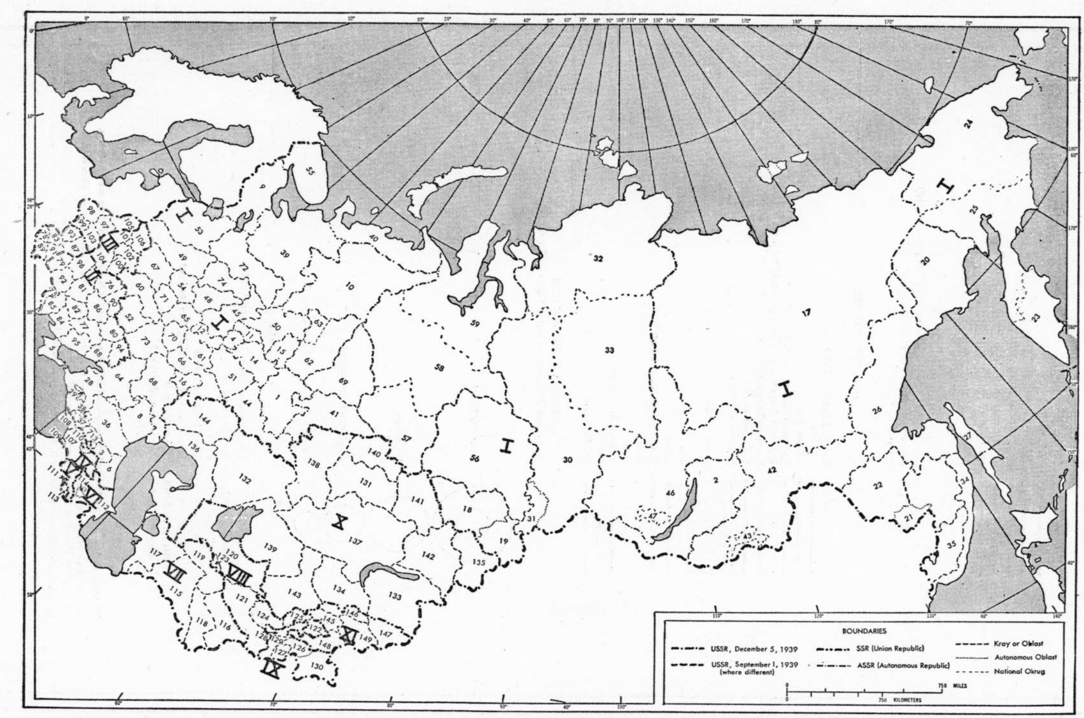

* Fig. 83. Administrative Divisions of the USSR, December 5, 1939 (when the text was written)

CONVENTIONAL SIGNS

BOUNDARIES

USRR 1947
USSR 1938 (where different)
SSR (Union Republic)
ASSR (Autonomous Republic), Oblast, or Kray
International Boundary Outside USSR

SETTLEMENTS

City, Town, or Other Inhabited Point (Undifferentiated)
Administrative Center of an Oblast or ASSR
Other City

TRANSPORT FEATURES

Railroad Existing 1939
Steam
Electrified
Railroad Under Construction 1939
Railroad Reported Built During World War II
Narrow-Gauge Railroad
Surfaced Road
Unsurfaced Road
Water Body
River
Canal
Canal Under Construction
Lock
Dam
Internal Sea Route
Port
Oil Pipe Line

POINTS OF PRODUCTION
(No value indicated except in Figures 27 and 28)

Most Important
Important
Moderately Important
Others (More Significant Ones Only)

NAMES

Moscow	City, Town, or Other Inhabited Point
CAUCASUS MTS.	Terrain Feature
Mt. Elbrus	Peak
Volga R.	River, Lake, or Canal
BALTIC SEA	Sea, Ocean, Strait, Gulf, Bay, or Inlet
CENTRAL ASIA	Regional Name
CHUVASH ASSR	Administrative Area
POLAND	Country

Variations of the above general symbols and special symbols are identified in the legends of the individual maps.

Data on most maps apply to 1937 or 1938, except on those showing distribution of manufactures, which in general are based on 1935 data revised in part by later information.

On nearly all maps data are limited to the 1938 area of the USSR.

Fig. 84. Conventional Signs Used on the Maps in this Book

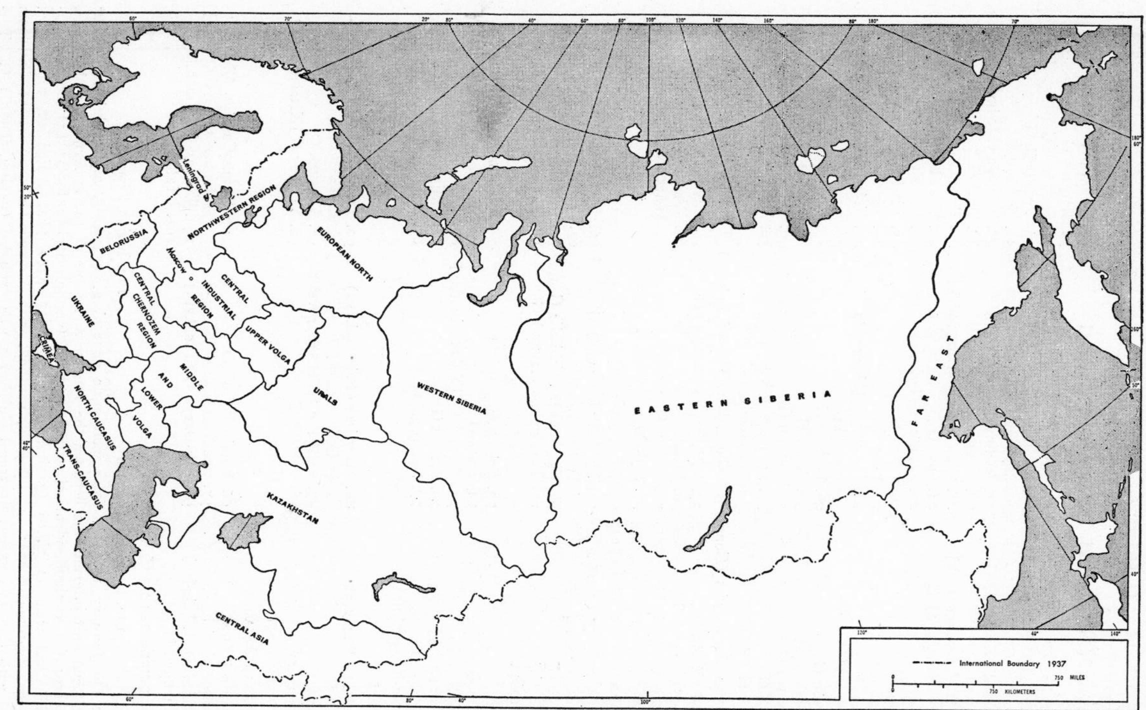

* Fig. 7. Statistical Regions, 1937. As far as can be ascertained these are the statistical regions used in Tables 33–35, 39, and A5–A8, data for which apply to 1937. For similar statistical regions used in 1926 see * Fig. 82.

KEY TO FIG. 22

Names given are those in use in 1914; alternate names are in parentheses. Location of the administrative center of each unit is indicated by a circle; The name of the capital or administrative center when not the same as that of the area is given in brackets. Abbreviations: G, Guberniya; O, Oblast; Ok, Okrug.

I. EUROPEAN RUSSIA

1. Archangel (Arkhangelsk) G
2. Astrakhan G
3. Bessarabia G [Kishinev]
4. Chernigov G
5. Courland (Kurland) G [Mitava]
6. Don O [Novocherkassk]
7. Estonia (Estland) G [Revel]
8. Grodno G
9. Kaluga G
10. Kazan G
11. Kharkov G
12. Kherson G
13. Kiev G
14. Kostroma G
15. Kovno G
16 Kursk G
17. Livonia (Lifland) G [Riga]
18. Minsk G
19. Mogilev G
20. Moscow (Moskva) G
21. Nizhny Novgorod G
22. Novgorod G
23. Olonets G [Petrozavodsk]
24. Orel G
25. Orenburg G
26. Penza G
27. Perm G
28. Podolsk G [Kamenets Podolsk]
29. Poltava G
30. Pskov G
31. Ryazan G
32. St. Petersburg (Petersburg) G
33. Samara G
34. Saratov G
35. Simbirsk G
36 Smolensk G
37. Tambov G
38. Tavrida G [Simferopol]
39. Tula G
40. Tver G
41. Ufa G
42. Vilna G
43. Vitebsk G
44. Vladimir G
45. Volyn G [Zhitomir]
46. Vologda G
47. Voronezh G
48. Vyatka G
49. Yaroslavl G
50. Yekaterinoslav G

II. VISTULA PROVINCES (Congress Poland, Kingdom of Poland)

51. Kalish (Kalisz) G
52. Keltsy (Kielce) G
53. Lomzha (Łomża) G
54. Lyublin (Lublin) G
55. Petrokov (Piotrków) G
56. Plotsk (Płock) G
57. Radom G
58. Sedlets (Siedlce) G
59. Suvalki (Suwałki) G
60. Warsaw (Varshava, Warszawa) G

III. GRAND DUCHY OF FINLAND

61. Åbo-Björneborg (Turku-Pori) G [Abo]
62. Kuopio G
63. Nyland (Uusimaa) G [Helsingfors]
64. S:t Michel (Mikkeli) G
65. Tavastehus (Häme) G
66. Uleåborg (Oulu) G
67. Vasa (Vaasa) G [Vaasa]
68. Viborg (Viipuri) G

IV. CAUCASIA

69. Baku G
70. Batum O
71. Black Sea G [Novorossiisk]
72. Dagestan O [Temir-Khay-Shura]
73. Erivan G
74 Kars O
75. Kuban O [Yekaterinodar]
76. Kutais G
77. Stavropol G
78. Sukhum-Kale Ok
79. Terek O [Vladikavkaz]
80. Tiflis G
81. Yelizavetpol G
82. Zakataly Ok

V. SIBERIA

83. Amur O [Blagoveshchensk]
84. Irkutsk G
85. Kamchatka O [Petropavlovsk]
86. Maritime (Primorskaya) O [Khabarovsk]
87. Sakhalin [Aleksandrovsk]
88. Tobolsk G
89. Tomsk G
90. Trans-Baikal (Zaibaikalskaya) O [Chita]
91. Yakutsk O
92. Yenisey G [Krasnoyarsk]

VI. CENTRAL ASIA

93. Akmolinsk O [Semipalatinsk]
94. Fergana O [Skobelev]
95. Samarkand O
96. Semipalatinsk O
97. Semirechensk O [Verny]
98. Syr-Darya O [Tashkent]
99. Trans-Caspian (Zakaspiiskaya) O [Ashkhabad]
100. Turgay O [Kustanay]
101. Uralsk O

VII. DEPENDENCIES IN CENTRAL ASIA

102. Bukhara Khanate
103. Khiva Khanate

Note: On January 1, 1914, there were nine general governments, an administrative but not statistical unit intermediate between the Empire and some of the guberniyas and oblasts. These were: (1) Finland, identical with III above (capital, Helsingfors); (3) Poland, virtually identical with II above (capital, Warsaw); (3) Kiev (Kiev, Podolsk, and Volyn guberniyas) (capital, Kiev); (4) Moscow, identical with Moscow Guberniya; (5) Caucasus identical with Caucasia except Stavropol Guberniya was excluded (capital, Tiflis); (6) Turkestan (Fergana, Samarkand, Semirechensk, Syr-Darya, and Trans-Caspian oblasts—capital, Tashkent); (7) Steppes (Akmolinsk and Semipalatinsk oblasts—capital, Semipalatinsk); (8) Irkutsk (Irkutsk and Yenisey guberniyas and Trans-Baikal and Yakutsk oblasts—capital, Irkutsk); and (9) Amur (Amur, Kamchatka, Maritime, and Sakhalin oblasts—capital, Khabarovsk).

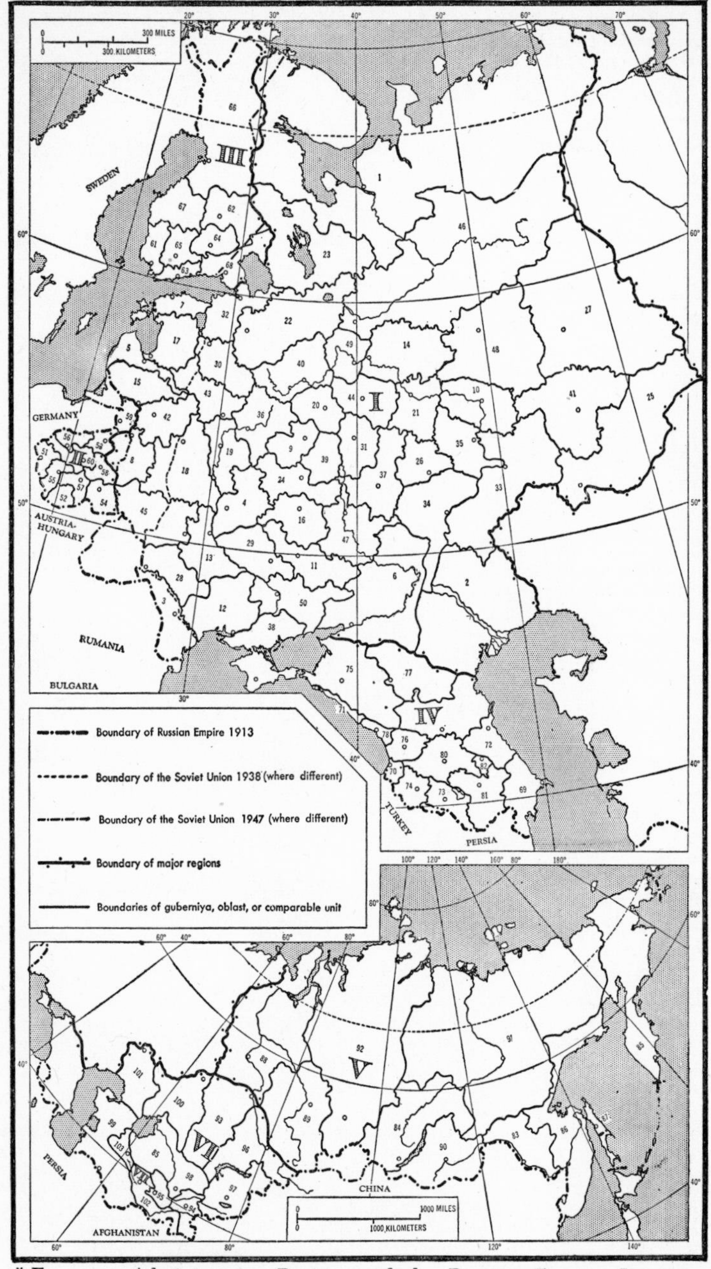

* FIG. 22. Administrative Divisions of the Russian Empire, January 1, 1913, Grouped by Major Statistical Regions (Adapted from *Great Soviet World Atlas,* Vol. I, Plate 168)

INDEX I. A: INDEX TO CITATIONS

References not in the original have been enclosed in brackets. Entries are in the form used by the Library of Congress or the University of Chicago Library except for the slightly different transliteration scheme (see Appendix IV, pp. 538–39). The edition to which page references in the text refer is given first; other editions or English translations follow.

The index entries following list any figure references first, preceded by the letter F; then any table references, preceded by the letter T (A1, A2, etc., appearing among these, refer to the tables so numbered in Appendix I); and, last, any page references, preceded by P.

mittee of the Communist Party of the Soviet Union), P159

Vsesoyuznaya Kommunisticheskaya Partiya (bolshevikov), Tsentralny Komitet, *Istoriya Vsesoyuznoy Kommunisticheskoy Partii (bolshevikov), Kratky Kurs* (*History of the Communist Party of the Soviet Union, Short Course*) (Moscow: Gosudarstvennoye Izdatelstvo Politicheskoy Literatury, 1938, 351 pp.—repr. 1943 with same paging), P112, 127, 133, 142. English ed.: *History of the Communist Party of the Soviet Union (bolsheviks), Short Course*, ed. by a Commission of the Central Committee of the C.P.S.U. (B.), authorized by the Central Committee of the C.P. S.U. (B.). (New York: International Publishers, 1939, 364 pp.)

Weber, Alfred (b. 1868), *Teoriya Razmeshcheniya Promyshlennosti* (*Theory of the Distribution of Industry*), Pxliii, 199. Original German ed.: Ueber den Standort der Industrien: I. Teil, Reine Theorie des Standorts (Tübingen: J. C. B. Mohr, 1909, 246 pp.). English ed.: *Alfred Weber's Theory of the Location of Industries*, ed. with Introduction and Notes by Carl J. Friedrich (Chicago: University of Chicago Press, 1929, 256 pp.).

[*Wirtschaft und Statistik*, vols. 20–21, 1940–41. T1]

B: BIBLIOGRAPHY ON THE GEOGRAPHY OF THE USSR

The following list contains only the major books in English, French, and German. For detailed bibliographies including periodical articles and works in Russian see (1) American Geographical Society, *Current Geographical Publications;* (2) *Bibliographie Géographique Internationale;* and (3) *Geographisches Jahrbuch*, vols. 17, 29, 37–38, 43, and 52–54.

Berg, Lev Semenovich (b. 1876), *Les Régions Naturelles de l'U.R.S.S.*, transl. G. Welter. Paris: Payot, Bibliothèque Géographique, 1941, 382 pp. American edition: *The Natural Regions of the USSR*, translated from the Russian by Olga Adler Titelbaum. New York: Macmillan, *in press*.

Camena d'Almeida, Pierre Joseph (1864–1943), *Etats de la Baltique, Russie* (Vol. 5 of *Géographie Universelle*, ed. by P. Vidal de Blache and L. Gallois). Paris: Librairie Armand Colin, 1932, 355 pp.

Cressey, George Babcock (b. 1896), *The Basis of Soviet Strength.* New York: McGraw-Hill Book Co., 1945, 287 pp.

Fichelle, Alfred, *Géographie Physique et Economique de l'U.R.S.S.* Paris: Payot (Bibliothèque Géographique), 1946, 223 pp.

George, Pierre (b. 1909), *U.R.S.S., Haute-Asie, Iran.* Paris; Presses Universitaires de France, 1947, 534 pp.

Gray, G. D. B., *Soviet Land: The Country, Its People, and Their Work.* London: Adam & Charles Black, 1947, 324 pp.

Gregory, James S. (b. 1912), and D. W. Shave, *The U.S.S.R.: A Geographical Survey.* London: George G. Harrap & Co., 1944, 636 pp.

Hettner, Alfred (1859–1941), *Russland: Eine Geographische Betrachtung von Volk, Staat und Kultur*, 3rd ed. Leipzig: B. G. Teubner, 1916, 357 pp.

Jorré, Georges, *L'U.R.S.S.: La Terre et les Hommes.* Paris: Société d'Editions Françaises et Internationales, 1946, 403 pp. (English edition. London: Longmans, Green, *in press.*)

Klute, Fritz (b. 1885), *Handbuch der Geographischen Wissenschaft.* Potsdam: Akademische Verlagsgesellschaft Athenaien, 1933, 1937. Especially in Vol. 3 (*Mitteleuropa-Osteuropa*), pp. 278–464 by Max Friederichsen and Bruno Plaetschke, and Vol. 6 (*Nordasien, Zentral- und Ostasien*), pp. 125–244 by Helmut Anger and Arved Schultz.

Leimbach, Werner, *Sowjetunion.* Stuttgart: Kosmos-Verlag, *in press,* ca. 320 pp.

Mikhailov, Nikolay Nikolayevich, *The Land of the Soviets: A Handbook of the U.S.S.R.*, transl. Nathalie Rothstein. New York: Lee Furman, 1939, 351 pp.

Mikhailov, Nikolay Nikolayevich, *Soviet Geography: The New Industrial and Economic Distributions of the U. S. S. R.*, 2nd ed. rev., London: Methuen & Co., 1937, 229 pp.

Mikhailov, Nikolay Nikolayevich, *Soviet Russia: The Land and Its People,* transl. George H. Hanna. New York: Sheridan House, 1948, 374 pp.

National Geographic Society, *Union of Soviet Socialist Republics.* Washington: National Geographic Society, 1944. Map scale 1:9,000,000. Index to Map, with 8,016 names.

Shabad, Theodore, *The Geography of the U.S.S.R.* New York: Columbia University Press, *in press.*

Tuckermann, Walther (b. 1880), *Osteuropa.* Breslau: F. Hirt, 1922, 2 vols., 116, 124 pp.

INDEX II. INDEX OF PERSONS
(With Biographical Notes)

INDEX III. INDEX OF PLANTS AND ANIMALS
(With Identification by Scientific Names)

(The abbreviation spp. indicates that the plant or animal is represented by more than one species.)

A. PLANTS

B. ANIMALS

INDEX IV. GAZETEER OR INDEX OF PLACE NAMES

Prepared by William Horbaly

Parentheses enclose former or alternate names.

Brackets enclose the form of the name according to the system of transliteration recommended by the U.S. Board on Geographic Names for official U.S. Government use. The individual names, however, have not been checked by the U.S. Board on Geographic Names.

Numbers preceded by an F refer to figures. Numbers preceded by a T refer to tables. Numbers preceded by a P refer to pages.

Abbreviations:

SSR—Soviet Socialist Republic [Sovetskaya Sotsialisticheskaya Respublika]
ASSR—Autonomous Soviet Socialist Republic [Avtonomnaya Sovetskaya Sotsialisticheskaya Respublika]
AO—Autonomous Oblast [Avtonomnaya Oblast']
O—Oblast [Oblast']
G—Guberniya
NOk—National Okrug [Natsional 'nyy Okrug]
Mt.—Mountain
R.—River